Examining a New Automobile Global Manufacturing System

Kakuro Amasaka
Aoyama Gakuin University, Japan

A volume in the Advances in Logistics, Operations, and Management Science (ALOMS) Book Series

IGI Global
PUBLISHER of TIMELY KNOWLEDGE

Published in the United States of America by
IGI Global
Business Science Reference (an imprint of IGI Global)
701 E. Chocolate Avenue
Hershey PA, USA 17033
Tel: 717-533-8845
Fax: 717-533-8661
E-mail: cust@igi-global.com
Web site: http://www.igi-global.com

Library of Congress Cataloging-in-Publication Data

Names: Amasaka, Kakuro, 1947- author.
Title: Examining a new automobile global manufacturing system / by Kakuro Amasaka.
Description: Hershey, PA : Business Science Reference, 2022. | Includes bibliographical references and index. | Summary: "In this book, the author predicts the form of next generation automobile manufacturing, presenting a "New Automobile Global Manufacturing System" (NAGMS) that contains the hardware system with five core elements - "TDS, TPS, TMS, TIS and TJS" (Total Development System, Total Production System, Total Marketing System, Total Intelligence Management System and Total Job Quality Management System) for transforming management technology into automobile management strategy-Surpassing JIT"-- Provided by publisher.
Identifiers: LCCN 2021059483 (print) | LCCN 2021059484 (ebook) | ISBN 9781799887461 (hardcover) | ISBN 9781799887478 (paperback) | ISBN 9781799887485 (ebook)
Subjects: LCSH: Automobile industry and trade--Management. | Offshore assembly industry. | Globalization--Economic aspects.
Classification: LCC HD9710.A2 A483 2022 (print) | LCC HD9710.A2 (ebook) | DDC 338.4/7629222--dc23/eng/20220119
LC record available at https://lccn.loc.gov/2021059483
LC ebook record available at https://lccn.loc.gov/2021059484

This book is published in the IGI Global book series Advances in Logistics, Operations, and Management Science (ALOMS) (ISSN: 2327-350X; eISSN: 2327-3518)

British Cataloguing in Publication Data
A Cataloguing in Publication record for this book is available from the British Library.

Advances in Logistics, Operations, and Management Science (ALOMS) Book Series

John Wang
Montclair State University, USA

ISSN:2327-350X
EISSN:2327-3518

Mission

Operations research and management science continue to influence business processes, administration, and management information systems, particularly in covering the application methods for decision-making processes. New case studies and applications on management science, operations management, social sciences, and other behavioral sciences have been incorporated into business and organizations real-world objectives.

The **Advances in Logistics, Operations, and Management Science** (ALOMS) Book Series provides a collection of reference publications on the current trends, applications, theories, and practices in the management science field. Providing relevant and current research, this series and its individual publications would be useful for academics, researchers, scholars, and practitioners interested in improving decision making models and business functions.

Coverage

- Decision analysis and decision support
- Organizational Behavior
- Information Management
- Production Management
- Finance
- Political Science
- Computing and information technologies
- Risk Management
- Networks
- Operations Management

IGI Global is currently accepting manuscripts for publication within this series. To submit a proposal for a volume in this series, please contact our Acquisition Editors at acquisitions@igi-global.com or visit: https://www.igi-global.com/publish/.

The Advances in Logistics, Operations, and Management Science (ALOMS) Book Series (ISSN 2327-350X) is published by IGI Global, 701 E. Chocolate Avenue, Hershey, PA 17033-1240, USA, www.igi-global.com. This series is composed of titles available for purchase individually; each title is edited to be contextually exclusive from any other title within the series. For pricing and ordering information please visit https://www.igi-global.com/book-series/advances-logistics-operations-management-science/37170. Postmaster: Send all address changes to above address.

Titles in this Series

For a list of additional titles in this series, please visit: www.igi-global.com/book-series

Empowering Sustainable Industrial 4.0 Systems With Machine Intelligence
Muneer Ahmad (University of Malaya, Malaysia) and Noor Zaman (Taylor's University, Malaysia)
Business Science Reference • © 2022 • 315pp • H/C (ISBN: 9781799892014) • US $225.00

Interdisciplinary and Practical Approaches to Managerial Education and Training
Luísa Cagica Carvalho (Polytechnic Institute of Setúbal, Portugal & CEFAGE, University of Évora, Portugal) Nuno Teixeira (Polytechnic Institute of Setúbal, Portugal) and Pedro Pardal (Polytechnic Institute of Setúbal, Portugal)
Business Science Reference • © 2022 • 353pp • H/C (ISBN: 9781799882398) • US $195.00

Handbook of Research on the Future of the Maritime Industry
Nihan Senbursa (University of Ordu, Turkey)
Business Science Reference • © 2022 • 465pp • H/C (ISBN: 9781799890393) • US $395.00

Handbook of Research on Museum Management in the Digital Era
Francesco Bifulco (University of Naples Federico II, Italy) and Marco Tregua (University of Naples Federico II, Italy)
Information Science Reference • © 2022 • 412pp • H/C (ISBN: 9781799896562) • US $245.00

Management Strategies for Sustainability, New Knowledge Innovation, and Personalized Products and Services
Mirjana Pejic-Bach (University of Zagreb, Croatia) and Çağlar Doğru (Ufuk University, Turkey)
Business Science Reference • © 2022 • 365pp • H/C (ISBN: 9781799877936) • US $215.00

Cases on Supply Chain Management and Lessons Learned From COVID-19
Ana Paula Lopes (Polytechnic of Porto, Portugal)
Business Science Reference • © 2022 • 238pp • H/C (ISBN: 9781799891406) • US $225.00

Key Factors and Use Cases of Servant Leadership Driving Organizational Performance
Maria Pressentin (International School of Management, France)
Business Science Reference • © 2022 • 368pp • H/C (ISBN: 9781799888208) • US $215.00

Handbook of Research on Innovative Management Using AI in Industry 5.0
Vikas Garg (Amity University, Greater Noida, India) and Richa Goel (Amity University, Noida, India)
Business Science Reference • © 2022 • 351pp • H/C (ISBN: 9781799884972) • US $295.00

Contemporary Challenges for Agile Project Management
Vannie Naidoo (University of Kwa-Zulu Natal, South Africa) and Rahul Verma (Delhi University, India)
Business Science Reference • © 2022 • 354pp • H/C (ISBN: 9781799878728) • US $225.00

IGI Global
PUBLISHER of TIMELY KNOWLEDGE

701 East Chocolate Avenue, Hershey, PA 17033, USA
Tel: 717-533-8845 x100 • Fax: 717-533-8661
E-Mail: cust@igi-global.com • www.igi-global.com

Table of Contents

Section 2
Expanding Japanese Automobile Uniform Quality and Production at Optimum Locations Through SCM Strategy in the World

Section 3
Development of Automobile Simultaneous QCD Fulfilment for Customer Value Creation

Section 4
Example Applications

Preface

A future successful global marketer must develop an excellent management technology system that impresses users and continuously provides excellent, quality products in a timely manner through strategic corporate management. To succeed in global production, achieving worldwide uniform quality and simultaneous launch is an urgent task.

One of the greatest contributions that Japan made to the world is Just in Time (JIT). The Japanese-style production system represented by Toyota Production System, called JIT, is a production system which has been developed by Toyota Motor Corporation. JIT is introduced in a number of enterprises in the United States and Europe as a key management technology.

However, Toyota's production system has already been developed as an internationally shared system, known as a Lean System and is no longer an exclusive technology of Toyota. The top priority issue of the industrial field today is the new deployment of global marketing for surviving the era of global quality competition. The pressing management issue particularly for Japanese manufacturers to survive in the global market is the uniform quality worldwide and production at optimum locations which is the prerequisite for successful global manufacturing.

In this book, against this background, by predicting the form of next generation automobile manufacturing, the author hereby examines a "New Automobile Global Manufacturing System" (NAGMS) that contains the hardware system with five core elements - "TDS, TPS, TMS, TIS and TJS" (Total Development System, Total Production System, Total Marketing System, Total Intelligence Management System and Total Job Quality Management System) for transforming management technology into automobile management strategy—Surpassing JIT.

To realize automobile manufacturing that places top priority on customers with a good QCD, the author, therefore, a high linkage model "Advanced TDS, TPS, TMS, TIS and TJS" for expanding "uniform quality worldwide and production at optimum locations". The focus of this book is thus the theory and application of strategic management technology through the application of NAGMS for the "Evolution of Japan automobile manufacturing foundation".

As these results, developing of NAGMS has proved to be effective in actual implementations. Concretely, the author introduces the application examples through "Expanding Japanese automobile uniform quality and production at optimum locations through SCM strategy in the world". Moreover, through "Automobile simultaneous QCD fulfilment for customer value creation" with "Example Applications", the validity of NAGMS is then verified at an advanced car manufacturer Toyota and others.

Aims and Structure

To develop the automobile manufacturing strategy in the world, it is essential to create a core principle capable of changing the technical development work processes of development and design divisions. Similarly, it is important to develop a new production technology principle and establish new process management principles to enable global production. Furthermore, new marketing activities independent from past experience are required for sales and service divisions to achieve firmer relationships with customers. Moreover, a new quality management technology principle linked with overall activities for higher work process quality in all divisions is necessary for an enterprise to survive.

To overcome these issues, therefore, the aim of this book is to develop the *Examining a New Automobile Global Manufacturing System* with the theory and application of strategic management technology. To realize this, then, the author has structured the development of NAGMS for customer relations, sales and marketing, product planning, research, and development (R&D), product design, production engineering, SCM, procurement, administration and management, for enhancing business process innovation and introduction of new concepts and procedures, as follows:

Section 1, "A New Automobile Global Manufacturing System," includes Chapter 1, "Introduction"; Chapter 2, "Today's Global Manufacturing Issues: Innovation of Manufacturing Fundamentals"; Chapter 3, "Foundation of Toyota Production System: JIT Fundamentals"; Chapter 4, "Importance of Japan's Global Manufacturing Strategies 21C: Surpassing JIT"; Chapter 5, "Establishment of New Japan Model Using Total Linkage of TDS, TPS, TMS, TIS, and TJS"; Chapter 6, "Creation of New Japan Automobile Global Manufacturing Model Using Advanced TDS, TPS, TMS, TIS, and TJS"; Chapter 7, "Evolution of Japan Automobile Manufacturing Foundation Using Dual Global Engineering Model."

Section 2, "Expanding Japanese Automobile Uniform Quality and Production at Optimum Locations Through SCM Strategy in the World," includes Chapter 8, "Strategic Stratified Task Team Model for Innovating Business Process"; Chapter 9, "Total Quality Assurance Networking Model for New Defect Prevention Technique"; Chapter 10, "Partnering Performance Measurement Model for Automobile Assembly Makers and Suppliers"; and Chapter 11, "New Global Partnering Production Model for Expanding Overseas Manufacturing Strategy."

Section 3, "Development of Automobile Simultaneous QCD Fulfilment for Customer Value Creation," includes Chapter 12, "Strategic Quality Management: Performance Measurement Model for QCD Strategy"; Chapter 13, "Automobile Exterior Design Model Using Customer Science Principle"; Chapter 14, "Automobile Optimal Product Design Model: Application to Study on Bolt-Nut Loosening Mechanism"; Chapter 15, "Strategic Development of Automobile New Manufacturing Management Technology"; and Chapter 16, "Developing New Japan Marketing Management Model for Customer Creation."

Section 4, "Example Applications," includes Chapter 17, "Strategic Patent Value Appraisal Model: To Strengthen Corporate Technological Strategy"; Chapter 18, "Automobile Exterior Color Design Development Model: Partnering of Both Auto-Maker and Paint-Maker"; Chapter 19, "Robot Reliability Design and Improvement Method: Using Advanced TPS"; Chapter 20, "Body Auto Fitting Model (BAFM): Developing NJ-GPM"; Chapter 21, "Comparing Experienced and Inexperienced Machine Workers: Improving the Skills of Technicians"; Chapter 22, "CS and CL for Boosting Marketing Effectiveness: To Strengthen Japanese Auto-Dealerships"; Chapter 23, "Scientific Mixed Media Model Developing NJ-MMM: For Boosting Auto-Dealer Visits"; and Chapter 24, Conclusion.

Organization of the Book

In this book, the author presents the "Examining a New Automobile Global Manufacturing System (NAGMS)" aimed at the evolution of automobile manufacturing, and demonstrates its effectiveness.

Section 1 gives an overview of the "Examining a New Automobile Global Manufacturing System (NAGMS)" for the next generation of management technology-Surpassing JIT. NAGMS is the basis of automobile manufacturing fundamentals 21C accomplished by innovating the conventional JIT such as typical Toyota Production System named Japan Production System.

Firstly, Chapter 1 states the outline of NAGMS as the characteristic, aim and validity.

In Chapter 2, the author focuses on the "Today's Global Manufacturing Issues: Innovation of Manufacturing Fundamentals" and asserts the need for evolution in manufacturing in order to deal with the management issues currently facing Japanese manufacturers.

In Chapter 3, the author explains the "Foundation of Toyota Production System: JIT Fundamentals," which aims to create the "simultaneous realization of quality and productivity via a Lean System" and "process control and process improvement" through fundamentals and applications of Toyota Production System.

In Chapter 4, furthermore, the author explains the viewpoint of "Importance of Japan's Global Manufacturing Strategies 21C: Surpassing JIT" to realize best quality of Japanese manufacturing in a rapidly changing core-technologies and environment

In Chapter 5, therefore, the author shows the establishment of the "New Japan Model (NJM): New Corporate Management Principle" for the realization of surpassing JIT. NJM employing New JIT and Science TQM consists of the total linkage of Total Development System (TDS), Total Production System (TPS), Total Marketing System (TMS), Total Intelligence Management System (TIS) and Total Job Quality Management System (TJS). This model aims to realize an integrated form of a next-generation corporate management strategy by focusing product quality management strategy.

In Chapter 6, furthermore, the author shows the "Creation of New Japan Automobile Global Manufacturing Model (NJ-AGMM)" for the strengthening of Japan automobile corporate management. Specifically, to evolution of Japan automobile manufacturing foundation, NJ-AGMM consists of a structured "Integrated 5 hold-core system - Advanced TDS, TPS, TMS, TIS & TJS" for expanding "uniform quality worldwide and production at optimum locations".

In Chapter 7, to advance the evolution of Japan automobile manufacturing foundation, the author shows the "Evolution of Japan Automobile Manufacturing Foundation Using Dual Global Engineering Model" by possessing the "New Japan Global Production Model" (NJ-GPM) and "New Japan Global Manufacturing Model" (NJ-GMM) surpassing JIT.

To realize NAGMS, Section 2 gives typical case studies of "TDS, TPS, TMS, TIS, and TJS" as the "Expanding Japanese automobile uniform quality and production at optimum locations through SCM strategy in the world".

In Chapter 8, the author refers to the significance and validity of "Strategic Stratified Task Team Model" employing "Strategic Cooperative Creation Team" (SCCT). The validity of SSTTM is verified by successfully applying it to the technological problem "Automobile transaxle oil seal leakage" of development design bottlenecks at auto manufacturers

In Chapter 9, the author creates and verifies the "Total Quality Assurance Networking Model" for the new defect prevention for the new manufacturing management. This model focus on integrated quality assurance spanning different departments from design to production in automobile manufacturing companies and extending further to part manufacturers.

In Chapter 10, to realize the "Worldwide Uniform Quality and Simultaneous Production Launch," the author creates and verifies the effectiveness of "Partnering Performance Measurement Model" (PPMM) for automobile assembly makers and suppliers in order to reinforce Japanese-style partnering, or Japan Supply Chain Management.

In Chapter 11, to improve quality at leading manufacturers' overseas production, the author has established a "New Turkish Production System" employing strategic NJM (New Japan Model) in the Republic of Turkey. Recently, moreover, the author has developed the NGP-PM for expanding overseas manufacturing strategy.

Furthermore, Section 3 gives the "Development of Automobile Simultaneous QCD Fulfilment for Customer Value Creation" in order to develop NAGMS strategy.

In Chapter 12, the "Strategic Quality Management: Performance Measurement Model," SQM-PMM was established to enhance the key elements of successful for QCD strategy, and ensuring future management results through strategic manufacturing quality management. The validity of SQM-PMM was verified in Japan manufacturing companies.

In Chapter 13, the author has created and verified a "Automobile Exterior Design Model" using "Customer Science Principle". To strengthen automobile exterior design, AEDM contains the "Improvement of Design Business Process Methods for Automobile Profile Design", "Creation of Automobile Profile Design using "Psychographics" Approach Methods", and "Actual studies on Automobile Profile Design, Form and Color Matching Methods".

In Chapter 14, the author has established an "Automobile Optimal Product Design Model" as part of principle - based research aimed at the innovation of development design processes in the automotive industry. Using the combination of various experiments and CAE, this model's validity is verified with application to study on loosening mechanism of bolt-nut tightening and others as the auto-manufacturers' bottleneck in the world.

In Chapter 15, the author has created and verified the "Strategic Development of Automobile New Manufacturing Management" using typical dual technologies: (i) Creation of the "Working Value Evaluation Model" (WVEM) to improve the performance of labor, and (ii) Developing intelligence operators by employing the "Human Integrated Assist System" (HIA).

In Chapter 16, the author has created and verified the "New Japan Marketing Management Model" for customer creation in order to innovate in marketing process management by correctly identifying customer demands. Specifically, NJ-MMM innovates the Japan's auto-dealers' sales activities employing "Intelligent Customer Information Marketing Model" (ICIMM) for the evolution of market creating.

In addition, Section 4 demonstrates "Effectiveness of NAGMS" employing "Examples and Applications".

In Chapter 17, the author has created and verified the strategic "Patent Value Appraisal Model to Strengthen Corporate Technological Strategy." PVAM consists of several elements each for "inventive technique" and "patent right" in order to explain the indispensable elements of inventive technique and patent right for engineers' value creation at work (invention).

In Chapter 18, the author has created the "Automobile Exterior Color Design Development Model (AECD-DM): Partnering of Auto-Maker and Paint-Maker." Specifically, to affect purchasing customer behavior, the author has developed the AECD-DM to body color development at a specific company, and has obtained the given results.

In Chapter 19, the author has structured and developed the author has established the "Robot Reliability Design and Improvement Method (RRD-IM) Using Advanced TPS". This method has been implemented worldwide in an advanced car manufacturer Toyota, and has produced a better operating life cycle for industrial robots.

In Chapter 20, the author has established the "Body Auto Fitting Model (BAFM) Developing NJ-GPM (New Japan Global Production Model)". This model illustrates the development of the following three items: (1) panel fitting accuracy, (2) automatic bolt tightening, and (3) integration into flexible assembly line at an advanced car manufacturer Toyota.

In Chapter 21, the author has developed the "Comparing Experienced and Inexperienced Machine Workers: Improving the Skills of Technicians." This study aims to clarify the factors involved in improving the skills of technicians by conducting a comparison of experienced and inexperienced workers engaged in lathe work, using statistical science and electroencephalography (EEG).

In Chapter 22, the author has developed the "CS and CL for Boosting Marketing Effectiveness: To Strengthen Japanese Auto-Dealerships." Specifically, as an application example, the author focuses on the development and effectiveness for CS and CL (Customer Satisfaction and Customer Loyalty) describing "Video Unites Customer Behavior and Maker's Designing Intentions" (VUCKMIN) and "Total Direct Mail Management Model" (TDMM).

In Chapter 23, the author has constructed the "Scientific Mixed Media Model (SMMM) by Developing NJ-MMM (New Japan Marketing Management Model) for Boosting Automobile Dealer Visits" in order to realize the automobile market creation. At present, SMMM is applied to a dealership representing an advanced car manufacturer Toyota, where its effectiveness is verified.

Finally, Chapter 24 provides overall conclusion of the topics covered in this book.

Acknowledgment

This book is a complication of past studies, new scientific books and major academic journals, and explains the comprehensive theory and practices of the author's "New JIT, new management technology principle", "Toyota: Production System, Safety Analysis and Future Directions", "New Manufacturing Theory: Surpassing JIT", "Science TQM, new quality management principle" and "Science SQC, new quality control principle" which has been widely used and is evolving as Japan's new management technology principle.

The author would like to acknowledge the generous support of the following researchers: All those at Toyota Motor Corporation, Toyota group of 12 leading enterprises, many affiliated / nonaffiliated suppliers, Study group of the Ideal Situation the Quality Management of Manufacturing Industry in JUSE (Union of Japanese Scientists and Engineers) called Amasaka's Forum, "Study group of 68QCS-Questionnaire analysis team of Toyota Group" in JUSE, Interim Report of WG4's Studies Research on Simulation and SQC in JSQC (Japanese Society for Quality Control), Nagoya QC study group in JSA (Japanese Standards Association), and Amasaka's New JIT Laboratory in Aoyama Gakuin University that assisted with the research.

Especially, Mr. Nagaya, A., Dr. Sakai, H., Mr. Kishimoto, M., Miss. Matsubara, W. (Toyota Motor Corporation), Mr. Ootaki, M. (NOK Corporation), Mr. Misawa, N. (Aishin Chemical Co., Ltd.), Mr. Murayama, T. and Mr. Ando, Y. (Nippon Research Center), Mr. Asami, H., Mr. Ishikawa, A., Mr. Ishiguro, H., Mr. Koyama, H., Mr. Okutomi, H., Mr. Yanagisawa, K., Mr. Uchida, K., Mr. Ebioka, K., Mr. Hashimoto, K., Mr. Anabiki, K., Mr. Yoshioka, K., Mr. Yamaji, M., Mr. Tsunoi, M., Mr. Ogura, M., Mr. Sakalsiz, M. M., Miss. Yamazaki, M., Mr. Hifumi, S., Mr. Takebuchi, S., Mr. Toyoda, S., Mr. Shimura, T., Mr. Onodera, T., Mr. Sakatoku, T., Mr. Ito, T., Mr. Kozaki, T., Mr. Kojima, T., Mr. Ueno, T., Mr. Takahashi, T., Mr. Nomura, R., Mr. Nozawa, Y., Mr. Sakurai, Y. and Mr. Morita, Y. (Aoyama Gakuin University), and others.

Section 1

A New Automobile Global Manufacturing System

Chapter 1
Introduction

ABSTRACT

In this book, by predicting the form of next generation automobile manufacturing, the author examines a new automobile global manufacturing system (NAGMS) that contains the hardware system with five core elements—TDS, TPS, TMS, TIS, and TJS (total development system, total production system, total marketing system, total intelligence management system, and total job quality management system)—for transforming management technology into automobile management strategy—surpassing JIT.

INTRODUCTION

The increasing sophistication and diversification of customers' wants are needed for the development of global production, which acts in concert with the overseas deployment of production bases, a pressing management issue (Amasaka, 2002, 2004). A future successful global marketer must develop an excellent management technology system that impresses users and continuously provides excellent, quality products in a timely manner through strategic corporate management (Amasaka, 2007a, 2008a).

To succeed in global production, achieving worldwide uniform quality and simultaneous launch (production at optimal locations) is an urgent task. The simultaneous achievement of QCD requirements that reinforce the product appeal is required to realize this global production system (Amasaka, 2008b) (Refer to Chapter 2 in Part I).

The Japanese management technology that made the biggest impact on the world in the latter half of the 20th century was the Toyota Production System. It is often also referred to as to Just-in-Time (JIT) or Total Quality Management (TQM) (Ohno, 1977; Amasaka, 1988, 2002). As Toyota Production System became practiced as Lean System around the world and was further developed, it lost its status as a Japanese production system. In recent years, the superior quality of Japanese products has rapidly lost ground (Womack et al., 1990; Goto, 1999; Taylor and Brunt. 2001; Amasaka, 2002, 2004, 2007, 2008) (Refer to Chapter 3 in Part I).

To be successful in the near future, a global marketer must develop an excellent management technology that can impress customers and continuously provide high value products in a timely manner (Refer to Chapter 4 in Part I).

DOI: 10.4018/978-1-7998-8746-1.ch001

Against this background, in this book, by predicting the form of next generation automobile manufacturing, the author hereby examines a "New Automobile Global Manufacturing System" (NAGMS) that contains the hardware system with five core elements - "TDS, TPS, TMS, TIS and TJS" (Total Development System, Total Production System, Total Marketing System, Total Intelligence Management System and Total Job Quality Management System) for transforming management technology into automobile management strategy—Surpassing JIT (Amasaka, 2002, 2004, 2007a,b, 2008a,b, 2010). (Refer to Chapter 5 in Part I),

To realize automobile manufacturing that places top priority on customers with a good QCD, the author, therefore, a high linkage model "Advanced TDS, TPS, TMS, TIS and TJS" for expanding "uniform quality worldwide and production at optimum locations" (Amasaka, 2007c,d, 2012, 2013; Ebioka et al., 2007; Yamaji et al., 2007; Sakai and Amasaka, 2007a,b, 2008). (Refer to Chapter 6 in Part I).

The focus of this book is thus the theory and application of strategic management technology through the application of NAGMS for the "Evolution of Japan automobile manufacturing foundation" (Refer to Chapter 7 in Part I). As these results, developing of NAGMS has proved to be effective in actual implementations. Concretely, the author introduces the application examples through "Expanding Japanese automobile uniform quality and production at optimum locations through SCM strategy in the world" (Refer to Chapter 8 to 11 in Part II).

Moreover, through "Automobile simultaneous QCD fulfilment for customer value creation" with "Application examples", the validity of NAGMS is then verified at an advanced car manufacturer Toyota and others (Amasaka, Ed., 2012; Amasaka, 2014a,b, 2015, 2017, 2019) (Refer to Chapter 12 to 24 in Part III to IV).

REFERENCES

Amasaka, K. (1988). Concept and progress of Toyota Production System (Plenary Lecture). The Japan Society of Precision Engineering, Hachinohe Regional Advance Technology Promotion Center Foundation, Hachinohe, Aomori, Japan.

Amasaka, K. (2002). *New JIT*, a new management technology principle at Toyota. *International Journal of Production Economics*, *80*(2), 135–144. doi:10.1016/S0925-5273(02)00313-4

Amasaka, K. (2004). Development of Science TQM, a new principle of quality management: Effectiveness of Strategic Stratified Task Team at Toyota. *International Journal of Production Research*, *42*(17), 3691–3706. doi:10.1080/0020754042000203867

Amasaka, K. (2007a). New Japan Production Model, an Advanced Production Management Principle: Key to Strategic Implementation of New JIT. *The International Business & Economics Research Journal*, *6*(7), 67–79.

Amasaka, K. (2007b). The validity of "TDS-DTM", a strategic methodology of merchandise: Development of New JIT, Key to the excellence design "LEXUS". *The International Business & Economics Research Journal*, *6*(11), 105–115.

Amasaka, K. (2007c). High Linkage Model - Advanced TDS, TPS & TMS-Strategic development of New JIT at Toyota. *International Journal of Operations and Quantitative Management*, *13*(3), 101–121.

Amasaka, K. (2007c). The validity of Advanced TMS, a strategic development marketing system utilizing New JIT. *The International Business & Economics Research Journal*, *6*(8), 35–42.

Amasaka, K. (2007d). Highly Reliable CAE Model, The key to strategic development of Advanced TDS. *Journal of Advanced Manufacturing Systems*, *6*(2), 159–176. doi:10.1142/S0219686707000930

Amasaka, K. (2008a). Science TQM, a new quality management principle: The quality management strategy of Toyota. *The Journal of Management & Engineering Integration*, *1*(1), 7–22.

Amasaka, K. (2008b). Strategic QCD studies with affiliated and non-affiliated suppliers utilizing New JIT. Encyclopedia of Networked and Virtual Organizations, 3(PU-Z), 1516-1527.

Amasaka, K. (2010). Changes in marketing process management employing TMS: Establishment of Toyota Sales Marketing System, China-USA. *Business Review*, *10*(7), 539–550.

Amasaka, K. (2012). Constructing Optimal Design Approach Model: Application on the Advanced TDS. *Journal of Communication and Computer*, *9*(7), 774–786.

Amasaka, K. (Ed.). (2012). Science TQM, new quality management principle: The quality management strategy of Toyota. Bentham Science Publishers.

Amasaka, K. (2013). *The strategic development of Advanced TPS based on the New Manufacturing Theory* (Plenary Lecture). The 1st WSEAS International Conference on Industrial and Manufacturing Technologies, Vouliagmeni, Greece.

Amasaka, K. (2014a). New JIT, new management technology principle. *Journal of Advanced Manufacturing Systems*, *13*(3), 197–222. doi:10.1142/S0219686714500127

Amasaka, K. (2014b). New JIT, new management technology principle: Surpassing JIT. *Journal of Procedia Technology*, *16*(special issues), 1135–1145. doi:10.1016/j.protcy.2014.10.128

Amasaka, K. (2015). *New JIT, new management technology principle*. CRC Press.

Amasaka, K. (2017). *Toyota: Production System, Safety Analysis, and Future Directions*. NOVA Science Publishers.

Amasaka, K. (2019). Studies on New Manufacturing Theory, *Noble. International Journal of Scientific Research*, *3*(1), 1–20.

Ebioka, K., Sakai, H., Yamaji, M., & Amasaka, K. (2007). A New Global Partnering Production Model "NGP-PM" utilizing Advanced TPS. *Journal of Business & Economics Research*, *5*(9), 1–8.

Goto, T. (1999). *Forgotten Management Origin*. Seisansei-shuppan.

Ohno, T. (1977). *Toyota Production System*. Diamond-Sha.

Sakai, H., & Amasaka, K. (2007a). The Robot Reliability Design and Improvement Method and the Advanced Toyota Production System. *Industrial Robot: International Journal and Service Robotics.*, *34*(4), 310–316. doi:10.1108/01439910710749636

Sakai, H., & Amasaka, K. (2007b). Human Intelligence Diagnosis Method utilizing Advanced TPS. *Journal of Advanced Manufacturing Systems*, *6*(1), 77–95. doi:10.1142/S0219686707000905

Sakai, H., & Amasaka, K. (2008). Demonstrative verification study for the Next Generation Production Model: Application of the Advanced Toyota Production System. *Journal of Advanced Manufacturing Systems*, *7*(2), 195–219. doi:10.1142/S0219686708001577

Taylor, D., & Brunt, D. (2001). *Manufacturing operations and supply chain management–The lean approach*. Thomson Leaning.

Womack, J. P., Jones, D., & Roos, D. (1990). *The machine that change the world – The story of Lean Production*. Rawson.

Yamaji, M., Sakai, H., & Amasaka, K. (2007). Evolution of technology and skill in production workplaces utilizing Advanced TPS. *Journal of Business & Economics Research*, *5*(6), 61–68.

Chapter 2
Today's Global Manufacturing Issues:
Innovation of Manufacturing Fundamentals

ABSTRACT

Global manufacturing is currently facing major transformations. First is the shortened life cycle of products due to the diversification and sophistication of customers' needs. Because of this, the manufacturers need to realize the shortest lead time possible in cooperation with their suppliers from the product development stage, through to manufacturing, and finally to sales, so that they are able to respond to this change. Second, it is essential to create a new corporate management technology necessary for the deployment of global production, worldwide uniform quality, and simultaneous production and to manage such production in a systematic and organized manner. Based on this, the author believes it necessary to establish a new management technology toward innovation of manufacturing fundamentals for all the business processes of each department from upstream to downstream.

INTRODUCTION

The leading Japanese management technology that contributed most to worldwide manufacturing from the second half of the 20th century was the "Japanese Production System". This is typified by the "Toyota Production System" (TPS) (Ohno, 1977; Totota Motor Corp., 1987; Amasaka, 1988, 2002, 2006). This system has been further developed as production systems called "Just in Time" (JIT) and Lean System (Hayes and Wheelwright, 1984; Roos, et al., 1990; Womack, et al., 1991; Womack and Jones, 1994). The Japanese manufacturing represented by TPS constitutes the basis for the manufacturing carried out today worldwide (Refer to Chapter 3 in detail).

Conventional Japanese manufacturing has developed from in-house production to cooperative relationships with suppliers (parts manufacturers), but since the beginning of the 21st century, the production bases have shifted from domestic to overseas sites and the management technology has become increasingly complicated (Amasaka, 2004c, 2008a).

DOI: 10.4018/978-1-7998-8746-1.ch002

The current task of today's manufacturing is to succeed in global production. A key to this is the deployment of supply chain management on a global scale that encompasses cooperative business operations, even with overseas suppliers, and the ever growing necessity for the systemization of such operation methods (Amasaka, 2000, 2004a,b, 2008a,b).

In particular, during the implementation stage the parallel use of partnering, Supply Chain Management (SCM), and digital engineering will become necessary as they are essential for the deployment of the main components of JIT, namely, TPS and Total Quality Management (TQM). Therefore, in-depth study of the kind of management technology that will be effective even for next-generation business operations is urgently needed as well. To realize this, specifically, the author believes it necessary to establish a new management technology toward "Innovation of manufacturing fundamentals" for all the business processes of each department from upstream to downstream (Amasaka, 2008b, 2009a).

On a concrete target, first is the shortened life cycle of products due to the diversification and sophistication of customers' needs (Amasaka, 2005; Amasaka Ed., 2007; Amasaka et al., 2008). Because of this, the manufacturers need to realize the shortest lead time possible in cooperation with their suppliers from the product development stage, through to manufacturing, and finally to sales, so that they are able to respond to this change (Amasaka, 2003, 2004c, 2005). Moreover, second, it is essential to create a new corporate management technology necessary for the deployment of global production, worldwide uniform quality, and simultaneous production and to manage such production in a systematic and organized manner (Amasaka, 2007a,b,c,e, 2014)

MANUFACTURING SHIFTING TO GLOBAL PRODUCTION

Advanced companies in the world, including Japan are shifting to global production to realize *uniform quality worldwide and production at optimum locations* for survival in fierce competition. To attain successful global production, technical administration, production control, purchasing control, sales administration, information system, and other administrative departments should maintain close cooperation with clerical and indirect departments while establishing strategic cooperative and creative business linkages with individual development, production and sales departments, and outside manufacturers (suppliers) (Amasaka, 2007a).

Today, consumers have quick access to the latest information in the worldwide market thanks to the development of Information Technology (IT), and strategic organizational management of the production control department has become increasingly important. Simultaneous attainment of quality, cost and delivery (QCD) requirements is the most important mission for developing highly reliable new products ahead of competitors (Amasaka, 2004a,b, 2005, 2008a,b).

This requires the urgent establishment of an innovative production control system for the next generation (called next-generation production control system). With a view to assuring that future management technology is a new leap forward for Japanese manufacturing, the progress of production control of plants in the manufacturing industry made so far by the manufacturing industry is summarized in Figure 1 (Amasaka, 2004a; Amasaka et al., 2008).

In the figure, the basis of the major production control methodologies, such as industrial engineering (IE), operations research, quality control, management of administration, marketing research, production control, and IT, are plotted along the vertical axis. Along the horizontal axis, some of the key elemental technologies, management methods, scientific methodologies, and so on are mapped out in a time series.

Since the beginning of the century, the operation of manufactures has shifted from domestic production in Japan to overseas production bases, and management technology has become increasingly complicated, as depicted in Figure 1.

Figure 1. Progress of management technology in the manufacturing industry

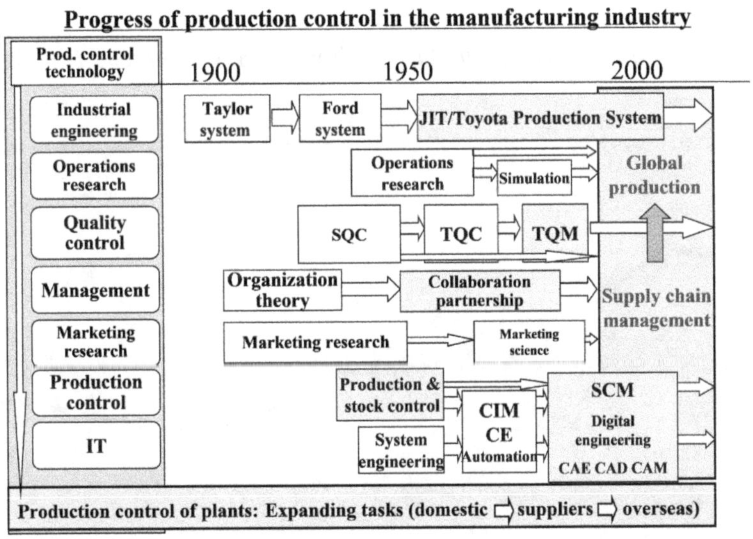

For the production control department, the key to success in global production is modeling strategic SCM for domestic and overseas suppliers with a systematization of its management methods. In the implementation stage, deep-plowing studies of the TPS called JIT, TQM, partnering (collaboration/ partnership), and digital engineering will be needed in the future (Amasaka, 2009).

IS JAPANESE MANUFACTURING ALL RIGHT?

A straightforward look at the recent management activities of Japanese manufacturers reveals a series of quality-related recalls that were totally unexpected by the top corporations in the industry and increasing delays in technological development that may even threaten the survival of these manufacturers (Nihon Keizai Shinbun, 1999, 2000, 2001, 2002, 2006: Nihon Sangyou Shinbun 2000a,b).

In recent years, both developed Western nations and developing nations have advanced the study of Japanese TPS and TQM and re-acknowledged the importance of the "quality" of administrative management technology. They have also promoted the reinforcement of "quality" in manufacturing on a national level. As a result of such efforts, the "superiority in quality" of Japanese products has been gradually compromised.

One distinctive example of this is shown in Figure 2., a comparison of the "quality of automobiles" sold in the United States. Although Toyota, a leading Japanese car manufacturer, can be seen to have achieved steady improvements in the quality of its automobiles (IQS, Initial Quality Study) up to now,

GM of the United States and Hyundai of Korea have also promoted quality improvements and achieved even more dramatic results (Gabor, 1990; Joiner, 1994; Nezu, 1995; JD Power, 2009).

The observations above indicate that in order for Japanese manufacturers to continue to play the leading role in the world, it is urgent to reform their management technology from a fresh standpoint, rather than simply clinging to the successful experiences they have enjoyed up to now (Amasaka, 2002, 2014; 2005, Yamaji and Amasaka, 2009; Sakai and Amasaka, 2013).

Figure 2. The comparative examples of automobile quality in U.S.A (Source: J.D Power and Associates)

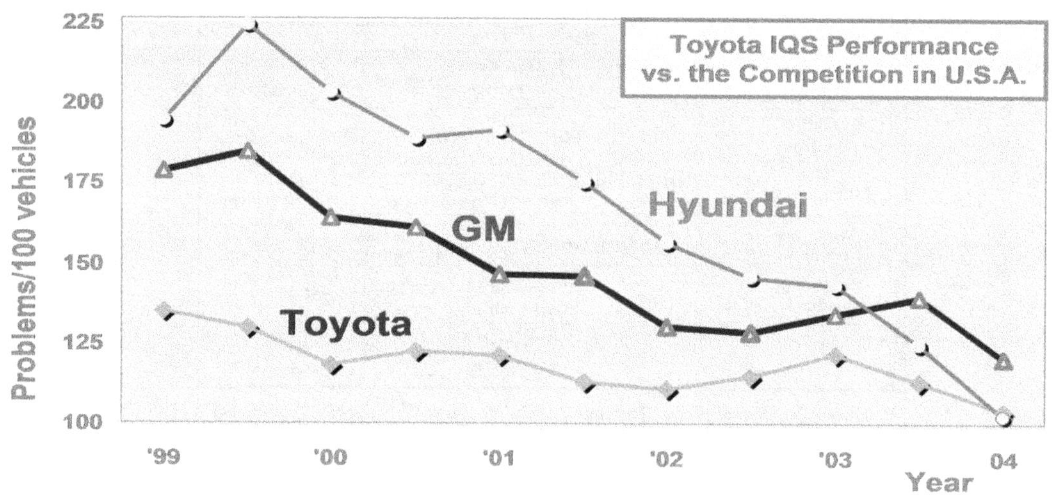

INNOVATION OF MANUFACTURING FUNDAMENTALS

Management Tasks for the Manufacturing Industry

The environmental changes that surround today's manufacturing industry are truly severe. The customers strictly judge the reliability of the manufacturer according to the reliability (quality and value gained from use) of their products (Amasaka, 1999). Therefore, for Japanese manufacturers to be successful and survive in the future marketplace, they must carry out global marketing that will focus on customers worldwide and then be able to quickly offer high quality products of the latest model that are designed to enhance the value to the customer (Amasaka, 2004a,b).

They need to precisely grasp the customers' preferences and advance their "manufacturing" so that it can respond to the demands of the times or they will be eliminated from the world market. In order to prevail in today's manufacturing industry, which is often referred to as a worldwide quality competition, the pressing management issue is to realize the kind of global production that can achieve the so-called "worldwide uniform quality and simultaneous production (production at optimal locations)". It is not an exaggeration to say that what will ensure Japanese manufacturers' success in global marketing is the realization of "competitive manufacturing – the simultaneous achievement of QCD" ahead of their competitors in an effort to offer high value-added products (Amasaka, 2006, 2008a; Amasaka Ed., 2007).

In the midst of the drastic changes taking place at the manufacturing site due to the use of "digital engineering", it is imperative not to fall behind in the advancement of administrative management technology that is so vital to manufacturing. The urgent mission for Japanese manufacturers is to reconstruct world-leading, uniquely Japanese "principles of management technology" and "administrative management technology", which will be viable even for next-generation manufacturing (Amasaka, 2004b, Amasaka et al., 2008).

To accomplish this, it will be vital for such management-related departments as technology management, production management, sales management, and information technology, which collectively comprise the core of corporate management, not only to cooperate closely with general affairs-related departments, such as personnel affairs, total planning, TQM promotion, and overseas business, but also to strategically collaborate with the on-site departments responsible for engineering, production and sales, as well as cooperate with their suppliers (Amasaka, 2000, 2004a,b, 2006).

Needs for the Reform of Japanese-Style Management Technology

The top priority issue of the industrial field today is the "new deployment of global marketing" for surviving the era of "global quality competition" (Kotler, 1999; Amasaka, 2004b).

The pressing management issue particularly for Japanese manufacturers to survive in the global market is the "uniform quality worldwide and production at optimum locations" which is the prerequisite for successful global production. To realize manufacturing that places top priority on customers with a good QCD and in a rapidly changing technical environment, it is important to develop a new production technology principle and establish new process management principles to enable global production (Amasaka, 2006, 2009; Amasaka et al., 2008).

Furthermore, a new quality management technology principle linked with overall activities for higher work process quality in all divisions is necessary for an enterprise to survive (Burke and Trahant, 2000; Amasaka, 2004b). The creation of attractive products requires each of the sales, engineering/design, and production departments to be able to carry out management that forms linkages throughout the whole organization (Seuring et al., 2003; Amasaka, 2004a).

From this point of view, the reform of Japanese-style management technology is desired once again. In this need for improvements, Toyota is no exception (Goto, 1999; Amasaka, 2004a,b). IT development has led to a market environment where customers can promptly acquire the latest information from around the world with ease. In this age, customers select products that meet their lifestyle and have a sense of value on the basis of a value standard that justifies the cost.

Thus the concept of "Quality" has expanded from being product quality, which is oriented to business quality, to becoming corporate management quality-oriented. Customers are strict in demanding the reliability of enterprises through the utility values (quality, reliability) of their products (Amasaka, 1999; Evans and Dean, 2003).

Advanced companies in countries all over the world, including Japan, are shifting to global production. The purpose of global production is to realize "uniform quality worldwide and production at optimum locations" in order to ensure company's survival amidst fierce competition (Doz and Hamel, 1998; Amasaka, 2004a,b).

For the manufacturing industry, the key to success in global production is systematizing its management methods when modeling strategic SCM for its domestic and overseas suppliers. In-depth studies of the Toyota Production System called *JIT* and Lean Production System (Ohno, 1977; Roos et al. 1994; Taylor, D., and Brunt, D. 2001; Amasaka, 2002),

TQM, partnering, and digital engineering will be needed when these methods are implemented in the future. Above all, manufacturers endeavoring to become global companies are required to collaborate not only with affiliated companies, but also with non-affiliated companies to achieve harmonious coexistence among them based on cooperation and competition. In other words, a so-called "federation of companies" is needed (Hamel and Prahalad, 1994; Amasaka, 2000, 2004a,b,c).

Innovation of Automobile Manufacturing Fundamentals

Based on this knowledge obtained above, therefore, the author believes it necessary to establish a new management technology toward "Innovation of manufacturing fundamentals" for all the business processes of each department from upstream to downstream as follows (Amasaka, Ed., 2007, 2012; Amasaka et al., 2008; Amasaka, 2015);

First is the shortened life cycle of products due to the diversification and sophistication of customers' needs. Because of this, the manufacturers need to realize the shortest lead time possible in cooperation with their suppliers from the product development stage, through to manufacturing, and finally to sales, so that they are able to respond to this change.

Second, it is essential to create a new corporate management technology necessary for the deployment of global production, worldwide uniform quality, and simultaneous production and to manage such production in a systematic and organized manner.

CONCLUSION

It is essential to realize manufacturing that gives top priority on customers with a good QCD and in a rapidly changing technical environment. Therefore, the author believes it necessary to establish a new management technology toward "Innovation of manufacturing fundamentals" for improving in the reliability of all the business processes from the upstream to downstream.

Then, in this book, the author perceives the "Importance of Japan's global manufacturing strategies 21C: Surpassing JIT", and verifies as the "Creation of New Japan Automobile Global Manufacturing Model and its validity" through the "Establishment of New Japan Model" (Amasaka, Ed., 2007, 2012, 2019; Amasaka et al., 2008; Amasaka, 2015, 2017, 2022).

REFERENCES

Amasaka, K. (1988). Concept and Progress of Toyota Production System (Plenary Lecture). Co-sponsorship: The Japan Society of Precision Engineering, The Japan Society for Technology of Plasticity, The Japan Society for Design & Drafting and Hachinohe Regional Advance Technology Promotion Center Foundation, Hachinohe, Aomori, Japan.

Amasaka, K. (1999). The TQM responsibilities for industrial management in Japan - The research of actual TQM activities for business management. *The Japanese Society for Production Management, The 10st Annual Technical Conference,* 48-54.

Amasaka, K. (2000). Partnering chains as the platform for Quality Management in Toyota. *Proceedings of the 1st World Conference on Production and Operations Management,* 1-13.

Amasaka, K. (2002). New JIT, a new management technology principle at Toyota. *International Journal of Production Economics, 80*(2), 135–144. doi:10.1016/S0925-5273(02)00313-4

Amasaka, K. (2003), A "Dual Total Task Management Team" involving both Toyota and NOK - A cooperative team approach for reliability improvement of transaxle. *Proceedings of the Group Technology / Cellular Manufacturing World Symposium,* 265-270.

Amasaka, K. (2004a). *The past, present, future of production management* (Keynote lecture). The Japan Society for Production Management, The 20th Annual Technical Conference, Nagoya Technical College, Nagoya, Aichi, Japan.

Amasaka, K. (2004b). Development of "Science TQM", A new principle of quality management: Effectiveness of Strategic Stratified Task Team at Toyota. *International Journal of Production Research, 42*(17), 3691–3706. doi:10.1080/0020754042000203867

Amasaka, K. (2004c), Strategic Quality Management and its new development for SCM: Example of Collaborative Task Team of Toyota and NOK.*Supply Chain Management; Theory and Practice of Cooperation between companies in Kuroda,* 79-109.

Amasaka, K. (2005). Constructing a Customer Science Application System "CS-CIANS"- Development of a global strategic vehicle "Lexus" utilizing New JIT. *WSEAS Transactions on Business and Economics, 2*(3), 135–142.

Amasaka, K. (2006). Development of New JIT, new management technology principle, Production Management. *Transaction of the Japan Society for Production Management, 13*(1), 143–150.

Amasaka, K. (Ed.). (2007). New Japan Model: Science TQM – Theory and practice for strategic quality management. Study group of the ideal situation the quality management of the manufacturing industry, Maruzen, Tokyo, Japan.

Amasaka, K. (2007a). High linkage model "Advanced TDS, TPS & TMS"-Strategic development of "New JIT" at Toyota. *International Journal of Operations and Quantitative Management, 13*(3), 101–121.

Amasaka, K. (2007b). The Validity of Advanced TMS, A strategic development marketing system utilizing New JIT. *International Business and Economics Research Journal, 6*(8), 35–42.

Amasaka, K. (2007c). The validity of "TDS-DTM", a strategic methodology of merchandise - Development of New JIT, Key to the excellence design "LEXUS". *International Business and Economics Research Journal, 6*(11), 105–115.

Amasaka, K. (2007e). New Japan Production Model, An Advanced Production Management Principle: Key to Strategic Implementation of New JIT. *The International Business & Economics Research Journal., 6*(7), 67–79.

Amasaka, K. (2008a). Strategic QCD studies with affiliated and non-affiliated suppliers utilizing New JIT. Encyclopedia of Networked and Virtual Organizations, 3(PU-Z), 1516-1527.

Amasaka, K. (2008b). Science TQM, A New Quality Management Principle: The Quality Management Strategy of Toyota. *The Journal of Management and Engineering Integration*, *1*(1), 7–22.

Amasaka, K. (2009). *New JIT, advanced management technology principle: The global management strategy of Toyota* (Invitation lecture). *International Conference on Intelligent Manufacturing and Logistics System, and Symposium on Group Technology and Cellular Manufacturing*, Kiitakyushu, Japan.

Amasaka, K. (Ed.). (2012). Science TQM, New Quality Management Principle: The quality management strategy of Toyota. Bentham Science Publishers.

Amasaka, K. (2014). New JIT, New Management Technology Principle: Surpassing JIT. *Journal of Procedia Technology*, *16*(Special Issues), 1135–1145. doi:10.1016/j.protcy.2014.10.128

Amasaka, K. (2015). New JIT, New Management Technology Principle. Taylor and Francis Group.

Amasaka, K. (2017). *Toyota: Production system, safety analysis and future directions*. Nova Science Publishers.

Amasaka, K. (Ed.). (2019). *Fundamentals for the management principle of manufacturing industries*. Sankei-Sha.

Amasaka, K. (2022). New Manufacturing Theory: Surpassing JIT (2nd ed.). Lambert Academic Publishing.

Amasaka, K., Kurosu, S., & Morita, M. (2008). *New Manufacturing Theory: Surpassing JIT-Evolution of Jusst In Time*. Morikita-Shuppan.

Burke, W., & Trahant, W. (2000). *Business climate shift*. Butterworth Heinemann.

Doz, Y. L., & Hamel, G. (1998). *Alliance advantage*. Harvard Business School Press, Boston.

Evans, J. R., & Dean, J. W. (2003). Total quality management, organization and strategy. Thomson, South-Western.

Gabor, A. (1990). *The Man Who Discovered Quality; How W. Edwards Deming Brought the Quality Revolution to America- The Stories of Ford, Xerox, and GM*. Random House, Inc.

Goto, T. (1999). *Forgotten origin of management–Management quality taught by G.H.Q, CSS management lecture*. Productivity Publications.

Hamel, G., & Prahalad, C. K. (1994). *Competing for the future*. Harvard Business School Press.

Hayes, R. H., & Wheelwright, S. C. (1984). *Restoring Our Competitive Edge: Competing Through Manufacturing*. Wiley.

Joinr, B. L. (1994). *Fourth generation management: The new business consciousness. Joiner Associates, Inc.*

Kotler, F. (1999). *Kotler Marketing*. The Free Press.

Nezu, K. (1995). *The scenario of the U.S. manufacturing industry: Remarkable progress aimed at by CALS*. Kogyo Chosakai.

Ohno, T. (1977). *Toyota Production System*. Diamond-sha.

PowerJD. (2009). http;//jdpower.com/

Roos, D., Womack, J. P., & Jones, D. (1990). *The Machine that Change the World – The Story of Lean Production*. Rawson.

Sakai, H., & Amasaka, K. (2013). Highly Reliable Production System for Expanding Global Production: Total Linkage of Planning, Preparation and Production. *International Journal of Operations and Quantitative Management*, *19*(3), 157–168.

Seuring, S., Muller, M., Goldbach, M., & Schneidewind, U. (Eds.). (2003). *Strategy and Organization in Supply Chains*. Physica-Verlag, Heiderberg.

Shimbun, A. (2005). *The manufacturing industry-Skill tradition feels uneasy*. Academic Press.

Taylor, D., & Brunt, D. (2001). Manufacturing Operations and Supply Chain Management - The Lean Approach. Thomson Leaning.

Toyota Motor Corporation. (1987). *The Toyota Production System and a Glossary of Special Teams at Production Job – Site at Toyota*. Toyota.

Womack, J. P., & Jones, D. (1994). *From Lean Production to the Lean Enterprise*. Harvard Business Review.

Womack, J. P., Roos, D., & Jones, D. T. (1991). *The machine that changed the World -The story of lean production*. Rawson.

Yamaji, M., & Amasaka, K. (2009). Strategic Productivity Improvement Model for white-collar Workers Employing Science TQM. *The Journal of Japanese Operations Management and Strategy*, *1*(1), 30–43.

Chapter 3
Foundation of the Toyota Production System:
JIT Fundamentals

ABSTRACT

The Japan production technology principle that contributed most to the world in the latter half of the 20th century was the Japanese-style production system typified by the Toyota Production System named Just in Time (JIT) and Lean System. The Toyota Production System aimed to improve product quality while pursuing maximum efficiency through the application of total quality management (TQM) into the manufacturing process, as well as applying the principle of cost reduction. In this chapter, the author introduces the core concept, basic philosophy, and development of the Toyota Production System of the manufacturing management in Toyota.

CORE CONCEPT OF TOYOTA PRODUCTION SYSTEM

In this section, JIT fundamentals that reformed the automobile manufacturing of Toyota are discussed. The basic principles and on-site implementation of manufacturing using the Toyota Production System, which has been adopted as a core concept of the world's manufacturing, will be illustrated here (Amasaka, Kurosu and Morita, 2008).

What is known as the JIT system, a Japanese production system typified by the Toyota Production System, is a manufacturing system that was developed by the Toyota Motor Corporation (Ohno, 1977; Toyota Motor Corporation, 1987). The basic philosophy of Toyota Production System is built upon the ideas of the company founder, Sakichi Toyoda, and his business mottos, (1) Be ahead of the times through endless creativity, inquisitiveness, and the pursuit of perfection, (2) A product should never be sold unless it has been carefully manufactured and has been tested thoroughly and satisfactorily. The philosophy also reflects Kiichiro Toyoda's ideas of improvement through inspection, (1) Grasp the demands of consumers firsthand and reflect them in your product, and (2) Investigate the product quality and business operations and then improve them.

DOI: 10.4018/978-1-7998-8746-1.ch003

These are the basic concepts of JIT which aims to realize "quality and productivity" simultaneously by effectively applying TQC (Total Quality Control) and TQM to the automobile manufacturing process. It also pursues maximum efficiency (optimal streamlining, which is called a Lean System) while also being conscious of the principles of cost reduction, and thereby improving the overall product quality (Ohno, 1977: Toyota Motor Corporation, 1987: Amasaka, 1988, 2002a). In JIT implementation stage, it is important to constantly respond to the customers' needs, promote flawless production activities, and conduct timely Quality, Cost and Delivery (QCD) research, as well as put it into practice (Amasaka, 2002a, 2008a). Therefore, Toyota has positioned Toyota Production System and TQM as the core management technologies for realizing "reasonable manufacturing" and these management technologies are often likened to being the wheels of an automobile (Amasaka, 1989, 1999a, 2000, 2002a: Hayashi and Amasaka, 1990). In Figure 1, these management technologies have been placed on the vertical and horizontal axes. As shown in the figure, the combination of these technologies reduces large irregularities in manufacturing to the state of "tiny ripples" where the average values are consistently improved in the process.

This strategy is an approach used by reasonable corporate management in which the so-called "leaning process" is consistently carried out. As indicated by the vertical and horizontal axes in the figure, when the hardware technology of the Toyota Production System and software technology of TQM (TQC) are implemented, the statistical quality control (SQC) is to be effectively incorporated to scientifically promote QCD research and achieve constant upgrading of the manufacturing quality (Amasaka, 2008b). The Aim of Toyota Production System is to create a highly functional production system that offers better products at lower prices more quickly through the timely application of QCD activities for strengthening Value Engineering (VR) using Value Analysis (VA) (Amasaka, 1988, 2009a). Another point is that TQM and SQC are the foundations of maintaining and improving the manufacturing quality, and both have also historically served as a basis for the advancement of JIT (Amasaka, 2003, 2004a).

In this way, the basic concept of JIT and the lean system approach have reformed the automobile manufacturing process used at Toyota. As a result of the JIT effectiveness has been recognized on a worldwide scale and it is now regarded as the "core concept of manufacturing" (Hayes and Wheelwright, 1984: Roos, et al., 1990: Womack and Jones, 1994: Taylor and Brunt, 2001).

BASIC PHILOSOPHY OF TOYOTA PRODUCTION SYSTEM

Simultaneous Realization of Quality and Productivity via a Lean System

The basic principle of manufacturing via the TPS (1) is lean system production. As shown in Figure 2. In this system manufacturing is conducted via *one-by-one* (single part) *production* and its aim is to achieve is the simultaneous realization of quality and productivity (Amasaka, 1988,

The first basic principle of manufacturing is thorough quality control by means of one-by-one production. As Figure 2(a) illustrates, this system of one-by-one production on a manufacturing line using an assembly conveyor gives the assembly worker the ability to conduct a self-check on each piece. If a defective item comes to their assembly point from the previous process, they can then stop the conveyor and detect the defect without fail. Therefore, the assembly workers can provide 100% quality products to the downstream processes. It is obvious that compared to lot production, this system can considerably improve the detection of from a probabilistic viewpoint. In this context, the one-by-one production is

Figure 1. Relationship between Toyota Production System and Total Quality Management

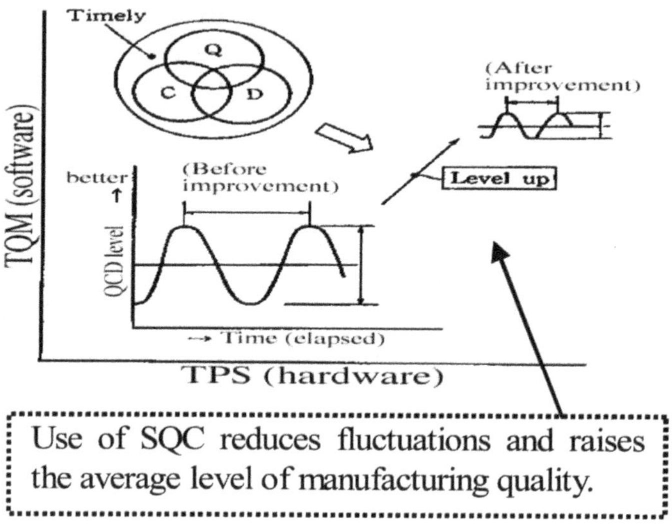

sometimes compared to a fine, quick, and pure flow of water upstream in a mountain stream, while lot production is likened to the broad, stagnant and slow water found downstream. The incorporation by the TPS of this one-by-one production deserves to be recognized as Lean System production.

The second basic principle of manufacturing is the thorough incorporation of quality into the process via one-by-one production. *One-by-one production* in a machining process is shown in Figure 2(b). The diagram illustrates an operation where a worker picks up a piece (work) from the parts box, conducts the machining process operation on it from processes #01-processes #04 in the order shown, and finally places the completed piece into the completed parts box.

Since the production operation is conducted according to a predetermined cycle time, the worker can consistently carry out the prepared standard operation in a rhythmical manner. Similar to the previous case of operation on an assembly conveyor, a self-check can be consistently performed and the incorporation of quality is ensured so that the stabilization of production can also be promoted.

Even in the case of a production operation that involves multiple types of work pieces, the intelligent application of production engineering and process designing can be used to support workers and allow them to conduct the standard operations in a rhythmical manner. A process like this is depicted in Figure 3(1). A process like this is depicted in Figure 3(2)., where the zigzag work flow interferes with the smooth performance of the standard operations each time a work piece changes. This causes the worker to become fatigued and triggers human errors, thus resulting in the lowering of quality and productivity.

Fundamentals of Toyota Production System

In this sub-section, the author shows the examples of fundamentals of Toyota Production System to actual strengthen the manufacturing management of Toyota, as follows;

(1) The aim of TPS, (2) Sale price and cost, (3) Manufacturing methods and costs, (4) Heijyunka (Levelled Production), (5) Standardized Work, (6) Standardized Work Chart, (7) Standardized Work Combination Table, (8) Working Sequence and Operation standards, (9) The exclusion of "Muda" (Non-

Value Added), (10) Examples of Production Lead Time, (11) True Efficiency and Apparent Efficiency, (12) The flow of the product and the information, (13) Examples of "Kanban", (14) Examples of "Andon", and (15) "Kaizen" (improvement) activities - Kaizen is eternity and infinity (Refer to the "Concept and progress of Toyota Production System" and "The basic principles of JIT" (Amasaka, 1988, 2000).

Figure 2. The basic principle of manufacturing via the Toyota Production System (1) - The simultaneous realization of quality and productivity

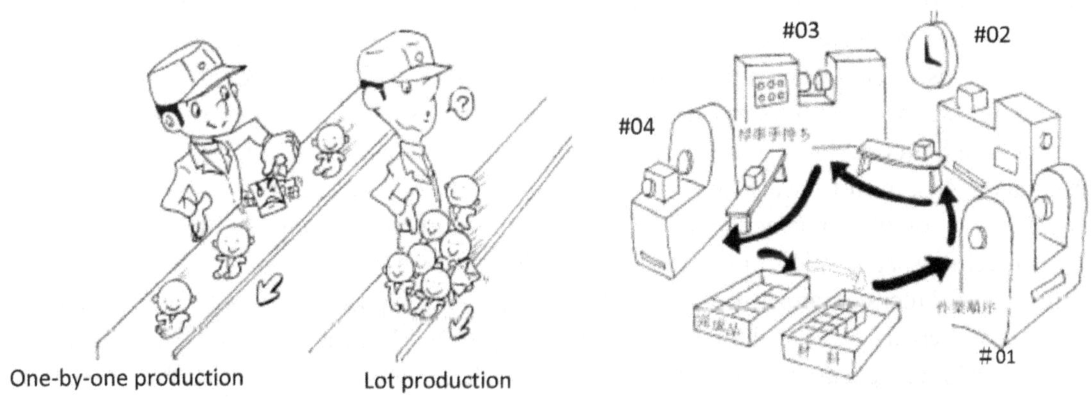

(a) Thorough quality control by means of one-by-one production

(b) Thorough incorporation of quality into the process via one-by-one production

Figure 3. The basic principle of manufacturing via the Toyota Production System (2) - The simultaneous realization of quality and productivity

Good and bad examples of work sequencing

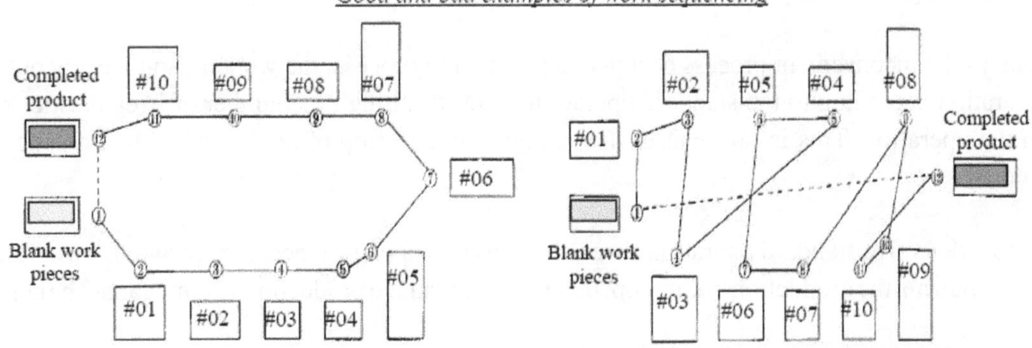

(1) Easy process of standard work

(2) Difficult process of standard work

Process Control and Process Improvement

The high productivity and high quality of manufacturing in Japan today are universally acknowledged (Toyota Motor Corp., 1987; Amasaka, 2000). At manufacturing sites, the process control and process improvement, mainly promoted by production workers under the supervision of their supervisors, and the QCD research, conducted by white-collar engineers, are equally valued in order to ensure the incorporation of design quality, which is demanded by customers (Amasaka, 1988, 2000, 2002b, 2008a, 2009b; Amasaka and Sakai, 2010).

Process Control and Process Improvement

Consideration is given here to the method of manufacturing an automobile and the resulting manufacturing cost (initial cost) and profit based on Figure 4. The main parts (heavy material parts) that compose an automobile are the skeletal structure, made up of the body and frame, and the parts that control the running functions, such as the engine and axles. These parts are made of steel plates and cast forged steel. Automobile manufacturers procure these materials from steel manufacturers. Parts such as tires, engine ignition batteries, brake units, power steering units, and a wide variety of other parts such as windshields, lights, mirrors, seats, and so on are purchased from specialized parts manufacturers.

In order to produce a complete automobile, the manufacturer also purchases a variety of machining tools for processing parts, welding machines for the body and frame, and assembling robots for assembling the vehicle, and other equipment from specialized machine or equipment manufacturers. Finally, the electric power needed to operate these machines and equipment is bought from power supply companies. Generally speaking, the manufacturing costs listed above that are borne by the automobile manufacturer do not differ very much from those of other manufacturers.

The labor cost (workers' wages) is also similar among manufacturers. Therefore, the manufacturing cost (initial cost) shown on the left half of the figure for automobiles of a similar design does not vary greatly from manufacturer to manufacturer. On the other hand, the right half of the figure shows the manufacturing cost that results from the method of manufacturing the vehicle at the production site, and this can very widely depend on how each manufacturer handles their manufacturing process control and process improvement.

The following are some poor cases of process control.

1. Due to the inconvenient process design and production process, the worker cannot carry out their operation according to the standard operation sheet, resulting in a number of irregularities result in the operation. This in turn causes the assembly line to stop often, lowering the line operating rate.

Due to a defective standard operation sheet, the worker's operation becomes strained, wasteful, and irregular, requiring the production line to stop: therefore the planned production volume cannot be ensured.

2. Due to insufficient maintenance and upkeep of the machines and equipment, malfunctions occur, lowering the equipment operating (availability) rate.
3. Although the production line is not operating during the break time, the production equipment's power is still on, resulting in wasteful power consumption.
4. Due to inadequate instructions from the supervisor or insufficient education and training provided to new workers regarding manual (skill required) operation or handling of machines, quality defects result from operation errors or improper machine manipulation. This causes pieces with machining defects, which entails their disposal or reworking of these pieces.

Figure 4. Manufacturing methods and costs

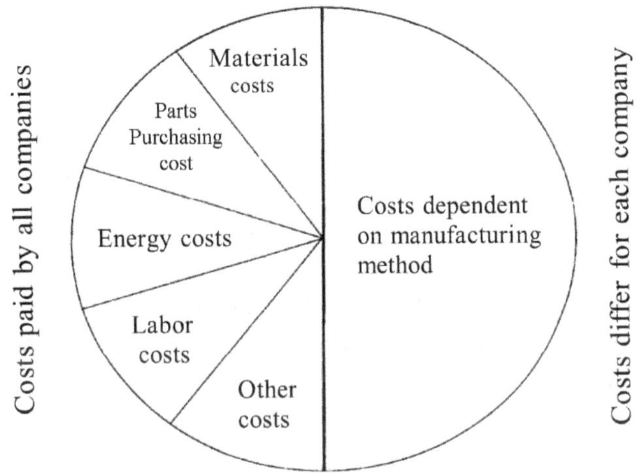

5. Due to a lot of waste materials (scrap for disposal) during the stamping process or excessive cutting processing that causes the blade to be damaged, the processing line has to be stopped or defective work pieces result. This increases the cost of replacing the stamping process blades.

For these and other reasons, the manufacturing cost can exceed the expected cost, and the profit rate per vehicle that was initially calculated can also decline substantially. Cases such as these should not be neglected, and the process control at the production site needs to be thoroughly reviewed. Process improvement and preventive measures need to be thoroughly reviewed. Process improvement and preventive measures need to be devised and implemented through ingenuity, and original suggestions should be obtained via the full participation of all the on-site staff.

If the efforts of the production site staff alone do not make progress, then the cooperation of the engineering staff from related departments should be obtained to thoroughly implement process improvements. The ultimate objective is to reduce the manufacturing costs and improve the profit rate. The accumulation of a variety of process improvements at the production site can also conserve resources, resulting in lower material cost, parts purchasing cost, and energy consumption (items on the left side of Figure 3). In turn, this will all lead to reduction in the number of quality defects and an improvement in the line operating rate. Furthermore, unnecessary labor cost can be eliminated by reducing excessive overtime work, and the manufacturing cost can be further improved.

In addition, continuous efforts to improve process control and process improvement will enhance the skills and motivation of the production workers and contribute greatly to the strengthening of the work environment and work culture at the production site.

Daily Control Activities at the Production Site

Daily control activities at the production site make a large difference in the level of finished quality and productivity. For this reason, the third basic principle of manufacturing is a thorough and continuous effort to employ daily control activities through cooperation between the supervisors and workers on the production site (Amasaka, 1988, 2000, 2007a).

The basic elements needed for daily control activities at the production site are the maintenance and improvement of what are called the four Ms: material, machine, man, and method (Amasaka, 2007). In the implementation stage of daily control activities, it is vital to organize work standards and thoroughly implement standard operations by using the check sheets, such as the standard operation sheet, important quality check sheet, worker process designation list, and new worker operation sheet. These are designed to help ensure quality and productivity. Setting up reminder boards designed to remind workers about major quality defects in the past is also an effective preventive measure (Amasaka and Kamio, 1985). In addition, an important quality control activity for ensuring manufacturing quality is the simultaneous confirmation of quality and incorporation of quality through utilization of control charts via a scientific process control method (Amasaka and Yamada, 1991).

Another factor that is vital to stably incorporate quality into the process is the control of conditions at the production facility. Condition controls take the following forms: (1) Condition controls for bolt tightening on the assembly line will indicate the operating pressure of air tools or the type of lubricating oil to be used. In the case of (2) Condition controls for the machining process line will be used to ensure the position and standard operation of quenching tempering equipment (visual control). Through daily control activities such as these, the reliability and maintainability of the production facility can be ensured, as well as the incorporation of quality (process capability (Cp) and machine capability (Cm)) and productivity by using a control chart (Amasaka, Ed., 2003).

Daily Improvement Activities at the Production Site

The fourth basic principle of manufacturing is daily improvement activities at the production site. The basis for simultaneous realization of quality and productivity via the Toyota Production System is improvement of the work environment to prevent errors, improvement of control through visual confirmation, and so on. These improvements are designed to help the workers to maintain their standard operations in a rhythmical flow. Concerted efforts are made to make small improvements that do not incur a large expense, such as safe work procedures, prioritizing quality, quickening the pace of work by one second, and so on (Amasaka and Kamio, 1985).

The main facilitators of these daily improvement activities are the workers themselves, who carry them out through small group activities, mainly in the form of QC Circles or through their own voluntary originality and ingenuity. In the implementation stage, activities such as having an improvement team support the production site or promoting greater cooperation between the supervisors and production staff are put into practice (Amasaka, 1999, 2003).

One characteristic example of such "daily improvement activities" is a process improvement that achieves work operations that are less tiring. Similarly, the second example is a process improvement made to an inconvenient work operation. As demonstrated by these daily improvement examples, carrying out process improvements on a daily basis gives the workers themselves the opportunity to develop more convenient work processes, make their work operations safer, and also ensure that quality is being incorporated. At the same time, redundant work processes can also be removed (Amasaka and Yamada, 1991).

Innovation of Production Process: QCD Research Activities by White-Collar Staff

The fifth basic principle of manufacturing that is capable of quickly responding to the stringent demands of today's customers is the innovation of the production process and advancements in manufacturing that result from the QCD research activities conducted by white-collar staff (Amasaka and Kamio, 1985; Amasaka and Yamada, 1991; Amasaka, 2002b, 2009a; Amasaka, Ed., 2003; Amasaka and Sakai, 2010).

First, the fundamental principle of Toyota Production System is to manufacture only what can be sold, when it can be sold, in the quantity that can be sold. To accomplish this, it is essential to establish a flexible production system that will produce and transport only what is needed, when it is needed, in the quantity that is needed, as a rational production measure. Second, as a production mechanism that will realize the conditions listed above, it is important to incorporate production leveling, shortening of the production lead time, and a pull system into the process planning and design. Third, with a view to reasonably carrying out the above, it is vital to always use signboards, facilitate small branch conveyance to raise precision, promote the flow of the production process, determine the tact time according to the needed volume, and then strictly adhere to these measures. Fourth, it is imperative to reinforce the capabilities of the production site and to advance Toyota Production System production by actively developing new production technologies that will solve the bottleneck technological problems in production and substantially improve the quality and productivity of the production site.

Having said the above, the following is an explanation of a small part of a QCD research activity that was promoted by the white-collar engineering staff (or engineers and managers responsible for manufacturing technology, production engineering development, process planning, process designing, and production management) that contributed to innovation of the production process. Figure 5 shows an example of a process improvement for a layout that facilitates the incorporation of quality by implementing a countermeasure for the *outlying island* called *Hanare Kojima* layout (Amasaka and Kamio, 1985). Before the improvement – *Kaizen*, as seen in the left of Figure 5(a), the six workers at the automatic table conveyor are separated from one another by the five parts feeders that supply the parts to the assembling machines (the five automated machines, marked as A–E) located at each of the preceding processes.

This process arrangement is the *outlying island* (*Hanare Kojima)* layout and when there is quality trouble or a small stop of the assembling machines, it is difficult for an expert worker (skilled worker) to provide instruction (assistance) to a newly assigned worker. In addition, each worker's standard operation time differs due to the variation in experience. Therefore, an expert worker is forced to wait for work from a new worker (creating wasted time), since their operation time is shorter than that of newly assigned workers. Moreover, in the case of a production line with this outlying island layout, the takt time cannot be set according to the fluctuations (increase and decrease) in production volume because the takt time is fixed according to the operation time of the workers. Therefore, the takt time cannot be changed in a flexible manner according to the number of workers.

Given this background, the engineering staff (white-collar engineers) reviewed the production line where the workers' manual operations and automated machining processes are combined, so that they could reform the production process. As seen in Figure 5(b), after the improvements - "*Kaizen*" were made, the automated machining processes were consolidated. In an effort to create a continuous processing operation from A to B to C, as well as from D to E, the set positions of the work pieces were changed and the processing jigs were altered. The parts feeders that supply the same parts were also integrated so that the number of parts feeders could be reduced from five to three. These improvement

Figure 5. Example of a production layout that facilities built-in quality by eliminating isolated worksites

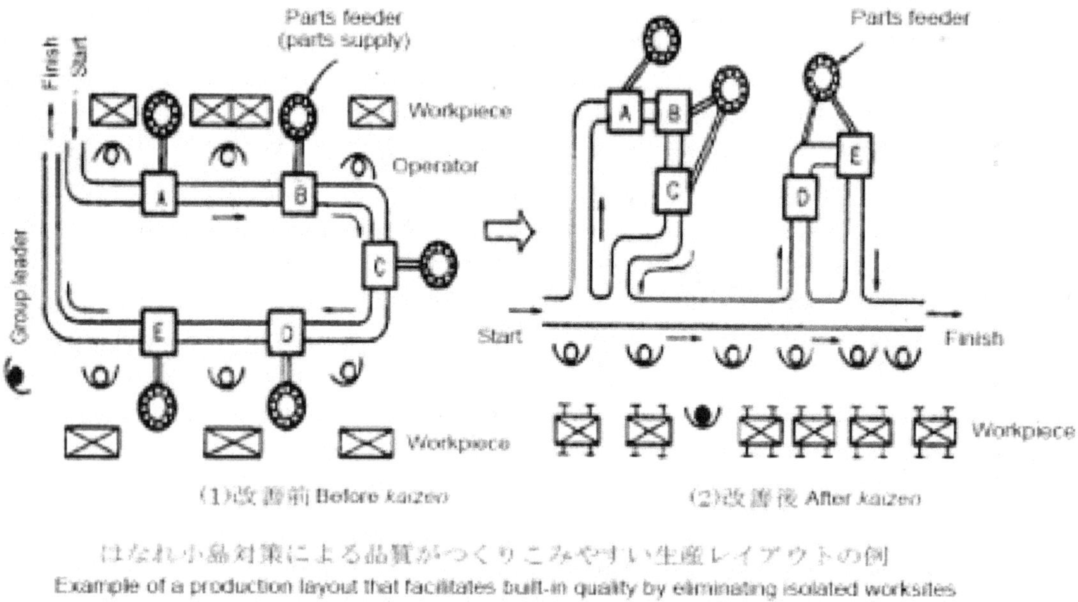

measures rearranged the automatic table conveyor into a single line and the old work layout that had separated the workers was discarded.

The above case is a characteristic example of a process improvement that realized flexible production that could react to fluctuations in production volume; it resulted in improvements in the line operating rate and stabilized the production quality. This all effectively contributes to meeting the QCD requirements. These improvement measures promoted (i) mutual confirmation between the workers on work progress; (ii) mutual assistance in case of any delay in work operation; (iii) observance of simultaneous confirmation of quality; (iv) improvement in the efficiency of material transport; (v) the ability to respond to the increase or decrease in the number of workers according to the changing production volume; (vi) the ability of supervisors to respond to short stops of the automated processing line outside of their own production line, to supply parts to the parts feeders, to provide work instructions and assistance to line workers, and to create greater efficiency in the replacement work between completed work pieces and materials, and so on. Below are a few examples of process improvements that have helped solve human errors. In recent years, it has become increasingly important to improve product quality in response to an increase in customers' sensitivity to quality;

The first example describes the efforts made to achieve high quality assurance for shock absorbers, a main part of the unit axle. Usually, the inspection to ensure the finished quality of assembled parts was dependent on the personal experience of the inspectors and their visual senses. Judgment of the *Lissajous waveforms* indicating the damping force characteristics (damping force and up-and-down strokes), which are displayed in rotation on the X-Y coordinates of an oscilloscope, is a difficult inspection process. It often induced human error and misjudgments, even when performed by expert workers. In addition, it was time-consuming to find where on the work piece (product) the problem was or to conduct a disassembly investigation, fault diagnosis, and correction. This was a problem that could not be solved easily. Then, the engineering staff and production site staff cooperated and developed an automatic diagnosis inspection device. This device simultaneously conducts a quantitative evaluation of the quality into what had been a bottleneck problem in this inspection process (Amasaka and Saito, 1983; Amasaka and Kamio, 1985).

The second example is of an improvement made to help solve unforced errors such as wrong or missing parts and misassembled pieces. Generally, automobile production involves manufacturing various models and, therefore, it is necessary for the vehicle or parts assembly line workers to conduct *parts assembly* while being alert to wrong or missing parts and mistaken assembly. As a process improvement measure to reduce these sorts of errors, IT was used to assist in accurately sorting out the work pieces on the assembly conveyor. In this system, production instructions, electronic signboards, and radio-frequency identification tags (IC tags) are used to detect the types of work pieces. Then it lights up the assembly parts shelf that corresponds to the intended work pieces and uses sensors and visualization equipment to match the work operation with the proper work pieces (Amasaka and Kamio, 1985).

The third example is the identification of work-piece types using this IT. Until now, the parts unit signboards were visually confirmed, and the unit numbers were written down manually, but this repeatedly resulted in human errors such as misidentification or mistaken descriptions. After the process improvement was carried out, a bar-code signboard-reading device was developed and the unit code was automatically identified. An automatic marking device that prints out the intended code on the work-piece surface was also developed, and these devices solved the human error-based problems in this process (Amasaka, and Kamio, 1985).

These examples of process improvement are the results of QCD research activities carried out through cooperation between the white-collar and production site workers or supervisors in an effort to solve the inconvenient work operations from the standpoint of human behavioral science.

DEVELOPMENT OF TOYOTA PRODUCTION SYSTEM

Application to Simultaneous Achievement of QCD

To realize manufacturing that places top priority on customers with good QCD in a rapidly changing the technical environment, it is essential to create a new manufacturing technology in order to reform super-short-term development production (Amasaka, 2008a). Furthermore, a new quality management technology linked with overall activities for higher work process quality in all divisions and SCM strategy is necessary for an enterprise to survive (Amasaka, 1988, 2000, 2004ab, 2008ab; Burke et al., 2000; Roger and Flynn, 2001; David and David, 2001).

Therefore, the author illustrates the foundation and effectiveness of applications of Toyota Production System (Amasaka, 2008a). This is based on effort to attain simultaneous achievement of QCD through innovative of manufacturing technology by having cooperation between on-site white-collar engineers and supervisors and workers with affiliated and non-affiliated suppliers. In these examples, the author has proved the effectiveness on development of Toyota Production System through innovation of the production line of automobile suspension and chassis parts.

ACTUAL HIGH QUALITY MANUFACTURING THROUGH INNOVATION OF MANUCTURING

Technology

In order to prevail in the worldwide quality competition and be successful in global production–worldwide uniform quality and simultaneous production launch (production at optimal locations), manufacturing with high quality assurance has to be realized at the manufacturing site (Amasaka, et al., 2008; Amasaka, 2009a, 2014).

Cooperation between On-Site Manufacturing Staff and White-Collar Engineers

The foundation for advancing TPS is based on efforts to attain simultaneous acheivement of QCD through inovation of manufacturing technology (Amasaka, 2008a). This in turn is accomplished by having on-site manufacturing (engineering) staff carry out innovation at the manufacturing site, as well as having white-collar engineers lead the innovation and improvement of the manufacturing technolgy (Amasaka, 2002, 2003, 2004ab, 2007b, 2008a; Amasaka and Yamada, 1991; Amasaka, et al., 2008). All this is done wth the aim of conducting manufacturing with high quality assurance.

Firstly, some of the features of Toyota Production System are the improvement of laborious work operations and the creation of a safe, worker-friendly manufacturing site in which the supervisors and workers take the initiative, while the manufacturing technology staff members (white-collar engineers) also cooperate. Through such a process, the improvement of daily management and maintenance can be reinforced, which realizes rhythmical and smooth work operations, thus enabling reliable manufacturing (ensuring the process capability (Cp) and machine capability (Cm)).

Secondly, Toyota Production System takes on the challenge of simultaneous achievement of QCD through innovation of manufacturing technology. In this case the initiative is taken by the white-collar engineers, while the supervisors and workers on the manufacturing site cooperate. This effort has contributed to drastically improve the manufacturing technology (for the working environment, production equipment, production management, production technology, quality management technology, etc.), which has been a bottleneck obstacle of the manufacturing site.

In the implementation stage, the innovations mentioned above are to be carried out by a Strategic Total Task Management Team led by the on-site manufacturing technical staff and production engineering development staff and production engineering development staff, while production designing and research development staff and even suppliers (parts manufacturers, production equipment, and machinery manufacturers, etc.) also participate (Amasaka, 2004c).

By means of these activities, wide-ranging business processes from the suppliers to the vehicle manufacturers can be linked in a highly efficient manner, and therefore manufacturing can be conducted while advancing Toyota Production System, enabling JIT production. Below is an example of the simultaneous achievement of QCD through innovation of manufacturing technology. In this example, innovation of the production line producing suspension and chassis-related parts for automobiles in Toyota's plant will be presented.

It will demonstrate an example of solving a bottleneck manufacturing technology problem that was inhibiting JIT production. (Amasaka, 1983, 1986; Amasaka, et al., 1982, 1988ab, 1990; Amasaka and Yamada, 1991).

Innovation of the Production Line of Auto-Suspension and Chassis Parts

In this example, innovation of the production line producing rear axle unit-related parts for automobiles in "Toyota's machining div. of Motomachi plant, will be presented (Amasaka, 1983, 1984ab, 1985, 1986, 1988, 1999b; Amasaka and Saito, 1983; Amasaka and Kamio, 1985; Amasaka and Sugawara, 1988; Amasaka and Yamada, 1991; Amasaka and Ishida. 1991; Amasaka and Yasuda, 1998; Amasaka, et al., 1982, 1988ab, 1990, 1993). It will demonstrate an example of solving a bottleneck manufacturing technology problem that was inhibiting JIT production.

1. Outline of the production process of the rear axle unit

A rear axle unit for an automobile underbody is manufactured in order of a production process that includes a welding process, machining process and assembly process based on TPS. These are performed in order by means of JIT production called *Tatenagashi production* at Toyota. This process is generally referred to as a lean production (production of one piece at a time) system.

After assembly is complete, the assembled rear axle unit is further combined together with various other products via a method called the *Jyunbiki or Jyunjyo hikitori* (sequential parts withdrawal system) and then it is taken to a vehicle assembly plant via the pull system production method. Figure 6 illustrates the machining and assembling process of a rear axle unit manufactured by a typical Toyota Production System (The previous process of welding is omitted here).

The main characteristic of Toyota Production System is to carry out production without keeping any excess parts in stock. Therefore, in this process, it is necessary to conduct assembly in an orderly manner according to the assembly sequence from the start of the conveyor driven assembly process (5) to the latter process in the vehicle assembly plant. This is done by utilizing an intra-process instruction *Kanban* called *Shikake Kanban* (Production instruction *Kanban*) that clearly indicates the order of the processes in coordination with the downstream pull system processes.

The main component parts of this product, namely the rear axle housing and rear axle tube, come in a wide variety of different types that are delivered from parts manufacturing suppliers. Both parts are put together through friction welding and are subjected to machining before being supplied to the beginning of the assembly process. Similarly, the various types of rear axle shaft delivered from a designated supplier are subjected to machining and then supplied to the beginning of the assembly conveyor.

For both products, what is required is synchronized production called *Douki-ka production* (Synchronized production), where finished processed parts of the needed types are supplied in a timely, JIT fashion to the head of the assembly conveyor, while minimizing the amount of intra-process parts and the number of finished products kept in inventory to the greatest extent possible.

As for the rear axle housing, after a variety of brackets are welded onto it mainly by CO_2 arc welding machines (involving a mixture of manual, exclusively automated, and robot welding processes), the finishing process is applied on a one-by-one (or unit-by-unit) basis via a transfer machine (1) in the downstream machining process.

The rear axle shaft is also subjected to machining one at a time (2 shafts per unit) according to the production sequence table. In the intermediate process for this part, (2) high frequency hardening, (3) tempering (4) stress relief, and other operations are conducted. As can be seen above, it is not easy to carry out synchronized production of either of these machined parts as they require a long lead time and there can be a large quantity of in-process inventory.

Moreover, what make these synchronized productions even more difficult are the considerable differences in the operation availability of each of the processes of machining and assembly. Generally, the operation availability of the assembly process is relatively high, but the previous machining process has low operation availability due to bottleneck problems and other reasons.

Similarly, the operation availability of the welding process is even lower as it requires the nozzles to be cleaned of weld spatters, the replacement of worn out welding tips, and so on. As discussed, the production line for the rear axle units is arranged in a one-unit-at-a-time production manner from welding, to machining, to assembly. Therefore, *Douki-ka production* is not easy, particularly in the case where in-process inventory is not held in each process or between processes.

2. Before process improvement–bottleneck-like manufacturing technical problems that inhibit JIT

In addition to the above, in each of the processes of machining, and assembly, bottleneck-like manufacturing technical problems that inhibit JIT exist, and these have not been solved for a long time as follows;

a. Bottleneck problems in the welding process for rear axle housing

The bottleneck problem of this process involves welding quality defects caused by forgotten welding operations, blow holes in welded areas, core deviation of the welding beads, and so on. In addition, these defects subsequently lower the operation availability due to discontinuation of equipment operation (Amasaka, 1988; Amasaka and Sugawara, 1988; Amasaka and Yasuda, 1998). In the CO_2 arc welding process, periodic cleaning is conducted to remove the weld spatter that sticks to the inner surface of the welding nozzle used for gas-shielding the welded areas as shown in Figure 7(a). Also, regular replacement is required to avoid causing welding core deviation, which is caused by wear on the inner surface of the welding tip that feeds to the welding wire. As a result, as indicated in Figure 7(b) the operation availability of the arc robot or automated welding equipment can be lower than that of the machining process or assembly process in the downstream processes.

Consequently, inventory of half-processed or finished products is kept within the welding process as shown in Figure 7. This bottleneck situation prevents production that is synchronized with the downstream assembly process (5) and has not been solved, so it has remained as a pending technical issue.

b. Bottleneck technology in the machining process for rear axle shaft

The bottleneck problems in this process are ensuring manufacturing quality and energy conservation, as well as the technical hindrances that prevent synchronized production. (Amasaka, et al., 1982; Amasaka, 1983).

As Figure 6 suggests, the upstream process of machining (#010-#030) and the downstream process conducted manually by production operators (#070-#170) are separated by the large-size, automated high frequency quenching equipment (#040) (2) and heat circulating-type tempering equipment (#050) (3), which consume a large amount of power and have a large amount of in-process inventory. For this reason, these processes are left like "remote islands" as it were. As a result, the one-operator work operations in the upstream process (#010-#030) require assistance from the supervisor in order to accommodate any extra cycle time in the case where the number of production units per day is increased. On the other hand, the operators are in standby mode when production volume per day is small.

Figure 6. Rear axle unit processes proceeding to assembly (before and after kaizen)

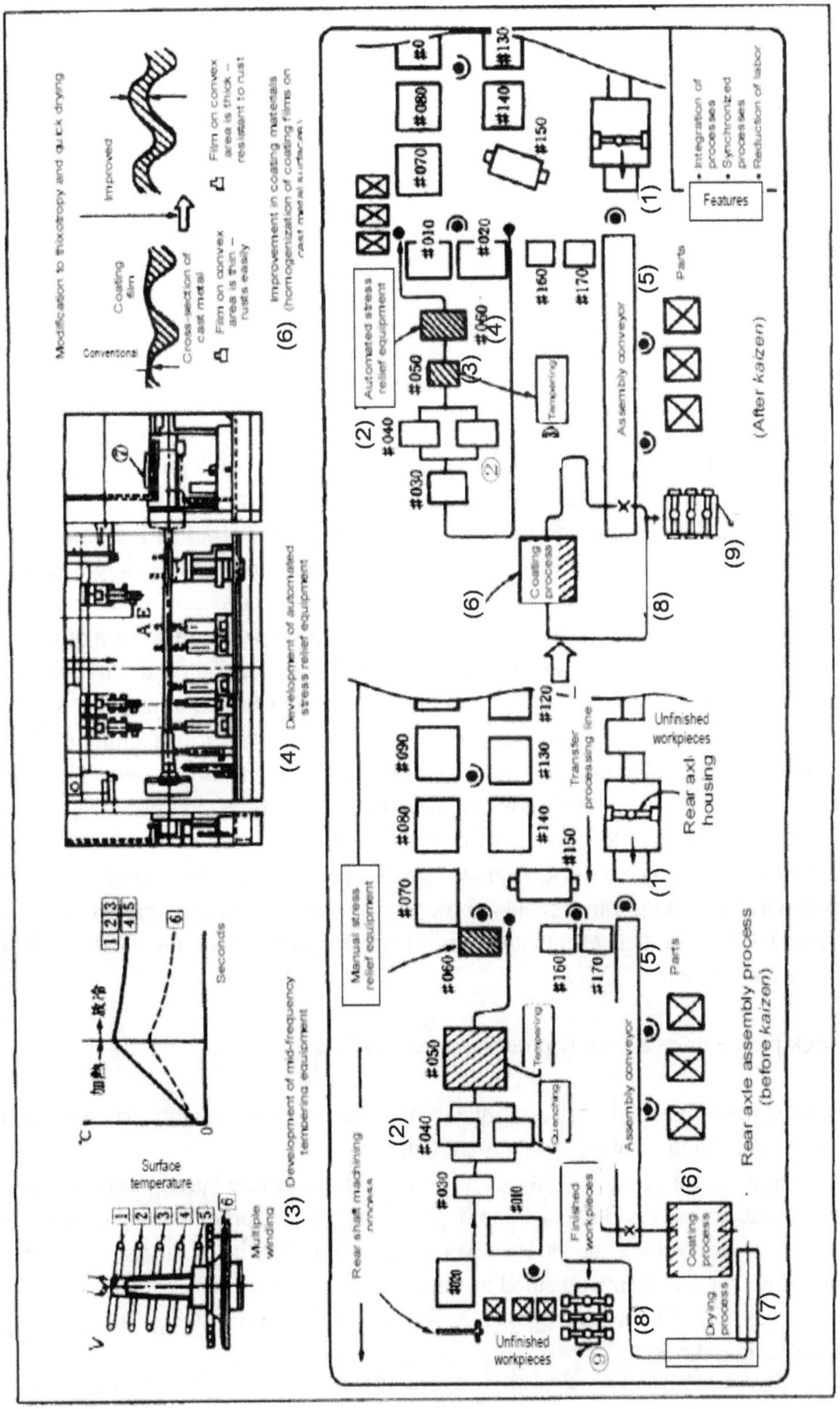

Figure 7. CO_2 gas shielded arc welding

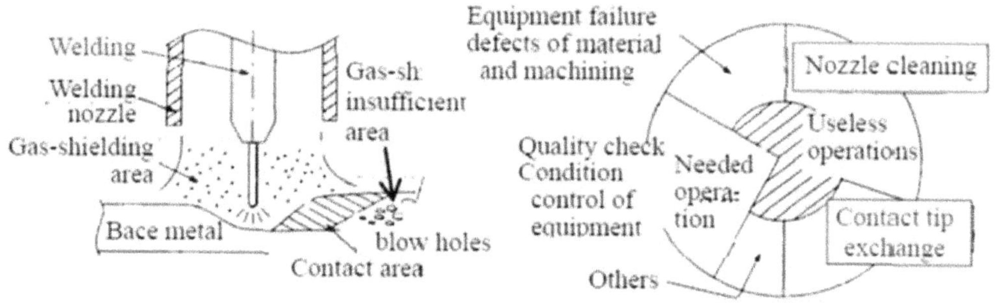

(a) Blow holes in welded areas (b) Lower factors of operation availability

In addition, the operation of manual stress relief equipment (marked as #060) is dependent on the emprical skills and abilities of expert production operators. The long work pieces (rear axle shafts) supplied from the upstream process (quenching and tempering equipment, #040-#050) have a stress profile of complicated spirals after heat treatment. Also, in cases where the required heat stress adjustment is large, the number of adjustment operations (time needed for adjustment) becomes larger, resulting in extra cycle time. When a production operator is overburdened and conducts excessive adjustment operations in order to avoid the above situation, cracks can be induced inside or on the surface of these long work pieces. Moreover, if the operator has not acquired sufficient skills, this can result in human error and a supply of defective long work pieces that do not satisfy the standard stress adjustment specifications to the downstream processes (#070-#170). This will then cause a number of machining process defects.

As discussed above, many problems such as defective quality, *Hanare Kojima* (Isolated jobsites) work area arrangement, wasteful power consumption, extra cycle time, and in-process inventory have not been solved, presenting bottleneck manufacturing technical problems. Due to this situation, half-processed or finished products are stuck within the processes as inventory and synchronized production in coordination with the downstream assembly process (5) cannot be realized, particularly in the case of the welding process. This bottleneck situation has not yet been solved and this prevents the realization of simultaneous achievement of QCD.

c. Bottleneck problems in assembly process for rear axle units

The bottleneck problems of this process range from ensuring product quality, to energy conservation, to production response to the downstream pull system.

The market requires that the quality of rust proofing of manufactured products be assured. The steel surface of a rear axle housing is flat and smooth. Therefore, the rustproof coating thickness can be ensured with (6) automated coating robots. However, the rustproof quality of the uneven areas on the cast metal surface cannot be sufficiently ensured as the coating on convex surfaces tends to be thinner due to the characteristics of the coating being used, as shown in (6) of Figure 3.6 (in the upper right corner) (Amasaka, 1986; Amasaka, et al., 1990).

To avoid such uneven coating, extra coating operations are conducted to ensure sufficient thickness, and these results in a higher coating cost. Furthermore, after the coating operation indicated by (6) in the figure, the work pieces are passed through the electric heater-type drying machine (7), which requires considerable power consumption, and are then cooled down to room temperature in the cooling process area. After this, the finished products are unloaded to the pull system cart (9). For this reason, excessive inventory remains on the overhead conveyor (8), and therefore, as in the cases of the upstream welding and machining processes, this process presents a hindrance to the realization of simultaneous achievement of QCD.

3. After process improvement–Simultaneous achievement of QCD by innovation of manufacturing technology

In order to solve the above mentione bottleneck problems of this production line, it is necessary to innovate the manufacturing technology. Given this background, The authors decided to take a systematic approach to the improvement of the fundamental process by taking into consideration the timing of production of a forthcoming new vehicle model (Amasaka and Kamio, 1985; Amasaka and Yamada, 1991; Amasak and Sugawara, 1988).

Before this plan was implemented, Amasaka (2004b, 2008) formed a Strategic Total Task Management Team led by the technical staff on the manufacturing site, as well as the production engineering development staff. The production development staff, parts manufacturers (affiliated and non-affiliated suppliers), and equipment machine manufacturers also participated, and the authors attempted to realize the simultaneous achievement of QCD with revolutionary approaches such as those introduced as follows;

a. Solution of bottleneck problems related to welding process for rear axle housing:

First solution is the resolving Issues of human error–Development of a weld bead coloration method. In this welding process, a lot of welding operations are conducted on large piece parts or brackets, which are important safety-related parts. For the purpose of solving problems related to human error, such as forgotten welding areas or missed welding defects during the visual inspection, development efforts were made in cooperation with several suppliers who deliver weld wire and a colored bead welding method was established. The conventional combination of black colored workpieces (without deoxidization treatment) and black weld bead was improved and changed by devising a method to add color to the weld bead (such as white, yellow, pink, etc.) and thereby this problem was solved (Amasaka, 1988; Amasaka, et al., 1988ab).

Furthermore, second solution is the improvement in operation availability and stabilization of quality –applying new ceramic materials to the welding nozzle and welding tip. The conventional welding nozzle has been made of a copper base alloy (Cr-Cu alloy), and therefore welding spatter can easily get stuck on it. Similarly, the welding tip is also made of copper base alloy, and therefore its inner surface, where the welding wire passes through, can quickly become worn out and welding spatter can get stuck to this tip area. In either case, periodic cleaning and replacement are frequently needed and when there is considerable adhesion of welding spatter, it can cause continuous quality defects, requiring the equipment to be stopped.

Given this background, the author and others collaborated separately with Noritake and Toshiba Tungaloy to improve the operation availability and assure the quality stability of the welding process. The author focused on the high strength wear resistance and heat resistance characteristics of new ceramics technologies in an effort to solve the above problems associated with the welding process.

As shown in Figure 8, for the lengthening the welding tip wear life by improving its surface, the conventional Cr-Cu alloy welding tip (Substrate (A) in the figure) has been improved to Zr-Cr-Cu alloy materials (Substrate (B)). Next, the authors developed a surface improvement technology, New Ceramics, that employed CVD (chemical vapor deposition) or PVD (physical vapor deposition) to the entire surface layer of the welding tip, as well as developed these manufacturing methods. Moreover, efforts were also put into improving technology by developing a variety of ceramic coating methods to be used as intermediate layers for a thick coating treatment that used plasma spraying (as indicated (C)-(G)in the figure).

These improvement measures increased the wear life by about a dozen times and the operation availability was also improved as expected. More recently, development of conductive ceramics substrates has also been promoted.

Figure 8. Improvement of the wear life of welding tip by new ceramics films

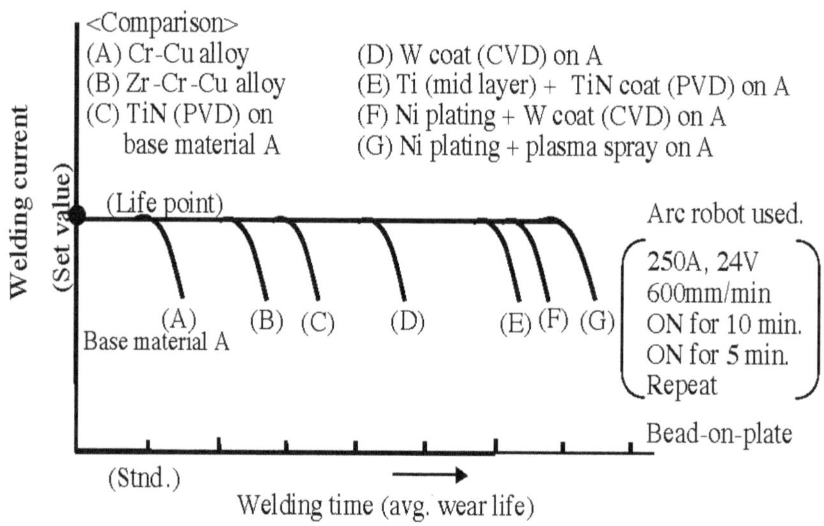

Similarly, for the development of all ceramic welding nozzle, the above surface improvement technology was also applied to welding nozzles, and the desired results were obtained. In addition to this, the author and others developed a substrate material for all ceramic welding nozzle, as well as its manufacturing method, and thereby solved the problem of weld spatter adhesion.

This eliminated the need for periodic cleaning maintenance and lengthened the life of the welding tip. These improvements substantially enhanced the operation availability of the welding process and consequently contributed to the simultaneous achievement of QCD and synchronized production (Amasaka, et al., 1988).

b. Solution to bottleneck problems related to processing of rear axle shaft

First solution is the Development of mid-frequency tempering equipment. In place of the aforementioned, large-scale, hot air circulating oven, panel-heater-type tempering equipment that consumes a lot of electric power (#050), a newly developed mid-frequency, heat induction coil-type, tempering equipment unit was installed (Amasaka, et al., 1982; Amasaka and Ishida, 1991).

As indicated in the upper section (3) in Figure 1 (Chapter 5), tempering is now conducted for one work piece at a time while concentrating on the high frequency quenching area. This meant that power consumption and in-process inventory are drastically reduced and the lead time is also substantially shortened (Amasaka, et al., 2008).

Furthermore, second solution is the Development of automated stress relief equipment. In addition to the above, the aforementioned manual stress relief equipment (#60) that depends on the empirical skills and abilities of an expert operator was replaced with a newly developed automated stress relief equipment unit (4). As indicated in the upper section (4) in Figure 6., the master skills commonly acquired by expert operators are simulated in order to conduct stress relief operations in an automatic and intelligent manner.

This equipment is capable of properly conducting stress adjustment operations on work pieces with a variety of different shape profiles (lengths and diameters). Even in the case of a sizable spiral adjustment, stress relief can be done in a cycle time that is comparable to that of skilled operators. Also, by installing a work piece crack detector, stable quality manufacturing was ensured and uneven cycle times were successfully eliminated.

These improvements in the facility equipment made it possible for the flow of work pieces from the high frequency quenching equipment (3), to the mid-frequency tempering equipment, to the automated stress relief equipment (#040→#050→#060), as shown in the Figure 6, to be connected in sequence along with automatic transportation of the work pieces. Consequently, these processes could be separated from the manual work processes.

Also, by integrating the upstream processes (#010→#030) and downstream processes (#070→#170) as illustrated in the Figure 6, the problem of work operations conducted over "remote island" work areas was also solved. These process improvement measures make it possible to flexibly arrange production operators according to the increase and decrease in production volume per day, and therefore enhance productivity.

As a result, manufactured quality was improved (Amasaka, et al., 1993), the lead time was considerably shortened, the problems associated with energy conservation, labor force minimization, and skill acquisition were solved, and synchronized production was realized. This substantially contributed to the simultaneous achievement of QCD.

4. Solution to bottleneck problems related to assembly process of rear axle unit

First solution is the simultaneous achievement of QCD for corrosion resistance coating. In recent years, in an aim to improve the product value of parts related to an automobile's suspension and chassis, efforts have been made toward the simultaneously achievement of QCD in the area of corrosion-resistant coating technology by drastically improving its rust proofing characteristics without raising the coating cost (Amasaka, 1986; Amasaka, et al., 1988b, 1990).

In order to implement this project, the authors organized a Total Task Management Team through collaboration with the on-site staff, production engineering staff, product development and designing staff, and coating material manufacturers (Aisin Chemical Co., Ltd., one of several affiliated coating manufacturers, and also non-affiliated manufacturer, Tokyo Paint Co., Ltd.). The manufacturing technical staff took the lead in this project.

Figure 9 shows the development procedure (rust proof quality and coating cost) that aimed for the simultaneous achievement of QCD by improving the coating materials, coating equipment, and drying equipment. In addition, the authors also aimed to solve the technical problems in order to enhance the product value (VA is indicated by the rust proof quality/cost) of the rear axle units to which the coating materials manufactured by Tokyo Paint are applied (Improvement (1)- (8) in Figure 2, Chapter 5) (Amasaka, et al., 1990). The coating cost in the figure indicates not the price of coating materials, but that of the coating operation, which includes the entire cost of the coating materials, energy consumed, cleaning, and maintenance cost of the coating equipment per one work piece.

Figure 9. Improvement process of the paint

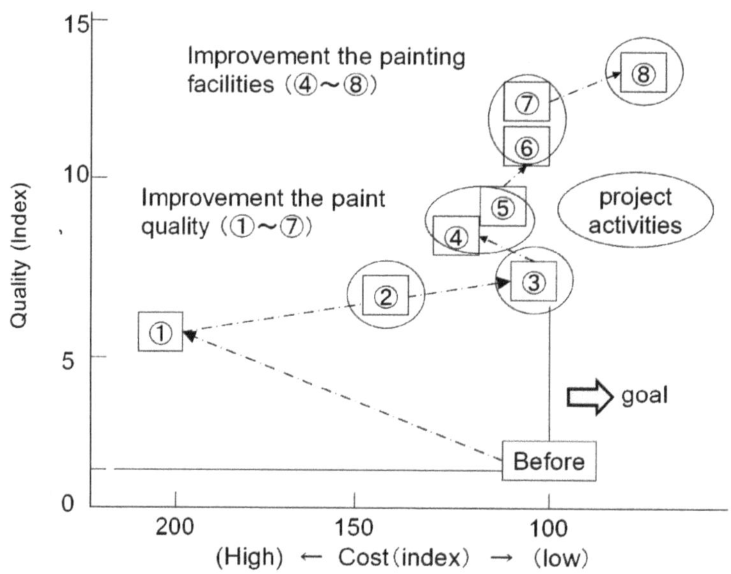

Conventionally, styrene modified alkyd resin solvent coating was used, but in an effort to prevent initial rusting caused by the spread of antifreeze agents, mainly used overseas, improved phenol modified alkyd resin (Improvement (1)) was adopted, and this resulted in an increase in the coating cost due to the high material cost. Given this background, a task team was formed that set development targets in several phases, while also anticipating the required quality improvements demanded by the market, which grow higher year after year, and systematically promoted the project through close monitoring of the process improvement.

In the early phases of improvement, mainly the coating materials were improved (Improvement (1)-(7)), and in the latter half, improvements in coating and drying equipment were promoted in parallel (Improvement (4)-(8)). More specifically, the following widely varied improvements were implemented as follows;

a. The aim of improving the solvent coating materials was better corrosion resistance characteristics. Air-drying alkyd resin provides drying and corrosion resistance characteristics and nonpolluting rustproof colorant and filling colorant were then properly mixed with the modified alkyd resin. These were used as the base materials and improvement of the corrosion resistance was achieved.
b. Another target was to improve the quick-drying characteristics and cost, corrosion resistance, quality of the coating films, storage stability of the coating materials, and safety (prevention of spontaneous ignition by the coating mist). Improved results were obtained by using a lacquer-type phenol alkyd resin that is resistant to oxidation polymerization.
c. In order to homogenize the coating films and enhance the finished exterior of the film surface, stearin acid and organic bentonite were added to the quick drying materials to improve thixotropy. This resulted in improvement of the finish quality, cost, and corrosion resistance characteristics
d. To improve the coating efficiency of the airless electrostatic coating, a polar solvent and nonpolar solvent having strong polarity and high permittivity were optimally composed in such a way as to satisfy the requirements of cost, drying characteristics, solubility, workability, and storage stability. As a result, the electric resistance of the coating materials was optimally adjusted.
e. The initial material cost was reduced through an optimal choice of the coating materials, filling colorants, thinners, and various compounding ingredients.
f. In order to improve the equipment for the coating and drying processes, irregularities in the coating efficiency and films were reduced by adapting dilution-adjusted coating materials to seasonal changes, hot sprays, and so forth, so that the amount of coating materials consumed per unit was reduced by over 30%. Moreover, by implementing collection and reuse of over spray coating and optimal compounding with new agents, the initial cost was further reduced. In addition, the adoption of robots to the coating operation realized a reduction in the running cost and improved the finish quality and coating efficiency in comparison with the conventional fixed multiunit airless electrostatic gun coating (Improvement (7)-(8)).

As a result, the final improved coating operation conducted 10 months later showed marked improvement. The rustproof characteristics were improved by 14 times (index based) and the visual quality was improved by 5 times (index based) by homogenizing the coating films. Moreover, the drying facility was abolished because of the development of the quick-drying coating materials with room temperature drying characteristics. These improvements reduced the in-process inventory within the process to one-third and drastically reduced the coating cost by over 30% compared to the conventional method. Even in the case of Aisin Chemical, similar improvement approaches have been taken and resulted in the simultaneous achievement of QCD (Amasaka, et al., 1988a).

Furthermore, second solution is the improvement of the bolt tightening tools. As shown in Figure 6 (on the right), the finished rear axle unit products are mounted on pull system carts located at the final process of the assembly conveyor (Amasaka, 1984ab: Amasaka and Yamada, 1991). The work hours needed for this operation have been reduced by improving the bolt-tightening tools for the brake units and disc wheel units that are assembled together with the rear axle units. The conventional bolt-tightening operations are conducted in three steps: tightening with an impact wrench via the emperical feel of the operators, additional tightening with a torque wrench, and torque checking. These operations have been very burdensome and difficult, even for expert production operators, and tightening operations were not always uniform in quality.

Given this background, the authors developed a high-precision tightening tool with torque control (tightening torque detector), which reduced this operation to only a single step, thereby reducing the manual work time and also improving and stabilizing the bolt-tightening quality at the same time. The efforts made through the task team activities of the on-site manufacturing staff and technical engineers introduced in this discussion were undertaken to realize the simultaneous achievement of QCD and in an aim to attain high quality assurance manufacturing by innovating the manufacturing technology. These activities have been positioned as the basis for advancement of the TPS, along with daily improvement activities at the manufacturing site (Amasaka, 2002b, 2004ab, 2007b, 2008a, 2015, 2017, 2022; Amasaka, et al., 2008; Amasaka, Ed. 2013).

CONCLUSION

In Section 1 and 2, Toyota Production System aimed to improve product quality while pursuing maximum efficiency through the application of TQM into the manufacturing process, as well as applying the principle of cost reduction. As for this chapter, the author introduced the "Fundamentals of Toyota Production System about the whole aspect of Toyota Production System (philosophy, theory and practice) which is the core principle of the manufacturing management in Toyota. In section 3, moreover, innovation of the production line producing suspension and chassis-related parts for automobiles in Toyota's Machining Div. of Motomachi plant presented by having cooperation between on-site white-collar engineers and supervisors and workers with affiliated and non-affiliated suppliers. In these examples, the author proved the effectiveness on advancing Toyota Production System through innovation of *t*he production line of automobile rear axle unit.

ACKNOWLEDGMENT

The author would like to acknowledge the generous support of the following researchers: All those at Toyota Motor Corporation, many affiliated / nonaffiliated suppliers, and those connected with the Amasaka New JIT laboratory at Aoyama Gakuin University that assisted with the research.

REFERENCES

Amasaka, K. (1983). Mechanization for operation depended on intuition and knack – Corrective method for distortion of rear axle shaft. *The Japanese Society for Quality Control, The 26th Technical Conference,* 5-10.

Amasaka, K. (1984a). Process control of the bolt tightening torque of automotive chassis parts (Part 1). *Standardization and Quality Control*, *37*(9), 97–104.

Amasaka, K. (1984b). Process control of the bolt tightening torque of automotive chassis parts (Part 2). *Standardization and Quality Control*, *37*(10), 71–76.

Amasaka, K. (1985). Management of the quenching process of the automotive chassis parts in case measurement takes time. *Standardization and Quality Control*, *38*(3), 93–100.

Amasaka, K. (1986). The improvement of the corrosion resistance for the front and rear axle unit of the vehicle - QCD research activities by plant production engineers. *The Japanese Society for Quality Control, The 30th Technical Conference,* 20-25.

Amasaka, K. (1988). Concept and progress of Toyota Production System (Plenary lecture). The Japan Society of Precision Engineering, Hachinohe Regional Advance Technology Promotion Center Foundation and others, Hachnohe, Aomori-ken, Japan.

Amasaka, K. (1988). Electrodes of Arc welding, Surface modification technology - A dry process and its application. The Japan Society for Precision Engineering, Editing of surveillance study subcommittee about surface modification, 304-311.

Amasaka, K. (1989). TQC at Toyota: Actual state of quality control activities in Japan (Special lecture). The 19th Quality Control Study Team for Europe, Union of Japanese and Engineers, Statistical Quality Control, 39, 107-112.

Amasaka, K. (1999a). A study on Science SQC by utilizing Management SQC, A demonstrative study on a new SQC concept and procedure in the manufacturing Industry. *International Journal of Production Economics, 60-61*, 591–598. doi:10.1016/S0925-5273(98)00143-1

Amasaka, K. (1999b). New QC circle activities at Toyota, A training of trainer's course on evidence-Based on participatory quality improvement (Special lecture). *The International Health Program (TOT Course on EPQI),* 1-7.

Amasaka, K. (2000). *Basic Principles of JIT – Concept and progress of Toyota Production System* (Plenary lecture). The Operations Research Society of Japan, Strategic research group-1, Tokyo, Japan.

Amasaka, K. (2002a). New JIT, A new management technology principle at Toyota. *International Journal of Production Economics, 80*(2), 135–144. doi:10.1016/S0925-5273(02)00313-4

Amasaka, K. (2002b). Intelligence production and partnering for embodying a high quality assurance (Plenary Lecture). The Japan Society of Mechanical Engineers, The 94th Course of JSME Tokai Branch, Nagoya, Japan.

Amasaka, K. (2003). Proposal and implementation of the Science SQC Quality Control Principle. *International Journal of Mathematical and Computer Modeling, 38*(11-13), 1125–1136. doi:10.1016/S0895-7177(03)90113-0

Amasaka, K. (Ed.). (2003). *The origin of manufacturing: Progress of the intelligence quality control chart: Digital engineering and high quality assurance*. Japanese Standards Association.

Amasaka, K. (2004a). The past, present, future of production management. *The Japan Society for Production Management, The 20th Annual Technical Conference,* 1-8.

Amasaka, K. (2004b). Development of "Science TQM", a new principle of quality management: Effectiveness of Strategic Stratified Task Team at Toyota. *International Journal of Production Research, 42*(17), 3691–3706. doi:10.1080/0020754042000203867

Amasaka, K. (2004c). Development of "Science TQM", A new principle of quality management: Effectiveness of strategic stratified task team at Toyota. *International Journal of Production Research, 42*(17), 3691–3706. doi:10.1080/0020754042000203867

Amasaka, K. (2007a). Developing the high-cycled quality management system utilizing New JIT. *Proceedings of the Seventh International Conference on Reliability and Safety, Beijing, China*, 248-253.

Amasaka, K. (2007b). *The forefront of manufacturing technology: Evolution of Toyota Production System - The quality technological strategy by Science TQM (Special lecture). The small and medium enterprises - Personnel training task utilizing the technical college etc. in the Heisei 19 fiscal year, Hachinohe intelligent plaza/Hachinohe Regional Advance Technology Promotion Center Foundation.*

Amasaka, K. (2008a). Strategic QCD studies with affiliated and non-affiliated suppliers utilizing New JIT. Encyclopedia of Networked and Virtual Organizations, 3(PU-Z), 1516-1527.

Amasaka, K. (2008b). Science TQM, a new quality management principle: The quality management strategy of Toyota. *The Journal of Management & Engineering Integration, 1*(1), 7–22.

Amasaka, K. (2009a, June). The foundation for advancing the Toyota Production System utilizing New JIT. *Journal of Advanced Manufacturing Systems, 80*(1), 5–26. doi:10.1142/S0219686709001614

Amasaka, K. (2009b). An Intellectual Development Production Hyper-cycle Model - *New JIT* fundamentals and applications in Toyota -. *International Journal of Collaborative Enterprise, 1*(1), 103–127. doi:10.1504/IJCENT.2009.026459

Amasaka, K. (Ed.). (2013). Science TQM, New Quality Management Principle, The quality management strategy at Toyota. Bentham Science Publishers.

Amasaka, K. (2015). New JIT, New Management Technology Principle. Taylor & Francis.

Amasaka, K. (2017). *Toyota: Production System, Safety Analysis, and Future Directions*. NOVA Science Publishers.

Amasaka, K. (2022). New Manufacturing Theory: Surpassing JIT (2nd ed.). LAP Lambert Academic Publishing.

Amasaka, K., & Ishida, T. (1991). *Tempered equipment, Aichi Invention Encouragement Prize*. Aichi Japan Institute of Invention and Innovation.

Amasaka, K., Iwata, M., & Fujii, M. (1988a). Development and the effect of the welding nozzle made from all ceramics, *Engineering Materials, 36*(10), 60–64.

Amasaka, K., & Kamio, M. (1985). Process improvement and process control: The example of axle-unit parts of the automobile. *Union of Japanese and Engineers Statistical Quality Control, 36*(6), 38–47.

Amasaka, K., Kurosu, S., & Morita, M. (2008). *New Manufacturing Principle: Surpassing JIT - Evolution of Just in Time*. Morikita-shuppan.

Amasaka, K., Mitani, Y., & Tsukamoto, H. (1993). Research into rust prevention quality assurance for plated components using SQC: Improvement of surface smoothness of rod pistons ground by centerless grinding machine. *Quality Japanese Society for Quality Control, 23*(2), 90–98.

Amasaka, K., Ohmi, H., & Murai, H. (1990). The improvement of the corrosion resistance for axle unit of the vehicle. *Coal Technology, 25*(6), 230–240.

Amasaka, K., Okumura, Y., & Tamura, N. (1988b). Improvement of paint quality for automotive chassis parts. *Standardization and Quality Control, 41*(2), 53–62.

Amasaka, K., & Saito, H. (1983). Mechanization of sensory evaluation-Example of the judgment of the Lissajous waveform indicating the damping force characteristics. *Proceedings of the Annual Conference of Central Japan Quality Control Association 1983,* 48-54.

Amasaka, K., & Sakai, H. (2010). Evolution of TPS fundamentals utilizing *New JIT* strategy: Proposal and validity of Advanced TPS at Toyota. *Journal of Advanced Manufacturing Systems, 9*(2), 85–99. doi:10.1142/S0219686710001831

Amasaka, K., & Sugawara, K. (1988). Q.C.D research activities of the engineer of the manufacture site: Improvement of paint corrosion resistance of shock absorber parts. *Quality Control Union Japanese Scientist and Engineers, 39*(11), 337–344.

Amasaka, K., Tsukada, H., & Ishida, M. (1982). Development of the tempering machine using mid-frequency of the rear axle shaft. *The Energy Conservation Center, Annual Technical Conference 1982,* 193-201.

Amasaka, K., & Yamada, K. (1991). Re-evaluation of the QC concept and methodology in auto-industry. *Union of Japanese and Engineers Statistical Quality Control, 42*(4), 13–22.

Amasaka, K., & Yasuda, K. (1998). *The coloring method of a welding bead.* Japanese Patent No. 2558493.

Burke, W., Trahant, W., & Koonce, R. (2000). *Business climate shift.* Butterworth-Heinemann.

David, T., & David, B. (2001). *Manufacturing operations and supply chain management: Lean approach.* Thomson Learning.

Hayashi, N., & Amasaka, K. (1990). Concept and progress of Toyota Production System: The physical distribution improvement in manufacture (Special lecture). *The Annual Conference of Japan Physical Distribution Management Association, 3,* 4-12.

Hayes, R. H., & Wheelwright, S. C. (1984). *Restoring our competitive edge: Competing through manufacturing.* Wiley.

Ohno, T. (1977). *Toyota Production System.* Diamond-sha.

Roger, G. S., & Flynn, B. B. (2001). *High performance manufacturing.* John Weiley & Sons, Inc.

Roos, D., Womack, J. P., & Jones, D. T. (1991). *The machine that change the world – The story of lean production.* Rawson.

Taylor, D., & Brunt, D. (2001). *Manufacturing operations and supply chain management - The Lean Approach.* Thomson Leaning.

Toyota Motor Corporation. (1987). *The Toyota Production System and a glossary of special terms used at production job-sites at Toyota.* Author.

Womack, J. P., & Jones, D. (1994). From Lean Production to the Lean Enterprise. *Harvard Business Review,* (March-April), 93–103.

Chapter 4
Importance of Japan's Global Manufacturing Strategies 21C:
Surpassing JIT

ABSTRACT

The top priority of the industrial field today is the new deployment of global marketing for surviving the era of global production competition. Therefore, to continue to play the leading role in the world, the reform of Japanese-style management technology is desired once again. To realize this, the urgent mission JIT evolution for Japanese manufacturers is to reconstruct world-leading, which will be viable for next-generation manufacturing. In such a viewpoint, the author states the importance of Japan's global manufacturing strategies 21C–surpassing JIT.

INTRODUCTION

All over the world, including in Japan, advanced automobile companies are shifting to global production to realize worldwide uniform quality and manufacturing at optimum locations to enable survival aimed fierce competition. In recent years, the Toyota Production System (TPS) representing Japanese manufacturing has been adopted as the JIT and Lean System and further developed in various international manufacturing systems (As the result, it is no longer exclusively Japanese (or Toyota's) system) (Amasaka, 1988a, 2002) (Refer to Chapter 2 and 3).

In this chapter, therefore, the author states the viewpoint of "Importance of Japan's global manufacturing strategies 21C–Surpassing JIT" to realize best quality of Japanese manufacturing in a rapidly changing core-technologies and environment, as follows (Amasaka, Ed., 2007; Amasaka et al., 2008; Amasaka, 2015, 2017, 2022).

Firstly, the author clarifies the "Today's management technology issues" as the highest priority to "suggestion-based new merchandise, product development and manufacturing" as the global manufacturing strategy "Next-generation management principle" through the survey of general managers and executives from Toyota, Fuji Xerox, Daikin and many other advanced companies. Specifically, this

DOI: 10.4018/978-1-7998-8746-1.ch004

principle is the based on the basis for new management technologies, and the technological elements required for linking these core technologies".

Secondly, to realize the success of global production strategies, the author clarifies the quality of the business processes of all divisions needs to be enhanced through clear-cut, rational TPS adopting JIT activities, as follows (Amasaka, 2002, 2008b, 2009, 2013, 2014). Specifically, in particular, in experiencing a drastic transition due to digital engineering, (i) the manufacturing technical capabilities are declining as a result of the stagnation in QC Circle activities and "hollowing-out" of transfer of production bases overseas. (ii) Consequently, a weakening in problem solving abilities and the incorporation of quality has become increasingly fragile.

Thirdly, moreover, from a viewpoint of advancement in technology and skill, the author has clarified the various problems of the "present condition of overseas starting in new products of production launches" for re-strengthening of high quality technology, drew its countermeasure as the "style of Japanese manufacturing that is required in overseas production plants and reinforcement of the production management function" (Amasaka et al., 2008; Amasaka, 2015).

WHAT ARE TOP MANAGEMENT'S CONCERNS?

New Evolution of Management Technology Surpassing JIT

For manufacturers to be successful in the future global market, they need to develop products that have a strong impression on consumers and supply these items in a timely fashion through effective corporate management. Then, the author shows that it is clearly impossible to continue to lead the next generation simply by adhering to and maintaining the Toyota Production System and TQM, which are the dual-pillars of traditional Japanese management technology. To overcome these problems, it is essential not only to advance the Japanese Production System, a core technology of the production processes, but to also establish a core technology for the sales-, design-, and development related divisions (Amasaka, 2002, 2004a, 2007a).

Given the above, the author (Amasaka, 2002, 2007b) has conducted an awareness survey of general management personnel and executives (a total of 72 people) from 12 advanced companies belonging to the Toyota Group. Similarly, based on another awareness survey of other companies (Fuji Xerox and Daikin among others, with a total of 153 participants) participating in the "Study Group for Manufacturing Quality Management (a.k.a. "The Amasaka Forum")", management technology issues have been investigated from the standpoint of corporate management (Amasaka, 1999, 2008a; Amasaka, Ed., 2007; Amasaka et al., 2008).

In Figure 1, by incorporating Quantification Class III, the overall management technology issues have been plotted in a chart. This confirms that managers responsible for development give the highest priority to "suggestion-based new merchandise and product development" as a global merchandise strategy, whereas production managers put efforts into establishing the "next-generation production system" in view of global production. Sales managers, on the other hand, prioritize the "development of new marketing methods" in order to be successful in global marketing. Moreover, the issue common to all was how to respond to globalization.

Figure 1. Management Technology Problems (: Positioning of Opinion)

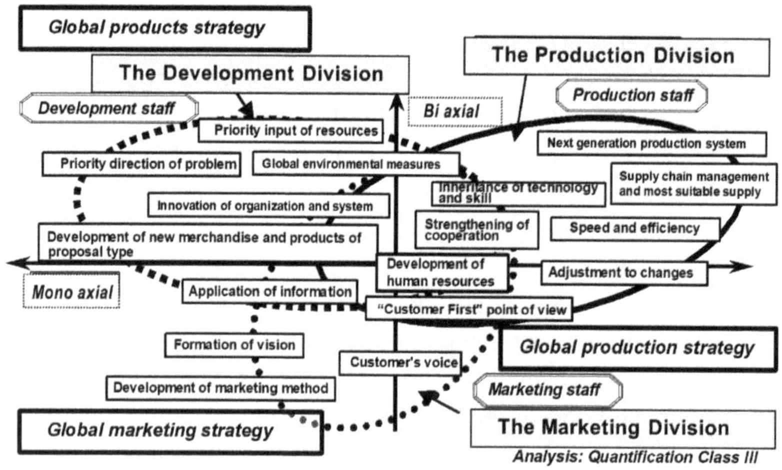

Therefore, to overcome these management issues, it will be necessary to carry out reforms of the human resources cultivation system through intelligent sharing of information, and create a new management technology for closer ties among the company's all divisions. The above awareness surveys and analysis clarified the core technologies necessary for the next-generation management technology principle, the basis for new management technologies, and the technological elements required for linking these core technologies. Thus, in the future, it will be important to create management technology equipped with a new concept that enables total linkage of QCD research conducted by each of the aforementioned divisions from the standpoint of strategic corporate management, and by so doing, to create a "New Manufacturing Theory: Surpassing JIT" (Amasaka et al., 2008; Amasaka, 2019, 2022).

Specifically, to offer customers high value-added products and prevail in the worldwide quality competition, it is necessary to establish the advanced production system that can intellectualize the production engineering and production management system. This will in turn produce high performance and highly functional new products. On a concrete target, the simultaneous achievement of QCD requirements that reinforce the product appeal is required to realize this global production system (Amasaka, 2002, 2008b, 2015). To succeed in automobile global production, worldwide uniform quality and simultaneous launch (production at optimal locations) is an urgent task.

Therefore, in increasing sophistication and diversification of customers' needs, the author has made the development of a form of global production that acts in concert with the overseas deployment of production bases into a pressing management issue.

JAPANESE MANUFACTURING – RESTRENGTHENING OF HIGH QUALITY TECHNOLOGY IN GLOBAL MANUFACTURING

The author believes that what determines the success of global production strategies is the advancement of technologies and skills that are capable of fully utilizing the above mentioned advanced production system in order to realize reliable manufacturing at the production sites (Amasaka, 2005, 2007b, 2015, 2017, 2020; Amasaka, Ed., 2003, 2012; Amasaka et al., 2008).

Necessity for Advanced Manufacturing-Advancement in Technology and Skill

In near future, to promote excellent quality management capable of contributing to global manufacturing, the quality of the business processes of all divisions needs to be enhanced through clear-cut, rational JIT activities, as follows. (Amasaka, 2002, 2008b, 2009, 2013, 2014).

First, at Japanese manufacturers that are experiencing a drastic transition in on-site manufacturing due to digital engineering, the technical capabilities of their on-site manufacturing are declining as a result of stagnation in QC Circle activities and the "hollowing-out" that occurs due to the transfer of production bases overseas. Consequently, a weakening in problem identification abilities and problem solving abilities at the production site has been revealed and the incorporation of quality has become increasingly fragile.

Second, the recent increase of recall cases happening to Japanese products, which are expected to lead the world, and the remarkable "quality improvement" of industrially developing nations are sending out a warning message about the need to reinforce Japanese quality technology capabilities in view of global production.

Third, Production launches of new products at Japanese domestic bases have been promoted through a concurrent system in which each production-related department conducts its own preparations based on their experience, while also taking into consideration a large number of design changes. However, in the case of overseas production, the experience, intuition, and know-how of the Japanese production staff are not conveyed to the local staff in each process, such as procurement, production preparation, and manufacturing.

Forth, from now on, it is urgent to establish "a new and original Japanese management technology system" that is suitable for the IT adopting production sites, instead of clinging to the conventional quality management or production management methods (Amasaka, 2007a,b, 2015; Amasaka, Ed., 2007, 2012).

Present Condition of Overseas Starting as the Production Launches of New Products

In particular the characteristic problem that should be prevented is correspondence to "Present condition of overseas starting" (Amasaka, 2007a, 2008b; Amasaka, Ed., 2007; Amasaka et al., 2008). In this case, the practical application problems as the "Production launches of new products" are often not solved.

Fifth, specifically, one countermeasure currently being taken is to launch at a production site in Japan first, solving various problems one by one, and then transferring the production as it is to an overseas site. If this current practice is continued even for a worldwide simultaneous launch, a large number of the Japanese production launch members will need to be dispatched to each of the overseas production bases.

Figure 2 shows conceptually what is stated above. The upper half of the figure d depicts the status of production launch in Japan, while the lower half shows the status at overseas sites. As shown in the figure, in a normal production launch in Japan, planning, development, prototyping, equipment and material procurement, and production preparation overlap with one another and as indicated in the upper half of the figure, the quality problems that occur after the production begins gradually decrease as the designing and manufacturing staff take the necessary measures to solve them. A widely observed case even now is for the transfer of manufacturing to an overseas production base to be carried out after these quality problems have been solved.

Figure 2. Production launches of new products - Present condition of overseas starting-(Japanese domestic production and overseas production) the project is promoted through trial and error.

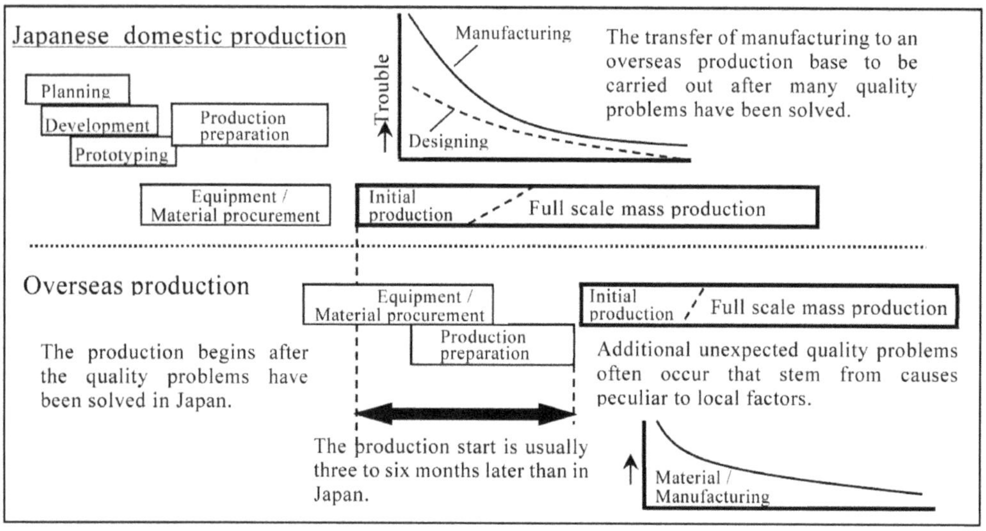

On the other hand, in the case of a launch at an overseas plant (or local production) from the start, equipment and material procurement as well as production preparation do not overlap with each other, rather, they are often promoted in sequence. For this reason, the production start is usually three to six months later than Japan.

Even though the production begins after the quality problems has been solved in Japan, once production starts overseas, additional unexpected quality problems often occur that stem from causes peculiar to local factors (procured materials or local workers). Such additional quality problems are handled as needed on a trial and error basis similarly to Japan, and often such troubles gradually diminish.

The Style of Japanese Manufacturing that is Required in Overseas Production Plants

1. Manufacturing products at overseas plants with same quality as Japan at the same time

Regardless of if it is a domestic or foreign market, the recent purchasing behavior of customers suggests that their consciousness of product value has been rapidly growing and they will only pay the price that they think matches the perceived value gained from the product.

True to the saying, "the price provides temporary satisfaction, but quality provides life-long satisfaction", even in the markets of developing nations, the product specifications and functional quality of older models surely cannot gain the upper hand, even if such products are priced more inexpensively.

From now on, the basis of global production and quality assurance will be to equalize the finished quality of products regardless of where they are manufactured, either overseas or domestically. Depending on the state of the country, it will not matter whether production is carried out by the latest automated factory or by workers' manual operation. Some manufactures might decide on their production system according to the location, product specifications, or volume of the products to be manufactured. However, in order to achieve worldwide uniform quality, it is increasingly important to create a high quality assurance system that gives top priority to the customers (Amasaka, 2001, 2003a, 2015; Amasaka Ed., 2007).

2. The reinforced inspection to enhanced process management

One of the measures that will equalize the product quality enjoyed by the customers is to implement a thorough inspection process. It is generally difficult however, to check in detail all the inspection items that must be assured for all products. In addition, when the daily management based on 4M-E (Man, Machine, Material, Method, and Environment) is not thoroughly carried out, production which matches the design drawing will be impossible and simply result in a mountain of defective products after all the items have been inspected. This will then require a large amount of reworking or disposal and will interfere with the original production plan.

Next, the factor of logistics needs to be given similar consideration. In Japanese domestic production, many of the assembly manufacturers conduct JIT production and therefore are able to supply what is needed, when it is needed, in the amount that is needed, through cooperation with their suppliers. However, in the case where JIT production is not fully implemented at an overseas base, what will happen when the products manufactured there are exported to Japan or to other foreign countries?

The general means of transporting products is by ship and this requires a longer lead time. It also means that holding a large stock is inevitable. If a quality problem occurs under such circumstances, the damage inflicted on the manufacturer will multiply in proportion to the volume of product in stock. Having said the above, it is not an exaggeration to say that overseas production requires a higher level of quality assurance manufacturing than Japanese domestic production. Reinforcing quality inspections is an important facet of quality assurance, but it alone is not sufficient and attention must also be given to how quality is being incorporated into the production process. In other words, in the end it is essential to implement enhanced process management (Amasaka and Sakai, 2009).

There are a great variety of different cultures, religions, and languages in the world. When thinking about the mission of trying to realize high quality assurance from a global standpoint, while also overcoming these sorts of barriers, one cannot help but think how easy it would be if all of the company's employees at least understood a single common language for communication. Luckily however, at the manufacturing site there is a universally common language. It is what is called probability and statistics in statistical terminology. The majority of people agree that the scientific process management method applying SQC (statistical quality control) can be a powerful tool for maintaining and improving the production process, as well as in determining the causes of a variety of quality problems and preventing them from recurring in the future (Amasaka, Ed., 1998, 2000a, 2003; Amasaka, 1999b, 2003b, 2004b).

3. The production system issues at the overseas production plants

In recent years, the limit of traditional Japanese manufacturing, or the so-called on-site capability, has been recognized at the overseas production sites. Up until now the general business practice has been to bring the local production staff to Japan to educate them in the Japanese production system and then transfer them back to their overseas sites after solving various problems. These production staff members would then implement the Japanese production system and quality assurance system.

The question is, "Does this achieve the overseas deployment of production that was originally intended?." There are several issues concerning the application of the current Japanese production system at overseas production sites. These issues include: correcting the declining on-site capabilities at Japanese domestic production sites, which are expected to be the model for the overseas bases, correcting the scattering of Japanese engineers to overseas bases and the subsequently decline in total technological capability, solving the concerns over the possibility of manufacturing products at overseas sites with the same level of quality as in Japan, establishing a new production system that will enable global production, and so on.

The author assumes that a simple extension of the current Japanese production system is not sufficient to overcome these issues, and therefore have decided that the top priority issue here is the further advancement of the Japanese production system in order to realize worldwide uniform quality and simultaneous launch (production at optimal locations) as the key to success in global production (Amasaka, 2000b, 2001, 2005a, 2007a; Ebioka et al., 2007).

ADVANCEMENT IN MANUFACTURING– REINFORCEMENT OF THE PRODUCTION

Management Functions

As already mentioned above, customers today select products that suit their lifestyle and personal values. In addition, they are strongly demanding manufacturing that will enhance customer value via the products' reliability (quality and value gained from use). For this reason, unless the manufacturer advances its manufacturing processes in such a way as to respond to these demands, while also accurately grasping the customers' preferences, it will be pushed out of the world market.

In this day and age when customers have quick and easy access to the latest information from every corner of the world due to the permeation of IT, the production management department, which is the command center of manufacturing, needs more than ever before to have a global view and deploy strategic production management as the core of corporate management (Amasaka, 2001, 2005a, 2007).

The new mission of the production management department is the deployment of strategic cooperation between the on-site departments of engineering, production and sales, and general administration departments, as well as the domestic and overseas suppliers. This is done in order to realize worldwide uniform quality and simultaneous launch (production at optimal locations) ahead of other competitors (Amasaka, 2000b; 2001; Ebioka et al., 2007).

In other words, to solve the various manufacturing problems both domestically and overseas, the experienced-based implicit knowledge (such as know-how, empirical rules, intelligent information, etc.) possessed by the white-collar and on-site production workers needs to be converted to "linguistically expressed knowledge" or "explicit knowledge" employing Customer Science Principle as shown in Figure 3 (Amasaka, 2002, 2005b; Yamaji and Amasaka, 2009).

Figure 3. Visualization of experienced-based implicit knowledge

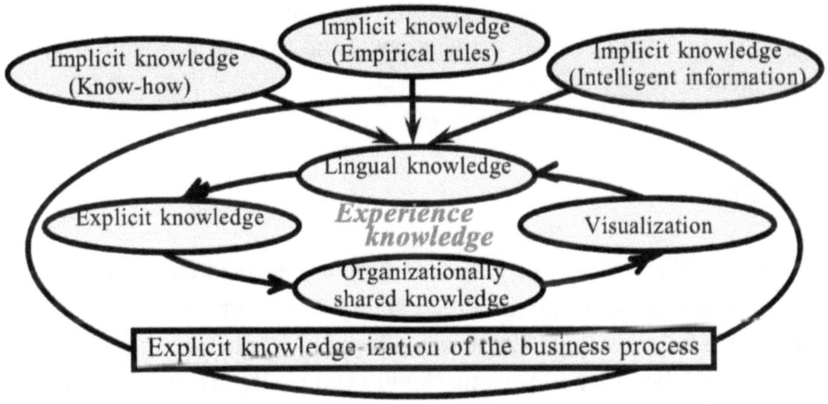

This will be done through the incorporation of the "Science TQM, new quality management principle" employing the "Science SQC, new quality control principle" that has been proven effective as a scientific problem solving method as shown in Figure 3, Chapter 5 (Amasaka, 1999a, 2000a, 2003b, 2004a,b) (Refer to Chapter 5 in detail).

Moreover, this is important for all divisions to turn implicit knowledge of their business process into explicit knowledge through integrated and collaborative activities by sharing awareness. To accomplish this, a new systematic and organized SQC propulsion cycle in the Toyota's strategy, established by the author was developed under a new concept using a new methodology that applied the four core principles that enabled jobs to be scientifically performed. This conceptual diagram shows the nucleus of Toyota's and its group's TQM activities based on a new quality principle "Science TQM" that is the secret of success for next-generation manufacturing (Amasaka, 2004a, 2008a; Amasaka Ed., 2012) (Refer to Chapter 5 in detail).

Particularly in the practical application, the gaps between principles and rules have to be clarified scientifically as engineering problems, and general solutions have to be approached by clarifying the gaps that exist in theory, testing, calculation, and actual application. For further details on Science SQC with four core principles, refer to Amasaka and Osaki (1999) and Amasaka (1998b, 2000a,b, 2002, 2003b; Amasaka, Ed., 2012).

CONCLUSION

In this chapter, the author stated a viewpoint of the Importance of Japan's global manufacturing strategies 21C–Surpassing JIT". Specifically, the author illustrated the necessity of JIT evolution from the viewpoint of the reform of Japanese-style management technology in overseas manufacturing strategy from a standpoint of "overseas manufacturing strategy". To continue to play the leading role in the world, particularly, the author focused on the necessity of the advanced production system, advancement in technologies and skills for the "Reinforcement of the production management functions" as follows; (1) Manufacturing products at overseas plants with the same quality as Japan at the same time, (2) The reinforced inspection to enhanced process management, and (3) The Production system issues at the overseas production plants.

ACKNOWLEDGMENT

The author would like to acknowledge the generous support received from the following researchers: all those at Study group of the Ideal Situation the Quality Management of Manufacturing Industry in JUSE (Union of Japanese Scientists and Engineers), Toyota Motor Corporation, and those connected with the Amasaka New JIT laboratory at Aoyama Gakuin University that assisted with author's research.

REFERENCES

Amasaka, K. (Ed.). (1998). Practice: SQC-key for beginner and professionals. QC Educational Study Group, Japanese Standards Association.

Amasaka, K. (1998a). *Concept and progress of Toyota Production System (Plenary lecture). Co-sponsorship: The Japan Society of Precision Engineering, Hachinohe Regional Advance Technology Center Foundation.*

Amasaka, K. (1998b). Application of classification and related methods to the SQC Renaissance in Toyota Motor. In *Data Science, Classification and Related Methods.* Springer.

Amasaka, K. (1999a). *The TQM Responsibilities for Industrial Management in Japan* (Lecture). The Japanese Society for Production Management, The 10th Annual Technical Conference, Fukuoka, Japan.

Amasaka, K. (1999b). A study on "Science SQC" by utilizing "Management SQC-A demonstrative study on a new SQC concept and procedure in the manufacturing industry-. *International Journal of Production Economics, 60-61*, 591–598. doi:10.1016/S0925-5273(98)00143-1

Amasaka, K. (2000a). A demonstrative study of a new SQC concept and procedure in the manufacturing industry-Establishment of a new technical method for conducting Scientific SQC-. *An International Journal of Mathematical & Computer Modeling, 31*(10-12), 1–10. doi:10.1016/S0895-7177(00)00067-4

Amasaka, K. (2000b). Partnering chains as the platform for quality management in Toyota. *Proceedings of the 1st World Conference on Production and Operations Management, Seville Spain*, 1-13.

Amasaka, K. (2001). Quality management in the automobile industry and practice of the joint activities of auto-maker and supplier. Japan Small Business Research Institute-A change in the order system such as a part in manufacturing industry: The condition of supplier continuance in the automobile industry, 74(2), 133-161.

Amasaka, K. (2002). New JIT, a new management technology principle at Toyota. *International Journal of Production Economics*, *80*(2), 135–144. doi:10.1016/S0925-5273(02)00313-4

Amasaka, K. (Ed.). (2003). *Manufacturing fundamentals: The application of intelligence control charts-Digital Engineering for superior quality assurance*. Japanese Standards Association.

Amasaka, K. (2003a). *Digital engineering and production control in a high quality assurance* (Special lecture). The Japan Society for Production Management, The 17th Annual Conference, Tutorial session: The Past, the present, and the future of quality creation-Logic and digital engineering of quality creation, Gakushuin University, Tokyo.

Amasaka, K. (2003b). Proposal and implementation of the "Science SQC", quality control principle. *International Journal of Mathematical and Computer Modeling*, *38*(11-13), 1125–1136. doi:10.1016/S0895-7177(03)90113-0

Amasaka, K. (2004a). Development of "Science TQM", a new principle of quality management: Effectiveness of strategic stratified task team at Toyota. *International Journal of Production Research*, *42*(17), 3691–3706. doi:10.1080/0020754042000203867

Amasaka, K. (2004b). *Science SQC, New Quality Control Principle: Quality Control Strategy at Toyota*. Springer-Verlag. doi:10.1007/978-4-431-53969-8

Amasaka, K. (2004c). *The past, present, future of production management* (Keynote Lecture). In The 20th Annual Technical Conference of the Japan Society for Production Management, Nagoya Technical College, Nagoya, Aichi, Japan.

Amasaka, K. (2005a). Next-generation Management Technology: Aim at establishment of the Japan Method (Lecture). *The Japan Society for Production Management, The 21st Annual Conference-10th anniversary symposium of the JSP foundation,* 1-16.

Amasaka, K. (2005b). Constructing a Customer Science Application System "CS-CIANS" - Development of a Global Strategic Vehicle "Lexus" Utilizing New JIT. *WSEAS Transformations in Business & Economics*, *2*(3), 135–142.

Amasaka, K. (Ed.). (2007). New Japan Model: Science TQM-Theory and practice for strategic quality management. Study group of the ideal situation on the quality management of the manufacturing industry, Maruzen, Tokyo.

Amasaka, K. (2007a). New Japan Production Model, An advanced production management principle: Key to strategic implementation of New JIT. *The International Business & Economics Research Journal*, *6*(7), 67–79.

Amasaka, K. (2007b). High Linkage Model "Advanced TDS, TPS & TMS": Strategic development of "New JIT" at Toyota. *International Journal of Operations and Quantitative Management*, *13*(3), 101–121.

Amasaka, K. (2008a). Science TQM, a new quality management principle: The quality management strategy of Toyota. *The Journal of Management & Engineering Integration, 1*(1), 7–22.

Amasaka, K. (2008b). Strategic QCD studies with affiliated and non-affiliated suppliers utilizing New JIT. Encyclopedia of Networked and Virtual Organizations, 3(PU-Z), 1516-1527.

Amasaka, K. (2009). The Foundation for Advancing the Toyota Production System utilizing New JIT. *Journal of Advanced Manufacturing Systems, 80*(1), 5–26. doi:10.1142/S0219686709001614

Amasaka, K. (Ed.). (2012). Science TQM, new quality management principle: The Quality Management Strategy of Toyota. Bentham Science Publisher.

Amasaka, K. (2013). The development of a Total Quality Management System for transforming technology into effective management strategy. *International Journal of Management, 30*(2), 610–630.

Amasaka, K. (2014). New JIT, New Management Technology Principle: Surpassing JIT. *Journal of Procedia Technology, 16*(special issues), 1135–1145. doi:10.1016/j.protcy.2014.10.128

Amasaka, K. (2015). New JIT, new management technology principle. Taylor & Francis Group.

Amasaka, K. (2017). *Toyota: Production system, safety analysis and future directions.* Nova Science Publishers.

Amasaka, K. (2019). Studies on New Manufacturing Theory. *Noble. International Journal of Scientific Research, 3*(1), 1–20.

Amasaka, K. (2022). New Manufacturing Theory; Surpassing JIT (2nd ed.). Lambert Academic Publishing.

Amasaka, K., Kurosu, S., & Morita, M. (2008). *New Manufacturing Theory: Surpassing JIT-Evolution of Just In Time*. Morikita-Shuppan.

Amasaka, K., & Osaki, S. (1999). The promotion of New Statistical Quality Control Internal Education in Toyota Motor-A Proposal of"Science SQC" for improving the principle of TQM. *European Journal of Engineering Education, 24*(3), 259–276. doi:10.1080/03043799908923561

Amasaka, K., & Sakai, H. (2009). TPS-QAS, new production quality management model: Key to New JIT-Toyota's global production strategy. *International Journal of Manufacturing Technology and Management, 18*(4), 409–426. doi:10.1504/IJMTM.2009.027774

Ebioka, K., Sakai, H., Yamaji, M., & Amasaka, K. (2007). A New Global Partnering Production Model "NGP-PM" utilizing Advanced TPS. *Journal of Business & Economics Research, 5*(9), 1–8.

Yamaji, M., & Amasaka, K. (2009). Strategic Productivity Improvement Model for white-collar workers employing Science TQM. *The Journal of Japanese Operations Management and Strategy, 1*(1), 30–43.

Chapter 5
Establishment of a New Japan Model Using Total Linkage of TDS, TPS, TMS, TIS, and TJS

ABSTRACT

In this study, the author has established the New Japan Model (NJM), new corporate management principle for the realization of surpassing JIT. NJM employing New JIT and Science TQM consists of the total linkage of total development system (TDS), total production system (TPS), total marketing system (TMS), total intelligence management system (TIS), and total job quality management system (TJS). This model aims to realize an integrated form of a next-generation corporate management strategy by focusing product quality management strategy. Furthermore, this study demonstrates how the utilization of Science SQC and the Strategic Stratified Task Team Model (SSTTM) contributes systematically and organically to solving product quality management problems. Its validity has also been verified through its application within the Toyota, Toyota Group, and other Japanese advanced corporations.

INTRODUCTION

Looking closely at the quality management issues facing advanced corporations both domestically and overseas in recent years, it has become clear that a new corporate management model by focusing product quality management strategy is being strongly sought after (Amasaka, 1999a,b, 2007a, 2008a,b; Nihon Keizai Shinbun, 1999, 2000, 2006; Asahi Shinbun, 2005).

This new model needs to employ a rational concept and methodology that will break away from the conventional ideas of quality management and contribute to the restoration of quality. In the main discussion of this study, the next generation of "New Japan Model (NJM), new corporate management principle" employing "New JIT, new management technology principle" and "Science TQM, new quality management principle" for the realization of surpassing JIT (Amasaka, 2000a, 2002a,b, 2004a, 2007, 2008a, 2014a,b, 2015, 2020; Amasaka, Ed., 2007, 2012), will be established and its effectiveness will

DOI: 10.4018/978-1-7998-8746-1.ch005

be demonstrated. NJM systematically and organizationally contributes to the solution of company-wide management technology problems.

NJM is composed of integrated five core elements: the (1) Total Development System (TDS), (2) Total Production System (TPS), (3) Total Marketing System, (TMS), (4) Total Intelligence Management System (TIS), and (5) Total Job Quality Management System (TJS). By implementing NJM, each work department will become equipped with the core technology and linked with one another cooperatively. This study demonstrates how the utilization of "Science SQC, new quality control principle" and the Strategic Stratified Task Team Model (SSTTM) contributes systematically and organically to solving quality management problems (Amasaka, 2000b, 2003a, 2004a, 2008a,b, 2013). Its validity will then be been verified through its application within the Toyota Motor Corp., Toyota group companies, and other Japanese advanced corporations (Amasaka, 1999a,b, 2004a,b, 2017, 2020, 2022; Amasaka, Ed., 2007a, 2012).

THE KEY TO SUCCESS IN GLOBAL PRODUCTION

What are the Critical Management Issues for Japanese Manufacturing?

In recent years, consumers (hereafter called, customers) have been selecting products that fit their lifestyles and their set of personal values. Consequently, a market environment was created in which customers strictly judge the reliability of manufacturers according to the reliability (quality and value gained from use) of their products.

For this reason, it is not an exaggeration to say that manufacturers' success or failure in global marketing will depend on whether or not they are able to precisely grasp the customers' preferences and are then able to advance their manufacturing to adequately respond to the demands of the times (Amasaka, 1999b,c, 2004a). This is being done in order to realize global production that will achieve the so-called "globally consistent levels of quality and simultaneous production worldwide (production at optimal locations)" ahead of other manufactures. Achieving this will allow the manufacturer to not be pushed out of the market (Amasaka, Ed., 2007a).

In the midst of the drastic changes taking place at the manufacturing site due to the use of digital engineering, the author (Amasaka, 1999b,c, 2008a) can say that the reconstruction of world-leading, uniquely Japanese principles of management technology and administrative management technology, which will be viable even for next-generation manufacturing, are urgently needed in order to keep up with this evolution in management technology. This is the mission imposed on Japanese manufacturers today (Amasaka, 1999b,c; Amasaka, Ed., 2007a).

In order to accomplish this, it is imperative that management related departments, such as technical management, production management, sales management, and information technology, which make up the core of corporate management, closely cooperate with the administrative departments, such as personnel affairs, general planning, TQM promotion, and overseas business. Furthermore, management-related departments also need to carry out strategic collaborations with on-site departments handling technical, production, and sales matters, as well as with suppliers (parts manufacturers) (Amasaka, 2004a; Amasaka, Ed., 2007a).

The Evolution of Administrative Management Technology is now being Demanded

In today's rapidly changing technological environment (Amasaka, 2004a, 2008a), one of the first management technology issues that needs to be addressed in order to realize the "simultaneous achievement of QCD" and place the customer first, is the creation of a new development designing system capable of reforming the technological development business processes of the development designing. Second, it is increasingly important for departments concerned with production to develop new production technologies and advance the "production management technology system" that enables global production. Third, it is necessary for sales-related departments to concentrate their view on global marketing and to establish a "new marketing system" that breaks away from the conventional systems in an effort to strengthen ties with the customers.

It is becoming increasingly necessary, moreover, even from the standpoint of assuring "corporate reliability", for the general administration departments and management-related departments to cooperatively establish and implement a new administrative management technology which enhances the business processes of all departments involved in corporate management (Amasaka, 2004a, 2008a). The above statements also apply, without exception, to Toyota's TPS, which has been adopted and further developed in various systems shared internationally, such as JIT or Lean Systems (Taylor and Brunt, 2001), and therefore, it is no longer Toyota's exclusive technology. In the United States as well, the importance of quality management has been increasingly recognized though studies of Japanese TQM. TQM has been actively promoted, thus encroaching on the quality superiority that Japanese products have previously enjoyed (Gabor, 1990; Joiner, 1994; Goto, 1999).

What can be deduced from these facts is that it is clearly impossible to continue to lead in the next generation of manufacturing simply by adhering to and maintaining the traditional, production-based "Japanese management technology". In order to overcome these problems, it is essential not only to advance TPS, a core technology of production processes, but to also establish a core technology for the service and sales, development designing, production, general administration, and management-related departments (Amasaka, 2004a; Amasaka, Ed., 2007).

Furthermore, for the purpose of ensuring the reform of the business process in all departments, as well as reinforcing inter-department cooperation, it is vital to reconstruct an intelligent system for sharing information. During the implementation stage of this system, it will be important to further upgrade the advantages of the *Japan Supply System* (Amasaka, 2000c, 2004a, 2007; Amasaka, Ed. 2007a), a cooperative system between the assembly parts manufacturers and the automobile manufacturers that has long been a part of Japanese manufacturing, to a "Partnering Chain Management System on Platforms", as well as to establish the method of this system's operation.

ESTABLISHMENT OF THE NEW JAPAN MODEL, NEW CORPORATE MANAGEMENT PRINCIPLE

The aim of corporate management activity in global manufacturing is to offer attractive products. To realize this goal, it is vital for all departments to share the same values toward work and improve the business quality of their work through internal and external cooperation in the world. This means because the existing corporate management activities are based on past successes brought about by each person's particular experience or skills, and it is not enough to encompass such diversified technologies. To create customer-oriented furthermore, attractive products which can truly satisfy the customer's demands, a core technology needs to be established.

Specifically, the author has established the New Japan Model (NJM), new corporate management principle employing New JIT, new management technology principle and Science TQM, new quality management principle for the realization of surpassing JIT as the global transforming management technology strategy in the world as shown in Figure 1 (Amasaka, 2000, 2002a,b, 2004a, 2007, 2008a, 2014a,b, 2015, 2020; Amasaka Ed., 2007a, 2012a).

NJM would allow, technological development designing, production engineering / manufacturing, the advertisement / promotion and sales related departments, which are organically linked together by the management department, and office personnel / indirect department having the role of utilizing human resources in all departments and thus activating the organization, to improve the quality of their work. It is imperative that all these are linked with one another systematically and organizationally.

This model rationalizes the high-linkage cycle for the improvement of business process of each department in a continuous circular ring employing information technology (IT) and statistical science named Science SQC, new quality control principle (Amasaka, 2003a, 2004b). Grasping the mission of each department involved in management technology, this new model is composed of a structured "Integrated five core elements": the Total Development System (TDS), Total Production system (TPS), Total Marketing System (TMS), Total Business Intelligence Management System (TIS) and Total Job Quality Management, System (TJS) as shown in Figure 2, so that each department is equipped with the core technology and linked with one another cooperatively. Each of TDS, TPS, TMS, TIS and TJS consists of organized "four sub-core elements (a)-(d)", as follows;

Figure 1. Outline of New Japan Model (NJM), new corporate management principle

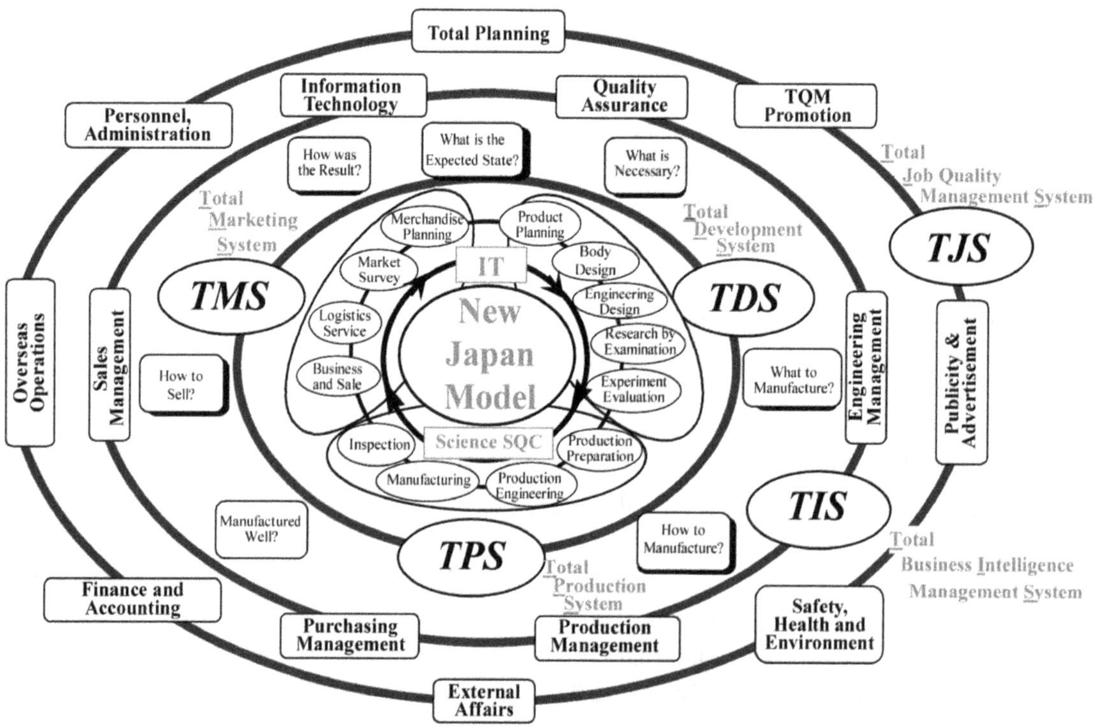

Figure 2. Outline of New Japan Model (NJM) using integrated "five core elements"

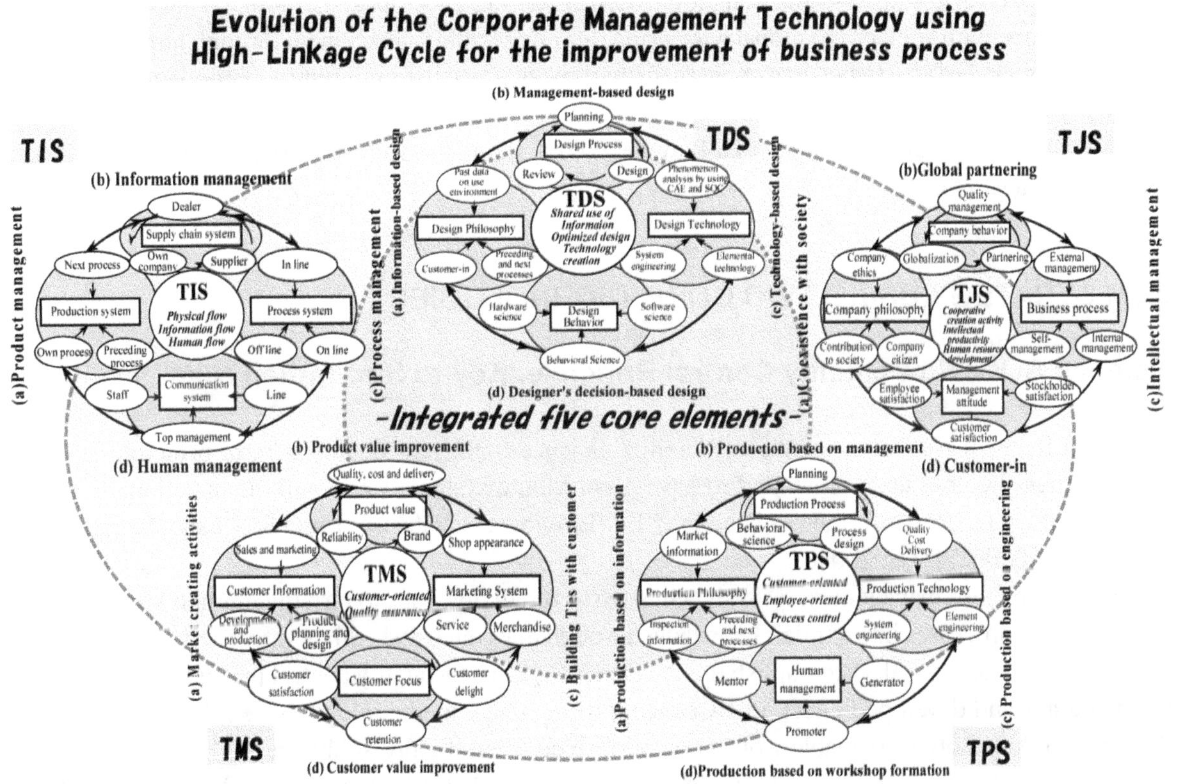

The significance of TDS is to create the optimum product design based on the common knowledge by shared use of information. TDS is to systematize the development design methodologies through (a) design based on the on internal and external information with stress laid on design philosophy, (b) development-design management aimed at a reasonable design process, (c) creating general solutions based on the most advanced design technologies, and (d) clarifying the design behavior based on the design policy of a development designer (: theory-action-decision making).

The main objective of TPS is process management laying stress on customers and employees to realize working environment leading to skill improvement. To improve the reliability of the entire production process, TPS is composed of indispensable sub-core elements: (a) production based on information, (b) production based on management, (c) production based on engineering, and (d) production based on workshop formation.

Similarly, TMS is to develop quality management to be relied on by customers through scientific marketing and sales not sticking to conventional concept. To realize quality assurance with an emphasis on the customer, TMS is composed of strategic sub-core elements: (a) market creating activities, (b) product value improvement, (c) building ties with customer, and (d) customer value improvement.

The aim of TIS has a function of new management technology system for the development design, production and sales departments in the inner circle by linkage with the indirect office department in the outer circle. TIS is composed of organized sub-core elements: (a) product management, (b) information management, (c) process management, and (d) human management based on the integrated cooperative activities.

Similarly, TJS has a function for improving intellectual productivity by employee training and internal/external partnering to strengthen global marketing. TJS is composed of intellectual sub-elements (a) coexistence with society, (b) global partnering, (c) intellectual management through human resource development, and (d) customer-in management activity, to grasp the importance of cooperative creation activity.

The development and validity of NJM are detailed to the references of Amasaka Ed. (2007a, 2012) and Amasaka (2008a).

NJM STRATEGY USING TWO CORE TECHNOLOGIES

Science SQC, New Quality Control Principle, Key to Strengthen NJM

The main focus of NJM is to strategically utilize Science SQC, new quality control principle in order to strengthen the core technology and to have it contribute systematically and organizationally to the activities of QCD, CS (Customer Satisfaction), ES (Employee Satisfaction), and SS (Social Satisfaction) (Amasaka, 2000b, 2003a, 2004b).

To achieve these management tasks, it is important for all divisions to turn the implicit knowledge of their business processes into explicit knowledge through integrated and collaborative activities and sharing objective awareness. To accomplish this, "Science SQC, anew quality control principle" was created by the author and developed under a new concept using a new methodology that applied the four core SQC principles in order to enable work to be performed scientifically as shown in Figure 3 (Amasaka and Azuma, 1991; Amasaka and Maki, 1992; Amasaka, 1992, 1993; Amasaka, 1999a, 2003a). (Refer to Amasaka (2004b) in detail).

The first of the four principles, Scientific SQC is the scientific and inductive approaches in addition to the conventional deductive method of tackling engineering problem, and the

second principle, SQC Technical Methods, is a methodology "Mountain-Climbing for Problem–Solving" by using the proactive combination of reliability analysis, new QC seven tools (N7), multivariate analysis design of experiment and other statistical science. The third principle, the Integrated SQC Network, which is called TTIS (Total SQC Technical Intelligence System) by using TPOS (Total TQM Promotional Original SQC Soft), TSIS (Total SQC Intelligence System), TIRS (Total Information Retrieval System) and TSML (Total SQC Manual Library), is designed to turn management technologies that deal with proprietary technologies or business processes into owned assets (Amasaka and Maki, 1992; Amasaka, 1997). The fourth principle, Management SQC, interprets the gap between the theory and reality of technical problems as the problems existing between departments and organizations. It then verbalizes the implicit understanding inherent in the business process in order to present it as explicit knowledge and also as a general solution to the technical problems (Refer to Amasaka (2004b) in detail).

Science SQC takes a scientific approach to work operations based on these four principles, and is not limited to an "individual solution", which only provides a special or partial solution to the problem. Rather, it is a new principle that describes a next generation quality management technique for the manufacturing business. It aims to provide a universal "general solution" and thereby create a new technology for problem solving (Amasaka, 1993, 2003a, 2004b).

Figure 3. Outline of Science SQC, new quality control principle

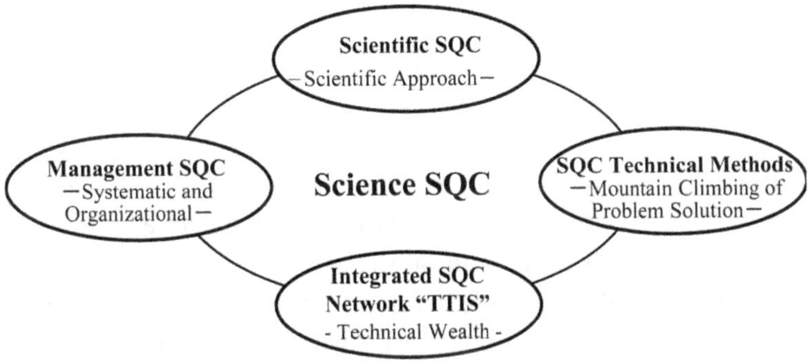

More specifically, as illustrated in Figure 4, it will be vital to collect and analyze product quality information gathered from outside and inside the company. Then use this information to create "wants" as part of the market creation activity and also to establish a structure for development and production that is capable of offering new products. In the implementation stage, it is important to apply the Science SQC and Science TQM, via a verifiable scientific business approach, to each step ((1) Input information, (2) Information for development, and (3) Output information) of the business process of development designing and manufacturing. This is done in order to effectively carry out the strategic integration of the five core elements and also to bring about the evolution of management technology that can ensure high reliability (Amasaka, 2008a).

Figure 4. The Business Process of product development & Design, and Manufacturing

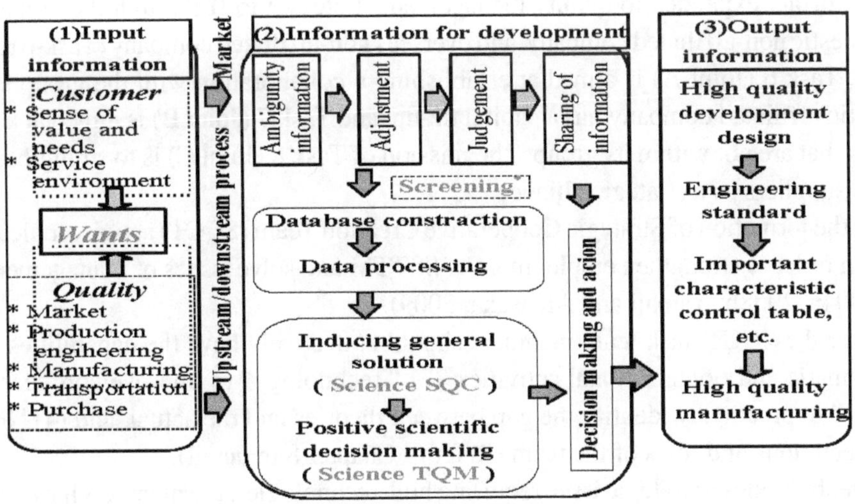

Strategic Stratified Task Team Model, Driving Force in NJM Strategy

In a general assembly industry like the automotive manufacturing, a thorough quality assurance (QA) plays an important role. It includes not only the parts and unit quality control, but also the optimization of adaptive engineering for assembly by the automobile manufacturers and the quality of production, sale and services. Therefore, when working on the solution of a pending engineering task, separate and independent team activities by the automobile manufacture or parts manufacturers alone often fail to clarify the engineering area, which exists in-between or across the two teams (both companies).

In this connection, it is important to zero-in on the end users from the view point of customer-in and to challenge for realizing simultaneous QCD fulfilment by mutually disclosing their software and hardware techniques to each other (Amasaka, 2000b). As a management technology strategy to enable smooth business management for realizing high-quality assurance, the author has created the Strategic Stratified Task Team Model (SSTTM) as shown in Figure 5 (Amasaka, 2004b, 2013). The expected role of the SSTTM and benefits it provides are not limited to cooperation among the departments inside the company. It also contributes to strengthening the ties among group manufacturing companies, non-group companies, and even overseas manufacturers. Two measures must be taken in order to realize SSTTM.

The first is to eliminate the work methods that rely too heavily on the techniques and experiences of individuals. The second is to revolutionize the business process through the SSTTM that places emphasis on cooperation among the departments, and that with suppliers. SSTTM formed from partnering linkages are developed systematically and organizationally to promote the strategic development of NMT. This model consists of Task 1 to Task 8 teams involving the group, department, division, field, whole company, affiliated companies, non-affiliated companies, and overseas affiliates (Refer to Chapter 8 in detail).

As indicated in Figure 5, the level of problem-solving technology rises in product development strategy I and II through joint task teams of intra-company departments and divisions (Task-1 to Task-5, Group Task team, Department task team, Division task management team, Field task management team and Total task management team) in proportion with the improvement of the stratified task level. This technology is further expanded to quality management strategy I to II through the domestic affiliated company, domestic non-affiliated company, and overseas non-affiliated company (Task-6 to Task-8, Joint A to Joint C). Task 6 (Joint A) is aimed at establishing a collaboration with the group suppliers with whom domestic affiliated company has a capital tie-up, and Task 7 (Joint B) is aimed at a collaboration with suppliers that are not within its group. The mission of Task 8 (Joint C) is to strengthen cooperation with overseas suppliers as a strategic alliance.

Moreover, the formation of Strategic Cooperative Creation Team (SCCT) activity indicated by Figure 6 is required in order to strengthen employment of SSTTM and solve issues of management technology (Amasaka, 2004a, 2008b; Yamaji and Amasaka, 2009).

To empower the SCCT, task team members should collectively have the capabilities in (1) "Strategy" for systematic and organizational activities, (2) "Technology" to improve core technologies, (3) "Methodology" to practically identify the gap between theories and the actual, and (4) "Promotion" to fulfill the expectations and roles of the team (Refer to Chapter 8 in detail).

If the task team tackles a strategic issue requiring high technologies, the members have to be ingenious as (i) "Generators," and at the same time they have to be able to perform strategic analysis as (ii) "Mentors". In addition, to infuse effective drive force in the team activities, creativity as (iii) "Producers" and leadership to orchestrate all members' ideas as (iv) "Promoters" toward target achievement are important. As the key to the successful team activities, the team leader (Administrator) should select the members who have at least one of the capabilities for (i) to (iv), commission authority and responsibilities to the members, and have himself/herself concentrate on risk management.

For this reason, as the leader, a person who has an experience of clearing business obstacles should be appointed, so that the leader is capable of leading the team overcoming difficulties (Amasaka, Ed., 2012a; Amasaka, 2015, 2020).

Figure 5. Outline of Strategic Stratified Task Team Model (SSTTM)

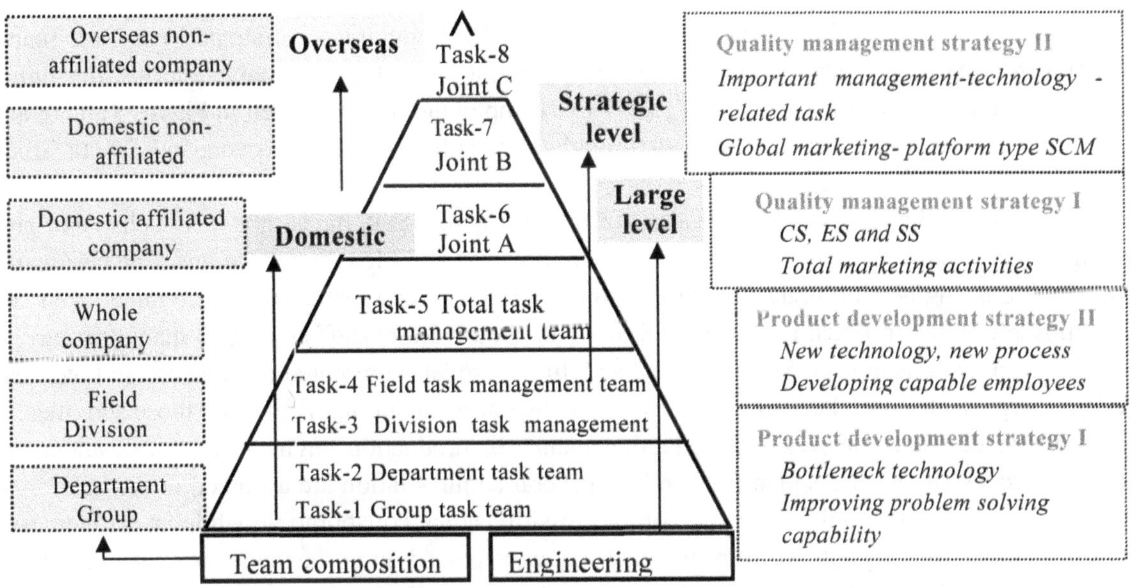

Figure 6. Formation of Strategic Cooperative Creation Team (SCCT)

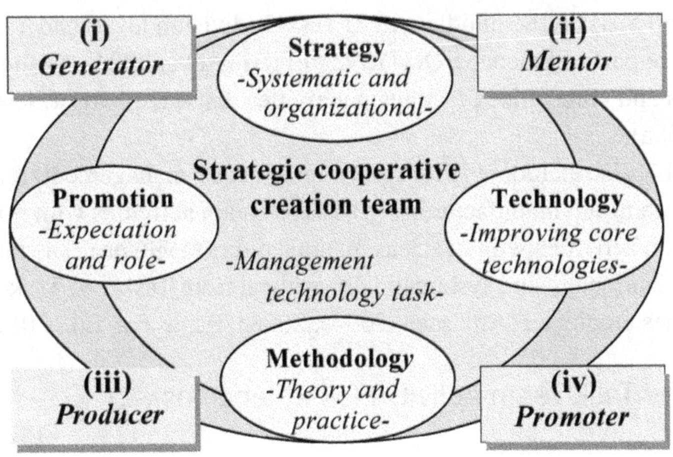

APPLICATION - PUTTING INTO PRACTICE AND VALIDITY OF NJM

In this section, the author introduces the typical research examples of how NJM improved the management technology at an advanced corporation, Toyota, Toyota Group companies and other Japanese advanced companies.

Transition and Validity of the Science SQC and Strategic Joint Task Team Activities Employing TDS, TPS, TMS, TIS and TJS in Toyota

The author will introduce the transition and validity of NJM through the "Strategic Joint Task Team" activities in order to advance the evolution of management technology. In concrete terms, the author has developed the formation of SSTTM (Task-1 to 8) employing SCCT as seen in Figure 5 and 6, and the validity of these task teams was verified through their application within Toyota and Toyota Group companies (Amasaka, 2004a, 2008a).

Particularly, as the stage of NJM creation (from 1988 up to 2000), the author was in charge of promoting strategic quality management, and therefore organized and led the task teams. The task teams tackled various engineering issues. Table 1 is a chart of the activity themes that were undertaken and accomplished by the task teams. From 1988 to 2000, about 15,000 staff and 5,000 managers carried out 4,000 task team activities. Some of these activities were later presented to Japanese and overseas academic organizations in the form of theses. The table covers about one-fifth of all those activities.

Corporate divisions such as (a) production plant, (b) production engineering, (c) development design, (d) sales and business planning, and (e) general administration are arranged in the horizontal direction. An "×" in the table is the symbol for cross-divisional collaboration, while an arrow means that the technical findings obtained from an activity were passed on to the next study (handing down of technologies). Tasks are stratified vertically from the top: (1) Task-1 (small group level) and Task-2 (group and department level) task team activities were part of the "SQC

Renaissance" (1988 on) (Amasaka, 1998; Amasaka and Azuma, 1991; Amasaka and Maki, 1992) based on "SQC Promotion Cycle" using "Stratified SQC Seminar and Growing Human Resource" (Refer to Appendix 5.A and 5.B). In the middle are (2) Task-3 (division level) and Task-4 (field level) task team activities that were part of Science SQC (1992 on) (Amasaka, 2003). At the bottom is (3) Task-5 (across different fields and companies), task team activities that were part of Science TQM (1996 on) (Amasaka, 2004a, 2008a).

Furthermore, the table also includes (4) Task-6, "joint total task management team" activities in which Toyota collaborated with group manufacturers, (5) Task-7, team activities with non-group manufacturers, and (6) Task-8, team activities with overseas manufacturers (1996 on). The table indicates how the technical themes organizationally and systematically evolved from Task-1 to Task-8, thereby enhancing the level of the strategies employed (Amasaka, 2004a, 2008a; Amasaka, Ed., 2012a).

The Effectiveness of Task Team Activity (Task-1 and Task-2)

In employing TDS, as the Table 1 shows, "SQC Renaissance" was triggered by (1) "analysis of fuel economy improvement factor" tackled by the development design (R & D) division and Amasaka, 1991). The R&D members of the division formed a task team (Task-1).

Table 1. Changes in the Strategic Task Team Activities of Toyota (1988-2000)

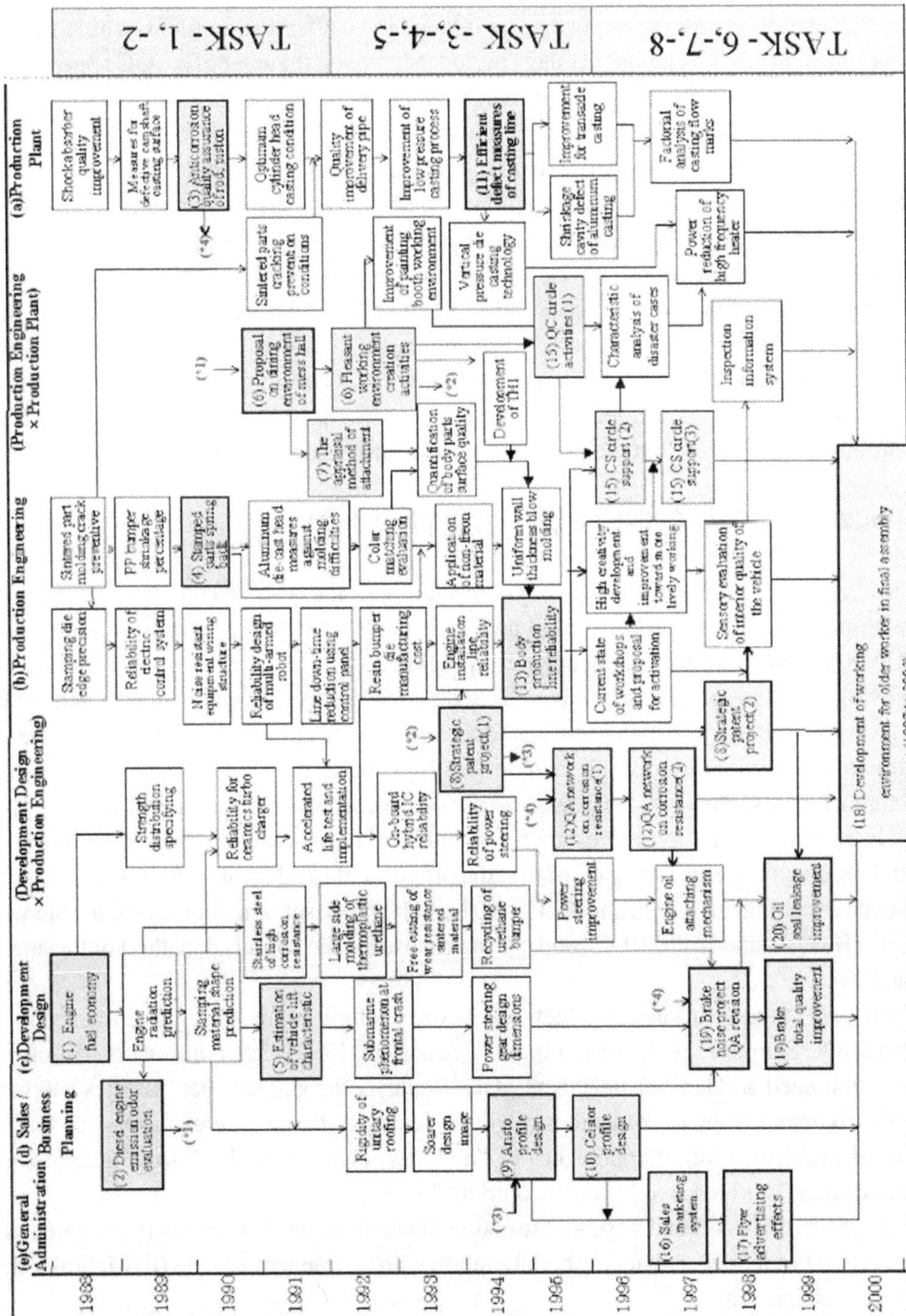

In Task-1, they performed multi-regression analysis of stratified curves based on existing engine fuel consumption data (N=22 units) and formulated a relation model of fuel consumption and design factors. By adjusting the identified design factors that were found to be effective for fuel saving, they succeeded in development of fuel-saving engine in a short period. Moreover, the scientific SQC approach triggered a pioneering laser engine study and a chain of new technology development shown in Table 5.1, including (2) "development of diesel emission odor evaluation method" (Tanaka, et al., 1990).

In employing TPS, similarly in the production engineering division and production plant divisions, a chain of technological development and production improvements occurred for production issues (1988-1989). A framework of task teams also expanded from a small group to group and department (1990-1991). For example, in Task-2, development of new process methods advanced such as (3) "studies on the rust preventive quality assurance of plated parts" (Amasaka et al., 1993) and (4) "analysis of total curvature spring back in stamped parts" (Kusune, et al., 1992).

These remarkable achievements were underpinned by "SQC promotion cycle" campaigns initiated by "generators and mentors" described in Figure 6 for tackling upskilling themes and human resource development through stratified SQC seminars (Amasaka and Osaki, 1999).

Task Management Team Activities (Task-3 and Task-4)

After confirming effectiveness of task team activities, the activities evolved into task management team activities within and across divisions (Task-3 and Task-4) (1992-1995) described in Table 5.2. For instance, R&D divisions unfolded "Science SQC" in Figure 3.

In employing TDS, a typical example is indicated by (5) "a study on estimation of vehicle lift characteristic" (Amasaka, et al., 1996), they enhanced the speed of development by improving the accuracy of CAE estimation. Activities to solve these important engineering issues took place in a divisional scale (Task-3). Moreover, cross-divisional task teams (Task-4) were also formed and significant improvements were made. In employing TPS, typical examples include collaboration between production engineering divisions and production plants for topics of (6) "the proposal of the desirable dining room environment at the employee restaurant" (Uchida and Maki, 1991), "The proposal of making comfortable workplace environment" (Hayashi and Kido, 1992), and (7) "a proposal of the appraisal method of the attachment" (Komuro and Ito, 1992).

One of the keys to these successful achievements was training of managers. The managers received "Management SQC Seminar" as shown in Figure 7 (Amasaka, 1999) (3,500 managers participated over 5 years), and embodied and led "Management SQC"—clarify the gap between theories and facts. As a result, in order to depart from work methods relying on a rule of thumb, the managers and staff applied straightforward problem solution approaches of "SQC technical methods (N7/multivariate analysis / experimental design)" and reached "general solutions".

In team activities of Task-3 and Task-4, a structure in which general managers ((iv) Promoters) manage managers ((iii) Producers), enhancing collaboration with "(i) Generators and (ii) Mentors" described in Figure 6 is essential.

Total Task Management Team Activity (Task-5)

The expansion and successful results of the team activities from Task-1 to Task-4 led company-wide activities where the management themselves assume the leadership. A methodology to provide what

Figure 7. Outline of Management SQC Seminar

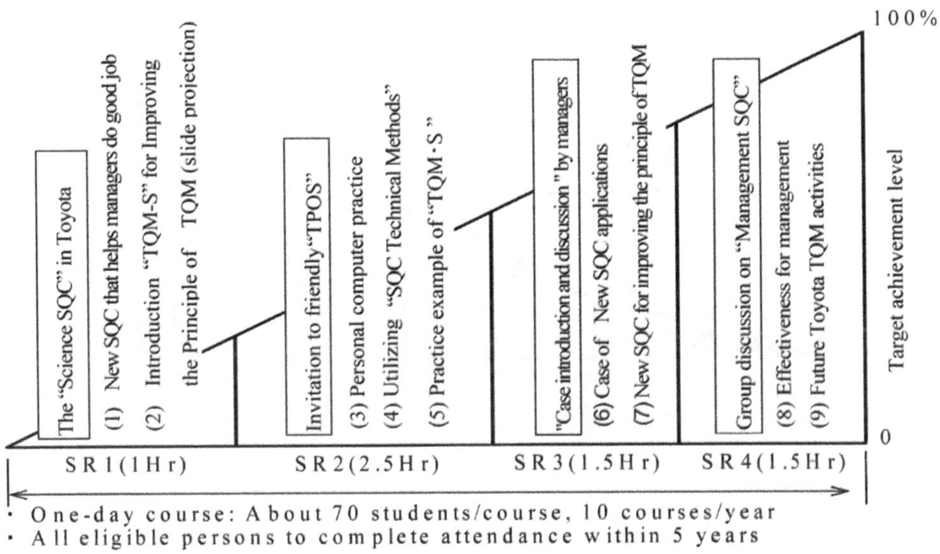

customers need before they notice their needs - "Customer Science" has created by the author (Amasaka, 2002a, 2005) - was utilized as management technology strategy in a form of company-wide activity (Task-5) described in Table 5.2 . Here, "SQC Technical Methods" was applied effectively for identification and solution of problems.

In employing TDS and TJS, typical examples of product technology strategies, (8) "strategic patent project" was jointly promoted with development design division, production engineering division and Intellectual Property Division (External Affairs Department) (Amasaka, et al., 1996). The project constructed a model of engineers' image concepts of good patent, enabling the Patent Value Appraisal Method (Amasaka, et al., 1996; Amasaka, 2009a). In employing TDS, moreover, the results and approaches adopted in this project for materializing images were also utilized in (9) "LEXUS GS400 and (10) LS430 profile design (Japanese name is Aristo and Celsior)" by body design division and "Higashifuji Technical Center" of design precedence development, and this model presently receives worldwide reputations. In the course of R&D for LEXUS profile design, the author has applied in combination with TDS-DTM (- Design Technical Method) by shown in Figure 8, in order to identify "proportion ratios" that explain the universal vehicle profile of world prestige vehicles (Amasaka, et al., 1999; Amasaka and Nagasawa, 2000; Amasaka, 2005, 2007a; Motor Fan, 1997, 2000; J. D, Power and Associates, 1998) (Refer to Chapter 13 in detail).

In employing TPS, similar approaches were taken in the joint promotion by production engineering division and production plant division for (11) "development of new engine casting method" (Amasaka, 2000a) and (12) "vehicle body rust prevention technology" (Amasaka, et al., 1995; Amasaka, 2004b). These studies led to an establishment of "QA network system". In addition, combination of (13) "production equipment operation and maintenance system" (Amasaka and Sakai, 1996, 1998) and (14) "IT control chart" (Amasaka and Sakai, 2002, 2009) achieved establishment of "TPS-QAS". These achievements affected other production engineering development and drove company-wide (15) "New QC Circle activities" (Amasaka, et al., 1995). These movements of the strategic task team activities largely contributed to evolution of "TPS" and high quality assurance of manufacturing.

Figure 8. TDS-DTM, the conception support methods for developing strategic product

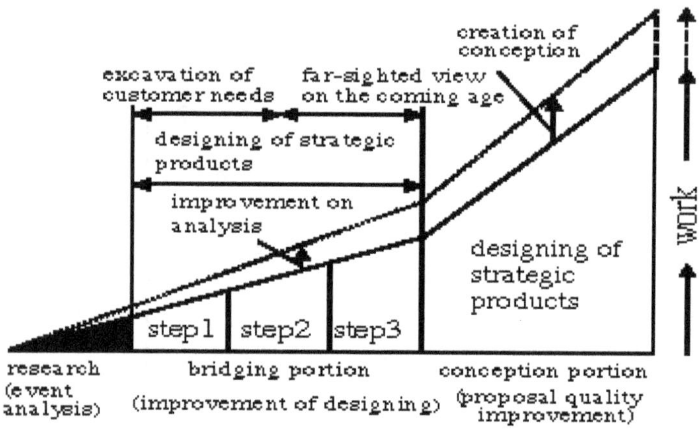

In employing TMS, particularly, the author has developed the "Marketing SQC" which utilizes Science SQC, in order to aim at improvement in quality of the business process of operating marketing and sales strategy (Amasaka, 2001a; Amasaka, et al, 2005). By implementing "Marketing SQC", the achievements by these team activities enhanced links with customers. Some examples include (16) "development of Toyota sales marketing system" (Amasaka, 2001b, 2007) that utilized IT and SQC as support tools and (17) "flyer advertising effects" (Amasaka, 2001c, 2009b) that contributed to effective advertisement (Refer to Chapter 15 in detail).

In this way, the task team activities also influenced sales and marketing activities and triggered their revision. Furthermore, in recent years, due to increasing number of aged and female employees, general administration division initiated a company-wide work environment improvement activity named (18) "AWD-6P/J" (Amasaka, et al., 1999a; Amasaka, 2007b) as a task team activity.

Each activity mentioned above achieved favorable results. Through these activities, core techniques of "TDS, TPS, TMS, TIS and TJS" were build up and these techniques were gradually integrated (Amasaka, 2002, 2004a, 2008a,b).

Joint Total Task Management Team Activity (Task-6 and Task-7)

For the survival of automotive manufacturer in a competitive business of comprehensive assembly in the global market, partnering with parts manufacturers is essential. For this reason, the authors extend the task team activity structure further to Task-6 and Task-7 in which a company collaborate with group or non-group suppliers.

As the Table 5.1 shows, in Task-6, the team tackled a global quality issue of (19) "brake quality improvement" employing TDS, TPS, TMS, TIS and TJS (Amasaka and Osaki, 1999, 2003) (Refer to Chapter 14 in detail). This Task-6 activity involved one of Toyota group companies, Aisin and succeeded in developing new materials and manufacturing methods that satisfies requirements for brake noise, braking performance and durability, which were regarded as being in mutual inverse relationship.

Similarly, another example of Task-7 was (20) "drive system oil seal leakage improvement" (Amasaka, 1999, 2003b; Amasaka and Osaki, 2003), for which Toyota worked jointly with NOK. The achievement of the team activity was unprecedented visualization of oil leakage phenomena. Regarding the organization of the two activities, the team in the former case was "QAT-6P/J" that consisted of members of Aisin divisions of R&D, production engineering, manufacturing, sales and service in addition to Toyota members for supporting innovation of total business process.

The project teams ("TDOS-Q5" and "NDOS-Q8") in the latter case invited NOK members. They also acted as "dual total task management team", orchestrating Toyota and NOK. The author led both teams and their activities are positioned as platform-based "supply chain management" for quality strategies. All activities utilized "Science SQC" to identify problem mechanisms and practiced "Customer Science", leading to an achievement of 90-95% reduction of quality problems, including field complaints and in-process defects.

Based on these achievements, since 1997, a task team activity as "Task-8" which involves collaboration with overseas companies has been steadily progressing. Using approaches similar to those utilized in Toyota's internal team activities and work, the team is seeing achievement of their activities for human resources development by "SQC promotion cycle" for problem-solving with "Science SQC" (Amasaka, et al., 1999; Amasaka, 2004b).

Expanding NJM Application to Toyota Group Companies and other Japanese Advanced Corporations

To strengthen NJM strategy in Toyota, particularly, the author has expanded the NJM application employing the Science SQC and SSTTM to Toyota Group companies and other Japanese advanced corporations as follows;

First, to strengthen quality management of the auto-industry, the author has developed NJM to the cooperation activities of automobile assembly maker and supplier, and proved the validity of scientific Total Quality Management called "TQM-S" by employing TDS, TPS, TMS, TIS and TJS (Refer to Amasaka (2001d) in detail).

Second, in Toyota Group's application, the author has developed the "All Toyota SQC Study Group" by Toyota and named "TQM-S" through the promoting "Stratified SQC Seminar" based on "SQC Promotion Cycle" activity in Toyota Group Companies named "Kyohokai" in Japan, and Toyota Motor Thailand as a model case of NJM application to overseas factory (Amasaka, et al., 1997, 1999b,c), Moreover, to expanding NJM application, the author has developed the "JSA-Nagoya QST Study Group in Toyota and Toyota Group" employing "SQC Technical Methods" for strengthen "Mountain-Climbing for Problem-Solving" (Refer to Kamio and Amasaka Eds. (2000) in detail).

Third, in other Japanese advanced corporations' application, the author has focused the "Establishment of the quality management technology of customer first" by developing "Study Group of the Ideal Situation the Quality Management of the Manufacturing Industry" named "Amasaka's Forum" (Amasaka, et al., 2004, 2005). As concrete deployment of NJM strategy, the author has worked the validity of the "New Japan Model: Science TQM-Theory and Practice for Strategic Quality Management" (Refer to Amasaka, Ed. (2007) in detail).

Brake Pad Quality Assurance using Total Task Management Team Activities

Here, the author introduces problem-solving of the "automobile brake pad quality assurance" to below as a typical example of bottleneck technology for which SSTTM was used. The brake pad quality assurance (QA) activity is adopted as a typical recent study for automobile manufacturing. As a case A, the main objective of this activity is to establish a technology for attaining satisfactory braking performance while minimizing squeal through exchange of the result of sensitivity analysis on the causes of squeal and braking performance.

Disk brakes work on a principle that the pressing of pads to the rotors by the calipers generate braking force. Brake noise is generated when the pad and the rotor are in contact with each other in a delicately unstable condition. The condition that allows noise or abnormal sound to be generated with ease and the response quality of brake are items contrary to each other. Therefore, it is important to analyze the properties of pads and the response quality of noises and brake, and reduce dispersions in the properties of pads that affect the generation of noises and the braking effect (Miller, 1978). The key point of this activity lies in establishing technologies that make sensitivity of factors on the braking effect and noise in the aspect of design engineering, and to make these mutually contrary braking performances compatible with each other through bi-directional interaction with the manufacturing engineering (Amasaka, 1999b, 2004a,b; .Amasaka and Osaki, 1999; Amasaka, Ed., 2007, 2012a).

1. Organizational outline of "Total Task Management Team" (TTMT)

The key to successful production is a joint task team activity between the manufacturer and affiliated suppliers as stated above Task-6 in SSTTM and evolution of quality management (: simultaneous QCD fulfilment) using Automobile Global Manufacturing Model (AGMM) using SCCT shown in Figure 2, Chapter 6 (Amasaka, 2004b, 2017a; Amasaka, Ed., 2012) (Refer to Chapter 6).

To embody the scheme of SCCT, forming an organization allowing use of know-how and information among the vehicle design, parts design, production process design, manufacture, inspection, maintenance, and marketing (service, marketing quality) departments for vehicle production including the final vehicle assembly manufacturer will lead to improvement of engineering capability through supporting conception by engineers, possibly resulting in improvement of the business quality.

To develop AGMM, this organization has been realized in the form of "Total Task Management Team" (TTMT) named Toyota's QAT (Total QA Network) by final vehicle assembly manufacturer (Toyota Motor Corporation), brake unit manufacturer (Aishin Seiki Co., Ltd. of tier-1 supplier in Figure 3, Chapter 8), and brake pad manufacturer (Aishin Chemical Co., Ltd. of tier-2 supplier in Figure 3, Chapter 8) as shown in Figure 9 (Amasaka, 1999a, 2004b, 2017a; Amasaka, Ed., 2012a).

By the top policy of Toyota and Kyohokai (Toyota, 1987), the author (a general manager of TQM promotion div. of Toyota) constitutes the following organizations as a supervisor of Task-6. Task-6 consists of (i) two general managers of the chassis design department, production engineering and development department in Toyota, (ii) two general managers of the chassis unit development department and quality assurance department in Aishin Seiki, and (iii) three general managers of the brake components development department, brake components manufacturing department and quality assurance department in Aishin Chemical.

In TTMT composed of the seven general managers of three companies, each general manager assigns several section chiefs, sub-section chiefs, technical staffs, and statistics analysis staffs named "SQC special adviser" (Amasaka, 2004b) as the TTMT members.

2. Development of QAT

Figure 9. Organizational outline of Total Task Management Team

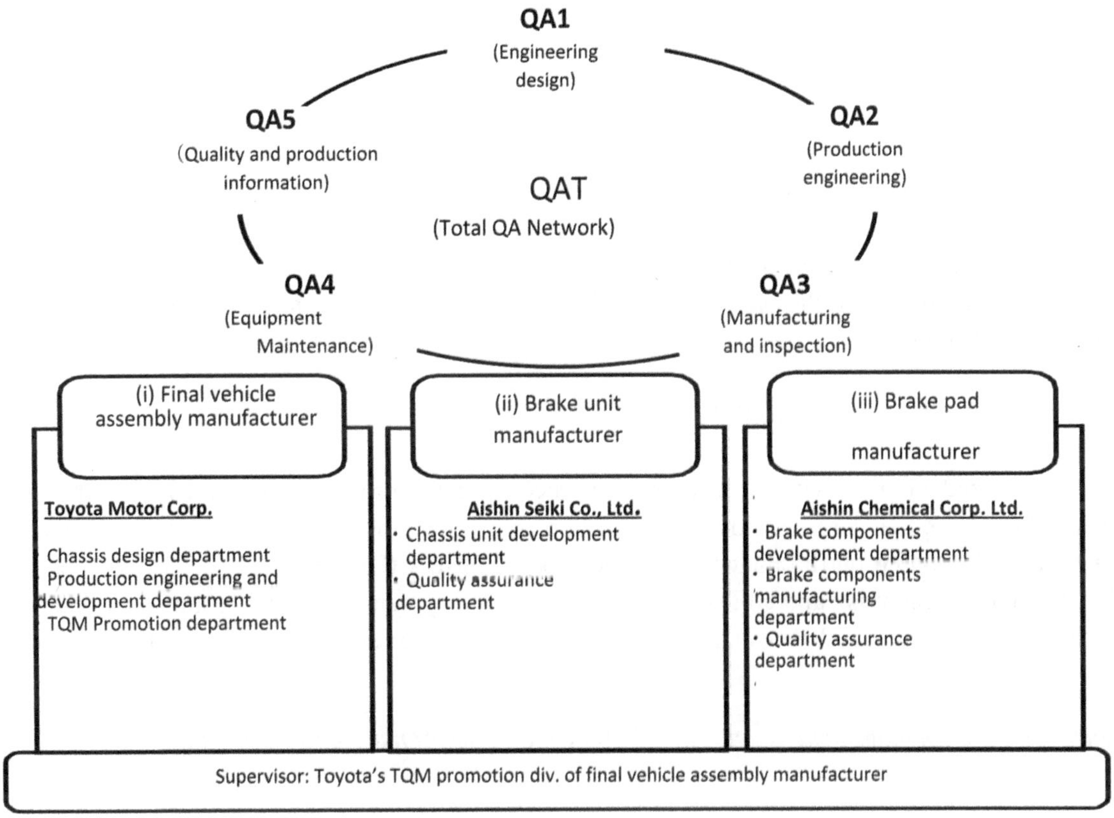

In Figure 9, Then, the author develops SCCT using (QAT) in enforcement of TTMT as follows; As embodiment of SCCT, five task teams, QA1 (engineering design), QA2 (production engineering), QA3 (manufacture and inspection), QA4 (equipment maintenance) and QA5 (quality and production information), are linked mutually for QAT activities.

The author commissions the general manager of the quality assurance department of Aishin Seiki and Aishin Chemical as "sub-supervisor" in order to rationalize progress management of QAT. Next, the author commissions each part chief as Generators of QA1 to QA5 as follows; QA1 is chassis design department of Toyota, QA2 is chassis unit development of Aishin Seiki, QA3 is brake components development department of Aishin Chemical, QA4 is Brake components manufacturing department, and QA5 is Production engineering and development department and TQM promotion department of Toyota.

Similarly, five teams of QA1 to QA5 arrange section chief as Mentors, sub-section chief as Promoters, and technical staffs and statistics analysis staffs as (d) Producers or every team, separately as indicated Figure 2, Chapter 6 (Refer to Chapter 6 in detail).

3. Three management activities for developing QAT

As a key technology for quality assurance, three management activities- "Total technical Management (TM)" by QA1 and QA2, "Total production management (PM)" by QA3 and QA4, and "Total information management (IM)" by corporation of QA5 and two quality assurance departments- were created to promote QAT and were promoted by integrating these activities as shown in Figure 10.

Five teams focus on reviewing the work method and control items in process conditions by clarifying how brake performance and squeal are affected by dispersions in raw material property and process condition through sensitivity analysis.

(3-1) Total technical management

Makes a sensitivity analysis of dispersion in both raw materials and the process condition for the brake response quality and the brake noise, and reviews the engineering method and clarifies process condition control items.

(3-2) Total product management (PM)

This is a production activity for realizing the process conditions and control items using the "Total Quality Assurance Networking Model" named "Process QAT table" (Amasaka, 2004b; Kojima and Amasaka, 2011) based on the matrix chart and process FMEA (Failure Mode and Effect Analysis), FTA (Fault Tree Analysis), and QFD (Quality Function Deployment) by utilizing statistical science, in which the research and development, production design, production engineering, production, equipment

Figure 10. Three management activities for Total Quality Assurance Network (QAT)

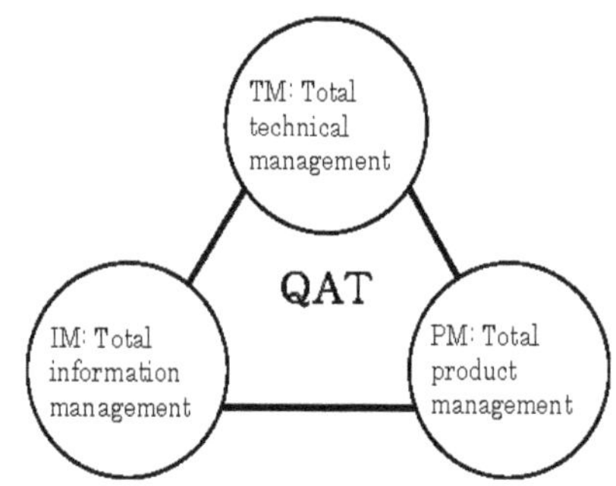

maintenance, quality assurance and others departments participate jointly (Refer to Chapter 11 in detail).

(3-3) Total information management (IM)

This activity focuses on establishing the system for timely feedback of the market quality information (from dealers), next process information (from vehicle assembly manufacture) and local process information (parts manufacturer) to respective processes.

4. Development of QAT using SQC Technical Methods

For quick systematic and organizational optimization of QAT as indicated in Figure 10, the "Development of QAT using SQC Technical Methods" as described in Figure 8 are used as the "Mountain-Climbing for Problem-Solving" utilizing Science SQC (Amasaka, 2004a,b). Each type of arrow in the figure represents the activity of each team among QA1 to QA5.

(4-1) Total technical management activities

Analyses of each raw material (TM1 in Figure 11) and market research (TM2 in Figure 11) were conducted, and factor analysis based on results (sensitivity analysis) was performed to screen the material in a short period. In the factor analysis I (TM3 in Figure 11) using principal component analysis, for example, it was found that the embedded material grain size and the inorganic fiber diameter are related to the abnormal sound characteristic and wear respectively as shown in Figure 12.

Each "a" region where abnormal sound or wear is very conspicuous, while each "b" represents a region where its influence remains. Each "c" has been found as a region where both characteristics are not contradictory.

Factor analysis I has shown variation in the production process conditions (PM1 in Figure 11). For the abrasive components (inorganic fibers and hard fine particles), technical analysis such as electron microscopy to observe the states of dispersion in each raw material and the pad was used in combina-

Figure 11. Development of QAT using SQC Technical Methods

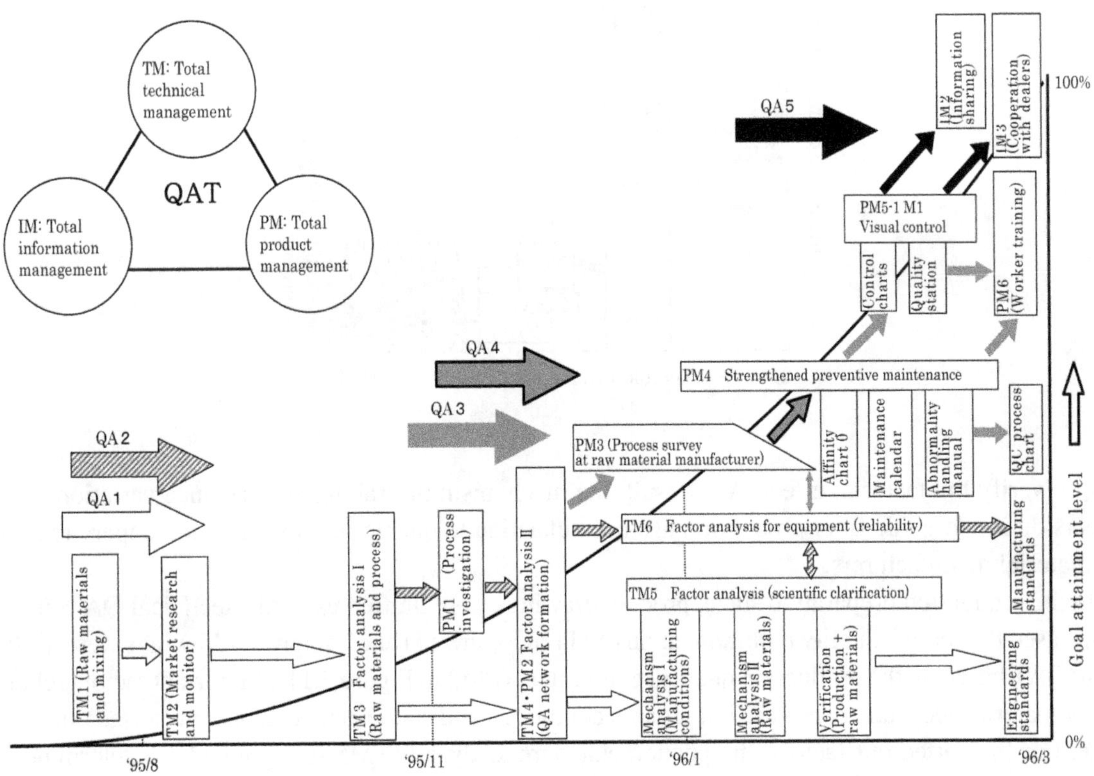

Figure 12. Example of analyzed influences of raw material properties

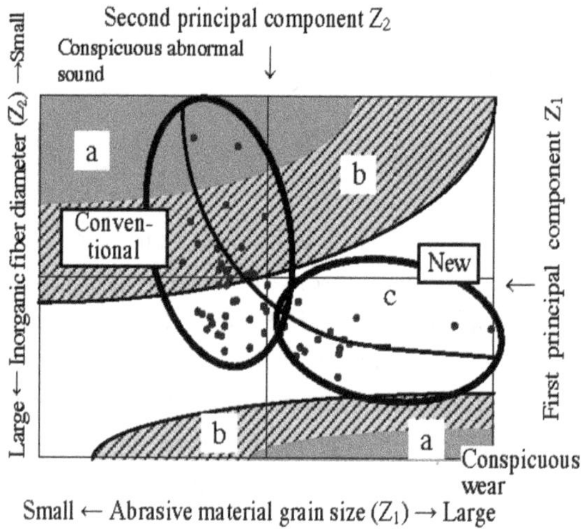

Figure 13. Causal relation between alternative characteristics of squeal and thermoforming temperature

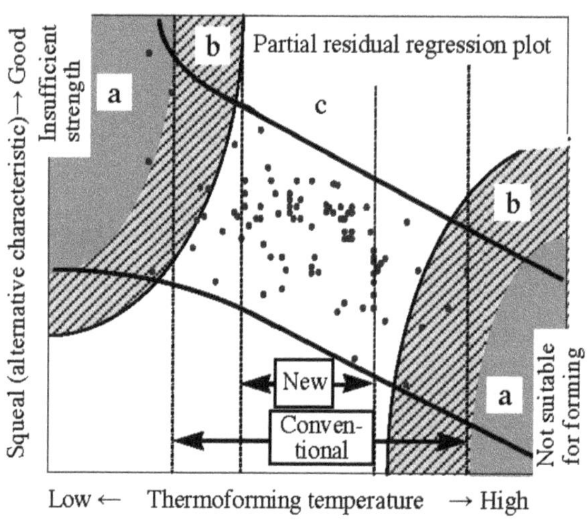

tion, to verify the factorial effect. As a result, the mechanism of braking performance variation due to dispersion in inorganic fiber production has been clarified to enable improvement in cooperation with the material manufacturers.

In the production preparation stage, product drawings were drafted using the technical QA Network table based the market quality requirement on (TM4 in Figure 11) and equipment drawings were drafted using QAT based on the production quality requirement (PM2 in Figure 5.11). Important factors relating to raw material acceptance, production process conditions and state management were sorted out at this stage. For the sorted out factors, the phenomena were analyzed (TM5 in Figure 11) to determine the equipment condition quantitatively and the product drawing tolerances were determined by combined use on the design experiments and multivariate analysis for scientific optimization.

For example, use of the partial residual regression plot has clarified that the thermoforming temperature has a causal relation with the alternative characteristic of squeal, as shown in Figure 13. Each "a" represents a region where the strength is insufficient or a region not suitable for forming, while each "b" representing a region where the influence remain. In consideration of the strength and formability, region "c" has been determined as the control conditions of thermoforming process. To ensure control conditions shown by region "c", factor analysis on the equipment side (TM6 in Figure 11) for the molding die temperature dispersion, for example, was conducted, thus enabling unification of the pad forming temperature.

(4-2) Total product management activities

To attain the process conditions clarified by "Total technical management", the defects causes were studied by process investigation (PM1 in Figure 11) and the relationships with the quality characteristics were checked by QAT (PM2 in Figure 11). Further, to complete QAT, the brake unit manufacturer, brake pad manufacturer and raw material manufacturers formed a TTMT for mutual quality reviewing (PM3 in Figure 11).

As the result, the current process capability was clarified with summarized recurrence and release prevention measures, leading to strengthened preventive maintenance (PM4: maintenance calendar in Figure 8), visual control (PM5: inline SQC in Figure 11) and worker training (PM6: abnormal quality handling manual in Figure 11).

(4-3) Total information management activities

A quality check station (IM1 in Figure 11) was formed to enable the process information as the result of "Total product management" to be seen immediately. The route for making the market information (DAS: Dynamic Assurance System for high reliability and quality) (Sasaki, 1972) owned by the final assembly manufacturer available to parts manufacturers (IM2 in Figure 11) and the route for obtaining the actual product information from dealers (IM3 in Figure 11).

5. Effect

Through practical use of Total Task Management Team, the effect of the QCD research activities is remarkable as follows;

- Estimated market claim ratio reduction to 1/6 (from 2.6% to 0.4%)
- In-process fraction defective: down 60% (from 0.5% to 0.2%)
- Short convergence of initial failures: (from 9 months to 3 months)
- Cost reduction: 9.4% (156 Yen/unit)

Other Cases

The author has applied the SSTTM using Task 6 to Task 8 to critical QCD studies of automobile manufacturing developing NJM strategy as follows;

(i) Preventing vehicles' rusting (Amasaka, 2004b), (ii) Intelligence production operating system (Sakai and Amasaka, 2006), (iii) Epoch-making Innovation of the work environment (Amasaka, 2007b), (iv) Partnering performance measurement of Japanese automobile assembly makers and suppliers (Yamaji et al., 2008), (v) High reliability assurance of the transaxle oil seal leakage (Amasaka, 2008d), (vi) Simultaneous fulfillment of QCD for improving automotive chassis (paint corrosion resistance and welding process) (Yamaji and Amasaka, 2009), (vii) Automobile Body Color Development Approach Model (Muto et al., 2011), (viii) Prevention of bolt looseness (Hashimoto et al., 2014), (ix) New Global Partnering Production Model (Ebioka et al., 2007), (x) New Turkish Production System, New Malaysia Production Model and New Vietnam Production Model (Siang et al., 2010; Huang et al., 2012; Miyashita and Amasaka, 2014), (xi) Joint task team activities between Toyota Motor Corporation and Toyota Motor Thailand (Amasaka, 2012), and (xii) Developing Advanced Toyota Production System at Toyota manufacturing USA (Amasaka, 2016).

Furthermore, the result of this research has spread in many other manufacturing industries.

In the "Study group of the ideal situation the quality management of the manufacturing industry" (Union Japanese Scientists and Engineers), and "Establishment of a needed design quality assurance framework for numerical simulation" (Japanese Society for Quality Control) which the author led., Bridgestone Corp., Daikin Industries LTD., Fuji Xerox Co. Ltd., Futaba Corp., Hino Motors LTD., NEC Corp., NHK Spring Co., NTT DATA Mathematical Systems Inc., Sanden Holdings Corp., Toyota Motor Corp., Mizuho Research Institute Ltd, etc. indicate the case studies which can hold the validity of SSTTM, and are indicating the predetermined result (Amasaka, Ed., 2007a, 2007b; Amasaka, 2015; Amasaka, 2022).

CONCLUSION

In this chapter, the author has established the NJM (New Japan Model) for the realization of surpassing JIT, NJM employing "New JIT and Science TQM" consists of the integrated "TDS, TPS, TMS, TIS and TJS". NJM aims to realize an integrated form of a next-generation corporate management strategy by focusing product quality management strategy.

In this study, furthermore, the author has verified the validity of NJM using Science SQC and SSTTM (Strategic Stratified Task Team Model). On a concrete target, It's validity of NJM has been verified through its application within the Toyota Motor Corporation, Toyota group companies and other advanced corporations in Japan. The validity of study obtained in this chapter is further mentioned in Chapter 6 for realization of a present global production strategy.

ACKNOWLEDGMENT

The author would like to acknowledge the generous support of the following researchers: All those at Toyota Motor Corporation, Toyota Group companies and many affiliated / nonaffiliated suppliers, Study group of the Ideal Situation the Quality Management of Manufacturing Industry in JUSE (Union of Japanese Scientists and Engineers), Nagoya QC study group in JSA (Japanese Standards Association), and those connected with the Amasaka New JIT laboratory at Aoyama Gakuin University that assisted with author's research.

REFERENCES

Amasaka, K. (1992). Application of SQC analysis soft in Toyota. *Quality Journal of the Japanese Society for Quality Control*, *22*(2), 79–85.

Amasaka, K. (1993). SQC development and effects at Toyota. *Quality Journal of the Japanese Society for Quality Control*, *23*(4), 47–58.

Amasaka, K. (1995). A construction of SQC Intelligence System for Quick Registration and Retrieval Library. *Lecture Notes in Economics and Mathematical Systems*, *445*, 318–336. doi:10.1007/978-3-642-59105-1_24

Amasaka, K. (1997). A construction of SQC Intelligence System for quick registration and retrieval library. *Lecture Notes in Economics and Mathematical Systems*, *445*, 318–336. doi:10.1007/978-3-642-59105-1_24

Amasaka, K. (1998). *Application of classification and related methods to the SQC Renaissance in in Toyota Motor. In Data Science, Classification and Related Methods*. Springer.

Amasaka, K. (1999b). A study on "Science SQC" by utilizing "Management SQC"-A demonstrative study on a new SQC concept and procedure in the manufacturing industry-. *International Journal of Production Economics*, *60-61*, 591–598. doi:10.1016/S0925-5273(98)00143-1

Amasaka, K. (1999c). The TQM responsibilities for industrial management in Japan (Lecture). *The Japanese Society for Production Management, The 10th Annual Technical Conference,* 48-54.

Amasaka, K. (2000a). Science TQM, a new principle for quality management. *Proceedings of the 2nd Euro-Japanese Workshop, Chamonix, France*, 6-14.

Amasaka, K. (2000b). A demonstrative study of a new SQC concept and procedure in the manufacturing industry. *An International Journal of Mathematical & Computer Modeling, 3*(10-12), 1-10.

Amasaka, K. (2000c). Partnering chains as the platform for quality management in Toyota. *Proceedings of the 1st World Conference on Production and Operations Management,* 1-13.

Amasaka, K. (2001a). Recommendation of "Marketing SQC" which reforms the business and sales-Demonstrative study of the Customer Science by using Science SQC. *Production Management Transactions of the Japan Society for Production Management*, *7*(2), 153–156.

Amasaka, K. (2001b). Proposal of Marketing SQC to revolutionize dealers' sales activities. *Proceedings of the 16th International Conference on Production Research, Czech Public*, 1-9.

Amasaka, K. (2001c). A study of flyer advertising affect when TMS-S at Toyota. *Proceedings of the 12th Annual Conference of the Production and Operations Management Society,* 1-8.

Amasaka, K. (2001d). The quality management and supplier in the auto industry: Actuality of cooperation activities of auto-maker and supplier. Japan Small Business Research Institute.

Amasaka, K. (2002a). New JIT, a new management technology principle at Toyota. *International Journal of Production Economics*, *80*(2), 135–144. doi:10.1016/S0925-5273(02)00313-4

Amasaka, K. (2002b). Science TQM, a new principle for quality management. *Proceedings of the 2nd Euro-Japanese Workshop on Stochastic Risk Modelling for France, Insurance, Production and Reliability,* 1-9.

Amasaka, K. (2003a). Proposal and implementation of the Science SQC quality control principle. *International Journal of Mathematical and Computer Modeling, 38*(11-13), 1125–1136. doi:10.1016/S0895-7177(03)90113-0

Amasaka, K. (2003b). New application of strategic quality management and SCM-A "Dual Total Task Management Team" Involving Both Toyota and NOK. *Proceedings of the Group Technology/ Cellular Manufacturing World Symposium,* 265-270.

Amasaka, K. (2004a). Development of "Science TQM", a new principle of quality management: Effectiveness of Strategic Stratified Task Team at Toyota. *International Journal of Production Research, 42*(17), 3691–3706. doi:10.1080/00207540420002003867

Amasaka, K. (2004b). *Science SQC, new quality control principle: The quality strategy of Toyota.* Springer-Verlag. doi:10.1007/978-4-431-53969-8

Amasaka, K. (2005). Constructing a Customer Science Application System "CS-CIANS"–Development of a global strategic vehicle "Lexus" utilizing New JIT. *WSEAS Transactions on Business and Economics, 2*(3), 135–142.

Amasaka, K. (2007a). The Validity of "TDS-DTM", A strategic methodology of merchandise -Development of New JIT, Key to the excellence design "LEXUS". *The International Business & Economics Research Journal, 6*(11), 105–115.

Amasaka, K. (Ed.). (2007a). New Japan Model - Science TQM: Theory and practice for strategic quality management. Study Group of the Ideal Situation the Quality Management of the Manufacturing Industry, Maruzen, Tokyo.

Amasaka, K. (2007b). Applying New JIT - Toyota's global production strategy: Epoch-making innovation in the work environment. *Robotics and Computer-integrated Manufacturing, 23*(3), 285–293. doi:10.1016/j.rcim.2006.02.001

Amasaka, K. (Ed.). (2007b). Establishment of a needed design quality assurance framework for numerical simulation in automobile production. Working Group No. 4 studies "Study group on simulation and SQC, in Japanese Society for Quality Control.

Amasaka, K. (2008a). Science TQM, a new quality management principle: The quality management strategy of Toyota. *The Journal of Management & Engineering Integration, 1*(1), 7–22.

Amasaka, K. (2008b). Strategic QCD studies with affiliated and non-affiliated suppliers utilizing New JIT. Encyclopedia of Networked and Virtual Organizations, 3(PU-Z), 1516-1527.

Amasaka, K. (2009a). Proposal and validity of Patent Value Appraisal Model "TJS-PVAM"-Development of "Science TQM" in the corporate strategy. *China-USA Business Review, 8*(7), 45–56.

Amasaka, K. (2009b). The effectiveness of flyer advertising employing TMS: Key to scientific automobile sales innovation at Toyota, China-USA. *Business Review, 8*(3), 1–12.

Amasaka, K. (2011). Changes in Marketing Process Management employing TMS: Establishment of Toyota Sales Marketing System, China & USA. *Business Review*, *10*(7), 539–550.

Amasaka, K. (2012). *Science TQM, New Quality Management Principle, The Quality Management Strategy of Toyota*. Bentham Science Publishers. doi:10.2174/97816080528201120101

Amasaka, K. (Ed.). (2012). Science TQM, new quality management principle: The quality strategy of Toyota. Bentham Science Publishers.

Amasaka, K. (2013). The development of a Total Quality Management System for transforming technology into effective management strategy. *International Journal of Management, 30*(2), 610-630.

Amasaka, K. (2014a). New JIT, New Management Technology Principle. *Journal of Advanced Manufacturing Systems*, *13*(3), 197–222. doi:10.1142/S0219686714500127

Amasaka, K. (2014b). New JIT, new management technology principle: Surpassing JIT. *Journal of Procedia Technology*, *16*(special issues), 1135–1145. doi:10.1016/j.protcy.2014.10.128

Amasaka, K. (2015). New JIT, new management technology principle. Taylor & Francis Group.

Amasaka, K. (2016). Innovation of automobile manufacturing fundamentals employing New JIT: Developing Advance Toyota Production System at Toyota Manufacturing USA. *Proceedings of the 5th Conference on Production and Operations Management,* 1-10.

Amasaka, K. (2017a). Strategic Stratified Task Team Model for realizing simultaneous QCD fulfilment: Two Case Studies. *Journal of Japanese Operations Management and Strategy*, *7*(1), 14–35.

Amasaka, K. (2017b). *Toyota: Production System, Safety Analysis and Future Directions*. NOVA Science Publishers.

Amasaka, K. (2020). New Japan Automobile Global Manufacturing Model: Using Advanced TDS, TPS, TMS, TIS & TJS. *Journal of Business Management and Economic Research, 6*(6), 499-523.

Amasaka, K. (2022). New Manufacturing Theory, Surpassing JIT (2nd ed.). Lambert Academic Publishing.

Amasaka, K., & Azuma, H. (1991). The practice of statistical quality control education at Toyota-For growing human resource and practical effort. *Quality Journal of the Japanese Society for Quality Control*, *21*(1), 18–25.

Amasaka, K., Eri, Y., Mitoma, T., & Fukumoto, K. (1999a). Development of working environment for older worker in final assembly process. *Proceedings of the 2nd Asia-Pacific Conference,* 129-132.

Amasaka, K., Igarashi, M., Yamamura, N., Soeda, S., & Nomasa, H. (1995). The QA Network activities for prevent rusting of vehicle by using SQC. *The Japanese Society for Quality Control, The 50th Technical* Conference, 35-38.

Amasaka, K., Kato, H., Yasuda, Y., & Kosugi, T. (1999b). Application of 'Science SQC' for corporate management—"TQM-S" in Toyota Group. *The Japanese Society for Quality Control, The 61st Technical Conference,* 57-60.

Amasaka, K., Maki, K., Koto, H., & Jittra, K. (1999c). SQC promotion activities in Thailand Toyota Motors-The Development of "Science SQC" in overseas company. *The Japanese Society for Quality Control, The 62nd Technical Conference,* 45-48.

Amasaka, K., Mitani, Y., & Tsukamoto, H. (1993). Studies on the rust preventive quality assurance of plated parts by using SQC. *Quality Journal of the Japanese Society for Quality Control, 23*(2), 90–98.

Amasaka, K., & Nagasawa, S. (2000). *Fundamentals and application of sensory evaluation: For Kansei Engineering in the vehicle*. Japanese Standards Association.

Amasaka, K., & Nagaya, A. (2002). Engineering of the new sensitivity in the vehicle: Psychographics of LEXUS, design profile, Development of articles over the sensitivity. In The method and practice. Japan Society of Kansei Engineering.

Amasaka, K., Nagaya, A., & Shibata, W. (1999). Studies on Design SQC with the application of Science SQC, Improving of business process method for automotive profile design. *Japanese Journal of Sensory Evaluations, 3*(1), 21–29. doi:10.9763/jjsse.3.21

Amasaka, K., Nagaya, A., & Shibata, W. (1999). Studies on Design SQC with the application of Science SQC improving of business process method for automotive profile design. *Japanese Journal of Sensory Evaluations, 3*(1), 21–29. doi:10.9763/jjsse.3.21

Amasaka, K., Nakaya, H., Oda, H., Oohashi, T., & Osaki, S. (1996). A study of estimating vehicle aerodynamics of lift-Combining the usage of neural networks and multivariate analysis. *Transaction of the Institute of Systems Control and Information Engineers, 9*(5), 227–235.

Amasaka, K., Nitta, S., & Kondo, K. (1996). An investigation of engineers recognition and feelings about good patents by new SQC method. *The Japanese Society for Quality Control, The 52nd Technical Conference,* 17-24.

Amasaka, K., & Osaki, S. (1999). The promotion of new statistical quality control internal education in Toyota Motor: A proposal of 'Science Statistical Quality Control' for improving the principle of Total Quality Management. *European Journal of Engineering Education, 24*(3), 259–276. doi:10.1080/03043799908923561

Amasaka, K., & Osaki, S. (1999a). The promotion of the New Statistical Quality Control Internal Education at Toyota Motor: A proposal of 'Science Quality Control' for improving the principle for Toyota Quality Management. *European Journal of Engineering Education, 24*(3), 259–276. doi:10.1080/03043799908923561

Amasaka, K., & Osaki, S. (2003). Reliability of oil seal for transaxle-A Science SQC approach in Toyota. Case Studies in Reliability and Maintenance, 571-588.

Amasaka, K., & Sakai, H. (1996). Improving the reliability of body assembly line equipment. *International Journal of Reliability Quality and Safety Engineering, 3*(1), 11–24. doi:10.1142/S021853939600003X

Amasaka, K., & Sakai, H. (1998). Availability and Reliability Information Administration System "ARIM-BL" by methodology in "Inline-Online SQC". *International Journal of Reliability Quality and Safety Engineering, 5*(1), 55–63. doi:10.1142/S0218539398000078

Amasaka, K., & Sakai, H. (2002). A Study on TPS-QAS when utilizing Inline-Online SQC. *Proceedings of the Production and Operations Management Society,* 1-8.

Amasaka, K., & Sakai, H. (2009). TPS-QAS, new production quality management model: Key to New JIT-Toyota's global production strategy. *International Journal of Manufacturing Technology and Management, 18*(4), 409–426. doi:10.1504/IJMTM.2009.027774

Amasaka, K., Tamoto, T., Oohashi, T., & Ihara, M. (1995). A study of qualitative estimation of Q.C.C activities. *The Japanese Society for Quality Control, The 49th Technical Conference*, 49-52.

Amasaka, K., Watanabe, M., Ohfuji, T., Matsuyuki, H., & Ebine, A. (2004). Establishment of the quality management technology of customer first: Study Group of the Ideal Situation the Quality Management of the Manufacturing Industry (Report 1). *The Japanese Society for Quality Control, The 74th Technical Conference,* 141-144.

Amasaka, K., Watanabe, M., & Shimakawa, K. (2005). Modeling of strategic marketing to reflect latent customer needs and effectiveness. *Fragrance Journal, The Magazine of Research & Development for Cosmetics Toiletries & Allied Industries*, *33*(1), 72–77.

Ebioka, K., Sakai, H., Yamaji, M., & Amasaka, K. (2007). A New Global Partnering Production Model "NGP-PM" utilizing Advanced TPS. *Journal of Business & Economics Research*, *5*(9), 1–8.

Gabor, A. (1990). *The man who discovered quality; How Deming W. E., brought the quality revolution to America.* Random House, Inc.

Goto, T. (1999). *Forgotten Management Origin–Management Quality Taught by GHQ*. Seisansei-shuppan.

Hashimoto, K., Onodera, T., & Amasaka, K. (2014). Developing a Highly Reliable CAE Analysis Model of the mechanisms that cause bolt loosening in automobiles. *American Journal of Engineering Research*, *3*(10), 178–187.

Hayashi, T., & Kido, T. (1992). Towards a pleasant working environment-Improvement of working environment using multivariate analysis. *The Japanese Society for Quality Control, The 22nd Annual Conference,* 65-68.

Huang, S., Siang, Y. Y., & Amasaka, K. (2011). Proposal of a New Malaysia Production Model "NMPM", A new integrated production system of Japan and Malaysia. *Proceedings of International Conference on Business Management 2011, Miyazaki Sangyo-Keiei University,* 235-246.

J. D. Power and Associates. (1998). https://www.jdpower.com/

Joiner, B. L. (1994). *Forth generation Management: The new business consciousness*. Joiner Associates, Inc.

Kamio, M., & Amasaka, K. (Eds.). (2000). Science SQC: The quality revolution of a business process. JSA-Nagoya QST Group, Japanese Standard Association.

Kojima, T., & Amasaka, K. (2011). The Total Quality Assurance Networking Model for preventing defects: Building an effective quality assurance system using a Total QA Network. *International Journal of Management & Information Systems*, *15*(3), 1–10. doi:10.19030/ijmis.v15i3.4637

Komuro, F., & Ito, S. (1992). A proposal of the appraisal method of the attachment. *The Japanese Society for Quality Control, The 39th Technical Conference,* 35-38.

Kusune, K., Suzuki, Y., Nishimura, S., & Amasaka, K. (1992). Analysis of total curvature spring back in stamped parts with large curvature. *Quality Journal of the Japanese Society for Quality Control, 22*(4), 24–30.

Kyohokai. (1990). Error! Hyperlink reference not valid.

Miller, N. (1978). *An analysis of disk brake squeal.* SAE Technical Paper 780332.

Miyashita, S., & Amasa, K. (2014). Proposal of a New Vietnam Production Model, NVPM: A new integrated production system of Japan and Vietnam. *IOSR Journal of Business and Management, 16*(12), 18–25. doi:10.9790/487X-161211825

Motor Fan. (1997). *All of new-model "Aristo", a new model prompt report, 213,* 24-30.

Motor Fan. (2000). *All of new-model "Celsior", a new model prompt report, 268,* 23-24.

Muto, M., Miyake, R., & Amasaka, K. (2011). Constructing an Automobile Body Color Development Approach Model. *Journal of Management Science, 2*, 175–183.

Sakai, H., & Amasaka, K. (2006). Strategic *HI-POS,* Intelligence production operating system: Applying *Advanced TPS* to Toyota's global production strategy. *WSEAS Transactions on Advances in Engineering Education, 3*(3), 223–230.

Shinbun. (2005). *The manufacturing industry – Skill tradition feels uneasy.* Academic Press.

Siang, Y. Y., Sakalsiz, M. M., & Amasaka, K. (2010). Proposal of New Turkish Production System (NTPS): Integration and evolution of Japanese and Turkish production system. *Journal of Business Case Study, 6*(6), 69–76. doi:10.19030/jbcs.v6i6.260

Takaoka, T., & Amasaka, K. (1991). Analysis of factor for specific fuel consumption Improvement. *Quality Journal of the Japanese Society for Quality Control, 21*(1), 64–69.

Tanaka, T., Kobata, K., Sato, H., & Inoue, K. (1990). Development of diesel engine emission odor evaluation method. *JUSE, The 20th Sensory Evaluation Symposium,* 183-188.

Taylor, D., & Brunt, D. (2001). *Manufacturing operations and supply chain management - Lean approach.* Thomson Learning.

Toyota Motor Corp. (1987). *Creation is infinite: The history of Toyota-50 years.* Toyota Motor Corporation.

Uchida, S. & Maki, K. (1991). The proposal of the desirable dining room environment at the employee restaurant. *Quality Control, 42*(11), 420-425.

Yamaji, M., & Amasaka, K. (2009). Strategic Productivity Improvement Model for white-collar workers employing Science TQM. *The Journal of Japanese Operations Management and Strategy, 1*(1), 30–43.

Yamaji, M., Sakatoku, T., & Amasaka, K. (2008). Partnering performance measurement "PPM-AS" to strengthen corporate management of Japanese automobile assembly makers and suppliers. *International Journal of Electronic Business Management, 6*(3), 139–145.

APPENDIX 1. THE SQC RENAISSANCE IN TOYOTA

Figure 14. SQC promotion cycle activities in Toyota

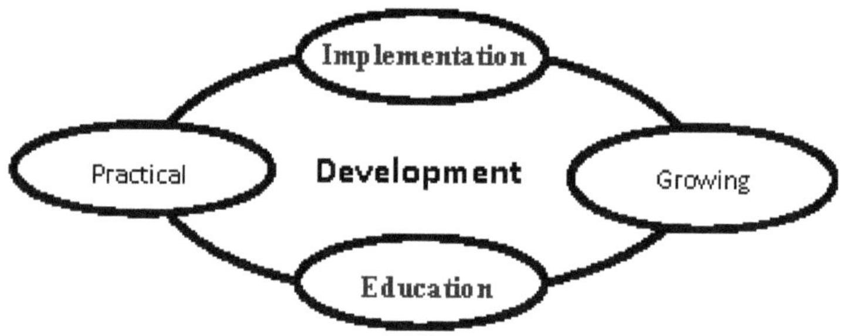

The author has been engaged in *SQC promotion cycle activity* (Implementation – Practical Effort – Education – Growing Human Resources) under the banner of the SQC Renaissance, as shown in Figure 12. This was done in order to capture the true nature of making products and in the belief that the best way to develop personnel is through practical research that will raise the technological level. The aim of SQC Promotion Cycle activity that is being promoted by Toyota is to take up the challenge of solving vital technological assignments (Amasaka, 1998, 2004b).

APPENDIX 2. THE STRATIFIED SQC SEMINAR AND GROWING HUMAN RESOURCE

To make the SQC Promotion Cycle shown in Figure 12, it is important to improve the contents of seminars to make them practically applicable to SQC education. To keep abreast of the times, it is important to apply SQC personal computer software “TPOS” (Amasaka and Maki, 1992; Toyota TQM Promotional Original SQC Software) and give importance to experimental, and analytical designs so as to prevent us from ending up merely conducting trial and error analyses. From the viewpoints of of SQC Promotion Cycle, the “Stratified SQC Seminar (education) for Growing human Resources” shown in Figure 13 is systematized as follows, and a step-up SQC seminar is implemented for six hierarchies of “Beginner SQC, Business SQC, Intermediate SQC, Lower Advanced, Upper Advanced, and SQC Advisor courses”. The seminar attendant ratio is set up as illustrated in the figure for a total of 17,000 businessmen from all departments to ensure full growth of human resources (Amasaka and Azuma, 1991; Amasaka and Osaki, 1999).

Figure 15. Outline of Stratified SQC Seminar and Growing Human Resources

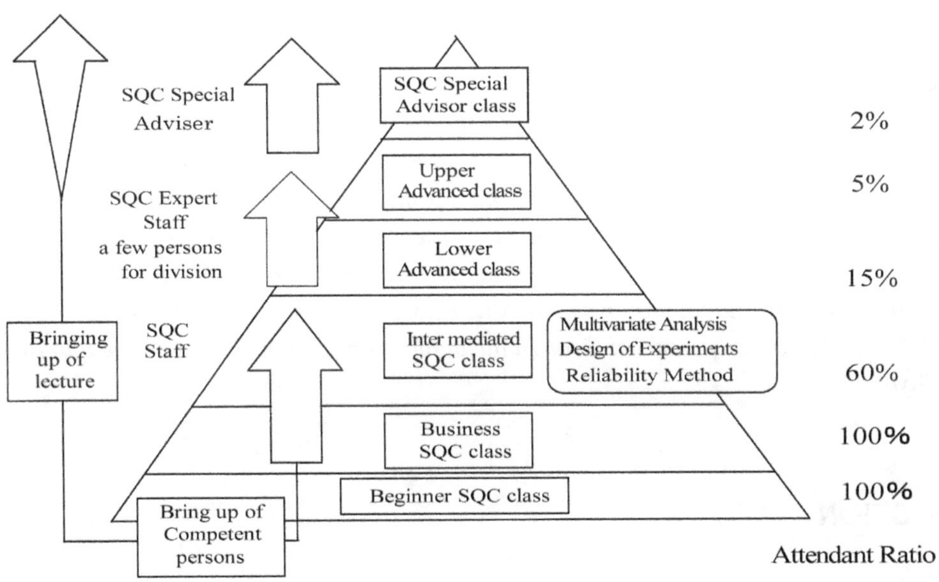

Chapter 6
Creation of a New Japan Automobile Global Manufacturing Model Using Advanced TDS, TPS, TMS, TIS, and TJS

ABSTRACT

This study mentions the New Japan Automobile Global Manufacturing Model (NJ-AGMM) for the strengthening of Japan automobile corporate management in advanced companies that surpasses traditional Toyota Production System. Specifically, to evolution of Japan automobile manufacturing foundation, NJ-AGMM consists of a structured integrated 5 hold-core system - advanced TDS, TPS, TMS, TIS, and TJS for expanding uniform quality worldwide and production at optimum locations. The validity of NJ-AGMM has been verified through the actual applications based on the author's research studies in Toyota.

INTRODUCTION

At present, leading automobile companies are promoting global production strategies to realize "same quality standards and simultaneous production startup worldwide". Advanced companies in particular are eagerly looking for a new quality management method to supply new attractive product models ahead of their competitors to ensure their survival in the worldwide market.

A future successful global marketer must develop an advanced manufacturing model that impresses users and continuously provides excellent products of high quality in a timely manner through corporate management. To realize global manufacturing that places top priority on customers with a good QCD (Quality, Cost and Delivery) in a rapidly changing manufacturing technical environment, it is essential to create the new core principles that are capable of changing the work process quality of all divisions

DOI: 10.4018/978-1-7998-8746-1.ch006

in order to reform super-short-term development production. Therefore, for the strengthening of Japan automobile corporate management, this study focuses on the New Japan Automobile Global Manufacturing Model (NJ-AGMM) for expanding "same quality worldwide and production at optimum locations".

Specifically, to evolution of automobile manufacturing foundation, NJ-AGMM consists of a structured "Integrated 5 hold-core system - Advanced TDS, TPS, TMS, TIS & TJS (TDS is the Total Development System, TPS is the Total Production System, TMS is the Total Marketing System, TIS is Total Management System, and TJS is Total Job Quality Management System) in advanced companies that utilize the author's research principles: the New Japan Model (NJM), new corporate management principle employing New JIT, Science TQM and New Manufacturing Theory in the world (Amasaka, 2002, 2007a,b, 2008a, 2014, 2019a; Amasaka Ed., 2007a).

The aim of NJ-AGMM is *the traditional Just in Time (JIT)* system for not only manufacturing, but also for customer relations, business and sales, merchandise planning and engineering design, product development design, product engineering, administration, and management for enhancing business process innovation. The validity of NJ-AGMM surpassing JIT has been verified through actual applications based on author's researches in Toyota Motor Corporation (Amasaka Ed., 2012, 2019; Amasaka, 2015, 2017a, 2018, 2019a,b, 2020a,b,c).

THE DEMAND FOR ACHIEVING JAPANESE AUTOMOBILE GLOBAL MANUFACTURING

Today's Japanese Global Manufacturing Issues

For manufacturers to be successful in the future global market, they need to develop products that give strong impressions to consumers and supply such items in a timely fashion through effective corporate management. In recent years however, the Toyota Production System representing Japanese manufacturing has been adopted as a called Just-in-Time and Lean System (Ohno, 1977; Amasaka, 1988; Taylor and Brunt, 2001), and further developed in various systems shared internationally. Therefore, it is no longer Japanese (or Toyota's) exclusive technology. In the United States and European countries also, the importance of quality control has been increasingly recognized through studies of Japanese TQM (Total Quality Management).

However, a close look at recent Japanese corporate management activities reveals various situations where an advanced manufacturer, which is leading the industry, is having difficulty due to unexpected quality related problems. Some companies have slowed down their production engineering development, and are thus facing a crisis of their own survival as a manufacturer. Against this background, improvement of the Japanese administrative management technology is sorely needed at this time (Goto, 1999: Amasaka, 1999: Nihon Keizai Shinbun, 1999, 2000, 2006: Asahi Shinbun, 2005). To be successful in the future Japanese global marketer must develop an excellent quality management system that can impress consumers and continuously provide excellent quality products in a timely manner through corporate management.

Given the above, the author has conducted an awareness survey of general management personnel and executives (a total of 72 people) from 12 advanced companies belonging to the Toyota Group (Amasaka Ed., 2007a). Similarly, based on another awareness survey of the companies (Fuji Xerox and Daikin among others, with a total of 153 participants) participating in the "Study Group for Manufacturing Quality Management (aka "The Amasaka Forum")", management technology issues have been investigated from the standpoint of corporate management (Refer to Chapter 4 in detail).

The result of analysis by incorporating Quantification Class III, it can be confirmed that managers responsible for development give the highest priority to "suggestion-based new merchandise and product development" as a global merchandise strategy, whereas production managers put efforts into establishing the "next generation manufacturing principle" in view of global production. Sales managers, on the other hand, prioritize the "development of new marketing methods" in order to be successful in global marketing. Moreover, the issue common to all was how to respond to globalization (Refer to Amasaka (2015, 2019b) in detail).

Needs for New Japanese Automobile Global Management Technology

At present, automobile advanced companies in the world are shifting to global manufacturing to realize "uniform quality worldwide and production at optimum locations" for survival in fierce competition (Amasaka, 2007a,b). To attain successful global manufacturing, technical administration, production control, purchasing control, sales administration, information system and other administrative departments should maintain close cooperation with clerical and indirect departments while establishing strategic cooperative and creative business linkages with individual development, as well as with outside manufacturers.

For a manufacturer to accurately grasp customer intentions in order to proceed with production that satisfies the demand of the times, it is important that all the departments play the leading role in company management with an advanced view of the world (Amasaka, 2008a,b, 2014). Because realizing "manufacturing at optimum locations with the same quality worldwide" ahead of competitors is the key to successful global manufacturing, it is not too much to say that strategic partnering between development design, engineering, production and sales operations as well as suppliers is essential (Amasaka, 2007a, 2008b). Specifically, in order to overcome these management issues, it will be necessary to reform the organization and system and innovate the human resources cultivation system through intelligent sharing of information and to create a new management technology for closer ties among the company's divisions.

The above awareness surveys and analysis clarified the core technologies necessary for the next generation management technology principle, the basis for the new management technologies, and the technological elements required for linking these core technologies. Consequently, what will be important in the future is the creation of a new Japanese automobile global management technology equipped with a new concept. That enables a total linkage of QCD research conducted by each of aforementioned divisions from the standpoint of strategic corporate management will be deemed possible (Amasaka, 2008b). Moreover, to promote excellent quality management capable of contributing to global manufacturing, the quality of the business processes of all divisions needs to be enhanced through clear-cut, rational JIT activities (Amasaka, 2010, 2011, 2014).

NEW JAPAN AUTOMOBILE GLOBAL MANUFACTURING MODEL

Creation of New Japan Automobile Global Manufacturing Model

(NJ-AGMM) using "Advanced TDS, TPS, TMS, TIS & TJS"

A future successful global marketer must develop an advanced management system that impresses users and continuously provides excellent products of high quality in a timely manner. In this sub-section, the author creates the New Japan Automobile Global Manufacturing Model (NJ-AGMM) using a structured "Integrated 5 hold-core system, Advanced TDS, TPS, TMS, TIS & TJS" based on the knowledge acquired by "Chapter 5" as shown in Figure 1.

The mission of NJ-AGMM in the automobile global deployment of NJM is aimed at the simultaneous achievement of QCD by high quality manufacturing which is essential to realize CS (Customer Satisfaction), ES (Employee Satisfaction), and SS (Social Satisfaction) (Amasaka Ed., 2007a, 2012; Amasaka, 2007b, 2008a, 2015, 2019b, 2020a).

Advanced TDS, Strategic Development Design Model

In the automobile business process from development design to production, the development cost is high and time period is prolonged due to the "scale-up effect" between the stages of experiments (tests and prototypes) and mass production. Against this background, it is vital not to stick to the conventional product development method, but to expedite the next generation development design business process in response to a movement toward digitizing design methods.

In Figure 1(1), to tackle this issue, the author has created the Advanced TDS, Strategic Development Design Model using "organized four sub-core elements (i)-(iv)" for the strategic application of automobile product design of further updates TDS, a core element of NJM (Amasaka, 2007a,b; Amasaka Ed., 2007a). In realizing global development strategy employing Advanced TDS, for same quality worldwide and production at optimal locations, customers' orientation (subjective implicit information) must be scientifically interpreted by means of Customer Science Principle, namely, converting the implicit information to explicit information by objectifying the subjective information using Science SQC (Amasaka, 2002, 2004a,b).

Specifically, the author has created the (i) Intelligence Product Design Management System so as to (ii) create the High Reliable Development Design System, thereby (iii) eliminating prototypes with accurate prediction and control by means of Intelligence Numerical Simulation. To this end, it is important to (iv) introduce the Intellectual Technology Integrated System which enables a sharing of knowledge and the latest technical information possessed by all related divisions (Amasaka, 2007c, 2012).

Advanced TPS, Strategic Production Management Model

As digital engineering transforms manufacturing in workshops, a reduction in the engineering capability of members is often a result. This weakens the scientific production control that ensures that quality is incorporated in processes.

In Figure 1(2), to solve this issue, the author has clarified the "Advanced TPS, Strategic Production Management Model" using organized "four sub-core elements (i)-(iv)" for the strategic application of automobile production of further updates TPS, a core element of NJM (Amasaka, 2007a,b, 2010, 2018). In developing global production strategy employing Advanced TPS, for same quality worldwide and production at optimal locations, the fundamental requirements are the "renewal of production management systems" to accommodate "digitized production" and the "creation of attractive workshop environments" tailored to the "increasing number of older and female workers".

Figure 1. Outline of New Japan Automobile Global Manufacturing Model (NJ-AGMM) using integrated "five core elements"

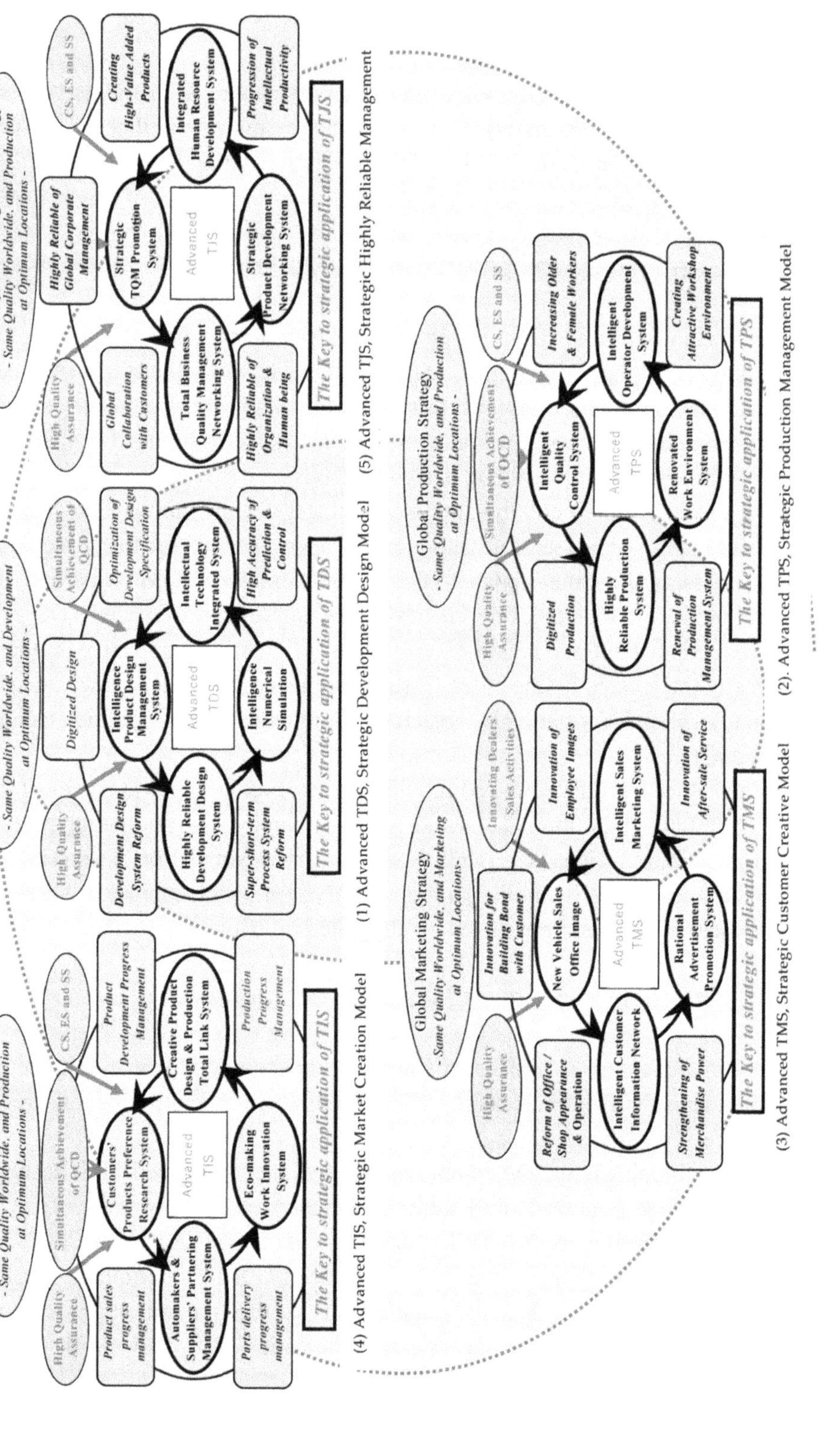

In more definite terms, what is needed is to (i) strengthen process capability maintenance and improvement by establishing Intelligent Quality Control System, (ii) establish the Highly Reliable Production System for high quality assurance, (iii) realize the Renovating Work Environment System in order to enhancement intelligent productivity, and (iv) develop the Bringing up Intelligent Operators through the establishing Intelligent Production Operating System. Particularly, accomplishing these objectives will achieve the higher-cycled business processes through the joint efforts of production technology, production preparation, manufacture and others (Amasaka et al., 2008; Amasaka and Sakai, 2011; Amasaka, 2018, 2020b,c; Amasaka Ed., 2019).

Advanced TMS, Strategic Customer Creation Model

When the author views recent changes in the marketing environment, what is needed now is to develop "Innovative business and sales activities" that are unconventional and correctly grasp the characteristics and changes of customers' tastes (Amasaka 2007b).

In Figure 1(3), therefore, the author has established the "Advanced TMS, Strategic Customer Creation Model" using organized "four sub-core elements (i)-(iv)" for the strategic application of automobile production of further updates TMS, a core element of NJM (Amasaka, 2007b,d, 2011; Yamaji and Amasaka, 2009a). In developing global Marketing strategy, for same quality worldwide and production at optimal locations, Advanced TMS aims to achieve the customer-oriented marketing strategy "Contact with customers" (Amasaka, 2007d) as follows;

Sub-core element (i), the New Vehicle Sales Office Image to achieve a high cycle rate for market creation activities by, "innovation for bond building with the customer" and "reform of shop appearance and operation", is particularly important. These constitute the basis for the development of "strengthening of merchandise power", "innovation of after sale service", and "innovation of the employee image". At a certain stage of execution, for example, it is more important to construct and develop (ii) the Intelligent Customer Information Network, (iii) "Rational Advertisement Promotion System" and (iv) "Intelligent Sales Marketing System" that systematically improves "Customer information software application know-how" (Amasaka Ed., 2007a, 2012; Amasaka, 2015, 2019b) .

Advanced TIS, Strategic Market Creation Model

The management departments of "quality assurance, engineering, production, purchasing, sales, and information technology" are the core of corporate activity so as to strengthen and enrich both internal and external management with the general administration department, and cooperate with the on-site departments, such as development designing, manufacturing and sales, as well as with business partners.

In Figure 1(4), to tackle this issue, the author has created the Advanced TIS, Strategic Market Creation Model using "organized four sub-core elements (i)-(iv)" for the strategic application of further updates TIS, a core element of NJM (Amasaka Ed., 2007a, 2012; Amasaka, 2004a, 2008a,b). In developing global production strategy, Advanced TIS aim to achieve the "simultaneous achievement of QCD" as follows; (i) Customers' Products Preference Research System for the development of "product sales progress management", (ii) Creative Product Design and Production Total Link System for the strengthening of "product development progress management", (iii) Eco-making Work Innovation System for the realization of "production progress management", and (iv) Automakers and Suppliers' Partnering Management System for the development of "parts delivery progress management". Particularly, these objectives achieve the strategic development of JIT involving "human resources, technical and product information and SCM" (Amasaka, 2007e, 2015, 2017a, 2019b; Yamaji et al., 2008; Okihara et al., 2014).

Advanced TJS, Strategic Highly Reliable Corporate Management Model

It is increasingly important for the general administration-related department to advance corporate management by grasping the changing domestic and overseas environment surrounding the industry so as to strengthen internal and external management.

In Figure 1(5), to enhance the "cooperative creation activity, intellectual productivity and human resource development", the author has created the Advanced TJS, Strategic Highly Reliable Corporate Management Model using "organized four sub-core elements (i)-(iv)" for the strategic application of further updates TJS, a core element of NJM (Amasaka Ed., 2007a, 2012; Amasaka, 2004b, 2007d, 2009a,b; Yamaji and Amasaka, 2007a,,b, 2009b).In developing global corporate management strategy, for same quality worldwide and production at optimal locations, Advanced TJS aims to enhance the corporate reliability" as follows;

(i) Strategic TQM Promotion System for the realization of highly reliable of global corporate management, (ii) Integrated Human Resource Development System for the strengthening of creating high-value added products, (iii) Strategic Product Development Networking System for the progression of intellectual productivity, and (iv) Total Business Quality Management Networking System for the development of highly reliable of organization and human being and global collaboration with customers. Particularly, to solve pressing problems inside and outside companies, this is done through cooperation with the development designing, production, customer and sales, and management-related departments (Amasaka, 2015, 2017a,b, 2019b).

APPLICATION EXAMPLES

In this section, the author illustrates typical research examples of Toyota's pioneering manufacturing foundation as the NJ-AGMM application employing Integrated Advanced TDS, TPS, TMS, TIS & TJS. NJ-AGMM is contributing to the evolution of automobile global manufacturing management at Toyota and suppliers, and is proving to be effective both in Japan and overseas (Amasaka, 2015, 2017b, 2019a,b, 2020a,b,c).

Automobile Global Manufacturing Management Model for the Simultaneous QCD Fulfilment: Key to the Customer Value Creation

To realize manufacturing that places top priority on customers with a good QCD and in a rapidly changing technical environment, it is essential to create a new global quality management technology linked with overall activities for higher work process quality in all divisions is necessary for an enterprise to survive (Burke and Trahant, 2000; Amasaka, 2007a, 2008b; Amasaka Ed., 2007a). To actualize the key to the customer value creation, the author has created an Automobile Global Manufacturing Management Model (AGM-MM) called Toyota's Global Intelligent Partnering Model for Corporate Strategy (GIPM-CS) for the strategic productivity improvement of White-Collar utilizing Advanced TDS, TPS, TMS, TIS & TJS as shown in Figure 4 (Yamaji and Amasaka, 2007a, 2009b; Amasaka, 2009a).

In Figure 2, the function of the (i) Quality Assurance (QA) and (ii) TQM promotion as corporate environment factors for succeeding in "global production are (1) CS, ES, and SS, (2) High Quality Assurance, (3) simultaneously achievement of QCD, (4) success in global partnering, and (5) evolution of quality management and intellectual productivity. More specifically, the (i) QA division needs to promote manufacturing of high reliable manufacturing, and cooperative activity across the organization is indispensable to achieve that. In the (ii) TQM promotion division, it is important to cultivate human resources that have even higher skills, knowledge, and creativity. Therefore, the value of intelligent human resources must be promoted in an effort to improve the productivity of White-Collar.

To realize AGMM, global partnering which enables a strategic cooperation among divisions, such as product development and design, production and manufacturing, marketing and administration as well as the entire company, affiliated and non-affiliated companies, and overseas corporations, must be achieved. Specifically, to increase the effectiveness of AGMMM, the author has established the Intelligence High-cycle System of Assembly Maker Production Process (HIS-AMPP) and Total Quality Assurance Networking Model (TQA-NM) for Toyota's new defect prevention (Amasaka and Sakai, 2010; Kojima and Amasaka, 2011).

Then, the author illustrates the typical case studies of AGMM deployment below.

Figure 2. Automobile Global Manufacturing Management Model (AGM-MM)

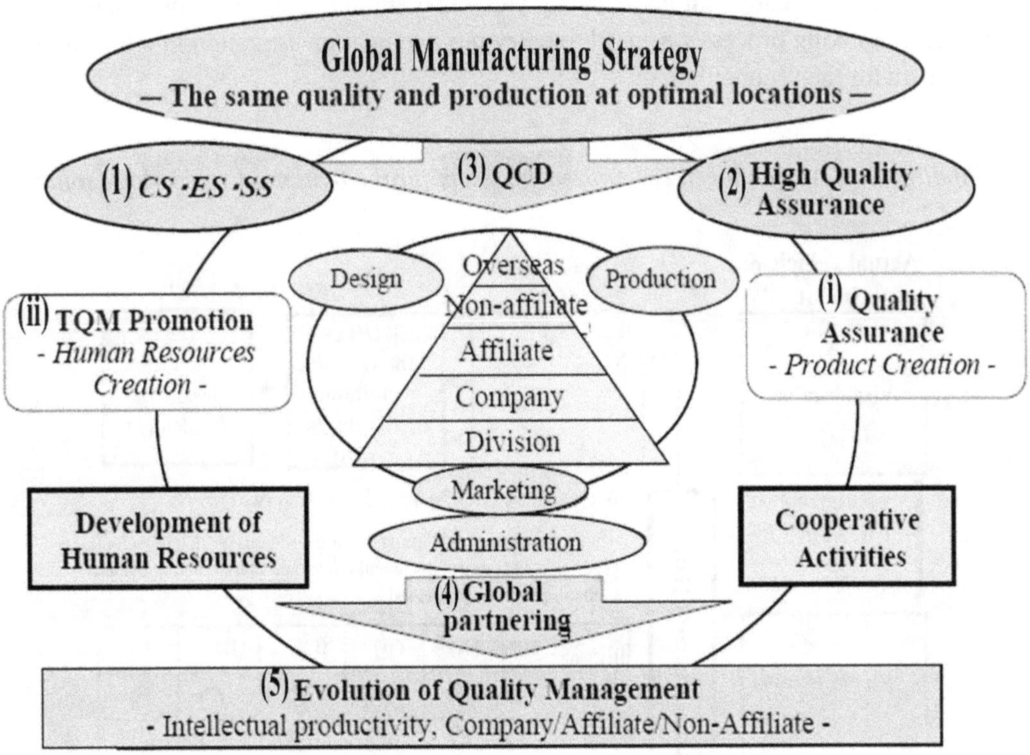

AUTOMOBILE PRODUCT DEVELOPMENT AND DESIGN FOR THE BOTTLENECK

Technology Solution

In general, experienced development and design staff and CAE engineers understand the mechanism that is causing the bottleneck technical problem (BTP) as the implicit knowledge (a rule of thumb or empirical rules). While many examples of calculation based on CAE analysis have been reported, the accuracy of estimation has not to be improved for satisfactory vehicle development (Amasaka Ed., 2007b). Therefore, as the development of "Optimal CAE Design Model", the author has created the "Intelligence CAE Management Approach System" in an effort to help solve the BTP that had become the global technological issue as shown in Figure 3 (Amasaka, 2007c, 2008c, 2017b).

To accomplish this, as the first stage, it was important to (A) the "Visualization - Visualize the dynamic behavior of the problem" by using "Actual vehicles and equipment" and carrying out testing. At this point the expertise of specialists from both inside and outside the company was brought together through the "Partnering" activities using Strategic Stratified Task Team Model (Amasaka, 2004a, 2017b). As the second stage, it was vital to deduce the (B) fault mechanism using various "Techniques". To carry out the precise fault analysis and factor analysis, new seven tools (N7), statistical quality control (SQC), reliability engineering (RE), multivariate analysis (MA) and design of experiment (DE) were combined and utilized to search out and identify previously unknown or overlooked latent causes. In this way a logical thinking process was used to carry out a logical investigation into the cause of fault (BTP) mechanism for the "Modelling".

Figure 3. Intelligence CAE Management Approach System for the bottleneck technology solution

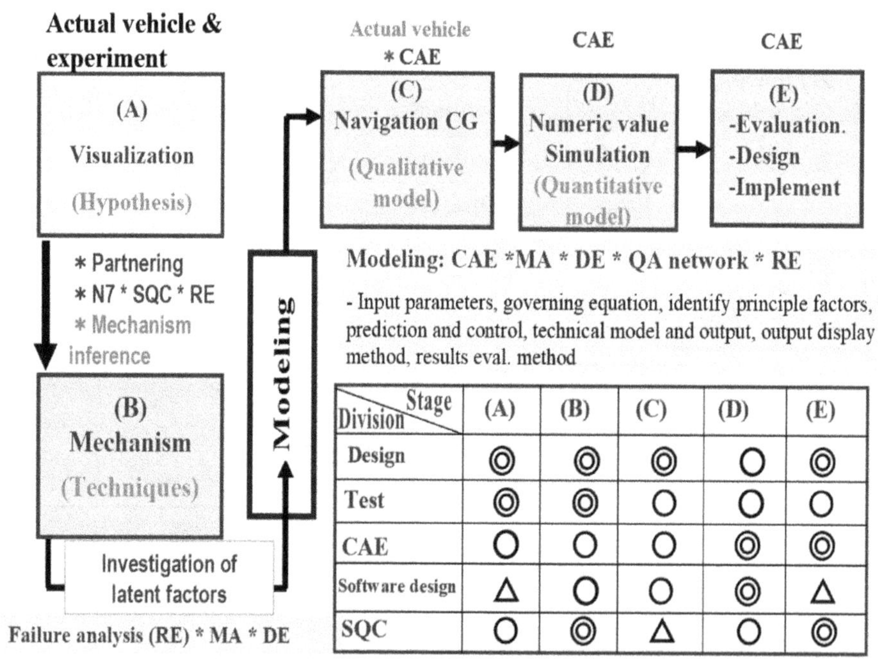

Moreover, all of this knowledge and information was then unified through (C) the creation of "CAE Navigation Software" that employs computer graphics (CG) to reproduce the visualization of the actual vehicle and testing data so that it can be made consistent to a "Qualitative Model (QM)". At this stage, where CAE Navigation Software is being created, it was important to carry out actual vehicle and testing work so that a QM could be made for the cause and effect relationships of the unknown mechanism. It would then become extremely important to use this model to reduce the divergence (gap) between the results from the actual vehicle testing and CAE to develop the "absolute value evaluation".

As the third stage, at the stage of developing the (D) "Numeric value simulation", exhaustive actual vehicle testing was carried out in order to convert the mechanism of BTP from implicit knowledge into precise explicit knowledge. The information gained from these work processes would then be unified and a "highly credible numerical simulation for the realization of QM" would be carried out to make absolute value prediction and control possible. In the final stage (E), the CAE analysis results are then verified by comparing them to the actual vehicle testing results. In the case of a decentralized organization and business process, it is essential that the specialists in the fields of design, testing, CAE analysis, CAE software design, and SQC carry out cooperative team activities, "partnering" (¥ Main, 0 Sub, △ Support) at each stage of the work process (A to E). By using the Intelligence CAE Management Approach System, the author has solved current technological problems in automotive product design (Amasaka, 2010, 2012, 2015; Amasaka et al., 2012).

As an actual case study, the BTP in the world is an unknown mechanism causing an oil seal leakage on the surface of the drive shaft during high-speed rotation (Lopez et al., 1997). The author discusses the application of Optimal CAE Design Model for drive train oil seal leaks through a partnership between

Figure 4. Highly Accurate CAE Analysis Approach Model to prevent automobile oil seal leaks

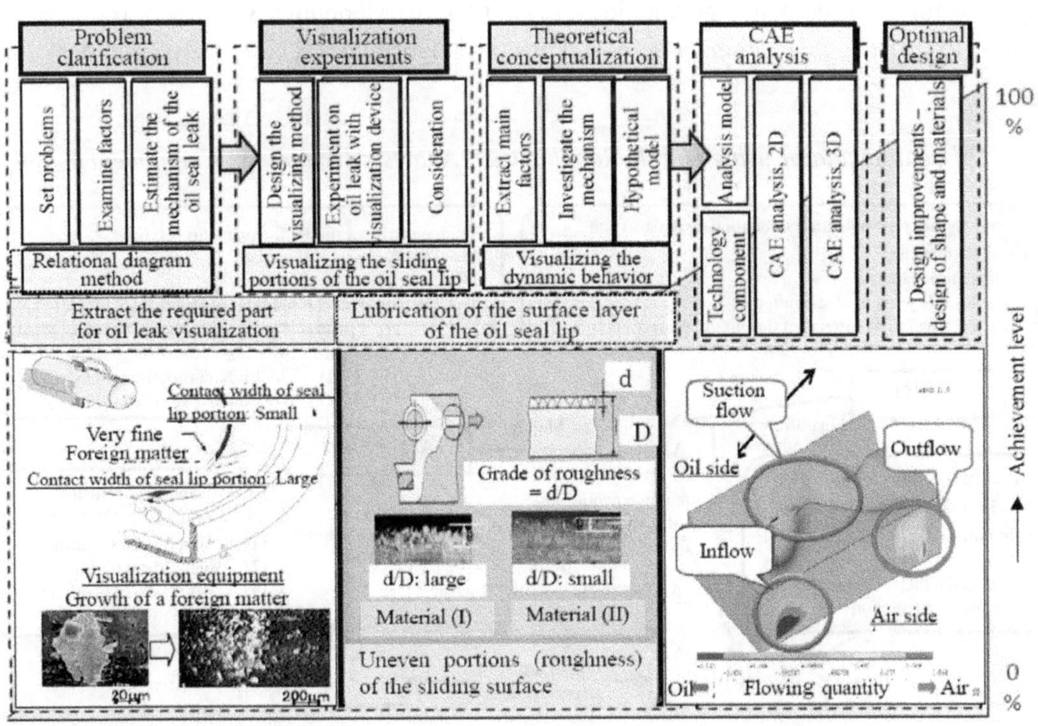

Toyota Motor Corp. and NOK Corp. as examples where the mechanism of technical problems is unknown (Amasaka, 2008b,c, 2010). As shown in Figure 4, the author has created the "Highly Accurate CAE Analysis Approach Model" to prevent automobile oil seal leaks, incorporating SQC technical methods (Amasaka et al., 2012).

The author has contributed to solving a problem of drive train oil seal leaks, which was the BTP for automotive manufacturers worldwide. This was achieved through an analysis process involving problem clarification, visualization experiments, theoretical conceptualization, CAE analysis and optimal design.

First, the authors have begun by developing a device for visualizing the ascertained phenomena in order to the estimate the unknown mechanisms involved in the leaks. This made it possible to estimate the mechanism of the oil seal leaks by visualizing the dynamic behavior involved in the process whereby metal particles (foreign matter) from gear rotation wear, found around the rotating and sliding portions of the oil seal lip, become mechanically fused and accumulate. Next, the findings obtained were used to formulate the following design countermeasures as follows.

1. Strengthen gear surfaces to prevent occurrence of foreign matter even after 100,000 km (improve quality of materials and heat treatments).
2. Formulate a design plan to scientifically ensure optimum lubrication of the surface layer of the oil seal lip (uneven portions of the sliding surface) where it rotates in contact with the drive shaft.

These design technology elements were incorporated into the "Oil Seal Simulator using Highly Reliable CAE Analysis Technology Component Model" to create highly-reliable CAE analysis software capable of accurately reproducing the oil seal leak phenomena, enabling them to be identified and controlled as describe in Figure 5 (Amasaka, 2010, 2012).

The following methods were proposed: (i) Identifying the problems: Simulation of variously converging physiochemical phenomena (methodology: (1) to (3)), (ii) Modeling: Building of problem-solving models ((1) to (3)), (iii) Algorithms: Useful and practical algorithms ((1) to (2)), (iv) Rational theories:

Figure 5. Oil Seal Simulator using Highly Reliable CAE Analysis Technology Component model

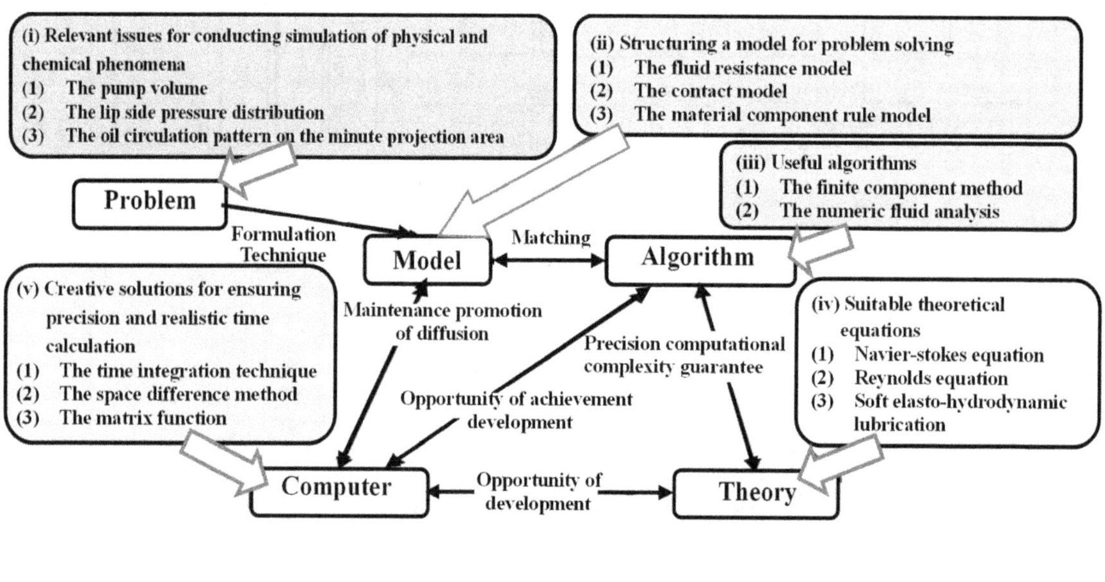

Creation of the suitable theoretical equations ((1) to (3))) and (v) Calculators: Innovations enabling calculations to be made accurately within a realistic period of time ((1) to (3)). As a result, it is now possible to implement highly-reliable numerical simulation (CAE analysis, 2D and 3D), enabling the realization of the quality assurance CAE analysis. The CAE analysis is an example of numerical simulation for pump flow volume (flow of lubricant: air side [atmosphere]–oil side [gears]) around the oil seal. Oil seal leaks (market claims) have now been reduced to less than 1/20 due to the product design improvements (design of shape and materials).

As the application examples to similar problem-solving, the author was able to apply the Intelligence CAE Management Approach System to critical development design technology for the automotive high quality production. This approach system includes the predicting and controlling the special characteristics of urethane foam molding of seat pads, aerodynamics of body lifting power, anti-vibration design of door mirrors, loosening bolt-nut tightening and others (Amasaka, 2007c, 2008b,c,d, 2010, 2012, 2019c; Amasaka Ed. 2007b; Sakai et al., 2011; Amasaka et al., 2012). In each of these cases as well, discrepancy was 3–5% versus prototype testing. Based on the achieved results, this model is now being used as an intelligent support model for optimizing product design.

These examples of AGMM development are detailed to Amasaka (2015, 2019b, 2020a).

Automobile Highly Reliable Production for the Global Manufacturing

Strengthening of the automobile highly reliable production becomes the most important of the strategic development of global manufacturing engineering employing Dual Global Engineering Model (DGEM) possessing the NJ-GPM and NJ-GMM (Amasaka and Sakai, 1998, 2009, 2011; Amasaka, 2009c,d, 2015, 2017a, 2018, 2019b, 2020a,b).

Specifically, the author has established the Human Digital Pipeline System (HDP) as the new production system suitable for the Total linkage of planning, preparation and production as shown in Figure 8 (Sakai and Amasaka, 2007a,, 2013a,b).

1. HDP creates, in advance, "Standard Work Sheets" on which production operators have recorded each task in the correct order for jobs such as assembly work, by using product design data for new products and facilities prepared from product design through to production technology, even if there are no production prototypes.
2. Next, HDP enables visualization training for machining processes step-by-step in the order that parts are built up, even if the actual product does not yet exist.

Actually, HDP is proving to be very effective in raising the level of proficiency for processes requiring skills and capabilities at the production preparation stage, as follows.

1. This system enables a real-time, total linkage of "Data print service (DPS) data" related to techniques and skills, from designing to manufacturing through a digital pipeline for the operators in both domestic and overseas production plants. By this means, the training for highly intelligent work with intellectual productivity can be realized before long.
2. Moreover, this system promotes the leveling of operators' workload in each process and then completes the building up of the production line even before launching it.

Concretely, the hardware configuring HDP is depicted in Figure 6 (Sakai and Amasaka, 2007a). The conventional work procedure manuals in which hand-written letters and drawings were used are to be done away with. Instead, intelligent, user-friendly operation manuals are prepared, which clearly present the items listed and instructed in an easily understandable manner, and offered to production operators.

The CAD data as well as CAE data used from development to production engineering are stored in ① Product D/B through the digital pipeline. Next, , Production Information D/B, containing the production management information, such as production scale and volume as well as the parts arrangement information regarding procurement status and locally procured parts is connected to *f* Work Procedure D/B, which accumulates typical examples of past work procedures, completing a total linkage.

Figure 6. Schematic diagram of Human Digital Pipeline system (HDP)

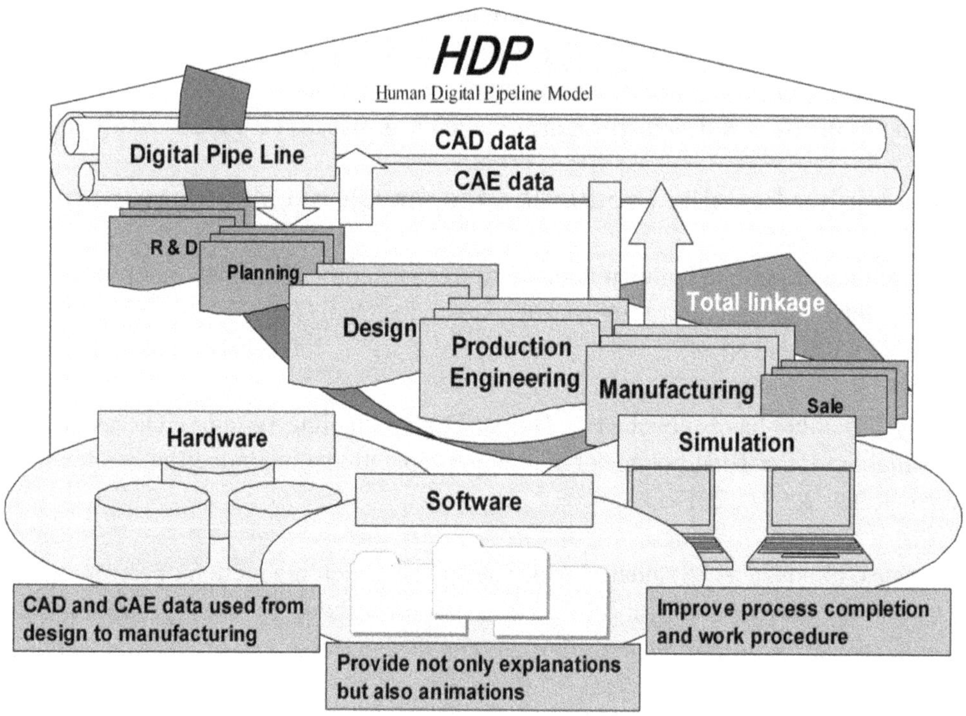

In such a procedure, a work procedure manual is prepared from work data and parts data in advance and offered to production operators. Also, at the same time, based on this work procedure manual, the routes which can be taken by the operators when moving in the production line are prepared. Then, from among these routes, the optimal combination of production operations is selected and arranged by utilizing simulation algorithm. As a result, the process setup which rearranges the work processes to correspond to multi-model production will be verified before the start of mass production. In addition, the workload of each process is totaled for comparison, so that an uneven distribution of the workload (uneven distribution of the work amount among differing vehicle models on the production line) is leveled out. The workload as well as the work posture of the operators are confirmed beforehand, which then is subjected to evaluation and fault finding.

Figure 7. Hardware and software configuration of "HDP"

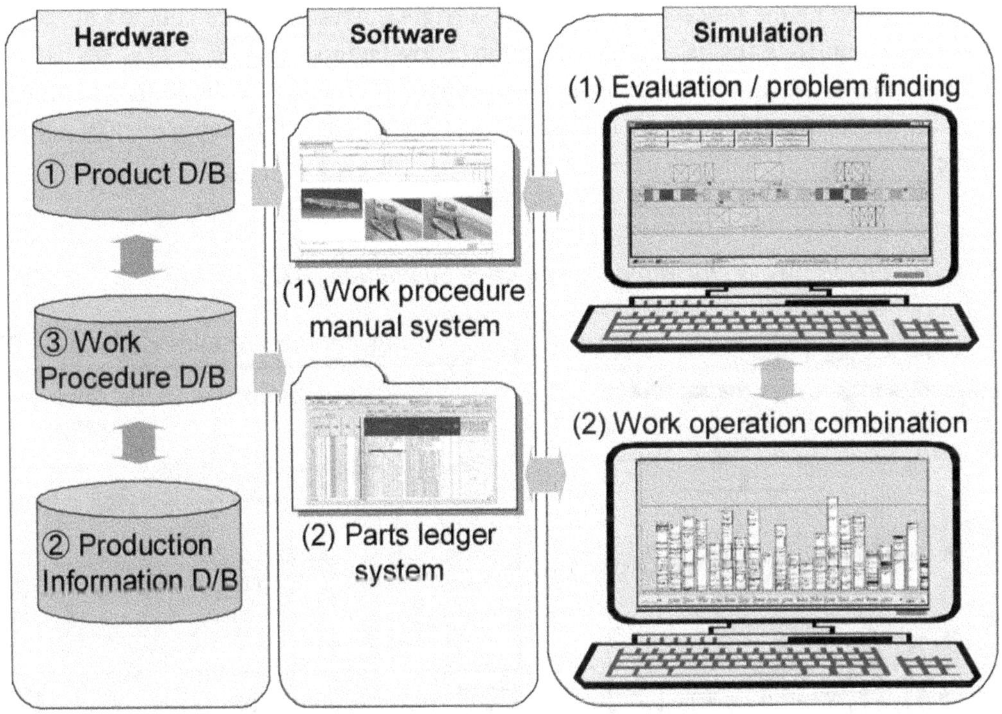

The software configuring HDP is depicted in Figure 7. The work procedure manual mentioned above is prepared using the (1) "Work Procedure Manual System." This system contains a wide range of information, such as the work data consisting of work names, times, locations, the specification data consisting of the specification, number, and quantity of parts, in addition to quality, work posture, instruments, safety, intuitive knacks and know-how, etc. Based on all this, the work procedure manual mentioned above is prepared. Next, the visual data of parts is generated by using the (2) "Parts Ledger System". In concrete terms, target parts are extracted using the information about their number, name, model, or quantity, and the associated 3-D shape data (CAD data) or verification data (CAE data) are searched.

Based on the above systems of (1) and (2), the linkage between work and parts is made, and the elemental instruction sheet is prepared for each of the parts in the order of the steps in which the parts are being assembled. For the types of work operations that cannot be fully instructed through explanations and photographs, video images are added to the visual manual to describe the acquired knacks and know-how. This is to ensure more accurate work operations by instructing the procedure to be followed and the things not to be performed by providing animation.

As the application case, HDP example is called the Work Operation Combination Simulation (WOCS). WOCS is the accumulated work operations for each process is shown in Figure 8. The work hours are accumulated for each assembling location, specification, and priority, and are colored for easy distinction. The walking time is automatically calculated from the traces connecting each part of a vehicle, and it is confirmed whether each operation is completed within the given takt time. An example of comprehending and confirming the network ratio, and the walking time is shown in Figure 8 (left). By sorting out the working time and walking time from the accumulated time results, the uneven distribution of the networking time and the non-working time, such as time spent walking, are stratified to serve as a guideline for reviewing the process layout. Figure 8 (right) shows the re-calculation of the work accumulation after reshuffling the basic work operations between processes. Such changes can be easily made on the accumulative simulation screen by dragging and dropping with the mouse, immediately confirming the work points of previous and subsequent operations while automatically adjusting the walking time involved.

Figure 8. HDP example: Work Operation Combination Simulation (WOCS)

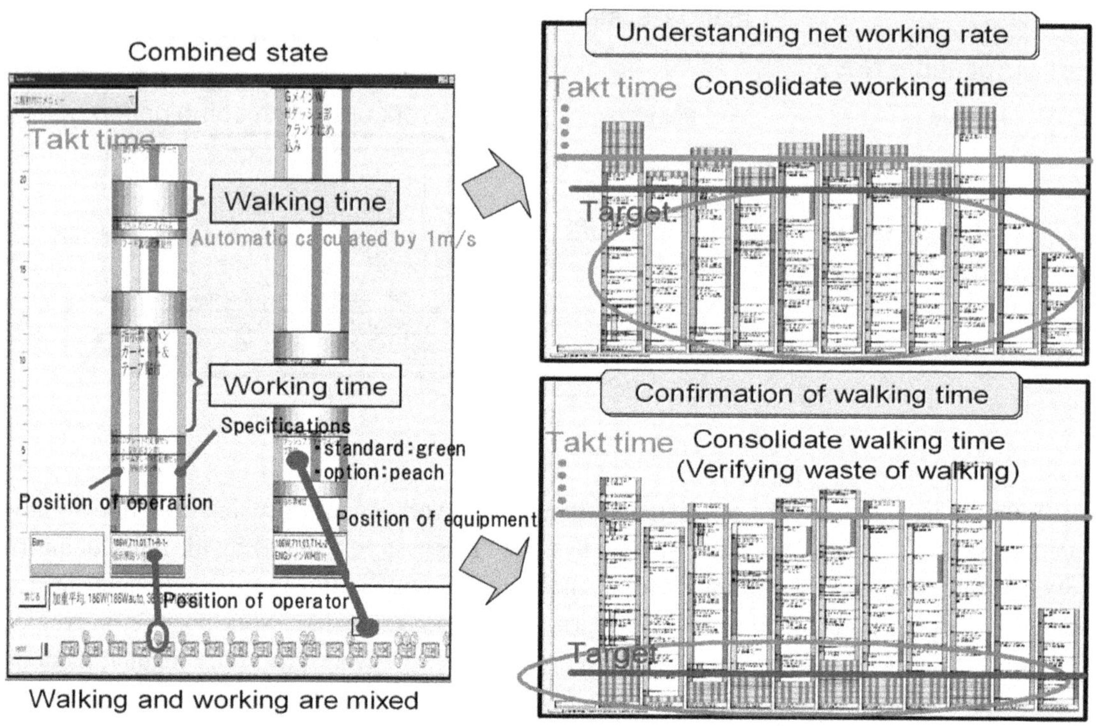

Furthermore, the author has developed the DGEM possessing the typical core systems for the simultaneous QCD fulfillment through the concrete examples as follows;

1. In Highly Reliable Production System (HRPS) as the reform of production planning and preparation: The author has created the (i) Virtual-Maintenance Innovated Computer System (V-MICS) for the globalization of production information, (ii) TPS Layout Analysis System (TPS-LAS) for the production optimization CAE system with the investigation of digital factory, robot control, workability, logistics and vehicle body auto fitting, and (iii) Human Intelligence Production Operating System (HI-POS) using Human Intelligence Diagnosis System (HID) and Human Integrated Assist System (HIA) for the intelligent work development (Sakai and Amasaka, 2011, 2013a,b).
2. In Intelligence Quality Control System (IQCS) as the reform of production process management: The author created the (iv) TPS Quality Assurance System (TPS-QAS) using Quality Control

Information System (QCIS) with quality control charts of abnormal diagnosis, and Availability & Reliability Information Monitor System (ARIM) with Weibull analysis of equipment failures in real-time (Amasaka and Sakai, 1998, 2009).

3. In Renovated Work Environment System (RWES) as the reform of work and labor: The author has created the (v) Aging & Work Development-Comfortable Operating System (AWD-COS) named Aging & Work Development 6 Programs Project (AWD6P/J) (Amasaka et al., 2000; Amasaka, 2007e). AWD6P/J contains the P/J-I (: Boost morale of worker), P/J-II (: Study work standards to reduce fatigue), P/J-III (: Build up physical strength), P/J-IV (: Alleviate heavy work by employing easy-to-use tools and equipment), P/J-V (: Thermal conditions suited to work characteristics), and P/J-VI (reinforce preventive measures against illness and injury).
4. In Intelligent Operators Development System (IODS) as the reform of technical skills level of production operators and further improving the reliability of their skills: The author has created the (vi) TPS-Intelligent Production Operating System (TPS-IPOS) to lead to a fundamental development of the work. TPS-IPOS is made up of two sub-systems: The Virtual-Intelligent Operator System (V-IOS) and Robot Reliability Design-Improvement Method (RRD-IM) (Sakai and Amasaka, 2007a,b, 2013b).
5. In Accelerated Technical Training System (ATTS) for the highly skilled operators: The author has realized the shortened training of highly skilled operators in auto-assembly line employing Intellectual Working Value Improvement Management Model (IWV-IMM), Working Value Evaluation Model (WVEM), and Inexperienced Machine Workers' Training Model (IWPM) for strengthening of manufacturing technology and making of "Creative workplace" (Yamaji et al., 2007b; Tsunoi et al., 2010; Uchida et al., 2012; Yanagisawa et al., 2013; Kawahara et al., 2016).

Recently, for expanding overseas manufacturing using DGEM, the author has created the New Global Partnering Production Model (NGP-PM) (Ebioka et al., 2007) employing AGMM. Concretely, the author has developed the New Turkish Production System (NTPS), New Malaysia Production Model (NMPS), New Vietnam Production Model (NVPM) and Advanced Toyota USA Manufacturing System by developing Partnering Performance Measurement to strengthen corporate management of Japanese automobile assembly makers and suppliers (PPM-AS) and TQM Promotion Diagnosis Model (TQM-PDM) (Shan, et al., 2007; Yamaji et al., 2008; Yeap, et al., 2010; Shan et al., 2011; Kozaki et al., 2012; Miyashita and Amasaka, 2014; Amasaka, 2016; Kozaki et al., 2012).

These studies of AGMM development are detailed to Amasaka (2015, 2017a, 2019b, 2020c).

Change in Automobile Marketing for Developing Customer Creation

One vital point of the strategic marketing structure is its definition; Sales marketing activities for developing should be defined from closed marketing activities that are limited to the business and sales divisions to open marketing activities that can be performed through steady linkage with all other divisions in a company-wide framework.

Then, the author has created the Scientific Customer Creative Model (SCCM) which takes the form of strategic marketing as shown in Figure 9 (Amasaka Ed., 2007a, 2012). The entire structure consists of three domains; (1) *Marketing Strategy*, (2) *Manufacturing Process* and (3) *Market and Customers*. In each domain, the key marketing items are linked by paths to show how they are associated.

First of all, in the (1) *Marketing Strategy*, the key point is how the market segment and the target market are determined. In general, the target market is determined based on the company's core competencies, competition strategy, and resource strategy over the medium and long term basis. By introducing a scientific analysis that uses IT, it clarifies a potential target market from the changing market or the customer structure analysis.

Secondly, in the (2) *Manufacturing Process*, the key point is to collect/analyze customers' demands and expectations precisely. At this time, it is important to consider what value the customer's want. When implementing information collection/analysis, customer value is described in numerical form from many different viewpoints, and a new product which is aimed at enhancing customer value is implemented through the flow of planning, development, and production.

Thirdly, in the (3) *Market and Customer*, the key point is to learn the structure of the customer's motivation to buy products. Concretely, it is important to develop an analysis tool for close examination of the marketing structure and a marketing structure analysis system that will support marketing activities in three domains stated above from a strategic market viewpoint.

In Figure 9, for realization of strategic employment of SCCM, the author has created the total linkage by four elements with (A) Intelligent Customer Information Network System (ICINS), (B) Rational Advertisement Promotion System (RAPS), (C) Intelligent Sales Marketing System (ISMS) and (D) New Sales Office Image (NSOI) as follows. To accomplish SCCM, as the first application of automobile market creative activities, the commanding of CS and CL (Customer Loyalty) in the (3) *Market and Customer domain* is a criterion for the strategic development of SCCM. As the prior research, the authors know of no studies that have been done on auto sales from a multidisciplinary perspective (Mikawa, 2008).

Figure 9. Outline of Scientific Customer Creative Model (SCCM)

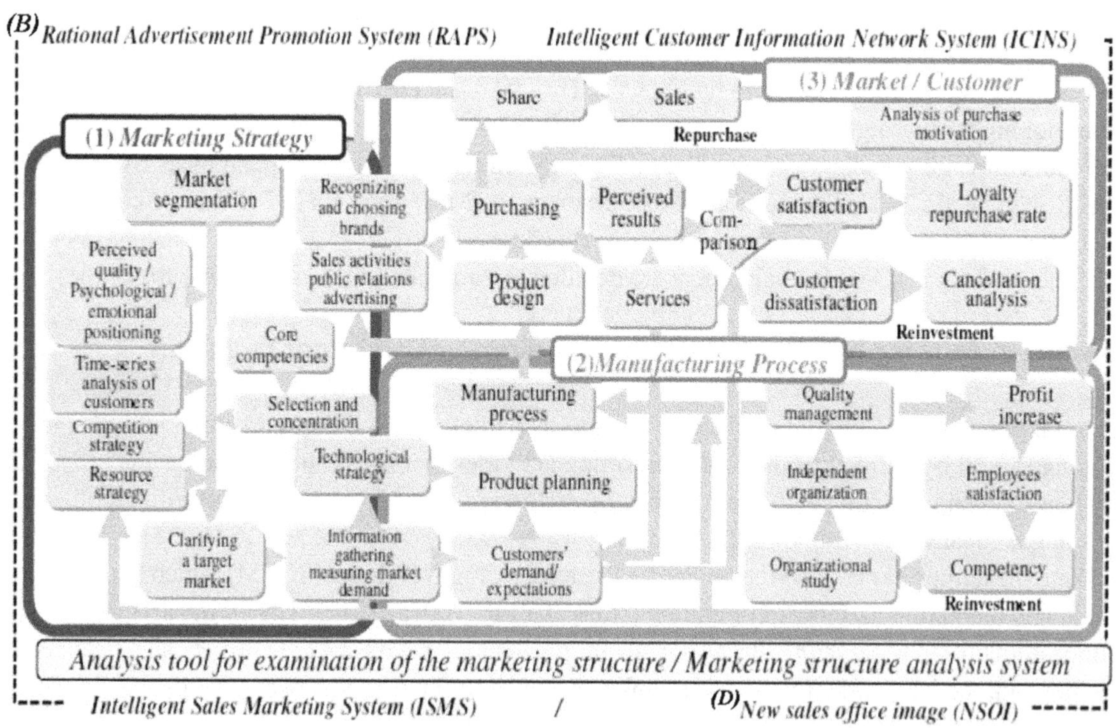

In above three domains of the *Marketing Strategy, Manufacturing Process* and *Market and Customer*, CL is the concept that will become increasingly critical in the future. It requires that dealerships work to boost satisfaction among their core customers by continuing to offer the products and services that these loyal customers want to take advantage of and purchase. Specifically, by employing the (a) Intelligent Customer Information Network System (ICINS), this research uses the statistics approach for focusing on CS as a way of boosting marketing effectiveness, clarifying the key factors that comprise CL (Ishikawa et al., 2011; Iida et al., 2013; Okutomi and Amasaka, 2013).

At a stage of execution, the key factors comprising CS and CL among core customers at the six target dealerships, each of whom represent major automakers in japan—four Japanese (Toyota, Nissan, Honda and Mitsubishi) and two foreign (Mercedes-Benz and Volkswagen) were identified in order to determine the level of impact each carries.

The author collected and analyzed sales information from core customers to identify the four key factors of CS and CL among them using covariance structure analysis as shown in Table 1.

In Table 1, these included 17 product factors, 3 employee factors, 6 dealership factors, and 3 corporate factors as an example of Toyota.

The 29 factors were rated on a seven-point scale along with CS and CL to identify the kinds of things that customers were looking for. In an example of Toyota, Table 1 shows the results of covariance structure analysis on each individual factor by using the data of the persons (: 226 in total 138 male and 88 female) who came to four typical auto-shops (affiliated dealerships).

Table 1. Example of covariance structure analysis (Ex. Toyota Motor Corporation)

Product	CS	CL
exterior	.612	.470
interior	.198	.217
Safety device	-.034	-.109
Handling	.087	.026
Cornering	.190	.149
Straight-line stability	.207	.213
High-speed stability	.106	-.077
Durability	-.045	-.064
pedal	-.458	-.257
seat	.519	.694
Engine displacement	.600	.343
fuel efficiency	.475	.270
Interior noise	.136	.188
Body shaking	.254	.506
Car navigation system	-.045	-.120
audio	.181	-.099
price	-.024	.119

Dealership	CS	CL
Appearance	.115	-.041
Opening Hours	.024	-.048
location	-.098	.169
mandatory inspection services	.203	.086
Emergency measure	.659	.559
Periodic contact	-.294	.278
Employee	**CS**	**CL**
polite	.291	.552
knowledge	.154	.316
Prompt customer service	.464	.077
Corporate	**CS**	**CL**
pamphlet・Website	.205	.057
TV commercials	.128	.502
corporate image	.776	.511

Note: The number of four key factors (: product, dealership, employee and corporate) in the table shows standardizing coefficient.

Under product, for example, the analysis results indicate that if auto manufacturers are to prioritize CS and CL during their sales and marketing activities, they need to enhance product development so that it focuses on performance quality (engine displacement, fuel efficiency, straight-line stability, body shaking and cornering, etc.), design quality (exterior design, seats comfort and interior design etc.) including body shape and paint color and others. At the same time, affiliated dealerships need to work to enhance customer handling during emergencies measure as well as mandatory inspection services. Under topic of employees, similarly, polite, prompt customer service was found to have the greatest impact on CL.

As the second application based on the above-mentioned knowledge, by employing the RAPS, ISMS and NSOI in order to strengthen automobile sales activities, usuful advertisement methods in the (1) *Market Strategy* domain is a fundamental for the strategic development of SCCM. Then, according to automotive dealers' empirical knowledge, number one in rank for major mass effect is TV-CM. But as far as the author knows, there are no studies on the quantitative effects of TV-CM, etc. as the strategic advertisement methods (Niiya and Matsuoka, Eds., 2001; Amasaka, 2003, 2009d).

Specifically, the author has developed the Customer Purchasing Behavior Model of advertisement effect (CPBM-AE) employing Scientific Mixed Media Model (SMMM) as shown in Figure 10 (Amasaka, 2011; Amasaka, Ed., 2012; Amasaka, et al., 2013). Here, the author has borne interest in quantitatively turning the purchasing behavior of customers, who visit dealers with intentions to buy after watching TV-CM etc., into explicit knowledge. Moreover, the visiting ratio of customers will rise, and the effect of marketing and sales activities will be drastically enhanced due to an improved understanding of the effects of TV-CM and the media-mix of newspaper ads, radio, flyers, magazine, direct mail (DM), direct hand (DH), poster, train car ad., internet and others.

Figure 10 Customer Purchasing Behavior Model of advertisement effect (CPBM-AE)

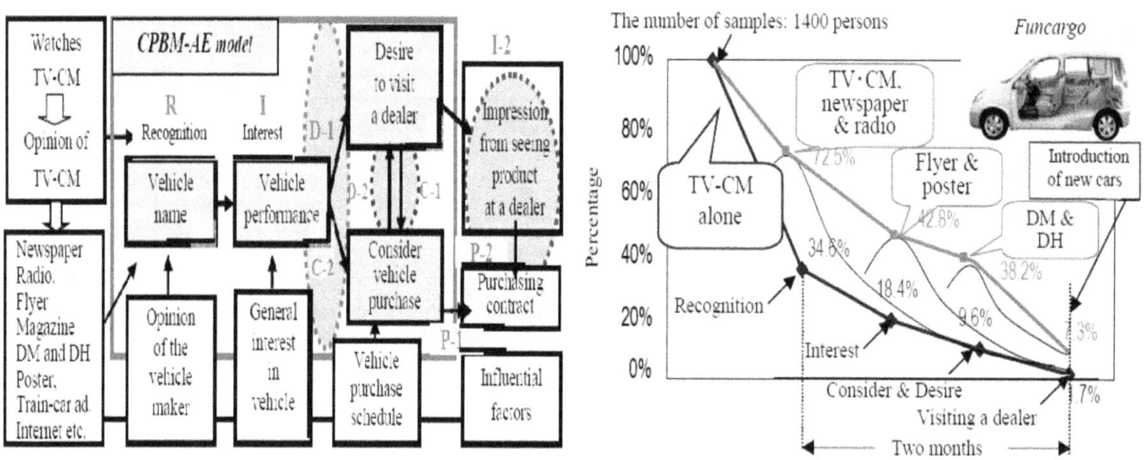

(i) Scientific Mixed Media Model (SMMM) (ii) Reality of SMMM of customer actions

Figure 10(i) indicates SMMM at the time of introduction of Toyota's new small-size vehicles "Japanese names: *Funcargo / Platz*" with the help in Toyota and Amasaka New JIT laboratory in Aoyama Gakuin University. As background for the influential factors, the author has established the following CPBM-AE: starting with recognition of the vehicle name (R)®interest in the vehicle (I)®desire to visit a dealer to see the vehicle (D-1)®consideration of purchasing (C-1)®visiting a dealer for purchasing contract (P-1). This was influenced by TV-CM, newspaper ad, radio, flyer, DM/DH, or presence/business talk over approximately 2 months. Moreover, the authors realized that the CPBM-AE exists, starting from considering purchasing the vehicle (C-2)®desire to visit a dealer (D-2)®impression from actually seeing the vehicle at the dealer (I-2)®purchasing contract (P-2). For example, supposing that customers have their purchasing desire aroused by watching TV-CM for a newly released vehicle.

What percentage of customers would visit their dealers? It is important for future marketing strategies to conduct a dynamic survey of customers' purchasing behavior. First, Figure 10(ii) (the lower line graph of figure) shows the results of analysis that applied the CPBM-AE. As the verification results of the investigation analysis of TV-CM alone in Toyota's new car sales, *Fancargo*. In Figure 10(ii), the total mean curve indicates that 1/3 (34.6%) of customers recognize the new car name (R) from TV-CM alone. The number of customers drops by half (18.4%) at the interest stage (I), dropping by a further a half (8.1%) at the desire to visit a dealer stage (D-1). At the considering purchase stage (C-1), the figure drops to 9.6% at best, even with the addition of D-2®I-2, as stated above. Moreover, at the visiting stage, the ratio of customers that visited a dealer fails to reach 1.7%. This implies the need to establish an effective media mix model in the future. It has been verified that this analysis has a similar dynamic trend for the *Platz* and does not vary for gender of purchasers, age or area.

Next, the author shows the most effective mix-media model for increasing the rate of dealer visits (the upper line graph in the middle of the figure). Compared to the effect of TV-CM alone, the media mix effect of TV-CM, newspaper ads, and radio improved vehicle name recognition (R) to 72.5%. Similarly, use of flyers and posters increased interest in the vehicle (I) to 42.8%. DM/DH increased the desire to visit the dealer, and also vehicle purchase consideration (D-2, C-2, I-2) to 38.2%. The cumulative effect produced an end result where the rate of dealer visits (P-2) increased greatly to 7.3%. To strengthen the CPBM-AE, the author proceeds with the qualitative improvement studies such as TV-CM, fliers, DM/DH, poster/pamphlet, motion picture and video for internet, catalog, train car ads. and mix-media effects of mid-size vehicle (Ishiguro and Amasaka, 2012; Ogura et al., 2014; Koizumi et al., 2014).

As the third application, furthermore, the author has established the Toyota's New Automobile Sales Marketing System (T-NASMS) named Japan's New Automobile Sales Marketing System (J-ANSMS) to strengthen three domains linkage using SCCM as a way to aid sales marketing through innovative bonding with customer as shown in Figure 11 (Amasaka, 2007d, 2011). As the CR investigation to enhance the validity of T-NASMS, the author dealt with the subject of improving sales rate for replacement Toyota vehicles, which involves setting up Netz dealers in a model case (Yamaji et al., 2010; Amasaka, Ed., 2007b, 2012)

Concretely, the Categorical Automatic Interaction Detector (CAID) and Cramer's Analysis are used to identify characteristics and variations in customer orientation through the analysis of user questionnaire data. Accordingly, specific models are developed for customers of high replacement probability (Amasaka, 2011, 2015, 2019b). The knowledge thus obtained is used to generate specific measures for increasing sales through CR based on customer type, enabling the construction of JASMS, an intelligent customer information network system. TNSMS employing the above CPBM-AE combines IT and statistical science to make practical use of customer data in order to (i) increase the rate of CR, and (ii) acquire new customers.

To increase the rate of dealer visits and vehicle purchases by current loyal users, they are stratified into high-probability customers (HPCs), medium-probability customers (MPCs) and low- probability customers (LPCs), and then a sample is taken of the marketing, sales, and service items that the customers demanded, and CS is taken as follows;

(1) The CR activities based on customer type are adopted by classifying HPCs and MPCs into those who visit the shop and those who must be visited by our staff, taking characteristics at new vehicle

Figure 11 Toyota's New Automobile Sales Marketing System (T-NASMS)

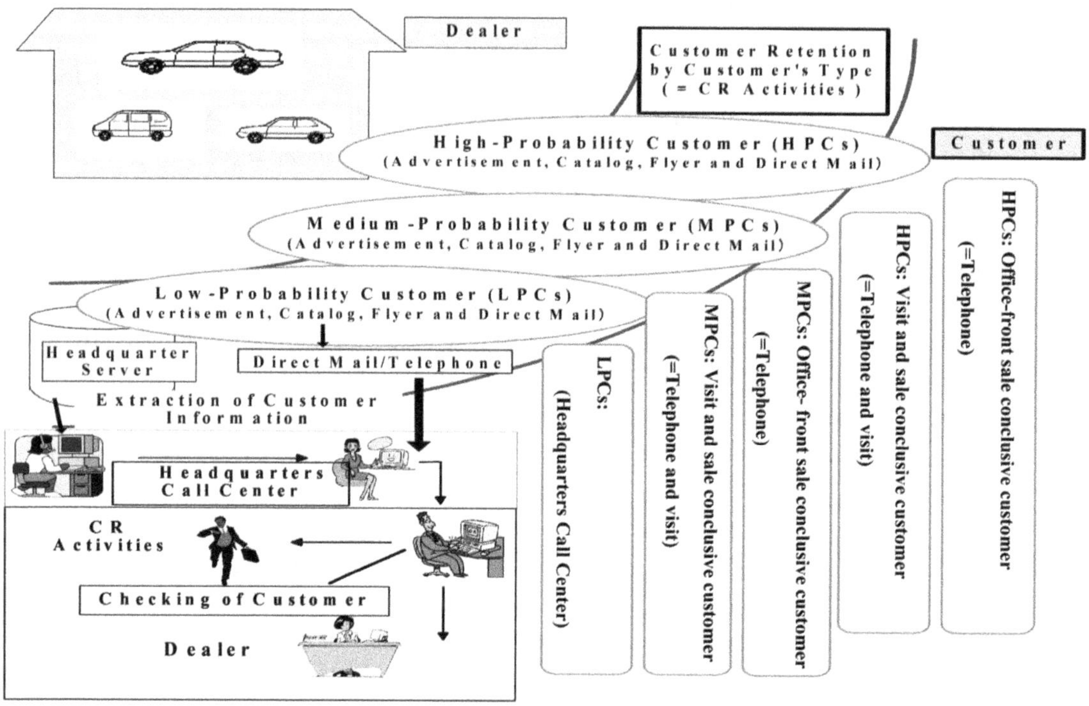

purchase into account. A system is established so that the shop manager directly receives MPCs when they visit to the shop without fail in order to promote visits to the shop by HPCs. Thus, the frequency of contact with customers is increased. Furthermore, sales and service focus on telephone calls for customers who visit the shop, and telephone calls and home visits for those who require visits.

(2) As for LPCs, who have less contact with the sales staff, a telephone call center is established within the dealer, to accumulate know-how related to the effective use of customer information software. The two-step approach is adopted as the practical sales policy where telephone calls are used to follow up on the effect of advertisements, catalogs, fliers and DM/DH. As expected, excellent results have been reported at Netz Chiba, Netz Ehime and other Toyota dealers who applied the TSMS described here.

SCCM operation using T-NASMS has recently contributed to an increase in the sales share of vehicles at Toyota in Japan (40%/1998 to 46%/2007) (Nikkei Business.1999; Toyota Motor Corp., 2013). Furthermore, as the typical case studies, SCCM can also be made use of when visiting customers, and to help acquire new customers at the time they visit a dealer through the raising capability of the employee of the car dealer, and developing long-term eco-friendly car in the logistics industry (Toyoda et al., 2015; Okihara et al., 2015).

Furthermore, as the concrete development of this Section 6.4.4, the author introduces in detail by Chapter 16, 23 and 24.

CONCLUSION

In this study, the author has created the NJ-AGMM (New Japan Automobile Global Manufacturing Model) for expanding "same quality worldwide and production at optimum locations". Specifically, to evolution of automobile manufacturing foundation, NJ-AGMM consists of a structured "Integrated 5 hold-core system - Advanced TDS, Advanced TPS, Advanced TMS, Advanced TIS and Advanced TJS in Toyota and advanced companies. The validity of NJ-AGMM surpassing JIT has been verified through the actual applications based on the author's researches in Toyota and others.

ACKNOWLEDGMENT

The author would like to acknowledge the generous support received from the following researchers. All these at Toyota Motor Corporation and other advanced companies, many affiliated/nonaffiliated suppliers, and those connected with the Amasaka New JIT laboratory at Aoyama Gakuin University that assisted with author's research.

REFERENCES

Amasaka, K. (1988). *Concept and progress of Toyota Production System (Plenary lecture). Co-sponsorship: Japan Society of Precision Engineering, The Japan Society for design and Drafting, and others,* Hachinohe, Aomori-ken.

Amasaka, K. (1999). The TQM responsibilities for industrial management in Japan (Special Lecture). *The 10st Annual Technical Conference of the Japanese Society for Production Management, Kyushu-Sangyo University,* 48-54.

Amasaka, K. (2000). *AWD6P/J Report of First Term Activity 1996-1999: Creation of 21C production line in which people over 60's can work vigorously.* Toyota Motor Corporation.

Amasaka, K. (2002). New JIT, a new management technology principle at Toyota. *International Journal of Production Economics, 80*(2), 135–144. doi:10.1016/S0925-5273(02)00313-4

Amasaka, K. (2003). A demonstrative study on the effectiveness of "Television Ad" for the automotive sales. *The Japan Society for Production Management, The 18th Annual Technical Conference,* 113-116.

Amasaka, K. (2004a). Development of "Science TQM", a new principle of quality management: Effectiveness of Strategic Stratified Task Team at Toyota. *International Journal of Production Research, 42*(17), 3691–3706. doi:10.1080/0020754042000203867

Amasaka, K. (2004b). *Science SQC, New Quality Control Principle: The quality strategy of Toyota.* Springer-Verlag. doi:10.1007/978-4-431-53969-8

Amasaka, K. (2007a). New Japan Production Model, an advanced production management principle: Key to strategic implementation of New JIT. *International Business & Economics Research Journal, 6*(7), 67–79.

Amasaka, K. (Ed.). (2007a). New Japan Model: Science TQM – Theory and practice of strategic quality management. Study group of the ideal situation quality management of the manufacturing industry, Maruzen, Tokyo.

Amasaka, K. (2007b). High Linkage Model "Advanced TDS, TPS & TMS": Strategic development of "New JIT" at Toyota. *International Journal of Operations and Quantitative Management*, *13*(3), 101–121.

Amasaka, K. (Ed.). (2007b). Establishment of a needed design quality assurance framework for numerical simulation in automobile production. Working Group No. 4 studies "Study group on simulation and SQC". Japanese Society for Quality Control.

Amasaka, K. (2007c). Highly Reliable CAE Model, The key to strategic development of *Advanced TDS*. *Journal of Advanced Manufacturing Systems*, *6*(2), 159–176. doi:10.1142/S0219686707000930

Amasaka, K. (2007d). The validity of Advanced TMS, A strategic development marketing system utilizing New JIT. *The International Business & Economics Research Journal*, *6*(8), 35–42.

Amasaka, K. (2007e). Applying New JIT - Toyota's global production strategy: Epoch-making innovation of the work environment. *Robotics and Computer-integrated Manufacturing*, *23*(3), 285–293. doi:10.1016/j.rcim.2006.02.001

Amasaka, K. (2008a). Science TQM, a new quality management principle: Quality management strategy of Toyota. *The Journal of Management & Engineering Integration*, *1*(1), 7–22.

Amasaka, K. (2008b). Strategic QCD studies with affiliated and non-affiliated suppliers utilizing New JIT. Encyclopedia of Networked and Virtual Organizations, 3(PU-Z), 1516-1527.

Amasaka, K. (2008c). An Integrated Intelligence Development Design CAE Model utilizing New JIT, Application to automotive high reliability assurance. *Journal of Advanced Manufacturing Systems*, *7*(2), 221–241. doi:10.1142/S0219686708001589

Amasaka, K. (2008d). Proposal and validity of the High Quality Assurance CAE Model for automobile development. *Journal of the Japanese Society for Quality Control*, *38*(1), 38–44.

Amasaka, K. (2009a). Establishment of Strategic Quality Management-Performance Measurement Model "SQM-PPM": Key to successful implementation of Science TQM. *China-USA Business Review*, *8*(12), 1–11.

Amasaka, K. (2009b). Proposal and validity of Patent Value Appraisal Model "TJS-PVAM" –Development of Science TQM in the corporate strategy. *China-USA Business Review*, *8*(7), 45–56.

Amasaka, K. (2009c). The foundation for advancing Toyota Production System utilizing New JIT. *Journal of Advanced Manufacturing Systems*, *80*(1), 5–26. doi:10.1142/S0219686709001614

Amasaka, K. (2009d). The effectiveness of flyer advertising employing TMS: Key to scientific automobile sales innovation at Toyota, China-USA. *Business Review*, *8*(3), 1–12.

Amasaka, K. (2010). Proposal and effectiveness of a High Quality Assurance CAE Analysis Model: Innovation of design and development in automotive industry. *Current Development in Theory and Applications of Computer Science, Engineering and Technology*, *2*(1/2), 23–48.

Amasaka, K. (2011). Changes in marketing process management: Employing TMS: Establishment of Toyota Sales Marketing System, China & USA. *Business Review*, *10*(7), 539–550.

Amasaka, K. (2012). Constructing Optimal Design Approach Model: Application on the Advanced TDS. *Journal of Communication and Computer*, *9*(7), 774–786.

Amasaka, K. (Ed.). (2012). Science TQM, new quality management principle: The quality management strategy of Toyota. Bentham Science Publishers.

Amasaka, K. (2014). New JIT, new management technology principle: Surpassing JIT, *Procedia Technology. Science Direct*, *16*, 1135–1145.

Amasaka, K. (2015). New JIT, new management technology principle. Taylor and Francis Group.

Amasaka, K. (2016). Innovation of automobile manufacturing fundamentals employing New JIT: Developing advance Toyota Production System at Toyota Manufacturing USA. *Proceedings of the 5th Conference on Production and Operations Management*, 1-10.

Amasaka, K. (2017a). *Toyota: Production System, Safety Analysis and Future Directions*. NOVA Science Publishers.

Amasaka, K. (2017b). Strategic Stratified Task Team Model for realizing simultaneous QCD fulfilment: Two case studies. *The Journal of Japanese Operations Management and Strategy*, *7*(1), 14–35.

Amasaka, K. (2018). Innovation of automobile manufacturing fundamentals employing New JIT: Developing Advanced Toyota Production System. *International Journal of Research in Business Economics and Management*, *2*(1), 1–15.

Amasaka, K. (Ed.). (2019). *Fundamentals of manufacturing industry management: New Manufacturing Theory – Operations management strategy 21C*. Sankei-Sha.

Amasaka, K. (2019a). Studies on New Manufacturing Theory. *Noble. International Journal of Scientific Research (Ahmedabad, India)*, *3*(1), 1–20.

Amasaka, K. (2019b). New Manufacturing Theory: Surpassing JIT. LAP Lambert Academic Publishing.

Amasaka, K. (2019c). Establishment of an Automobile Optimal Product Design Model: Application to study on bolt-nut loosening mechanism. *Noble International Journal of Scientific Research*, *3*(9), 79–102.

Amasaka, K. (2020a). New Japan Automobile Global Manufacturing Model: Using Advanced TDS, TPS, TMS, TIS & TJS. *Journal of Business Management and Economic Research*, *6*(6), 499–523.

Amasaka, K. (2020b). Studies on New Japan Global Manufacturing Model: The innovation of manufacturing engineering. *Journal of Economics and Technology Research*, *1*(1), 42–71. doi:10.22158/jetr.v1n1p42

Amasaka, K. (2020c). Evolution of Japan manufacturing foundation: Dual Global Engineering Model surpassing JIT. *Journal of Business Management and Economic Research*, *6*(6), 499–523.

Amasaka, K., Ito, T., & Nozawa, Y. (2012). A New Development Design CAE Employment Model. *The Journal of Japanese Operations Management and Strategy*, *3*(1), 18–37.

Amasaka, K., Kurosu, S., & Morita, M. (2008). *New Manufacturing Theory: Surpassing JIT – The evolution of Just-In-Time*. Morikita-Shuppan.

Amasaka, K., Motoi, O., & Ishiguro, H. (2013). Constructing a Scientific Mixed Media Model for boosting automobile dealer visits: Evolution of market creation employing TMS. *International Journal of Business Research and Development, 3*(4), 1377–1391.

Amasaka, K., & Sakai, H. (1998). Availability and Reliability Information Administration System "ARIM-BL" by methodology of Inline-Online SQC. *International Journal of Reliability Quality and Safety Engineering, 5*(1), 55–63. doi:10.1142/S0218539398000078

Amasaka, K., & Sakai, H. (2009). TPS-QAS, new production quality management model: Key to New JIT – Toyota's global production strategy. *International Journal of Manufacturing Technology and Management, 18*(4), 409–426. doi:10.1504/IJMTM.2009.027774

Amasaka, K., & Sakai, H. (2010). Evolution of TPS fundamentals utilizing New JIT strategy – Proposal and validity of Advanced TPS at Toyota. *Journal of Advanced Manufacturing Systems, 9*(2), 85–99. doi:10.1142/S0219686710001831

Amasaka, K., & Sakai, H. (2011). The New Japan Global Production Model "NJ-GPM": Strategic development of Advanced TPS. *The Journal of Japanese Operations and Strategy, 2*(1), 1–15.

Burke, W., & Trahant, W. (2000). Business Climate Shift. Academic Press.

Ebioka, K., Sakai, H., Yamaji, M., & Amasaka, K. (2007). A New Global Partnering Production Model "NGP-PM" utilizing Advanced TPS. *Journal of Business & Economics Research, 5*(9), 1–8.

Goto, T. (1999). *Forgotten Management Origin – Management Quality*. Taught by GHQ.

Iida, T., Mihara, R., & Amasaka, K. (2013). Constructing Business Process Network System "A-BPNS-NPD". *Journal of Business Case Studies, 9*(4), 343–352.

Ishiguro, H., & Amasaka, K. (2012). Establishment of a Strategic Total Direct Mail Model to bring customers into auto dealerships. *Journal of Business & Economics Research, 10*(8), 493–500. doi:10.19030/jber.v10i8.7177

Ishikawa, A., Morita, Y., & Amasaka, K. (2011). Constructing Measures of CS Effectiveness to boost subjective quality at manufacturers. *International Business & Economic Research Journal, 10*(11), 55–62.

Kawahara, F., Kogane, Y., Amasaka, K., & Ouchi, N. (2016). Work procedure manual incorporating experienced workers' intuition and knowhow. *IOSR Journal of Business and Management, 18*(12), 80–85.

Koizumi, K., Muto, M., & Amasaka, K. (2014). Creating Automobile Pamphlet Design Method: Utilizing both biometric testing and statistical science. *Journal of Management Research, 6*(1), 81–94. doi:10.5296/jmr.v6i1.4569

Kojima, T., & Amasaka, K. (2011). The Total Quality Assurance Networking Model for preventing defects: Building an effective quality assurance system using a Total QA Network. *International Journal of Management & Information Systems, 15*(3), 1–10. doi:10.19030/ijmis.v15i3.4637

Kozaki, T., Oura, A., & Amasaka, K. (2012). Establishment of TQM Promotion Diagnosis Model "TQM-PDM" for strategic quality management. *China-USA Business Review, 10*(11), 811–819.

Mikawa, K. (2008). A study of quantification method for important factors based on customer loyalty structure diagram. *Journal of Japan Industrial Management Association*, *59*(5), 365–375.

Miyashita, S., & Amasaka, K. (2014). Proposal of a New Vietnam Production Model, "NVPM", a new integrated production system of Japan and Vietnam. *IOSR. Journal of Business and Management*, *16*(12), 18–25.

Niiya, T., & Matsuoka, F. (Eds.). (2001). *Foundation lecture of the new advertising business*. Senden-kaigi.

Nikkei Business. (1999). Renovation of shop, product and selling method-Targeting young customers. *NETS.*

Ogura, M., Hachiya, T., Masubuchi, K., & Amasaka, K. (2014). Attention-Grabbing train car advertisements. *International Journal of Engineering Research and Applications*, *4*(1), 56–64.

Ohno, T. (1978). *Toyota Production System: Beyond Large-Scale Production*. Diamond-sha.

Okihara, D., Fujita, K., Murakami, K., & Amasaka, K. (2015). The introductory plan model of the long-term eco-friendly car in the logistics industry. *Scheduling Symposium of the Scheduling Society of Japan*, 139-144.

Okihara, D., Takada, S., & Amasaka, K. (2014). Constructing a model for selecting improvement actions to gain mutual trust between logistics providers and shippers. *Journal of Japanese Operations Management and Strategy*, *5*(1), 74–85.

Okutomi, H., & Amasaka, K. (2013). Researching customer satisfaction and loyalty to boost marketing effectiveness. *International Journal of Management & Information Systems*, *17*(4), 193–200.

Sakai, H., & Amasaka, K. (2007a). Human Digital Pipeline Method using total linkage through design to manufacturing. *Journal of Advanced Manufacturing Systems*, *6*(2), 101–113. doi:10.1142/S0219686707000929

Sakai, H., & Amasaka, K. (2007b). The robot reliability design and improvement method and Advanced Toyota Production System. *International Journal of Industrial and Service Robotics*, *34*(4), 310–316. doi:10.1108/01439910710749636

Sakai, H., & Amasaka, K. (2013a). Highly Reliable Production System for expanding global production: Total linkage of planning, preparation and production. *International Journal of Operations and Quantitative Management*, *19*(3), 157–168.

Sakai, H., & Amasaka, K. (2013b). Construction of "V-IOS" for promoting intelligence operator: Development and effectiveness for visual manual format. *The Japan Society for Production Management, The 18th Annual Conference, Nagasaki Institute of Applied Science*, 173-176.

Sakai, H., Waji, Y., Nakamura, M., & Amasaka, K. (2011). Establishment of "A-PPNS", A navigation system for regenerating the software development business. *An International Journal. Industrial Engineering & Management System*, *10*(1), 43–53. doi:10.7232/iems.2011.10.1.043

Shan, H., Yeap, Y. S., & Amasaka, K. (2011). Proposal of a New Malaysia Production Model "NMPM": A new integrated production system of Japan and Malaysia. *Proceedings of the International Conference on Business Management 2011, Miyazaki Sangyo-Keiei University*, 235-246.

Shinbun. (2005). *The manufacturing industry – Skill tradition feels uneasy*. Academic Press.

Taylor, D. & Brunt, D. (2001). *Manufacturing Operations and Supply Chain Management - Lean Approach*. Thomson Learning.

Toyoda, S., Miyashita, S., Murakami, K., & Amasaka, K. (2015). A study on assignment at the dealer-shop in consideration of the capability of the employee of the car dealer. *The Japanese Operations Management and Strategy Association, The 7th Annual Conference*, 249-260.

Toyota Motor Corp. (2013). *75 Years of Toyota*. www.toyota-global.com/company/history_of _ Toyota/75years/

Tsunoi, M., Yamaji, M., & Amasaka, K. (2010). A study of building an Intellectual Working Value Improvement Model "IWV-IM". *International Business & Economics Research Journal*, *9*(11), 79–84. doi:10.19030/iber.v9i11.33

Uchida, K., Tsunoi, M., & Amasaka, K. (2012). Creating Working Value Evaluation Model, WVEM. *International Journal of Management & Information Systems*, *16*(4), 299–306.

Yamaji, M., & Amasaka, K. (2007a). Proposal and validity of Global Intelligence Partnering Model for corporate strategy, "GIPM-CS". *Advances in production* management systems, *International IFIP TC 5, WG 5.7 Conference on Advanced in Production Management System*, 59-67.

Yamaji, M., & Amasaka, K. (2009a). Proposal and validity of Intelligent Customer Information Marketing Model: Strategic development of Advanced TMS. *China-USA Business Review*, *8*(8), 53–62.

Yamaji, M., & Amasaka, K. (2009b). Strategic Productivity Improvement Model for White - Collar Workers employing Science TQM. *The Journal of Japanese Operations Management and Strategy*, *1*(1), 30–43.

Yamaji, M., Hifumi, S., Sakalsis, M. S., & Amasaka, K. (2010). Developing a Strategic Advertisement Method "VUCMIN" to enhance the desire of customers for visiting dealers. *Journal of Business Case Studies*, *6*(3), 1–11. doi:10.19030/jbcs.v6i3.871

Yamaji, M., Sakatoku, T., & Amasaka, K. (2008). Partnering Performance Measurement "PPM-AS" to strengthen corporate management of Japanese automobile assembly makers and suppliers. *International Journal of Electronic Business Management*, *6*(3), 139–145.

Yamaji, N., Sakai, H., & Amasaka, K. (2007b). Evolution of technology and skill in production workplaces utilizing Advanced TPS. *Journal of Business & Economics Research*, *5*(6), 61–68.

Yanagisawa, K., Yamazaki, M., Yoshioka, K., & Amasaka, K. (2013). Comparison of experienced and inexperienced machine workers. *International Journal of Operations and Quantitative Management*, *19*(4), 259–274.

Yeap, Y. S., Sakalsis, M. S., & Amasaka, K. (2010). Proposal of New Turkish Production System, NTPS: Integration and evolution of Japanese and Turkish Production System. *Journal of Business Case Study*, *6*(6), 69–76.

Chapter 7
Evolution of the Japan Automobile Manufacturing Foundation Using Dual Global Engineering Model

ABSTRACT

Today, digital engineering is bringing about radical changes in manufacturing. To advance the evolution of Japan automobile manufacturing foundation, this study mentions the New Japan Production Management Model (NJ-PMM) that surpasses conventional JIT practices in order to re-construct world-leading management technologies. On a concrete target, the author focuses on the strategic development of Dual Global Engineering Model (DGEM) by possessing the New Japan Global Production Model (NJ-GPM) and New Japan Global Manufacturing Model (NJ-GMM) surpassing JIT. The effectiveness of DGEM was verified through the actual applications to automobile manufacturing in Toyota and suppliers.

INTRODUCTION

Recently, Japanese Production System, which is typified by the Toyota Production System (TPS) has been further developed and spread in the form of internationally shared global production systems such as Just in Time (JIT), and therefore it is no longer a proprietary technology of Japan (Ohno, 1977; Womack et al., 1990; Amasaka, 1988, 2002, 2007a). Furthermore, today, digital engineering is bringing about radical changes in the way manufacturing is carried out at manufacturing sites (Amasaka, 2007b; Amasaka, Ed., 2007; Amasaka and Sakai, 2010).

To overcome this issue, it is now necessary to re-construct world-leading management technologies so that they will be viable even for the next generation of automobile manufacturing which is represented by the Total Production System based on core principle for the New Manufacturing Theory (NMT) based

DOI: 10.4018/978-1-7998-8746-1.ch007

on New JIT principle (Amasaka, 2002, 2007a, 2014, 2019a, 2020a; Amasaka et al., 2008). By concrete deployment for automobile global production employing NMT, the author has created the New Japan Production Management Model (NJ-PMM) in Toyota.

With this mind, as the keys to successful global production, this study mentions the evolution of Japan automobile manufacturing foundation in order to develop NJ-PMM named Advanced TPS that surpasses conventional JIT practices (Refer to Chapter 6). On a concrete target, the author focuses on the strategic development of Dual Global Engineering Model (DGEM) by possessing the New Japan Global Production Model (NJ-GPM) and New Japan Global Manufacturing Model (NJ-GMM) surpassing JIT (Amasaka and Sakai, 2011; Amasaka, 2020a,b,c). The aim of DGEM is to realize a highly reliable production system suitable for global production by reviewing the production process from production planning, preparation and manufacturing through production itself and process management.

Specifically, first, six core management technologies of NJ-GPM consist of the TPS Layout Analysis System (TPS-LAS), Human Intelligence-Production Operating System (HI-POS), TPS Intelligent Production Operating System (TPS-IPOS), TPS Quality Assurance System (TPS-QAS), Human Digital Pipeline (HDP), and Virtual-Maintenance Innovated Computer System (V-MICS) (Amasaka and Sakai, 2011). Similarly, second, six core management technologies of NJ-GMM consist of the Intellectual Working Value Improvement Management Model (IWV-IMM), Partnering Performance Measurement Model (PPMM), Strategic Stratified Task Team Model (SSTTM), Intelligence High-cycle System of Assembly Maker Production Process (IHS-AMPP), Strategic Quality Management using Performance Measurement Model (SQM-PMM), and Working Value Evaluation Model (WVEM).

Concretely, the author has verified the effectiveness of DGEM through the actual applications of automobile manufacturing in Toyota and suppliers (Amasaka et al., 2008; Amasaka, 2015, 2017a, 2019a,b,c; Amasaka, Ed., 2012, 2019).

NEED FOR ADVANCES IN GLOBAL MANUFACTURING ENGINEERING

The Demand for Advances in Manufacturing Technology

The environmental changes that surround today's manufacturing industry are truly severe. It is vital for Japanese manufacturing not to fall behind in the advancement of management technologies. In order for manufacturers to succeed in the future world market, they need to continue to create products that will leave a strong impression on customers and to offer them in a timely fashion (Amasaka, 2002).

At present however, the TPS which is representative of Japanese manufacturing, has been further developed and spread in the form of internationally shared global production systems such as JIT and Lean System and therefore it is no longer a proprietary technology of Japan (Hayes and Wheelwright, 1984; Doos et al., 1991; Womack and Jones, 1994; Taylor and Brunt, 2001). It is not an exaggeration to say that what will ensure Japanese manufacturers' success in global marketing is the realization of simultaneous achievement of QCD (quality, cost and delivery)–ahead of their competitors (Amasaka, 2004a, 2007a,b, 2008).

The urgent mission for Japanese manufacturers is to reconstruct world-leading, uniquely Japanese principles of management technology, which will be viable even for next-generation manufacturing as the evolution system of JIT (Amasaka et al., 2008; Amasaka, 2009, 2014; Amasaka and Sakai, 2010). To prevail in today's competitive manufacturing industry, which is often referred to as a worldwide quality competition, the pressing management issue is to realize the kind of global production that can achieve called the "worldwide uniform quality and production at optimal locations" (Amasaka and Sakai, 2011; Amasaka, 2015, 2018).

Innovation of Japan's Global Manufacturing Fundamentals

To offer customers high value-added products and prevail in the worldwide quality competition, it is necessary to establish an advanced production system that can intellectualize the production engineering and manufacturing management system. This will in turn produce high performance and highly functional new products. The author believes that what determines the success of global production strategies is the advancement of technologies and skills that are capable of fully utilizing the above mentioned advanced production system in order to realize reliable Japan's global manufacturing fundamentals at the production sites (Amasaka, 2007a).

Then, the author posed the question, "What are some of the issues that need to be addressed in order to prevail in the 21st century?" to a total of 154 respondents chosen from the top management class (board members) and managers (of divisions and departments) of the six manufacturers that participated in the "Workshop on Quality Management of Manufacturers" (hosted by Kakuro Amasaka, Professor of Aoyama Gakuin University from May 2004 to March 2006). The survey revealed the interests of the top management and manager classes (Amasaka Ed., 2007). Figure 1 is an example of the summary and analysis results of these interests (or the free opinions gathered from the survey). As shown here, their interests center on technological development, human resources development, globalization, product differentiation, quality, safety, organization, and management.

Consolidating these items, the management technology issue that they commonly share is the establishment of the kind of global production system that can achieve worldwide uniform quality and simultaneous launch (production at optimal locations). Among other things, what they give top priority to is the realization of manufacturing with high quality assurance. This is achieved through high cycleization of the business process related to manufacturing at overseas production plants (or production sites) in industrialized nations in the West or developing nations, not to mention in the Japanese domes-

Figure 1. What is the important issue which should be tackled?

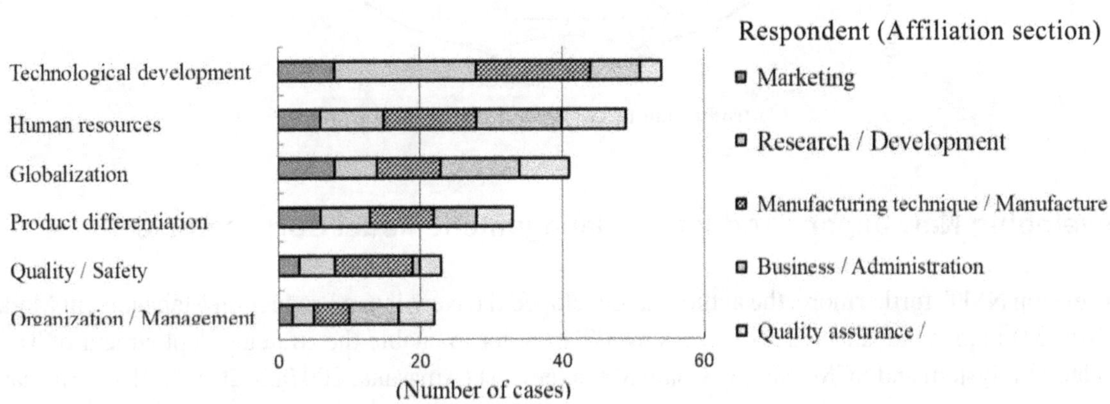

tic market. In particular, they are concerned about the current situation in which the production sites are undergoing drastic changes due to the use of digital engineering and IT (Information Technology). Moreover, it was seen as critical to realize the intellectualization of the production sites so that they do not lag behind the advancements being made in technology and skills.

EVOLUTION OF JAPAN MANUFACTURING FOUNDATION SURPASSING JIT

Creation of Total Production System based on New Manufacturing Theory

To develop the Advances in Global Manufacturing Engineering above, the author has created the Total Production System which is one of core principles of the New Manufacturing Theory (NMT) called New JIT, new management technology principle (Amasaka and Sakai, 2011; Amasaka et al., 2008; Amasaka, 2014, 2019a,b).

In Figure 2, the aim of Total Production System is to enable a focus on customers and employees as well as the reinforcement and improvement of production process control through incorporation of four sub core elements as follows; (a) production based on information to require the reformation of the production philosophy, (b) production based management to reform the workplace configuration, (c) Production based on engineering to reinforce the production technology and (d) production based on workshop formation to create the highly creative and active workplace (Refer to Chapter 6).

Figure 2. Schematic Drawing of Total Production System

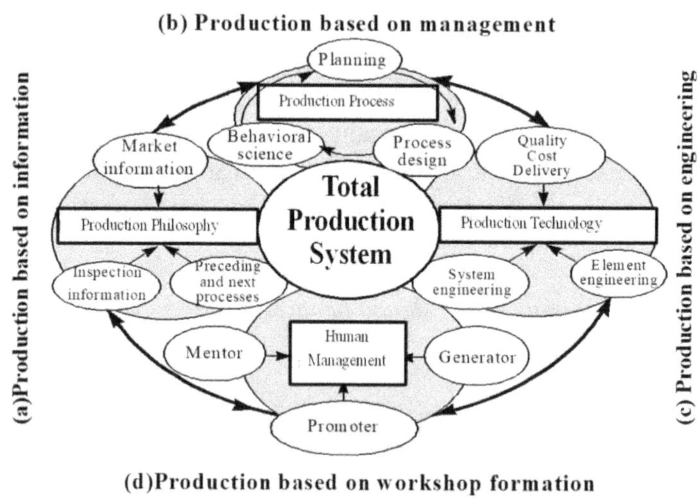

Developing New Japan Production Management Model Surpassing JIT

To develop NMT, furthermore, the author has developed the New Japan Production Management Model (NJ-PMM) named Advanced TPS surpassing JIT in order to enable the strategic deployment of Total Production System and SCM (Supply Chain Management) (Amasaka, 2007a,b, 2008, 2019a; Amasaka and Sakai, 2010, 2011). In Figure 3, the mission of NJ-PMM is to contribute the worldwide uniform quality and production at optimal locations as the strategic deployment of global production and to realize Customer Satisfaction (CS), Employee Satisfaction (ES), and Social Satisfaction (SS) through high quality assurance manufacturing.

Figure 3. Schematic Drawing of New Japan Production Management Model (NJ-PMM)

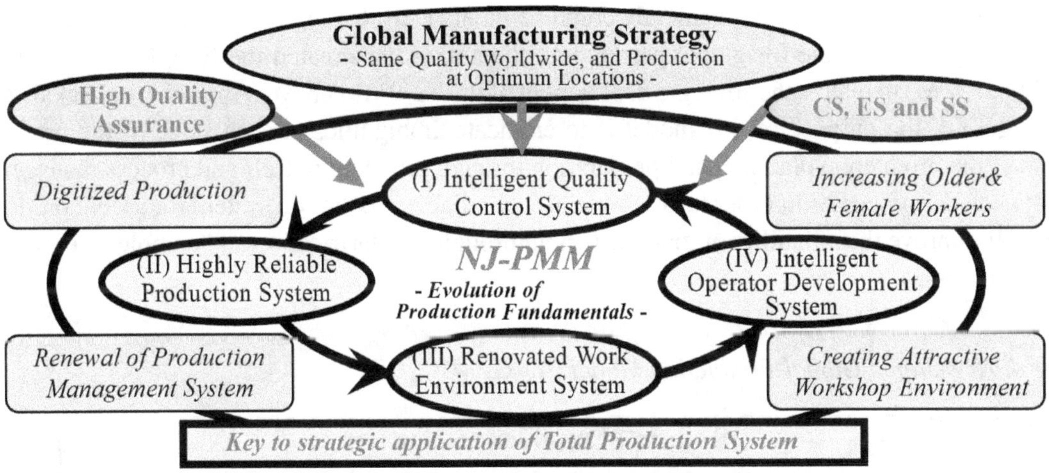

On a concrete target, this model is the systemization of a new, next-generation Japanese production management system and this involves the high-cyclization of the production process for realizing the simultaneous achievement of QCD requirements. To make this model into a reality it will be necessary to adapt it to handle digitalized production and reform it to realize a renewal production management system. Moreover, other prerequisites for realizing this include the need to create an attractive working environment that can accommodate the increasing number of older and female workers at the production sites and to cultivate intelligent production operators.

One of the technical elements necessary for fulfilling these requirements is the reinforcement of maintenance and improvement of process capabilities by establishing an intelligent quality control system. Second, a highly reliable production system needs to be established for high quality assurance. Third, reform is needed for the creation of a next generation working environment system that enhances intelligent productivity. Fourth, intelligent production operators need to be cultivated that are capable of handling the advanced production system and an intelligent production operating development system needs to also be established.

DUAL GLOBAL ENGINEERING MODEL TO ADVANCE NJ-PMM

Then, to advance NJ-PMM, the author has created the Dual Global Engineering Model (DGEM) by processing the New Japan Global Production Model (NJ-GPM) and New Japan Global Manufacturing Model (NJ-GMM) as the dual global engineering on the production plan, production preparation, manufacturing, inspection and SCM.

New Japan Global Production Model (NJ-GPM)

Global production must be deployed in order to establish the kind of manufacturing that is required to gain the trust of customers around the world by achieving a high level of quality assurance and efficiency and shortening lead times to reinforce the simultaneous achievement of QCD requirements. The vital key to achieving this is the introduction of a production system that incorporates production machinery automated with robots, skilled and experienced workers (operators) to operate the machinery and, further, production information to organically combine them. Thus, having recognized the need for a new production system suitable for global production, the author has created the New Global Production Model (NJ-GPM) to realize the strategic deployment of the NJ-PMM above (Amasaka and Sakai, 2011).

In Figure 4, the purpose of this model is to eradicate ambiguities at each stage of the production process as the production planning and preparation through production itself and process management, and between the processes in order to achieve a highly reliable production system for global production which will improve the reliability of manufacturing through the clarification and complete coordination of these processes.

Figure 4. New Japan Global Production Model (NJ-GPM)

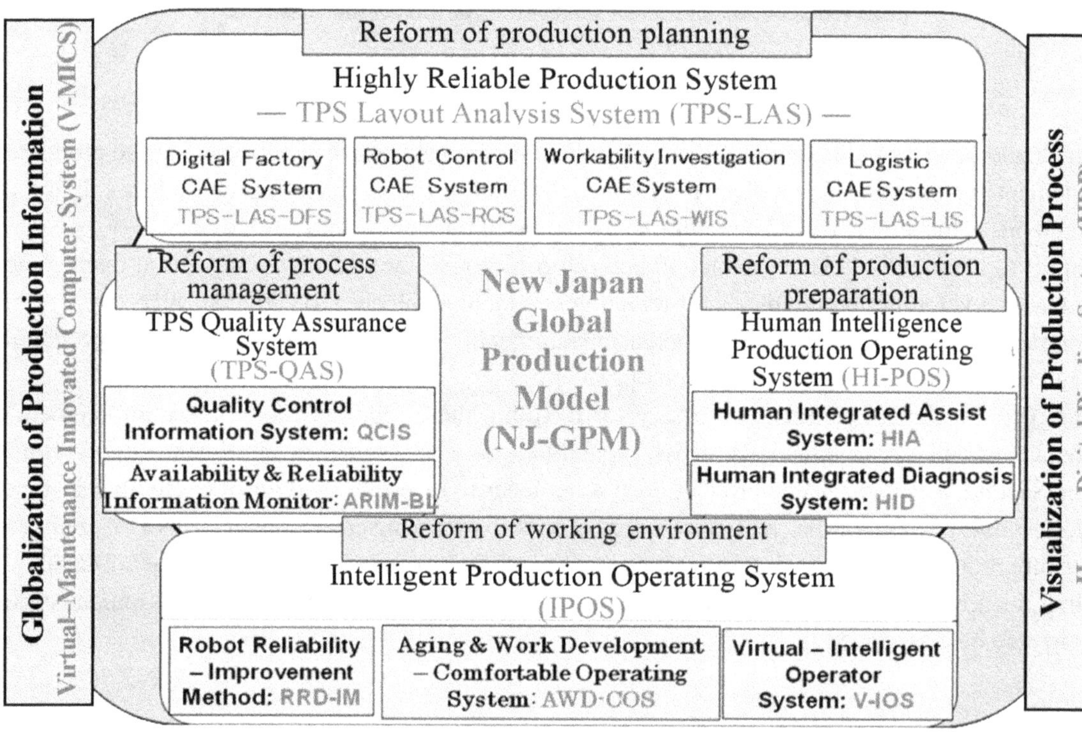

More specifically, the model is intended to (i) employ numeric simulation (Computer Aided Engineering, CAE) and computer graphics (CG) right from the production planning stage to resolve technical issues before they occur, (ii) reinforce production operators' high-tech machine operating skills and manufacturing capabilities, and (iii) visualize the above using IT in order to reform production information systems to create a global network of production sites around the world.

The six core management technologies that constitute this model and their characteristics are described below (Amasaka, 2017a, 2020b, 2022).

1. Reform of production planning: TPS Layout Analysis System (TPS-LAS) is a production optimization intended to realize a highly reliable production system by optimizing the layout of both the production site as a whole and each production process with regard to production lines (logistics and transportation), robots (positioning), and production operators (allocation and workability) through the use of numeric simulation (Sakai and Amasaka, 2006a).
2. 2. Reform of production preparation: Human Intelligence – Production Operating System (HI-POS) is an intelligent operator development system intended to enable the establishment of a new people-oriented production system whereby training is conducted to ensure that operators develop the required skills to a uniform level, and diagnosis is then carried out to ensure that the right people are assigned to the right jobs (Sakai and Amasaka, 2006b). HI-POS is made up of two sub-systems: Human Integrated Assist System (HIA) and Human Intelligence Diagnosis System (HID).
3. Reform of the working environment: Intelligent Production Operating System (IPOS) is intended to lead to a fundamental reform of the work involved in production operations by raising the technical skills level of production operators and further improving the reliability of their skills for operating advanced production equipment within an optimized working environment. TPS-IPOS is made up of three sub-systems: Virtual – Intelligent Operator System (V-IOS), Aging & Work Development – Comfortable Operating System (AWD-COS), and Robot Reliability Design - Improvement Method (RRD-IM) (Sakai and Amasaka, 2003, 2007a; Amasaka, 2007c).
4. Reform of process management: TPS Quality Assurance System (TPS-QAS) is an integrated quality control system intended to ensure that quality is built into production processes through scientific process management that employs statistical science to secure process capability (Cp) and machine capability (Cm) (Amasaka and Sakai, 1998, 2009). TPS-QAS is made up of two sub-systems: Quality Control Information System (QCIS) and Availability & Reliability Information Monitor System (ARIM).
5. Visualization of production processes: Human Digital Pipeline System (HDPS) ensures that top priority is given to customers through manufacturing with a high level of quality assurance (Sakai and Amasaka, 2007b). This involves the visualization of intelligent production information throughout product design, production planning and preparation, and production processes, thereby facilitating the complete coordination of these processes. This system enables the high-cyclization of business processes within manufacturing.
6. Globalization of production information: Virtual – Maintenance Innovated Computer System (V-MICS) is a global network system for the systemization of production management technology necessary to realize a highly reliable production system, which is required to achieve worldwide uniform quality and production at optimal locations (Sakai and Amasaka, 2005).

New Japan Global Manufacturing Model (NJ-GMM)

To be successful of global manufacturing in the near future, the Japanese manufacturing industry must develop an excellent manufacturing management technology employing the advances in manufacturing engineering that can continuously provide high value products in a timely manner surpassing "Kaizen" (improvement) of manufacture site symbolized by TPS based on the three actuals of the actual place, actual part and actual situation (Amasaka, 1988, 2009).

Moreover, a key of global manufacturing is the systematic deployment of SCM on a global scale that encompasses cooperative manufacturing operations with overseas suppliers employing a newly global partnering model (Amasaka, 2004a, 2008; Ebioka et al., 2007).

To realize the world uniform quality-simultaneous model launches, the author has created the New Japan Manufacturing Management Model (NJ-GMM) by using six core models based on the structure of manufacturing engineering as shown in Figure 5 (Amasaka, 2020a).

Figure 5. New Japan Global Manufacturing Model (NJ-GMM)

In NJ-GMM, the main characteristics of each core model contribute to the advancement of manufacturing management through actual QCD research by using statistical science, as follows (Amasaka, 2017a, 2022);

1. Intellectual Working Value Improvement Management Model (IWV-IMM) as the basic principle of working value intends that the design, production, quality assurance, marketing, human resource development, and administration cooperate and must reform the technologies and skills of the workers for the revolution of operating technology and skill in workplaces (Yamaji et al., 2007a; Tsunoi et al., 2010). In particular, boosting morale, reduction of fatigue, development of physical strength, development of tools & devices, improvement of thermal environment, and prevention of illness & injury are required for evolution.
2. Partnering Performance Measurement Model (PPMM) for assembly makers and suppliers serves as a formulation model using radar chart for visualization and evaluation in the actual status of Japanese partnering between automobile assembly makers and parts suppliers, which has been somewhat implicitly carried out in the past (Yamaji et al., 2008). In connection with the PPMM development, the author creates PPMM-A for assembly makers, PPM-S for suppliers, and PPM-AS for assembly makers and suppliers, as a comprehensive dual performance measurement.
3. Strategic Stratified Task Team Model (SSTTM) for the driving force of problem-solving contributes to the strengthening of the ties among group manufacturing companies, non-group companies, and even overseas manufacturers (suppliers) (Amasaka, 2004a,b, 2008). To realize this, the level of problem-solving technology rises in product development strategy I and II through joint task teams of intra-company departments and divisions (Task-1 to Task-6, Group task team, Department task team, Division task management team, Field task management team, Total task management team) called "Internal Partnering". This technology is further expanded to quality management strategy I to II through the domestic affiliated company, domestic non-affiliated company, and overseas non-affiliated company (Task-6 to Task-8, Joint A to Joint C) called "External Partnering".
4. Intelligence High-cycle System of Assembly Maker Production Process (IHS-AMPP) for preventing defects and achieving quality is effective management of the advanced production process (Amasaka et al., 2008; Amasaka and Sakai, 2010; Amasaka, 2018). To improve the intelligent productivity of production operators and to consolidate the information about highly cultivated skills and operating skills, IHS-AMPP contains the advanced facilities into commonly shared fore core systems as follows; (I) Highly Reliable Production System (HRPS), (II) Intelligent Quality Control System (IQCS), (III) Renovated Work Environment System (RWES), and (IV) Intelligent Operators Development System (IODS).
5. Strategic Quality Management using Performance Measurement Model (SQM-PMM) is the criterion of strategic development of NJ-GMM. At a stage of creation of SQM-PMM, specifically, and a survey of top management at Japanese manufacturers was conducted in order to investigate the management achievements as a key to strategic global manufacturing (Survey targeted 898 companies) (Amasaka et al., 1999; Amasaka, 2009; Kozaki et al., 2012). First, the author conducted the graphical modeling method based on the correlations among the 28 practice items of six categories–TQM methods, technological development, CS, quality assurance, corporate culture, and total participation activities. Second, the author performed the formulation of SQM-PMM through canonical correlation analysis. Moreover, the author verified the validity of SQM-PMM standardization.
6. Working Value Evaluation Model (WVEM) for strengthening of manufacturing technology makes the basic of "Creative workplace" as moving power of SQM-PMM, and evaluates the awareness of the working value of workers by statistically analyzing data collected through actual condition survey on Toyota, Nissan and other three companies (Uchida et al., 2012). This model systemati-

cally covers 20 key factors based on the fatigue reduction, disease prevention, comfort, organizations, and intelligence ability. Then, the author received 25 sets of answers from workers in the manufacturing industry, and analyzed their weightings using covariance structure analysis. Also, standardization of evaluation formulas made it possible to compare the strength of each working value evaluation axis in order to deployment and verify the validity of WVEM.

EXAMPLE APPLICATIONS

In this section, the author illustrates some research examples of Toyota's pioneering technology as applications of the NJ-PMM based on the NMT. NJ-PMM is contributing to the advancement of automobile management technology at Toyota and suppliers by developing DGEM with NJ-GPM and NJ-GMM, and is proving to be effective both in Japan and overseas (Amasaka and Sakai, 2011; Amasaka, 2015, 2017a, 2018, 2019a, 2020a,b, 2022).

Innovation of Automobile Production Engineering based on the NJ-GPM

Production Planning Employing TPS-LAS, HDP and HI-POS

In TPS-LAS application based on production engineering, the author has developed a simulation of main body conveyance using its four constitute sub-systems ((1)-(4)) to illustrate a highly liable production process that has contributed to the reform of production planning as shown in Figure 6 (Sakai and Amasaka, 2006a).

Firstly, specifically, a hypothetical production line is set up within a "digital factory" on a computer. (1) TPS-LAS-DFS is then used to reproduce the flow of people and parts within the production site. This enables any interference between production machinery and production cycle times to be checked in advance using simulations. One type of advance simulation uses (2) TPS-LAS-RCS for the optimum placement of welding robots for the main body to ensure that no interference occurs. Next, advance verification is performed using (3) TPS-LAS-WIS to ensure that the predetermined work (standardized work) is carried out within the predetermined cycle time with no waste (*muda*) or overburdening (*muri*). Then, (4) TPS-LAS-LIS is used to establish optimized conveyance routes between processes and determine optimum buffer allocations.

In addition, in HDP application using production engineering, the author has carried out the image training of production processes in actual order of assembly automobile operations in order to the innovation of production planning as shown in Figure 7 (Sakai and Amasaka, 2007b). To intellectual training, this is done at the preparatory stage before beginning mass production without having a real product on hand. HDP promotes the leveling of the workload of operators in each process, and then completes the building up of production line even before launching it using Total Linkage System (TLS) of intellectual production information through the product design, production engineering and manufacturing.

Firstly, specifically, HDP creates and supplies in advance "Standard Work Sheets" on which production operators have recorded each task in the correct order for jobs such as assembly work, by using design data for new products and facilities prepared from design through to production technology, even if there are no production prototypes. Next, HDP enables visualization training for machining processes step-by-step in the order that parts are built up, even if the actual product does not yet exist. This sys-

Figure 6. TPS-LAS, Developing the simulation of main body conveyance

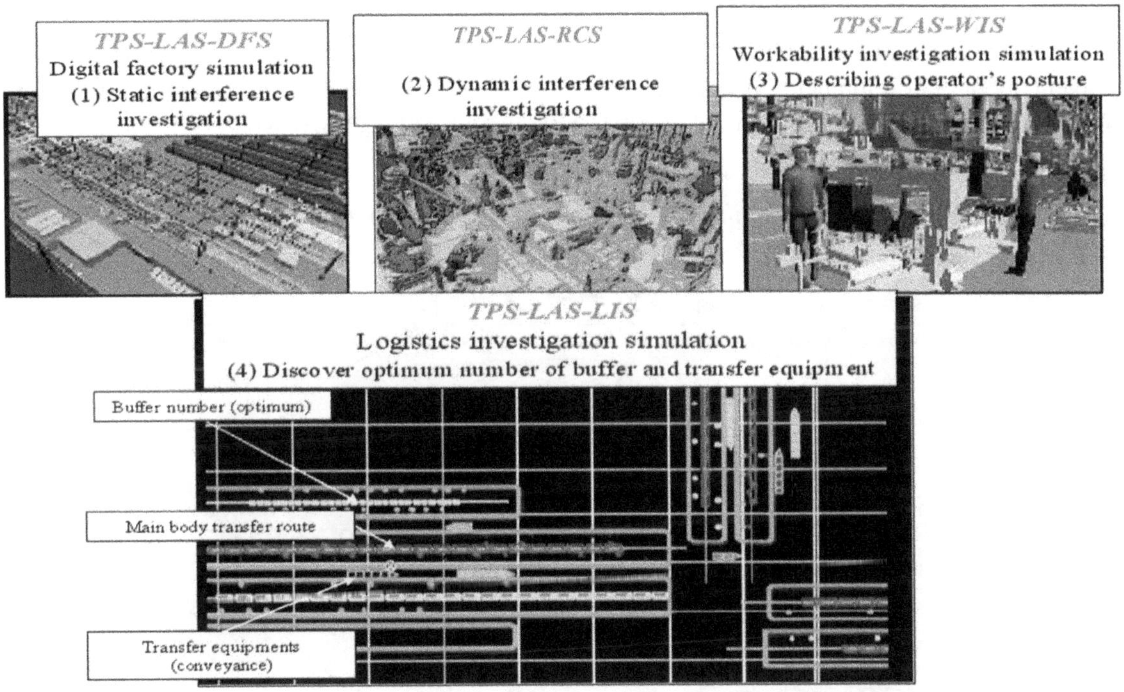

Figure 7. HDP system, raising the level of skills and capabilities

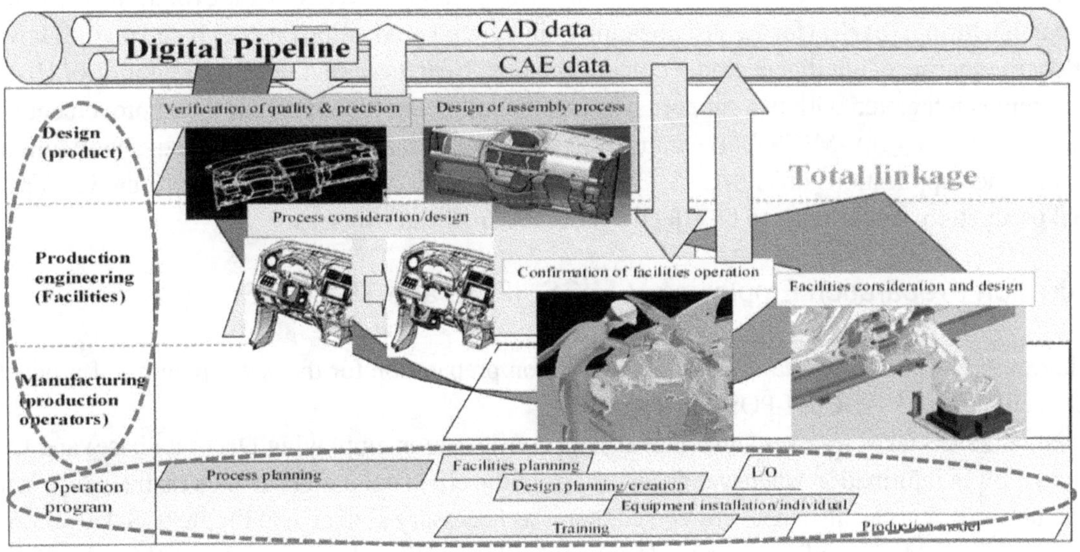

tem is proving to be very effective in raising the level of proficiency for processes requiring skills and capabilities at the production preparation stage.

Furthermore, in HI-POS application employing production engineering, the author has created the intelligent operator development system intended to establish a new people - oriented production system as shown in Figure 8 (Sakai and Amasaka, 2003, 2005, 2006b, 2007a,b, 2008).

Figure 8. HI-POS, strengthening of the intelligent operator development system

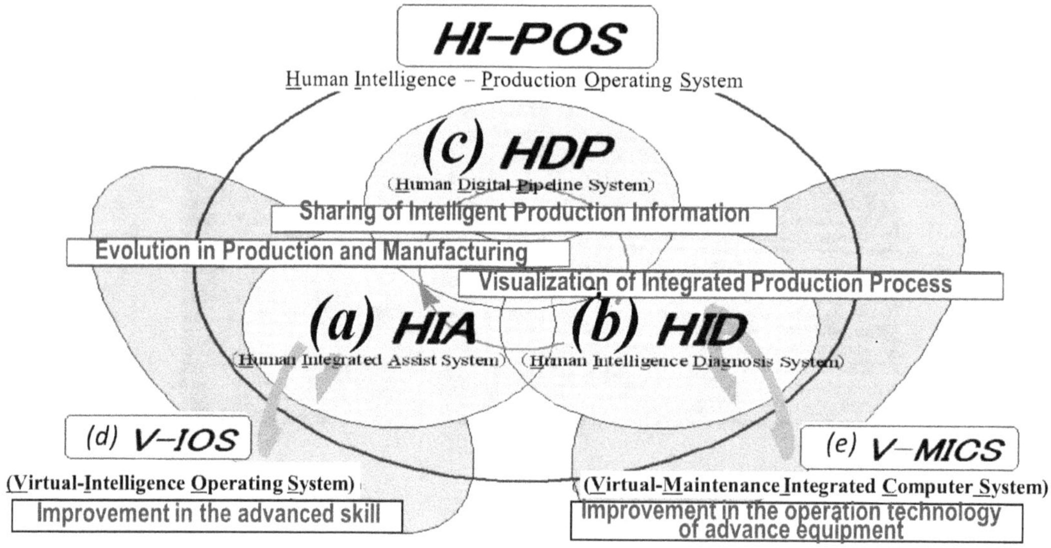

Firstly, the author has developed three constituent sub-systems–(a) HIA for the evolution in production and manufacturing, (b) HID for the visualization of integrated production process based on the above (c) HDP for the sharing of intelligent production information. Next, to strengthen the integration of HI-POS, this system is integrated with two support systems–the following (d) V-IOS for the improvement in the advanced skill, and (e) V-MICS for the improvement in the operation technology of advance equipment. The combined applications of TPS-LAS, HDP and HI-POS are currently being contributed as a part of global production, and proving to be effective both in Japan and overseas.

Production Preparation Employing V-MICS, IPOS and TPS-QAS

Furthermore, the author has developed the production preparation for the strengthening of production process employing V-MICS, I-POS and TPS-QAS.

First, V-MICS takes a server and client system configuration employing DB (data base) and CG in order to browse information whenever necessary from the client computers at each maintenance station via the network, and can also input any special items as necessary as shown in Figure 9 (Sakai and Amasaka, 2005). In V-MICS application using HDP, TPS-LAS, HI-POS, V-IOS and RRD-IM, the author has developed combining both the (1) Production Process Optimization Simulation (PPOS) and (2) Work Operation Combination Simulation (WOCS) for the high productivity (Sakai and Amasaka, 2007a,b).

Figure 9. V-MICS, systematizing managerial technique of production facilities

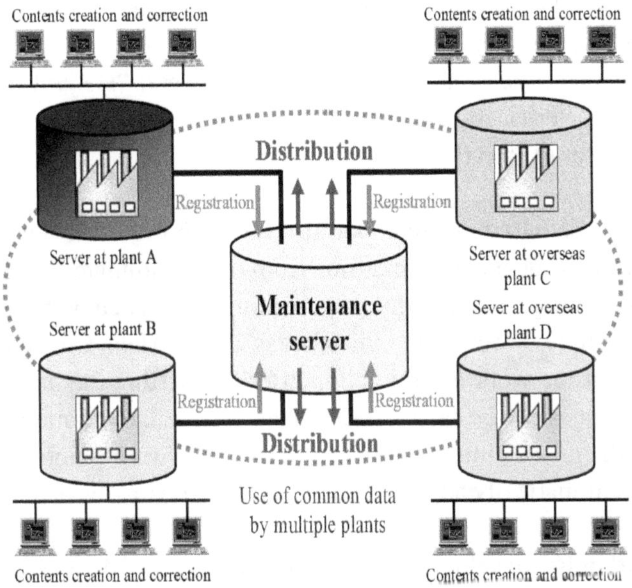

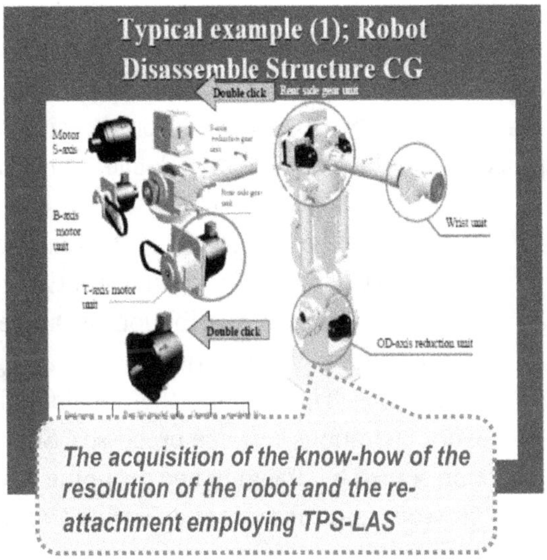

Ex. Robot Maintenance using Visual Manual Format based on RRD-IM

1. PPOS shows the verification of the operators interfering with one another when determining which combinations of vehicle models cause the overlapping of operators in the time series in order to evaluation and problem finding as shown in Figure 10. This is an aerial view of the process in which a vehicle is carried on the conveyor at a fixed speed, and the walking routes of the operators performing assigned work operations are displayed in real time in straight lines.

Figure 10. PPOS example of verification of operators' interfering with one another

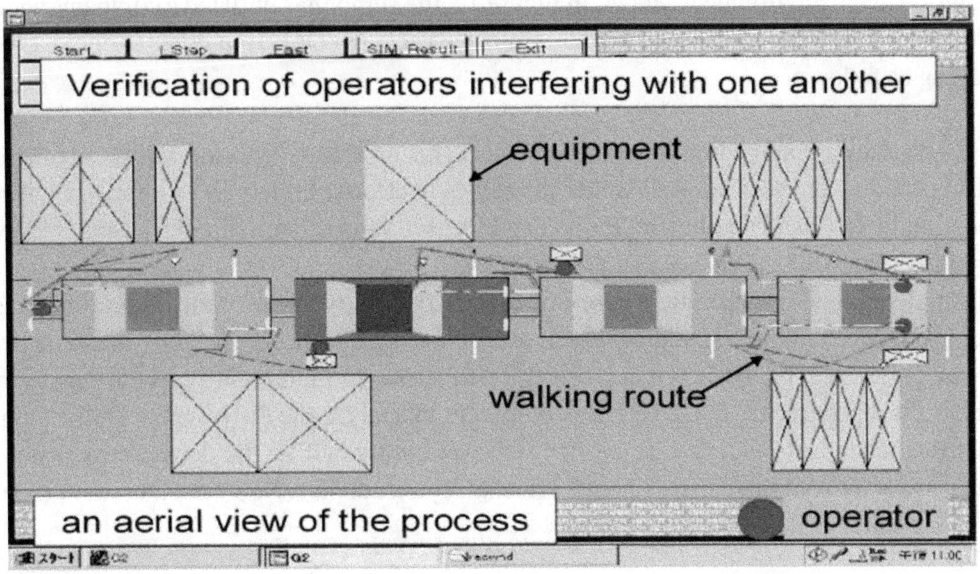

When multiple operators performing different operations in one process are overlapped (that is when operators' interference occurs), it is displayed instantly, and the information on which combination of models is also output immediately. Verification will be conducted through simulation as to whether operators can complete their entire operation of one process in the set "Takt-Time" and "Heijunka" (Amasaka, 1988, 2009). Based on the simulation, verification results are displayed showing which process, on which vehicle model, caused the operator to stop the conveyor.

2. W-COS can be carried out in the real Takt-Time based on Heijunka. In Chapter 6 Figure 8, (left) (Refer to Chapter 6), by sorting out the working time and walking time from the accumulated time results, the uneven distribution of the net-working time and the non-working time, such as time spent walking, are stratified to serve as a guideline for reviewing the process layout. Then, Chapter 6 Figure 8, (right) shows the re-calculation of the work accumulation after reshuffling the basic work operations between processes. Such changes can be easily made on the accumulative simulation screen by dragging and dropping with the mouse, immediately confirming the work points of previous and subsequent operations while automatically adjusting the walking time involved.

Second, to employ I-POS strategically, the author has developed the (i) V-IOS, (ii) RRD-IM and (iii) TTD-IM employing HDP, HI-POS and TPS-LAS, as follows;

(i) V-IOS and (ii) RRD-IM using HID and Visual Manual is intended to improve the skills of new (inexperienced) production operators both in Japan and overseas. In Figure 11, at special training centers with simulations of actual assembly lines, (a) training processes for assembly work, and (b) work training systems for assembly work are employed in the training of operators. Then, once a certain level of skills has been mastered, operators progress to actual assembly lines where they are promptly and methodically developed as highly skilled and experienced technicians using (c) standard work sheets extracted (Sakai and Amasaka, 2003).

(ii) AWD-COS constitutes a fundamental reform of work and labor named Toyota's Epoch-Making Evolution in the Environment Model. In Figure 12, the author has initiated a company-wide project called Aging & Work Development 6 Programs Project (AWD6P/J) in order to combat the effects of aging as follows;

Project I is arousing motivation in workers, Project II is reviewing working styles to reduce fatigue, Project III is creating physical strength under the self-help efforts, Project IV is improving heavy work with user-friendly tools and equipment, Project and Project VI is reinforcing illness and injury prevention (Amasaka et al., 2000c; Amasaka, 2004a, 2007c).

For example, Figure 13 illustrates a result of Project II activity as the "Study work of changing the rest pattern to reduce fatigue". In Figure 13(a), fatigue during operation gradually increases with time and decreases after each break shown in Normal Rest Pattern. In Figure 13(b), as the way to minimize fatigue, new 2 rest patterns (A & B) were tested in order to analyze the difference with the fatigue level of Normal Rest Pattern. In Figure 13(c), a line stop was cut by half by the decrease in quality defects and human error (⬇ from these experimental effects, Toyota adopts a New Rest Pattern A in Japan and overseas at present).

Figure 11. V-IOS example for the skill strengthening of operators using virtual operation

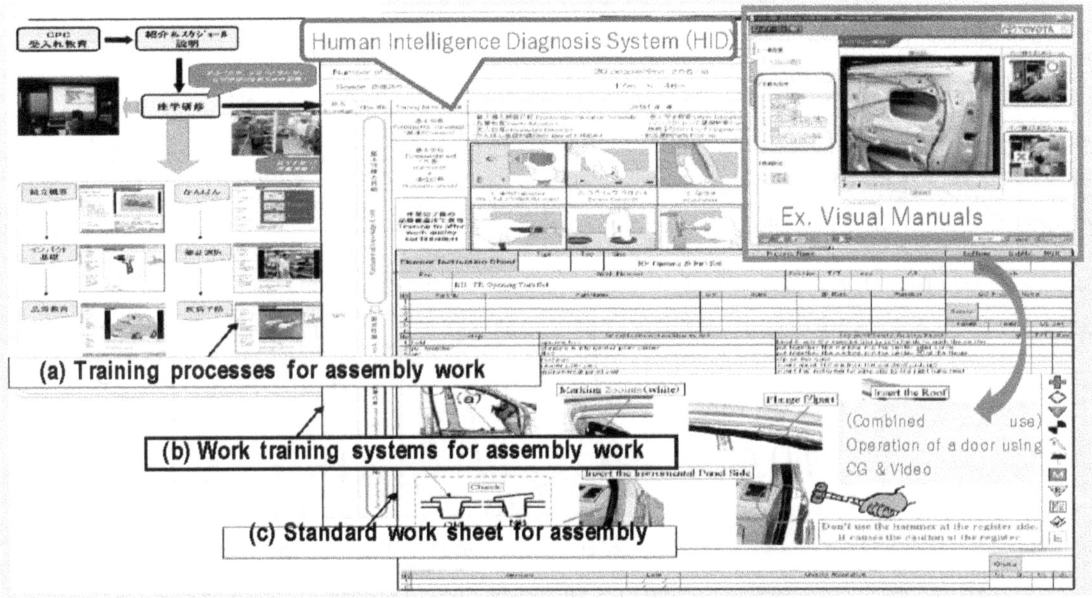

Figure 12. AWD-COS example for the Aging & Work Development 6 Programs Project

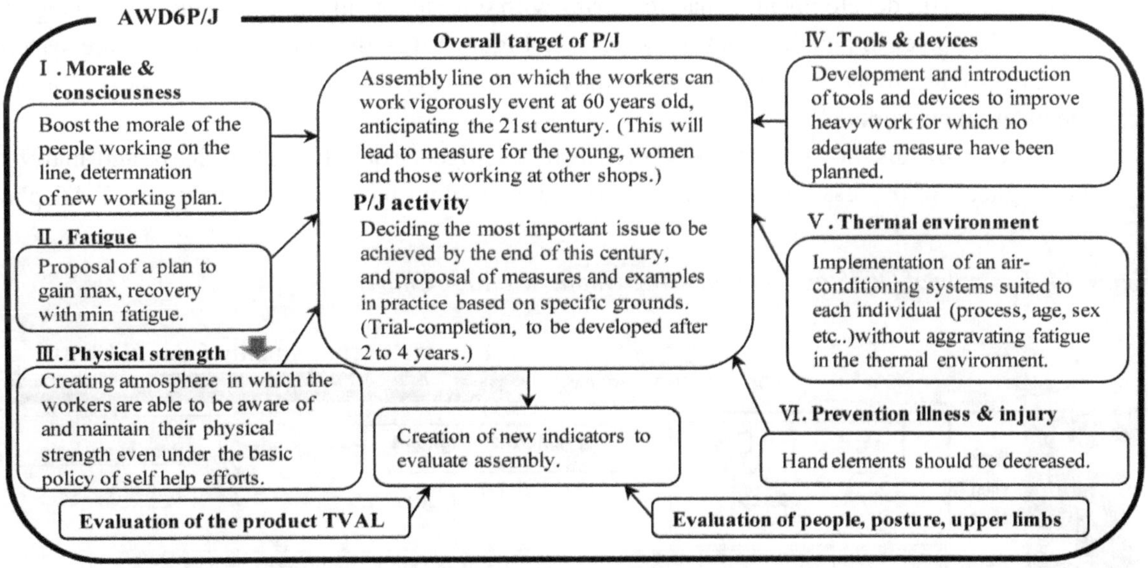

Third, the author has established the TPS-QAS with two sub-systems – (i) QCIS and (ii) ARIM for the automobile high quality assurance (Amasaka and Sakai, 1996, 1998, 2009; Amasaka, Ed., 2003) as follows;

Figure 13. Example of Project II - Study work of changing the rest pattern to reduce fatigue

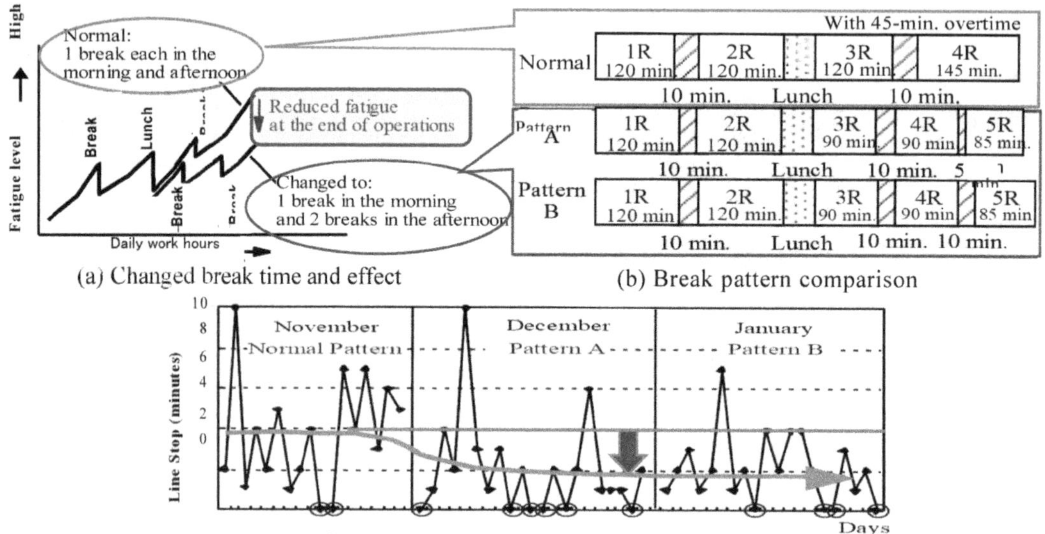

(a) Changed break time and effect

(b) Break pattern comparison

(c) Example of line stop time between 12:25 and 13:25 that causes work delays

Notes: Two assembly lines at Motomachi plant, where the Crown and IPSUM car models, were selected as the experimental lines for 2-month trial. Fatigue level was calculated by both subjective and objective indicators (e.g., physiological).

(i) QCIS enables the development of manufacturing with superior quality and productivity by integrating the high-precision quality control systems. In Figure 14(a), this illustrates a hardware system of trans-axle assembly line holding the (a) main-system, (b) sub-system and (c) connects internal and external networks.

In Figure 14(b), this shows a software system using intelligence quality control charts, and analyzes the diagnosis of process management abnormalities holding the (1) Scroll-function, (2) Display

Figure 14. Example of QCIS application using Quality Control Charts

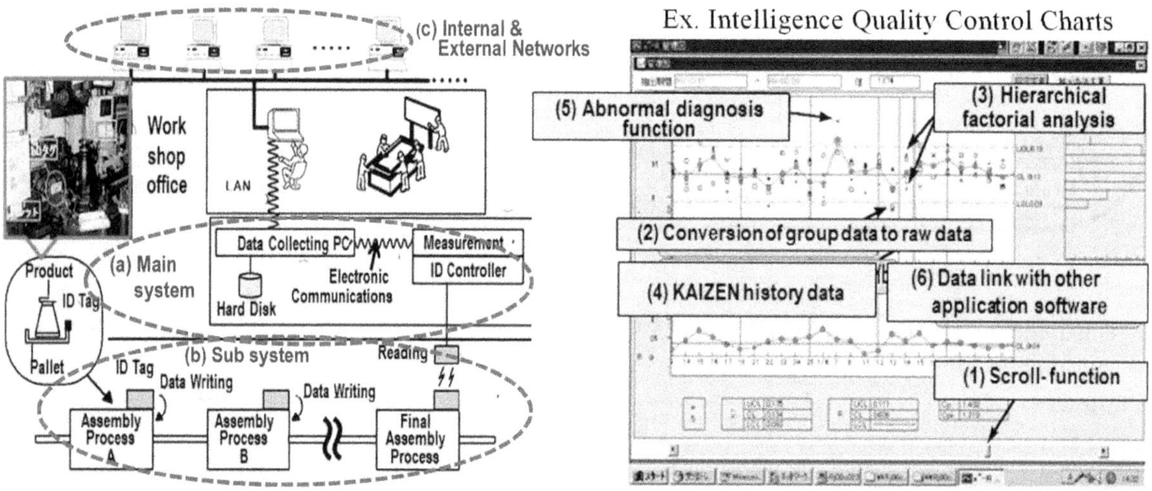

(a) Outline of hardware system (Trans-axle unit)

(b) Outline of software system

of grouped and raw data, (3) Hierarchical factorial analysis, (4) Kaizen, improvement of history database, (5) Abnormal diagnosis and (6) Data link with other application software.

(ii) ARIM enables the strengthen reliability analysis of facility operation and maintenance of information management. In Figure 15(a), this illustrates a hardware system for gathering the operating efficiency and failures using Andon system, and clusters of machinery on each production line in Japan and overseas. In Figure 15(b), for developing the preventive maintenance, this software system performs the Weibull analysis, failure diagnosis and failure life predicting employing Table 1 based on the reliability engineering.

Figure 15. Example of ARIM application using "Weible analysis"

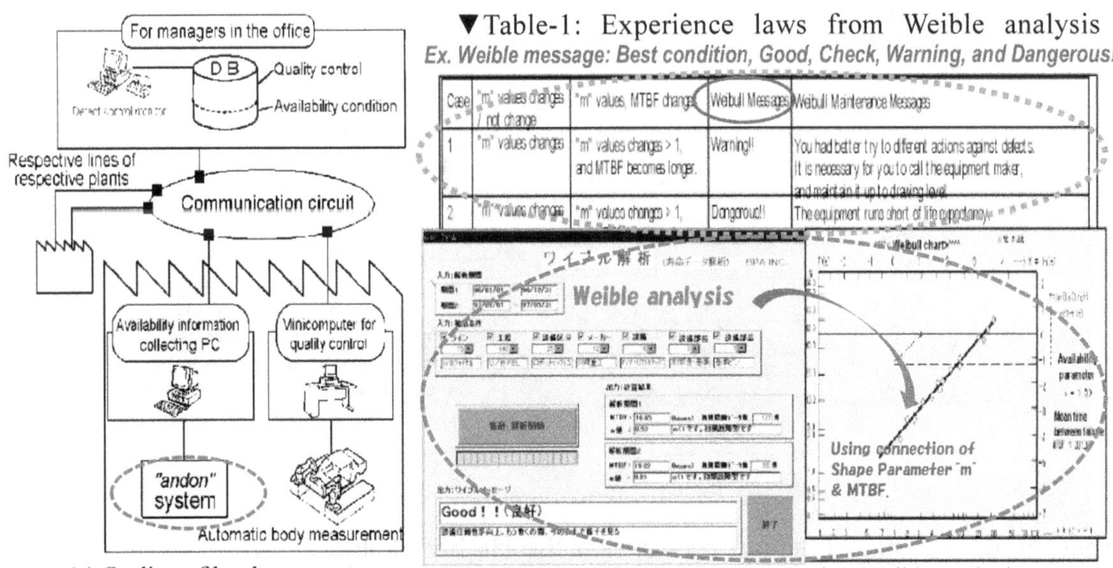

(a) Outline of hardware system (b) Outline of software system using Weible analysis

Innovation of Automobile Manufacturing Engineering Based on the NJ-GGM

Improving the Skills of Experienced and Inexperienced Machine Workers

To develop IWV-IMM and WVEM based on the NJ-GGM, the author has clarified the factors involved in improving the skills of experienced and inexperienced machine workers engaged in typical lathe work with 6 processing stages of setup, rough cutting, semi finishing, making adjustments, finishing and completion by using S45C workpiece (Yanagisawa, et al., 2013).

Specifically, using electroencephalography (EEG) and statistical science, the physical and mechanical characteristics of a workpiece are those tensile strength, elongation, hardness, thermal conductivity, density, Young's modulus, shear elasticity modulus and yield strength, and the relative influence of these characteristics are clarified in accordance with the cutting conditions. Through these investigations, the author clarified the important criteria for making decisions based on the chip color and chip shape.

For example, using covariance structure analysis, Figure 16 illustrates an example of clarifying factors for the "chip color during finishing" by experienced machine workers, and clarifies the influence these elements receive from each factor. This research clarifies points where inexperienced workers need guidance such as cutting tool selection, which is beneficial for both the person giving guidance and the person receiving guidance. Moreover, the author has investigated how intuition and knowhow make a difference between the skills of experienced and inexperienced workers based on the validity of other researches (Kawahara et al., 2016). These studies have contributed to technical training of inexperienced workers.

Figure 16. Chip color during finishing using Covariance Structure Analysis

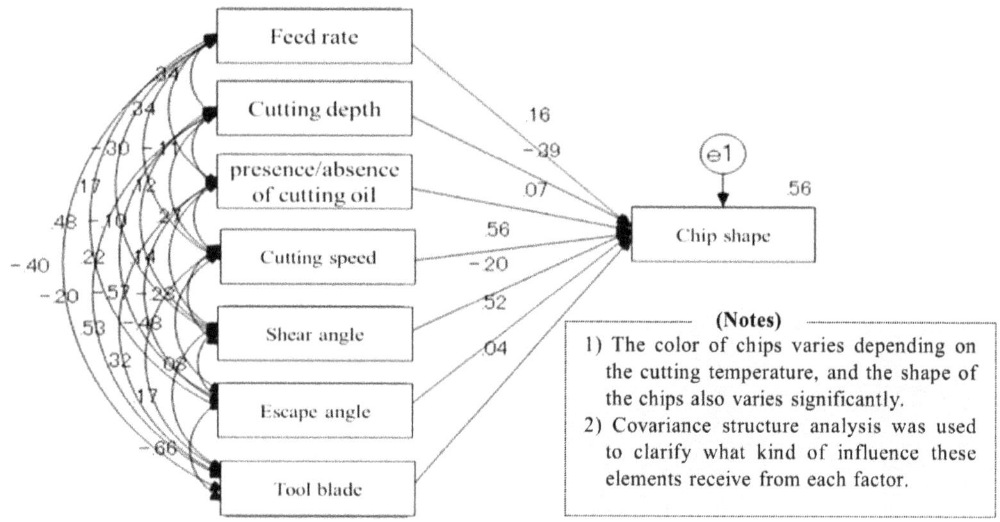

Accelerated Technical Training System for the Highly Skilled Operators

To realize the shortened training of highly skilled operators in auto-assembly line employing IWV-IMM and WVEM, the author has developed an Accelerated Technical Training System (ATTS) by development of HI-POS with HIA and HID above (Sakai and Amasaka, 2006b, 2007b, 2008; Amasaka et al., 2008).

Specifically, ATTS contains the four sub-system of vehicle assembly process – (i) Assessment system of aptitude/inaptitude using aptitude test with eight categories of fundamental skills (: tightening, screw grommet, attachment, connector, hose, plug hole, tube and fitting), (ii) Optimization system of training steps with flowchart of training program, (iii) Skill training system for newly employed production operators, and (iv) Shortened training system for new overseas production operators.

In Figure 17, the author illustrates an application case of "Toyota's shortened training for the new overseas production operators" with four step program based on the courses during 5 courses during five days from "Day 1" to "Day 5"– Classroom lecture, Skill training, Dynamic training with simulating movement and actual line training.

The deployment of ATTS for training newly employed production operators at domestic and overseas manufacturing plants reduced the conventional training period by more than half, from two weeks to five days, leading the full-scale production to a good start. In this case, the launch of an overseas production plant, the target operating rate was achieved in four months after the start-up.

Figure 17. Toyota's shortened training for the new overseas production operators in ATTS

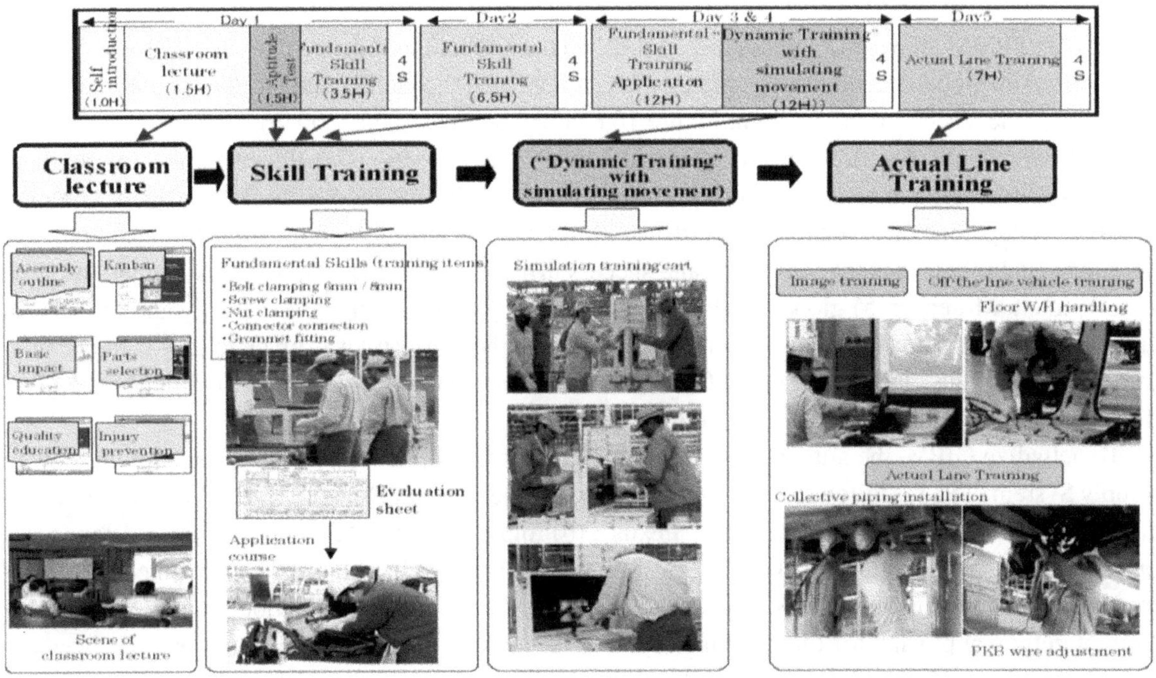

Figure 18. GIPM for the global manufacturing strategy

Global Intelligence Partnering Model for the Global Manufacturing Strategy

To develop PPMM above, the authors has established the Global Intelligence Partnering Model (GIPM) for automobile global manufacturing strategy which improves the intellectual productivity of the affairs and management sections as shown in Figure 18 (Yamaji and Amasaka, 2007b).

GIPM shows the functions of the affairs and management sections as the corporate environment factors for succeeding in global marketing, customer-first, 1) CS, ES and SS, for 2) high quality product and as a strategic factor to realize it, in order to 3) product reliability (high quality assurance) and corporation reliability (excellent company), and success in 4) intellectual productivity and human resource development. Moreover, 5) global production is realized by these. So the same quality and production at optimal locations are achieved. For that purpose, the highest priority was given to the "i) Intellectual information sharing" and "ii) Strategic Co-Creative Action" so that the "Strategic intelligence application system", and "Business process high linkage system" can effectively function.

To actualize GIPM, the author has developed the strategic application examples employing Toyota Supply System (TSS) as follows; (a) Creation of Automobile Exterior Design Model (AEDM) for raising customers' worth of world's prestige car "Lexus", (b) Improvement of "Paint corrosion resistance and protect plating parts from corrosion" for raising auto-unit-axle reliability, (c) Development of "Mid-frequency tempering equipment using the heating coil of electromagnetic induction" and (d) "Automated straightening equipment" for the realizing high productivity of auto-unit-axle shaft, and (e) "New ceramic materials to the welding nozzle and welding tip" for the improving high operational availability of auto-unit-axle housing" as the epoch-making improvement of QCD (Toyota, 1993; Amasaka, 2004b, 2009, 2018, 2019b).

Strategic Cooperative Task Team Model for Raising Management Technology

To strengthen promotion of SSTTM and SQM-PMM above, the author has structured the Strategic Cooperative Task Team Model (SCTTM) between the auto-maker and affiliated/non-affiliated suppliers as shown in Figure 19 (Amasaka, 2004a, 2008, 2017b). To purchase the necessary parts, it will be important for the manufacturer (maker) to mutually cooperate with (a) Supplier I (in-house parts maker (own company)), (b) Supplier II, affiliated maker (capital participation), (c) Supplier III, non-affiliated maker, and (d) Supplier IV, overseas maker (capital participation). In the actual deployment, it is important to strategically organize the stratified task teams for raising management technology as follows: (i) Product strategy, (ii) Engineering strategy, (iii) Quality strategy, (iv) QCD effect, (v) Value of the task teams, and (vi) Human resource strategy.

In SCTTM for the evolution of automobile manufacturing, the important job for the manufacturer's general administrator is to select jointly from his own company and suppliers: (1) Generators gifted with a special capacity for creating ideas, (2) Mentors having the ability to give guidance and advice, (3) Producers with the capability to achieve and execute, and (4) Promoters capable of implementing things as an organization. Then, as the key to successful SCTTM, the team leader (administrator) should select the members who have at least one of the capabilities for (1) to (4), commission authority and responsibilities to the members, and has himself / herself concentrate on risk management.

To develop this, the author presents typical case studies as the improving of the bottleneck problems of worldwide auto-makers employing SCTTM called Toyota's Total Task Management Model (TTMTM)

Figure 19. SCTTM for the evolution of Japanese automobile manufacturing

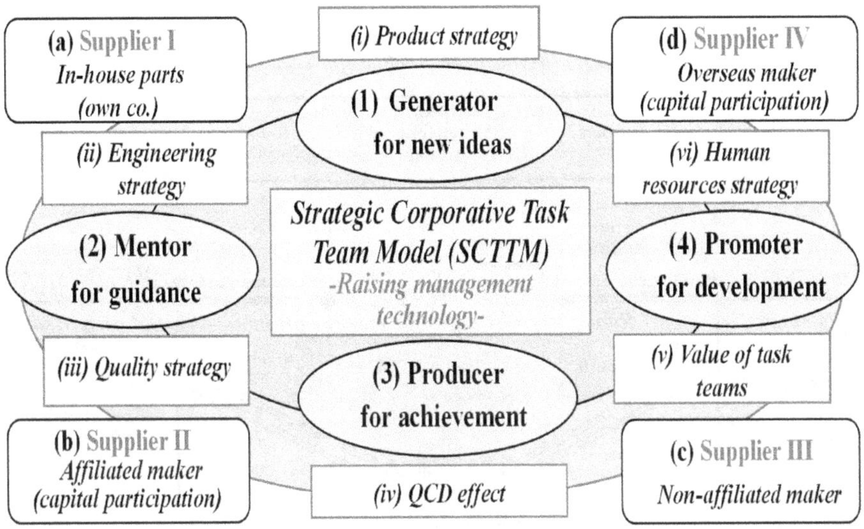

for realizing simultaneous QCD fulfilment (Amasaka, 2004a, 2017b). In Suppliers I, II and III, the author developed the establishment of "Brake pad quality assurance" using Total QA network activity (QAT) by Toyota, Aishin Seiki, Aishin Chemical and Akebono Brake Industry.

The main objective is to establish a technology for attaining satisfactory braking performance while minimizing squeal through the result of sensitivity analysis on the causes of squeal and braking performance. The result of QAT is remarkable effects as follows; (i) Estimated market claim ratio reduction to 1/6 (from 2.6% to 0.4%), (ii) In-process fraction defective: down 60% (from 0.5% to 0.2%), (iii) Short convergence of initial failures: (from 9 months to 3 months), and (iv) Cost reduction: 9.4% (156 Yen/unit).

Moreover, in other cases of Suppliers I-IV, the author was able to apply the SCTTM (TTMTM) as follows; (i) TQM and SQC training for growing human resources of Toyota group in Japan and overseas, (ii) Specific engine fuel consumption improvement, (iii) High reliability assurance of the transaxle oil seal leakage, (iv) Rust preventive quality assurance of rod piston plating parts, (v) Various anti-rusting methods to various section of the vehicle body, (vi) Improvement of total curvature spring back in stamped parts with large curvature, (vii) Improving the reliability of body assembly line equipment, and (viii) Bolt-nut loosening solution by developing Automobile Optimal Product Design Model (AOPDM) (Toyota, 1993; Amasaka, 2004b, 2019a,b; Amasaka et al., 2012).

New Global Partnering Production Model for Expanding Overseas Manufacturing

To develop IHS-AMPP using IWV-IMM and WVEM above, the author has established a New Global Partnering Production Model (NGP-PM) for Japan's expanding overseas manufacturing strategy as

Figure 20. NGP-PM for Japan's Expanding Overseas Manufacturing Strategy

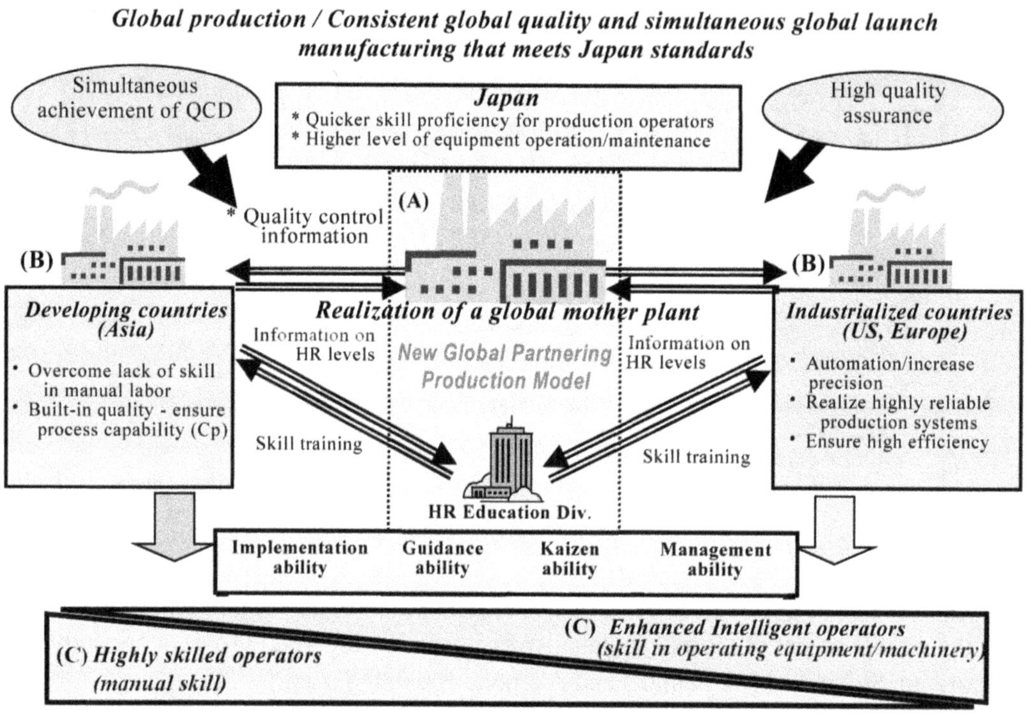

shown in Figure 20 (Ebioka et al., 2007; Amasaka and Sakai, 2010, 2011). The mission of NGP-PM is the simultaneous achievement of QCD in order to realize high quality assurance. The essential strategic policies include the following items:

First of all, (A) establishment of a foundation for global production, "realization of global mother plants-advancement of Japanese production sites"; Second, (B) achieving the "independence of local production sites" through the incorporation of the unique characteristics (production systems, facilities, and materials) of both developing countries (Asia) and industrialized countries (US, Europe); Third, (C) necessity of developing intelligence operators to promote knowledge sharing among the production operators in Japan and overseas as well as for the promotion of higher skills and enhanced intelligence.

To actualize NGP-PM, it is essential to create a spiraling increase in the four core elements by increasing their comprehensiveness and high cycle-ization. Specifically, in realizing global mother plants, if Japanese and overseas manufacturing sites are to share knowledge from their respective viewpoints, the core elements must be advanced.

To achieve this, a necessary measure is to design separate approaches suited to developing and industrialized countries. Concretely, in developing countries (1), the most important issue is increasing the autonomy of local manufacturing sites. At these sites, "training for highly skilled operators" that is suited to the manual-labor based manufacturing sites is the key to excellent QCD studies. Similarly, in industrialized countries (2), where manufacturing sites are based on automatization and increasingly high-precision equipment, "training of intelligence operators" resulting in "realizing highly reliable production control systems and ensuring high efficiency" is the key to excellent QCD studies.

Moreover, production operators trained at "global mother plants" (3) can cooperate with operators at overseas production bases, and in order to generate synergistic results, can work to "localize global mother plants" in a way that is suited to the overseas production bases.

As the typical examples of NGP-PM deployment, the author describes the typical case studies of new integrated local production by partnering Toyota and overseas as follows; (i) New Turkish Production System (NTPS), an integration and evolution of Japanese and Turkish Production System, (ii) New Malaysia Production Model (NMPM), a new integrated production system of Japan and Malaysia, (iii) New Vietnam Production Model (NVPM), developing hybrid production of Japan and Vietnam, and (iv) Developing Advanced TPS at Toyota Manufacturing USA (Amasaka, 2007c, 2016; Yeap et al., 2010; Shan, et al., 2011: Miyashita and Amasaka, 2014, 2016). Deployment and validity of these studies are detailed to Amasaka (2015, 2017a, 2020b, 2022).

Total Quality Assurance Networking Model for Toyota's New Defect Prevention

To survive globalization and worldwide quality competition, Japanese manufacturing must work in order to shorten development times, ensure high quality and lower costs for the shift response to market changes (Amasaka, 2007a). To develop the IHS-AMPP above, therefore, the author has created the Total Quality Assurance Networking Model (TQA-NM) (Amasaka, 2004b; Kojima and Amasaka, 2011).

In Figure 21, TQA-NM focuses on the subject of (A) Clear QA standards that make use of quantitative values (process capability, Cp), (B) Systematic use of know-how and experience resolving part issue, (C) Development of staff (workers) and managers familiar with the site, (D) QA tools for staff (workers) and managers and (E) Process visualization enabled" which turned their attention especially to the "stronger partnerships between assembly manufacturers and suppliers".

Figure 21. TQA-NM for Toyota's new defect prevention technique

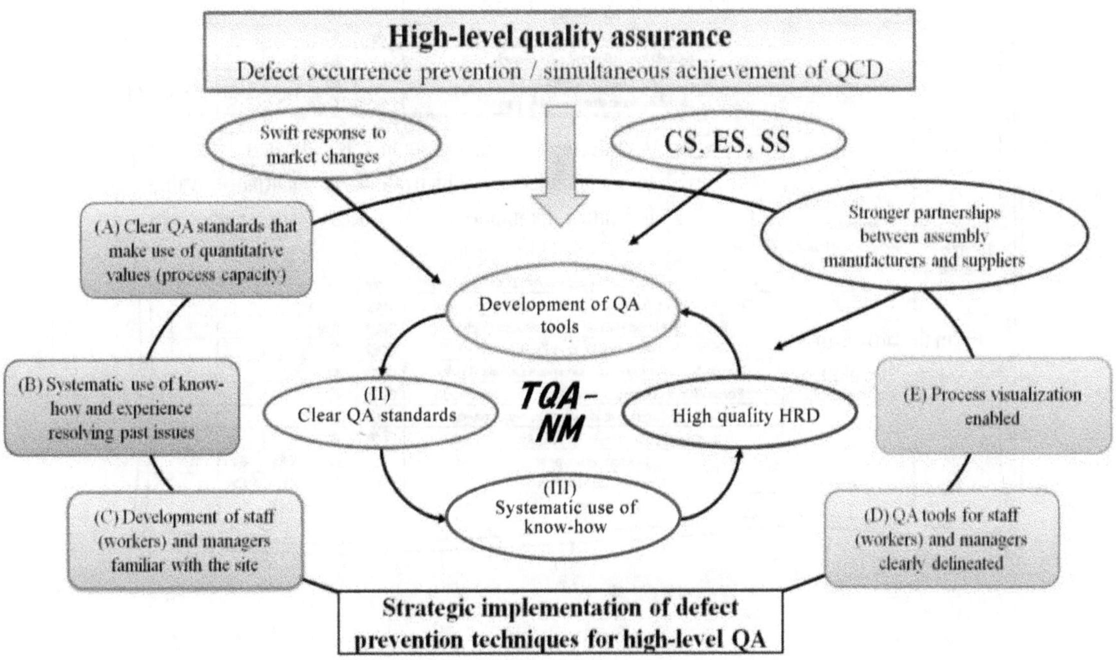

Then, this model is done through the prevention of defect occurrence and by supporting the simultaneous achievement of QCD that come from strategically deploying a high-level quality assurance process as follows; (I) One of the technological components in achieving these goals is strengthening QA networks, and deploying QA tools, (II) Second is establishing clear quantitative QA standards that are not affected by worker experience, (III) Third is creating a system that can

make use of worker expertise and information on past defects in an organized manner, and (IV) Fourth is the development of workers and frontline staff as the high quality HRD (Human Resource Development) who are familiar with the site.

To realize TQA-NM, specifically, the Total QA Networking Chart shown in Figure 22 is a defect occurrence prevention technique featuring a combination of QA tools. It also uses the Quality Function Deployment (QFD) or Failure Mode and Effect Analysis (FMEA), and matrix diagrams to deploy partnerships. The vertical axis identifies joint processes by suppliers and assembly manufacturers, from the arrival of goods to shipment. The horizontal axis lists individual defects. The degree of QA is indicated where the two axes intersect, which allows a quantitative value indicating the importance of process management tasks to be assigned to each.

Figure 22. An example of the Total QA Networking Chart

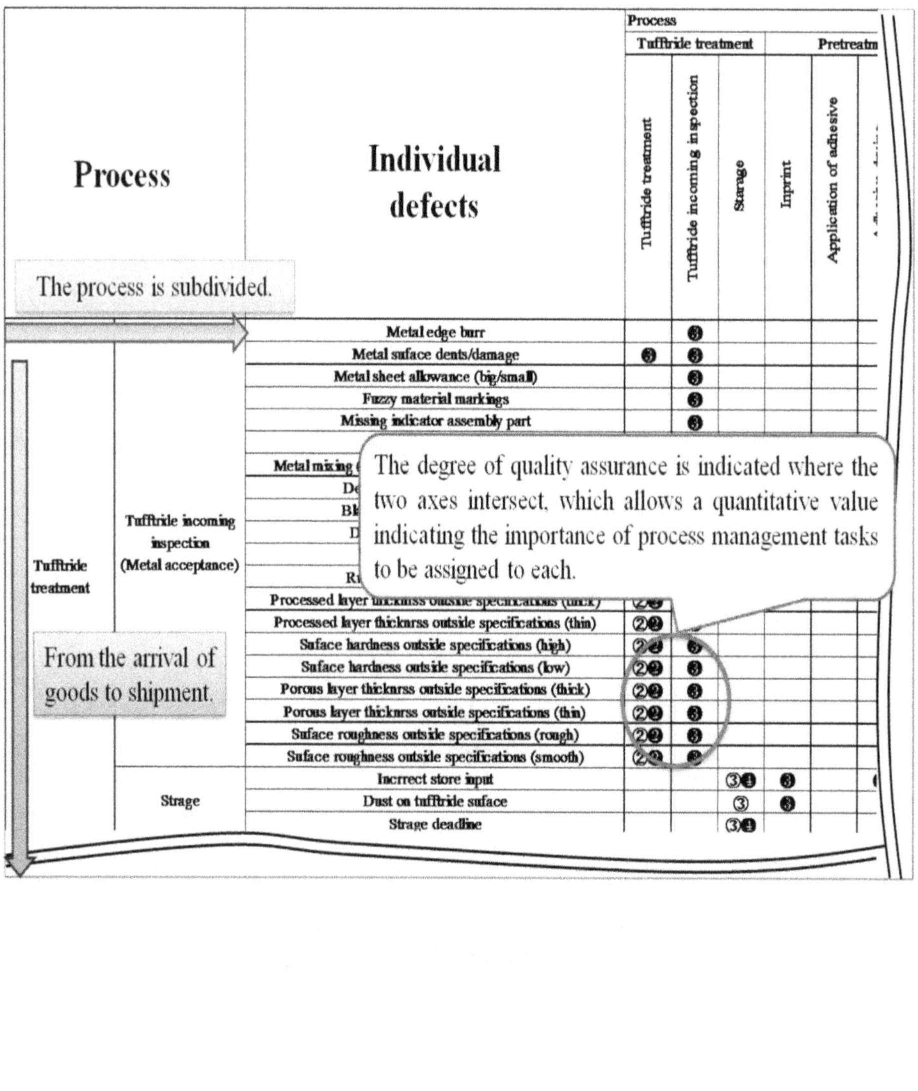

Each process is comprehensively evaluated on the basis of what the defect occurrence prevention tasks are for that process and how highly they are ranked in terms of QA level using QA matrix. The task of this chart is ensured based on the "Ranking Occurrence and Outflow prevention", and is established a high-level QA system.

As the pioneering examples of TQA-NM deployment of Toyota and Toyota's SCM strategy, the author presents as follows; (i) Establishment of optimum casting conditions for compact DOHC cylinder head, (ii) Development of ferrite heat resistant cast steel, (iii) Measures to be taken for difficulties in the manufacture of aluminum die-casted head cover, (iv) Rust prevention quality assurance of plated components, (v) Improving the brake pads quality of trans-axle unit, (vi) CAE analysis for oil leakage mechanism of transaxle oil seal, and others (Toyota, 1993; Amasaka, 2004b, Amasaka Ed.,2012; Amasaka, et al., 2012). Deployment and validity of these studies are detailed to Amasaka (2015, 2017a, 2022).

CONCLUSION

To re-construct world-leading management technologies, this study mentioned the evolution of Japan manufacturing foundation that surpasses conventional JIT practices. On a concrete target, the author focused on the strategic development of DGEM (Dual Global Engineering Model) possessing the NJ-GPM (New Japan Global Production Model) and NJ-GMM (New Japan Global Manufacturing Model) surpassing JIT. Concretely, the effectiveness of DGEM was verified through the actual applications to automobile manufacturing in Toyota and suppliers.

ACKNOWLEDGMENT

The author would like to acknowledge the generous support received from the following researchers: all those at the "Study group of 68QCS-Questionnaire analysis team of Toyota Group" in JUSE (Union of Japanese Scientists and Engineers), "Study group of the Ideal Situation the Quality Management of Manufacturing Industry" called Amasaka's Forum in JUSE, Toyota and other advanced assembly makers, many affiliated / nonaffiliated suppliers, and those connected with the Amasaka New JIT Laboratory at Aoyama Gakuin University that assisted with author's research, especially, Dr. Sakai, H., Mr. Yamaji, M., Mr. Ebioka, K., Yanagisawa, K., Kojima, T. and others.

REFERENCES

Amasaka, K. (1988). *Concept and progress of Toyota Production System (Plenary lecture). Co-sponsorship: Japan Society of Precision Engineering and others*, Hachinohe, Aomori-ken.

Amasaka, K. (1999). *The preliminary survey in 68QCS: Questionnaire result of TQM which creates Japan (Special Lecture)*. Union of Japanese Scientists and Engineers.

Amasaka, K. (2000c). *AWD6P/J Report of First Term Activity 1996-1999: Creation of 21C production line in which people over 60's can work vigorously*. Toyota Motor Corporation.

Amasaka, K. (2002). New JIT, a new management technology principle at Toyota. *International Journal of Production Economics*, *80*, 135–144.

Amasaka, K. (2004a). Development of Science TQM, a new principle of quality management: Effectiveness of strategic stratified task team at Toyota. *International Journal of Production Research*, *42*(7), 3691–3706.

Amasaka, K. (2004b). *Science SQC, New Quality Control Principle: The quality strategy of Toyota*. Springer-Verlag Tokyo.

Amasaka, K. (Ed.). (2007). New Japan Model "Science TQM"– Theory and practice for strategic quality management. Study group of ideal situation on quality management at manufacturing industry, Maruzen, Tokyo.

Amasaka, K. (2007a). New Japan Production Model, an advanced production management principle: Key to strategic implementation of New JIT. *The International Business & Economics Research Journal*, *6*(7), 67–79.

Amasaka, K. (2007b). High Linkage Model "Advanced TDS, TPS & TMS: Strategic development of "New JIT" at Toyota. *International Journal of Operations and Quantitative Management*, *13*(3), 101–121.

Amasaka, K. (2007c). Applying New JIT–Toyota's global production strategy: Epoch-making innovation in the work environment. *Robotics and Computer-integrated Manufacturing*, *23*(3), 285–293.

Amasaka, K. (2008). Strategic QCD studies with affiliated and non-affiliated suppliers utilizing New JIT. Encyclopedia of Networked and Virtual Organizations, 3(PU-Z), 1516-1527.

Amasaka, K. (2009). The foundation for advancing Toyota Production System utilizing New JIT. *Journal of Advanced Manufacturing Systems*, *80*(1), 5–26.

Amasaka, K. (Ed.). (2012). Science TQM, new quality management principle: The quality management strategy of Toyota. Bentham Science Publishers.

Amasaka, K. (2014). New JIT, new management technology principle. *Journal of Advanced Manufacturing Systems*, *13*(3), 197–222.

Amasaka, K. (2015). New JIT, New Management Technology Principle. Taylor and Francis Group.

Amasaka, K. (2016). Innovation of automobile manufacturing fundamentals employing New JIT: Developing advance Toyota Production System at Toyota Manufacturing USA. *Proceedings of the 5th Conference on Production and Operations Management*, 1-10.

Amasaka, K. (2017a). *Toyota: Production system, safety analysis and future directions*. NOVA Science Publishers.

Amasaka, K. (2017b). Strategic Stratified Task Team Model for realizing simultaneous QCD fulfilment: Two case studies. *The Journal of Japanese Operations Management and Strategy*, *7*(1), 14–35.

Amasaka, K. (2018). Innovation of automobile manufacturing fundamentals employing New JIT: Developing Advanced Toyota Production System. *International Journal of Research in Business, Economics and Management*, *2*(1), 1–15.

Amasaka, K. (Ed.). (2019). *Fundamentals of manufacturing industry management: New Manufacturing Theory – Operations management strategy 21C*. Sankei-sha.

Amasaka, K. (2019a). Studies on New Manufacturing Theory. *Noble*. *International Journal of Scientific Research (Ahmedabad, India)*, *3*(1), 1 20.

Amasaka, K. (2019b). Establishment of an Automobile Optimal Product Design Model: Application to study on bolt-nut loosening mechanism. *Noble International Journal of Scientific Research*, *3*(9), 79–102.

Amasaka, K. (2020a). Studies on New Japan Global Manufacturing Model: The innovation of manufacturing engineering. *Journal of Economics and Technology Research*, *1*(1), 42–71.

Amasaka, K. (2020b). Evolution of Japan Manufacturing Foundation: Dual Global Engineering Model Surpassing JIT. *International Journal of Operations and Quantitative Management*, *26*(2), 101–126.

Amasaka, K. (2022). *New Manufacturing Theory: Surpassing JIT* (2nd ed.). Lambert Academic Publishing.

Amasaka, K., Ito, T., & Nozawa, Y. (2012). A New Development Design CAE Employment Model. *The Journal of Japanese Operations Management and Strategy*, *3*(1), 18–37.

Amasaka, K., Kurosu, S., & Morita, M. (2008). *New Manufacturing Theory: Surpassing JIT – The evolution of Just-In-Time*. Morikita-Shuppan.

Amasaka, K., & Sakai, H. (1996). Improving the reliability of body assembly line equipment. *International Journal of Reliability Quality and Safety Engineering*, *3*(1), 11–24.

Amasaka, K., & Sakai, H. (1998). Availability and Reliability Information Administration System "ARIM-BL" by methodology of Inline-Online SQC. *International Journal of Reliability Quality and Safety Engineering*, *5*(1), 55–63.

Amasaka, K., & Sakai, H. (2009). TPS-QAS, new production quality management model: Key to New JIT–Toyota's global production strategy. *International Journal of Manufacturing Technology and Management, 18*(4), 409–426.

Amasaka, K., & Sakai, H. (2010). Evolution of TPS fundamentals utilizing New JIT strategy–Proposal and validity of Advanced TPS at Toyota. *Journal of Advanced Manufacturing Systems, 9*(2), 85–99.

Amasaka, K., & Sakai, H. (2011). The New Japan Global Production Model "NJ-GPM": Strategic development of Advanced TPS. *The Journal of Japanese Operations Management and Strategy, 2*(1), 1–15.

Doos, D., Womack, J. P., & Jones, D. T. (1991). *The Machine that Change the World – The Story of Lean Production*. Rawson.

Ebioka, K., Sakai, H., Yamaji, M., & Amasaka, K. (2007). A New Global Partnering Production Model "NGP-PM" utilizing Advanced TPS. *Journal of Business & Economics Research, 5*(9), 1–8.

Hayes, R. H., & Wheelwright, S. C. (1984). *Restoring Our Competitive Edge: Competing through Manufacturing*. Wiley.

Kawahara, F., Kogane, Y., Amasaka, K., & Ouchi, N. (2016). A skill map based on an analysis of experienced workers' intuition and knowhow. *IOSR Journal of Business and Management, 18*(12), 80–85.

Kojima, T., & Amasaka, K. (2011). The Total Quality Assurance Networking Model for preventing defects: Building an effective quality assurance system using a Total QA Network. *International Journal of Management & Information Systems., 15*(3), 1–10.

Kozaki, T., Oura, A., & Amasaka, K. (2012). Establishment of TQM Promotion Diagnosis Model "TQM-PDM" for strategic quality management. *China-USA Business Review, 10*(11), 811–819.

Miyashita, S., & Amasaka, K. (2014). Proposal of a New Vietnam Production Model (NVPM), a new integrated production system of Japan and Vietnam. *IOSR. Journal of Business and Management, 16*(12), 18–25.

Ohno, T. (1977). *Toyota Production System*. Diamond-sha.

Sakai, H., & Amasaka, K. (2003). Construction of "V-IOS" for promoting intelligence operator: Development and effectiveness for visual manual format. *The Japan Society for Production Management, The 18th Annual Conference, Nagasaki Institute of Applied Science,* 173-176.

Sakai, H., & Amasaka, K. (2005). V-MICS, Advanced TPS for strategic production administration: Innovative maintenance combining DB and CG. *Journal of Advanced Manufacturing Systems, 4*(6), 5–20.

Sakai, H., & Amasaka, K. (2006a). TPS-LAS Model using process layout CAE system at Toyota, Advanced TPS: Key to global production strategy New JIT. *Journal of Advanced Manufacturing Systems, 5*(2), 1–14.

Sakai, H., & Amasaka, K. (2006b). Strategic HI-POS, intelligence production operating system: Applying Advanced TPS to Toyota's global production strategy. *WSEAS Transactions on Advances in Engineering Education*, *3*(3), 223–230.

Sakai, H., & Amasaka, K. (2007a). The robot reliability design and improvement method and Advanced Toyota Production System. *International Journal of Industrial and Service Robotics*, *34*(4), 310–316.

Sakai, H., & Amasaka, K. (2007b). Human digital pipeline method using total linkage through design to manufacturing. *Journal of Advanced Manufacturing Systems*, *6*(2), 101–113.

Sakai, H., & Amasaka, K. (2008). Human-Integrated Assist Systems for intelligence operators, Encyclopedia of Networked and Virtual Organizations, 2(G-Pr), 678-687.

Shan, H., Yeap, Y. S., & Amasaka, K. (2011). Proposal of a New Malaysia Production Model "NMPM": A new integrated production system of Japan and Malaysia. *Proceedings of International Conference on Business Management 2011, Miyazaki Sangyo-Keiei University,* 235-246.

Taylor, D. & Brunt, D. (2001). *Manufacturing Operations and Supply Chain Management - Lean Approach.* Thomson Learning.

Toyota Motor Corporation. (1993). Toyota Technical Review. *SQC at Toyota*, *43*(Special issue), 1–172.

Tsunoi, M., Yamaji, M., & Amasaka, K. (2010). A study of building an Intellectual Working Value Improvement Model, IWV-IM. *International Business & Economics Research Journal*, *9*(11), 79–84.

Uchida, K., Tsunoi, M., & Amasaka, K. (2012). Creating Working Value Evaluation Model, WVEM. *International Journal of Management & Information Systems*, *16*(4), 299–306.

Womack, J. P., Jones, D., & Roos, D. (1990). *The machine that change the world – The story of Lean Production*. Rawson.

Womack, J. P., & Jones, D. T. (1994). From Lean Production to the Lean Enterprise. *Harvard Business Review*, (March-April), 93–103.

Yamaji, M., & Amasaka, K. (2007b). Proposal and validity of Global Intelligence Partnering Model for Corporate Strategy, GIPM-CS. *International IFIP-TC 5.7 Conference on Advanced in Production Management System,* 59-67.

Yamaji, M., Sakai, H., & Amasaka, K. (2007a). Evolution of technology and skill in production workplaces utilizing Advanced TPS. *Journal of Business & Economics Research*, *5*(6), 61–68.

Yamaji, M., Sakatoku, T., & Amasaka, K. (2008). Partnering Performance Measurement "PPM-AS" to strengthen corporate management of Japanese automobile assembly makers and suppliers. *International Journal of Electronic Business Management*, *6*(3), 139–145.

Yanagisawa, K., Yamazaki, M., Yoshioka, K., & Amasaka, K. (2013). Comparison of experienced and inexperienced machine workers. *International Journal of Operations and Quantitative Management*, *19*(4), 259–274.

Yeap, Y. S., Murat, M. S., & Amasaka, K. (2010). Proposal of New Turkish Production System, NTPS: Integration and evolution of Japanese and Turkish Production System. *Journal of Business Case Study*, *6*(6), 69–76.

Section 2
Expanding Japanese Automobile Uniform Quality and Production at Optimum Locations Through SCM Strategy in the World

Chapter 8
Strategic Stratified Task Team Model for Innovating Business Processes

ABSTRACT

To gain the position of a top runner of the 21st century, the author introduces the application study of driving force in New Japan Model (NMT) strategy that contributes to the evolution of Japanese automobile manufacturing strategy. In this chapter, the author refers to the significance and validity of Strategic Stratified Task Team Model (SSTTM) employing Strategic Cooperative Creation Team (SCCT) between the auto-assembly maker Toyota and typical non-affiliated supplier NOK. The validity of SSTTM is verified by successfully applying it to the technological problem automobile transaxle oil seal leakage of development design bottlenecks at auto manufacturers.

INTRODUCTION

Today's management challenge of manufacturer is to provide high QCD (Quality, Cost, and Delivery) products ahead of competitors through market creating activities, with priority given to customers. To accomplish manufacturing that places top priority on customers with a good QCD in a rapidly changing technical environment, it is important to develop a new production technology and establish new process management to enable global production. For the automobile manufacturing industry, the key to success in global production is systematizing its management methods when modeling strategic SCM.

The author analyzes and proves the significance of strategically employing NMT (New Manufacturing Theory, Refer to Chapter 4 and 5) at Japanese automobile manufacturing (Amasaka, 2000a, 2002, 2007a, 2009a, 2011, 2013, 2014abc, 2015, 2016, 2022). In the implementation stage, automobile manufacturers endeavoring to become global companies are required to collaborate with not only affiliated companies, but also non-affiliated companies to achieve harmonious coexistence among them based on cooperation and competition called "Japan Supply System" (Amasaka, 2000b, 2008a).

DOI: 10.4018/978-1-7998-8746-1.ch008

Particularly, as white-collars are prone to be obsessed with their daily work, the business process is likely to become routine. It is a crucial task of today to innovate the business process through creation of value, for which strategic team activities where related fields can collaborate autonomously and mutually are indispensable. Specifically, to actualize manufacturing of excellent quality as the application study of driving force in NMT strategy, the author employs the Strategic Stratified Task Team Model (SSTTM) for strengthening SCM strategy by a typical case study (Amasaka, 1999, 2004a,b, 2008b, 2012a,b,c, 2015, 2008a,b, 2017).

Concretely, the author verifies the validity of SSTTM by Strategic Cooperative Creation Team (SCCT) activity between auto-assembly maker Toyota and non-affiliate supplier NOK through the solution of bottleneck problem "automobile trans-axle oil seal leakage" of the worldwide automobile manufactures for realizing simultaneous QCD fulfilment (Amasaka, 2004c,e, 2015b, 2012c, 2017, 2020; Amasaka et al., 2007; Amasak, Ed., 2007a,b, 2012).

REFORM OF JAPANESE-STYLE FOR INNOVATING BUSINESS PROCESS

Needs for the Reform of Japanese-style Management Technology

Looking at the recent automobile recall problems, the author see rapidly increasing

manufacturing quality issues with their roots in technological product design and product (Joiner, 1994; Nihon Keizai Shinbun, 2000, 2006; Amasaka Ed., 2007ab; Amasaka, 2008c). The author cannot be content with simply resolving individual technical issues. Rather, it is necessary to evolve core technologies that result in the overhaul of every business process from development and production to SCM, and establish and systematically apply a new management technology model that intelligently links them together (Amasaka, 2004a). The top priority issue of the industrial field today is the "new deployment of global marketing" for surviving the era of global quality competition (Kotler, 1999; Amasaka, 2004a). The pressing management issue particularly for Japanese manufacturers to survive in the global market is the "uniform quality worldwide and production at optimum locations" which is the prerequisite for successful global production.

To realize manufacturing that places top priority on customers with a good QCD and in a rapidly changing technical environment, it is essential to create a core principle capable of changing the technical development work processes of development and design divisions (Amasaka, 2004b, 2005a). Furthermore, a new quality management technology principle linked with overall activities for higher work process quality in all divisions is necessary for an enterprise to survive (Burke and Trahant, 2000; Amasaka, 2004b). The creation of attractive products requires each of the sales, engineering/design, and production departments to be able to carry out management that forms linkages throughout the whole organization (Seuring et al., 2003; Amasaka, 2000b, 2004a). From this point of view, the reform of Japanese-style management technology is desired once again. In this need for improvements, Toyota is no exception (Goto, 1999; Amasaka, 2004a).

Similarly, it is important to develop a new production technology principle and establish new process management principles to enable global production. Furthermore, new marketing activities independent of past experience are required for sales and service divisions to achieve firmer relationships with customers. In addition, a new quality management technology principle linked with overall activities for higher work process quality in all divisions is necessary for an enterprise to survive (Amasaka, 2007b).

Business Management and Development of Creative Corporate Climate

When the author views recent business management activities, the author see from time to time, cases where leading enterprises are busy with unexpected product quality problems inside and outside the companies or other cases where they are confronted with the risk of going out of business due to delays in developing technologies. On the other hand, not a few enterprises have continued to grow vigorously for these past several decades through company-wide total marketing activities and management reliability enhancements (Amasaka, 2002a).

These enterprises have consolidated their footing, fixing their gaze upon world market trends and developed human resources with problem solving capabilities. What background brings forth such a difference among enterprises? Isn't management concerned with "quality management giving importance to customer satisfaction" and the achievement of streamlined management through the "creation of a corporate climate that makes the most of individual human resources and energizes the organization"? For some time, a number of Japanese enterprises have been recruiting students who have both brains and capabilities from universities and other institutions across the country. Therefore it is apparent that the fate of an enterprise depends on how these young people grapple with creative work and become the forerunners of corporate climate innovation (Amasaka, 2002a; 2004b; Amasaka, Ed., 2007, 2012; Amasaka et al., 2008).

Reliability of Job and Importance of Team Activities

This section reviews the job quality that constitutes the key for corporate management reliability and the importance of systematic and organizational collaboration of all fields. Figure 1 shows a typical corporate organizational chart (Amasaka, 2004b; Amasaka, Ed., 2007; Amasaka et al., 2008). This figure shows a typical corporate organizational chart with 13 business fields from upstream to downstream and their mission. Table 1 shows 6 cases of job quality in terms of reliability per field (Amasaka, 2004b). In Case 1, one field has a reliability level of 99.9%, yet market claims of 1.3% are generated in terms of total reliability. Similarly, as the reliability lowers sequentially to 99.0% for Case 2, 95.0% for Case 3 and 90.0% for Case 4, total reliability rapidly drops leading to the inevitable generation of a recall. In Case 5, a similar problem occurs merely because of a mistake made by one field. In addition, it is apparent that total reliability further drops if inter-field collaboration is lost.

To upgrade the intellectual level of individuals and enhance organizational performance within a decentralized organization, the authors restudy the significance of mutually collaborating team activities and touch on their effectiveness. Incorporating team activities into strategy is important from the viewpoint of key business management factors such as human resources and organization, knowledge and value, product quality and information, development and systems and so forth. In the future, it will be necessary for us to develop a new methodology for achieving a high reliability exceeding Case 6 (99.99%).

Significance of Team Activities and Requirements for their Promotion

When considering the association between an organization and individuals, there would be few people who could not reply to the questions "Which field in an enterprise requires no creativity? Which field does not need team activities?" In corporate activities, individuals could easily lose their objective when given complete freedom or if they managed to achieve the target, they might be mutually disassociated without being stimulated by others.

Figure 1. A typical corporate organization chart

Table 1. Job reliability of 13 departments

Case 1: 99.9 % / department
→ 0.999^{13} = 0.987 (1.3 % problems)
Case 2: 99.0 % / department
→ 0.990^{13} = 0.878 (12.2 % problems)
Case 3: 95.0 % / department
→ 0.950^{13} = 0.513 (48.7 % problems)
Case 4: 90.0% / department
→ 0.900^{13} = 0.254 (4.6 % problems)
Case 5: When 12 departments are 99.99 %
but 1 department is 50.0%:
→ 0.999^{12}x 0.500 =0.4999 (50.01% problems)
Case 6: 99.99 % / department
→ 0.9999^{13} = 99.88% (0.12 % problems)

It is not a restriction of freedom but it raises breakthrough productivity for management to give direction to the whole organization by presenting a clear vision to individuals and for the managers to guide them with a proper mission. This raises the knowledge of individuals and the organization and leads to improved human and product reliability. The author thinks that team activities signify an opportunity for "improving business process quality" and "realizing business achievement" through mutual contact and enlightenment.

To obtain such effects, in the implementation stage of team activities, three factors - special knowledge, thinking capability and the value of job as shown in Figure 2 - are required (Amasaka, 2004b, 2015b; Amasaka et al., 2008). To promote them, it is important to develop four requirements (mission, promotion cycle, performance measure, and pleasure of working). Through spiral-up cycles by meeting these requirements, the team members can steadily mountaineer for problem solution (advance from step (1) to step (4)).

Figure 2. Three elements for team activities and requirements for promotion

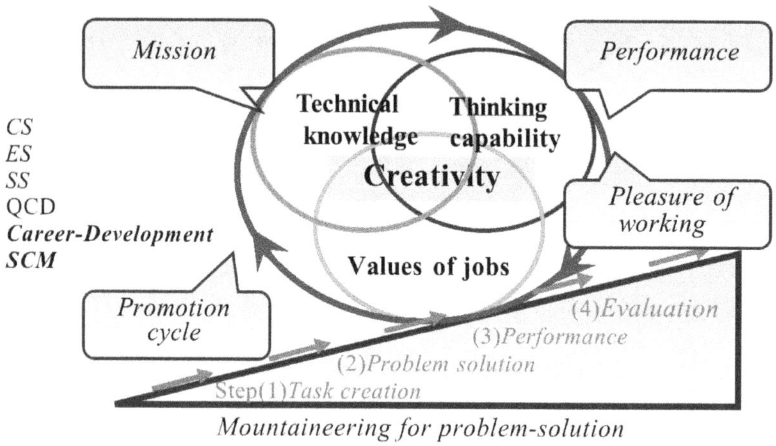

Creativity and Strategy Necessary for Team Activities

The recent business environment surrounding Japanese enterprises is quite severe. Above all, manufacturing requires a high reliability of business management in order to cope with the globalization of manufacturing, the use of information and communications technologies and the protection of the environment, etc. To do this, management has to carry out streamlined business operation (SS, Social satisfaction), improvement of customer value (CS, Customer satisfaction), improvement of employees' value (ES, Employee satisfaction), and mutual trust and collaboration with the group enterprises (SCM, Supply chain management) (Amasaka, 2002a).

In the implementation stage, it will become necessary to improve human reliability through team activities with creativity and strategy and consolidate merchandise power in the form of total marketing activities (Amasaka, 2001, 2004b). Team activities comprise task (force) teams as frequently observed with the engineering and/or administration fields (knowledge-intensive type), project teams, QC circle activities among blue-collar workers (labor-intensive type) and various other forms of activities (Amasaka, 2001).

In particular, to survive in the above-mentioned environment, today's task is to innovate team activities of the so-called white-collars or knowledge-groups. It is particularly important to innovate the business process, which is prone to become routine, as white-collars are busy with daily work, creating value. Strategic team activities where related fields can collaborate autonomously and mutually are needed (Amasaka, 1999a).

In addition to enhancing cross-functional collaboration of their own company, strategic team activities reinforce collaboration among group, non-group, and overseas. To the author's knowledge, there have been no studies that presented a strategic team activity model systematically designed from the above point of view to contribute to the advancement of management technology and verified the effectiveness of the model (Doz and Hamel, 1998; Burke and Trahant, 2000: Evans and Lindsay, 2001; Gryna, 2001; Stefan et al., 2003).

CREATION OF THE STRATEGIC STRATIFIED TASK TEAM MODEL

Japan Supply System-Partnering Chains as the Platform-Type

Toyota group consists of a total 14 enterprises (Toyota, 1987). Twelve enterprises, which branched from Toyota Automatic Loom Works, Ltd. form the nucleus of the primary group parts manufacturers (called "Kyohokai") that supply parts directly to Toyota. In addition, Hino Motors, Ltd. and Daihatsu Motor Co., Ltd. jointed the group. Each of the group companies is closely linked to Toyota in a wide and solid supplier-assembler relation called "Toyota Supply System." Amasaka (2000b, 2008a) generalizes it as the Japan Supply System (JSS) as shown in Figure 3.

An automobile is assembled with some 20,000 parts. Since it is not economical for the assembler to manufacture all the parts in-house, considerable portion of the parts are normally purchased from outside suppliers (parts manufacturers). This situation still remains unchanged. If parts purchased from the supplier (parts manufacturer) have low dependability, vehicles assembled with them have also low dependability naturally.

This is exactly the reason why "performance of a vehicle almost depends on the parts" (Amasaka, 2000b; Amasaka, Ed., 2007; Amasaka et al., 2008; Amasaka, 2015b). In this sense, the assembly makers (automobile manufactures) and parts manufacturers (suppliers) are the inhabitant of the same fate-sharing community. Actual supplier-assembler relation is generally quite complex and many-sided.

Relationship between Toyota and its suppliers is unique in many points compared with those of other assemblers. There is the saying that "Toyota wrings a towel even when it is dry." indicating Toyota's strict demand to suppliers for their prices and quality. At the same time, no other assemblers are so enthusiastic as Toyota in raising strong suppliers through education and training. As early as in 1939, Toyota established its basic concept of the purchasing activities for promoting coexistence and co-prosperity.

To realize this, Toyota strengthened its suppliers by making it a rule to continue transaction forever once started. No other assemblers have their supplier groups as powerful as those of Toyota. The 14 Toyota group companies form the nucleus of the powerful supplier system. As thus far stated, close relation between Toyota and its group members is quite cooperative in one sense while simultaneously very competitive in another. This represents the supplier- assembler relation unparalleled elsewhere.

There is no denying that the strength of Toyota that can keep on supplying popular vehicle model such as "Lexus" of high dependability originates from within Toyota's own. But one part of Toyota's strength comes from the strength of its supply system consisting of Toyota group and thousands of other suppliers, and the other comes from Toyota's skill in managing such powerful supply system. In the following, the authors intend to zero in on Toyota's quality management activities in exploring the secret of the strength of Toyota that continues to manufacture vehicles of high dependability. This is because

Figure 3. Outline of Japan Supply System (JSS)

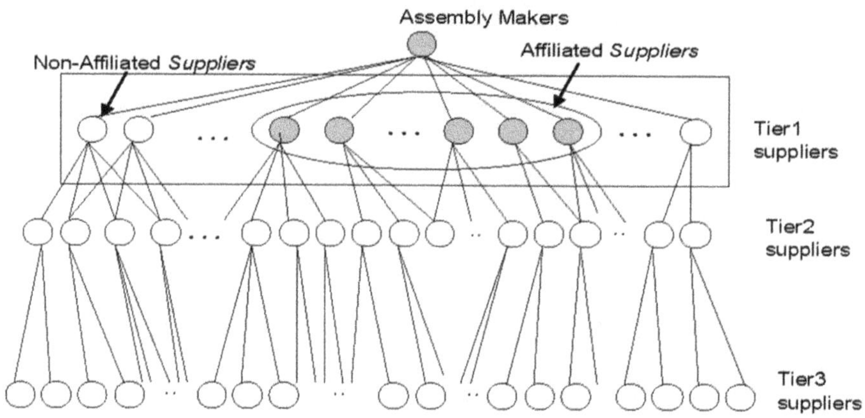

it is quality management activities themselves that provide important bonds to cooperation or partnering between Toyota and its group companies (Amasaka, 2000b, 2001).

Strategic Stratified Task Teams Model, the Driving Force in Developing Japan Supply System

In a general assembly industry like the automotive manufacturing, a thorough quality assurance (QA) plays an important role. It includes not only the parts and unit quality control, but also the optimization of adaptive engineering for assembly by the automobile manufacturers and the quality of production, sale and services.

Therefore, when working on the solution of a pending engineering task, separate and independent team activities by the automobile manufacture or parts manufacturers alone often fail to clarify the engineering area, which exists in-between or across the two teams (both companies). In this connection, it is important to zero-in on the end users from the view point of customer-in and to challenge for realizing simultaneous QCD fulfilment by mutually disclosing their software and hardware techniques to each other (Amasaka, 2000b; 2001).

As a management technology strategy to enable smooth business management for realizing high-quality assurance, the author has created a Strategic Stratified Task Team Model (SSTTM) as shown in Figure 5, Chapter 5 (Refer to Chapter 5) (Amasaka, 1999, 2004b, 2013, 2015b; Amasaka, Ed., 2007b, 2012). The expected role of the SSTTM and the benefits it provides are not limited to cooperation among the departments inside the company. It also contributes to strengthening the ties among group manufacturing companies, non-group companies, and even overseas manufacturers. Two measures must be taken in order to realize this proposal.

The first is to eliminate the work methods that rely too heavily on the techniques and experiences of individuals. The second is to revolutionize the business process through the SSTTM that places emphasis on cooperation among the departments, and that with suppliers. SSTTM formed from partnering linkages are developed systematically and organizationally to promote the strategic development of New Japan Model (NJM) (Refer to Chapter 5 in detail). In Figure 5, Chapter 5, SSTTM consists of Task 1 to Task 8 teams involving the group, department, division, field, whole company, affiliated companies, non-affiliated companies, and overseas affiliates.

As indicated in the Figure 5, Chapter 5, the level of problem-solving technology rises in product development strategy I and II through joint task teams of intra-company departments and divisions (Task-1 to Task-5, Group Task team, Department task team, Division task management team, Field task management team and Total task management team) in proportion with the improvement of the stratified task level. This technology is further expanded to quality management strategy I to II through the domestic affiliated company, domestic non-affiliated company, and overseas non-affiliated company (Task-6 to Task-8, Joint A to Joint C).

In particular, to strengthen employment of SSTTM, the author has developed the formation of Strategic Cooperative Creation Team (SCCT) indicated by Figure 6, Chapter 5 (Refer to Chapter 5). In Figure 6, Chapter 5, to empower the team, team members should collectively have the capabilities of (1) "Strategy" for systematic and organizational activities, (2) "Technology" to improve core technologies, (3) "Methodology" to practically identify the gap between theories and the actual, and (4) "Promotion" to fulfill the expectations and roles of the team. If the task team tackles a strategic issue requiring high technologies, the members have to be ingenious enough as (i) "Generators" and at the same time they have to be able to perform strategic analysis as (ii) "Mentors". In addition, to infuse effective drive force in the team activities, creativity as (iii) "Producers" and leadership to orchestrate all members' ideas as (iv) "Promoters" toward target achievement is important.

As the key to the successful team activities, the team leader (Administrator) should select the members who have at least one of the capabilities for (i) to (iv), commission authority and responsibilities to the members, and have himself/herself concentrate on risk management. For this reason, as the leader, a person who has an experience of clearing business obstacles should be appointed, so that the leader is capable enough to lead the team overcoming difficulties.

Specifically, to develop as the driving force in JSS (Japan Supply System) Task 6 (Joint A) is aimed at establishing a collaboration with the group suppliers with whom domestic affiliated company has a capital tie-up, and Task 7 (Joint B) is aimed at a collaboration with suppliers that are not within its group. The mission of Task 8 (Joint C) is to strengthen cooperation with overseas suppliers as a strategic alliance.

EXAMPLE APPLICATIONS

This section presents a case of "automotive transaxle oil seal leakage", a technical reliability problem that generates bottlenecks for auto-manufacturers around the world. The author has applied SSTTM to resolve this issue, and its validity was verified within auto-assembly maker Toyota and its typical non-affiliate supplier NOK (Amasaka, 2004e, 2012, 2017, 2015b, 2020).

Needs for the High Reliability Assurance of Transaxle Oil Seal Leakage

An oil seal is a machine part built into machinery that plays an important role in preventing oil from leaking and foreign matters from entering the machinery. An oil seal on an automobile's transaxle prevents the oil lubricant within the drive system from leaking from the drive shaft as shown in Figure 4.

Figure 4. Outline of automotive transaxle oil seal

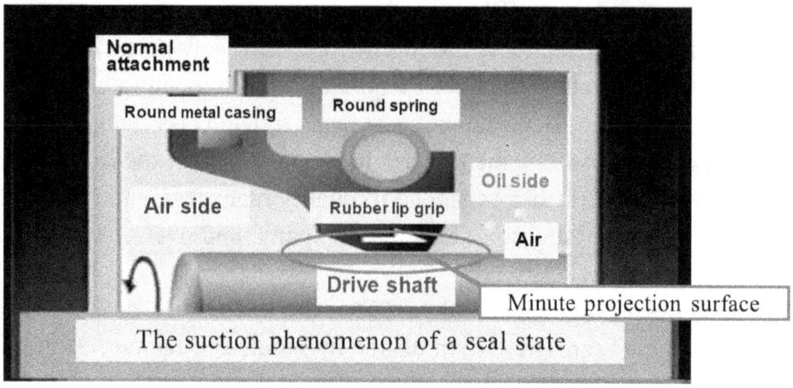

Its basic components include a sealing lip (rubber lip grip), which consists of both a metal case providing rigidity to the outside surface and synthetic rubber (round metal casing), and a garter spring (round spring). The sealing edge has direct contact with the drive shaft to prevent leakage of oil. Why doesn't the fluid on the oil side leak out to the air side?

A correctly installed oil seal takes in a small amount of air from the air side into the oil side. In this case the sealing ability (sealing performance) of microscopic roughness on the rubber lip grip (minute projection surface) is of primary importance (Lopez et al., 1997).

The key to resolving problems where the faulty mechanism is unclear is to use an empirical approach and apply technology that allows visualization of the dynamic behavior at the moment the problem occurs. The structure of the problem must then be unraveled so that an accurate model of cause-and-effect relationships can be built (NOK Corp., 2000).

The problem is an unknown mechanism causing an oil seal leakage on the surface of the drive shaft during high-speed rotation. To achieve this, the authors applied the following analytical process (Amasaka and Ootaki, 1999: Amasaka, 2004c, 2005b, 2008d, 2010, 2012a, 2012b: Amasaka, Ed., 2007a, 2007b: Ito et al, 2010a, 2010b: Nozawa et al., 2012, 2013): (1) understand the phenomenon, (2) conduct a visualization experiment, (3) conceptualize the problem logically, (4) apply CAE analysis, and (5) optimize the design.

The result was a plan to resolve oil leaks caused by age-related wear to the transaxle oil seal lip. Figure 5 uses a relational diagram to organize related causes and knowledge previously collected on the problem.

Because the mechanism causing the oil leak was unknown, the pathway by which it was generated is not clearly shown. Areas of dynamic behavior that needed to be visualized were specified and tested using a visualization device.

Figure 5. Estimation of the oil leakage mechanism

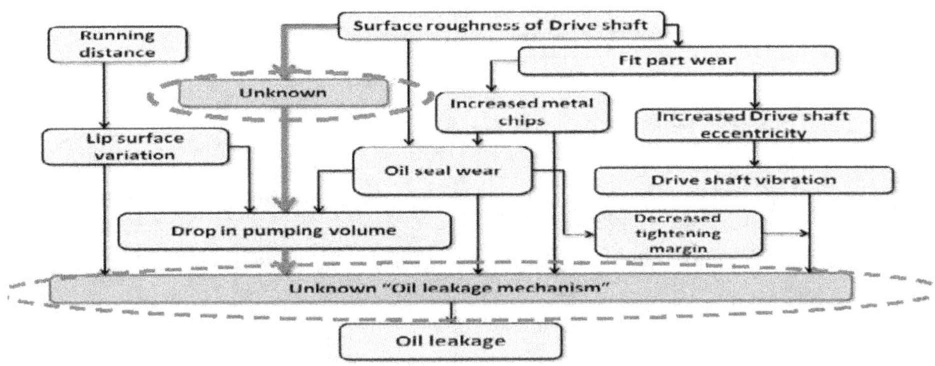

DUAL TOTAL TASK MANAGEMENT TEAM USING SSMMT

Organizational outline of "Dual Total Task Management Team"

This case study is a joint task team activity between manufacturer and non-affiliated supplier as the Task-7 based on the SSTTM in Figure 5, Chapter 5, (Refer to Chapter 5) for problem-solving (simultaneous QCD fulfilment) as the Automobile Global Manufacturing Model (AGMM) in Figure 2, Chapter 6, (Refer to Chapter 6). Effective solution of technical problems requires also the formation of Strategic Cooperative Creation Team (SCCT) in Figure 6, Chapter 5, (Refer to Chapter 5) and understanding of the essence of problems by the teams as a whole.

To ensure high reliability of product design and quality assurance, the author develops the "TDS-D" (Total Design System for drive-train development) as a core element "TDS" of NJM (New Japan Model) named the Dual Total Task Management Team (D-TTMT) in Toyota. This organization has been realized in the form of D-TTMT consisting of the final vehicle assembly manufacture (Toyota Motor Corporation) with transaxle unit, and oil seal manufacture (NOK Corporation) of tier-1. Deployment of D-TTMT consists of SCCT named "DOS-Q" (Drive-train Oil Seal - Quality Assurance Team: "T DOS-Q5" of Toyota and "N DOS-Q8" of NOK) is as shown in Figure 6 (Amasaka, 2003, 2004b, 2004c, 2015b).

In "DOS-Q", the author commissions the thirteen general managers of two companies, each general manager assigns several section chiefs, sub-section chiefs, technical staffs, and statistics analysis staffs named "SQC adviser" as D-TTMT members "T DOS-Q5" consists of Q1 (Unit

manufacturer quality team), Q2 (Oil leakage mechanism study team), Q3 (Design improvement team), Q5 (Shaft manufacturer quality improvement team) and Q5 (install-ability improvement team). Similarly, "N DOS-Q8" consists of Q1 (Production engineering team), Q2 (Mechanism study team), Q3 (Design improvement team), Q4 (Quality assurance team), Q5 (Receiving/Shipping team), Q6 (Affiliated company), Q7 (Production team) and Q8 (Production design team). Concretely,

In T DOS-Q5 and N DOS-Q8, the author also develops SCCT utilizing three management activities utilizing TM, PM and IM named QAT in enforcement of D-TTMT as indicated in Figure 6.

Figure 6. Dual Total Task Management Team using "T DOS-Q5" and "N DOS-Q8"

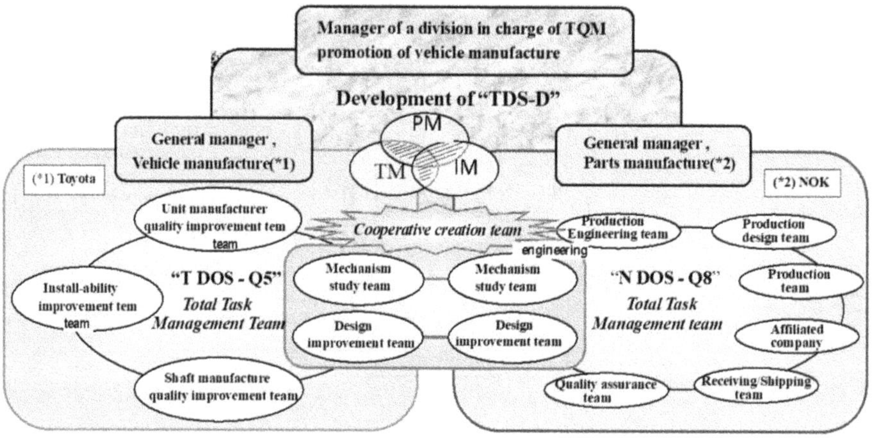

Thereby, D-TTMT was created to transform the implicit knowledge (relating to product and processes in both organization) into explicit knowledge, and to create new technology of interest to both organizations of "T DOS-Q5" and "N DOS-Q8". By the top policy of Toyota and NOK, the author constitutes the following organizations as a supervisor of Task-7 as follows; In SCCT, five teams of "T DOS-Q5" constitute Q1 (Chassis design department), Q2 (Drive train engineering department), Q3 (Product evaluation and engineering department) for TM, Q4 (Production engineering and development department) for PM and Q5 (Quality assurance department and TQM promotion department) for IM (Fukuchi et al., 1998). Eight teams of "N DOS-Q8" are also the same organization and formation of Q1-Q8 (Amasaka and Otaki, 1999).

Specifically, "T DOS-Q5" constituting teams comprise Q1 and Q2 in charge of investigation into the cause of the oil leakage and Q3-Q5, which handled manufacturing problems relating to drive shafts, vehicles and transaxles. Similarly, "N DOS-Q8" formed teams Q1 through Q8. Q1 and Q2 at Toyota interacted closely with their counterparts at NOK to improve the reliability of the oil seal as a single unit and, likewise, Q3-Q8 handled the manufacturing problems for quality assurance.

Furthermore, in order to strengthen the cooperation activities of A and B, the author forms "Cross-functional team" of Q2 and Q3 of Toyota, and Q2 and Q3 of NOK, solves the mechanism of an oil seal leak, and strives for an improvement of quality of design. Further, the author forms the cross-functional team between Q2 and Q3 of both companies, and, thereby, strengthens improvement of transaxle design by the clarification of oil leakage mechanism.

Accordingly, the thirteen teams shared their individual knowledge (relating to empirical techniques and other technical information) to apply them to solving the problems under consideration. Each team had a general manager and the joint team was led by the general manager of Toyota's TQM promotion division for the vehicle reliability assurance. The methodology of "TDS-D" involving TM, PM and IM was used by utilizing three management activities for QAT in Figure 9, Chapter 5 (Refer to Chapter 5).

Moreover, to realize optimization of the DOS-Q business process, problem-solving is formulated using the "Problem-solving by utilizing SQC Technical Methods" (Amasaka and Osaki, 1999; Amasaka, 2001; Amasaka and Osaki, 2003) by using the same approach

Highly Accurate CAE Analysis Approach Model using Science SQC

The problem is an unknown mechanism causing an oil seal leakage on the surface of the drive shaft during high-speed rotation (Lopez et al., 1997). Now, the author will discuss the application of highly accurate CAE analysis for trans-axle oil seal leak of automobile drivetrain through a partnership between Toyota and NOK as an example of cases where the mechanism of technical problems is unknown.

As shown in Figure 4, Chapter 6, the author has applied a Highly Accurate CAE Analysis Approach Model (Refer to Chapter 6) to prevent automobile oil seal leaks by using Highly PRECISE CAE Analysis Model in Figure 4, Chapter 14 (Refer to Chapter 14), incorporating Science SQC methods (Amasaka, 2008d,e, 2012a,b; Takahashi et al., 2010). As the figure shows, the author has contributed to solving the problem of drive train oil seal leakage, which is a bottleneck technological problem for automotive manufacturers worldwide. This was achieved through an analysis process involving problem clarification, visualization experiments, theoretical conceptualization, CAE analysis, and optimal design.

First, the author has adapted by developing a device for visualizing the ascertained phenomena in order to estimate the unknown mechanisms involved in the leaks. This made it possible to estimate the mechanism of the oil seal leaks by visualizing the dynamic behavior involved in the process whereby metal particles (foreign matter) from gear rotation wear, found around the rotating and sliding portions of the oil seal lip, become mechanically fused and accumulate. Next, the findings obtained were used to formulate the following design countermeasures. (i) Strengthen gear surfaces to prevent occurrence of foreign matter even after 100,000 km (improve quality of materials and heat treatments), and (ii) Formulate a design plan to scientifically ensure optimum lubrication of the surface layer of the oil seal lip (uneven portions of the sliding surface) where it rotates in contact with the drive shaft.

Fault Analysis and Factor Analysis

In the conventional cases of oil seal unitary sample collection process, it was observed from time to time that there was no information on the mating part or the collected sample was attached with foreign matters which hampered the determination of the cause of leakage. To prevent this, recovery process was improved along with the acquisition of the background or the history of the market recovery. Thus Weibull analysis for the fault analysis could be made in Figure 7 with credibility based on the comparison result with the actual parts by recovering non-defectives as well as defectives or by recovering whole of the trans-axle unit in order to reproduce oil leakage.

As the result, the author has obtained a new knowledge that the failure type of "oil leakage" is a mixed model of three failures of the "Decreasing failure rate", "Constant failure rate" and "Increasing failure rate" which was not found in the rule of thumb. Moreover, the author could understand the correct particle size distribution and the composition of foreign matters attached to the oil leaking parts by recovering them in a special recovery case. It was also newly discovered that two oil seals of apparently similar degree of wear produce difference in pumping quantity depending on the mileage.

For the factor analysis to research the oil leakage phenomenon and mechanism of the failure type, not only defective parts (oil leaking parts) but non-defectives (non-oil leaking parts) were used. As the result, the difference of two parts was detected through the discriminating analysis as shown in Figure 6. For example, it is known that the factor analysis to the design factor of hardness of oil seal rubber has the largest influence among explanatory factors evaluated. Such survey and analysis could not be made with the conventional separate investigation activities of the vehicle manufacturer or the parts manufacturer.

This was accomplished through the D-TTMT activities between the companies of Toyota and NOK (Fukuchi et al., 1998; Amasaka and Ootaki, 1999; Amasaka and Osaki, 1999, 2003; Amasaka, 2004c).

Figure 7. Result of Weibull analysis

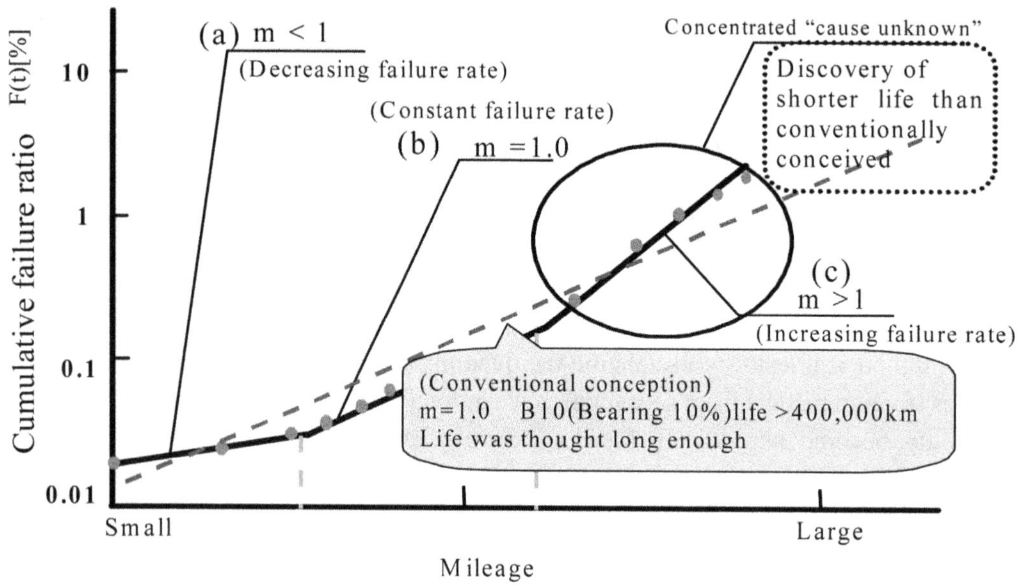

Figure 8. Influential effect of each Factor

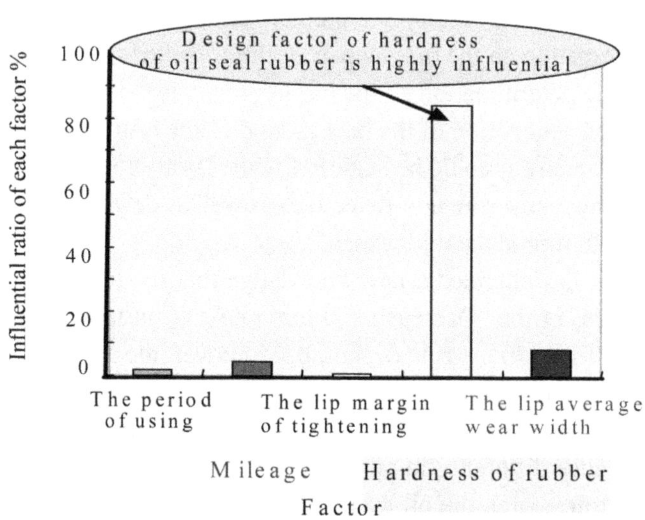

Relation between the Condition of Sliding Surface and Sealing Performance

In the stage of problem clarification, the author has investigated the relation between the condition of the sliding surface and the sealing performance of the oil seal (Amasaka and Ootaki, 1999; NOK Corp., 2000; Amasaka, 2005b, 2007f, 2010a, 2012a,b). To grasp the features of the sliding and surface condition, the author takes a quantification approach. First of all, the authors will consider two typical characteristic values (A_R and X_G).

The Figure 9 shows roughness in the form of contour lines on a map, and the shaded area indicates the area which is actually in contact with the drive shaft. As the characteristic value representing the degree of roughness, the author defines A_R which is the ratio of the actual (real) contact area to the apparent contact area. A_R is a characteristic value indicating roughness on the seal sliding side level, and shows the proportion of the visible touch area that is the real contact area shown in equation (1). The smaller A_R values signify minute roughness on the sliding surface, and conversely, larger A_R values show evenly flat contact.

Next, the author defines the characteristic value X_G, which indicates whether the real contact area (dA_i) is closer to the oil side or the air side as show in Figure 10. X_G is the distance that the true contact area center of gravity is biased from the sliding side center to either the oil side ($1>X_i>0$) or the air side (atmospheric side) ($-1<X_j<0$); it is the characteristic value that shows the extent true contact area distribution bias axially shown in equation (2). X_G can be interpreted as the maximum pressure position of the contact pressure distribution. If the X_G value is positive, it means that the actual contact area is biased toward the oil side. On the other hand, if the X_G value is negative, it is biased toward the air side.

Figure 9. Ratio of the real contact area A_R

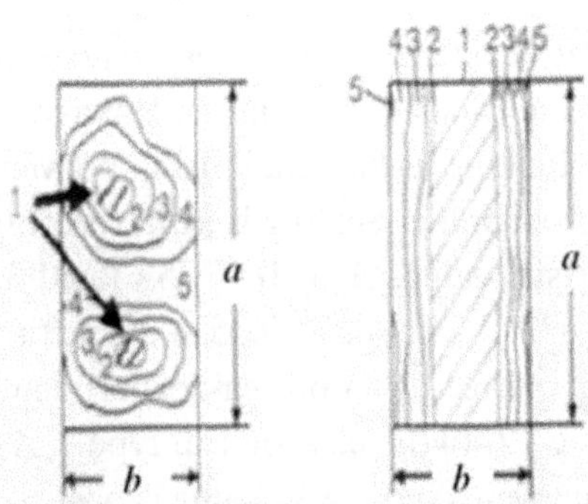

$$A_R = \frac{\text{The real contact area}}{\text{The visible touch area}} = \frac{(\text{Shaded area})}{(a \times b)} \tag{1}$$

$$X_G = \frac{\sum dAi\left(\frac{Xi}{b/2}\right) - \sum dAj\left(\frac{Xj}{b/2}\right)}{\sum dAi + \sum dAj} \tag{2}$$

Figure 10. Bias of the true contact area X_G

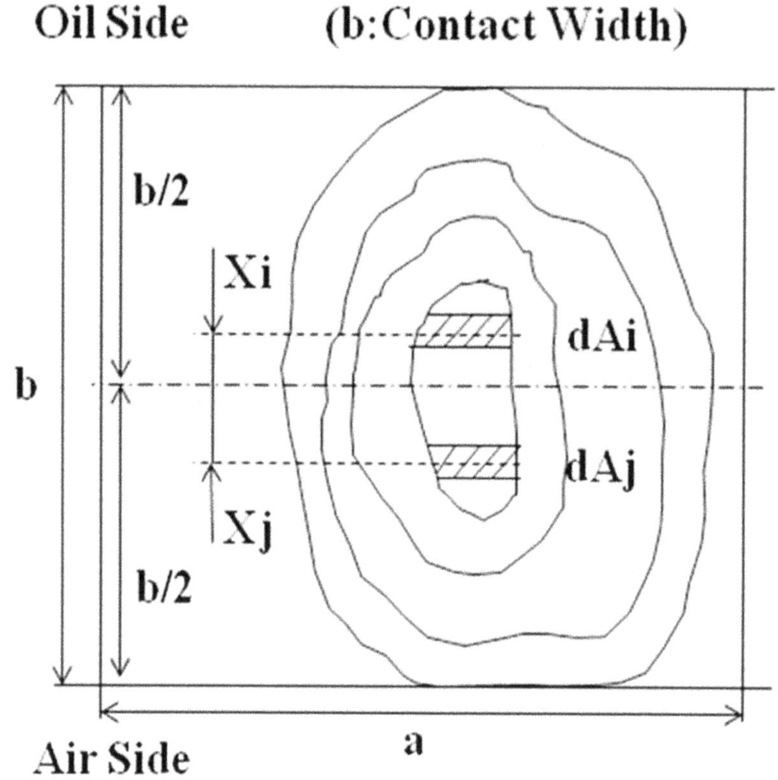

Figure 11 shows the characteristic seal values and the outcome of the experiments for the four types of seals made of different materials and shapes. In addition, leakage stopping can be classified according to both characteristic values by looking at the relationship between these two characteristic values and the observed state of the leakage stopping. Sealing is achieved only in Seal type 1 in Figure 11, and sliding surfaces show the characteristic values $A_R < 0.05$ (5%) and $X_G > 0$. The domain representing complete seal is defined as having an A_R value under 0.05 and a positive X_G value.

Then, the author observes the existence of an oil leak experimentally using the two characteristic values, A_R and X_G as shown in Figure 12. In the case of seal type 1, A_R shows a small value, indicating that the sliding surface is minutely uneven. And the X_G value is positive, meaning that the actual contact area is closer to the oil side. Under such a sliding surface condition, there will be no oil leak (sealing). In the case of seal type 3, although the A_R value is small with an uneven sliding surface, the X_G value is negative, suggesting that the actual contact area is inclined toward the air side.

Under such a sliding surface condition, oil can easily leak through. It follows that the sliding surface must be slightly uneven and the actual contact area should be biased toward the oil side in order to realize absolute sealing. It is evident that the unique sliding side structure to ensure sealing has minute surface roughness (existence of minute projections) and the true contact area is biased towards the oil side (Sato et al., 1999: Kameike et al., 2000).

Understanding of the Oil Seal Leakage Mechanism through Visualization

In the stage of visualization, the oil leaks and similar problems can result in immediate and critical vehicle defects. One of the primary causes of oil seal leaks is wear to convex areas of the oil seal) where it comes into contact with the surface of the drive shaft, which is rotating at high speeds. The author is applying Optimal CAE Design Approach Model in Figure 11, Chapter 14 (Refer to Chapter 14) to this issue in order to resolve it.

Figure 11. Two seal characteristic values, A_R and X_G, and outcome of the experiments

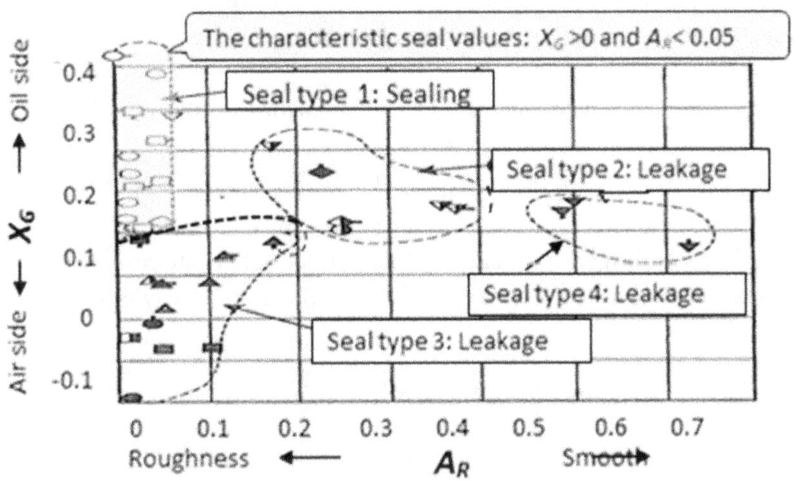

Figure 12. Relation between the characteristic values, A_R and X_G, and the seal condition

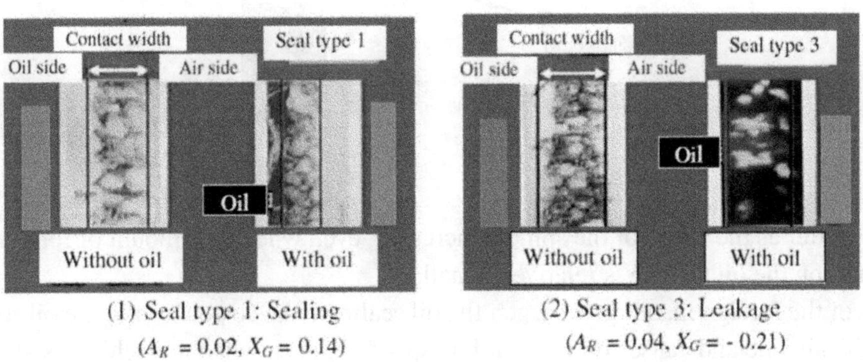

This subsection addresses a second unexplained problem: metal particles (foreign matter) generated from rotation wear in drive train gears (Amasaka, 1997, 2005b, 2007f, 2010a; Amasaka and Ootali, 1999; Amasaka and Osaki, 1999, 2003; NOK Corp., 2000; Amasaka, Ed., 2012). The dynamic behavior of the faulty oil seal leak mechanism causing these metal particles to form was outlined using the developed visualization device (equipment) in Figure 13(a), in order to turn this “unknown oil leak mechanism” into explicit knowledge.

In Figure 13(a), the oil seal was immersed in the lubrication oil in the same manner as the transaxle, and the drive shaft was changed to a glass shaft that rotated eccentrically via a spindle motor so as to reproduce the operation that would occur in an actual vehicle. The sealing effect of the oil seal lip was then visualized using an optical fiber. It was conjectured that in an eccentric seal with one-sided wear, the foreign matter becomes entangled at the place where the contact width changes from small to large.

Three trial tests were carried out to ascertain if this was true or not. Based on the examination of faulty parts returned from the market and the results of the visualization experiment, it was observed that very fine foreign matter (which was previously thought to not impact the oil leakage problem) grew at the contact section, as shown in Figure 13(b) (test-1). It was also confirmed from the results of the component analysis that the fine foreign matter was a powder produced during gear engagement inside the transaxle gear box.

This fine foreign matter on top of microscopic irregularities on the lip sliding surface resulted in microscopic pressure distribution which eventually led to the degrading of the sealing performance as shown in Figure 14 (test-2). Also, the presence of this mechanism was confirmed from a separate observation that foreign matter had cut into the lip sliding surface, thereby causing aeration (cavitations) to be generated in the oil flow on the lip sliding surface. This caused deterioration of the sealing performance, as shown in Figure 15 (test-3). The figure indicates that cavitations occur in the vicinity

Figure 13. Oil seal visualization and oil seal leak mechanism

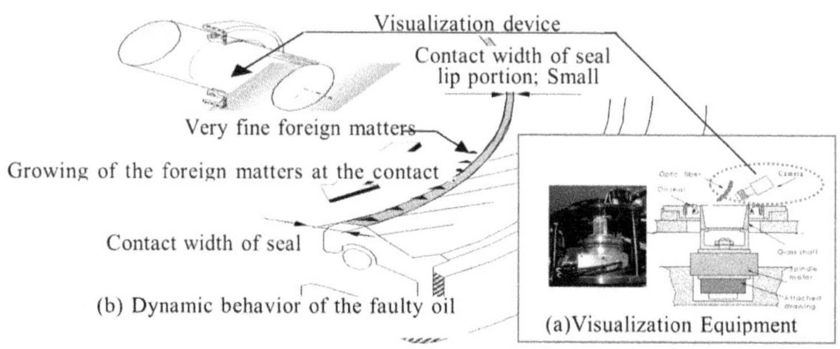

of the foreign matter as the speed of the spindle increases, even when the amount of foreign matter that has accumulated on the oil seal lip is relatively small.

As the size of the foreign matter gets bigger, the oil sealing balance position of the oil seal lip moves more toward the air side and causes oil leaks at low speeds or even when the vehicle is at rest.

This fact was unknown prior to this study, and therefore was not incorporated into the original product design of the oil seals. As a result of these efforts, the author was able to investigate the mechanism generating the oil seal leaks and use factor analysis to pinpoint the design elements in the oil seal and drive train gears that should have controlled the problem. The oil seal leakage mechanism involved cavitation occurring in rotating parts when foreign matter got wedged between sliding surfaces (on the lip surface). This happened in areas where there was variation in the size of the contact surface (from small to large) on the oil seal lip, caused by irregular wear and assembly variations.

The author used the knowledge obtained from the visualization experiment to logically outline the faulty oil seal leakage mechanism. This was done in order to capture the problem using Highly Reliable CAE Analysis Technology Component Model as shown in Figure 3, Chapter 14 (Refer to Chapter 14). Using this process, the author was able to arrive at a hypothesis for why the cavitation was occurring; namely, factors like low pump volume and seal damage had compromised the tightness of the seal and lead to oil leaks.

Figure 14. Growing of the foreign matter (test-2)

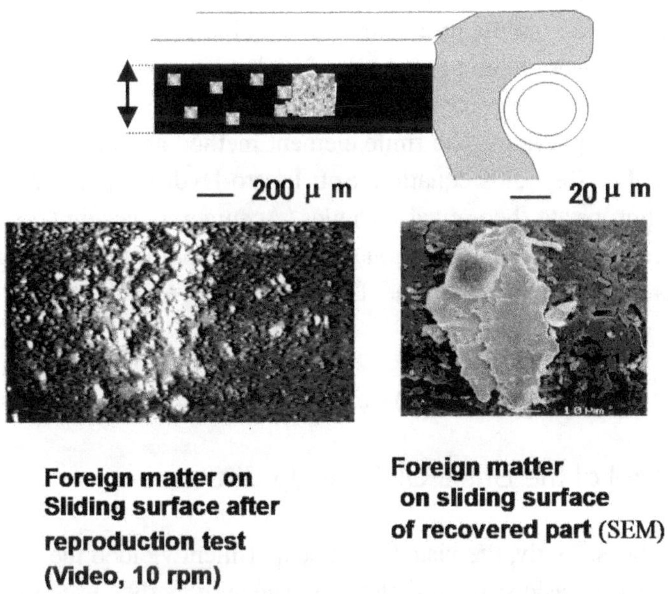

Figure 15. Causing cavitation (Test-3)

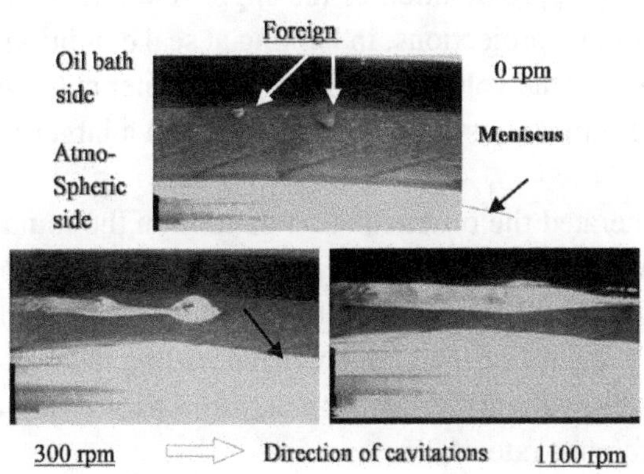

Oil Seal Simulator using Highly Reliable CAE Analysis Technology Component Model

In the stage of theoretical conceptualization, in order to conduct a numerical analysis based on the knowledge gained from the visualization experiment, it is necessary to select the kinds of technological elements involved. Appropriate selection of technological elements (*defining the problem, modeling, algorithms, theory, and computer technology*) is a critical part of generating Highly Accurate CAE Analysis Approach Model (Figure 4, Chapter 6). Organically linking these technological elements is what will make the CAE analysis a success.

The author thus has added the needed technological component to the Oil Seal Simulator using Highly Reliable CAE Analysis Technology Component Model as shown in Figure 5, Chapter 6 (Amasaka, 2005b, 2007f, 2010a; Amasaka, Ed., 2012) (Refer to Chapter 6). In addressing the oil leakage phenomenon, the problem is researching the pump volume and lip side pressure distribution that directs the behavior and the oil circulation pattern on the minute projection area of sliding surfaces. The fluid resistance model, the contact model, and the material component rule model were used to solve these problems.

The Rayleigh Plesset Model for controlling steam and condensation was used as a CAE analysis model that could explain the problem. The finite element method and numeric fluid were analyzed as a convenient algorithm. The Reynolds equation, Soft Elasto-Hydrodynamic Lubrication, and Navier-Stokes equation were appropriate theoretical formulas. Accuracy is ensured, and the time integration method, space difference method, and procession method were appropriate computer technologies used to perform calculations in a realistic timeframe. Each of the above elements was used to construct the "Oil Seal Simulator".

Highly-Accurate CAE Analysis for Drivetrain Oil Seal Leakage

CAE Qualitative Model of the Basic Oil Seal Lip Structure

In the stage of CAE analysis, firstly, the visualization experiment yielded the conditions on the sliding surface of the oil seal lip as a basic structural element. The authors then used this element to construct the CAE Qualitative Model of the basic oil seal lip structure shown in Figure 16 in order to demonstrate sealing conditions (Amasaka, 2005b, 2007f, 2008d, 2010a; NOK Corp., 2000; Amasaka, Ed., 2012) (Refer to Appendix 8.A).

This model uses a statistical approximation of the slight roughness on the sliding surface to show the wedge effect created by minute projections. In looking at seal conditions on the sliding surfaces as a whole, the authors concluded that the volume of inflow was greater at QAA' than the outflow at QBB', based on the fact that minute projections in section AA' created a larger wedge effect than the minute projections in section BB'.

These conditions also generated the oil circulation pattern on the minute projection area of sliding surfaces, which meant that wear could be prevented by separating the two surfaces (Sato et al., 1999: Kameike et al., 2000: Dong et al., 2011). The result obtained from incorporating "CAE Qualitative Model" has helped to identify and refine the high precision sealing mechanism of oil seals. The validity of the CAE Qualitative Model–sealing mechanism analysis was verified against the results of actual vehicles and tests with a difference rate of 2%.

Figure 16. CAE Qualitative Model of the basic oil seal lip structure

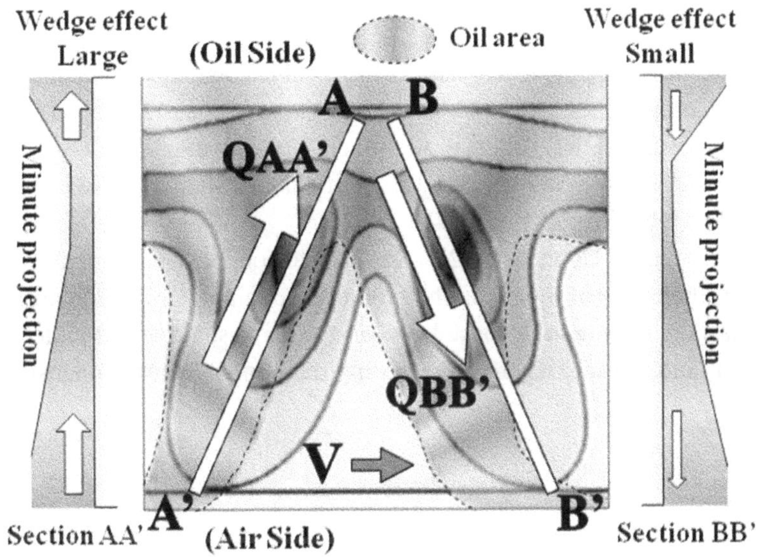

Figure 17. A two-dimensional analysis

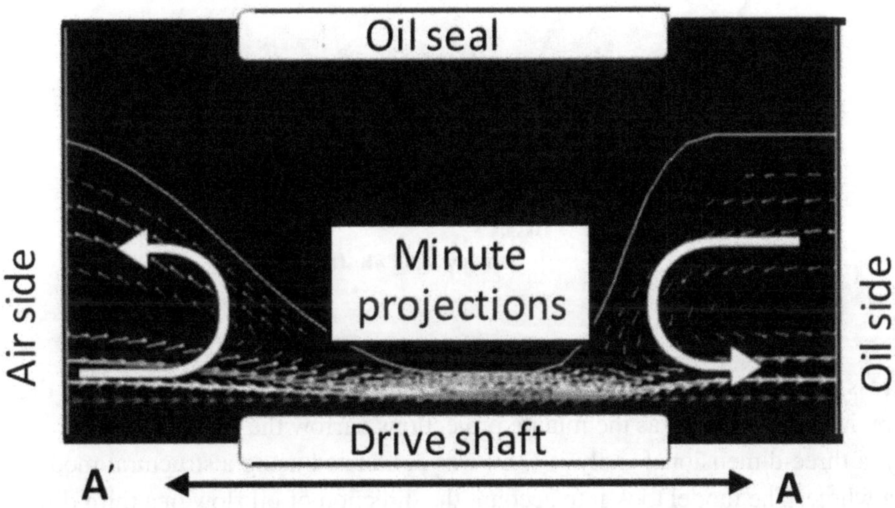

The study conducted by the authors has established this as a predictive engineering method for functional designing of oil seal parts (Amasaka and Ootaki, 1999; NOK Corp., 2000; Amasaka, 2005b, 2007f, 2010; Amasaka, Ed., 2012).

Development of Highly Accurate CAE Analysis Approach Model using 2D and 3D CAE Analysis

Based on the knowledge acquired by visualization of oil seal leakage mechanism, Highly Reliable CAE Analysis Technology Component Model and CAE Qualitative Model mentioned above, the author has developed the Highly Accurate CAE Analysis Approach Model using **2D** and 3D CAE analysis (NOK Corp., 2000; Ito, et al., 2010a,b,; Amasaka, 2012a; Amasaka et al., 2012; Nozawa et al., 2012, 2013; Amasaka, 2012a,b) (Refer to Chapter 6 and 14).

Firstly, a two-dimensional CAE analysis (2D) was used to conduct a numerical simulation that would accurately describe the behavior of the oil on the problematic minute projection areas. Figure 17 shows the results of this analysis. It shows the space between the drive shaft near minute projection AA' and minute projection BB' and the seal where oil is getting trapped. This two-dimensional analysis shows

Figure 18. A three-dimensional analysis

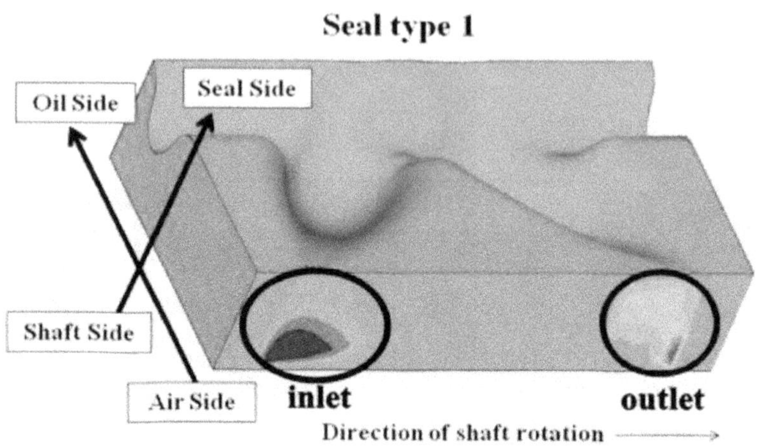

that shear stress is being generated by the fluid (oil) due to the rotation of the shaft and that the seal side flow direction is being reversed as the minute projections narrow the fluid channel.

Secondly, a three-dimensional analysis (3D) was conducted using a structural model of the sliding surfaces as a whole. The model took into account the direction of oil flow in a third dimension (depth) based on the knowledge gained from the visualization experiment and the two-dimensional CAE analysis. The model was used to do a numerical simulation of the oil film present on the sliding surfaces. The analytical model shown in Figure 18 was constructed based the CAE qualitative model of the basic oil seal lip structure indicated in Figure 16. By imposing conditions such as shaft rotation speed, the amount of oil flow on the oil side and air side could be calculated. The oil flow to the seal side and to the air side was compared, producing similar results to the visualization experiment.

Thirdly, a cavitation is generated at the following steps; Oil collides with a foreign matter - The flow velocity rise near a foreign matter - The fall of pressure - Decreased pressure is carried out to below saturated vapor pressure - Emasculation of oil - Generating of a cavitation. The fluid speed analysis like the one in Figure 19(1) was then conducted in order to look more closely at the mechanism causing cavitation. The analysis revealed that rapid changes in fluid speed were occuring in the vicinity of foreign particles, and that fluid speed drops immediately before the oil collides with foreign matter. This led to the conclusion that the presence of foreign particle was having an effect on oil flow.

Comparing cavitation and the fluid speed analysis results against the results of the pressure analysis shown in Figure 19(2) reveals that in areas of reduced pressure, oil was disappearing inside the cavities being formed—meaning that drops in pressure were likely being caused by these concave areas. Figure 19(3) shows the CAE analysis results at a rotation speed of 1100 rpm. This analysis confirmed the

Figure 19. Analysis of cavitation generating around foreign matter using 2D & 3D

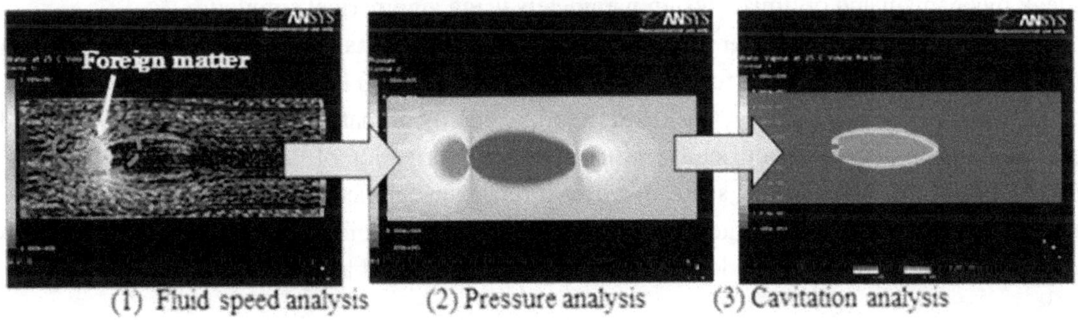

cavitation occurring around foreign matter, thus replicating the results of the visualization experiment.

At the same time, the finding that cavitation becomes more significant as the rotation speed of the drive shaft increases was similarly replicated.

The above CAE analysis allowed the authors to clarify the faulty mechanism causing cavitation: namely, the presence of metal foreign particles was affecting the strength of the oil flow, causing drops in pressure in areas with faster oil flow and creating cavities. In addition, a similar analysis of changes in the shape and size of the foreign particles revealed that these changes were also causing changes in cavitation. These CAE analysis results indicate a close link between particle size/shape and cavitation.

Preproduction and testing/evaluation of prototypes adds a significant amount of time and cost to the development process. However, precise CAE allowed manufacturers to eliminate preproduction (as well as prototype testing/evaluation) and still predict the mechanism causing cavitation and oil leaks. Though gaps such as minute surface variations caused by foreign particles and the shape of the oil film model exist, the CAE analysis allowed the authors to recreate the changes in flow speed and pressure around the foreign metal particles that were causing cavitation—changes which typically cannot be identified.

The deviation between the CAE analysis results and the results of the prototype testing were less than 5%, attesting to the usefulness of precise CAE analysis in certain cases.

Quality Improvement using Intellectual Customer Data Collection/Analysis Integrated System

In the stage of optimal design, the author has developed Intellectual Customer Data Collection/Analysis Integrated System to improve oil seal leak reliability for transaxle quality improvement (Amasaka, 2005c,

2010b). The result of a wear test on oil seal indicates a running distance of 400,000km (equivalent to 10 years or more vehicle life) is regarded as a sufficiently reliable development design (Amasaka and Osaki, 2003). Moreover, the oil seal leakage from the failure repair history of the DAS (Toyota Dynamic Assurance System) made possible Weibull analysis of the market claim (Sasaki, 1972: Amasaka, 2003b).

The visualization experiment above allowed the dynamic behavior of the transaxle oil seal leakage to be visualized; more specifically, the dynamic behavior involved in the process whereby metal particles (foreign matter) from gear rotation wear, found around the rotating and sliding portions of the oil seal lip, become mechanically fused and accumulate. This phenomenon was then reproduced in a two- and three-dimensional CAE analysis with high precision (with a deviation of around 3% versus prototype testing evaluations). This information made it possible to gain an approximate understanding of the oil seal leak mechanism and optimize design parameters using a numerical simulation.

These results led to two measures to improve design quality (shape and materials): strengthen gear surfaces to prevent occurrence of foreign matter even after the B10 life (L10 Bearing to MTBF (Mean Time Between Failures)) to over 400,000 km (improve quality of materials and heat treatments) and (2) formulate a design plan to scientifically ensure optimum lubrication of the surface layer of the oil seal lip (uneven portions of the sliding surface) where it rotates in contact with the drive shaft. As shown in Figure 20, the result of these countermeasures was a reduction in oil seal leaks (market complaints) to less than 1/20th their original incidence (Amasaka, 2008d; Amasaka, Ed., 2012).

Figure 20. Reduction in market complaint rate

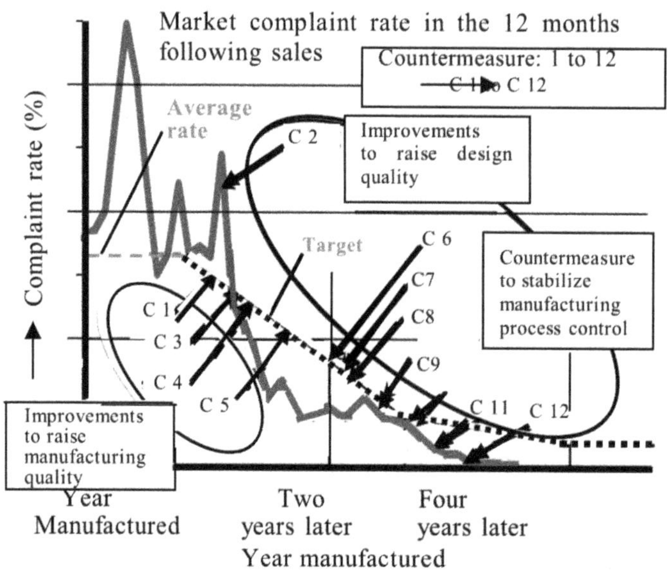

Application to Similar Problems

With its effectiveness verified, the authors were able to apply the New Development Design CAE Employment Model to critical development design technologies for automotive production, including predicting and controlling the special characteristics of Automobile lifting power (Amasaka et al., 1996;

Amasaka, 2004c), Automobile transaxle disk brake (Amasaka, 2004c, 2017), Anti-vibration design of door mirrors (Amasaka, 2010a), Urethane seat foam molding (Amasaka, 2007c), and Loosening bolt-nut (Amasaka, 2019).

In each of these cases as well, discrepancy was 3–5% versus prototype testing. Based on the achieved results, these studies employing a typical Highly Accurate CAE Analysis Approach Model are now being used as an intelligent support tool for optimizing product design processes.

CONCLUSIONS

In this chapter, the author has described the development of SSTTM (Strategic Stratified Task Team Model), and verified within advanced automobile manufacturer Toyota and its affiliate/non-affiliate supplier by a typical case study for realizing simultaneous QCD fulfilment, necessary for the driving force in the development of NJM (New Japan Model). Specifically, through the positivism research taken up by this application, to solution of a peculiar technical problem, the systematic business approach and problem-solving using SSTTM has dynamism and pliability, and the author believes that all have expressed the technical general solution as the transaxle oil seal leakage of automobile bottleneck problem in the world.

Actually, this case study addresses the necessity reforming the business processes associated with development design, a critical component of manufacturing, by creating a New Development Design CAE Employment Model that takes manufacturers away from conventional preproduction and prototype testing methods and towards a better predictive evaluation method. The validity of this model through the problem-solving of transaxle oil seal leakage was verified by successfully applying it to the technological problem of development design bottlenecks at the auto-assembly maker Toyota and typical non-affiliate supplier NOK.

ACKNOWLEDGMENT

The authors would like to acknowledge the generous support received from the following researchers. All those at WG'4 (Working Group No. 4) studies in JSQC (Japanese Society for Quality Control), Study group on Simulation and SQC – "A study of the high quality assurance CAE model for automobile development design", Toyota Motor Corporation and NOK Corporation, and those connected with the Amasaka laboratory at Aoyama Gakuin University that assisted with author's research, especially, Mr. Ito, T., Nozawa, Y., Takahashi, T. and others.

REFERENCES

Amasaka, K. (2000a). New JIT, a new principle for management technology 21C: Proposal and demonstration of "TQM-S" in Toyota (special lecture). *The 1st World Conference on Production and Operations Management,* 15-27.

Amasaka, K. (2000b). Partnering chains as the platform for quality management in Toyota. *Proceedings of the 1st World Conference on Production and Operations Management,* 1-13.

Amasaka, K. (2001). Quality management in the automobile industry and the practice of the joint activities of the auto maker and the supplier. Japan Small Business Research Institute - A change in the order system such as a part in the manufacturing industry: The condition of the supplier continuance in the automobile industry, 74(2), 135-163.

Amasaka, K. (2002a). New JIT, A New Management Technology Principle at Toyota. *International Journal of Production Economics, 80*(2), 135–144. doi:10.1016/S0925-5273(02)00313-4

Amasaka, K. (2002b). Reliability of oil seal for Transaxle –A Science SQC approach at Toyota. In *Case Studies in Reliability and Maintenance*. John Wiley & Sons, Inc.

Amasaka, K. (2003). A "Dual Total Task Management Team" involving both Toyota and NOK - A cooperative team approach for reliability improvement of transaxle. *Proceedings of the Group Technology/Cellular Manufacturing World Symposium-Year 2003,* 265-270.

Amasaka, K. (2004a). The past, present, future of production management (Keynote lecture). *The Japan Society for Production Management, The 20th Annual Technical Conference, Nagoya Technical College,* 1-8.

Amasaka, K. (2004b). Development of "Science TQM", A new principle of quality management -Effectiveness of Strategic Stratified Task Team at Toyota. *International Journal of Production Research, 42*(17), 3691–3706. doi:10.1080/00207540420000203867

Amasaka, K. (2004c). *Science SQC, New Quality Control Principle, The Quality Strategy of Toyota.* Springer-Verlag. doi:10.1007/978-4-431-53969-8

Amasaka, K. (2004d). Applying New JIT—A Management Technology Strategy Model at Toyota - Strategic QCD studies with affiliated and non-affiliated Suppliers. *Proceedings of the 2nd World Conference on Production and Operations Management Society*, 1-22.

Amasaka, K. (2004e). Strategic Quality Management and its New Development for SCM: Collaborative Task Team of Toyota and NOK. *Supply Chain Management; Theory and Practice of Cooperation between companies,* 79-109.

Amasaka, K. (2005a). New Japan Production Model, An innovative production management principle: Strategic Implementation of New JIT. *Proceedings of the 16th Annual Conference of the Production and Operations Management Society*, 1-17.

Amasaka, K. (2005b), Interim Report of WG4's studies in JSQC research on simulation and SQC(1) - A study of the high quality assurance CAE model for car development design. *Transdisciplinary Federation of Science and Technology*, 93-98.

Amasaka, K. (2005c). Constructing a Customer Science application system "CS-CIANS". *WSEAS Transactions on Business and Economics*, *2*(3), 135–142.

Amasaka, K. (2007a). High Linkage Model "Advanced TDS, TPS & TMS: Strategic development of New JIT at Toyota". *International Journal of Operations and Quantitative Management*, *13*(3), 101–121.

Amasaka, K. (Ed.). (2007a). New Japan Model – "Science TQM": Theory and practice for strategic quality management. Study group of the ideal situation the quality management of the manufacturing industry, Maruzen, Tokyo.

Amasaka, K. (2007b). New Japan Production Model, An Advanced Production Management Principle: Key to strategic implementation of New JIT. *The International Business & Economics Research Journal*, *6*(7), 67–79.

Amasaka, K. (Ed.). (2007b). Establishment of a needed design quality assurance framework for numerical simulation in automobile production. Working Group No. 4 studies "Study group on simulation and SQC", in Japanese Society for Quality Control, Tokyo.

Amasaka, K. (2007c). Highly Reliable CAE Model, the key to strategic development of *Advanced TDS. Journal of Advanced Manufacturing Systems*, *6*(2), 159–176. doi:10.1142/S0219686707000930

Amasaka, K. (2007f). Final report of WG4's studies in JSQC research activity of simulation and SQC (Part-1)-Proposal and validity of the High Quality Assurance CAE Model for automobile development Design. *Transdisciplinary Science and Technology Initiative, The 2nd Annual Technical Conference,* 321-326.

Amasaka, K. (2008a). *Simultaneous fulfillment of QCD - Strategic collaboration with affiliated and non-affiliated suppliers. In New theory of manufacturing - Surpassing JIT: Evolution of Just-in-Time.* Morikita-Shuppan.

Amasaka, K. (2008b). Strategic QCD studies with affiliated and non-affiliated suppliers utilizing New JIT. Encyclopedia of Networked and Virtual Organizations, Information Science Reference, 3(PU-Z), 1516-1527.

Amasaka, K. (2008c). Science TQM, A New Quality Management Principle: The Quality Management Strategy of Toyota. *The Journal of Management & Engineering Integration*, *1*(1), 7–22.

Amasaka, K. (2008d). An Integrated Intelligence Development Design CAE Model Utilizing New JIT. *Journal of Advanced Manufacturing Systems*, *7*(2), 221–241. doi:10.1142/S0219686708001589

Amasaka, K. (2008e). Proposal and validity of the High Quality Assurance CAE Model for automobile development. *Journal of the Japanese Society for Quality Control*, *38*(1), 38–44.

Amasaka, K. (2009a). New JIT, Advanced Management Technology Principle: The global management strategy of Toyota (special lecture). *International Conference on Intelligent Manufacturing & Logistics Systems and Symposium on Group Technology and Cellular Manufacturing*, 1-16.

Amasaka, K. (2010a). Proposal and effectiveness of a High Quality Assurance CAE Analysis Model. *Current Development in Theory and Applications of Computer Science, Engineering and Technology*, *2*(1/2), 23–48.

Amasaka, K. (2010b). Product design. In Quality Assurance Guide Book (New Edition). The Japanese Society for Quality Control.

Amasaka, K. (2011). *New JIT, new management technology principle* (Plenary Lecture). In VIII Siberian Conference "Quality Management-2011, Krasnoyarsk, Russia, Siberian Federal University.

Amasaka, K. (Ed.). (2012). Science TQM, New Quality Management Principle, The Quality Management Strategy of Toyota. Bentham Science Publishers. doi:10.2174/97816080528201120101

Amasaka, K. (2012a). Constructing Optimal Design Approach Model: Application on the Advanced TDS. *Journal of Communication and Computer*, *9*(7), 774–786.

Amasaka, K. (2012b). A New Development Design CAE Employment Model. *The Journal of Japanese Operations Management and Strategy*, *3*(1), 18–57.

Amasaka, K. (2013). The development of a Total Quality Management System for transforming technology into effective management strategy. *International Journal of Management*, *30*(2), 610–630.

Amasaka, K. (2014a). New JIT, new management technology principle. *Journal of Advanced Manufacturing Systems*, *13*(3), 197–222. doi:10.1142/S0219686714500127

Amasaka, K. (2014b). New JIT, new management technology principle: Surpassing JIT. *Journal of Procedia Technology*, *16*(Special Issues), 1135–1145. doi:10.1016/j.protcy.2014.10.128

Amasaka, K. (2015a). Global manufacturing strategy of New JIT: Surpassing JIT (keynote lecture). *International Conference on Information Science and Management Engineering, Phuket, Thailand*, 1-12.

Amasaka, K. (2015b). New JIT, new management technology principle. Taylor & Francis Group.

Amasaka, K. (2016). Innovation of automobile manufacturing fundamentals employing New JIT: Developing Advance Toyota Production System at Toyota Manufacturing USA. *Proceedings of the 5th Conference on Production and Operations Management*, 1-10.

Amasaka, K. (2017). Strategic Stratified Task Team Model for realizing simultaneous QCD fulfilment: Two case studies. *The Journal of Japanese Operations Management and Strategy*, *7*(1), 14–36.

Amasaka, K. (2019). Establishment of an Automobile Optimal Product Design Model: Application to study on bolt-nut loosening mechanism, *Noble International Journal of Scientific Research. Nobel Academic Publisher*, *3*(9), 79–102.

Amasaka, K. (2022). New Manufacturing Theory; Surpassing JIT (2nd ed.). Lambert Academic Publishing.

Amasaka, K., Kurosu, S., & Morita, M. (2008). *New Manufacturing Theory: Surpassing JIT-The evolution of Just-in-Time*. Maruzen.

Amasaka, K., Nakaya, H., Oda, K., Oohashi, T., & Osaki, S. (1996). A study of estimating vehicle aerodynamics of lift-Combining the usage of neural networks and multivariate analysis. *The Institute of Systems Control and Information Engineers*, *40*(5), 27–35.

Amasaka, K., & Ootaki, M. (1999). Development of New TQM by Partnering – Effectiveness of "TQM-SP" by collaborating Total Task Management Team activities. *Journal of the Society for Production Management,* 69-74.

Amasaka, K., & Osaki, S. (1999). The promotion of the New Statistical Quality Control Internal Education at Toyota Motor: A proposal of 'Science Quality Control' for improving the principle of Toyota quality Management. *European Journal of Engineering Education*, *24*(3), 259–276. doi:10.1080/03043799908923561

Amasaka, K., & Osaki, S. (1999). The promotion of New Statistical Quality Control Internal Education in Toyota Motor. *European Journal of Engineering Education, 24*(3), 259–276. doi:10.1080/03043799908923561

Amasaka, K., & Osaki, S. (2003). Reliability of oil seal for transaxle - A Science SQC approach in Toyota. In Case Studies in Reliability and Maintenance. John Wiley & Sons, Inc.

Burke, W., & Trahant, W. (2000). *Business Climate Shift*. Oxford Butterworth–Heinemann.

Corp, N. O. K. (2000). *The Hitory of NOK's Oil Seal - Oil Seal Mechanism*. Promotion Video.

Dong, Y., Fan, X., & Liu, B. (2011). Numerical simulation and technology optimization of rear oil seal bearing die casting based on procast. *Advanced Materials Research, 189-193*, 4008–4013. doi:10.4028/www.scientific.net/AMR.189-193.4008

Doz, Y. L., & Hamel, G. (1998). *Alliance advantage*. Harvard Business School Press.

Evans, J. R., & Dean, J. W. (2003). *Total quality management, organization and strategy*. Thomson/South-Western.

Fukuchi, H., Arai, Y., Ono, M., Suzuki, S. T., & Amasaka, K. (1998). A proposal *TDS-D* by utilizing *Science SQC*: An improving design quality of drive-train components. *The Japanese Society for Quality Control, The 60th Technical Conference*, 29-32.

Goto, T. (1999). *Forgotten origin of management–Management quality taught by G.H.Q: CSS management lecture*. Productivity Publications.

Gryna, F. M. (2001). *Quality planning and analysis*. McGraw-Hill.

Ito, T., Matsuura, S., & Amasaka, K. (2010b). Optimized design using high quality assurance CAE. *The Japanese Society for Quality Control, The 40th Annual Technical Conference*, 189-192.

Ito, T., Sato, M., Yamaji, M., & Amasaka, K. (2010a). An Analysis of Bottleneck Technology by using experiments and CAE. *International Business & Economics Research Journal, 9*(12), 123–129.

Joiner, B. L. (1994). Fourth generation management: The new Business consciousness. Joiner Associates, Inc.

Kameike, M., Ono, S., & Nakamura, K. (2000). The Helical Seal: Sealing Concept and Rib Design. *Sealing Technology International, 77*(77), 7–11. doi:10.1016/S1350-4789(00)88559-1

Kotler, F. (1999). *Kotler marketing*. The Free Press, Simon & Schuster Inc.

Lopez, A. M., Nakamura, K., & Seki, K. (1997). A study on the sealing characteristics of lip seals with helical ribs. *Proceedings of the 15th International Conference on British Hydromechanics Research Group Ltd., Fluid Sealing*, 1-11.

Nozawa, Y., Ito, T., & Amasaka, K. (2013). High precision CAE analysis of automotive transaxle oil seal leakage. *The China Business Review, 12*(5), 63–374.

Nozawa, Y., Yamashita, R., & Amasaka, K. (2012). Analyzing cavitation caused by metal particles in the transaxle: Application of High Quality Assurance CAE Analysis Model. *Journal of Energy and Power Engineering., 6*(12), 2054–2062.

Sasaki, S. (1972). Collection and analysis of reliability information on automotive industries. *The 2nd Reliability and Maintainability Symposium, Union of Japanese Scientists and Engineers,* 385-405.

Sato, Y., Toda, A., Ono, S., & Nakamura, K. (1999). *A study of the sealing mechanism of radial lip seal with helical robs–measurement of the lubricant fluid behavior under sealing contact.* SAE Technical Paper Series, 1999-01-0878.

Seuring, S., Muller, M., Goldbach, M., & Schneidewind, U. (Eds.). (2003). *Strategy and organization in supply chains*. Physica-Verlag-Springer.

Stefan, S. (2003). *Strategy and organization in supply chains*. Physica-Verlag- Springer.

Takahashi, T., Ueno, T., Yamaji, M., & Amasaka, K. (2010). Establishment of Highly Precise CAE Analysis Model -An example the analysis of automotive bolts-. *The International Business & Economics Research Journal, 9*(5), 103–113.

Toyota Motor Corp., (1987). *Creation is infinite*: *The history of Toyota-50 years.* Toyota.

APPENDIX: CAE QUALITATIVE MODEL

The author combined the CAE Qualitative Model function that explains the dynamic behavior of the oil leak (Amasaka, 2008d). Figure 16 shows a typical example of the modeling of the basic oil seal lip structure that has been created for the purpose of reducing the weight of the sliding surface of the oil seal contact part. Judging from what has been observed up to this point, it is necessary to have the sliding surface minutely irregular and the parts that are actually in contact biased toward the oil side. This is done in order to maintain a good sealing condition that will prevent oil leaks from occurring at the contact part of the oil seals. As described in Figure 16, the upper section of the sliding surface is the oil side and the lower section is the air side. The darkest black part indicates the areas that are actually in contact. Among the conditions of characteristic values necessary for sealing, the minute roughness of the sliding surface or the small black area representing the actual contact area can be described in this way. Next, another condition is that this black area is biased toward the oil side, which can be incorporated in the sliding surface model like this. Here, the two black areas are not completely parallel, but rather the upper ends are found to be pointing inward. This takes into account the condition of a real oil seal. The actual sliding surface of the oil seal consists of countless tiny projections, which are represented by the black area, pointing in random directions. However, statistically speaking, the directional orientation of these projections shows counterbalancing characteristics.

In this model such factors have been taken into consideration. In other words, the two model projections representing the random projections are arranged to face each other at the same angle, so that a directionless model is presented. The authors actually photographed an oil seal reproducing this model sliding surface and observed the behavior of the oil. The upper section in the figure is the oil side and the lower section is the air side, while the rotating axis of the drive shaft rotates in the direction of the arrows. As the drive shaft rotates, a flow of oil in the same direction as the rotation is generated and it flows along the two tiny projections. With this situation in mind, let's consider the cross sections of the tiny projections, A-A and B-B. First of all, let's look at the cross section A-A. At the oil inlet, the angle between the shaft and the microscopic projection is small. Because of this, a strong (large), hydrodynamic wedge effect is produced, causing the oil film to become thicker and increasing the amount of flow to the oil side. On the other hand, at the cross section B-B, the angle at the oil inlet is larger. Consequently, the wedge effect is small and the oil film does not get thick, resulting in a smaller amount of flow to the air side. Comparing the inlet flow (QAA') and outlet flow (QBB') here, the flow rate into the oil side is larger and achieves sealing. This leak prevention phenomenon has been reproduced and confirmed by an actual oil seal having the same characteristic values as the above model, and therefore the validity of this sliding surface model has been verified.

It is this phenomenon that creates a circulation of the oil flowing in and out of the sliding surface against the direction of the shaft rotation (V) when sealed, as shown in the figure. This circulation, which is promoted by the tiny projections, is the very factor that separates the lip sliding surface and the shaft and maintains a favorable fluid lubrication condition. This is in line with the phenomenon explained at the beginning, and explains why the wear on the oil seals is limited. The series of discussions to this point has sufficiently explained why the newly designed oil seal suffers little wear and maintains it's sealing effect for a long period of time. The author has confirmed the leak proof phenomenon utilizing actual model seals. This clarified concept of Numerical Simulation by CAE – the CAE Qualitative Model has been applied to the development design engineering of high precision oil seals. That is to say, as a result of incorporating the CAE Qualitative Model, the minute roughness on the sliding surface has been controlled by regulating the composition of the materials. The next factor concerning the biased distribution of roughness toward the oil side can be interpreted as the bias of contact pressure distribution toward the oil side. Therefore, this factor has been controlled by shape designing technology used for designing the seal lip.

Chapter 9
Total Quality Assurance Networking Model for New Defect Prevention Techniques

ABSTRACT

In order to survive globalization and worldwide quality competition, Japanese manufacturing must work towards the simultaneous achievement of quality, cost, and delivery (QCD) in order to shorten development times, ensure high quality, and lower production costs. Therefore, in this chapter, the author creates the Total Quality Assurance Networking Model (TQA-NM) for the new defect prevention that uses the product quality assurance tools for the new manufacturing management. This model focuses on integrated quality assurance spanning different departments from design to production in automobile manufacturing companies and extending further to part manufacturers. TQA-NM is developed, and its effectiveness is verified at Toyota and its suppliers.

INTRODUCTION

In order to survive globalization and worldwide quality competition, Japanese manufacturing must work towards the simultaneous achievement of quality, cost and delivery (QCD) in order to shorten development times, ensure high quality and lower production costs (Amasaka, 2007).

At the concrete stage of implementation until now, there are many tools, such as Quality Function Deployment (QFD) that can be used to ensure manufacturing quality, but they do not always produce sufficient results. As for the actual situation, there are three key technological components needed to take product quality assurance to the next level: (1) the experience and skill of technical personnel, (2) the combined use of methods that take a scientific approach, such as Failure Mode and Effect Analysis (FMEA) and Fault Tree Analysis (FTA), and (3) partnerships—both internal partnerships that extend from design through production and external partnerships built with suppliers.

Therefore, the author has created the Total Qualty Assurance Networking Model (TQA-NM) includes the above key technological components as the new manufacturing management of the product

DOI: 10.4018/978-1-7998-8746-1.ch009

quality assurance, and is introduced for the new defect prevention (Amasaka, 2004a,b, 2015; Kojima and Amasaka, 2011; Amasaka, Ed., 2012). This model focus on integrated quality assurance spanning different departments from design to production in manufacturing companies and extending further to part manufacturers by employing Total Task Management Team (TTMT). The TQA-NM for preventing defects is then outlined and its effectiveness verified at the leading corporation Toyota and its suppliers (Amasaka, 2004a,b, 2015, 2017a,b, 2022; Kojima and Amasaka, 2011).

BACKGROUND

Manufacturing in Japan Today

Product lifecycles are getting shorter as customers present more sophisticated and diverse needs. Japanese manufacturing needs to address these issues by shortening lead times throughout development, production and sales (Amasaka, 2004a,b; Yamaji and Amasaka, 2008). However, recent quality issues such as the large-scale recalls of the markets and manufacturing quality problems have raised social concerns, and the number of incidents as well as the number of vehicles recalled is on the rise (Ministry of Land, 2009a,b).

These quality issues have naturally compromised user trust in addition to a loss in social standing for the companies themselves (Ministry of Economy, 2009). Quality issues are not limited simply to manufacturing quality issues or manufacturing reliability—it has become increasingly important to treat them as corporate organizational issues as well (Amasaka, K. 2004a,b; Amasaka et al., 2008).

Necessity of Preventing Defects

In order to grasp actual quality assurance conditions, the researchers conducted 204 interviews and surveys at the quality assurance departments of ten manufacturing companies (assembly manufacturers and suppliers), which included some major corporations. The investigation revealed that while many manufacturing companies are looking to shorten development times, they are also spending a great deal of their defect prevention efforts on preventing outflow rather than preventing occurrence itself (Amasaka, 2007).

It was discovered that one reason for this is that developers believe that focusing on preventing outflow contributed more to shortening development times than focusing on occurrence prevention. Occurrence prevention uses quality assurance tools like QFD or FMEA to predict what underlying factors are causing defects. But research indicated that these tools are currently not being sufficiently implemented. By putting effort into outflow prevention rather than occurrence prevention, fundamental solutions for reducing defects are never reached. Instead, it is critical that companies make the transition from quality assurance measures that prevent outflow to those that prevent occurrence as shown in Figure 1 (Kojima et al., 2011; Amasaka, 2015, 2017b, 2020).

Figure 1. Quality assurance process transitions

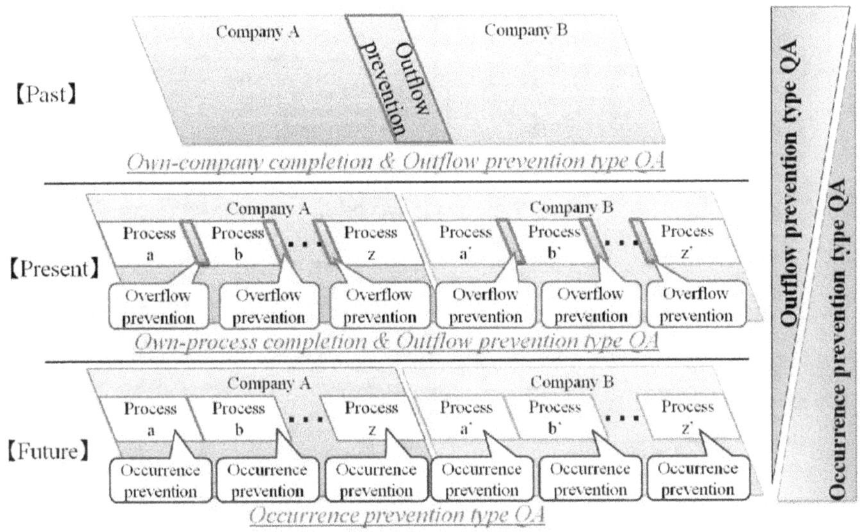

Issues Faced by Quality Assurance Departments

A statistical analysis using type III quantification method was conducted on the data collected in "Necessity of preventing defects" to identify the issues faced by quality assurance departments as shown in Figure 2 (Kojima ans Amasaka, 2011; Amasaka, 2015, 2017b, 2022).

The figure indicates two levels of problems: those faced by managers (i) and those faced by staff members (workers) (ii). The three problems faced by managers (i) are: (1) development and deployment of quality assurance tools, (2) visualization of processes, and (3) transmission of know-how and expertise. These are the quality assurance issues from the perspective of management. The next three problems are those faced by staff members (ii). They are: (4) clear quality assurance standards, (5) quality of human resources, and (6) swift response to changing market conditions. These are the quality assurance issues from the perspective of the plant workers themselves.

As a result of the investigation and analysis, the researchers were able to clarify the critical components of achieving a high degree of quality assurance from the perspective of both managers and staff members (workers).

CREATING THE TOTAL QUALITY ASSURANCE NETWORKING MODEL

Total Quality Assurance Networking Model (TQA-NM)

Putting effort into outflow prevention is necessary to fundamentally resolve defect issues. Effective partnerships—both internal partnerships that extend from design through production and external partnerships built with suppliers—are necessary to address quality issues as organizational issues within the company (Amasaka et al., 2008).

Figure 2. Issues faced by qualiy assurance departments

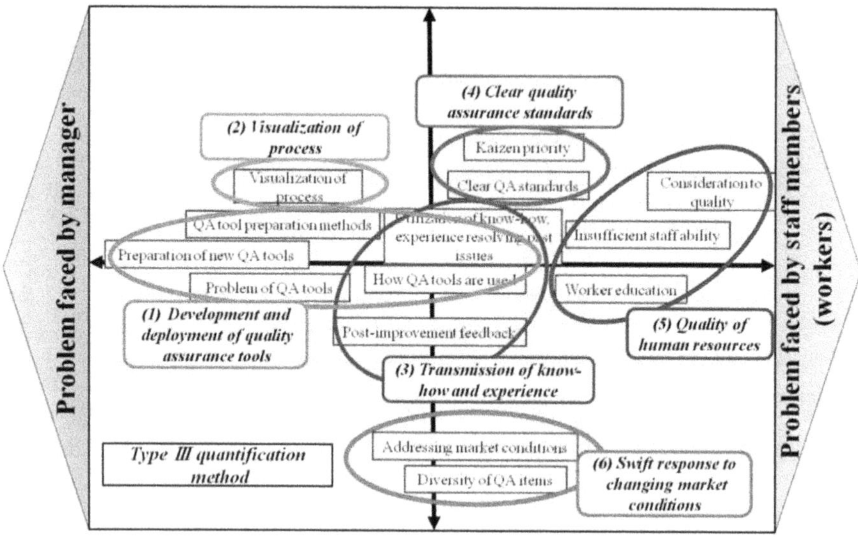

To establish a total quality assurance system and strategically deploy it, the author has created the Total Quality Assurance Networking Model (TQA-NM) as shown in Figure 2, Chapter 7 (Kojima and Amasaka. 2011) (Refer to Chapter 7). The purpose of the model is to create a new quality assurance system that can be used to comprehensively carry out quality assurance. The TQA-NM indicates the cycling total quality assurance process for achieving defect prevention by employing the Total Task Management Team (TTMT) activity with Strategic Stratified Task Team Model (SSTTM) (Amasaka et al., 1995: Takahashi, 1997: Takahashi et al., 1997; Amasaka, 2004a,b, 2015,2017a,b, 2020; Kojima and Amasaka. 2011) (Refer to Chapter 8).

The ultimate goal of the TQA-NM is to achieve customer satisfaction (CS), employee satisfaction (ES), and social satisfaction (SS) through high quality manufacturing. This is done through the prevention of defect occurrence and by supporting the simultaneous achievement of QCD that come from strategically deploying a high-level quality assurance process, as follows;

(I) One of the technological components in achieving these goals is strengthening quality assurance networks by developing and deploying quality assurance (QA) tools. (II) A second component is establishing clear quantitative quality assurance (QA) standards (such as process capacity) that are not affected by worker experience. (III) A third component is creating a system that can make use of worker expertise and information on past defects in an organized manner. (IV) A fourth component is the development of workers and frontline staff as the High Quality HRD (Human Resource Development) who are familiar with the site.

The strategic implementation of these components will allow companies to prevent defect occurrence and simultaneously QCD.

TQA-NM Approach

1. Creating the Total QA Networking Chart

The author has applied the TQA-NM by developing Total QA Networking Chart by employing Strategic Stratified Task Team Model (STTM) (Amasaka, 2004a,b, 2017a,b) (Refer to Chapter 8 in detail). Specifically, as the pioneering examples by using QA Network Matrix Table in Toyota as follows; (i) Establishment of optimum casting conditions for compact DOHC cylinder head (Miyamoto and Ishimoto, 1991) and (ii) Solutions for shrinkage cavities in low-pressure die-casting process: Establishment of optimum casting conditions (Kurumiya. and Miyamoto, 1991),

The Total QA Networking Chart was created in order to deploy the TQA-NM based on the Total Task Management Team activity by advanced assembly maker Toyota Motor Corp., and non-affiliated supplirer Aishin Seiki Co., Ltd., and Aishin Chemical Co.., Ltd. as shown in Figure 2, Chapter 7 (Amasaka et al., 1997) (Refer to Chapter 7). The chart is a defect occurrence prevention technique featuring a combination of quality assurance tools for automobile disk brake manufacturing process. It also uses FMEA and matrix diagrams to deploy partnerships. The vertical axis of the chart identifies joint processes by suppliers and assembly manufacturers, from the arrival of goods to shipment.

This creates a quality assurance network named Toyota's QA Network that eliminates gaps in quality assurance. The horizontal axis lists individual defects. The degree of quality assurance is indicated where the two axes intersect, which allows a quantitative value indicating the importance of process management tasks to be assigned to each. Each process is comprehensively evaluated on the basis of what the defect occurrence prevention tasks are for that process and how highly they are ranked in terms of the level of quality assurance (Amasaka et al., 1995, 1997; Amasaka, 1999, 2000a, 2004a,b, 2015, 2017a,b, 2022; Amasaka, Ed. 2007a,b; Kojima and Amasaka, 2011).

Moreover, the result of TQA-NM which uses Toyota's QA Network was reflected in deployment of defect prevention " transaxle oil seal leakage» (Amasaka and Ootaki, 2000) (Refer to Chapter 8).

2. Ranking occurrence and outflow prevention

Table 1 assigns rankings to occurrence and outflow prevention using "TQA Net – Level 1, 2 and 3". The importance of process management tasks is ensured based on the ranks shown for occurrence prevention and outflow prevention. This allows companies to carry out total quality assurance and establish a high-level quality assurance system (Kojima and Amasaka, 2011; Amasaka, 2015, 2020).

Table 1. Occurrence and outflow prevention rankings

TQA Net-Level	Level 1	Level 2	Level 3
Assignment of QA level	○, ●	Subjective 1-5	According to clear standards 1-4
User	Staff (workers)	⇔	Managers
Development task	Full model change	Model change	Minnor change
Level of technology at the company	Undeveloped	In transition	Advanced

3. Level-based application

Some participants in the investigation conducted in Subsection 9.2.2 "Necessity of preventing defects" felt that quality assurance tools did not match the scope or content of product development; they were not being used effectively, but simply being created as an empty exercise.

Level-based application of the Total Quality Asurance Networking Chart as shown in Table 2 can resolve this issue, because it allows companies to deploy the chart in a way that matches the development of each product. Level-based application also allows quality assurance tools to be created in less time and contributes to the simultaneous achievement of QCD (Kojima and Amasaka, 2011; Amasaka, 2015, 2022).

Table 2. Level-based application chart

		Lank of outflow prevention			
		❹	❸	❷	❶
Lank of occurrence prevention	④			1	2
	③	1	2	3	4
	②	1	3	4	5
	①	2			6

The degree of quality assurance (Low) → The degree of quality assurance (High)

Deployment of TQA-NM to Systematize High-Level Quality Assurance

Japanese companies manufacture some of the highest quality products in the world, making successful defect occurrence prevention a top priority. The author has indicated the deployment of TQA-NM as shown in Figure 3 as a way to systematize high-level quality assurance (Kojima and Amasaka, 2011). This was done to address the importance of quality assurance through partnerships between assembly manufacturers and suppliers for strategic distribution (Amasaka et al., 1995, 1997; Takahashi et al., 1997; Amasaka, 2000b, 2015, 2022; Amasaka, Ed., 2007a,b).

The ultimate goal of the TQA-NM is to achieve high-level quality assurance through defect occurrence prevention as well as the simultaneous achievement of QCD by developing Science TQM (Amasaka, 2004b) (Refer to Chapter 5 and 7 in detail). There are four essential guidelines that must be followed to achieve this goal.

The first is quality assurance that makes use of the TQA-NM (A). The second is further improving partnerships between assembly manufacturers and suppliers by considering the way their respective quality assurance systems are set up (B). The third requirement is establishing a quality assurance database for the TQA-NM in order to share quality assurance information. The fourth requirement is making use of quality assurance tools in subsequent product development in order to pass on know-how and experience resolving past issues.

Figure 3. Deployment of TQA-NM

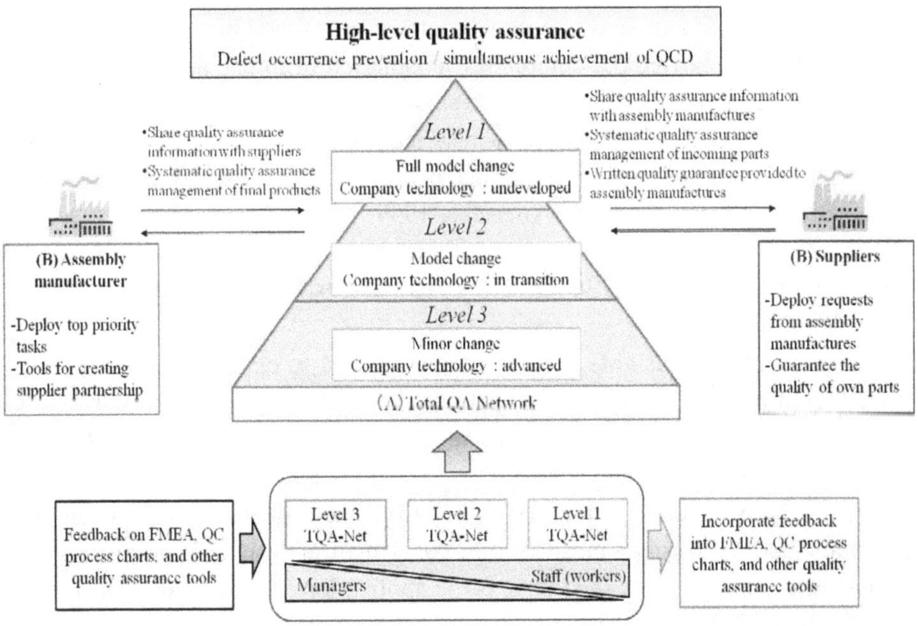

EXAMPLE APPLICATIONS

Improving Automobile Quality of Transaxle Brake Pads (Example-1)

The effectiveness of the TQA-NM was verified at a leading corporation. In this example-1, the automobile assembly maker Toyota, affiliated supplier Aishin Seiki Co., Ltd., and Aishin Chemical Co.., Ltd., and other suppliers partnership (jointly developed activities) using the TQA-NM with the goal of improving the automobile quality of transaxle brake pads to reduce the squel noise and abnomal noise (Amasaka et al., 1997; Amasaka, 1999, 2004a,b, 2017a,b, Amasaka and Osaki, 1999) (Refer to Chapter 5).

1. Technical management activity

Technical Management activities took a technical approach to reducing the variations in quality that resulted in disk brake noise. The activities searched for a mechanism by conducting a variable factor analysis, which included consideration of quality evaluation techniques.

2. Product management activity

A variable factor analysis was conducted on the brake pad products from a manufacturing perspective. The analysis sought to clarify the causal relationships leading to variations in process requirements and final products.

3. Deployment of TQA-NM using Total QA Networking Chart

The researchers aimed to create more efficient business processes by taking full advantage of member expertise in technical management and in product management—and by carrying out these two activities side by side. If they are carried out completely in isolation from one another, it will be difficult for all participating members to have an awareness of shared goals. The two activities have therefore been deployed using Total QA Networking Chart shown in Figure 4. In same approach of TQA-NM, moreover, the author has expressed the high quality assurance using TTMT activity by Toyota and non-affiliated suplier Akebono Brake Industry Co. Ltd. (Amasaka, 1999, 2004a).

Rust Prevention for Automobile Quality Assurance (Example-2)

In this example-2, the author was able to apply the TQA-NM to critical QCD studies of automobile manufacturing, including predicting and controlling the special characteristics for product process management as the vehicles' anti-rusting (Amasaka, 2004a, 2015, 2017a,b, 2020). One of the subjects for technological development of higher quality, longer life vehicles is the quality assurance of anti-rusting of the vehicle body (Amasaka et al., 1995, 2004b; Takahashi et al., 1997). From the engineering viewpoint of vehicle body, it involves consideration for structural design, adoption of anti-rusting steel, adoption of local anti-rusting processing (such as the application of wax, sealer, etc.), and paint design (conversion treatment and improvement of electrodeposition coating, etc.).

On the implementation stage of the research, these anti-rusting measures are adopted singularly or in combination of multiple measures as may be required by construction of subject section or corrosion factors. In order for us to proceed with advanced and timely QCDS (quality, cost, delivery and safety) study activities, it is necessary to conduct variable factor analysis of vehicle's anti-rusting and the optimization with strategic collaboration of suppliers. In this sense, Science SQC centering around the multivariate analysis has much to contribute as a scientific approach. In this connection, this research describes a characteristic case for study (Amasaka et al., 1995; Amasaka, 2004a).

1. Anti-rusting methods and how to outline their characterisics

To establish a superior quality assurance system, it is important to set up the network of automobile quality assurance on the job processing stage so as to raise reliability technology of whole the sectors including product planning, design, review, production engineering, process design, administration, inspection and so on. Such a quality assurance activity under the cooperation of all the sectors has been established as Toyota's QA Network Matrix Table, where SQC plays an important role as the behavioral science for enhancing quality performance.

Toyota has been incorporating various anti-rusting methods to various sections of the vehicle. To outline the deployment of quality performance, the application of matrix diagram method is effective. For example, Table 3 outlines complex correlationship, between corrosive environmental factors of 72 sections of a vehicle divided for the ease of arrangement of anti-rusting measures and the manufacturing

Figure 4. The Example of the Total QA Network Chart for Improving Quality to Reduce Brake Squeal noise and abnomal nose

Process		Individual defects	Process							Present quality assurance level													
			Tufftride treatment			Pretreatment				Occurrence prevention						Outflow prevention							
										Desigh specifications			Standardized work			Equipment specifications		Standardized work					
			Tufftride treatment	Tufftride incoming inspection	Starage	Inprint	Application of adhesive	Adhesive drying	Starage	Abnormality detected Interlock function	Abnormality detected Alarm	Sufficient process capacity	Regular equipment inspections	Sufficient standardization	Lank	Total automatic judgment Defective parts separation	Sufficient process capacity Regular sampling assessment	Regular gauge inspection	Can be determined at delivery inspection	Can be determined during total in-process inspections	Lank		Total Lank
Tufftride treatment	Tufftride incoming inspection (Metal acceptance)	Metal edge burr		❸								O			③				❸	O	❸		4
		Metal suface dents/damage	❸	❸																			5
		Metal sheet allowance (big/small)		❸																			3
		Fuzzy material markings		❸																			4
		Missing indicator assembly part		❸										O	③				❸	O	❸		4
		Unprocessed V-hole	❸	❸		❸								O	③				❸	O	❸		4
		Metal mixing (Different markings on the same shape)	③❸	❹		❸		❸						O	③					O	❸		4
		Defect of metal suface degree		❹								O			③		O	O			❷		3
		Blackening of the metal suface	③❸	❸		❸						O			③				❸	O	❸		4
		Dirty tufftride suface (Dust)	③❸	❸		❸								O	③				❸	O	❸		4
		Oily tufftride surface	③❸	❸		❸								O	③				❸	O	❸		4
		Rust spots on tufftride suface	③❸	❸		❸								O	③				❸	O	❸		4
		Processed layer thicknrss outside specifications (thick)	②❷	❸								O			②		O	O	❸		❸		2
		Processed layer thicknrss outside specifications (thin)	②❷	❸							O		O		②		O	O	❸		❷		2
		Suface hardness outside specifications (high)	②❷	❸							O		O		②		O	O	❸		❷		2
		Suface hardness outside specifications (low)	②❷	❸							O		O		②		O	O	❸		❷		2
		Porous layer thicknrss outside specifications (thick)	②❷	❸							O		O		②		O	O	❸		❷		2
		Porous layer thicknrss outside specifications (thin)	②❷	❸							O		O		②		O	O	❸		❷		2
		Suface roughness outside specifications (rough)	②❷	❸							O		O		②		O	O	❸		❷		2
		Suface roughness outside specifications (smooth)	②❷	❸							O		O		②		O	O	❸		❷		2
	Strage	Incrrect store input			③❸	❸		❸						O	③					O	❸		4
		Dust on tufftride suface			③	❸								O	③				O	O	❸		4
		Strage deadline			③❸									O	③				O		❸		4

Occurrence prevention

Outflow prevention

processes factors, and the respective anti-rusting methods adopted in an anti-rusting QA network table so called Toyota's Q.A. Matrix Table. This table is a summary of objective facts inductively arrested by engineers from multiple engineering sectors, which are then arranged deductively in the subjective point of view.

Table 3. Anchi-corrosion Q. A. Matrix Table

Part \ Category			Rest Prevent			
Large Classification	Small Classification	No.	Electro-deposited coating	Corrosion Prevented Steel Sheet	Adhesive	
Heming Of Shell Parts	Lower part of door	1.		1	1	
	Lower part of luggage	2		1	1	
	Lower part of fuel filler lid	3		1		
	Door, the others	4		1	1	
Shell Parts * R/F	Hood * Lock R/F	5	1	1		
	Door * Lock R/F	6		1		
	Door * Side Protection Bar	7	1	1		
	Back Door * Lock R/F	8		1		
Front Floor	General Surface	9		1		
	Under R/F	10		1		
	Exhaust Pipe R/F					

↓ 72 parts
Every parts of body shell

→ 28 categories
Anti-corrosion factor
Process influence factor
Corrosion factor etc.

} Yes 1, No blank

To make this table more effective, it is necessary to provide it with the ease of visual recognition so that it shows at a glance where Toyota stands in its present activities for rust prevention quality assurance. Table 4 enables staff and engineers to make the engineering judgment more accurately, subsequently contributing much to the strategic decision making on the part of the management.

To proceed with such an aim and make it much easier to understand complex entanglements of cause and effect relationships, they will be summarized visually as shown in Figure 5 by using quantification method type III by developing Science SQC (Refer to Chapter 5 in detail). From a scatter diagram of vehicle section (axis I x axis II), it is apparent that Toyota's anti-rusting measures are taken mainly against the steel sheet joint portions and that the local anti-rusting processing and many other methods tend to be adopted as the measures reach the underbody sections. The diagram indicates that the combination of several types of anti-rusting methods is applied to the doors and underbody members positioned in the upperbody sections.

Adoption of such an analytical method makes it easy to evaluate the vehicles of competition, enabling the reactive bench marking for additional advantages. In addition, insight into proprietary technologies with the knowledge acquired from the result of this analysis enables us to grasp proactively our responses to the future quality assurance including the trends of anti-rusting measures and techniques of competition that reflect thethe target quality and the counter-marketability of anti-rusting materials.

Figure 5. Characteristic of Toyota's anchi-corrosion measures

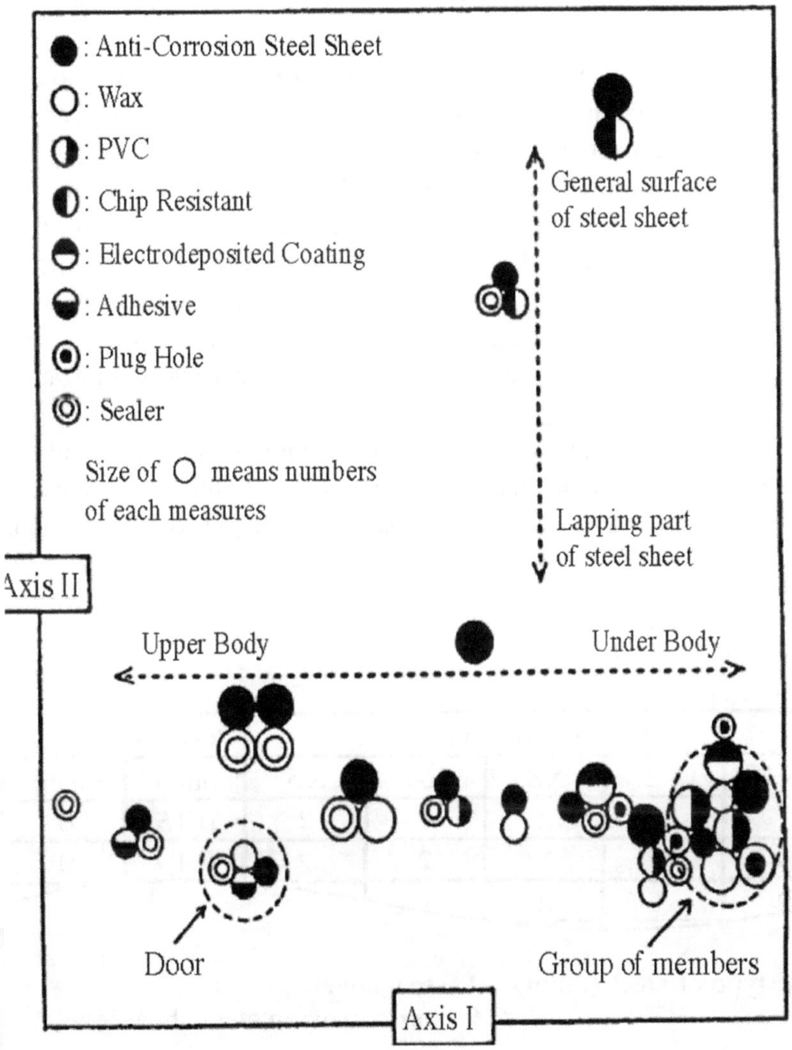

2. Factorial analysis methods for an optimal anti-rusting of vehicle bodies

This subsection takes up the door hemming sections to which application of anti-rusting technique meets particular difficulties based on QA network. Spraying of snow melting salts during winter to prevent the roads from freezing allows the filtration of salt water, a corrosive factor, to the hemmed joint portions of door outer-panels and inner-panels of rust prevention steel sheet. To prevent this, wax and/or sealer are adopted or the joint portions of the door outer-panels and inner-panels are sealed with adhesive agent for the dual purpose of adhesion and anti-rusting.

To evaluate the performance of various anti-rusting measures, we conduct a market monitor test using actual vehicles, in-house accelerated corrosion test, and the accelerated corrosion test on the bench using testpieces and/or parts. For any of these tests, it is imperative to conduct analysis of sources of variation for the optimization of anti-rusting of vihicle body.

An example indicated in Table 4 outlines the test data showing the result of analysis on the relationship between the (combined) rust prevention specifications of a testpiece and the depth of corrosion. A dendrogram can be generated as shown in Figure 6 by subjecting the above data to a cluster analysis. This dendrogram is used to hierarchically outline the degree of effect from the factors of anti-rusting measures by grouping the experiment numbers of a corrosion test.

Moreover, analysis using quantification method type I enables us to verify quantitative degree of effect from the factors of anti-rusting measures by category-scores and the size of partial correlation coefficient, as shown in Figure 7. From this diagram, it is possible to grasp the effect of anti-rusting steel sheets used to the door hemming sections and the validity of quantitative effect of local anti-rusting processing A, B, and C from the engineering point of view, which in concurrent application with the analytical results of other testing methods using actual vehicles enables the optimization of the vehicle body rust prevention.

The author has applied comprehensive and technical insight into these results of analyses. And by adopting controllable factors effective for anti-rusting measures in addition to the environmental factors in consideration of market environments, the author has been able to verify deftly the factorial effects

Table 4. Experiment data of test piece

Factor and Level					Corrosion depth	
X1	X2	X3	X4	X5	outer*	inner
1	1	2	2	2	0.15	0
1	1	1	2	2	0.10	0
2	1	2	1			

X1: type of steel (outer) 1: steel sheet
2: anti corrosion steel sheet level 1

X2: type of steel (inner) 1: anti corrosion steel sheet level 1
2: anti corrosion steel sheet level 2

X3: spot anti-corrosion steel process A (1: no 2: yes)

X4: spot anti-corrosion steel process B (1: no 2: yes)

X5: spot anti-corrosion steel process C (1: no 2: yes)

*: 21 combinations

Figure 6. Cluster Analysis

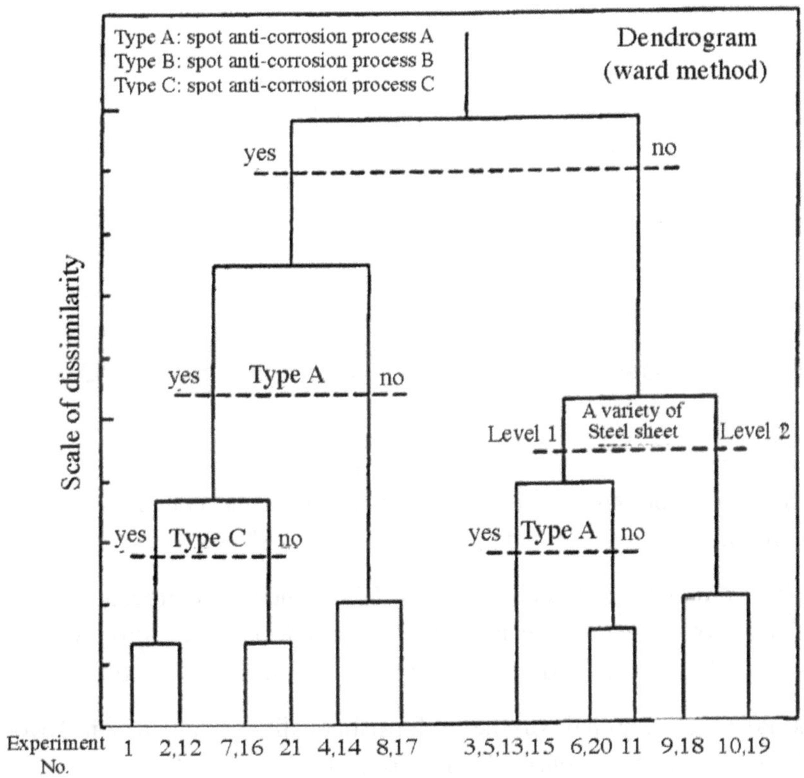

Figure 7. Influence of anchi-corrosion measures by Quantification Method (type I)

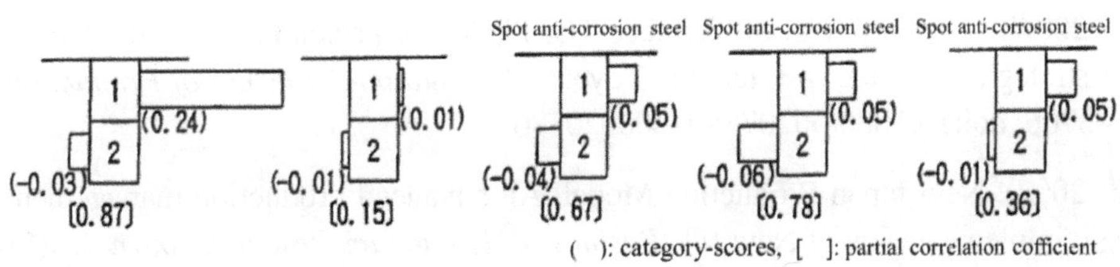

with the application of the design of experiment. The author has thus succeeded in the embodiment of production with good QCDS performance through the optimization of the vehicle body rust prevention.

CONCLUSION

The author focused on quality assurance activities that are integrated across different departments (from design through production) and extended to suppliers as well. The author has created the TQA-NM (Total Quality Assurance Networking Model) for new defect occurrence, and its validity was verified through application at the advanced assembly maker Toyota and its suppliers.

ACKNOWLEDGMENT

The author would like to acknowledge the generous support of the following researchers: All these at Toyota Motor Corporation, many suppliers, and Amasaka New JIT Laboratory at Aoyama Gakuin University that assisted with author's research, especially, Igarashi, M., Miyamoto, M., Kurumiya, N., Shirasawa, H. (Toyota Mortor Corporation), Misawa, N. (Aishin Chemical Co., Ltd.), Ootaki, M. (NOK Corporation), Kojima, T. (Aoyama Gakuin University), and others.

REFERENCES

Amasaka, K. (1996). Application of classification and related methods to SQC renaissance in Toyota Motor. *Data Science, Classification and Related Methods,* 684-695.

Amasaka, K. (1999). A study on "science SQC" by utilizing "management SQC" – A demonstrative study on a new SQC concept and procedure in the manufacturing industry. *International Journal of Production Economics, 60-61*, 591–598. doi:10.1016/S0925-5273(98)00143-1

Amasaka, K. (2000a). A demonstrative study of a new SQC concept and procedure in the Manufacturing Industry-Establishment of a New Technical Method for conducting Scientific SQC. *An International Journal of Mathematical & Computer Modeling, 31*(10-12), 1–10. doi:10.1016/S0895-7177(00)00067-4

Amasaka, K. (2000b). Partnering chains as the platform for quality management in Toyota. *The 1st World Conference on Production and Operations Management,* 1-13.

Amasaka, K. (2004a). *Science SQC, New Quality Control Principle: The quality strategy of Toyota.* Springer-Verlag. doi:10.1007/978-4-431-53969-8

Amasaka, K. (2004b). Development of "Science TQM", A new principle of quality management: Effectiveness of strategic stratified task team at Toyota-. *International Journal of Production Research, 42*(17), 3691–3706. doi:10.1080/0020754042000203867

Amasaka, K. (2007). New Japan Production Model, An advanced production management principle: Key to strategic implementation of New JIT. *Business & Economics Research Journal, 6*(7), 67–79.

Amasaka, K. (Ed.). (2007). New Japan model - Science TQM: Theory and practice for strategic quality management. Study group of the ideal situation: the quality management of the manufacturing industry, Maruzen, Tokyo.

Amasaka, K. (2015). New JIT, new management technology principle. Taylor and Francis Group.

Amasaka, K. (2017a). Strategic Stratified Task Team Model for realizing simultaneous QCD fulfillment: Two case studies. *The Journal of Japanese Operations Management and Strargy, 7*(1), 14–36.

Amasaka, K. (2017b). *Toyota: Production system, safety analysis and future directions.* Nova Science Publishers.

Amasaka, K. (2022). New Manufacturing Theory, Surpassing JIT (2nd ed.). Lambert Academic Publishing.

Amasaka, K., Igarashi, M., Yamamura, N., Fukuda, S. & Nomasa, H. (1995). The QA Network activity for prevent rusting of vehicle by using SQC. *Journal of the Japanese Society for Quality Control*, 35-38.

Amasaka, K., Kurosu, S., & Michiya, M. (2008). *New Theory of Manufacturing - Surpassing JIT: Evolution of Just-in-Time*. Morikita-Shuppan.

Amasaka, K., & Ootaki, M. (1999). Development of New TQM by Partnering – Effectiveness of "TQM-SP" by collaborating Total Task Management Team activities. *Journal of the Society for Production Management,* 69-74.

Amasaka, K., & Osaki, S. (1999). The promotion of new statistical quality control internal education in Toyota Motor - A proposal of "Science SQC" for improving the principle of TQM. *The European Journal of Engineering Education, Research and Education in Reliability, Maintenance, Quality Control Risk and Safety*, *24*(3), 259–276.

Amasaka, K., Shirasawa, H., & Misawa, N. (1997). The Development of Total QA Network by utilizing Management SQC - Example of Brake Pad's Quality Assurance Activity (Part 2). *The Japanese Society for Quality Control, The 55th Annual Technical Conference*, 17-20.

Kojima, T., & Amasaka, K. (2011). The Total Quality Assurance Networking Model For preventing defects: Building an effective quality assurance system using a Total QA Network. *International Journal of Management & Information Sytems*, *15*(3), 1–10. doi:10.19030/ijmis.v15i3.4637

Kurumiya, N., & Miyamoto, M. (1991). Solutions for shrinkage cavities in low-pressure die-casting process – Establishment of optimum casting conditions. *Union of Japanese Scientists and Engineers Quality Control*, *42*(5), 394–399.

Ministry of Economy. (2009b). *Trade and Industry, Recovery of trust in manufacturing, Manufacturing base paper.* Author.

Ministry of Land. (2009a). *Infrastructure, transport and tourism, Recall trouble information on car.* https://www.mlit.go.jp/jidosha/carinf/rcl/index.html

Miyamoto, M., & Ishimoto, Y. (1991). Establishment of optimum casting condition for compact DOHC cylinder head. *Union of Japanese Scientists and Engineers Quality Control*, *42*(5), 183–189.

Takahashi, A. (1997). *The Quality Month Textbook-Meaning of TQM at Toyota*. Union of Japanese Scientists and Engineers.

Takahashi, H., Tsukeshiba, Y., Soeda, S., Hosono, H., Kosugi, T., & Kaji, Y. (1997). A study for optimum prevention rusting of vehicle (Part 2). *The Japanese Society for Quality Control, The 57th Aannual Technical Conference,* 45-69.

Yamaji, M., & Amasaka, K. (2008). New Japan Quality Management Model: Implementation of New JIT for Strategic Management Technology. *International Business & Economic Research Journal*, *7*(3), 107–114.

Chapter 10
Partnering Performance Measurement Model for Automobile Assembly Makers and Suppliers

ABSTRACT

In the midst of the rapid advancement of globalization–worldwide quality competition, Japanese manufacturers are struggling to realize the simultaneous achievement of QCD (quality, cost, and delivery), reduction in product development periods, assurance of high quality, and production at low cost. It can be said that they are truly facing an era of new manufacturing in the process of simultaneous achievement of QCD. In recent years, the management issue in the Japanese automobile industry playing a key role in Japanese manufacturing is worldwide uniform quality and simultaneous production launch, in response to current globalization. To realize this, it is vital to reinforce Japanese-style partnering, or Japan Supply Chain Management, between automobile manufacturers and parts suppliers. Against this background, this chapter creates and verifies the effectiveness of Partnering Performance Measurement Model (PPMM) for automobile assembly makers and suppliers.

INTRODUCTION

In the midst of the rapid advancement of "globalization–worldwide quality competition", Japanese manufacturers are struggling to realize the "simultaneous achievement of QCD (quality, cost and delivery)", "reduction in product development periods", "assurance of high quality" and "production at low cost". It can be said that they are truly facing an era of new manufacturing in the process of "simultaneous achievement of QCD" (Amasaka, 2008a, 2009a,b; Amasaka, Ed., 2007; Amasaka and Sakai, 2010).

For a total assembly industry like auto manufacturing, not only is quality management for parts and units essential, but optimizing manufacturer assembly technology, as well as assuring consistent quality from manufacturing through to sales and service, is a must. If a vehicle manufacturer or supplier wants

DOI: 10.4018/978-1-7998-8746-1.ch010

to improve the reliability of products manufactured in-house, quality management is crucial to jointly improving the reliability of both members' business processes. It is safe to say that cooperative activities using Strategic Stratified Task Team (SSTTN) requiring the ability to solve problems will remain important in the future (Amasaka, 2004a) (Refer to Chapter 8) .

In this corporate management environment, the "key to success in global production" is the reinforcement of product power, or "simultaneous achievement of QCD" (Amasaka, 2008a). To realize this, it is vital to reinforce Japanese-style partnering, or Supply Chain Management (SCM) between automobile manufacturers and parts suppliers (Amasaka, 2008a, 2009a). This is also called the Japan Supply System (JSS) (Amasaka, 2000). Against this background, in this section, the author has created the Partnering Performance Measurement Model (PPMM) for assembly makers and suppliers and verifies its effectiveness as the application study of driving force in NMT (New Manufacturing Theory) strategy (Sakatoku, 2006: Yamaji, et al., 2008; Amasaka, 2008b, 2013, 2019). The purpose of PPMM is to formulate the actual status of "Japanese partnering" between automobile manufacturers and parts suppliers for clearer evaluation and diagnosis.

This PPMM has been somewhat implicitly carried out in the past, and it is viewed as the basis for deploying "Global SCM", and applying "Constructing measures of CS effectiveness at manufactures" and others (Ebioka et al., 2007; Yamaji and Amasaka, 2007; Amasaka, 2009a,b,c; Ishikawa et al., 2011; Nakamura et al., 2011; Uchida et al., 2012; Ishiguro and Amasaka, 2012; Okihara et al., 2014).

SIGNIFICANCE OF STRENGTHENING THE CORPORATE MANAGEMENT OF JAPANESE AUTOMOBILE ASSEMBLY MAKERS AND SUPPLIERS

In recent years, the management issue in the Japanese automobile industry playing a key role in Japanese manufacturing is "worldwide uniform quality, simultaneous production launch" in response to current globalization (Amasaka, 2004a, 2007a). In this corporate management environment, the "key to success in global production" is the reinforcement of product power, or the "simultaneous achievement of QCD" (Amasaka, 2008, 2009a). To realize this, it is vital to reinforce Japanese-style partnering, or "partnering of competition and collaboration - Japan Supply Chain Management" between automobile manufacturers (hereafter termed "assembly makers") and affiliated or non-affiliated parts manufacturers (hereafter termed "suppliers") (Amasaka, 2008a, 2009a). This is also called the Japan Supply System (JSS) as shown in Figure 3, Chapter 8 (Refer to Chapter 8 in detail).

For further advancement in this area, assembly makers should not only reinforce internal partnering with their own operational departments (such as engineering, production, and sales), but must also strengthen "external partnering". This means establishing cooperative relationships with other companies while advancing and establishing "global partnering" through strategic collaboration with both foreign and domestic Suppliers. To implement such reinforcements, it is fundamental that a new "Partnering Performance Measurement" be deployed. This measurement should serve as a formulation model (radar chart for visualization) for evaluating the actual status of "Japanese Partnering" between assembly makers and parts suppliers, which has been somewhat implicitly carried out in the past.

PARTNERING PERFORMANCE MEASUREMENT MODE FOR AUTOMOBILE ASSEMBLY MAKERS AND SUPPLIERS

The author creates the Partnering Performance Measurement Model (PPMM) for automobile assembly makers and suppliers, which evaluates employment and justification of Japan Supply System (JSS) for developing global SCM and approach as the application study of driving force in NMT strategy below (Ishizuka, 2005; Sakatoku, 2006; Yamaji, et al., 2008; Amasaka, 2008b, 2009a, 2013, 2019).

According to a survey conducted by the author, assembly makers in general assessed that they are "performing SCM with their suppliers well overall". On the other hand, suppliers' answers indicate that they are "not necessarily conducting SCM the way they would like to with some of their assembly makers", revealing a difference in evaluation, or so-called "disparity (deviation or gap) in evaluator awareness".

These SCM evaluations are often based on the evaluators' own implicit empirical knowledge, and (as far as the author know) evaluation scales are not usually shared (formulated as a model) between them. The author therefore attempts to "formulate evaluation causes and effects" that account for the difference in implicit evaluations on both sides - the so-called "gap in awareness".

The author then has attempted to carry out "diagnosis through visualization methods" by utilizing "Science SQC, New Quality Control Principle" (Amasaka, 2004b, 2009a). Under such a circumstance, there are many studies abroad for globalization (Gabor, 1990; Lagrosen, 2004; Ljungström, 2005; Manzoni and Islam, 2007) and SCM (Joiner, 1994; Taylor and Brunt, 2001; Pires and Cardoza, 2007). According to the author's investigation, a quality management survey (JUSE, 2006) is being jointly conducted by Nihon Keizai Shinbun and the Union of Japanese Scientists and Engineers.

It targets 528 corporations, mainly manufacturers, and does not cover the topic of partnering with Suppliers. The OEM-Supplier Working Relations Index (WRI) (Milo Media, 2006) defines the relationship between automobile manufacturers and their suppliers using index numbers, but specific evaluation items are not indicated. In connection with the PPMM creation, the author develops (1) PPMM-A, Partnering Performance Measurement Model for assembly makers, and (2) PPMM-S, Partnering Performance Measurement Model for suppliers.

The author also integrates the two and develops (3) PPMM-AS, Partnering Performance Measurement Model for assembly makers and suppliers, as a comprehensive Dual Performance Measurement to be shared by both.

Preparation of Evaluation Sheets for PPMM-A, PPMM-S, and PPMM-AS

The author extracted "evaluations of cause and effect elements" necessary for the preparation of the three types of evaluation sheets (PPMM-A, PPMM-S, and PPMM-AS), based on the response of staff members engaged in practical affairs at SCM-related departments (both assembly makers and suppliers). More specifically, evaluators from related departments on both sides were given a survey. The questions (evaluation sheet) are shown in Table 1.

The survey comprised of a total of 19 evaluation factors (Factor X_1 to X_{19}, with evaluation contents) extracted from an affinity diagram. The diagram was made based on meetings with assembly makers and suppliers.

1. Evaluators of assembly makers:
   Toyota Motor Corporation (Sales div. 1, Production Preparation div. 2, TQM Promotion div. 1), Hino Motors Ltd. (Procurement div. 1, TQM Promotion div. 1), Fuji Heavy Industries Ltd. (TQM Promotion div. 1, Procurement div. 2), Honda Motors Co., Ltd. (Quality Assurance div. 1), Nissan Motor Co., Ltd. (Procurement div. 1), GM (Procurement div. 1), Ford (TQM Promotion div. 1)
2. Evaluators of suppliers:
   Jatco (Quality Assurance div. 2), JFE (Quality Assurance div. 2, Procurement div. 1), NHK Spring Co., Ltd. (Quality Control div. 1, SQC Promotion div. 1)

Table 1. Evaluation Sheet

Factor	Contents	Factor	Contents
X_1	Corporate strategy	X_{11}	Price setting considering labor
X_2	Bias in selection of Suppliers	X_{12}	Parts inspection standards
X_3	Selection of affiliated Supplier	X_{13}	Parts inspection items
X_4	Weakening of group affiliation	X_{14}	Response to recalls
X_5	Weight of Suppliers' opinion	X_{15}	Response to contractual failure
X_6	Spirit of cooperation	X_{16}	Ability to improve
X_7	Appropriate evaluation	X_{17}	Technical capabilities
X_8	Considerate relation	X_{18}	Total satisfaction rate
X_9	Demand on discounting	X_{19}	Gained technology and know-how
X_{10}	Methods of price setting		

Formulation model of PPMM-A, PPMM-S and PPMM-AS

Using this evaluation sheet, the author attempted to derivate a formulation model that incorporated multivariable statistical analysis. First, "cause and effect relationships" were extracted by conducting cluster analysis (Ward method and Euclidean distance squared) and principal component analysis.

Next, using categorical canonical correlation analysis, formulation models for PPMM-A, PPMM-S and PPMM-AS were derived, while coefficients of each group's factors were calculated and a radar chart was designed for each group. One hundred (100) was set as the highest score.

1. Derivation of PPMM-A

PPMM-A for assembly makers was derived, with the results of cluster analysis and principal component analysis shown in Figure 1 and 2. Based on these results, evaluation factors could be categorized into five elements: "Supplier follow-up", "Degree of quality inspection", "Corporate capability", "Supplier decisions", and "Price setting".

Consideration was then given to PPMM-A, PPMM-S, and PPMM-AS so that formulation models could be derived. With that in mind, categorical canonical correlation analysis was conducted, employing optimum scaling methods in an effort to grasp the relationship between the five evaluation elements and seventeen evaluation factors.

Figure 1. Grouping by Cluster Analysis

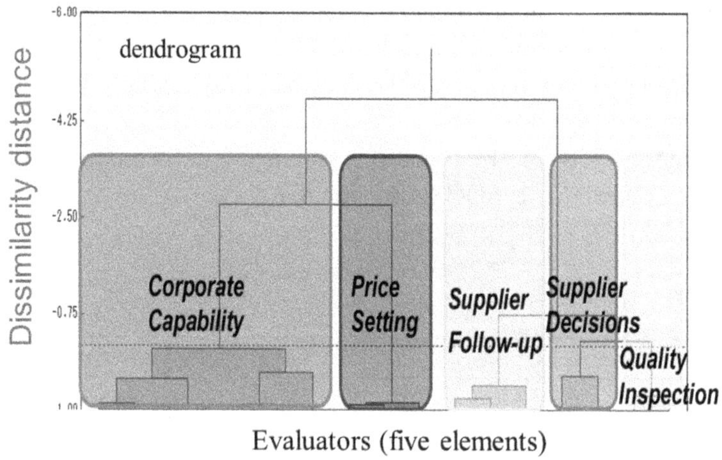

Figure 2. Grouping by Principle Component Analysis

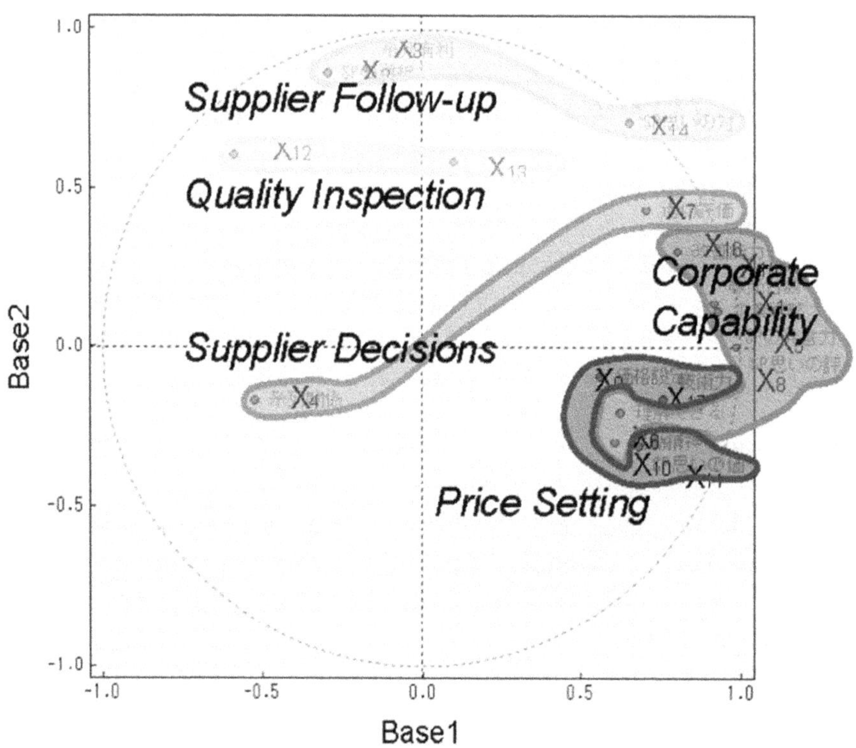

A calculation was conducted for PPMM-A using evaluation element axes (a) through (e). The weighted coefficients shown here were calculated based on component loading values for each of the five evaluation elements, resulting in a full score of 100 points.

a. Supplier follow-up = $5.24X_4 + 8.86X_7$
b. Degree of quality inspection = $2.28X_{12} + 12.01X_{13}$
c. Corporate capability=$1.91X_1 + 2.44X_{16} + 1.85X_6 + 2.46X_{17} + 1.89X_5 + 1.81X_8 + 1.91X_{15}$
d. Supplier decisions = $5.39X_2 + 7.23X_3 + 1.67X_{14}$
e. Price setting = $6.80X_9 + 5.84X_{10} + 1.64X_{11}$

Using the above equations, evaluation points for each of the five evaluation elements were calculated and visualized in a radar chart, as seen in Figure 3.

Figure 3. PPMM-A radar chart

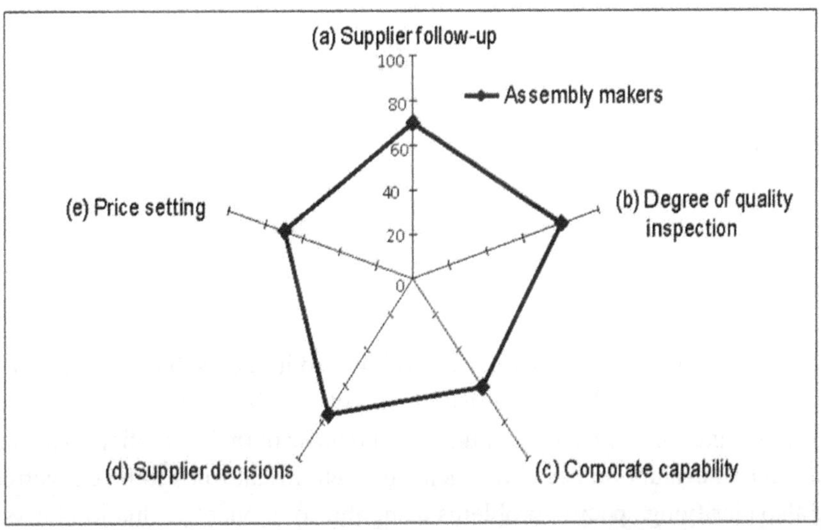

2. Derivation of PPMM-S

Derivation was conducted in a similar way for Suppliers' PPMM-S. As a result, the relationship between the five evaluation elements [(f) Assembly maker follow-up, (g) Degree of quality inspection, (h) Corporate capability, (i) Spirit of cooperation, (j) Price setting and the seventeen evaluation factors was grasped. Calculation was conducted for PPMM-S using the five evaluation element axes (f) through (j).

f. Assembly maker follow-up = 5.83X1 + 5.59X4 + 2.75X14 + 0.12X15
g. Degree of quality inspection = 1.54X12 + 12.75X13
h. Corporate capability = 5.23X2 + 2.27X3 + 1.34X7 + 0.63X16 + 4.81X17
i. Spirit of cooperation = 6.46X5 + 3.26X6 + 4.56X8
j. Price setting = 4.17X9 + 5.41X10 + 4.70X11

Using the above equations, evaluation points for each of the five evaluation elements were similarly calculated and visualized by a radar chart, as shown in Figure 4.

Figure 4. PPMM-S radar chart

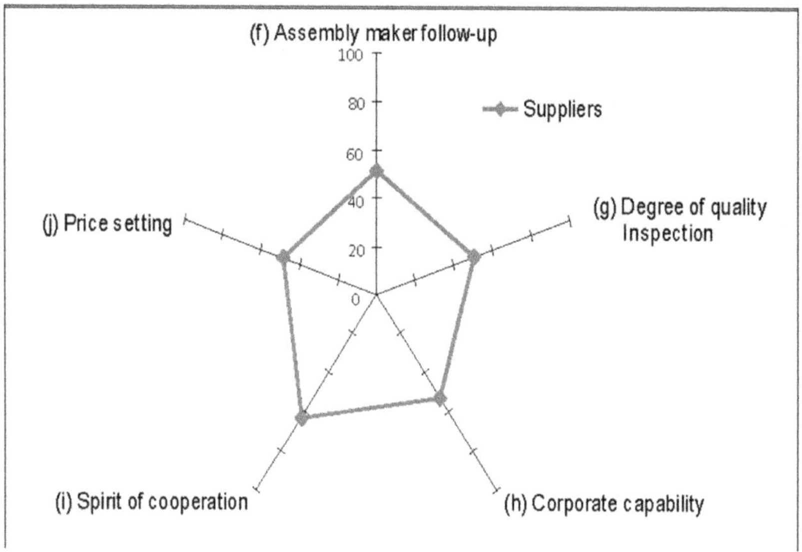

3. Derivation of PPMM-AS

The PPMM-AS was derived in order to visualize the gap in the evaluations of both sides. This was done by closely comparing the evaluation measurements of PPMM-A and PPMM-S. Corporations using PPMM-AS can see the gap between their evaluations and those of their Suppliers at a glance. This allows conventional subjective evaluation based on each side's empirical rules to be converted into objective analysis, while also clarifying specific problems using the component evaluation factors.

One of the features of the PPMM-AS formulation model is the overlapping of the five evaluation element axes of PPMM-A and PPMM-S. This is due to the fact that both PPMM-A and PPMM-S thus far consist of five evaluation elements and seventeen evaluation factors.

The three axes of Degree of quality inspection, Corporate capability and Price setting are common to both, allowing these elements to be overlapped for direct comparison. In addition, the two new axes, Assembly manufacturer follow-up and Supplier follow-up are integrated to create a new axis of Spirit of mutual support. Similarly, Spirit of cooperation and Supplier decisions are integrated to establish a new axis of Relationship with business partners.

As a result, these evaluation elements, made up of (k) Spirit of mutual support, (l) Degree of quality inspection, (m) Corporate capability, (n) Relationship with business partners and (o) Price setting are visualized in a radar chart as shown in Figure 5. The figure presents example evaluations of assembly makers and suppliers.

Figure 5. PPMM-AS radar chart

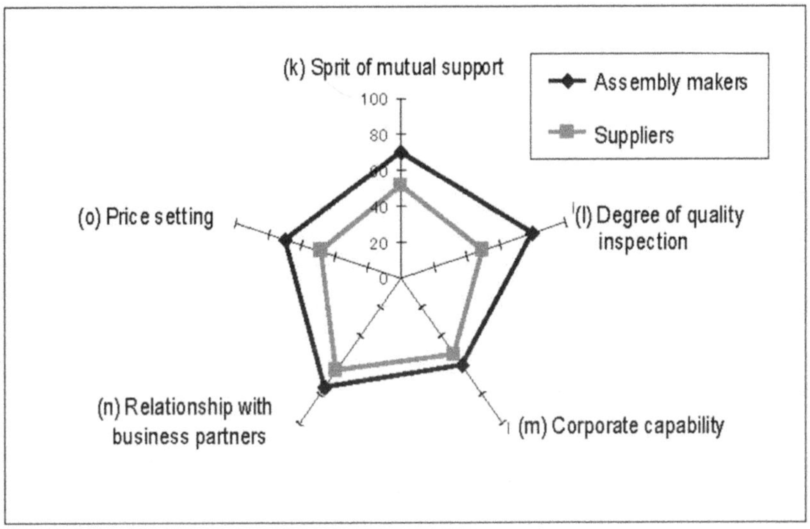

Verification of PPMM-AS

The author applied the created PPMM-AS to three Japanese assembly makers (Toyota Motor Corporation and Nissan Motor Co., Ltd.), one overseas Assembly Manufacturer (General Motors), and two Suppliers (Jatco and NHK Springs Co., Ltd.). Its effectiveness was thereby verified. As pointed out in subsection 10.3.1, it can be generally confirmed that assembly makers' evaluations are higher than those from suppliers. The suppliers' evaluations are more severe than the Assembly Manufacturer evaluations assume.

The following subsections provide examples of PPMM-AS evaluations at various corporations.

1. Toyota Motor Corporation

The survey results used for verification are shown in Table 2 (Toyota Motor Corporation), Table 3 (NHK Springs Co. Ltd. (hereafter, NHK)) and Figure 6 (Toyota and NHK) based on the evaluation sheet in Table 1. The evaluation example of Toyota Motor Corporation and NHK Springs Co., Ltd. is further described in Figure 7. As the figure indicates, evaluations on both sides are generally high. There are no large differences between elements, but a slight gap can be observed in Spirit of mutual support and Price setting.

The following subsections provide an interpretation of the obtained evaluation results. NHK's low evaluation in Price Setting and Spirit of Mutual Support stems from thorough cost price reduction carried out by Toyota, based on the company's Customer First principle. However, there is almost no gap is in the Relationship with Business Partners category. NHK evaluates Toyota's attitude towards problem-solving and QCD improvement highly, and these activities are carried out with mutual support.

Therefore, NHK names Toyota as the corporation they would most like to do business with.

Figure 6. Questionnaire result of Toyota and NHK

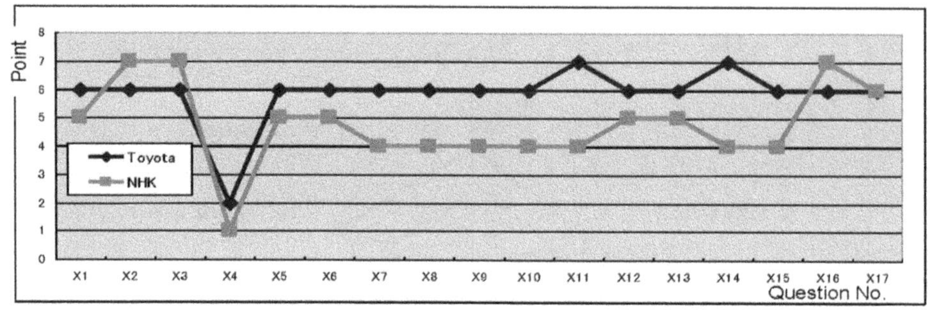

Figure 7. Radar chart of Toyota and NHK

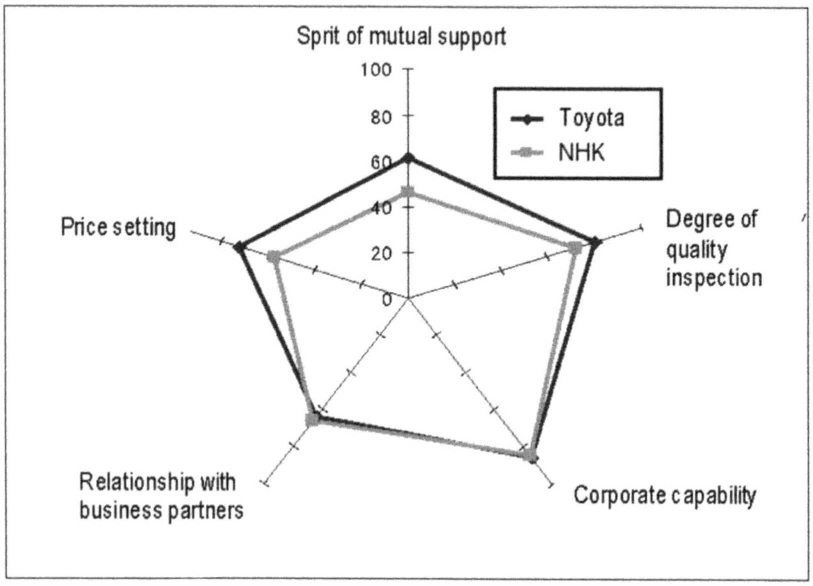

Nissan Motor Co., Ltd.

The evaluation example of Nissan and Jatco is shown in Figure 8. One outstanding feature is a generally lower evaluation than in the case of Toyota above. Gaps can be observed in both Price Setting and Corporate Capability. These results can be interpreted as showing partnering activity that is not necessarily based on mutual trust, thus generating gaps in Price Setting and Corporate Capability.

General Motors, Fuji Heavy Industries and Honda Motors

Figure 9 shows the examples of Genral Mortors (GM) and Jatco. Characteristic of these results is a large gap in the relationship between Price Setting and Relationship with Business Partners. This is because Jatco cannot fully respond to GM's severe, one-sided demands regarding QCD. This leads to a gap in awareness regarding good business partnerships based on mutual trust.

Table 2. Evaluation Sheet of Toyota

	Excellent	Very Good	Good	Fair	Poor	Bad	Very Bad
Corporate strategy	7	**6**	5	4	3	2	1
Bias in selection of Suppliers	7	**6**	5	4	3	2	1
Selection of affiliated Supplier	7	**6**	5	4	3	2	1
Weakening of group affiliation	7	6	5	4	3	**2**	1
Weight of Suppliers' opinion	7	**6**	5	4	3	2	1
Spirit of cooperation	7	**6**	5	4	3	2	1
Appropriate evaluation	7	**6**	5	4	3	2	1
Considerate relation	7	**6**	5	4	3	2	1

Table 3. Evaluation Sheet of NHK

	Excellent	Very Good	Good	Fair	Poor	Bad	Very Bad
Corporate strategy	7	6	**5**	4	3	2	1
Bias in selection of Suppliers	**7**	6	5	4	3	2	1
Selection of affiliated Supplier	**7**	6	5	4	3	2	1
Weakening of group affiliation	7	6	5	4	3	2	**1**
Weight of Suppliers' opinion	7	6	**5**	4	3	2	1
Spirit of cooperation	7	6	**5**	4	3	2	1
Appropriate evaluation	7	6	5	**4**	3	2	1

Similarly, evaluation was implemented in Fuji Heavy Industries Ltd. and Honda Motors Co., Ltd., and the expected results were obtained with regard to its effectiveness (Sakatoku, 2006).

APPLICATIONS UTILIZING PPMM

Constructing Measures of CS Effectiveness at Manufacturers

In recent years, consumers have been placing more importance on subjective quality factors such as the feel or design of a product. This has made it more important for automobile product planning and design departments and sales marketing, which form the core of product manufacturing at corporations, to work towards achieving subjective quality (Amasaka, 2002, 2007b, 2009c).

Figure 8. Radar chart of Nissan and Jatc

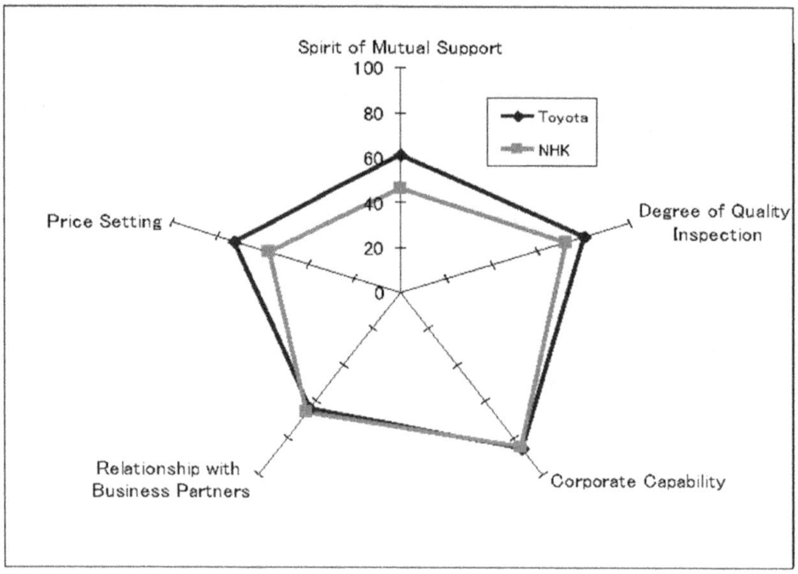

Figure 9 Radar chart of GM and Jatco

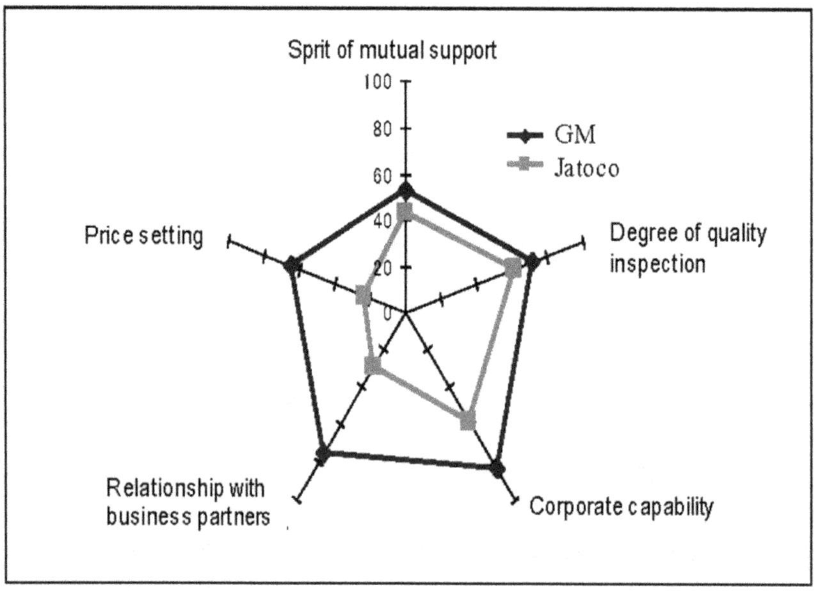

This subsection defines the "Customer Satisfaction (CS) effectiveness" as the ability of manufacturers' product planning and design departments to utilize customer information and effectively communicate (Ishikawa et al., 2011). The researchers developed Measures of CS Effectiveness to quantitatively evaluating the level of CS effectiveness in each department, enabling companies to immediately identify any gaps between their approaches to subjective quality.

The researchers thus offer a way to quantitatively assess the planning and design departments' approaches to subjective quality and pinpoint problem areas at a corporate or departmental level.

1. Background

Today, new product planning tends to be based on new product concept ideas, and fails to take customer needs into account. According to interviews with members of the design department at a certain domestic automaker, the development of new designs continues to be based only on the designers' rules of thumb (Ishizuka, 2006; Anabuki et al., 2011). The experiential rules of expert designers are an important factor in generating fresh, innovative ideas, but a design process based exclusively on this method poses high risks for companies in terms of cost and marketability.

Customers typically judge current products in terms of whether they are good or bad, but they rarely have a clear image of the kind of things they might want in the future. Offering the products customers want even before they want them will be particularly important in developing and manufacturing future products. In order to do this, it is essential that companies clearly grasp the vague, subjective notions of their customers.

Expressing the images formed through customers' words (implicit knowledge) as a shared language (linguistic knowledge) and appropriately translating (turning into explicit knowledge) technical words (e.g. design drawings) using a correlation technique—in other words, changing the subjective into the objective—will be an important part of future product development. At the same time, it is important to use a correlation technique to change the objective data back into subjective information in order to use the diagrammed data to create physical objects that customers want.

2. Identifying key factors in improving subjective quality

Product planning and design departments were surveyed in order to identify what components to evaluate in judging CS effectiveness. The survey consisted of a single free response question that asked participants what they thought were the key factors in boosting customer satisfaction. They were asked to give their answers from two perspectives: utilization of customer information and communication between product planning and design departments (Kuniyoshi, 2006; Kaneta, 2006: Sakatoku, 2006; Amasaka, 2009c).

Interviews were conducted at six manufacturers. Three were given in person during company visits, and three were done via email. The collected data was organized, eliminating duplicate responses, and used to construct an affinity diagram. This yielded eight groups of key factors that product planning and design department members felt were important in terms of utilizing customer information and communication: business process, information gathering, information analysis, reliability and trust, transmitting information, sharing/centralizing information, infrastructure, and collaborative tasks between departments. Twenty specific factors were then identified in the eight groups. A summary of these key components can be found in Figure 10.

Figure 10. Extraction of important factor

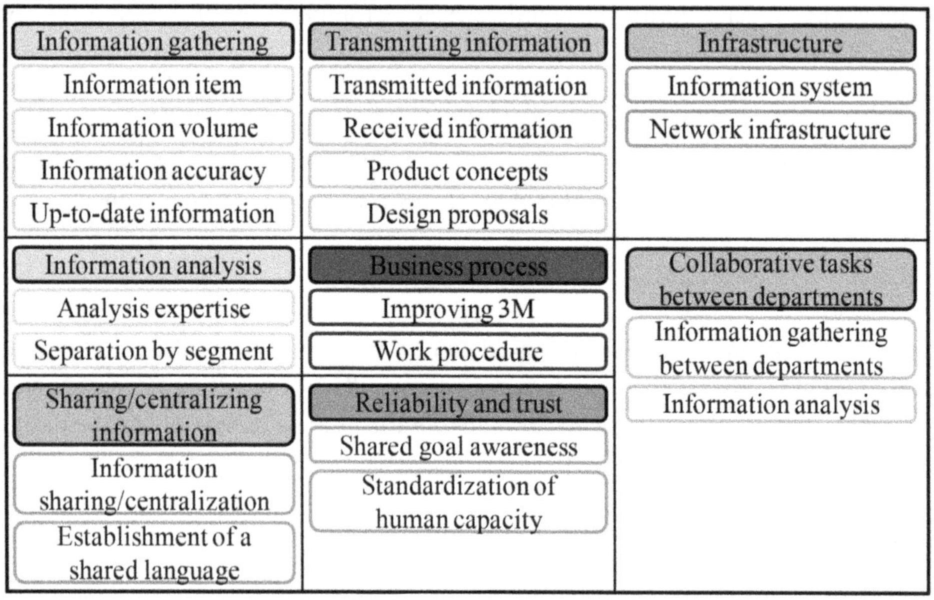

3. Core component of subjective quality improvement
    a. Groups of factors that boost CS effectiveness

In order to determine which customer information utilization and communication factors product planning and design departments consider to be most important in boosting customer satisfaction, it is necessary to weight each of the items for each department.

To do this, staff working in departments in charge of product planning and design at manufacturing companies were given a survey where they were asked to rate each factor on a seven-point scale in terms of importance. Specifically, they were asked how important each of 20 evaluation items were in response to the question "Do you think that X is important in increasing subjective product quality?"

The resulting data was then separated into two categories, depending on which department it was collected from (product planning or design). This was done in order to find out which factors were considered important in terms of improving subjective product quality in each department—in other words, to identify the keys to boosting CS effectiveness in both divisions. Here, we'll look for the factors that design departments considered important in improving subjective quality.

A cluster analysis was conducted on the 23 responses obtained from design department personnel. The purpose of the analysis was to categorize the 20 factors by looking at correlations in their level of importance. The results of this analysis are shown in Figure 11.

The cluster analysis revealed that the 20 factors that design departments considered to be important in boosting CS could be grouped into five categories: awareness/process, information gathering / analysis, business operations, understanding of information, and updated information.

Figure 11. The cluster analysis result of design departments

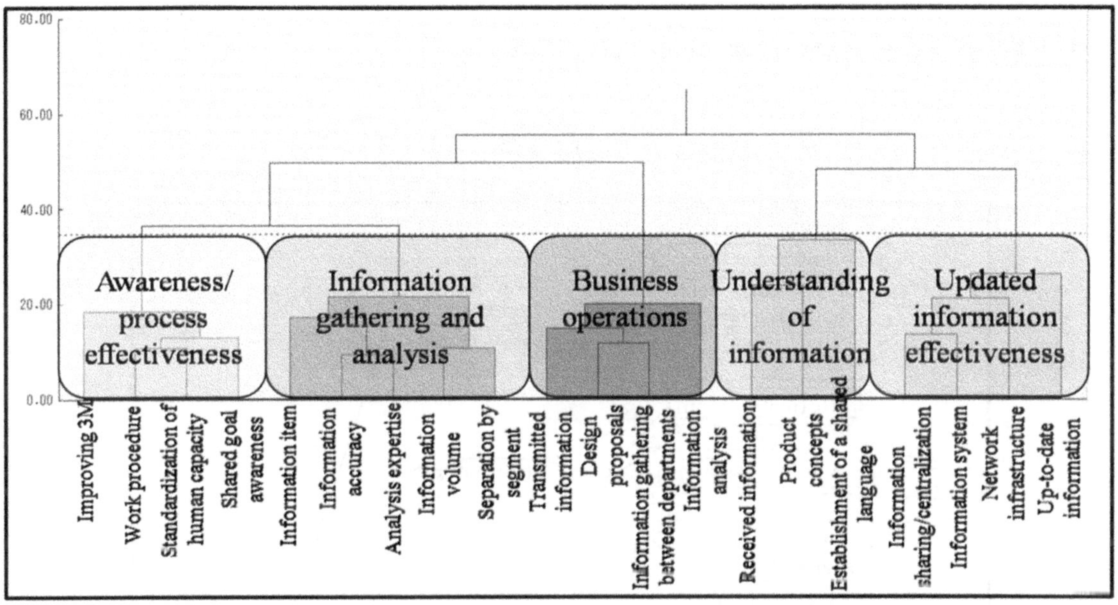

b. Covariance structure analysis

Next, a covariance structure analysis was conducted to ascertain which factors or groups both departments think contribute most to boosting CS effectiveness. Figure 12 shows a model of the covariance structure analysis and extracted results for design departments. This model diagram shows the 20 factors (observed variables), five groups (latent variables), and CS effectiveness (latent variable). The 20 variables are considered a subordinate concept, the five groups an intermediate concept, and CS effectiveness a superordinate concept.

This model is structured around the latent variables G1 through G5. Because each of the factors shows multicollinearity, Measures of CS Effectiveness that allow accurate scoring could not be generated. Adding latent factors G1 through G5 to eliminate multicollinearity in the subordinate concept made it possible to extract the separate influence of the intermediate concept.

The goodness of fit index (GFI) for the covariate structure analysis model was 0.821, and the adjusted goodness of fit index (AGFI) (an index that adjusts for instability in the model) was 0.785. Here, the GFI is greater than or equal to the AGFI—and though this does not present a problem in this case because the difference is not great—a model where the AGFI is significantly lower than the GFI cannot be considered a good model.

First, the influence of the 20 factors that make up the subordinate concept on the five groups that make up the intermediate concept will be examined using the example of the awareness/process effectiveness group. This group is made up of four factors and each has a coefficient of around 0.25—indicating a balanced influence. Higher coefficients indicate stronger influence. The influence of the subordinate concept on the intermediate concept was identified by calculating the coefficients for the other four groups (information gathering and analysis, business operations, understanding of information, and updated information effectiveness).

Next, the influence of the intermediate concept (the five groups) on the superordinate concept (CS effectiveness) was identified. The information gathering and analysis group had a coefficient of 0.58, making it the most descriptive of any of the five groups.

Figure 12. The covariance structure analysis model

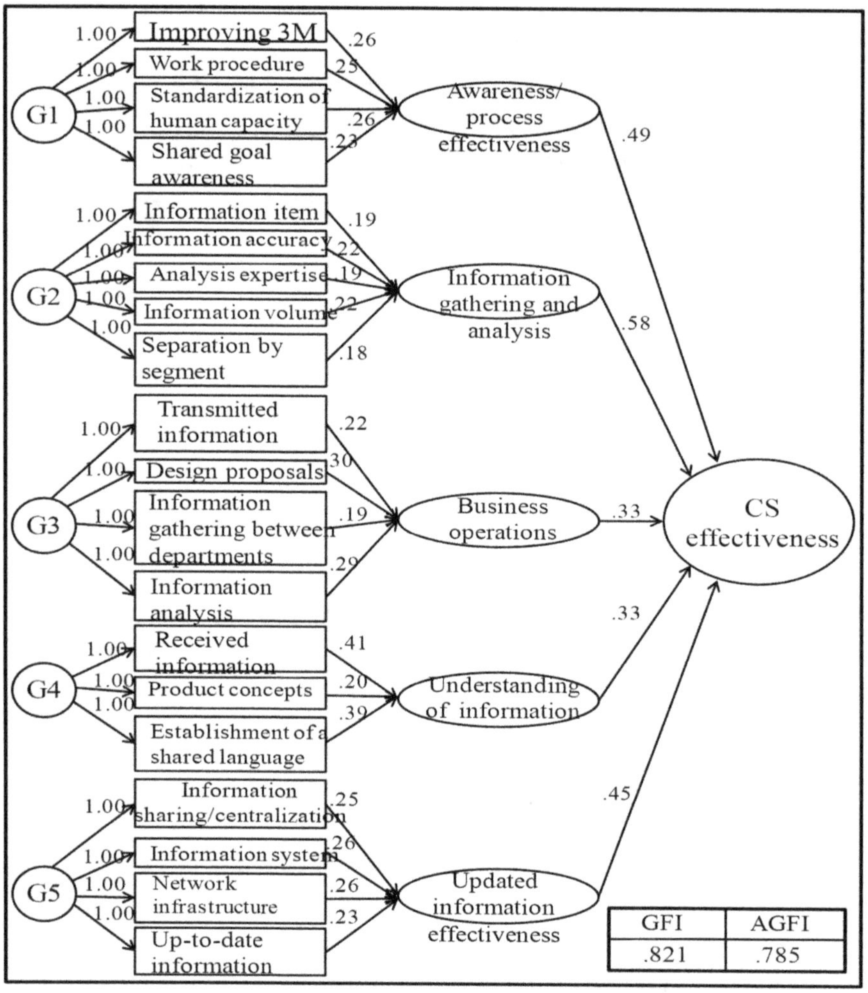

Using this method, the influence of the 20 factors on the five groups, and then the influence of the five groups on CS effectiveness in terms of what design departments felt improved subjective quality were quantitatively identified. In order to identify the keys to evaluating CS effectiveness at product planning departments, a cluster analysis and principle component analysis were conducted in the same way to categorize the factors into groups, which were then weighted using covariance structure analysis according to their degree of influence on CS effectiveness.

4. Creating measures of CS effectiveness to boost subjective quality

Measures of CS Effectiveness were created by combining the evaluation coefficients obtained in the previous chapter with their current level of applicability.

First, Measures of CS Effectiveness were shown in Figure 13 was created for design departments. In order to express CS effectiveness using a 100-point scale, each of the five group coefficients were adjusted by multiplying them all by 6.553. Then, Measures of CS Effectiveness were shown in Figure 14 was created for product planning departments. In order to express CS effectiveness using a 100-point scale, each of the five group coefficients were adjusted by multiplying them all by 6.583. In this way, the researchers were able to arrive at a method of evaluating CS effectiveness based on the opinions of product planning and design departments.

Figure 13. Constructing measures of CS effectiveness of design departments

CS effectiveness = 3.21 × [Awareness/process effectiveness] + 3.80 × [Information gathering and analysis] + 2.16 × [Business operations] + 2.16 × [Understanding of information] + 2.95 × [Updated information effectiveness]
[Awareness/process effectiveness] = 0.26 × (Improving 3M) + 0.25 × (Work procedure) + 0.26 × (Standardization of human capacity) + 0.23 × (Shared goal awareness)
[Information gathering and analysis] = 0.20 × (Information item) + 0.22 × (Information accuracy) + 0.22 × (Information volume) + 0.20 × (Analysis expertise) + 0.18 × (Separation by segment)
[Business operations] = 0.22 × (Transmitted information) + 0.30 × (Design proposal) + 0.19 × (Information gathering between departments) + 0.29 × (Information analysis)
[Understanding of information] = 0.41 × (Received information) + 0.29 × (Product concept) + 0.39 × (Established of a shared language)
[Updated information effectiveness] = 0.22 × (Information sharing/centralization) + 0.30 × (Network infrastructure) + 0.19 × (Information systems) + 0.29 × (Up-to-date information)

5. Verification

The Measures of CS Effectiveness were actually applied at companies in order to measure current levels of CS effectiveness. Three manufacturers participated in the verification process. Participants were asked to rate their current level in terms of a total of 20 evaluation items in response to the question "Is X currently being achieved in order to boost customer satisfaction?"

Figure 14. Constructing measures of CS effectiveness of product planing departments

CS effectiveness = 2.76 × [Awareness/process effectiveness] + 4.02 × [Information gathering and analysis] + 3.15 × [Business operations] + 1.65 × [Understanding of information] + 2.90 × [Updated information effectiveness]
[Awareness/process effectiveness] = 0.27 × (Improving 3M) + 0.23 × (Work procedure) + 0.24 × (Standardization of human capacity) + 0.25 × (Shared goal awareness)
[Information gathering and analysis] = 0.17 × (Information item) + 0.21 × (Information accuracy) + 0.26 × (Information volume) + 0.15 × (Analysis expertise) + 0.20 × (Separation by segment)
[Business operations] = 0.14 × (Transmitted information) + 0.28 × (Product concept) + 0.40 × (Information gathering between departments) + 0.18 × (Information analysis)
[Understanding of information] = 0.25 × (Received information) + 0.38 × (Design proposal) + 0.37 × (Established of a shared language)
[Updated information effectiveness] = 0.27 × (Information sharing/centralization) + 0.16 × (Network infrastructure) + 0.28 × (Information systems) + 0.29 × (Up-to-date information)

Figure 15 shows the results of "Company P" (with three product planning departments and two design departments).First, the average values for the 20 question items were calculated for each division and multiplied by the group coefficients to calculate a total score for each group. Next, each group score was multiplied by the CS effectiveness coefficient to calculate a score for each group. These scores were plotted on a radar chart in order to visualize the gaps between the product planning and design departments at Company P and identify problem areas.

a. Characteristics of Company P:
    i. Understanding of information effectiveness scores were low for both departments
    ii. There is a large gap between product planning and design departments in terms of information gathering and analysis effectiveness

Based on the above issues, it was determined that Company P should institute the following policies. To combat the first issue, Company P should establish a shared language that can also be understood by the product planning department and simplify product concepts. To address the second issue, Company P should require that improvements be made to problem areas in its information-gathering network and clarify the meaning of essential information from the design department.

Figure 15. The measures of CS effectiveness of Company P

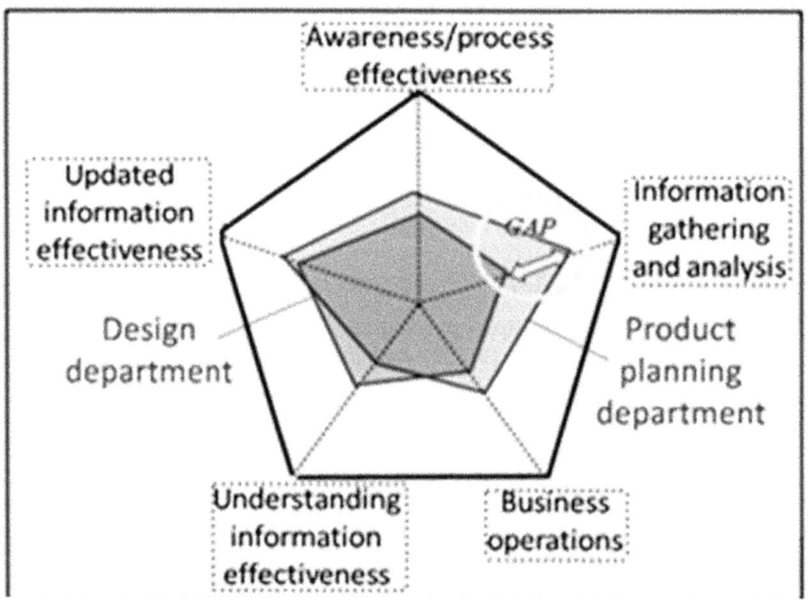

a. Characteristics of Company N:

The Measures of CS effectiveness were also applied at "Company N" (with two product planning departments and two design departments)and Company H (with two product planning departments and three design departments), enabling problem areas and policies to combat these issues to be determined

(. As the results, the development of Measures of CS effectiveness enabled the gaps between product planning departments and design departments to be visualized. By actually applying these measures at three companies, the researchers were able to identify problem areas at each as well as offer policies that companies could use to address them (Ishikawa et al., 2011).

Other Cases

The author was able to apply the PPMM to critical QCD studies of automobile manufacturing developing NMT strategy as follows; (i) Partnering to strengthen Japanese quality management (Ishizuka, 2005), (ii) Partnering Performance Measurement "PPM-AS" to strengthen corporate management (Yamaji et al., 2008), (iii) Patent value Measurement Model (Amasaka, 2009c; Anabuki et al., 2011), (iv) Strategic Quality Management - Performance Measurement Model (Amasaka, 2009a), (v) Success of information sharing between customers and vendors (Nakamuta et al., 2011), (vi) Highly Compelling Direct Mail Method (Ishiguro and Amasaka, 2012), (vii) Working Value Evaluation Model (Uchida et al., 2012), and (viii) A model for selecting improvement actions to gain mutual trust between logistics providers and shippers (Okihara et al., 2014).

CONCLUSION

In Chapter 10, the author has created PPMM for the driving force in the development of NMT strategy. The purpose of PPMM is to formulate (or visualize) the actual status of Japanese partnering between automobile manufacturers and parts suppliers for clearer evaluation and diagnosis. This partnering has been somewhat implicitly carried out in the past, and it is viewed as the basis for deploying "Global SCM" and applying "Constructing measures of CS effectiveness at manufactures" and others. PPMM has allowed visualization of gaps in assembly manufacturer and supplier evaluations of partnering among affiliated companies. The evaluation was implemented in advanced companies, and the expected results were obtained with regard to its effectiveness.

ACKNOWLEDGMENT

The author would like to acknowledge the generous support of the following researchers: All these at many automobile assembly makers and affiliated / nonaffiliated suppliers, and Amasaka New JIT laboratory at Aoyama Gakuin University that assisted with the researches, especially, Mr. Sakatoku, T., Mr. Yamaji, M., Ishizuka, T., Mr. Kaneta, H., Mr. Kuniyoshi, K., Mr. Ishikawa, A., Mr. Morita, Y. and others.

REFERENCES

Amasaka, K. (2000). Partnering chains as the platform for quality management in Toyota. *Proceedings of the 1st World Conference on Production and Operations Management,* 1-13.

Amasaka, K. (2002). *Quality of engineer's work and significance of patent application* (Lecture). The 2nd patent seminar, Aoyama Gakuin University, Sagamihara, Knagawa, Japan.

Amasaka, K. (2004a). Development of "Science TQM", a new principle of quality management: Effectiveness of Strategic Stratified Task Team at Toyota. *International Journal of Production Research, 42*(17), 3691–3706. doi:10.1080/0020754042000203867

Amasaka, K. (2004b). *Science SQC, New Quality Control Principle: The quality strategy of Toyota.* Springer–Verlag Tokyo. doi:10.1007/978-4-431-53969-8

Amasaka, K. (Ed.). (2007). New Japan Model: Science TQM – Theory and Practice for strategic quality management. Study group of the ideal situation the quality management of the manufacturing industry, Maruzen, Tokyo.

Amasaka, K. (2007a). Applying New JIT – Toyota's global production strategy: Epoch-making Innovation in the Work Environment. *International Journal of Robotics and Computer-Integrated Manufacturing, 23*(3), 285-293.

Amasaka, K. (2007b). Proposal of Marketing SQC to revolutionize dealers' sales activities – A demonstrative study on Customer Science by utilizing Science SQC. *Proceedings of the 16th International Conference Production Research. Praha Czech Public*, 1-9.

Amasaka, K. (2008a). Strategic QCD studies with affiliated and non-affiliated suppliers utilizing New JIT. Encyclopedia of Networked and Virtual Organizations, 3(PU-Z), 1516-1527.

Amasaka, K. (2008b). New Manufacturing Theory: Surpassing JIT – Evolution of Just-In-Time. Academic Press.

Amasaka, K. (2009a). Establishment of Strategic Quality Management – Performance Measurement Model "SQM-PPM": Key to successful implementation of Science TQM. *China-USA Business Review, 8*(12), 1–11.

Amasaka, K. (2009b). An Intellectual Development Production Hyper-cycle Model – *New JIT* fundamentals and applications in Toyota –. *International Journal of Collaborative Enterprise, 1*(1), 103–127. doi:10.1504/IJCENT.2009.026459

Amasaka, K. (2009c). Proposal and validity of Patent Value Appraisal Model "TJS-PVAM" –Development of "Science TQM" in the corporate strategy–. *Journal of China-USA Business Review, 8*(7), 45–56.

Amasaka, K. (2013). The strategic development of Advanced TPS based on the New Manufacturing Theory. *Recent Advances in Industrial & Manufacturing Technologies, The 1st WSEAS International Conference on Industrial and Manufacturing Technologies,* 248-261.

Amasaka, K. (2019). Studies on New Manufacturing Theory, *Noble. International Journal of Scientific Research, 3*(1), 1–20.

Amasaka, K., & Sakai, H. (2010). Evolution of TPS fundamentals utilizing New JIT strategy – Proposal and validity of Advanced TPS at Toyota. *Journal of Advanced Manufacturing Systems, 9*(2), 85–99. doi:10.1142/S0219686710001831

Anabuki, K., Kaneta, H., & Amasaka, K. (2011). Proposal and validity of Patent Evaluation Method "A-PPM" for corporate strategy. *International Journal of Management & Information Systems*, *15*(3), 129–137. doi:10.19030/ijmis.v15i3.4649

Ebioka, K., Sakai, H., Yamaji, M., & Amasaka, K. (2007). A New Global Partnering Production Model "NGP-PM" utilizing "Advanced TPS". *Journal of Business & Economics Research*, *5*(9), 1–8.

Gabor, A. (1990). *The Man Who Discovered Quality; How Deming W. E., Brought the quality revolution to America*. Random House, Inc.

Ishiguro, H., & Amasaka, K. (2012). Proposal and effectiveness of a Highly Compelling Direct Mail Method – Establishment and deployment of PMOS-DM. *International Journal of Management & Information Systems*, *16*(1), 1–10.

Ishikawa, A., Morita, Y., & Amasaka, K. (2011). Constructing measures of CS effectiveness to boost subjective quality at manufacturers. *International Business & Economics Research Journal*, *10*(11), 55–61. doi:10.19030/iber.v10i11.6405

Ishizuka, T. (2006). *One research on partnering to strengthen Japanese quality management* (Master's thesis). Amasaka New JIT Laboratory, Graduate School of Science and Engineering, Aoyama Gakuin University, Sagamihara, Kanagawa, Japan.

Joiner, B. L. (1994). *Forth generation management: The new business consciousness*. Joiner Associates, Inc.

JUSE. (2006). *Quality management survey: JUSE Home page*. http://www.juse.or.jp/

Kaneta, H. (2006). *The Research on constructing of the Patent Evaluation Model* (Master's thesis). Amasaka New JIT Laboratory, Graduate School of Science and Engineering, Aoyama Gakuin University, Sagamihara, Kanagawa, Japan.

Kuniyoshi, K. (2006). *The product development business model's new proposal* (Master's thesis). Graduate School of Science and Engineering, Aoyama Gakuin University, Sagamihara, Kanagawa, Japan.

Lagrosen, S. (2004). Quality management in global firms. *The TQM Magazine*, *16*(6), 396–402. doi:10.1108/09544780410563310

Ljungström, M. (2005). A model for starting up and implementing continuous improvements and work development in practice. *The TQM Magazine*, *7*(5), 385–405. doi:10.1108/09544780510615915

Manzoni, A., & Islam, S. (2007). Measuring collaboration effectiveness in globalized supply networks: A data envelopment analysis application. *International Journal of Logistics Economics and Globalization*, *1*(1), 77–91. doi:10.1504/IJLEG.2007.014496

Media, M. (2006). *WRI: MRO today Home page*. http://www.Progressivedistributor. com/mro_ today_body.htm

Nakamura, M., Enta, Y., & Amasaka, K. (2011). Establishment of a model to assess the success of information sharing between customers and vendors in software development. *Journal of Management Science*, *2*, 165–173.

Okihara, D., Takada, S., & Amasaka, K. (2014). Constructing a model for selecting improvement actions to gain mutual trust between logistics providers and shippers. *Journal of Japanese Operations Management and Strategy*, *5*(1), 74–85.

Pires, S., & Cardoza, G. (2007). A study of new supply chain management practices in the Brazilian and Spanish auto-industries. *International Journal of Automotive Technology and Management*, *7*(1), 72–87. doi:10.1504/IJATM.2007.013384

Sakatoku, T. (2006). *Partnering performance measurement for assembly makers and suppliers* (Master's thesis). Graduate School of Science and Engineering, Aoyama Gakuin University, Sagamihara, Kanagawa, Japan.

Taylor, D., & Brunt, D. (2001). Manufacturing operations and supply chain management- Lean Approach. Thomson Learning.

Uchida, K., Tsunoi, M., & Amasaka, K. (2012). Creating Working Value Evaluation Model "WVEM". *International Journal of Management & Information Systems*, *16*(4), 299–305.

Yamaji, M., & Amasaka, K. (2007). Proposal and validity of Global Intelligence Partnering Model for corporate strategy "GIPM-CS". *Proceedings of the International IFIP TC 5.7 Conference on Advanced in Production Management Systems,* 59-67. 10.1007/978-0-387-74157-4_8

Yamaji, M., Sakatoku, T., & Amasaka, K. (2008). Partnering Performance Measurement "PPM-AS" to strengthen corporate management of Japanese automobile assembly makers and suppliers. *International Journal of Electronic Business Management*, *6*(3), 139–145.

Chapter 11
New Global Partnering Production Model for Expanding Overseas Manufacturing Strategies

ABSTRACT

To improve quality at leading manufacturers' overseas production bases from the perspective of global production, a New Global Partnering Production Model (NGP-PM) is created, and its effectiveness discussed for expanding overseas strategy. The aim is to increase global quality by generating a synergetic effect that organically connects and promotes continual evolution of the production plants in Japan and overseas, as well as greater cooperation among production operators. As an example of concrete deployment, the author has established a New Turkish Production System (NTPS) employing strategic NJM (New Japan Model) in the Republic of Turkey. Recently, moreover, the author has developed the NGP-PM for expanding overseas manufacturing strategy.

INTRODUCTION

In recent years, leading manufacturers in Japan have been deploying a new production strategy called "globally consistent levels of quality and simultaneous global launch" in order to get ahead in the worldwide quality competition, and high quality assurance in manufacturing - simultaneous achievement of QCD (Amasaka, 2006, 2017a; Yamaji and Amasaka, 2006, 2007a,b,; Yamaji et al.,. 2006; Amasaka and Sakai, 2010, 2011). This is the key to successful global production, and has become a prerequisite for its accomplishment employing New Japan Model (NJM) (Amasaka, Ed., 2007, 2012) (Refer to Chapter 5).

The greatest concern of corporate managers is the success of "overseas production strategy - local production" as well as "to bring overseas manufacturing to Japan standards". Therefore, to increase the skills of production workers at local manufacturing sites (hereafter referred to as production operators),

DOI: 10.4018/978-1-7998-8746-1.ch011

the key to successful global production is necessary to realize manufacturing suited to the actual situation at production sites of various overseas production bases.

Against this background, the author has have established a New Global Partnering Production Model (NGP-PM) employing New Japan Production Management Model (NJ-PMM) for Toyota's expanding overseas manufacturing strategy (Amasaka, 2007a, 2015, 2016, 2017a, 2019, 2022; Ebioka et al., 2007). NGP-PM generates a synergetic effect that organically connects and promotes continual evolution of the production plants in Japan and overseas, as well as greater cooperation among production operators. As an example of concrete deployment, the author has established a New Turkish Production System (NTPS) employing strategic NJM in the Republic of Turkey. Recently, moreover, the author has developed the NGP-PM for expanding overseas manufacturing strategy (Sakalsiz, 2009; Yeap et al., 2010; Siang et al., 2010; Shan et al., 2011; Shan, 2012; Miyashita Amasaka, 2015, 2016, 2017, 2018, 2022).

PROBLEMS WITH SUCCESS IN GLOBAL PRODUCTION

Recently leading companies aim to succeed in localizing production as a global production strategy; the key to this is success in global production. However, it has been observed that, despite the fact that overseas plants have the relevant production systems, facilities, and materials equivalent to those that have made Japan the world leader in manufacturing, the "building up of quality - assuring of process capability (Cp)" has not reached a sufficient level due to the lack of skills of the production operators at the manufacturing sites. Under such a circumstance, there are many studies abroad for globalization (Lagrosen, 2004; Ljungström, 2005) and TQM (Burke et al., 2005; Hoogervorst et al., 2005).

As a countermeasure to such a problem, and in order not to lag behind the "evolution of digital engineering – the transition to advanced production systems at production plants", the Japanese manufacturers expect the production plants in Japan to serve as "mother plants". They would welcome overseas production operators to these plants, and promote "a local production program - transplanting the know - how of Japanese manufacturing" (Sakai and Amasaka, 2006). However, it is by no means easy to transfer the "know-how of Japanese manufacturing" directly to overseas production bases as mentioned above.

In other words, there is always "an obstacle to overcome - a suitable production system for each production base", due to the difference in ability (level of skill and education) or national characteristics between the local production site and Japan. Therefore, to cope with this situation, an environment in which the creation of labor values–ES (employee satisfaction), advanced skills, a sense of achievement, and self-development can be realized must be urgently considered (Amasaka et al., 2006; Yamaji et al., 2006, 2007).

To accomplish the above, the author surmises that it is necessary to develop a type of manufacturing which fits the local circumstances of various overseas production bases and to advance from "Japanese mother plants" to "global mother plants".

STRATEGIC USE OF NEW JAPAN MODEL, THE KEY TO GLOBAL PRODUCTION

Current Situation of Quality Management in the Japanese Manufacturing

Taking a careful look at the repeated cases of market recall happening in the manufacturing sector recently, it can be deduced that it is not only an "issue of quality of products", but also a severe challenge presented to the "reliability of products – the way of quality management" of Japanese manufacturing.

The author surmises that such a situation is pointing to the brittle fatigue of the "function of quality assurance - reliability of products", which once was a strong point of Japanese manufacturing. Also it suggests a possible idling of the "function of quality management – reliability of human resources" (Amasaka 2008a,b). Under such a circumstance, there are many studies abroad for globalization (Lagrosen 2004; Ljungström 2005) and TQM (Hoogervorst 2005; Burke 2005; Kakkar and Narag 2007; Prajogo 2007). Basically, the Quality Assurance Div. and TQM Promotion Div. work in harmony as a cornerstone of "quality management" which "manages the quality" of each of the related divisions so as to keep circulating normally the business cycles for quality management.

However, since the burst of the bubble economy, as if epitomizing the advantage of a Japanese production system as follows;

1. super mass production–automation of production and automation of inspection has been promoted,
2. as quality defects were reduced in the production process, it was thought that, relatively speaking
3. quality assurance and inspection do not produce added value, and therefore, and therefore,
4. the organization /operation of Quality Assurance Div. or Inspection Div. was scaled down or mere routine work was introduced therein, and
5. activities for creating new functions for quality assurance or TQM have been stagnating.

For the past 10 plus years, efforts for promoting customer-first "manufacturing – high quality assurance" which enhances the customer value as well as "human resource development – high reliability of total business process" have been neglected and therefore are lagging behind (Goto 1999: Amasaka and Sakai, 2010). Though overseas local production has been advancing recently along with a rapid expansion of global production, an uphill battle has been fought for the "building up of quality" which can match Japanese manufacturing. Quality Assurance related divisions are busy with cleaning up the mess of "quality defect" cases, and TQM Promotion Div. has been slack in functioning as a cultivator of human resources with fighting potential, giving too much "emphasis on TQM education for TQM promotion" (Evans and Lindsay 1995).

Having said the above, it is deemed necessary now to go back to the "Basic principle of quality management" as shown in Figure 1, and to reform the quality assurance function as well as the TQM promotion function which advances the former (Evans and Lindsay 1995; Yamaji and Amasaka 2006). This basic principle involves, as a management philosophy, establishment of mission, methodology, promotion, organization, and technology, and realization of CS (Customer Satisfaction), ES (Employee Satisfaction), SS (Social Satisfaction), high added value products, product development / technology development, creative corporate environment, human reliability, and full participation. It is vital to strategically deploy this basic principle.

Figure 1. Basic principle of quality management

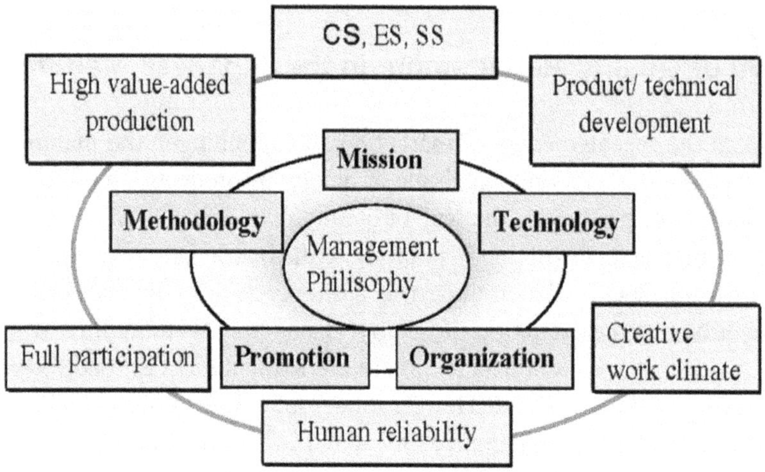

11.3.2 Development of New Japan Quality Management Model employing NJM

To realize the key to global production, globally consistent levels of quality and production at optimal locations, it is absolutely essential that manufacturing via "global partnering" is precisely developed to suit actual conditions and skill levels at production sites of the various overseas production bases. In working towards these urgent issues, the authors constructed the use of NJM (New Japan Model) (Amasaka, 2002, 2004a,b, 2007a,b,a,d, 2015, 2022; Amasaka, Ed. 2007) (Refer to Chapter 5).

Considering the importance of scientific quality management, and on the basis of the NJM which has verified the effectiveness of the Strategic Stratified Task Team Model (SSTTM) in the TQM promotion and Quality Assurance, as well as the universality of "basic principle of quality management" presented in Chapter 8 (Refer to Chapter 8 in detail), the author has established the New Japanese Quality Management Model (NJ-QMM) as the advanced model of quality management for the strategic cooperation indicated in Figure 2, Chapter 6, (Amasaka, 2004a, 2017a,b; Yamaji et al., 2006; Yamaji and Amasaka, 2007).

In Figure 2, Chapter 6, the following are the functions of the Quality Assurance and TQM Promotion related divisions: as corporate environment factors for succeeding in "global production", "Customer-first", (1) CS, ES, SS, (2) for high quality assurance and as a strategic factor to realize it, (3) in order to simultaneously achieve QCD, and (4) success in global partnering. Intellectual productivity, company/ affiliate/ non-affiliate linkage is realized by these. So (5) evolution of quality management is achieved. More specifically, the (i) Quality Assurance Div. needs to promote manufacturing of high reliability, and cooperative activity across the organization is indispensable to achieve it. In the (ii) TQM Promotion Div., it is important to cultivate human resources having even higher skills, knowledge, and creativity. It is a must to continue to upgrade working the value or by promoting the cultivation of intelligent human resources in an effort to improve the productivity of white collar workers.

To realize the above, global partnering which enables the strategic cooperation among divisions, such as designing, production, marketing and administration as well as the entire company, affiliated companies, non-affiliated companies, and overseas corporations, must be achieved. Improvement of intellectual productivity is simultaneous achievement of QCD utilizing this model (Refer to Chapter 8, 9 and 10).

NEW GLOBAL PARTNERING PRODUCTION MODEL FOR EXPANDING OVERSEAS MANUFACTURING STRATEGY

Significance of Global Partnering Research

The author has defined "global partnering" as knowledge sharing in order to promote continual evolution of the production plants in Japan and overseas, as well as greater cooperation among production operators (Amasaka, 2004a). In other words, global partnering means that Japanese companies no longer stick to a one-sided promotion of Japanese concepts and systems onto overseas plants as they have in the past, but that Japanese and overseas plants exchange opinions, accept each other, and share knowledge in order to continue developing the best-suited manufacturing system for each environment (Sakai and Amasaka, 2005: Ebioka et al., 2007).

Therefore, for expedient achievement of globally consistent levels of quality and simultaneous global launch (production at optimal locations), the author considers global partnering through cooperation from fresh standpoints to be the key to "achieving worldwide quality competitiveness—the simultaneous achievement of QCD" (Amasaka, 2007c, 2008a,b; Amasaka and Sakai, 2011).

New Japan Production Model for Overseas Strategically

To strengthen "global partnering", the author has proposed a new concept the New Japan Production Model (NJ-PM) for overseas strategically (Amasaka, 2005, 2015) (Refer to Chapter 7). The aims of NJ-PM is realization of digitized production, renewal of production management system, creating attractive workshop environment and Increasing older and female workers in the embodiment of four core elements ((a),(b), (c) and (d)).

Figure 2. New Japan Production Model (NJ-PM)

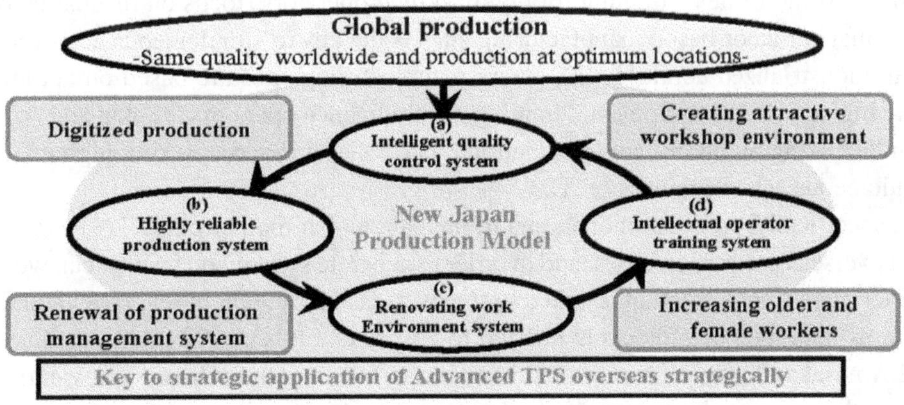

New Global Partnering Production Model for Bringing Overseas Manufacturing to Japan Standards

For advanced Japanese companies in the process of developing global production employing NJ-PM, the most important issue is how to "bring overseas manufacturing to Japan standards" at overseas plants. Therefore, to develop the New Japan Production Management Model (NJ-PMM) using Dual Global Engineering Model: "New Japan Global Production Model (NJ-GPM) and New Japan Global Manufacturing Model (NJ-GMM) (Refer to Chapter 7). the author has established the New Global Partnering Production Model (NGP-PM) which generates a synergetic effect that organically connects and promotes continual evolution of the production plants in Japan and overseas, as well as greater cooperation among production operators as shown in Figure 2, Chapter 7 (Ebioka et al., 2007).

The mission of NGP-PM is the simultaneous achievement of QCD in order to realize high quality assurance. The essential strategic policies include the following three items: first of all, the (A) establishment of a foundation for global production, "realization of global mother plants-advancement of Japanese production sites"; second, (B) achieving the "independence of local production sites" through the incorporation of the unique characteristics (production systems, facilities, and materials) of both developing countries (Asia) and industrialized countries (US, Europe); and third, (C) necessity of a "developing intelligence operators employing HI-POS (Human Intelligence – Production Operating System)" (Sakai and Amasaka, 2006) to promote knowledge sharing among the production operators in Japan and overseas as well as for the promotion of higher skills and enhanced intelligence (Refer to Chapter 7 and 15).

To realize this, with above NJ-PM as the foundation, it is essential to create a spiraling increase in the four core elements by increasing their comprehensiveness and high cyclization. Specifically, in "realizing global mother plants", if Japanese and overseas manufacturing sites are to share knowledge from their respective viewpoints, the core elements must be advanced. To achieve this, a necessary measure is to design separate approaches suited to developing and industrialized countries.

First, in developing countries (1), the most important issue is increasing the autonomy of local manufacturing sites. At these sites, "training for highly skilled operators (focus on manual laborers)" that is suited to the manual-labor-based manufacturing sites is the key to simultaneous achievement of QCD. Similarly, in industrialized countries (2), where manufacturing sites are based on automatization and increasingly high-precision equipment, "training of intelligence operators" (Sakai and Amasaka, 2005) resulting in "realizing highly reliable production control systems and ensuring high efficiency" is the key to simultaneous achievement of QCD.

Second, specifically, production operators trained at "global mother plants" (3) can cooperate with operators at overseas production bases, and in order to generate synergistic results, can work to "localize global mother plants" in a way that is suited to the overseas production bases. HIA (Human-Integrated Assist Systems) can then be effectively utilized to ensure that this contribution continues indefinitely (Sakai and Amasaka, 2008). HIA is critical in ensuring the smooth exchange of essential information in order to realize overseas manufacturing at Japan standards.

This essential information includes quality control information for each production base as well as facilities planning information, kaizen information, and information on the level of skill of human resources.

Developing Strategic Productivity Improvement Model for global production strategy

1. Global production strategy for expanding manufacturing

The management values shared by so-called winning companies are shifting from emphasis on materials to human resources. The companies have amassed human resources, materials, and finances. It is easy to procure materials as well as finances. However, human resources take time to develop, and therefore, is not as easy as the foregoing to procure. The companies are endeavoring to grasp the information on human resources, take hold of the work, and formulate the vision in order to compete at a higher level.

It has been increasingly difficult to differentiate companies only in terms of high product quality, cost performance, and superiority in the business process. It is imperative therefore to improve the value of human resources, but only a few companies have actually constructed a mechanism for improving human resources. Up until now, each department has acquired information on human resources from the personnel affairs division, and systems for offering such information have been insufficient. By improving the system for sharing information on human resources, similar to sharing information on materials and finances, the business assets of companies can be effectively utilized.

Moreover, the information of in-company systems has not been completely updated until the end of fiscal terms. Therefore, the accuracy of the information provided has been inferior, and the judgments regarding management tend to rely on personal experience or inspiration. In other words, information sharing has not been speedy enough. From now on, it is necessary to offer information with high precision based on the PDCA (plan, do, check and action) cycle so that decision-making on management matters will be based on facts.

In this application, information system, engineering control, production control and purchasing control are defined as management layer of functional division. The management layers are the core of corporate activity and therefore it is vital for it to reinforce the functions of "business management technology" so as to strengthen and enrich both internal and external management. This is also done in order to create a business linkage with the general administration department and cooperate with the on-site departments, such as development designing, production, and sales departments, as well as with business partners.

Total planning, personal division, etc. are defined as administrative divisions. It is increasingly important for the general administration-related department to advance corporate management by grasping the changing domestic and overseas environment surrounding the industry. It should also cooperate with the management layers so as to strengthen internal and external management.

To achieve this, it is urgently necessary to position human resource development at the core of management policy in order to enhance corporate, organizational, and human reliability as the basis of strategic quality management. It is also necessary, at the stage of utilizing human resources, to strengthen the function of improving intelligent productivity through cooperation with all the related departments.

Administrative and management layers are defined as white-collar sections, and the human resources working within the divisions are defined as white-collar workers. Additionally, the results produced by these divisions are referred to as intellectual productivity (Yamaji and Amasaka, 2009).

2. Establishment of the Strategic Productivity Improvement Model (SPIM)

In recent years, Japanese companies have introduced the Western-style division of labor. Such a western labor division system is designed for easy replacement of labor forces and is achievement-oriented, it evaluates the degree of personal contribution to target achievement. Therefore, when a problem arises, it is dealt with not as a personal problem, but only within their responsibility range. Consequently, many activities and actions based on such a principle have been criticized by society. On the other hand, in the former Japanese system, problems were handled by all members across departments, which was a strong point of the Japanese way.

In this subsection, an investigation has been carried out on problems and administrative issues currently facing a number of manufacturers, including automobile manufacturers. A questionnaire survey yielded feedback from 12 division managers at 10 companies. The survey was carried out from May to June in 2008. The responses to the survey questions have been summarized and categorized into 238 issues. These issues have been further categorized into 10 groups using an affinity diagram, and cluster analysis (word method, normalized data) has been carried out as shown in Figure 3 (Yamaji and Amasaka, 2007).

Figure 3. Result of the cluster analysis

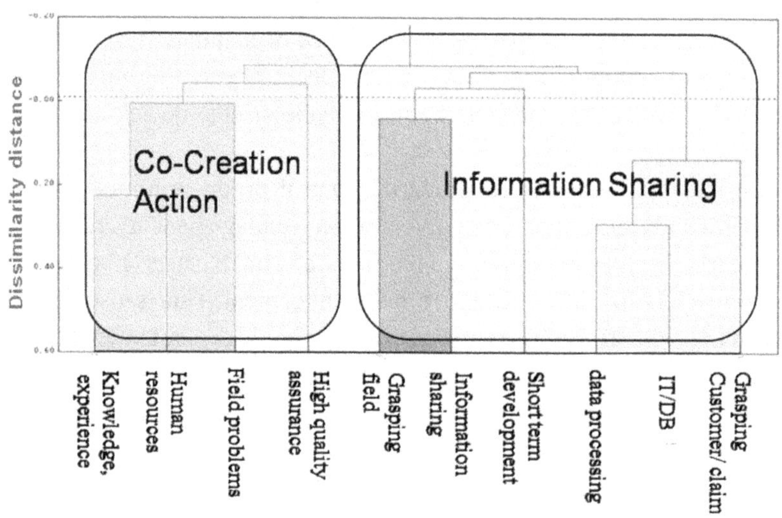

Therefore, the author has established the "Strategic Productivity Improvement Model" (SPIM) so called Toyota's NJQMM (New Japan Quality Management Model) for global production strategy as shown in Figure 4 (Yamaji and Amasaka, 2007). In Figure 4, the following are the functions of the white-collar sections as corporate environment factors for succeeding in "global marketing," customer-first, 1) high quality product for 2) CS, ES, SS and as a strategic factor to realize it, in order to 3) high white-collar productivity and human resource development. 4) Global production is realized by these. So the same quality and production at optimal locations are achieved.

For that purpose, the highest priority was given to the i) Strategic information sharing and ii) Strategic co-creative action so that the "Strategic Intelligence Application System and Business Process High Linkage System" can effectively function. When implementing a high cyclization of a business flow that consists of the setup of management policy, creation of a business plan, budget establishment, business deployment, optimal workforce distribution, task management, and evaluation, the relevant information needs to be shared among many departments and they need to also grasp the numerical values that show company-wide trends. In that way, upon confirming abnormal numerical indications, the problem can be identified and solved at an early stage.

For example, if overtime labor cost shows an unusual figure, the project manager should find out the cause by checking which division, as well as which position or which process, is showing such a trend. In the administrative division, consideration needs to be given to possible deterioration of the work environment or lack of labor force, and in the sales division, care must be exercised to not delay delivery. Each division exchanges information with the other divisions to solve the problem as a whole company. The solutions shall be evaluated so that the information sharing of both problems and solutions can become a preventive measure and food for thought for the next plan.

Figure 4. Outline of Strategic Productivity Improvement Model (SPIM)

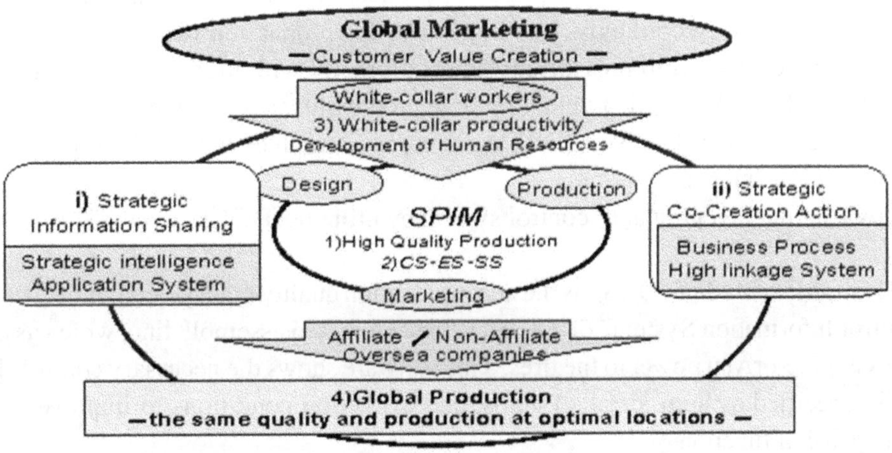

Such a partnership among divisions, involves creation of a system to visualize information flow as well as its effective and practical application. To that end, a leader who links human resources is indispensable, and therefore, the cornerstone of corporate management is to foster leaders who have the understanding of the vision of management directors, a broad view of world trends, and communication skills to create a network of personnel inside the company.

Simply putting, the cultivation of an entrepreneurial mind or professional mind is what the authors are intending by proposing this business model of strategic productivity improvement for the white-collar sections. In the following chapter, the effectiveness of the created SPIM is verified through application cases at the successful companies

3. Effectiveness of SPIM

The effectiveness of the established SPIM is verified through application cases at the successful companies by employing NJ-GPM as follows;

a. Strategic information sharing

"V-MICS" (Virtual-Maintenance Innovated Computer System) (Sakai and Amasaka 2005) for a global maintenance network system, and "TPS-QAS" (TPS-Quality Assurance System) for a quality control system (Amasaka and Sakai 2009) will be introduced as successful applications of Strategic Information Sharing, one of the core technologies of the proposed SPIM.

Both cases embody the successful sharing of the kind of information that cannot be expressed in words in order to achieve advances in global quality management. Additionally, similar activities at other companies will be introduced. Administrative divisions play the role of taking a proactive leadership role in putting together all the related divisions and built these systems.

i. V-MICS, a highly reliable production system by combining DB and CG Japanese automotive industries are grappling with the global marketing, simultaneous new vehicle start-up globally and other major propositions under our policy of production where customers need the product and the quantity needed. Accordingly, it is imperative for production plants to carry out production without breakdown so as to provide customers promptly with high quality products. The author has established the "V-MICS, a highly reliable production system", which has been systematized and practiced by using data base (DB) and computer graphics (CG), which form the nucleus of this advanced maintenance system.
ii. TPS-QAS, an intelligent quality control system by utilizing T-QCIS

The application line of "TPS-QAS" as the new production quality management model using "Toyota's Quality Control Information System" (T-QCIS) is the automated assembly line, which assembles a part that transmits engine-driven power to the tires. This software shows the necessary control characteristics hierarchically specified as item, detailed items, and extraction conditions to improve operability and provide an expansion function.

b. Strategic co-creative action

The key to success in global production is the reinforcement of product power, or the "simultaneous achievement of QCD" (Amasaka 2004a). To realize this, it is vital to reinforce Japanese-style partnering, or "partnering of competition and collaboration—Japan Supply Chain Management" between automobile manufacturers (hereafter termed Assembly Makers) and affiliated or non-affiliated parts manufacturers (hereafter termed Suppliers). This is also called the Japan Supply System (JSS).

For further advancement in this area, Assembly Makers should not only reinforce internal partnering with their own operational departments (such as engineering, production, and sales), but must also strengthen external partnering. This means establishing cooperative relationships with other companies while advancing and establishing global partnering through strategic collaboration with both foreign and domestic suppliers.

The author presents global development of SPIM employing NGP-PM between Toyota and a group of cooperation companies as case of internal partnering, and "Improvement in painting quality of chassis parts of automobiles" as case of external partnering in Toyota and suppliers. In these examples, management layers play the role of taking a proactive leadership role in putting together all the related divisions and solve problems.

i. Global development of Science TQM between Toyota and a group of cooperation companies Toyota's quality management, in 1st example, the Science SQC (Amasaka 2004b), which is the administrative staff's activity for improving quality management technology by utilizing Science TQM (Amasaka, Ed., 2012), became popularized and expanded through joint task team activities with affiliated and non-affiliated suppliers (Amasaka, 2008a, 2017b).
ii. Improvement in painting quality of chassis parts of automobiles: cooperative activities with affiliated and non-affiliated companies

Moreover, the 2nd examples are typical case studies where the quality of appearance and paint corrosion resistance (resistance to Salt Spray Test (SST)) were improved without increasing cost, in order to improve the market strength of automotive chassis parts (front and rear axles). Making a global initiative to achieve simultaneous fulfillment of QCD, Toyota formed joint task teams with Aisin Kako Co., an affiliate, and Tokyo Paint Co., a non-affiliate. For example, the author shows an example where the joint task team of Toyota and Tokyo Paint raised the product value (VA=performance/cost) of the front axle (Amasaka, 2008a).

APPLICATION EXAMPLES

New Turkish Production System, Integration Production of Japan and Turkish

A midst the rapid progress of globalization, the Republic of Turkey, one of the most prominent of Europe's newly emerging economies, is expected to achieve significant growth, centering on its manufacturing industries. Given its strong international competitiveness in terms of labor and raw materials, the country's automobile industry has particular potential for growth.

Therefore, as an opening move in Turkey's new global production strategy, the author has created a New Turkish Production System (NTPS). The NTPS has been developed by integrating Toyota Production System (traditional TPS and Advanced TPS), itself an evolved model of the current Toyota manufacturing strategy, the leading Japanese production system, with Advanced Turkish Production System, which is an evolved model of current Traditional Turkish Production System cultivated to date (Sakalsiz, 2009; Siang et al., 2010).

1. Current Status of Turkey's automobile industry

Turkey currently ranks 16th in the world for production of automobiles, one of the highest rankings among the newly industrialized countries. The strategic advantages of its location in terms of production and distribution have enabled the Turkish automobile industry to establish its own unique production system of which reflects local industries, known as the Traditional Turkish Production System, while achieving steady growth at the same time.

In recent years, in an opening move in the global production strategy of the Turkish automobile industry, leading overseas companies have become increasingly active in local production. For example, since 1994, Toyota Motor Manufacturing Turkey (TMMT) has been conducting training in "The Toyota Way" (Jeffrey, 2004) at Toyota in Japan, and has introduced the traditional Toyota Production System called JIT (Refer to Chapter 3). In the background to this is an undercurrent that Turkey has an environment that is amenable to the introduction of a Japanese style production system, given the similarities in character between the Turkish and Japanese people and their belief that success will come if one works hard.

2. Creation of a New Turkish Production System

Having investigated the actual situation in Turkey, the author creates a "New Turkish Production System" (NTPS) with the objective of integration and evolution of traditional Turkish Production System and the aforementioned Toyota Production System (traditional TPS and Advanced TPS) for the growth of the next-generation automobile industry in the Republic of Turkey (Sakalsiz, 2009; Yeap et al., 2010).

a. Concept of NTPS

Based on the research of Ramarapu et al (1995) and of Amasaka et al. (Amasaka, 2004a, 2007a,b,c,d, 2008a,b, 2009; Ebioka et al., 2007; Yamaji, et al., 2007, 2008; Amasaka and Sakai, 2010), the author creates a concept for NTPS as shown in Figure 5.

Figure 5. Concept of a New Turkish Production System (NTPS)

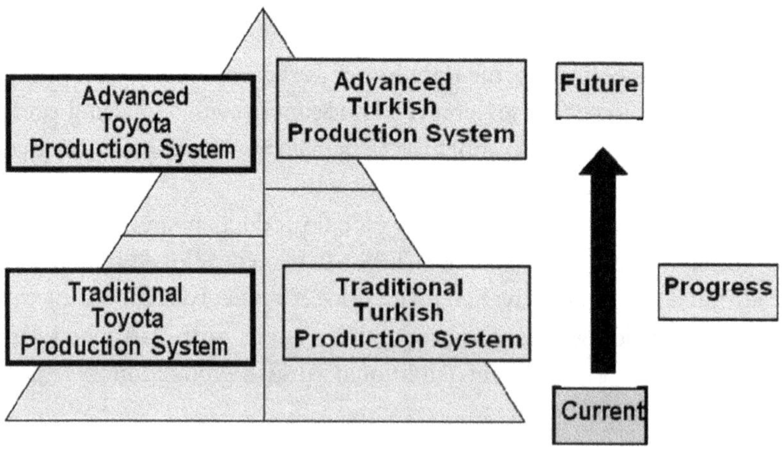

b. Extraction of important keywords for NTPS

In order to extract the common factors (elements) and the Turkey-specific unique factors (elements) required for a NTPS, the authors conduct field surveys of Japanese (Toyota, Honda, Denso, Central Motors, Nihon Spring, and others) and Turkish local manufacturers (TOFAS, OYAK-Renault, FORD OTOSAN, TOYOTA Turkey, and DENSO Turkey).

In these surveys, approximately 500 language data were obtained from interviews, findings obtained from manufacturing plant tours, on-site case studies and reference literature. An affinity diagram of the data thus obtained, based on 5M-E (man, machine, material, manufacturing, measuring, and environment), was used to investigate the relationships between the data based on empirical technologies. As shown in Figure 6, the author was able to extract, as important keywords for the NTPS, ten common factors - four unique factors specific to Turkey, and two unique factors specific to Japan as follows.

Figure 6. Important NTPS keywords obtained from affinity diagram

i. The factors common to Turkey and Japan are (1) quality assurance, (2) SQC education, (3) QCD activities, (4) kaizen activities, (5) creative proposal programs, (6) improvements through environmental regulations, (7) automatic management methods, (8) global partnering, (9) safety, and (10) definition, awareness and elimination of "*muda*" (waste).
ii. The Turkey-specific factors are (11) Turkish-style human resources education, (12) production, quality, logistics and informational harmony with European manufacturers, (13) focused kaizen, and (14) production management through world-class manufacturing (WCM).
iii. The Japan-specific factors are (15) digital engineering / CAE (computer aided engineering), and (16) new, people-focused production approaches.

c. Text mining analysis

The authors further used text mining analysis to explore in more detail the relationships between the language data obtained based on Figure 6. Examples of the results of analysis of the 5M-E keywords for the NTPS are explained below.

Specifically, the relationships between TPS and Advanced TPS (necessary keywords that each should possess) are shown clearly in Figure 7. Further, in a similar manner, the relationships between the Traditional Turkish Production System and Advanced Turkish Production System are shown clearly in Figure 8.

Figure 7 shows that TPS, JIT, workplace environment, SQC (statistical quality control), and standard work orientation have a high degree of relationship and that the key elements (factors) that should be present in Advanced TPS include worker education, assurance of high quality, DE (design of experiment), CG (computer graphics), TQM (total quality management), global production, virtual plant, simulation and partnering.

Figure 7.

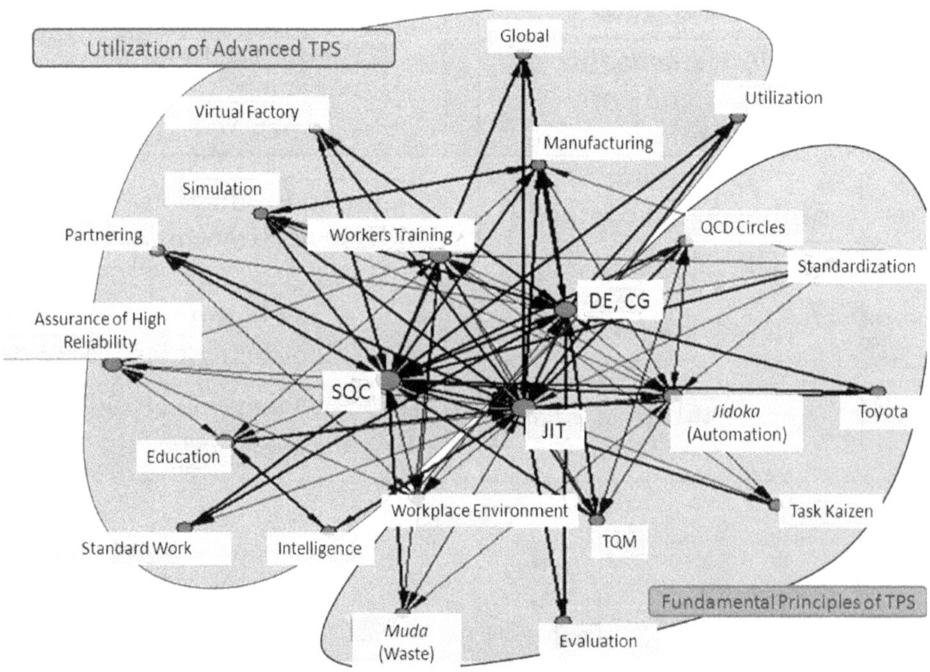

Similarly, Figure 8 shows that in the Traditional Turkish Production System, "safety, cost and quality control" essential to global production, "line supervision, environmental improvement and problem-solving methods" essential to Turkish style human resources development and utilization have a high degree of relationship.

The key elements (factors) that should be present in the Advanced Turkish Production System are "motivated and flexible workers and line, and kaizen activities" have a high degree of relationship with focused kaizen by sections, and "reinforcement of the influence and collaboration between Turkish and European manufacturers," which is essential to localized production that is in harmony with European manufacturers.

Figure 8. Connections of "Traditional Turkish Production System" and "Advanced Turkish Production System"

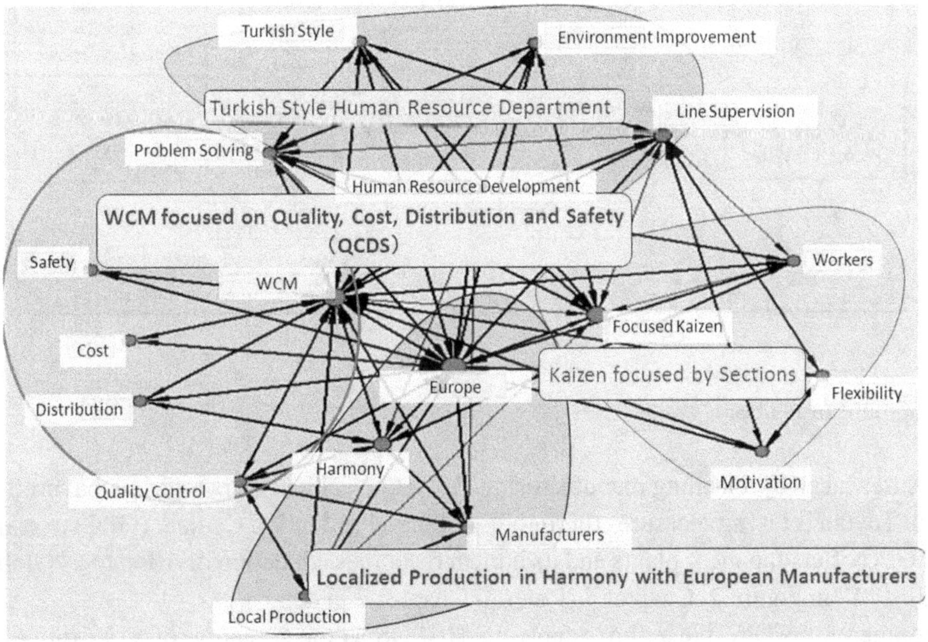

d. Outline of NTPS

Based on the results of analysis obtained, as described above, and the findings from same, the authors have created a New Turkish Production System (NTPS). This system represents the integration and evolution of the Advanced TPS, which is itself an evolved model of the current "Toyota Production System," and "Advanced Turkish Production System," which is an evolved model of "Traditional Turkish Production System" cultivated to date.

As shown in Figure 9, from the perspective of 5M-E, factors that are common to Japan and Turkey, Turkey-specific factors, and Japan-specific factors have been considered as the technological elements (factors) required for production. Not only will this enable the Turkish automobile industry to enhance its technological capabilities and increase production, but it will also lead to expectations of the production of high-quality products and the development of flexible production systems in the future.

Figure 9. Outline of a New Turkish Production System (NTPS)

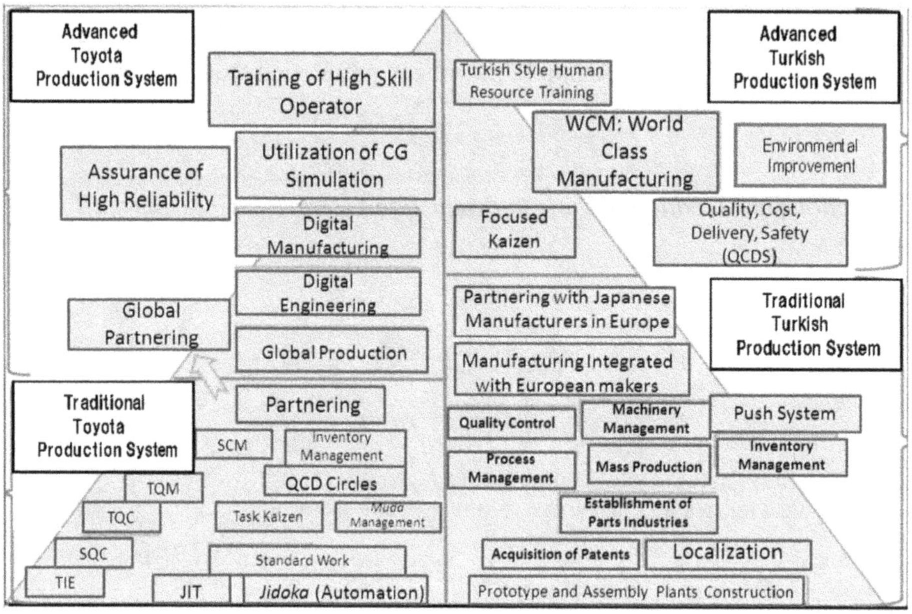

e. Development of NTPS

The measures taken by a leading manufacturing Toyota, to achieve successful global production will be discussed. Toyota is taking measures through its "Global Production Center" (GPC) to realize global production. GPC offers Japanese plants and its human resources education division to a "Global Mother Plant in NGP-PM" in Figure 2, Chapter 7 (Refer to Chapter 7 in detail).

In development of NTPS, the author adapts the HI-POS as the "creation of a person-centered new production system" to increasingly realize improvements in skills and proficiency (Refer to Figure 8, Chapter 7) An important part of this system is the HIA which allows human wisdom to be translated into increased skills and oral tradition. Within this, the skill training curriculum for overseas production operators and the important tools will be discussed.

i. Operator training process for assembly works

The skill training for newly hired domestic and overseas production operators, which used to take more than two weeks, has been shortened to just 5 days—less than half the time—and has ensured a stable mass production system. Specific content of the skill training curriculum for overseas production operators is shown in Figure 10. This figure shows an example of operator training process for automobile assembly works.

After everything from (1) Class room training (basic skills training) and (2) Skill training to a competency evaluation test are completed, (3) Off-line training (utilizing tools such as the Visual Manual and the HIA-Intelligent IT system) is conducted repeatedly until a certain standard is achieved on an evaluation sheet. Finally, (4) actual training on the line is conducted, and achievement of a set skill level was shown to be achieved in half the time previously needed.

Figure 10. Operator training processes for assembly works

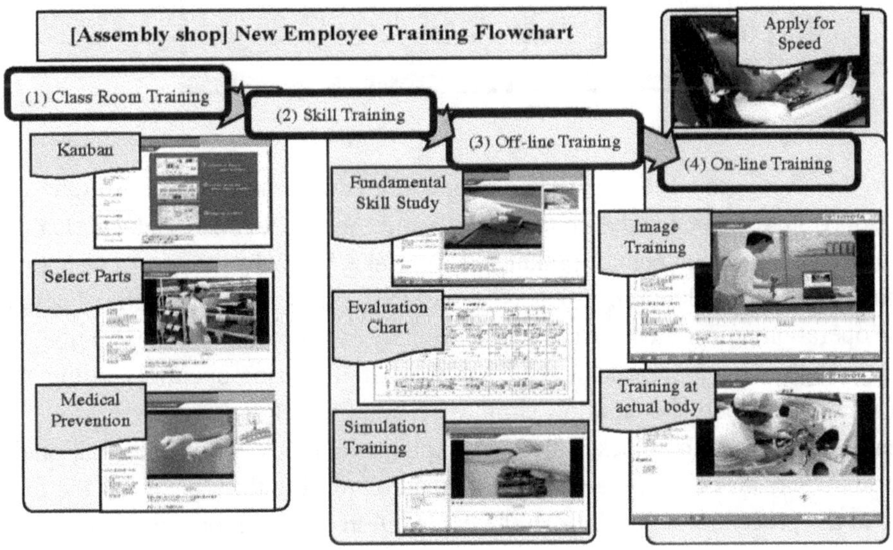

As an example, Figure 11 shows the screen setup of the Hyper Visual Manual (HVM) a communication tool that allows for increased exchange of knowledge and information regarding production processes as follows; (i) shows the process (Procedure of tighten training), while the section in (ii) shows video, animation, or pictures (Display image-main screen) and (iii) describes the process in words (Description, know-how). In Figure 11, HVM allows the operator to follow along, clicking the continue button to turn the pages as needed.

With this tool, production operators can be guided using shared content worldwide, and operators can also engage in self-study between actual skill training sessions. Through repeated image training, skill level can drastically improve at the initial stages, contributing significantly to proficiency improvement in highly skilled operators.

ii. Bringing up intelligent operators:

As mentioned earlier, the authors (Sakai and Amasaka, 2005) has established the V-MICS (Virtual–Maintenance Innovated Computer System–for Educational Management) (Refer to Chapter 7), which improves production operators' operational technology abilities in regard to integrated equipment, in preparation for global production (Sakai and Amasaka, 2005). This system works to make possible support for improvements in production operators' operating skills and techniques, such as equipment availability administration, defect analysis (Amasaka and Sakai, 1996, 1998), and other intelligence-based functions.

Figure 11. Example of Hyper Visual Manual (HVM) (Concerning bolt feeding operation)

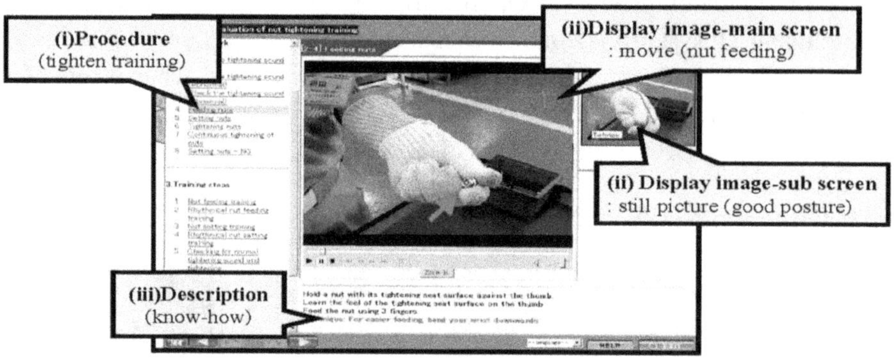

The author, therefore, proposed the intelligent operator educational system "V-IOS" (Virtual-Intelligence Operator System) (Sakai and Amasaka, 2002) and "V-MICS-EM" (–Educational Management) for the robot operation and maintenance (Sakai and Amasaka, 2009) by utilizing a visual manual format exemplified in Figure 12, which improves levels of mastered skills among production operators. Manuals describing the operation procedure have so far been kept by each operator or shop station, and the know-how obtained through use is a personal asset. To make manufacturing operators strong, the equipment (manufacturing) manual itself should allow simple revision by each handling person.

The screen consists of paging block, procedure explanation block, visual information display block, and explanation display block. The manual is to be read by turning the page using the forwarding button according to the procedure. Especially in the explanation display block, the key point representing the know-how of each operator is written and the visual information not indicated on the main screen is shown in details in the sub screen.

Figure 12. Example of the Visual Manual Format (VMF) using V-IOS

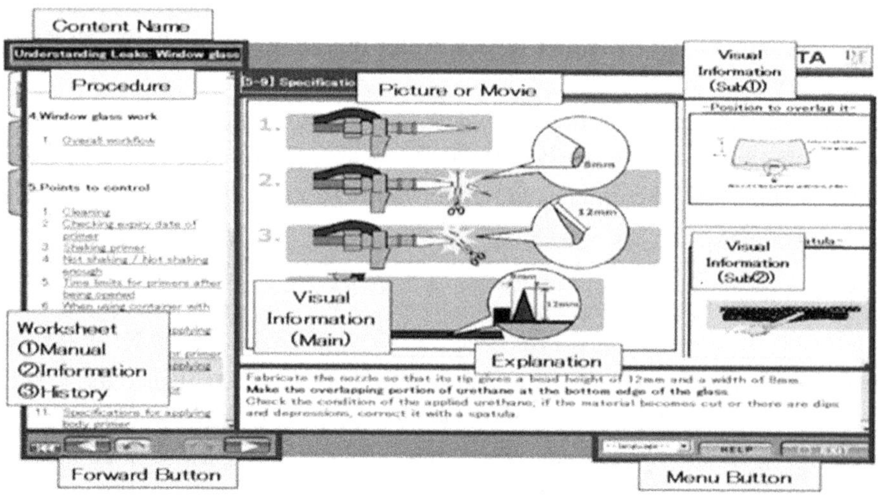

The contribution these systems make to the evolution and dissemination of production operators' mastered skills leads to improved productivity among production operators when setting up a new overseas plant, and the given benefits have already been acknowledged. As a result of execution using the engine block line at K plant as a model line, the target of zero failures was attained after a lapse of two years since the start of the activity in fiscal 2000, thereby establishing a new autonomous production line. Deployment to production lines in Japan and abroad has been promoted with satisfactory results.

Other Cases

The author was able to apply the NJ-GPM to critical QCD studies of automobile manufacturing developing NJM strategy as follows; (i) New Malaysia Production Model (Shan et al., 2012), (ii) New Vietnam Production Model (Miyashita and Amasaka, 2014), (iii) New China Production System (Shan. 2012), (iv) Advanced Toyota Production System at Toyota manufacturing USA (Amasaka, 2016), and (v) Advanced Peugeot Toyota Production System: Arc de Triomphe Production System (Amasaka, 2018) and others.

CONCLUSION

The author has established a model and conducts verification for the strategic development of Advanced TPS through the strategic use of NGP-PM (New Global Partnering Production Model) with the aim of establishing basic principles and realizing a Japan standard of quality in overseas manufacturing employing the SPIM (Strategic Productivity Improvement Model) for global production strategy, which improves the intellectual productivity.

As the concrete examples of NGP-PM deployment, the author describes some case studies of the New Turkish Production Model, Integration production of Japan and Turkish (NTPM) and others.

ACKNOWLEDGMENT

The author would like to acknowledge the generous support of the following researchers: all those at Toyota Motor Corporation, and Amasaka New JIT laboratory at Aoyama Gakuin University that assisted with the research, especially, Mr. Ebioka, K., Dr. Sakai, H., Mr. Miyashita, S, Mr. Sakalsiz, M. M., Mr. Shan, H., Mr. Yeap, Y. S., Mr. Siang, Y. Y., Mr. Yamaji, M., and others.

REFERENCES

Amasaka, K. (2002). New JIT, A New Management Technology Principle at Toyota. *International Journal of Production Economics*, *80*(2), 135–144. doi:10.1016/S0925-5273(02)00313-4

Amasaka, K. (2004a). Development of "Science TQM", a new principle of quality management: Effectiveness of strategic stratified task team at Toyota. *International Journal of Production Research*, *42*(17), 3691–3706. doi:10.1080/0020754042000203867

Amasaka, K. (2004b). *Science SQC, New Quality Control Principle: The quality strategy of Toyota.* Springer-Verlag. doi:10.1007/978-4-431-53969-8

Amasaka, K. (2005). New Japan Production Method, An innovative production management principle, *Proceedings of the 16th Annual Conference of the Production and Operations Management Society,* 1-22.

Amasaka, K. (2006). Evolution of TPS fundamentals utilizing New JIT strategy: Toyota's simultaneous realization of QCD Fulfillment Models. *Proceedings of the International Manufacturing Leaders Forum, Taipei, Taiwan,* 1-6.

Amasaka, K. (2006). The evolution of technology and skill, the Key to success in global production: Latest implementation of new Japan model "Science TQM." *The Japan Society for Production Management, the 23rd Annual Technical Conference*, 81-84.

Amasaka, K. (Ed.). (2007). New Japan Model - Science TQM: Theory and practice for strategic quality management. Study Group of the Ideal Situation the Quality Management of the Manufacturing Industry, Maruzen, Tokyo.

Amasaka, K. (2007a). High Linkage Model "Advanced TDS, TPS & TMS": Strategic development of "New JIT" at Toyota. *International Journal of Operations and Quantitative Management, 13*(3), 101–121.

Amasaka, K. (2007b). Applying New JIT-Toyota's global production strategy: Epoch-making innovation in the work environment. *Robotics and Computer-integrated Manufacturing, 23*(3), 285–293. doi:10.1016/j.rcim.2006.02.001

Amasaka, K. (2007c). New Japan Production Model, an advanced production management principle: Key to strategic implementation of New JIT. *The International Business & Economics Research Journal, 6*(7), 67–79.

Amasaka, K. (2007d). *New Japan Model, Science TQM: Theory and application of strategic quality management.* Maruzen publishing. (in Japanese)

Amasaka, K. (2008a). Strategic QCD studies with affiliated and non-affiliated suppliers utilizing New JIT. Encyclopedia of Networked and Virtual Organizations, 3(PU-Z), 1516-1527.

Amasaka, K. (2008b). Science TQM, a new quality management principle: The quality management strategy of Toyota. *The Journal of Management & Engineering Integration, 1*(1), 7–22.

Amasaka, K. (2009). The foundation for advancing the Toyota Production System utilizing New JIT. *Journal of Advanced Manufacturing Systems, 8*(1), 5–26. doi:10.1142/S0219686709001614

Amasaka, K. (Ed.). (2012). Science TQM, New Quality Management Principle: The quality management strategy of Toyota. Bentham Science Publisher.

Amasaka, K. (2013). The development of a Total Quality Management System for transforming technology into effective management strategy. *International Journal of Management, 30*(2), 610–630.

Amasaka, K. (2015). New JIT, New Management Technology Principle. Taylor & Francis Group.

Amasaka, K. (2016). Innovation of automobile manufacturing fundamentals employing New JIT: Developing Advanced Toyota Production System at Toyota Manufacturing USA. *Proceedings of the 5th Conference on Production and Operations Management,* 1-10.

Amasaka, K. (2017a). *Toyota: Production System, safety analysis and future directions.* Nova Science Publishers.

Amasaka, K. (2017b). Strategic Stratified Task Team Model for realizing simultaneous QCD fulfilment: Two case studies. *Journal of Japanese Operations Management and Strategy, 7*(1), 14–35.

Amasaka, K. (2018). Toyota Production System: Arc de Triomphe Production System in France (Lecture). Academic Press.

Amasaka, K. (2019). Studies on New Manufacturing Theory, *Noble. International Journal of Scientific Research, 3*(1), 1–20.

Amasaka, K. (2022). New Manufacturing Theory, Surpassing JIT (2nd ed.). Lambert Academic Publishing.

Amasaka, K., & Sakai, H. (1996). Improving the reliability of body assembly line equipment. *International Journal of Reliability Quality and Safety Engineering, 3*(1), 11–24. doi:10.1142/S021853939600003X

Amasaka, K., & Sakai, H. (1998). Availability and Reliability Information Administration System "ARIM-BL" by methodology in Inline-Online SQC. *International Journal of Reliability Quality and Safety Engineering, 5*(1), 55–63. doi:10.1142/S0218539398000078

Amasaka, K., & Sakai, H. (2009). TPS-QAS, New Production Quality management Model: Key to New JIT-Toyota's global production strategy. *International Journal of Manufacturing Technology and Management, 18*(4), 409–426. doi:10.1504/IJMTM.2009.027774

Amasaka, K., & Sakai, H. (2010). Evolution of TPS fundamentals utilizing New JIT strategy- Proposal and validity of Advanced TPS at Toyota. *Journal of Advanced Manufacturing Systems, 9*(2), 85–99. doi:10.1142/S0219686710001831

Amasaka, K., & Sakai, H. (2011). The New Japan Global Production Model "NJ-GPM": Strategic development of *Advanced TPS. The Journal of Japanese Operations Management and Strategy, 2*(1), 1–15.

Burke, R. J., Graham, J., & Smith, F. (2005). Effects of reengineering on the employee satisfaction-customer satisfaction relationship. *The TQM Magazine, 17*(4), 358–363. doi:10.1108/09544780510603198

Ebioka, K., Sakai, H., Yamaji, M., & Amasaka, K. (2007). A New Global Partnering Production Model "NGP-PM" utilizing Advanced TPS. *Journal of Business & Economics Research, 5*(9), 1–8.

Ebioka, K., Yamaji, M., & Amasaka, K. (2006). Strategic Development of *Advanced TPS* to bring overseas manufacturing to Japan standards-Proposal of a new global partnering production model and effectiveness. *Proceedings of the 11th Annual International Conference on Industrial Engineering-Theory, Application and Practice*, 262-267.

Evans, J. R., & Lindsay, W. M. (1995). *The Management and Control of Quality.* South-Western.

Goto, T. (1999). *Forgotten the origin of management.* Seisansei-syuppan.

Grundspenkis, J. (2007). Agent based approach for organization and personal knowledge modeling: Knowledge management perspective. *Journal of Intelligent Manufacturing, 18*(4), 451–457. doi:10.100710845-007-0052-6

Halevi, G., & Wang, K. (2007). Knowledge based manufacturing system (KBMS). *Journal of Intelligent Manufacturing, 18*(4), 467–474. doi:10.100710845-007-0049-1

Hoogervorst, J. A. P., Koopman, P. L., & Flier, H. (2005). Total quality management: The need for an employee-centered coherent approach. *The TQM Magazine, 17*(1), 92–106. doi:10.1108/09544780510573084

Jeffrey, K. L. (2004). *The Toyota way*. McGraw-Hill.

Kakkar, S., & Narag, A. S. (2007). Recommending a TQM model for Indian organizations. *The TQM Magazine, 19*(4), 328–353. doi:10.1108/09544780710756232

Lagrosen, S. (2004). Quality management in global firms. *The TQM Magazine, 16*(6), 396–402. doi:10.1108/09544780410563310

Ljungström, M. (2005). A model for starting up and implementing continuous improvements and work development in practice. *The TQM Magazine, 17*(5), 385–405. doi:10.1108/09544780510615915

Miyashita, S., & Amasaka, K. (2014). Proposal of a "New Vietnam Production Model" (NVPM), a new integrated production system of Japan and Vietnam. *IOSR Journal of Business and Management, 16*(12), 18–25. doi:10.9790/487X-161211825

Prajogo, D. (2006). Progress of quality management practices in Australian manufacturing firms. *The TQM Magazine, 18*(5), 501–513. doi:10.1108/09544780610685476

Ramarapu, N. K., Mehra, S., & Frolick, M. N. (1995). A comparative analysis and review of JIT implementation research. *International Journal of Operations & Production Management, 15*(1), 38–49. doi:10.1108/01443579510077188

Sakai, H., & Amasaka, K. (2002). Construction of "*V-IOS*" for promoting Intelligence Operator. *Proceedings of the 18th Annual Technical Conf.*, 173-176.

Sakai, H., & Amasaka, K. (2005). V-MICS, Advanced TPS for strategic production administration: Innovative maintenance combining DB and CG. *Journal of Advanced Manufacturing Systems, 4*(6), 5–20. doi:10.1142/S0219686705000540

Sakai, H., & Amasaka, K. (2006). Strategic HI-POS, Intelligence Production Operating System: Applying Advanced TPS to Toyota's Global Production Strategy. *WSEAS Transactions on Advances in Engineering Education, 3*(3), 223–230.

Sakai, H., & Amasaka, K. (2007). Development of a robot control method for curved seal extrusion for high productivity in an advanced Toyota production system. *International Journal of Computer Integrated Manufacturing, 20*(5), 486–496. doi:10.1080/09511920601160262

Sakai, H., & Amasaka, K. (2008). Human-Integrated Assist Systems for intelligence operators. Encyclopedia of Networked and Virtual Iorganizations, 2(G-Pr), 678-687.

Sakai, H., & Amasaka, K. (2009). Proposal and demonstration of V-MICS-EM by digital Engineering: Robot operation and maintenance by utilizing Visual Manual. *International Journal of Manufacturing Technology and Management*, *18*(4), 344–355. doi:10.1504/IJMTM.2009.027769

Sakalsiz, M. M. (2009). *The proposal of New Turkish Production System utilizing Advanced TPS, Graduate School of Science and Engineering* (Master's thesis). Aoyama Gakuin University, Amasaka New JIT laboratory.

Shan, H. (2012). *The proposal of China Local Automobile Manufacturer's Production System.* Graduate School of Science and Engineering, Aoyama Gakin University, Amasaka New JIT Laboratory.

Shan, H., Yeap, Y. S., & Amasaka, K. (2011). Proposal of a New Malaysia Production Model "NMPM": a new integrated production system of Japan and Malaysia. *Proceedings of International Conference on Business Management 2011,* 235-246.

Siang, Y. Y., Sakalsiz, M. M., & Amasaka, K. (2010). Proposal of New Turkish Production System (NTPS), Integration and evolution of Japanese and Turkish production system. *Journal of Business Case Study*, *6*(6), 69–76. doi:10.19030/jbcs.v6i6.260

Yamaji, M., & Amasaka, K. (2006). New Japan Quality Management Model, Hyper-cycle model "QA & TQM Dual System" - Implementation of New JIT for strategic Management technology. *Proceedings of the International Manufacturing Leaders Forum,* 1-6.

Yamaji, M., & Amasaka, K. (2007). Proposal and validity of Global Intelligence Partnering Model for Corporate Strategy, "GIPM-CS". *Advances in Production Management Systems, International IFIP TC 5.7 Conference on Advanced in Production Management System,* 59-67.

Yamaji, M., & Amasaka, K. (2008). New Japan Quality Management Model: Implementation of New JIT for strategic management technology. *The International Business & Economics Research Journal*, *7*(3), 107–114.

Yamaji, M., & Amasaka, K. (2009). Strategic Productivity Improvement Model for white-collar workers employing Science TQM. *The Journal of Japanese Operations Management and Strategy*, *1*(1), 30–46.

Yamaji, M., Sakai, H., & Amasaka, K. (2006). Intellectual Working Value Improvement Model utilizing Advanced TPS: Applying New JIT: Toyota's global production strategy. *Proceedings of the International Applied Business Research Conference,* 1-10.

Yamaji, M., Sakai, H., & Amasaka, K. (2007). Evolution of technology and skills in production workplaces utilizing Advanced TPS. *Journal of Business & Economics Research*, *5*(6), 61–68.

Yeap, Y. S., Murat, M. S., & Amasaka, K. (2010). Proposal of New Turkish Production System, NTPS, Integration and evolution of Japanese and Turkish Production System. *Journal of Business Case Study*, *6*, 69–76.

Section 3

Development of Automobile Simultaneous QCD Fulfilment for Customer Value Creation

Chapter 12
Strategic Quality Management-Performance Measurement Model for QCD Strategy

ABSTRACT

This study presents the Strategic Quality Management-Performance Measurement Model (SQM-PMM) as a new methodology for enhancing the key elements of successful for enhancing QCD strategy and ensuring future manufacturing results through strategic quality management. SQM-PMM was developed based on the actual company management practices of top management employing Science TQM. The validity of SQM-PM as the key to maintaining competitive corporate management was verified. Through the establishment of SQM-PMM, quality management techniques for the Japan manufacturing activity are maximized, thus bringing in a new phase of strategic quality management.

INTRODUCTION

In the current manufacturing, where "worldwide quality competition" continues to intensify, production of equal quality in optimum locations is essential for successful global marketing of quality, cost and delivery (QCD) by developing the Toyota Production System (TPS) and Total Quality Management (TQM) (Refer to Chapter 2). With this in mind, the "Science TQM, new quality management principle" was established for improving quality management techniques to strengthen manufacturing using "Science SQC, new quality control principle," and its validity was verified for corporate QCD activity (Amasaka, 2004a, 2008; Amasaka, Ed., 2012).

This study presents the Strategic Quality Management—Performance Measurement Model (SQM-PMM) as a new methodology for enhancing the key elements of successful for enhancing QCD strategy, and ensuring future manufacturing results through strategic quality management. SQM-PMM was developed based on the actual company management practices of top management employing Science TQM. The validity of SQM-PM as the key to maintaining competitive corporate management was verified. Through the establishment of SQM-PMM, quality management techniques for the Japan manufacturing activity

DOI: 10.4018/978-1-7998-8746-1.ch012

are maximized, thus bringing in a new phase of strategic quality management (Amagai and Amasaka, 2003; Amasaka, 2004bc, 2009, 2020; Wakaizumi, 2005; Kozaki et al., 2012; Amasaka, Ed., 2012).

BACKGROUND

Amidst increasingly fierce competition in the manufacturing industry both at home and abroad, developing a renewed awareness of how the industry is approaching quality management is critical. Companies must use this awareness when tackling recent quality problems—problems so severe that they have seriously undermined customer satisfaction (CS). Increasing recalls among the major corporations that should be leading the world in global production are a wake-up call for the manufacturing industry to reinforce the strength of their quality-related technologies (Goto, 1999; Nihon Keizai Shinbun, 2000, 2006; Amasaka, Ed., 2007; Amasaka, 2008).

In recent years, digital engineering has resulted in a dramatic shift in how manufacturing worksites operate. One occasionally sees a phenomenon where scientific quality management methods designed to "build in" quality during the manufacturing process are becoming diluted due to several factors—including a decline in manufacturing (worksite) technology, the realization that employees' ability to discover and solve problems is weakening, and a general fading of the concept of building in quality. Companies cannot afford to limit themselves by their past successes or cling to outdated forms of quality management; setting up new quality management methods appropriate to production sites equipped with digital engineering technology is an urgent task (Joiner, 1994; Amasaka, 1999, 2004a).

As worldwide quality competition has come to define the new century, success in producing consistent global quality at optimum locations has become a crucial part of deploying the new global marketing strategy that is key to corporate survival (Amasaka, 2004a, 2008). There is thus a need for strategic quality management performance measures: they allow companies to solidify their management achievements and are the key to maintaining competitive superiority in the years to come. Furthermore, these measures must contribute to the strategic deployment of quality management technologies for the next generation (Amasaka, 2004bc).

SCIENCE TQM, NEW QUALITY MANAGEMENT PRINCIPLE FOR THE QCD STRATEGY

When the author looked at recent corporate activities both inside and outside Japan, he found cases where leading companies had lost customer trust. The loss of customer trust was due to stagnant R&D activities for enhancing QCD strategy, an issue stemming from chronic internal and/or external quality problems. As a result, the companies lost sight of customer needs and fell behind in technological development. At the same time, other companies are focusing on the "customer first" principle while actively innovating in product development, sales and marketing. These companies are conducting company-wide quality management activities, successfully enhancing CS (Amasaka, 2004a, 2005).

The author strongly believes that the key difference between the successful and unsuccessful companies lies in strategic quality management based on a "customer first" principle that allows them to grasp future trends. With this in mind, the author has proposed a new quality management principle named Science TQM, new quality management principle (Amasaka, 2004b, 2008: Amasaka, Ed., 2012), which also referred to as the New Japan Model (Amasaka, Ed., 2007), to many leading Japanese companies, including Toyota Motor Corp., and others.

Implementing Science TQM utilizing Science SQC, new quality control principle (Amasaka, Ed., 2000; Amasaka, 2003). The author therefore endeavored to create strategic quality management performance measures to respond to the top concern of corporate management: how to solidify management achievements in the years to come. As the key to maintaining competitive superiority, these measures serve as a compass for corporate management activities. This process is outlined in the following sections.

ESTABLISHMENT OF THE STRATEGIC QUALITY MANAGEMENT — PERFORMANCE MEASUREMENT MODEL (SQM-PMM)

The Strategic Quality Management – Performance Measurement Model (SQM-PMM) was established as a key to the strategic manufacturing application of TPS and TQM in order to ensure superior corporate management achievements (Amasaka, 1999, 2004bc, 2009, 2022; Amasaka, Ed., 2000, 2012; Amagai and Amasaka, 2003; Wakaizumi, 2005; Kozaki et al., 2012).

Significance of Constructing SQM-PMM

The present study is based upon the viewpoints of management at leading companies (actual quality management activities undertaken by management and the resulting achievements), rather than existing international standards or awards (Refer to references: Chowdhury and Zimmer, 1996; Amasaka et al., 1999; Furuya, 1999; ISO9004, 2000; Boesen, 2000; Deming Prize Committee, 2003; Japan Quality Award Committee, 2003; EFQM, 2003).

The factors of quality management systems and practices were extracted and a model of causal relationships between these factors and QCD management achievements was constructed. The ultimate aim was to establish an SQM-PMM that ensures effective application of Science TQM and strategic quality management. This cause and effect analysis, which directly links performance measurement to corporate management performance, is unprecedented.

Questionnaire Overview

A survey of top management at Japanese manufacturers as shown in Table 1 was conducted in order to investigate (I) TQM Activity Structures and Practices and (II) TQM Achievements (quality, CS and productivity) and future tasks (Survey targeted 898 companies and resulted in 354 valid responses for a rate of 39.4%).

Questions in the TQM Activity Structures and Practices section (I) fell into the following categories as shown in Table 2: [1] Quality assurance and CS (8 items), [2] Product and technological development (3 items), [3] Lively corporate culture (10 items), and [4] Conventional TQM methods (7 items). For these items, the respondents were asked to evaluate their existing activity structure and practices on a 5-point scale and state their reasons for that evaluation. Questions in the TQM Achievements (quality, CS and productivity) and future Tasks section (II) included those in the [1] Quality and CS (5 items) and [2] Productivity (4 items) categories. The respondents evaluated their achievements and future tasks on a 3-point scale with an explanation of their reasons for that evaluation and future plans (see Table **2**).

Table 1. Sample composition

	Number of replies	Type of industry								Total
		Machinery	Primary metals	General materials	Natural resources	Direct materials	Service	Electricity	Petrochemistry	
Number of employees	Below 100	1	1	1	0	3	0	0	0	6
	100 – 299	15	4	8	0	6	6	2	5	46
	300 – 499	9	3	6	0	6	4	0	1	29
	500 – 999	29	1	13	0	12	11	0	5	71
	1,000 – 4,999	63	6	20	1	28	5	0	6	129
	5,000 – 9,999	18	1	6	0	9	0	1	3	38
	10,000 or more	23	0	1	0	6	3	1	1	35
Total		158	16	55	1	70	29	4	21	354

Table 2. Questionnaire content

I. TQM Activity Structure and Practice	II. TQM Achievements and Future Tasks
[1] Quality assurance, CS (1) Quality assurance to (8) CR structure [2] Product and technological development (1) Planning analysis and results incorporation to (3) Technological development and product planning [3] Lively corporate culture (i) Total participation activities (1) Decision making speed to (5) Intra-divisional team activity (ii) Creative workplace (1) Improvement motivation to (5) ES [4] Conventional TQM methods (1) Vision and strategy to (7) Top assessment and audit	[1] Quality and CS achievement (1) Customer complaint resolution cost reduction (2) Customer complaint reduction (3) CS improvement (4) New product development (5) Sales and marketing share enhancement [2] Productivity achievement (1) Sales per head (2) Hourly productivity (3) Cost reduction (4) Lead time reduction

Analytical Survey Results

1. State of TQM implementation (Question 1, see Figure 1)

Figure 1. TQM structure and practice

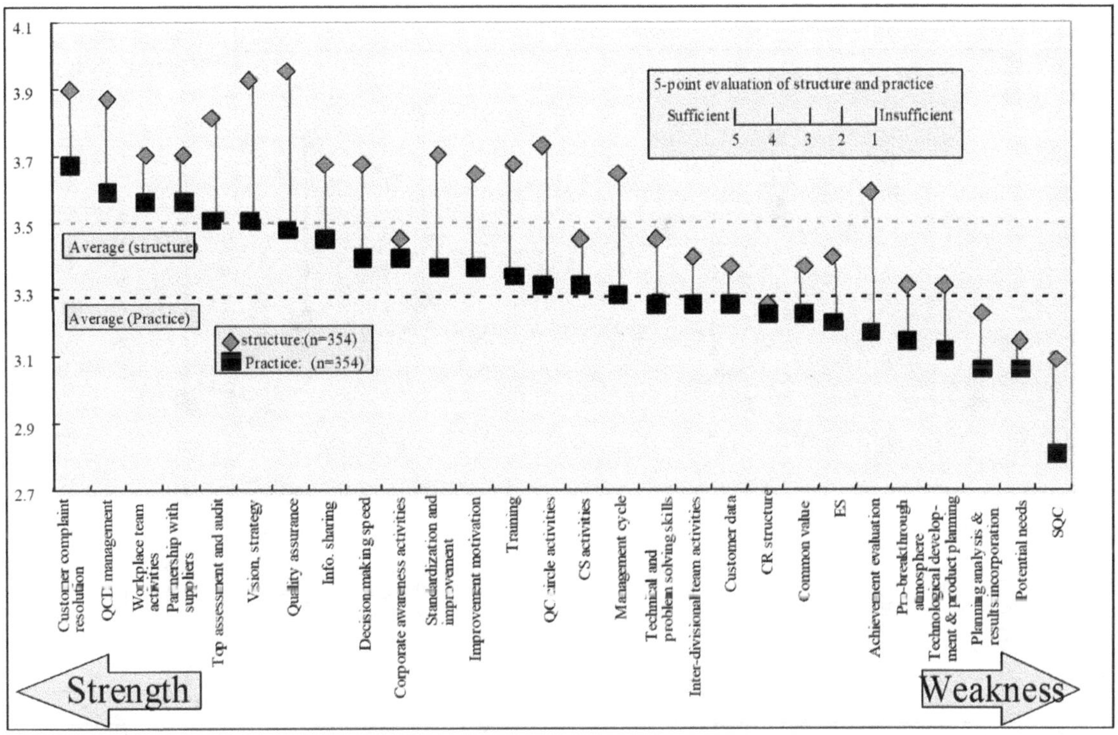

The current state of TQM activities in Japan can be summarized by looking at the following common shortcomings: (i) expected product quality has been retained; (ii) improvements aimed at more attractive quality are lacking; (iii) low division-to-division coordination and organizational vitality; (iv) structures exist for developing vision and strategies, but implementation and/or evaluation of achievements is weak; (v) organizations only partly utilize SQC and do not accumulate techniques; and (vi) a TQM structure exists, but is not sufficiently implemented.

2. TQM achievements and future tasks (Question 2, see Figure 2) and are summarized as follows:
   a. TQM, in principle, contributes to improvement of quality, cost and delivery; and
   b. current TQM activities do not contribute much to promote sales, improve CS, or address other important management issues.

12.4.4 Categorical Automatic Interaction Detector (CAID) analysis

Based on these findings, the author conducted a Categorical Automatic Interaction Detector (CAID) analysis (Murayama, et al. 1982; Amasaka, et al. 1998; Amasaka, 1999) in order to identify the major elements of TQM that lead a company to success. The results of this analysis are shown in Figure 3. For example, companies that rated CS, CR (Customer Retention), and product and technological development as important contributors to sales and market share growth showed excellent achievements in terms of QCD.

Figure 2. TQM achievements and future tasks

Figure 3. Causal analysis for sales and increased market share - CAID analysis

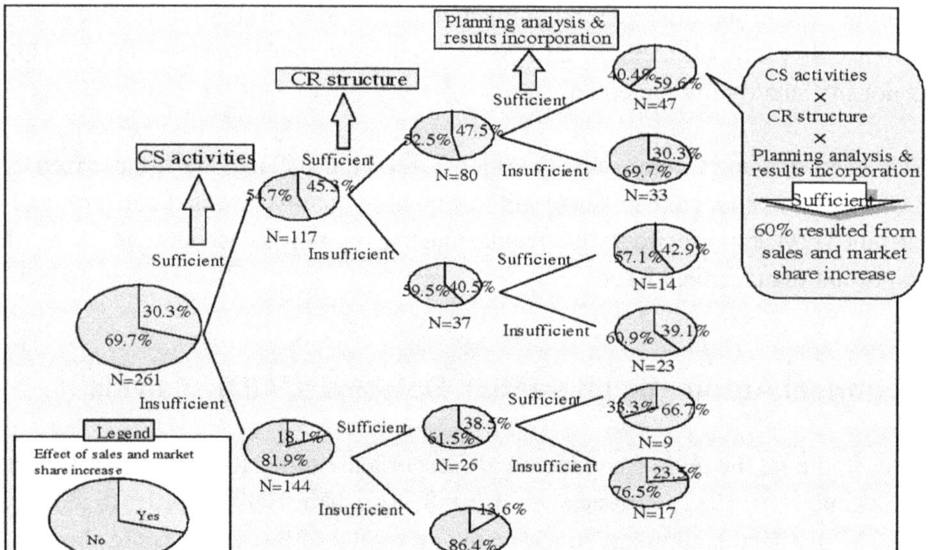

These results underscore the necessity of quality management performance measurements that enable top management to evaluate their company's quality management status and strategically utilize TQM activities in the future. Among the companies that implemented sufficient CS activities (N=117), 45.3% were able to increase their sales and/or market share. Furthermore, among the companies that put a sufficient CR structure in place, performed a results analysis, and incorporated these results into their technological development and merchandise planning (N=47), about 60% were able to increase their sales and market share.

These results make it clear that companies must devote themselves to CS, CR, and results analysis, and then reflect the results in technological development and merchandise planning to improve sales and market share.

Graphical Modeling Method

In the course of SQM-PMM formulation, further analysis was conducted using the graphical modeling method. Based on the correlations among the 28 TQM activity practice items (confirmed using a partial correlation coefficient), interrelation of the six categories—quality, CS, product and technological development, total participation, creative workshops, and TQM methods using SQC—and their contribution to corporate achievements was confirmed visually through the relation chart method shown in Figure 4.

In Figure 4, the author suggests that TQM methods, technological development, CS, quality assurance, and corporate culture are all modeling associated with management achievement. In particular, a strong

Figure 4. Relationships among TQM practices and achievements-Graphical modeling

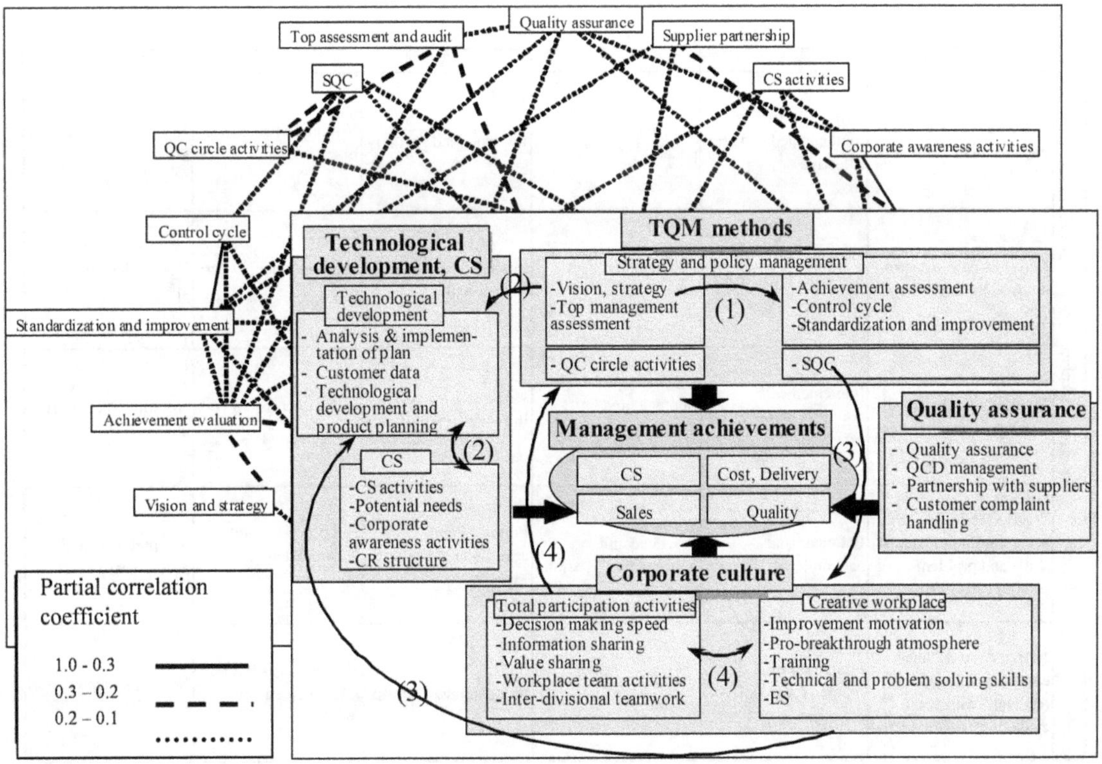

correlation was found between quality assurance and product quality as well as between technological development/CS and sales.

For example, the relationship marked with Arrow (1) indicates that in order for their vision/strategy and top management to function effectively, companies must enhance achievement assessment, control cycles, and standardization/improvement. The two arrows marked with (2) indicate that a correct vision/ strategy is necessary for technological development and CS to effectively contribute to sales.

The arrows marked (3) signify that a creative workplace, backed by SQC, is necessary as a foundation for effective technological development. The arrows marked (4) illustrate the relationship between total participation activities and a creative workplace, as well as the importance of QC circle activities as participation opportunities for all employees.

Formulation of the SQM-PMM through Canonical Correlation Analysis

Finally, canonical correlation analysis was conducted to clarify the correlation between the two main variables (practice items and management achievement items). The analysis focused on weighing factors of the selected first canonical variable. As a result, a SQM-PMM was successfully formulated as below: The 28 items for (I) TQM Activity Structure and Practice were sequentially determined as x_1 to x_{28}.

The first canonical variable f_1 (f_{11} to f_{16}) was divided into six categories, of which the relational expressions are indicated in (1) through to (6). Items x_1 to x_4 are quality assurance, x_5 to x_9 are CS, x_{10} to x_{12} are product and technological development, x_{13} to x_{17} are total participation activities, x_{18} to x_{22} are creative workshops, and x_{25} to x_{28} are conventional TQM methods.

Table 3. Example of SQM-PM standardization (Creative workshop)

	Evaluation Item	5	4	3	2	1
Creative workplace	Activities to maintain improvement motivation	Original activities implemented and are effective	Implemented generally	Implemented partially	Not implemented very much	Not implemented at all
	Activities to create pro-innovation atmosphere	Original activities implemented and are effective	Implemented generally	Implemented occasionally	Not implemented very often	Not implemented at all
	Training to enhance all employees' capabilities	Implemented regularly and is effective	Implemented generally	Implemented partially	Not implemented very much	Not implemented at all
	Practice and accumulation of special skills and problem solving capabilities	Practiced and accumulated	Practiced and accumulated generally	Practiced and accumulated to some extent	Not practiced and accumulated very much	Not practiced and accumulated at all
	Activities to enhance employee satisfaction (e.g. self realization, evaluation, treatment)	Implemented regularly and is effective	Implemented generally	Implemented partially	System exists but not implemented very much	Not implemented at all

1. $f_{11}=0.418x_1+0.232x_2+0.530x_3+0.160x_4$
2. $f_{12}=0.160x_5+0.878x_6+0.156x_7+0.494x_8+0.533x_9$
3. $f_{13}=0.335x_{10}+0.712x_{11}+0.063x_{12}$
4. $f_{14}=0.089x_{13}+0.477x_{14}+0.064x_{15}+0.058x_{16}+0.332x_{17}$
5. $f_{15}=0.230x_{18}+0.316x_{19}+0.259x_{20}+0.052x_{21}+0.210x_{22}$
6. $f_{16}=0.105x_{23}+0.254x_{24}+0.254x_{25}+0.251x_{26}+0.119x_{27}+0.190x_{28}$

Standardization of SQM-PMM

These six categories—(i) Quality Assurance (ii) TQM Methods (iii) Creative Workshops (iv) Total Participation Activities (v) Product and Technological Development, and (vi) CS—were standardized using formulas (1) to (6) and evaluated using a radar chart.

Table 3 shows the 5-point scale evaluation of category (iii), Creative Workshops. Practical application of the SQM-PMM has begun using the Amasaka New JIT Laboratory (http://133.2.218.195/~amalab/H) website (see Table 4 and Figure 5).

Table 4. An example of SQM-PMM (Source: Amagai and Amasaka, 2003)

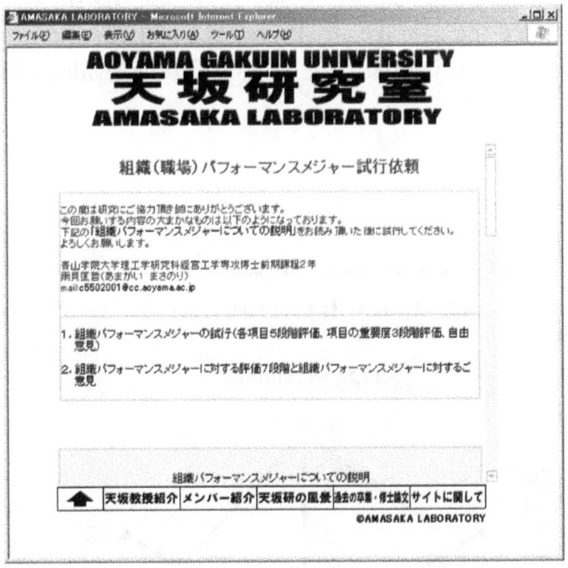

VERIFING THE VALIDITY OF SQM-PMM

Subsequent to the development of the model, the author asked top management and division general managers of leading companies in Japan to use the SQM-PMM in order to examine its validity (Amagai and Amasaka, 2003; Amasaka, 2004bc, 2009; Wakaizumi, 2005; Kozaki et al., 2012; Amasaka Ed., 2012).

Verification Objectives and Method

Verification was conducted to see whether SQM-PMM correctly reflected the evaluators' (management of leading companies) understanding of quality management. The extent of dispersion was also verified as a function of the evaluators' positions in their organizations. Furthermore, if evaluators made appropriate evaluations with SQM-PMM when calculating the results for (1) to (6) in 4.6, it was possible to identify the evaluation items (x_1 to X_{28} in 4.6) that should be improved to enhance management achievement items (f_{11} to f_{16} in 4.6) (Amagai and Amasaka, 2003).

SQM-PMM was utilized on a trial basis at five companies (A: Fuji-Xerox, B: Nihon-Hatsujyo, C: Yanma, D: Kawasaki-Seitetsu, and E: Sanden) and evaluated by eight evaluators (A_1, B_1–B_3, C_1, D_1–D_2 and E_1). Five evaluators were in positions that allowed them to grasp company-wide quality management status (top management: A_1, B_1, C_1, D_1, and E_1), while three evaluators were in positions that allowed them to observe business category–level quality management status (general managers: B_2, B_3, and D_2). Possible dispersions based on evaluator position and the validity of SQM-PM were examined.

Implementation Results and Discussion

Figure 5 is a radar chart prepared by evaluator A_1 indicating the results of the SQM-PMM trial at Company B. The chart is based on relationships (1) to (6) using the SQM-PMM. As shown in the figure, results were balanced, exceeded the average in all aspects, and corresponded to the evaluator's prior evaluation that product development is relatively strong. Similar evaluations were also obtained from other evaluators.

Figure 5. Radar chart Sample-1

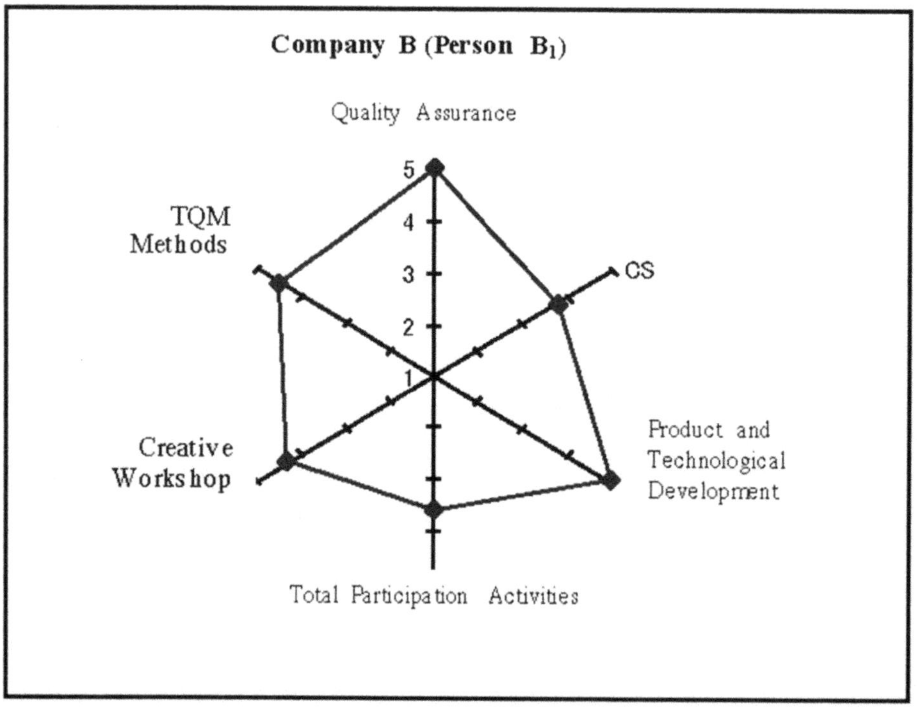

Figure 6. Evaluator positions

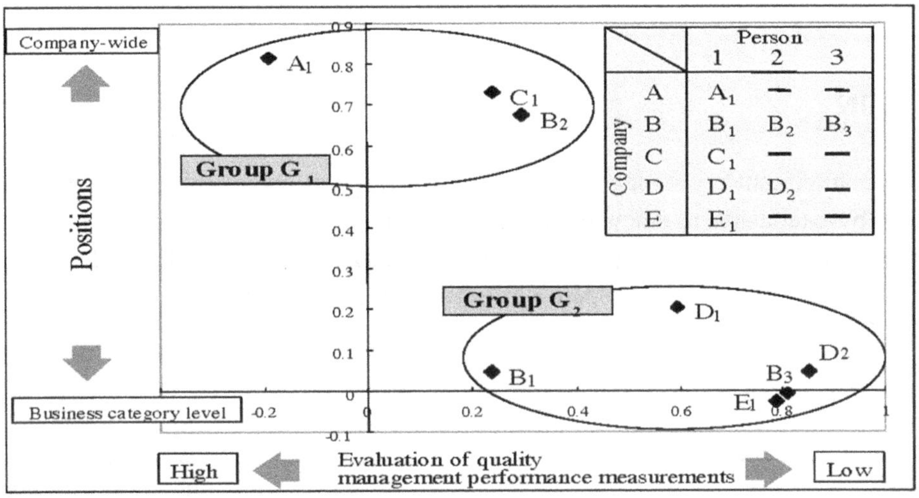

In addition, evaluator positions were analyzed using the principal component analysis shown in Figure 6. This analysis was based on the SQM-PMM evaluation and performance measurement results. The analysis classified the evaluators into two groups—one (Group G_1) made up of those who confirmed the validity of performance measurement for company-level quality management performance (positions where it was possible to grasp company-wide quality management status), and the other (Group G_2) made up of those who wanted performance measurement designed exclusively for each business category (positions where it was possible to observe business category–level quality management status).

In Figure 6, the primary component axis (horizontal axis) represents the evaluation scores (SQM-PMM) and the secondary main component axis (vertical axis) represents the evaluation focus (company-wide perspective or business category–oriented). Judging from the positioning shown in the figure, the G_1 group (company-wide level) tended to give higher ratings while the G_2 group (business category level) tended to give lower ratings.

Moreover, business category–oriented evaluations were confirmed. While evaluator B_2, a division general manager, made his evaluation from a company-wide standpoint, even the top management evaluators B_1, D_1, and E_1 showed a business category–oriented viewpoint. Upon presenting these findings (see the positioning in Figure 7) to all evaluators, it was proven that the results correctly reflect the evaluators' implicit prior evaluation, thus demonstrating the general validity of SQM-PM. Based on the evaluation guidelines (e.g. an evaluation sheet for each of the six categories and a radar chart for the evaluation results), top management evaluated the state of their company's quality management.

As a result, the strengths and weaknesses of quality management recognized in advance were expressed objectively.

Verification of SQM-PMM Validity

To verify the validity of SQM-PMM, additional investigations were conducted at companies A (Fuji-Xerox: 2 persons, 2 sections), B (Nihon-Hatsujyo: 5 persons, 2 sections), E (Sanden: 13 persons, 3 sections), F (Calsonic-Kansei: 6 persons, 3 sections) and G (Daikin-Kogyou: 17 persons, 6 sections) in the same way. The validity of SQM-PMM was reconfirmed as shown in Figure 7, proving the effectiveness of SQM-PM as a tool to identify what TQM actions are necessary for strategic quality management.

CONCLUSION

SQM-PMM is an important key to maximizing manufacturing activity for enhancing QCD strategy. This model was hereby established as a new methodology to enable top management to accurately evaluate corporate quality management for corporate QCD activity. The validity of SQM-PMM was proven successfully as the key to maintaining competitive corporate management.

Figure 7. Radar chart Sample-2

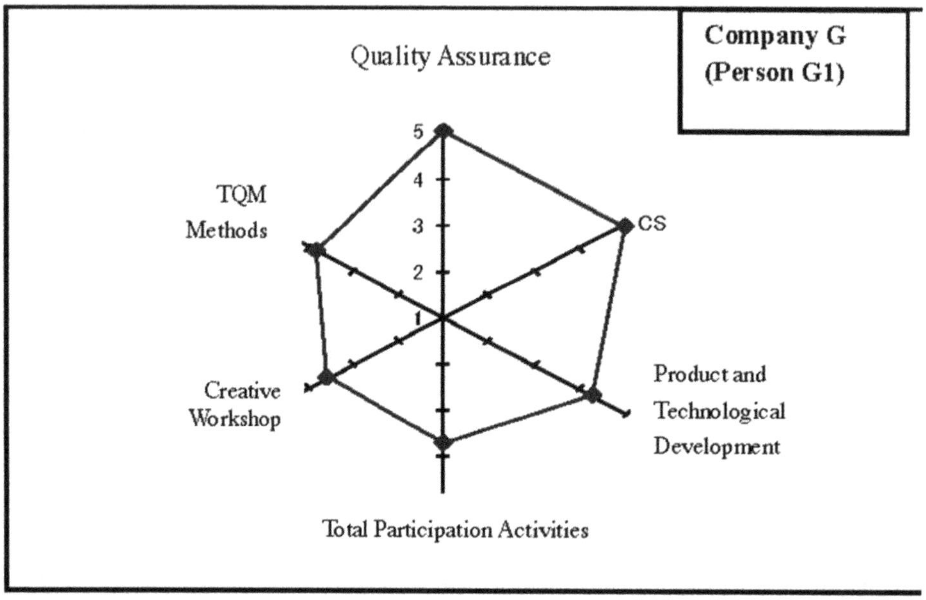

ACKNOWLEDGMENT

The author would like to acknowledge the generous support of the following researchers: Union of Japanese Scientists and Engineers (JUSE), Toyota Motor Corp., (: JUSE-68QCS "Questionnaire analysis team of Toyota Group," and the Amasaka New JIT laboratory at Aoyama Gakuin University that assisted with the research, especially, Mr. Kosugi, T., Mr. Maki, K., Mr. Iwamoto, N., Mr. Arai, Y., Mr. Kunishima, T., Mr. Koto. H., Mr. Hanamura, K., Mr. Amagai, M.,Mr. Wakaizumi, T., Mr. Kozaki, T., Miss. Oura, A and others.

REFERENCES

Amagai, M., & Amasaka, K. (2003). A study for the establishment of the quality management performance measure. *Proceedings of the 17th Asia Quality Symposium, Beijing Jiuhua Country Villa, Beijing, China*, 243-250.

Amasaka, K. (1999). The TQM responsibilities for industrial management in Japan: The actual condition survey of TQM activity seen from the viewpoint of management (Special Lecture). *Journal of the Japanese Society for Production Management,* 48-54.

Amasaka, K. (1999). *The preliminary survey in 68QCS: The questionnaire result of "TQM which creates Japan (1st report). In Union of Japanese Scientists and Engineers, 68QCS symposium.* Hakone.

Amasaka, K. (Ed.). (2000). The aim of Science SQC - Deployment as a new TQM methodology from a management perspective. In Science SQC: The reform of quality within business processes. Japan Standards Association.

Amasaka, K. (2003). Proposal and implementation of the *Science SQC* quality control principle. *An International Journal of Mathematical and Computer Modelling, 38*(11-13), 1125–1136. doi:10.1016/S0895-7177(03)90113-0

Amasaka, K. (2004a). Development of Science TQM, a new principle of quality management. *International Journal of Production Research, 42*(17), 3691–3706. doi:10.1080/0020754042000203867

Amasaka, K. (2004b). Establishment of performance measurement toward strategic quality management: Key to successful implementation of new management principle, Science TQM. *Proceedings of the 4th International Conference on Theory and Practice in Performance Measurement*, 515-522.

Amasaka, K. (2004c). Establishment of strategic quality management - Performance Measurement Model – Key to successful implementation of *Science TQM* (Part 6). *The Japan Society for Production Management, The 20th Annual Technical Conference,* 95-98.

Amasaka, K. (2005). Constructing a Customer Science application system "CS-CIANS" – Development of a global strategic vehicle "Lexus" utilizing New JIT. *WSEAS Transactions on Business and Economics, 3*(2), 135–142.

Amasaka, K. (Ed.). (2007). New Japan Model – Science TQM: Theory and practice for strategic quality management. Study group of the ideal situation the quality management of the manufacturing industry, Maruzen, Tokyo.

Amasaka, K. (2008). Science TQM, a new quality management principle: The quality management strategy of Toyota. *The Journal of Management & Engineering Integration, 1*(1), 7–22.

Amasaka, K. (2009). Establishment of Strategic Quality Management – Performance Measurement Model "SQM-PPM": Key to successful implementation of Science TQM. *China-USA Business Review, 8*(12), 1–11.

Amasaka, K. (Ed.). (2012). Science TQM, new quality management principle: The quality management strategy of Toyota. Bentham Science Publisher.

Amasaka, K. (2022). New Manufacturing Theory: Surpassing JIT (2nd ed.). LAP Lambert Academic Publishing.

Amasaka, K., Kishimoto, M., Murayama, T., & Ando, M. (1998). The development of Marketing SQC for dealers' sales operating system. *Journal of the Japanese Society for Quality Control, The 58th Technical Conference,* 76-79.

Boesen, T. (2000). *Creating budget - less organizations with the balanced scorecard, Balanced scorecard report.* Harvard Business School Publishing.

Chowdhury, S., & Zimmer, K. (1996). *QS-9000 PIONEERS.* Irwin Professional Pub.

Deming Prize Committee. (2003). *The bookmark of Deming Prize.* Union of Japanese Scientists and Engineers Press.

EFQM. (2003). *The EFQM excellence model.* www.EFQM.org

Furuya, Y. (1999). TQM which creates Japan (2nd report): Results of the investigation of the questionnaire analysis team-The proposal of TQM which will aim at the 21 C based on the viewpoint of management. *Union of Japanese Scientists and Engineers, 68QCS symposium.*

Goto, T. (1999). *Forgotten management origin - Management quality taught by GHQ.* Seisansei-shuppan.

ISO 9004. (2003). *Quality Management System - Guideline for performance.* Japan Quality Award Committee.

Joiner, B. L. (1994). *Fourth generation management: The new business consciousness.* Joiner Associates, Inc.

Kozaki, T., Oura, A., & Amasaka, K. (2012). Establishment of TQM Promotion Diagnosis Model "TQM-PDM" for strategic quality management. *China-USA Business Review, 10*(11), 811–819.

Murayama, T. (1994). *Analyzing CAID, Marketing Review.* Japan Research Center.

Nihon Keizai Shinbun. (2000). *Worst record: 40% increase of vehicle recalls.* Author.

Nihon Keizai Shinbun. (2006). *Risky "Quality": apart from production increase, it is recall rapid increase.* Author.

Wakaizumi, T. (2005). *Proof theory research on the Japanese Quality Management Consultation Model (A-QMDS) construction* (Master's thesis). Graduate school of Science and Engineering, Amasaka New JIT Laboratory.

Chapter 13
Automobile Exterior Design Model Using Customer Science Principles

ABSTRACT

As customer values become increasingly diverse, automobile exterior design is becoming one of the most critical elements influencing customer purchase behavior for automakers. The author develops a scientific approach to identifying customers' tastes, called Automobile Exterior Design Model (AEDM). To address this issue, the author uses Customer Science Principle aiming to achieve Intelligence Design Concept Method (CS-IDCM) developed elsewhere. AEDM improves the design business process so that implicit knowledge on customer is turned into explicit knowledge. To strengthen automobile exterior design, AEDM contributes to the following: (1) improvement of design business process methods for automobile profile design, (2) creation of automobile profile design using "psychographics" approach methods, and (3) actual studies on automobile profile design, form, and color matching methods. The validity of the proposed model was verified through case studies of the actual application of AEDM.

INTRODUCTION

At present, global marketing of automobile industry is growing rapidly. It is important for mapping up exterior design strategies to study on "what style of vehicles would lead the world market in the future?" However, in many cases, automaker's vehicle designers do not have a clear idea of future vehicle styling (Nunogaki et al., 1996). In order to respond to such a trend of vehicle exterior design, it is essential to conduct a scientific approach to customers' tastes whereby the customers' tastes are accurately grasped and reflected in the vehicle designing process by means of statistical science named Science SQC (Amasaka, 1999a, 1999b).

A specific commercialization study was conducted through academic-industrial cooperation, and substantial results have been obtained in the innovation of the vehicle designing process for 4-wheel vehicles (Amasaka et al., 1999; Nagaya et al., 1998; Okazaki et al., 2000; Amasaka and Nagaya, 2002).

DOI: 10.4018/978-1-7998-8746-1.ch013

This task is to be undertaken by the vehicle designing department. It is deemed important to determine the customers' desires in a precise manner, and to provide the vehicle designers with a clear-cut styling concept based on research of psychographics by the viewpoint of customers' life stage and lifestyle. As customer values become increasingly diverse, an automobile exterior design becomes an important element for automakers. Unfortunately, as people's values and subjective preferences become more varied and complex, it becomes increasingly difficult to accurately define their wants and needs.

As providing what customer's desire before they notice their wants becomes an essential part of any successful vehicle designing business, the author creates Automobile Exterior Design Model (AEDM) for customer value creation. To do the development of ADEM, the author applies "Customer Science Principle" that captures the customers' tastes by employing profile design concept support tool named "Customer Science aiming to achieve Intelligence Design Concept Method" (CS-IDCM). CS-IDCM utilizes SQC Technical Methods, which is one of the core methods of Science SQC (Amasaka et al., 1999; Nagaya et al., 1998).

AEDM takes a scientific approach to customer preferences and verbalizes (imagines or conceptualizes) the customers' feelings (which is implicit information). It conducts intelligence designing (i.e., converting implicit information into explicit information) in such a way that it reflects the information onto the design drawings. As an original idea, the author has developed a vehicle proportion, form, and color matching methodology based on AEDM. AEDM combines (A) Improvement of Design Business Process Methods for Automobile Profile Design, (B) Creation of Automobile Profile Design using "Psychographics" Approach Methods, and (C) Actual studies on Automobile Profile Design, Form and Color Matching Methods.

As research examples of the actual application of AEDM, the authors applied this model to the product design process and obtained the results in the development of Toyota Lexus and others (Amasaka and Nagaya, 2002; Nakamura et al., 2008; Amasaka, 2004a,b, 2015, 2018, 2022).

CUSTOMER SCIENCE PRINCIPLE

Issue in Automobile Marketing, Product Planning and Designing

Today, an increasing number of companies both in Japan and abroad try to grasp the unprejudiced desires of their customers from the viewpoint of customer-oriented business management and to reflect these desires in future product development (Amasaka, 1995; Evans et al., 2004). However, the actual behavioral patterns of designers in trying to grasp latent customer desires depend heavily on their empirical skills (Amasaka, 1999a, 1999b, 2003b, 2004b). Designers of vehicle designing department often proceed with product development using implicit business processes (Amasaka et al., 1999; Amasaka, Ed., 2007).

Accordingly, their performance is measured by sales results, and their efforts to improve business processes for future jobs may be insufficient as implicit prescriptions. Furthermore, designers often worry that their current business approaches are likely to depend on job performing capabilities and on the sensitivity (or intuition or knack) of individual persons, which does not improve the probability of success in future (Mori, 1991: Shinohara et al., 1996: Moriya and Sugiura, 1999). It is, therefore, important to establish a scientific approach that improves powers of product conception or a new model that assists the conception of strategic product development and tests its validity (Amasaka et al., 1999; Yamaji and Amasaka, 2009).

Developing New Japan Development Management Model for raising Customer Value

For strategic product development, it is important to explore consumer values, which are the basis for creating “wants”. Therefore, the author develops the New Japan Development Management Model (NJ-DMM) named “Advanced TDS, strategic development design model” as shown in Figure 1 (Amasaka, 2007a, b) (Refer to Chapter 6).

Specifically, to realize this, it is necessary to develop first core element “Intelligence Product Design Management System for the “Optimization of Development design Specification” as the development of “Development Design System Reform” by described in Figure 1.

Figure 1. New Japan Development Management Model (NJ-DMM)

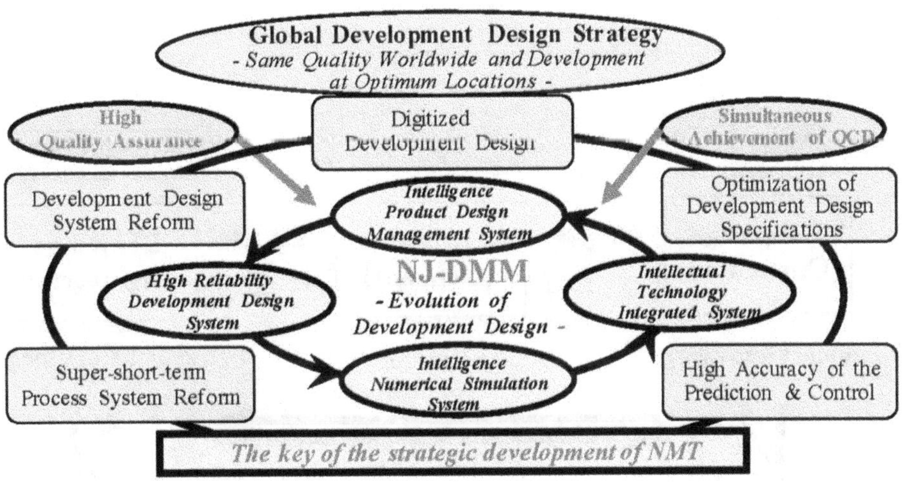

Customer Science Principle Aiming Customer Scientific Analysis

The mission of manufacturers is to offer products that please customers, and make it serve as a basis for sustainable growth. In this new era when product development is required as a basis of global marketing, it is important to establish a “behavior science principle” for strategic product development, which can dig deep into the customers’ needs and thus preempt the trend of times (Amasaka, 2003a, 2005).

Customers express their desires in words. Therefore, the product planners or designers engaging in product development must properly interpret these words and draw up accurate plans accordingly. The “Customer Science Principle” aims for customer value creation in an automobile exterior design with a clear-cut styling concept, which is based on psychographics by the viewpoint of customers’ life stage and lifestyle, as shown in Figure 2 (Amasaka, 2002, 2005, 2007b; Takimoto et al., 2010). It is intended to indicate the desirable state of new business processes for creating wants indispensable to the development of attractive products.

In Figure 2, the image of customer’s words (implicit knowledge) is translated first into common language (lingual knowledge) and then into engineering language (design drawings as explicit knowledge) by means of appropriate correlation. In other words, objectification of subjective information is realized in product development. It is also important to transform objective drawing into subjective information through correlation to check where engineering successfully reflects customer requirements. This refers to the Customer Science Principle that converts subjective information, y, to objective information, $\hat{y}$, and vice versa with a two-way application of correlation technology.

The author surmises that the implementation of Customer Science Principle improves the precision of "idea - product creation" in the business process of product development and designing and thus further ensures the accumulation of successful cases as well as the failure cases more than ever before. Taking an approach using Customer Science Principle can convert a variety of issues - why the customers are pleased with this particular product, why they complain about it, what is the underlying factor in this expression from the customers, what type of products must be offered next time, and in what situations defective products are manufactured - into a common language as well as the technical terms relevant to the manufacturing field.

Figure 2. Schematic drawing of Customer Science Principle

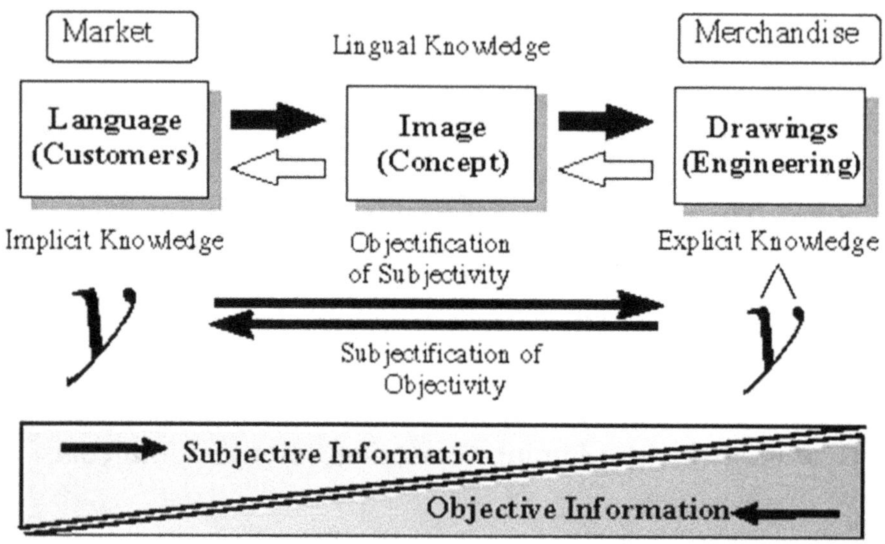

Figure 3. Systematic utilization levels of customer information for Customer Science activities

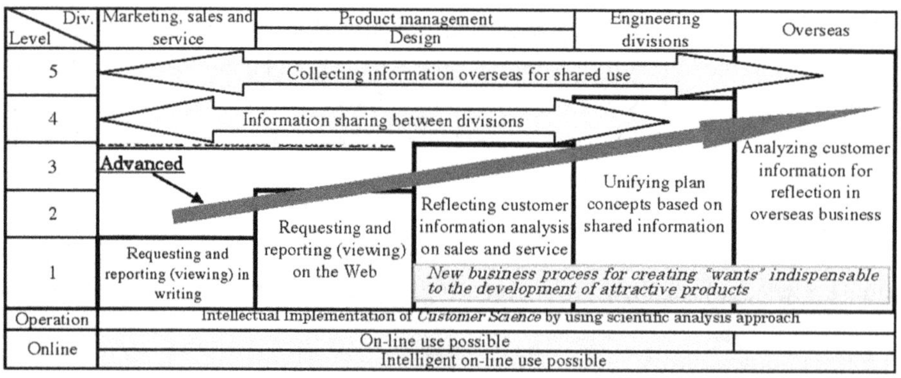

The designing or development staff can convert such verbal expressions into numerical terms using correlation techniques in their laboratory or experiment room in order to confirm whether the customers' demands are satisfied. Moreover, in order to double-check whether the objectification is properly conducted, it is vital for them to subjectify the results of objectification using correlation techniques. It has been observed that thriving manufacturers, today in Japan and in the world, endeavor to convert implicit knowledge into explicit knowledge in an effort to grasp the customers feelings, and to feed-back what has been drawn up to consider whether the original objective has been realized. That is, subjectifying the objectification is done: Such a humble attitude seems to be the manufacturers' essential growth base.

Customer Science Application System "CS-CIANS"

1. New Vehicle Model for Assisting the Conception of Strategic Product Development

Today, growing companies both in Japan and abroad try to grasp the unprejudiced desires of their customers from the viewpoint of customer-oriented business management and to reflect these desires in future product development. However, the actual behavioral patterns (conception methods) of designers (new product planners and designers) in trying to grasp latent customer desires depend heavily on the designers' empirical skills. Accordingly, designers often worry that their current business approaches are likely to depend on job performing capabilities and on the sensitivity (intuition or knack) of individual persons, which will not improve the probability of success in the future, regardless of whether or not they have "lucky success" or "unlucky failure".

For the realization of strategic products, the collection as well as intellectual analysis of customer information for creating customer "wants" is the core essence for success in Customer Science. Figure 3 shows the levels of systematic utilization of customer information and the modes of intellectual information-sharing among the related divisions inside and outside the company that are necessary to achieve this objective. To advance the level of execution of Customer Science activities, it is necessary to evolve customer information-sharing among the Marketing/Sales/Service, Product Management/Design, and Engineering/Production divisions from off-line to on-line (Amasaka, 2004c).

2. CS-CIANS, Networking of Customer Science Application System

For strategic product development, it is important to explore consumer values, which are the basis for creating "wants," through the collection/analysis of customer information, and to reflect as well as exteriorize such values in product development. Against this background, the author has constructed the "CS-CIANS, Networking of *Customer Science* Application System" for strategic product development, as shown in Figure 4 (Amasaka, 2005). This is designed to analyze customer information incorporating the optimal scientific approach, Science SQC, and to serve as a navigation system for the acquired analysis results.

Figure 4 shows the CS-CIANS networking system to which the customer science method is applied. As indicated therein, this system enables (1) the Merchandise Planning Div. which explores customer values and (2) each division of Product Planning and Design to regularly receive "Customer Data" from (3) domestic and overseas dealers which are exposed to the front line of the customer desires through their marketing/sales/service activities.

Figure 4. CS-CIANS, Networking of Customer Science Application System for strategic product development

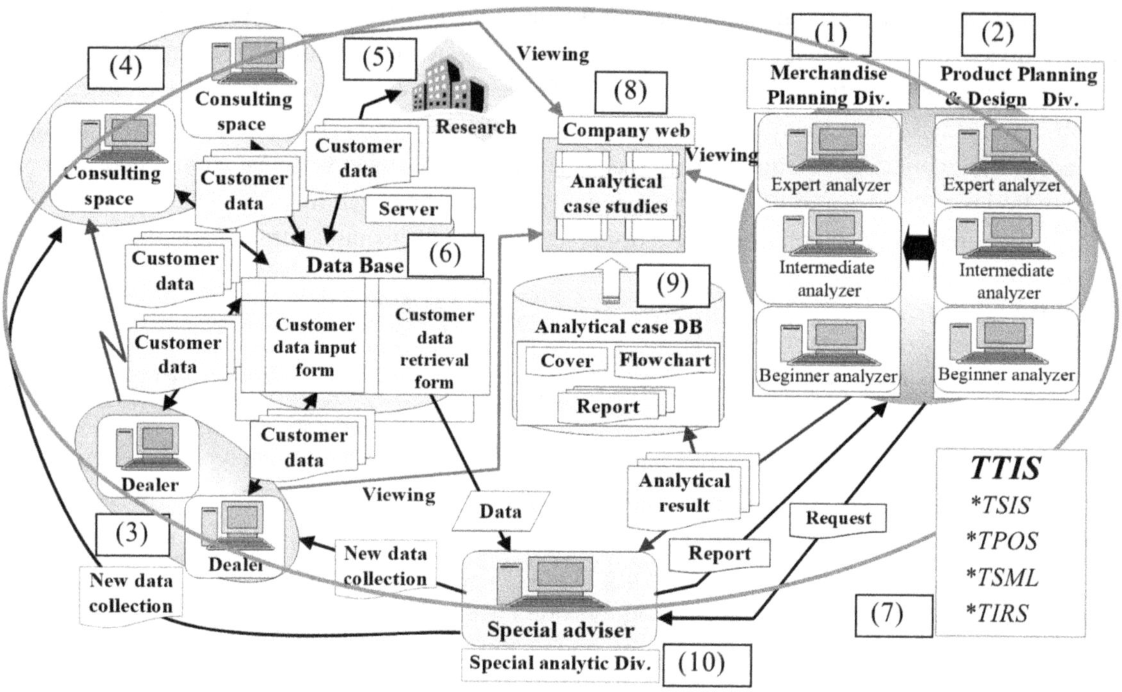

Similarly, the collection of "Customer Data" is also possible through (4) Consulting Spaces, namely, the showrooms promoting the company's own products or public facilities for discussions and consultations from the customers. Moreover, (5) the domestic/overseas marketing research companies (Research) conducting analyses of market trends and customer preferences are also a source of information for feeling out customer values.

All these sections are connected through on-line networking for building (6) a Database via a server of the company's own information system division. Into this system, (7) the core system of SQC integration network system, "TTIS" (Total SQC Technical Intelligence System) (Amasaka, 2000), namely, "TSIS-QR" (Total SQC Intelligence System for Quick Registration and Retrieval Library) (Amasaka, 1995), which has been developed by the author and others and already utilized by Toyota, is incorporated so that registration or search of customer information can be carried out in real-time using the data input/output form.

Another feature of CS-CIANS is that (1) the Merchandise Planning and (2) Design can conduct in a timely manner market investigations of the company's own products as well as benchmarking of competitors through cooperation with (3) Dealers, (4) Consulting Spaces, and (5) Marketing Research Companies via (8) an exclusive company WEB. In particular, it can carry out an SQC analysis of the acquired data by incorporating (7) "TPOS" (Total TQM Promotional Original SQC Soft) (Amasaka, 2000), that is, the second core system developed by the author and others for creating "wants". In practice, an advanced analyzer skilled in SQC analysis (Expert) gives instructions to an inexperienced analyzer "Beginner", while collaborating with mid-level analyzer "Intermediate analyzer" who has a certain level of experience (Amasaka, 2003a).

What serves as the guide for this scientific approach is the core system of TTIS, such as (7) "TSML" (Total SQC Manual Library) (Amasaka, 2000), the guidebook of SQC analytical results, and "TIRS" (Total Technical Information System) (Amasaka, 2000), the technical references and reports. These are accessible for search and utilization from (9) Analytical case Data Base. As seen in the figure, each of the data consists of (i) an A4-sized cover page with overview summary (Cover), (ii) step flow charts of SQC analytic processes on the sheets of the same size, called "Flow charts", and (iii) the main contents of the report on customer information analysis "Report", designed with high user-friendliness.

Particularly for highly complicated customer information analysis, cooperation requests for analysis can be submitted to (10) a "Special Adviser" in an exclusive SQC analysis division. The system is designed in such a way that the collection of "Analytical Results" created by (1) Merchandise Planning, (2) Design, and (10) Special adviser are registered and kept in (9) Analytical case DB for the successive development of analytical technology (Amasaka, 2003a).

AUTOMOBILE EXTERIOR DESIGN TOOL "CS-IDCM" UTILIZING SQC TECHNICAL METHODS

Guidelines and Approaches to the Study

In the 1980s, the small-size cars made in Japan had the merit of excellent run performance for reasonable price, and were exported successfully to Western countries. Thereafter, the development of the first noted car (i.e., stylish flag ship car as a world car), made in Japan, and accepted in Western countries, became pressing need.

In general, the automobile exterior design of new model car depended on the empirical rules and knowledge of experienced designers. Designers collected the surface reputation of the visitors in the car shops, and then attempted the conception and analysis in exterior design based on the implicit language information.

The creation of new methodology with the precise design idea process was a pressing need (Nunogaki et al., 1996). Therefore, the author generalized this conversion of "implicit knowledge and know how that is dependent on individual expertise" (Nagaya et al., 1998). Although the automobile exterior design is a creative artistic activity, there must be some part to which a scientific approach can be applied as long as the authors deal with manufacturing. An objective grasp of customer tastes and sense of values for practical application to the exterior design process is important in predicting the vehicle styles that are liked well in future.

The author has conducted and reported several studies to reach the following design development methodology (Suzuki et al., 2000). In this study, the author describes the Automobile Exterior Design Tool (CS-IDCM) utilizing SQC Technical Methods, with an example of the development of "Lexus exterior design" for raising customers' worth of world's prestige car.

Conception and Analysis in Automobile Exterior Design

A concept of "Kansei Engineering" (Shinohara et al., 1996: Amasaka and Nagasawa, 2002) has been in recognition for a long time. Examples of study are introduced (see e.g., Mori, 1991, 1993; Amasaka et al., 1999; Amasaka and Nagaya, 2002; Amasaka, 2004b) where it is possible to apply a statistical method to the development business of exterior design. When it comes to the application to actual business, however, there are few concrete examples of analysis worthy of introduction as an exterior design development story of new vehicles model.

This is attributable to the fact that the exterior design business (hereinafter referred to as designing) often ends up paying more importance to the end result, and that proposing good exterior designs in the design planning or development process is based on the conception, which is not closely related to the analysis. It is apparent that the higher the analysis develops, the more important the conception becomes. But the key point to the matter is how to yield a new conception, and the process of developing conception becomes critical.

In the advanced information society where identical conditions and/or data are shared, it hardly occurs to have remarkable difference in the environment. Under the circumstances, the method for proposing a leading conception cannot be the same as before. One may be prone to use human power for what a machine can handle, and may commit an error of misunderstanding that a conception has been gained.

Positioning of CS-IDCM

It is the objective of this study to find a guideline for establishing a method for scientifically supporting the designing so as to establish it expressly as a more creative activity from the state of tacit knowledge. It is considered that the analysis process for establishing it as an activity would be the key to the successful conception making. It is necessary for us to create a particular live solution that catches the liking of the next generation. In this connection, "Science SQC" with a core method "SQC Technical Methods" is applied to the flow designing to enhance the quality of the designer's job called "Design SQC" actually in Toyota (Amasaka et al., 1999; Amasaka, 1996, 2003a, 2004a, 2007; Amasaka and Nagasawa, 2002).

Figure 5. Automobile exterior design concept tool "CS-IDCM" using SQC Technical Methods

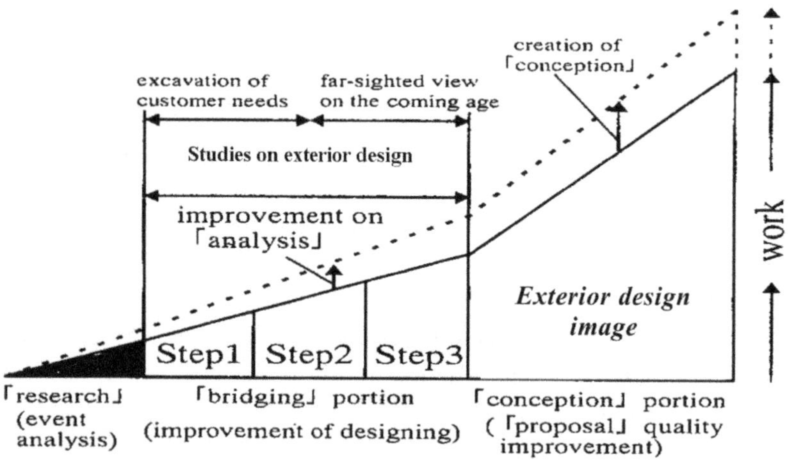

In this section, SQC Technical Methods is applied as the scientific new methodology "Mountain-Climbing for Problem-Solving," which is an effective solution to the various business tasks, by analyzing the bridge portion between analysis (research) and conception (creation of contour images)

(Amasaka, 2003b, 2004a, b, 2007, 2015; Amasaka and Nagasawa, 2002; Amasaka Ed., 2007). Designing is applied as the automobile exterior design conception tool named "Customer Science aiming to achieve Intelligence Design Concept Method" (CS-IDCM) as shown in Figure 5 (Amasaka et al., 1999).

In Figure 5, the analysis process that turns implicit knowledge into explicit knowledge constitutes a secret to the conception. In this connection, the author utilizes CS-IDCM as an automobile exterior design concept tool for developing strategic product design by the SQC

Technical Methods. Actually, bridging is attempted to span the research-oriented analysis as the event analysis to the exterior design in Steps 1 to 3 in Figure 5.

Step 1 analyzes relationships between images of vehicles desirable to customers and those actually selected to research, and it actualizes apparent relevancy whereby a vehicle type can be specified by the desirable image. Step 2 grasps what part of a vehicle customers observe to evaluate it. By coming down from the overall assessment, partial assessment and detailed assessment, this report clarifies which design factor should better be given priority to satisfy customers. By thinking that true customer-in is to propose a desirable thing before it is desired. In Step 3, the designers research the excellent exterior design by grasping the relevance of vehicle images and profile design (called proportion) data. CS-IDCM improves the designing process (work) for creation of exterior design image involving the matching profile design, form, and color. By accumulating the improvement processes, this study intends to improve the quality of designing - "creation of conception" as the dotted line indicates in Figure 5.

STUDIES ON AUTOMOBILE EXTERIOR DESIGN MODEL FOR CUSTOMER VALUE CREATION

To realize the above CS-IDCM, the author conducted the "Advanced Exterior Design Project by using Science SQC called ADS" for raising customers' worth in Toyota Motor Corporation described in the following (Nunogaki et al., 1996; Amasaka, 1999ab).

As for the development of ADS, the author as the Chief Examiner of TQM Promotion Div. (1992-2000), and the Head of Amasaka's New JIT Laboratory of Aoyama Gakuiin University (2000-2017) organized the (i) Design Div. I of Vehicle Development Center I for the development of new world car "Lexus," Design Div. II of Vehicle Development Center II for other model change of various mid-size cars, and Toyota Design Research Laboratory Tokyo for Advanced design cars, (ii) Marketing Service Div., Dealer Marketing System Div., Autosalon Amulux Tokyo, U.S. Office, Europe Office and others for the internal and external customers information gathering, and (iii) TQC Promotion Div. for developing Science SQC.

In the ADS project, the author developed an Automobile Exterior Design Model (AEDM). This model combines three core methods as follows; (A) Improvement of business process methods for automobile profile design, (B) Creation of automobile profile design "Psychographics" approach methods, and (C) Automobile profile design, form and color matching support methods, as shown in Figure 6 (Amasaka, 2017). As developing Customer Science Principle, the actual studies for AEDM have been applied to Toyota and others (Nunogaki et al., 1996; Nagaya et al., 1998; Amasaka et al., 1999; Okazaki et al., 2000).

In core technology (A), the first of the aims of the author and others was to grasp the characteristic of the profile design of the famous cars of the world such as "Benz, BMW, etc.," rationally by the concrete development of AEDM utilizing CS-IDCM. To realize the above knowledge, in core technology (B), the second aim was the realization of the profile design, which is the main elements of exterior design of

Figure 6. Outline of an Automobile Exterior Design Model (AEDM)

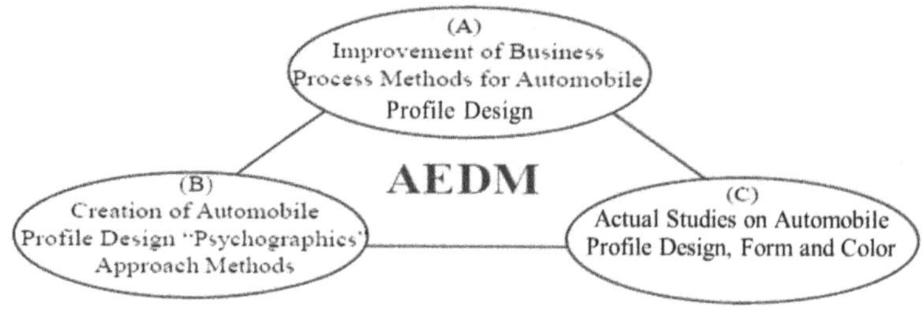

Toyota's strategic prestige car "new-model, Lexus GS400/LS430" by utilizing "psychographics" approach methods. In core technology (C), the third aim was the realization of the profile design development of various mid-size cars by the application of Lexus exterior design development.

The author has expanded AEDM for raising attractiveness to consumers by employing Customer Science utilizing Customer Information Analysis and Navigation System (CS-CIANS) (Amasaka, 2005), and describe it in the next Sections (A), (B) and (C).

IMPROVEMENT OF BUSINESS PROCESS METHODS FOR AUTOMOBILE PROFILE DESIGN (A)

To enhance the design planning quality, the present study aims at achieving the following: (1) To materialize vehicle images as desired by customers, (2) To analyze causal relations between the customer satisfaction assessment and the vehicle appearance review factors on the basis of the appearance style assessment, and (3) Based on the knowledge acquired, to understand the relevancy between vehicle images and proportion data and to reflect the results to the exterior design planning (Amasaka et al., 1999; Amasaka and Nagasawa, 2002).

Understanding Correlation between Customers' Desirable Images of the Vehicles and the Most Favored Vehicles (Step 1 in Figure 5)

Questionnaire was used for 157 customers (domestic panel) various in personality. First, their desirable images were determined for the vehicles in the panel without indicating the appearance shown in Table 1.. Then, the photographs of four representative vehicle models, consisting of domestic and imported models (BMW850i/1990 model, BENZ 300-24/1989 model, Legend Coupe/1991 model and Soarer 4.0GT/1991 model), without indicating vehicles' brand and name were presented to answer their most favorite vehicle as shown in Table 2.

In Tables 1 and 2, the design image words (1)-(20) reveal the customers' impressions on the four models. These image words are not independent enough to be able to reply exactly, and some similarity of words exists (Nunogaki et al., 1996; Okazaki et al., 2000; Suzuki et al., 2000). Using the desirable images and the most favored vehicle data from the questionnaire, the author conducted four-group discriminant analysis. As a result, it was found that all four models are roughly discriminated with a discrimination ratio of around 70%, and that the desirable panel images selected for individual models are almost similar. On the basis of the obtained data, the panel groups belonging to BMW, BENZ, Legend and Soarer are specifically extracted.

Table 1. Questionnaire on "desirable images"

1. desirable images	Name:	
(1) sophisticated	undesirable	desirable
(2) composed	undesirable	desirable
(3) high class	undesirable	desirable
(4) sporty	undesirable	desirable
(5) high status	undesirable	desirable
(6) safety	undesirable	desirable
(7) advanced	undesirable	desirable
(8) luxurious	undesirable	desirable
(9) simple	undesirable	desirable
(10) traditional	undesirable	desirable
(11) conservative	undesirable	desirable
(12) powerful	undesirable	desirable
(13) intellectual	undesirable	desirable
(14) high performance	undesirable	desirable
(15) urban	undesirable	desirable
(16) novel	undesirable	desirable
(17) high quality	undesirable	desirable
(18) intrepid	undesirable	desirable
(19) elegant	undesirable	desirable
(20) characteristic	undesirable	desirable

Table 2. Questionnaire on "desirable images" and "most favored

	name			
1. vehicle with most favored appearance	Legend 1	Soarer 2	BENZ 3	BMW 4
2. desirable images				
(1)sophisticated	undesirable 1	desirable 2		
(2)composed	undesirable 1	desirable 2		
(3)high class	undesirable 1	desirable 2		
(4)sporty	undesirable 1	desirable 2		
(5)high status				

Figure 7 shows a scatter diagram of individual scores obtained as the result of the analysis using the quantification method of the third type to more clearly understand the correlation between the desirable images and the most favored vehicle. It is understood from Figure 4 in Chapter 9, that a panel group in favor of Soarer has desirable vehicle images such as sophistication and/or sportiness as embodied by Soarer. Furthermore, the characteristics of BMW is composed of individuality, advanced, intellectual etc., while that of Benz is composed of intrepid, novel, safe, composed, etc. Since similar results are verified with other vehicle models, it is possible to conclude that customers' liking is consistent.

It was found that the customers' words can be materialized as the concrete contour of the vehicle. The knowledge of the above (A) corresponds to the automobile exterior designer's values and experienced intellect. Results of these analyses become great guidelines to the stylish "flag ship car" as a world car for the Japanese automakers, based on "Target area BMW and Target area BENZ" in Figure 7. These results gave sufficient knowledge for concept creation of the exterior design of "global car - prestige Lexus" (Amasaka et al., 1999; Amasaka, 2004a,b, 2007).

Figure 7. Correlation between "desirable images" and "the most favored vehicle"

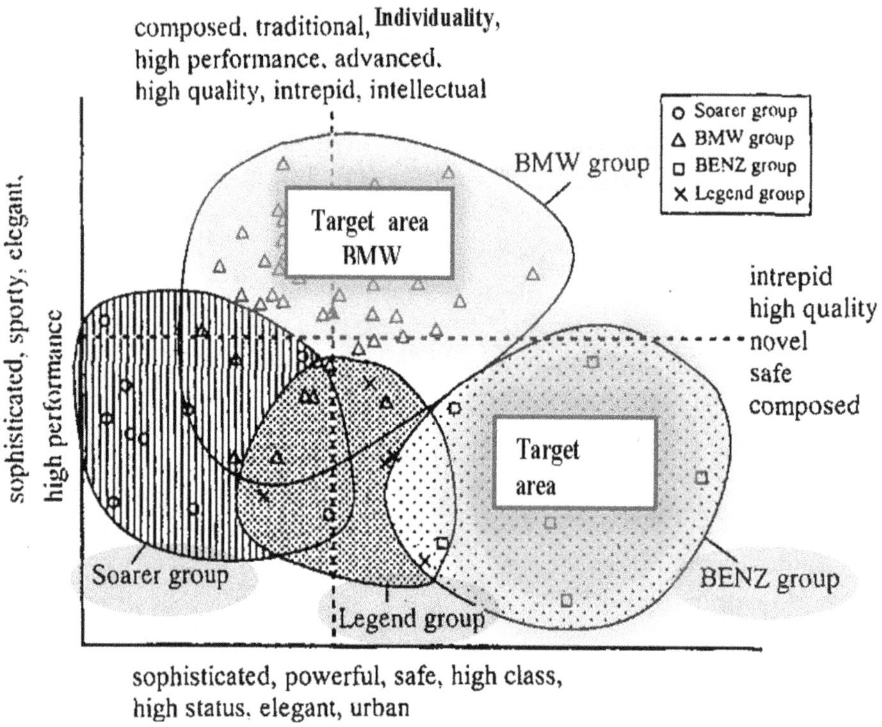

Method for Exploring the Factors that Customers Emphasize in Vehicle Appearance Evaluation (Step 2 in Figure 5)

The task taken up here is to objectify the above established theories (implicit knowledge) as qualitative and empirical rules for the professional designers who plan automobile profile designs. It is a well-known fact that the design of vehicle appearance has considerable weight in the customer's decision to make a purchase. To which part of vehicle appearance design do customers, domestic and overseas (regardless of age and sex), pay attention?

Professional automotive profile designers have a theory (or a rule of thumb) that, in general, Japanese customers tend to focus on the front design while North American customers look at the overall design of front, side and rear. Our challenge here was to give an objective analysis of the theory. To the authors' knowledge, no report has been made for objective verification of the theory in the academic world.

Quantitative evaluation on the sections of vehicle appearance is expected to advance a customer-in design strategy. For designing the new "Lexus GS400/LS430," 157 customers (young and old, and male and female panels) of various personality are asked to evaluate the appearance of the four major, mutually-competing models (BMW 850i/1990, Benz 300-24/1989, Legend coupe/1991 and Soarer 4.0GT/1991) and the priority of three appearance factors: front, side and rear views.

In analysis (1), the correlation between the evaluation and the priority is verified by multi-regression analysis. The three appearance factors are further divided into the design balance (profile) and detailed elements (4, 9, and 5 sections, respectively) for a similar study on their causal relationships as analysis (2). A preliminary cluster analysis shows that the customers can be stratified, in terms of the overall liking of the vehicle appearance, into a group lower in age and annual income and a group higher in age and annual income for all four models (Amasaka, 1996, 1999a; Amasaka et al., 1999; Amasaka, 2004a,b, 2007).

Figure 8 shows an example of analytical results on a vehicle model specified to the group higher in age and annual income. In analysis (1), the contributory factor adjusted for the degree of freedom (R^{*2}) representing the degree of influence on the overall evaluation of vehicle appearance (X1) is 0.62, indicating a high causal relationship. The breakdown is as follows: The influence of the front view is even higher at Bfv=0.59 while the influence of the side and rear views (X7 and X17) are relatively low at Bsv=0.18 and Brv=0.17.

Figure 8. Causal relationships between customer satisfaction assessment and vehicle appearance assessment factors by multiple regression analysis

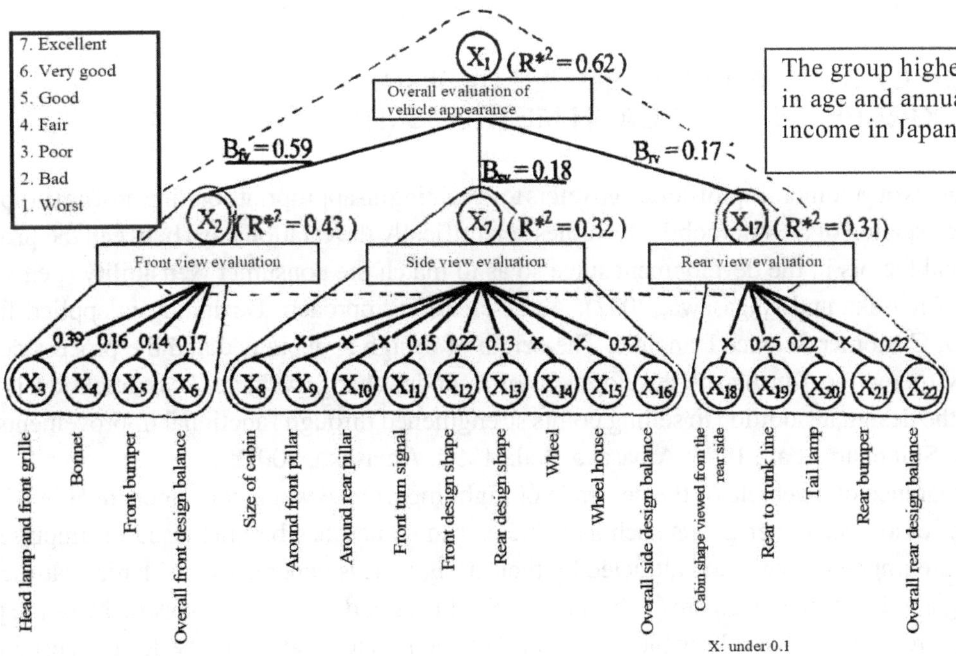

In analysis (2), the analytical results are similar to those for the group with lower age and annual income, but the influence of bonnet (X4) is high on the front view (X2). It is verified that the vehicle appearance is evaluated in a wider range; for example, the influence of the line (X19) from the rear to the trunk and the design balance (X22) of the rear as a whole are high on the side view (X7). This trend also applies to other three models. On the other hand, in the group lower one, though not illustrated in analysis (1), the overall evaluation of vehicle appearance (X1) is 0.74, indicating a high causal relationship. The breakdown is as follows: The influence of front view (X2) is fairly high at Bfv=0.46 while those of the side and rear views (X7 and X17) are at Bsv=0.30 and Brv=0.29, respectively, showing their positive influence. Moreover, in analysis (2), the head lamp and grille (X3) have a high degree of influence on the front view (X2). The overall side view and design (X16) exert much influence on the side view (X7). And, the tail lamp (X20) and rear bumper design (X21) exert much influence on the rear view (X17).

A similar survey and analysis were conducted in North American market. While the front view is generally high priority in Japan, it is known that the front, side and rear views are equally valued in North America. Another noticeable input is that Japanese customers are likely to provide individual evaluation for each front, side and rear view at a dealer. In contrast, North American customers evaluate the front view while looking at a moving car on the opposite lane, evaluate the side view while looking at a car driving pass, and evaluate the rear view similarly on the street. The authors confirmed that, as they evaluate the three appearance factors, their focus is the total balance of the design.

Through this analytical study approach, designers understood the need for the customer-in design strategy that gives consideration to the different characteristics in each country. These findings were the result of verification of the designer's theory (or rule of thumb), which greatly contributed to the designing of the global strategic vehicle Lexus GS400/LS430.

CREATION OF AUTOMOBILE PROFILE DESIGN "PSYCHOGRAPHICS" APPROACH METHODS (B)

Psychographics of automobile profile design refers to obtaining an appropriate outline profile (proportion), which is the skeleton of an automobile. It studies scientifically the relationships between the profile and psychological factors in the development stage so as to match the consumer' sensibility (i.e., so called "Kansei") (Amasaka and Nagasawa, 2002). As a scientific approach, Designing is applied from the viewpoint of Customer Science Principle. The origin of design is explained and the process described sequentially thereafter. During the development of a model-change vehicle, keen attention is paid to changes in the design in addition to selling points strengthened through functional improvements (Mori, 1991, 1993; Shinohara et al., 1996; Amasaka et al., 1999; Amasaka, 2007b).

The appearance of a vehicle or the design is of high importance when consumers decide which one to buy. The reason consumer goods such as vehicles can sometimes be purchased on impulse is that consumers are impressed with and attracted by their designs. It is generally considered that the factors determining good or poor design are (1) beauty, (2) freshness and (3) appearance worthy of the price. It seems that there is a universal rule on the correlation between beauty and product value to a certain extent. Freshness, changes and latest design are the main factors in selling a product by stimulating consumption.

Without these factors, there is no reason for customers to purchase new cars. Freshness of design has an important meaning for demonstrating functional improvements. The reason is that a consumer is not motivated to try unless functional improvements can be seen at a glance. For this reason, the spotlight is cast on design freshness. The factors that make the appearance and design of an automobile feel "fresh" are largely classified into (1) proportion, (2) form and (3) surface. It seems that most people note these points in forming a visual impression. It was considered that (1) proportion has a significant weight since it can be recognized from a considerable distance, and a new proportion cannot be realized without technical innovation.

This study focused on freshness not as transitory fashion (fad) but as evolutionary freshness, which should be made explicit to a certain degree. The author paid attention to proportion since it typically represents this characteristic. As in the expression of "form over substance," the form and surface generally represented by angles and roundness are considered to represent transitory fashions (Nagaya et al,, 1998; Amasaka and Nagaya, 2002)

Studies on the Customer-Orientedness of Profile Design (Step 2 in Figure 5)

Based on the above mentioned survey and analysis results, it can be assumed that "purchase because it is worth the price" and "purchase because it is newer than the model owned at present" can be represented by "high grade feel: price" and "freshness: year model." Here, analysis is done with the following approaches to estimate what would be the proportion of a vehicle that would sell in future. If we study why customers buy merchandise, the following two factors may be listed: They buy because they get what they pay for, and they buy because the product is newer than what they have now.

By supposing that these two factors represent "class feeling being equal price" and "newness being equal model year," the following relationships between these and profile design are analyzed: ① hood ratio: hood length/overall length, , trunk ratio: trunk length/overall length, ƒ cabin ratio: cabin skirt length/ overall length, „ roof ratio: roof length/overall length, … front overhang ratio: front overhang length/ overall length, † rear overhang ratio: rear overhang length/overall length, ‡ wheel base ratio: wheel base length/overall length, ˆ roof/cabin ratio: roof length/skirt length, overall height ratio, ‰ overall width ratio: overall height/overall length, and Š overall width ratio: overall width/overall length.

The data used for the analysis was measured with the autograph (measurement diagram). A total of 62 vehicle models, domestic and imported (sedans), are selected to measure their proportions (ratios), and a scatter diagram using principal component score is obtained as Figures 9 and 10. Figures 9 and 10 in Chapter 9, show the result of stratified classification by the class and the model year, respectively.

In Figure 9, the class drops toward the right of the scatter diagram. In Figure 10, Chapter 9, the model year is younger toward the right. For example, if one of these two sheets of scatter diagrams is placed on top the other, it is understood that it is hard to realize a combination of the highest class and the latest model.

When the scatter diagrams on these two principal components are overlapped, old and high class vehicles with a coach-type cabin (with long hood and luggage compartment length) such as Rolls Royce, Benz W123, BMW518, Jaguar X16, etc., are laid in the second quadrant. In the opposite fourth quadrant, late-model vehicles with a long cabin and shorter hood and luggage compartment are positioned. From the results of these analyses, it is quantitatively clarified that seemingly highest class "luxury" and latest newer "newness" are mutually contradictory elements (Amasaka et al., 1999; Amasaka and Nagaya, 2002; Amasaka, 2003b, 2004a,b, 2007). The customers wish the luxury and newness with advanced technology (fuel consumption, driving power and delightful cabin, etc.).

To create the "Lexus profile design," the authors had to realize the excellent proportion ratio by combining the short hood length (small size engine) and long cabin (large wheel base and small overhang unit-axle), excellent streamline (short roof length, large slope front/rear window by enlarging the area of window glass and cabin space spreads out) and low vehicle height (thin top and floor). Through these

Figure 9. Classification of vehicle model by the class grade "degree of luxury"

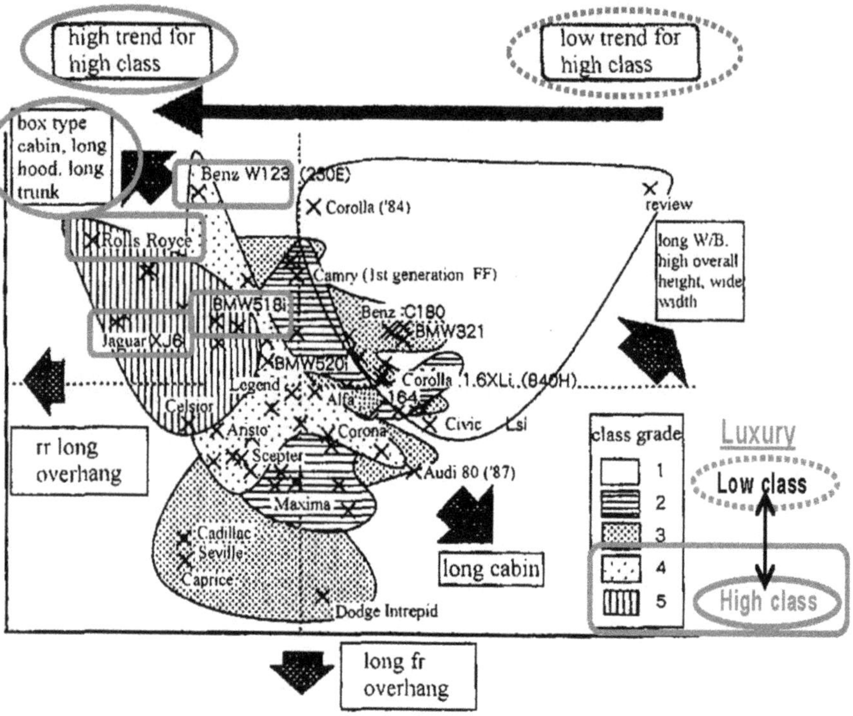

Figure 10. Classification of vehicle model by the year model "degree of newness"

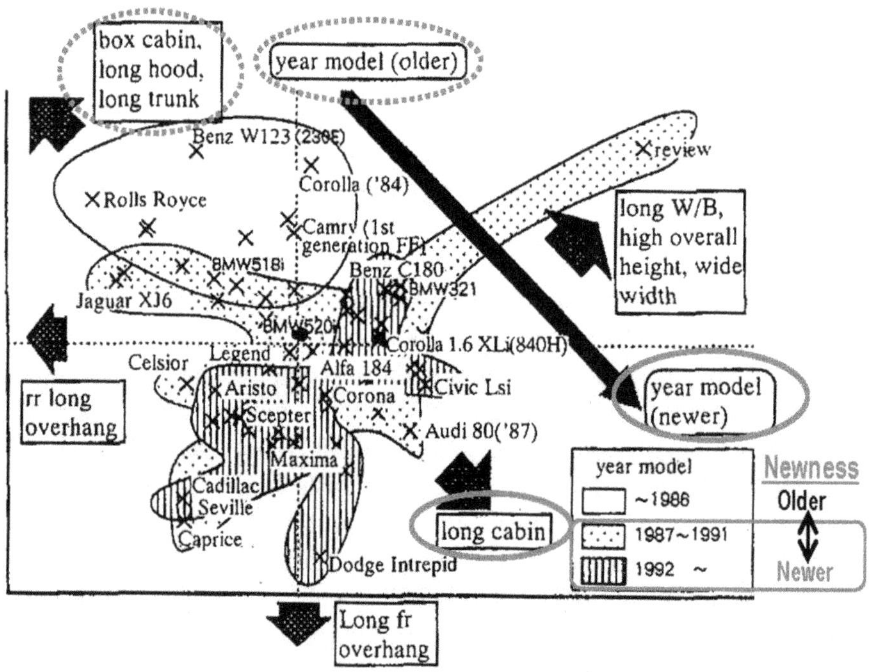

realizations, being compatible with "luxury" and "newness" became possible. In other words, it can be quantitatively verified that the luxury (high class) and the newness are contrary to each other, which is a newly found knowledge.

From these studies, the author has been able to obtain a desirable direction for the study to forecast the liking of future users, not of current users, by incorporating into analysis a factor containing the concept of time axis that the customers' liking can change in terms of newness. These findings are the result of verification of the designer's theory (a rule of thumb), which greatly contributed to the designing of the global strategic vehicle "Lexus GS400/LS430."

This enabled us to propose a desirable thing to customers before they want it, thereby obtaining a guideline that helped us improve the processing of design business. The author and others then identified the general rule (that was not the intentional but the natural consequence of designers' works) of the common proportional ratio (highest class) that was inherited in the world's prestigious vehicles and insusceptible to change over five or ten years.

Actual Proof Research of the Lexus GS400/ LS430 Development (Step 3 in Figure 5)

Upon designing a global strategic car "Lexus," the matter of primary concern was how to catch the target customers' heart. Taking advantage of the knowledge acquired in core technology (A) of Figure 6, the author realized the profile design of highest class and latest car "Lexus GS400/LS430". Particularly, the development target of the first Lexus was the realization of the profile design of high trend/high class vehicle "BMW/BENZ/Jaguar luxury" as shown in Figures 9, 10 and 11. The target of GS400 was the profile design surpassing middle grade class for lower in age (youth and middle age). In the same way, the target of LS4300 was the profile design surpassing upper grade class for higher in age (middle and advanced age).

To verify the above Steps 1 and 2 of Section B, the authors showed that side views with typically different proportion ratios A through F, which arrange the combination of proportion ratio of ①-Š in Figure 11, were selected for evaluation purposes (comparison of ratio data) (Amasaka and Nagaya, 2002). The direction toward ratio A was judged to be fresh, as expected (plan with shorter hood, longer cabin skirt length and shorter roof). On the other hand, ratios D and F (ratios opposite to those of A) were judged to be "newness" (GS400 adopted a model "ratio D" by the final judgement) (Amasaka and Nagaya, 2002).

The above survey results proved that the scientific approach yields a good match with sensory evaluations by consumers. Based on the knowledge obtained using the scientific approach, GS400 was developed successfully, named Toyota "new model Aristo" in Japan (Motor Fan, 1997).

Similarly, the survey shown in Figure 12 was implemented for the development of the Lexus LS430 named Toyota "Celsior" in Japan (Motor Fan, 2000). Proportion ratios A through F of the LS430 were determined in the same way as for the GS400 (LS430 adopted a model "ratio B" by the final judgement "Newness"). Both proportion ratios definitions of GS400/LS430 are illustrated in Amasaka et al. (1999), Amasaka and Nagaya (2002), and Amasaka (2005, 2007a, 2018). Lexus (APFC-MSM) GS400/LS430 obtained satisfactory evaluation from the customers, and was successful as a flag ship car "Lexus" of Toyota sedan vehicles (Motor Fan, 1997, 2000; JD Power Associates, 1998).

Figure 11. Side views for survey purposes using dimensional ratios for Lexus GS400 development

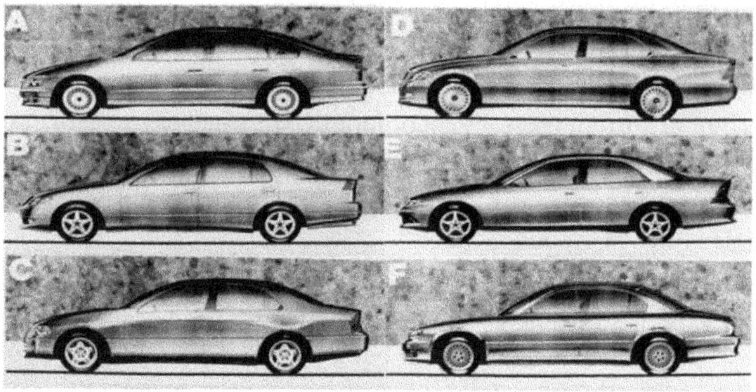

Lexus GS400 adopted proportion ratio "D"
(Source: Amasaka and Nagaya, 2002).

Figure 12. Side views for survey purposes using dimensional ratios for Lexus LS430 development

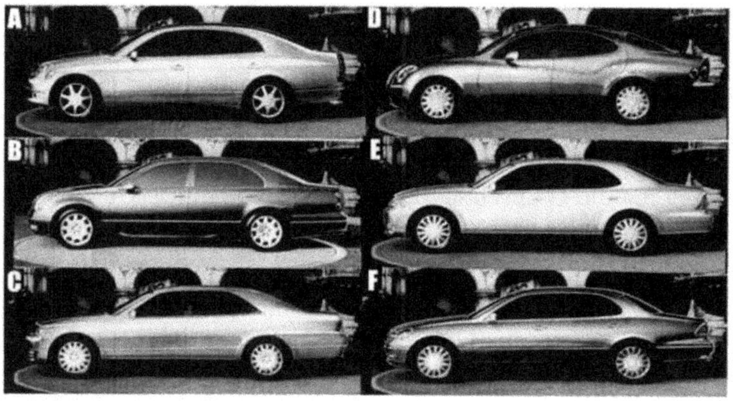

Lexus LS430 adopted proportion ratio "B"
(Source: Amasaka and Nagaya, 2002).

Figure 13. Automobile Proportion, Form and Color Matching Support Methods

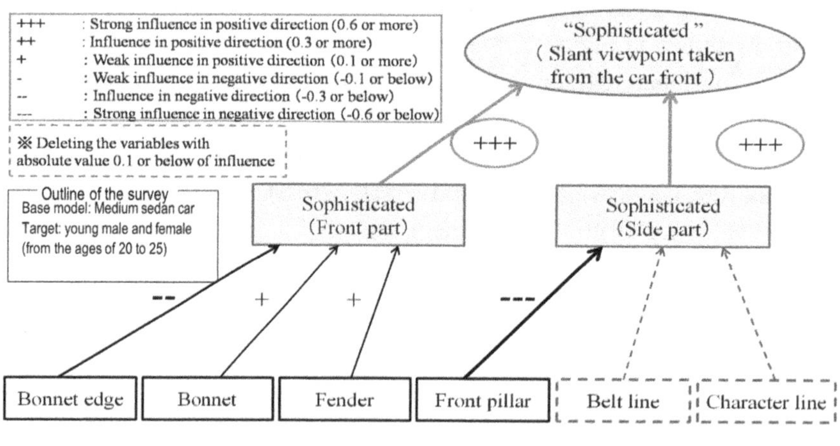

ACTUAL STUDIES ON AUTOMOBILE PROFILE DESIGN, FORM AND COLOR MATCHING SUPPORT METHODS (C)

Increasingly diverse consumer values have made an automobile exterior design the most important factor influencing purchasing decisions in recent years. For this reason, identifying customers' unspoken senses (values) and scientifically presenting them from an objective standpoint have become an absolute requirement in automobile exterior design processes for mid-size car. These processes involve successfully matching profile design (proportion), form, and color from the perspective of an objective Science SQC approach with SQC Technical Methods in AEDM (Amasaka et al., 1999; Amasaka, 2002, 2004a,b, 2015, 2018).

Developing Automobile Profile Design, Form and Color Matching Support Methods

The author has created the Automobile Profile Design, Form and Color Matching Support Methods (APFC-MSM) based on the customers' value elements of automobile exterior design work in developing AEDM as shown in Figure 12 (Toyoda et al., 2015a; Amasaka, 2018).

APFC-MSM starts with three elements (1) profile design, (2) form, and (3) color. Recent design work strategies make it a point to optimize business processes so that they are in line with the vehicle design concept from the product planning stage. Next, each element must be matched: (4) profile design and form, (5) form and color, and (6) profile design and color. Finally, (7) all three elements - profile design, form, and color - must be integrated harmoniously to address modern market demands.

Based on the knowledge acquired by the above-mentioned Sections (A) and (B), the authors developed AEDA by using APFC-MSM. These studies were carried out in the Amasaka New JIT laboratory by collaboration with Toyota Motor Corp., Toyota Design Research Laboratory Tokyo, Nissan Motor Corp., Honda Motor Co., Ltd., Mazda Motor Corp., Nippon Paint Co., Ltd., Kansai Paint Co. Ltd. and others.

In Figure 12, the synthetic optimization studies of the three elements - profile design, form and color - of exterior design are indispensable in making the knowledge of core technology (A) and (B) evolving further. Examples of actual case studies, corresponding to (1)-(7) for the business process innovation that addresses optimizing the automobile exterior design for customer creation, are as follows; (1) compatibility of profile design and package design (interior space) (Okabe et al., 2007;Yamaji and Amasaka, 2009), (2) form design (Asami et al., 2010; Yazaki et al., 2013), (3) color design (Muto et al., 2011; Takebuchi et al., 2012a), (4) profile design and form matching (Takimoto et al., 2010), (5) form and color matching (Takebuchi et al., 2012b; Muto et al., 2013), (6) profile design and color matching (Asami et al., 2011), and (7) integrated profile design, form and color matching (Toyoda et al., 2015a; Kobayashi et al., 2016).

The author now illustrates some pioneering case studies for the development of APFC-MSM in the following.

Creation of an Automobile Exterior Form Design Optimization

In this study, by paying attention to the automobile form, the details that were previously ambiguous, such as "roundness between bonnet and fender" and "angle," are represented numerically. With the aim of measuring the degree of influence of customer sensibility, the authors developed an automobile

Table 3. Form shape parameters for nine car model types (front view and side view)

Car type / Form shape	Angle of the bonnet edge (°)	Angle of the bonnet (°)	Angle of the fender (°)	Angle of the front pillar (°)	Angle of the belt line (°)	Angle of the character line (°)
Type A	40	40	40	45	2	25
Type B	15	20	25	30	0	15
Type C	15	25	60	30	0	55
Type D	25	50	20	30	5	15
Type E	25	50	60	30	5	55
Type F	30	25	20	60	0	15
Type G	30	25	60	60	0	55
Type H	45	50	20	60	5	15
Type I	45	50	60	60	5	55

exterior form design optimization (Asami et al., 2010). The authors created a model of a form-altered automobile to quantitatively evaluate the degree of influence of customer sensitivity by utilizing above mentioned CS-IDCM.

As a means of associating customer sensitivity (as expressed through words) with form, a car model, including several types of determined parameters, is created by design CAD, which performs a sensitivity evaluation. The form shape parameters and corresponding customer impressions are shown in Table 3 for each car model type (ex. front view and side view). Similarly, a model for investigating nine car types (Type A-Type I) was created for the front part and side part using numerical form representation.

The purpose of the sensitivity evaluation questionnaire was to explore the differences in the impressions felt by customers, regarding nine models in which the forms of the front and side had been changed. Accordingly, subjects were asked using the same questionnaire form for all models. These data were analyzed to determine the relationships between subjective impressions and forms. In addition, the younger age group (the 20's) was targeted for the investigation.

In the questionnaire, a seven-step evaluation (disagree=1 vs. agree=7) using sensitivity words was performed. In order to select suitable sensitivity words, a bibliographic search and an investigation hearing with the designer were conducted, and 42 sensitivity words related automobile appearance were extracted. This set of words was then narrowed to those having a close relationship, yielding the 12 sensitivity words (sophisticated, intellectual, elegant, traditional, advanced, high class, characteristic, simple, composed, cute, powerful and sporty).

In visualization of the front/side part of relationships, covariance structural analysis was conducted to obtain an overall sensitivity evaluation by combining separate sensitivity evaluations for the front/side part into a synthetic variable in order to examine their mutual influence. As an example, the shape parameter ~ sensitivity path diagram is shown in Figure 13 in Chapter 9, from the standardized partial regression coefficient for "sophisticated." In this figure, the strength of the relationship for the shape parameter with a strong weight is expressed by the thickness of the arrow, regardless of the positive and negative sign of the coefficient.

From the path diagram in Figure 14, one front part and one side part each exert large degrees of influence, and the angle of the front pillar conveys the sensitivity evaluation "sophisticated" as the shape parameter with the largest degree of influence. By conducting the same analysis for all sensitivity words, the front/side part of relationships can be comprehensively evaluated. Based on the above information, it is clear that, to the younger generation, the concept of "advanced," conveys a sense of stylishness.

Figure 14. Path diagram for "Sophisticated" using covariance structural analysis

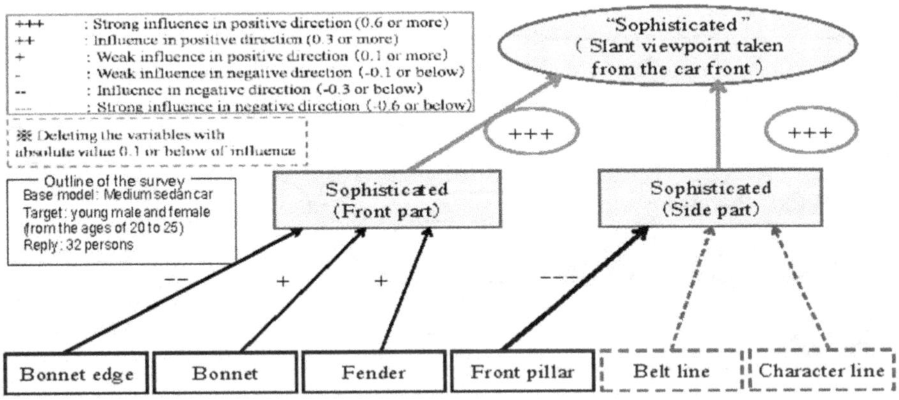

As a result, it is clear that an "advanced" image can be expressed via a specific combination of five points: (i) deep bonnet edge, (ii) bonnet with swelling, (iii) front pillar in an acute angle, (iv) upward belt line, and (v) strengthened character line, each parameterized and materialized by design CAD. The effectiveness of this study was considered to be verified.

Creation of an Automobile Exterior Color Design Optimization

The quality of the exterior colors of automobiles has become a major aesthetic factor (preference) influencing the car buying process. In this study, the authors created an automobile exterior color design optimization based on above mentioned CS-IDCM, and verified this study's effectiveness throughout the application of medium sedan car (Takebuchi et al., 2012a).

The author conducted a survey using 11 painted panels with varying color elements to determine how customers are influenced aesthetically by color variations including the textural expressions. For this study, the panels were shaped and painted like car panels to show the relevant textural expressions. First, the painted panels were selected. Three panels were initially prepared for the survey, using three colors (red, black and brown) with minimal opacity and graininess. Then, a further eight panels were prepared, varying the effect of the opacity and graininess equally to produce a total of 11 panels as shown in Figure 14(i). The six elements of color (hue, luminosity, intensity, shine, opacity and graininess) of each panel were measured.

The results are shown in Table 4. Then, the participants were asked to look at each painted panel and evaluate according to a seven-point scale, the extent to which each panel gave the desired impression for the above four preferences (classy, luxurious, dignified and sporty).

Aesthetic evaluation data was obtained from the results. The survey was aimed at men and women in their twenties, and the answers were obtained from a total of 94 men and women. This path diagram of covariance structure analysis was conducted to determine the correspondence relationship between color elements and preferences as shown in Figure 14(ii).

The results were then used to provide information to contribute to the development of exterior colors appealing to people who value self-expression. The coefficients of each path are standardized coefficients. The absolute values of these standardized coefficients indicate the degree of influence while the direction of influence is indicated by positive or negative numbers (Figure 14(ii)).

Figure 15. An example for matching of form and color optimization using front fender panels (Collaboration with Nippon Paint Co. Ltd.)

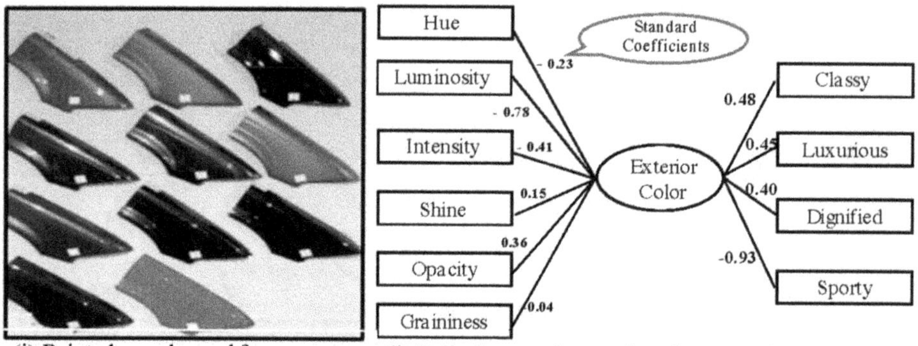

(i) Painted panels used for surveys. (ii) Path diagram from color elements of exterior color

Table 4. Six elements of color of each panel

Panel No.	Hue (H45°)	Luminosity (L45°)	Intensity (C45°)	Shine (60°)	Opacity (L15-110°)	Graininess (HG)
1	35.00	83.89	41.17	1.79	0	89.90
2	16.79	39.00	32.00	33.90	75.70	91.50
3	23.54	60.10	33.00	4.01	53.60	90.40
4	27.49	56.55	28.06	35.70	59.20	89.10
5	6.19	2.10	342.00	34.79	89.70	96.50
6	3.44	2.80	31.00	19.94	17.90	90.80
7	30.45	10.96	44.15	59.85	29.20	95.90
8	9.90	8.04	10.56	0.59	0	94.50
9	5.48	1.10	255.50	19.05	51.20	93.00
10	2.77	0.70	260.00	11.90	4.00	89.60
11	1.66	0.12	93.07	3.64	0	92.60

This model was subjected to a goodness-of-fit test once it was corrected using a modification index, resulting in reasonable scores of 0.979GFI and 0.895AGFI. In this path diagram used for this covariance structure analysis, the "exterior color" latent variable was chosen as the latent variable that would satisfy the four vehicle design preferences of those who value self- expression.

Respondents in the self-expression group were asked to freely evaluate the three developed colors. The respondents gave positive evaluations, saying they liked how classy the colors were and that they would like a car with colors such as these. This shows that the target users were satisfied with the exterior colors developed by employing AECD-AM.

Creation of an Automobile Profile Design, Form and Color Matching Model

Furthermore, the authors created an Automobile Profile Design, Form and Color Matching Model (APFC-MM) based on the investigation of "optimum profile design and form matching, form and color matching, and proportion and color matching" as shown in Figure 15 in Chapter 9. The development of the APFC-MM outlined above was applied to young people in their 20s to see whether the model selected by the method would match their preferences. The effectiveness of the research was thus confirmed (Toyoda et al., 2015a; Amasajka, 2018).

In Step 1, the authors began by conducting interviews with key automakers and dealers as well as with customers. They also consulted prior research to see which issues had already been addressed and which had yet to be clearly identified.

In Step 2, the authors conducted a customer preference survey based on the key issues identified above. In this step, customers were given a questionnaire to find out which vehicles they were interested in, and to pinpoint the main factors they considered when purchasing a vehicle. Once the data was collected, the authors subjected it to a principal component analysis and a cluster analysis in order to quantitatively determine the relationships between different customer senses.

In Step 3, the authors used the insights gained from the customer preference survey in Step 2 to recruit test subjects that resembled target customers. Once the test subjects were selected, they were each fitted with an eye camera to analyze line-of-sight information. This told the authors where the subjects placed their attention when looking at vehicles. At the same time, an electroencephalogram (EEG) was used to measure brain waves. This device ascertained how the subjects were feeling when they looked at certain parts of the car.

In Step 4, the authors continued to build upon the information gained in the previous steps in order to identify the relationship between the profile design and the form, two of the critical elements in exterior automotive design. To do this, they used 3D-CAD software to actually convert vehicle characteristics into numerical specifications, thus actually creating the vehicle designs that customers wants.

Figure 16. Automobile Profile Design, Form and Color Matching Model (APFC-MM)

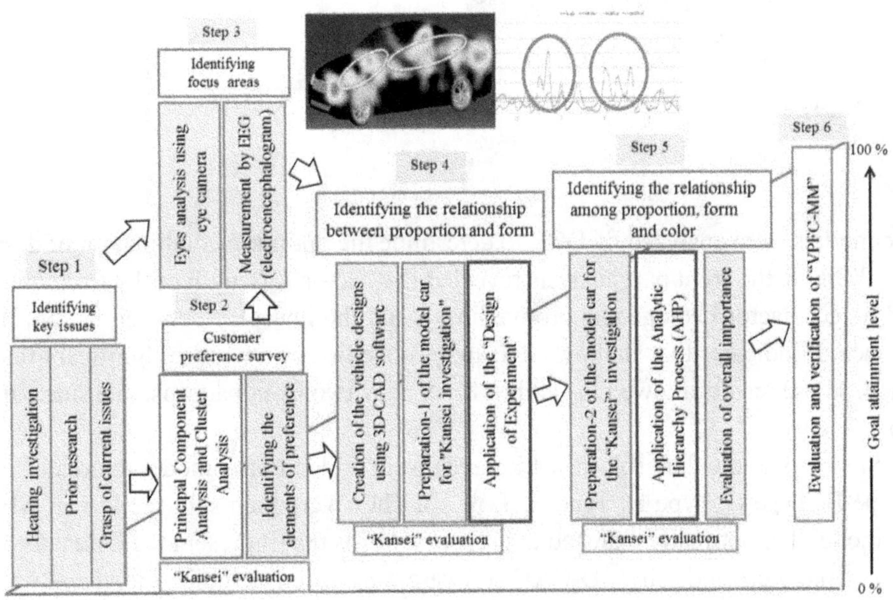

In Step 5, the models designed in Step 4 were then analyzed using statistics (Design of Experiments (DOE) and Analytic Hierarchy Process (AHP)) to select the model that had the optimum combination of design elements.

In Step 6, the authors evaluated the success of the model selected in Step 5. Test subjects were again fitted with EEG equipment as the authors compared their reactions to the selected model and other vehicle designs.

Concretely in Step 3, the authors used 3D-CAD software to actually design a vehicle exterior that reflected the critical proportion and form element as indicated in Figure 16. The study used a mid-size sedan and selected standard proportion and form dimensions based on collections of dimensional body drawings as shown in Table 5, and then numerically represented them at three levels based on the knowledge of the Steps 1- 2. The authors then created models that combined different front part (length of the front windshield glass, edge and groove lines), side part (hood bulge and strength of character lines), and rear part (rear pillar angle and rear bumper width) form elements.

Figure 17. Designing a vehicle exterior design (outline of proportion and form)

Table 5. Selected standard proportion and form dimensions

Model	Length of the front windshield (mm)	Hood bulge (°)	Edge and groove line (°)
A	730	40	45
B	[illegible]	25	15
C	[illegible]	[illegible]	[illegible]
D	[illegible]	[illegible]	15
E	805	50	15
F	655	25	45
G	[illegible]	[illegible]	[illegible]
H	655	50	45
	[illegible]	[illegible]	[illegible]

The nine models were analyzed by DOE to determine the optimum combination of design elements. As shown in Table 6, the front part analysis revealed that factor A (length of the front windshield), factor B (hood bulge), factor C (edge and groove lines), and the interplay between factors B and C had a 5% significance. It indicates that shallow edge and groove lines were more significant than differences in hood bulge. These results allowed the author to identify two front patterns, one side pattern, and one rear pattern.

Next, in Step 4, Three colors (black, white, red) were added to the model to create six alternatives (Type A, Type B, Type C, Type D, Type E, Type F). They were then subjected to an AHP in order to identify the model that optimally matched the sensory words that represent the demands of the exterior design group. Models created using 3D-CAD software were given to subjects to visually compare using a paired comparison method in order to assign priority levels to the different standards and alternatives.

The test subjects' subjective responses were gathered using a questionnaire. Table 7 shows the relative priority of each standard (sensory word) and alternative (CAD model). This information was then comprehensively evaluated to identify the model with the best proportion, form, and color combination.

Table 6. Analysis result (Front part)

Factor	Sum of Squares	Flexibility	Variance	Variance Ratio	Test
A	20.816	1	20.816	21.575	**
B	11.391	1	11.391	11.806	**
C	5.348	1	5.348	5.543	*
AB	0.660	1	0.660	0.684	
AC	1.266	1	1.266	1.312	
BC	7.223	1	7.223	7.486	*
ABC	2.250	1	2.250	2.332	
Error	7.719	8	0.965	0.558	

Table 7. The relative priority (standard)

Subject	Alternative 1	Alternative 2	Alternative 3	Alternative 4	Alternative 5	Alternative 6
1	0.13	0.17	0.12	0.10	0.16	0.32
2	0.13	0.15	0.10	0.13	0.18	0.30
3	0.09	0.10	0.26	0.39	0.06	0.11
4	0.25	0.29	0.03	0.04	0.15	0.24
5	0.33	0.31	0.19	0.09	0.02	0.06
6	0.31	0.34	0.16	0.10	0.06	0.03
7	0.31	0.34	0.16	0.10	0.06	0.03
8	0.06	0.11	0.08	0.07	0.21	0.48
9	0.17	0.16	0.06	0.08	0.31	0.21
10	0.10	0.23	0.09	0.25	0.11	0.13

The analysis indicated that, among young men in their 20s within the exterior design group (the target of the study), two models created using this method (Type B, Type F) received the highest evaluation (Toyoda et al., 2015a). The results indicate that the Type B model, with a front windshield length of 805mm, a hood bulge of 50°, an edge and groove lines of 45°, emphasized strong character lines, a front pillar angle of 30°, and black paint, has the "cool" sensory word as its main focus. The Type F model had the same proportions and form as Type B in red, and it had the luxurious|| sensory word as its main focus develop the APFC-MM. Here, EEG equipment was used to measure the subjects' alpha waves as they looked in random order at the models that they were asked about in the Step 4 questionnaire. The results of this test; namely, that the models triggering the highest alpha wave values were the same models that the study predicted through the APFC-MM. The effectiveness of the model was thus confirmed (Toyoda et al., 2015a; Amasaka, 2018).

The models identified in Step 4 were verified in Step 5, and the authors were then able to

Expanding Customer Science Principle for Raising Attractiveness to Consumers

Furthermore, the authors have been advancing the new deployments of AEDA employing Customer Science Principle for mid-size and small-size cars as follows.

The first research area is the development of automobile exterior color and interior color matching (Koizumi et al., 2013a; Shinogi et al., 2014) and auto instrumentation design (Yazaki et al., 2012). The second is the application to automobile exterior design for the women customers (Asami et al., 2011). The third is the development of exterior design research of a motor scooter and a bicycle (Nakamura et al., 2008: Koizumi et al., 2013b; Toyoda et al., 2015b).

These have been developed in Toyota Motor Corp., Yamaha Motor Co. Ltd., Nippon Research Center Ltd., and others

CONCLUSION

The author verified the validity of AEDM as the key to implementation of Design SQC for the innovation of business process and designing attractive vehicles by employing Customer Science Principle. As definite deployment of AEDM utilizing automobile exterior design concept support tool "CS-IDCM" using SQC Technical Methods, the author focused on three vehicle design elements that were handled separately in the past (proportion, form, and color) and attempted to match them all while pinpointing their correlations to customer senses.

As actual examples for customer value creation, this model was applied in the development of Toyota Lexus and others. Furthermore, the application of ADEM is currently advancing new areas such as automobile exterior color and interior color matching, package design, auto instrumentation design, motor scooter and bicycle.

ACKNOWLEDGMENT

The author would like to acknowledge the generous support received from the following researchers: all those at Toyota Motor Corp., and those connected with the Amasaka New JIT laboratory at Aoyama Gakuin University that assisted with author's research, especially, Mr. Nagaya, A., Miss. Matsubara, W., Miss. Suzuki, M., Mr. Okazaki, R., Mr. Nunogaki, N., Mr. Toyoda, S.., Nishio, Y., Mr. Takebuchi, S., Asami, H. and others.

REFERENCES

Amasaka, K. (1995). A Construction of SQC Intelligence System for quick registration and retrieval library: A visualized SQC report for technical wealth. *Lecture Notes in Economics and Mathematical Systems, Springer*, *445*, 318–336. doi:10.1007/978-3-642-59105-1_24

Amasaka, K. (1996), Application of classification and related method to the SQC renaissance in Toyota Motor. Data Science, Classification, and Related Methods, 684-695.

Amasaka, K. (1999a). A demonstrative study of a new SQC concept and procedure in the manufacturing industry: Establishment of a New Technical Method for conducting Scientific SQC. *An International Journal of Mathematical & Computer Modeling*, *31*(10-12), 1–10.

Amasaka, K. (1999b). A study on Science SQC by utilizing Management SQC: A demonstrative study on a new SQC concept and procedure in the manufacturing industry. *International Journal of Production Economics*, *60-61*, 591–598. doi:10.1016/S0925-5273(98)00143-1

Amasaka, K. (2000). A Demonstrative Study of a New SQC Concept and Procedure in the Manufacturing Industry. *An International Journal of Mathematical & Computer Modelling*, *31*(10-12), 1–10. doi:10.1016/S0895-7177(00)00067-4

Amasaka, K. (2002). New JIT, a new management technology principle at Toyota. *International Journal of Production Economics*, *80*(2), 135–144. doi:10.1016/S0925-5273(02)00313-4

Amasaka, K. (2003a). Proposal and implementation of the Science SQC, Quality Control Principle. *International Journal of Computer Modeling*, *38*(11-13), 1125–1136. doi:10.1016/S0895-7177(03)90113-0

Amasaka, K. (2003b). Development of "New JIT", Key to the excellence design "LEXUS": The validity of "TDS-DTM", a strategic methodology of merchandise. *Proceedings of the Production and Operations Management Society,* 1-8.

Amasaka, K. (2004a). *Science SQC, New Quality Control Principle: The quality strategy of Toyota.* Springer-Verlag. doi:10.1007/978-4-431-53969-8

Amasaka, K. (2004b). Customer Science: Studying consumer values. *Japan Journal of Behavior Metrics Society,* 196-199.

Amasaka, K. (2004c). Applying *New JIT*, A Management Technology Strategy Model at Toyota. *Proc. of the 2nd World Conference on Production and Operation Management, Mexico*, 1-12.

Amasaka, K. (2005). Constructing a Customer Science application system "CS-CIANS": Development of a global strategic vehicle "Lexus" utilizing New JIT. *WSEAS Transactions on Business and Economics*, *2*(3), 135–142.

Amasaka, K. (Ed.). (2007). *New Japan Model: Science TQM: Theory and practice for strategic quality management, The quality management of the manufacturing industry*. Maruzen.

Amasaka, K. (2007a). High Linkage Model -Advanced TDS, TPS & TMS-Strategic development of New JIT at Toyota. *International Journal of Operations and Quantitative Management*, *13*(3), 101–121.

Amasaka, K. (2007b). The validity of "TDS-DTM", A strategic methodology of merchandise: Development of New JIT, Key to the excellence design "LEXUS". *The International Business & Economics Research Journal*, *6*(11), 105–115.

Amasaka, K. (2015). New JIT, New Management Technology Principle. Taylor and Francis Group.

Amasaka, K. (2018). Automobile Exterior Design Model: Framework development and Supporting case studies. *The Journal of Japanese Operations Management and Strategy*, *8*(1), 67–89.

Amasaka, K. (2022). New Manufacturing Theory: Surpassing JIT (2nd ed.). Lambert Academic Publishing.

Amasaka, K., & Nagasawa, S. (2002). *Fundamentals and application of sensory evaluation: For Kansei Engineering in the vehicle*. Japanese Standards Association.

Amasaka, K., & Nagaya, A. (2002). Engineering of the new sensitivity in the vehicle: Psychographics of LEXUS design profile. In Development of articles over the sensitivity: The method and practice. Nihon Shuppan Service Press.

Amasaka, K., Nagaya, A., & Shibata, W. (1999). Studies on Design SQC with the application of Science SQC: Improving of business process method for automotive profile design. *Japanese Journal of Sensory Evaluations*, *3*(1), 21–29. doi:10.9763/jjsse.3.21

Asami, H., Ando, T., Yamaji, M., & Amasaka, K. (2010). A study on Automobile Form Design Support Method "AFD-SM". *Journal of Business & Economics Research*, *8*(11), 13–19. doi:10.19030/jber.v8i11.44

Asami, H., Owada, H., Murata, Y., Takebuchi, S., & Amasaka, K. (2011). The A-VEDAM for approaching vehicle exterior design. *Journal of Business Case Studies*, *7*(5), 1–8. doi:10.19030/jbcs.v7i5.5598

Evans, R. J., & Lindsay, M. W. (2004). *The management and control of quality*. South-Western College Publishing.

J. D. Power (1998). https://www.jdpower.com/

Kobayashi, T., Yoshida, R., Amasaka, K., & Ouchi, N. (2016). A statistical and scientific approach to deriving an attractive exterior vehicle design concept for indifferent customers. *Journals International Organization of Scientific Research*, *18*(12), 74–79.

Koizumi, K., Kanke, R., & Amasaka, K. (2013a). Research on automobile exterior color and interior color matching. *International Journal of Engineering Research and Applications*, *4*(8), 45–53.

Koizumi, K., Kawahara, S., Kizu, Y., & Amasaka, K. (2013b). A Bicycle Design Model based on young women's fashion combined with CAD and Statistical Science. *Journal of China-USA Business Review*, *12*(4), 266–277.

Mori, N. (1991). *The design plan of the engineering soft system of a designing*. Asakura-shoten.

Mori, N. (1993). *The research of the scientific method of a left brain designing*. Kaibundou.

Moriya, A., & Sugiura, K. (1999). *Collage Therapy: Esprit of Today*. Shibundou.

Motor Fan. (1997). All of new-model "Aristo," A new model prompt report, 213, 24-30.

Motor Fan. (2000). All of new-model "Celsior," A new model prompt report, 268, 23-24.

Muto, M., Miyake, R., & Amasaka, K. (2011). Constructing an Automobile Body Color Development Approach Model. *Journal of Management Science*, *2*, 175–183.

Muto, M., Takebuchi, S., & Amasaka, K. (2013). Creating a New Automotive Exterior Design Approach Model: The relationship between form and body color qualities. *Journal of Business Case Studies*, *9*(5), 367–374. doi:10.19030/jbcs.v9i5.8061

Nagaya, A., Matsubara, K. & Amasaka, K. (1998). *A Study on the customer tastes of automobile profile design* (Special Lecture). Union of Japanese Scientists and Engineers, The 28th Sensory Evaluation Symposium, Tokyo.

Nakamura, M., Kuniyoshi, M., Yamaji, M., & Amasaka, K. (2008). Proposal and validity of the product planning business model "A-POST": The application of the text mining method to scooter exterior design. *Journal of Business Case Studies*, *4*(9), 61–71. doi:10.19030/jbcs.v4i9.4808

Nunogaki, N., Shibata, K., Nagaya, A., Ohashi, T., & Amasaka, K. (1996). A study of customers' direction about designing vehicle's profile: A deployment of "Design SQC" for design business process. *The Japanese Society for Quality Control, The 26th annual conference*, 23-26.

Okabe, Y., Yamaji, M., & Amasaka, K. (2007). Research on the Automobile Package Design Concept Support Methods "CS-APDM": Customer Science approach to achieve CS for vehicle exteriors and package design. *Journal of Japan Society for Production Management*, *13*(2), 51–56.

Okazaki, R., Suzuki, M., & Amasaka, K. (2000). Study on the sense of values by age using Design SQC. *The Japan Society for Production Management, The 11th Annual Technical Conference*, 139-142.

Shinogi, T., Aihara, S., & Amasak, K. (2014). Constructing an Automobile Color Matching Model (ACMM). *IOSR Journal of Business and Management*, *16*(7), 7–14. doi:10.9790/487X-16730714

Shinohara, A., Sakamoto, H., & Shimizu, Y. (1996). *Invitation to Kansei Engineering*. Morikita-Shuppan.

Suzuki, M., Okazaki, R., & Amasaka, K. (2000). The research studies of the value by the generation by employing Design SQC: The development of Customer Science by utilizing Science SQC. *The Japan Society for Production Management, The 11th Annual Technical Conference, Okayama University*, 139-142.

Takebuchi, S., Asami, H., & Amasaka, K. (2012b). An Automobile Exterior Design Approach Model linking form and color. *Journal of China-USA Business Review*, *11*(8), 1113–1123.

Takebuchi, S., Nakamura, T., Asami, H., & Amasaka, K. (2012a). The Automobile Exterior Color Design Approach Model. *Journal of Japan Industrial Management Association*, *62*(6E), 303–310.

Takimoto, H., Ando, T., Yamaji, M., & Amasaka, K. (2010). The proposal and validity of the Customer Science Dual System, *China-USA. Business Review (Federal Reserve Bank of Philadelphia)*, *9*(3), 29–38.

Toyoda, S., Koizumi, K., & Amasaka, K. (2015b). Creating a Bicycle Design Approach Model based on fashion styles. *IOSR Journal of Computer Engineering*, *17*(3), 1–8.

Toyoda, S., Nishio, Y., & Amasaka, K. (2015a). Creating a Vehicle Proportion, Form, and Color Matching Model. *Journals International Organization of Scientific Research*, *17*(3), 9–16.

Yamaji, M., & Amasaka, K. (2009). An Intelligence Design Concept Method utilizing Customer Science. *The Open Industrial and Manufacturing Engineering Journal*, *2*(1), 10–15. doi:10.2174/1874152500902010021

Yazaki, K., Takimoto, H., & Amasaka, K. (2013). Designing vehicle form based on subjective customer impressions. *Journal of China-USA Business Review*, *12*(7), 728–734.

Yazaki, K., Tanitsu, H., Hayashi, H., & Amasaka, K. (2012). A model for design auto instrumentation to appeal to young male customers. *Journal of Business Case Studies*, *8*(4), 417–426. doi:10.19030/jbcs.v8i4.7035

Chapter 14
Automobile Optimal Product Design Model:
Application to Study the Bolt-Nut Loosening Mechanism

ABSTRACT

In this chapter, the author establishes an Automobile Optimal Product Design Model (AOPDM) as part of a principle-based research aimed at the innovation of development design processes in the automotive industry. As strategic deployment of Advanced TDS, this model's validity is verified with application to study on loosening mechanism of bolt-nut tightening and others as the auto-manufacturers' bottleneck in the world. To enable the high-quality assurance and simultaneous achievement of QCD to satisfy the requirements of developing automobile product design, it is necessary to initiate the transition from the conventional prototype testing method to predictive evaluation method by the combination of various experiments and CAE.

INTRODUCTION

The technological challenge currently facing Japanese auto-manufactures is to enable the high quality assurance and simultaneous achievement of QCD (quality, cost and delivery) by innovating product design processes, in order for them to prevail in the worldwide quality competition. Therefore, as the strategic deployment of Advanced TDS, it is necessary to undertake principle - based research in design and development (Amasaka, 2012, 2015a, 2019a) (Refer to Chapter 6).

Concretely, the author has conducted actual application case studies and established an Automobile Optimal Product Design Model (AOPDM) by combination of various experiments and numerical simulation (computer aided engineering, CAE) with statistical science based on their findings (Amasaka, 2007, 2008, 2010a, 2012, 2015b, 2019b; Amasaka Ed., 2007a, 2012; Amasaka et al., 2012, 2014).

DOI: 10.4018/978-1-7998-8746-1.ch014

To make the transition from the conventional prototype testing method to predictive evaluation method, this model contains four core models: (i) Total Intelligence CAE Management Model, (ii) Intelligence CAE System Approach Model, (iii) Highly Precise CAE Technology Element Model, and (iv) Highly Reliable CAE Analysis Approach Model. The author has succeeded in helping to overcome the current technological challenge through the unified application and systematic development of these core models for the innovation of product design in automotive industry.

The validity of this creative model was verified with application to study on bolt-nut loosening mechanism and others as the auto-manufacturers' bottleneck in the world automotive industries (Ueno et al., 2009; Takahashi, T, 2010; Yamada and Amasaka, 2011; Kozaki et al., 2012; Onodera and Amasaka, 2012; Amasaka et al., 2014; Hashimoto et al., 2014; Nomura et al., 2015, 2016; Shimura and Sakurai, 2015; Amasaka, 2015a,b, 2019c, 2022).

SIGNIFICANCE OF THE RESEARCH

Automotive Product Design and Production

In response to harsh competition, Japanese automotive enterprises have recently been promoting global production to realize uniform quality worldwide and production at optimal locations (Amasaka, 2007). The mission of the automotive manufacturers in this rapidly changing management technology environment is to be fully prepared for worldwide quality competition so as not to be pushed out of the market, and also to establish a new management technology model that enables them to offer highly reliable products of the latest design that are capable of enhancing value for the customer.

In terms of management technology for development and production processes, it is clear that there has been excessive repetition in prototyping, testing, and evaluation for the purpose of preventing the "scale-up effect" in the transitional stage between design / development and mass production. This has resulted in unstable built-in quality assurance in the product design stage, as well as an increase in development times and cost. Therefore, it is now vital to reform conventional product design processes (Nihon Keizai Shinbun, 2000, 2012). This can be achieved by shifting from so-called "product design through actual product confirmation and improvement" to a process of predictive evaluation–oriented development through the effective use of the latest numerical simulation (CAE) (Amasaka, 2007, 2008, 2010, 2015a).

Figure 1 shows the developments in the automotive product design process in Japan. In the past, model changes required approximately four years from development of product design to production. Once the design process was complete, problem detection and improvements were repeated mainly through the process of prototyping, testing, and evaluation. In some current automotive development processes, vehicle prototypes are not manufactured in the early stage of product design due to the utilization of CAE and simultaneous engineering (SE), resulting in a substantially shorter development periods.

It is now possible to utilize CAE for comparative evaluation, rather than the conventional supplementary "observation" role during prototypes testing. This improvement means that CAE is now utilized to the same extent as prototype testing. The vehicle product design and production processes have been shortened to one year, and there has been a transition to a super short-term concurrent product design process based on the utilization of CAE and Solid CAD, allowing individual processes to progress si-

Figure 1. Transitions in the automotive product design processes in Japan

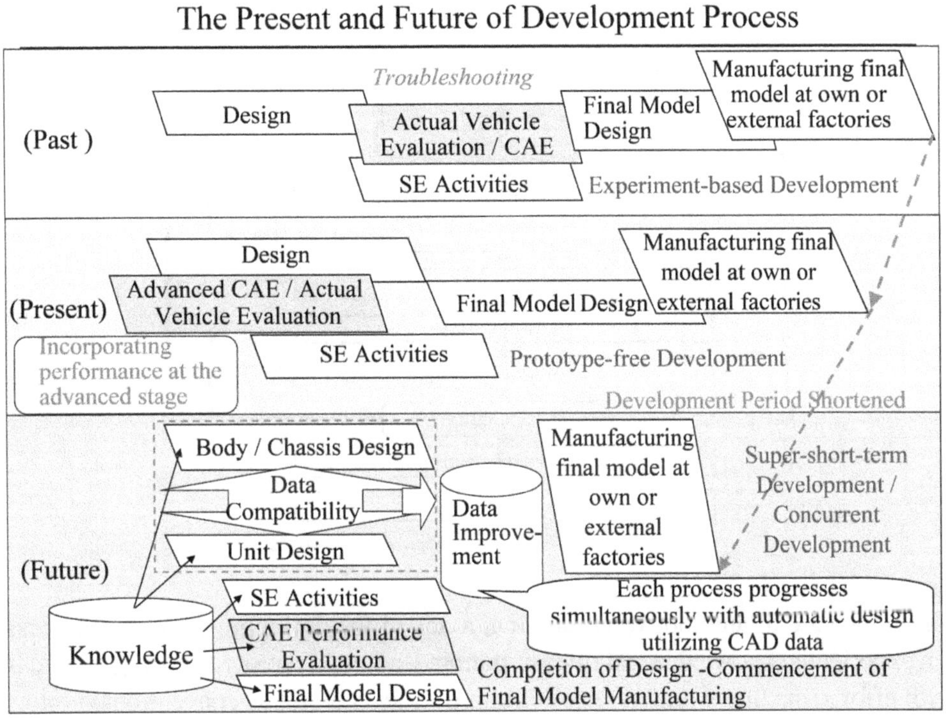

multaneously. This would be virtually impossible using the conventional repetitive testing of prototypes (Amasaka Ed., 2007a).

CAE in Development Design – Application and issue

The time between product design and production has been drastically shortened in recent years with the rapid spread of global production. Quality assurance, or QA, has become increasingly critical, making it essential that the development design process—a critical component of QA—be reformed to ensure quality (Kume, 1999: Amasaka, 2010b).

Figure 2 shows the typical product development design process currently used by many companies (Amasaka, Ed., 2007a). The figure shows that companies first create product development design instructions based on market research and planning. They then use these instructions to make specific development design specifications (drawings) and to promptly convert them to digital format so that they can be suitably processed and applied. The data is primarily used in numerical simulations known as computer-aided engineering, or CAE.

CAE and other numerical simulations have been applied to a wide variety of business processes in recent years, including research and development, design, preproduction and testing/evaluations, production technology, production preparation, and manufacturing. These and other applications are expected to have effective results (Magoshi, et al., 2003: Leo, et al., 2004: Amasaka, 2010b). In this age of global quality competition, using CAE for predictive evaluation method in design work is expected to contribute a great deal to shortening development design time and improving quality (Amasaka, 2007, 2008, 2010a).

Figure 2. CAE in the development design process

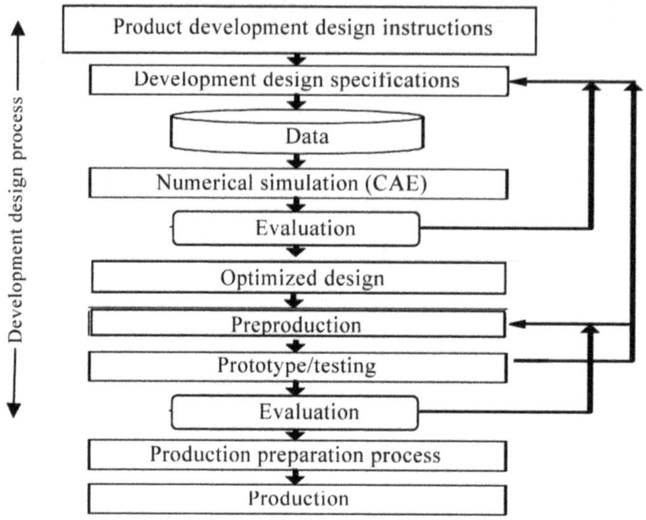

However, in the case of automotive production, much of the development design process is guided by unspoken experiential knowledge and rules of thumb, leading to prototype testing guided by repeated trial-and error efforts; in other words, a series of improvements based on conventional prototype testing methods. This not only draws out the development design process, but also results in enormous testing costs.

Previous forms of CAE analysis were not sufficiently precise, yielding figures that deviated as much as 10–30% from prototype testing evaluations (absolute values). This meant that CAE was hardly reliable enough to be an adequate substitute for prototype testing (Amasaka, 2007, 2008). As a result, manufacturers were not able to cut out preproduction and prototype testing (a necessity for shortening development design time) despite the enormous amount of funds they invested in CAE development. This means that many companies are now stuck with applying CAE only to the monitoring task of comparative evaluations of old and new products.

The only way get CAE analysis to function at a sufficient level and firmly establish it as part of (1) preventing recurrence of the pressing technical problem of bottlenecking and (2) the development design process for new products, is to make it more precise. Specifically, this means setting up highly reliable CAE analysis that reduce the deviation, or gap, with prototype testing evaluations (absolute values) to 5% or less (Amasaka, 2008, 2010b).

Problems when Applying CAE to Product Design Reform

Therefore, the author has identified problems when applying CAE to product design (design and development) reform and have summarized the main points as shown in Figure 3 from the standpoint of the simultaneous achievement of QCD (Amasaka, 2007).

Figure 3. Problems when applying CAE to automobile product design reform: From the experiment evaluation to the CAE prediction evaluation

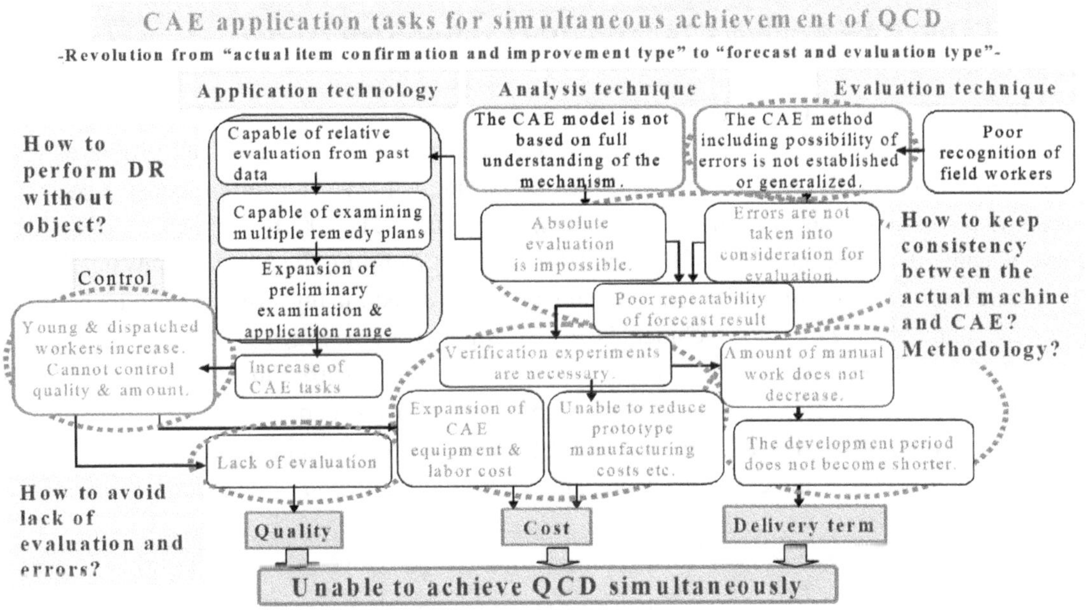

In Figure 3, specifically, it is clear that it is necessary to eradicate the tendency towards prototypes and experimental evaluation in favor of predictive evaluation based on CAE analysis.

To achieve this, however, the gap between analysis data and experimental evaluation data (analysis error) must be reduced from over 10 percent to 1-2 percent. Therefore, the author has conducted factorial analysis from the perspective of CAE technology for application, analysis, evaluation, and management (Amasaka, 2007, 2010a).

To realize the simultaneous achievement of QCD, it is necessary to enhance CAE analysis technology (Whaley et al., 2000; Amasaka, 2007; Amasaka Ed., 2007a). It is therefore important to determine the mechanisms behind the main technological problems, and accurately represent them with numerical calculations (simulation) as shown in the figure. Specifically, this means that it is vital to improve CAE analysis in order to more accurately and precisely reproduce the results of prototype testing (Amasaka, 2007, 2008).

CREATING NEW DEVELOPMENT DESIGN CAE MODEL

Therefore, as a way of overcoming these pressing problems in development design, technical issues that must be resolved by development design departments include development design process reform, design process reform, high accuracy of the prediction and control, computerization of business process, and optimization of development design specifications.

In terms of methodologies for resolving these issues, the author has created three core models as the new development design CAE model as the strategic development of Advanced TDS: the Highly Reliable CAE Analysis Technology Component Model, Highly Precise CAE Analysis Model, and Total

QA High Cyclization Business Process Model. The organically integrated and intelligent application of these models is essential. An overview of each model is given below.

Highly Reliable CAE Analysis Technology Component Model

The Highly Reliable CAE Analysis Technology Component Model (*problem-model- algorithm-theory-computer*) as shown in Figure 4 was designed to make the shift from conventional prototype testing methods to effectively applying CAE in predictive evaluation methods. The comprehensive issuance of this model is essential to achieving the desired shift. (Amasaka, Ed., 2007b: Amasaka, 2008, 2010a). More specifically, the critical aspects of this model include (i) *Defining the problem* (physically checking the actual item) in order to clarify the mechanism of the defect, using visualization technology to identify the dynamic behavior of the technical issue; (ii) full use of *formulization techniques* to generate logical modeling (statistical calculations, model application); (iii) constructing compatible *algorithms* (calculation methods); (iv) developing *theories* (establishing theories required to clarify problems) that ensure the precision of numerical calculations and sufficient computational capability; and (v) comprehensively putting the above processes in action using *computer* (*selection of calculation technology*).

Figure 4. Highly Reliable CAE Analysis Technology Component Model

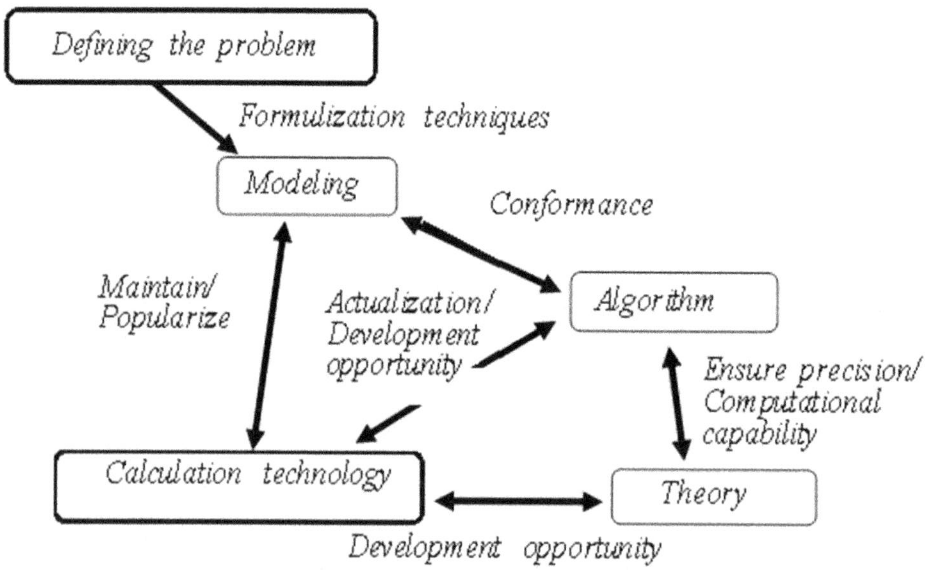

Highly Precise CAE Analysis Model

In order to minimize discrepancies in results obtained from testing of actual products and CAE, it is necessary to properly formalize the expertise of the many technical analysts required for CAE analysis. To achieve this, the authors (Amasaka, 2008: Takahashi, et al., 2010) propose the use of the Highly Precise CAE Analysis Model shown in Figure 5 to enable highly precise absolute analysis.

Functional failures are a recurring cause of market claims in automotive development design, making it necessary to clarify relevant technical issues such as the reasons and mechanisms by which such failures occur. This should be done according to the following steps.

STEP 1 Extracting the problem: Investigate and analyze the causal relationships that become apparent and infer the mechanisms through which failures occur, employing the latest "statistical science methods" backed up by expertise accumulated through the cooperative efforts of internal and external specialists (Amasaka, 2003).

STEP 2 Visualizing the problem: Test actual products demonstrating the failure mechanisms to visualize the dynamic behavior of the problem. In order to accurately analyze the failure and its causes, it is necessary to uncover any underlying factors that were not evident from previous findings and may have been overlooked. A logical reasoning process must be applied to demonstrate the mechanisms of the failure, employing tools and principles such as statistical science methods.

STEP 3 Testing & CAE analysis: Consolidate the findings and apply statistical simulation to create a two-dimensional model integrated on a qualitative level where the visualization produced through actual testing can be reproduced. When creating this two-dimensional model, it is necessary to conduct tests to produce a model (qualitative modeling) of the causal relationships involved in undefined failure mechanisms.

Precise calculation methods, analysis models and algorithms must be properly selected in order to clarify boundary conditions and contact situations, as well as to enable highly accurate statistical simulation. It is essential to use such tools to minimize discrepancies between actual testing and CAE absolute evaluation. The findings from such analysis should then be used for more detailed three-dimensional analysis.

STEP 4 Highly reliable CAE: Conduct accurate testing of actual products based on the findings from STEP 3 to gain a more explicit understanding of the failure mechanisms. Consolidate the findings from the processes involved and conduct statistical simulation (quantitative modeling) with a high level of credibility to enable the prediction and control of absolute values.

Figure 5. Highly Precise CAE Analysis Model using Highly Reliable CAE Analysis Technology Component Model

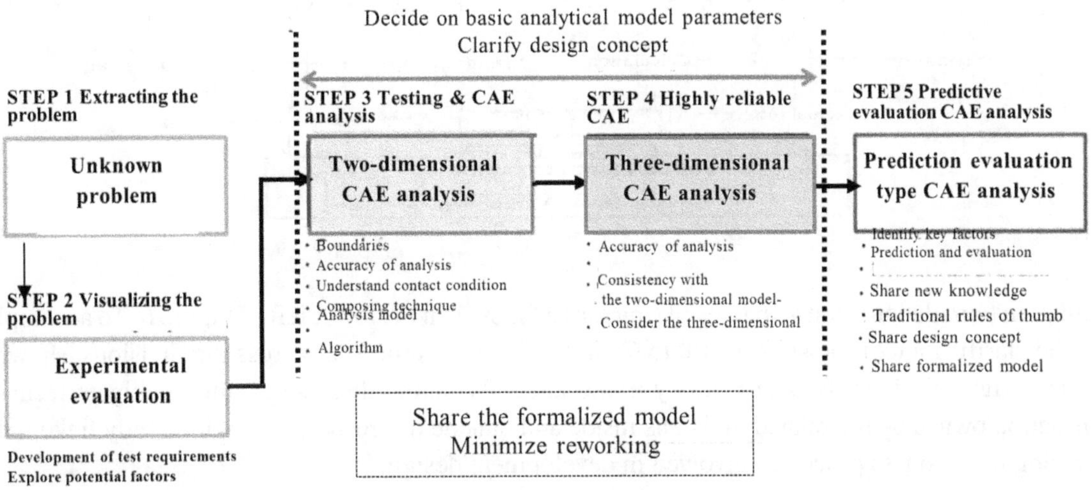

STEP 5 Predictive evaluation CAE analysis: In this final step, identify the primary factors from the results of the statistical simulation in STEP 4 to be used for prediction and evaluation. The new findings obtained, design concepts, and formulation models should be shared and disseminated. Utilizing models with a higher level of analytic accuracy enables manufacturers to move from relative evaluation to absolute evaluation of analysis results in the actual development process.

The author believes that this will lead to the future establishment of design frameworks involving predictive evaluation.

Total QA High Cyclization Business Process Model

As the first step, the author creates the development design business process model. This model is created from the standpoint of Verification/Validation (divergence of CAE from theory and divergence of CAE from testing) in order to make highly reliable CAE analysis that is consistent with the market testing theory profile possible. The authors (Amasaka, 2008) therefore recommend the introduction and utilization of the Total QA High Cyclization Business Process Model, which systematically and strategically realizes high quality assurance by incorporating analyses made via the core technologies of *Science SQC* as shown in Figure 6.

For example, in order to solve the pending issue of a technology problem in the market, it is necessary to create a universal solution (general solution) by clarifying the existing six gaps (① to ⑥ in Figure 6) in the process consisting of theory (technological design model), experiment (prototype to production),

Figure 6. Total QA High Cyclization Business Process Model

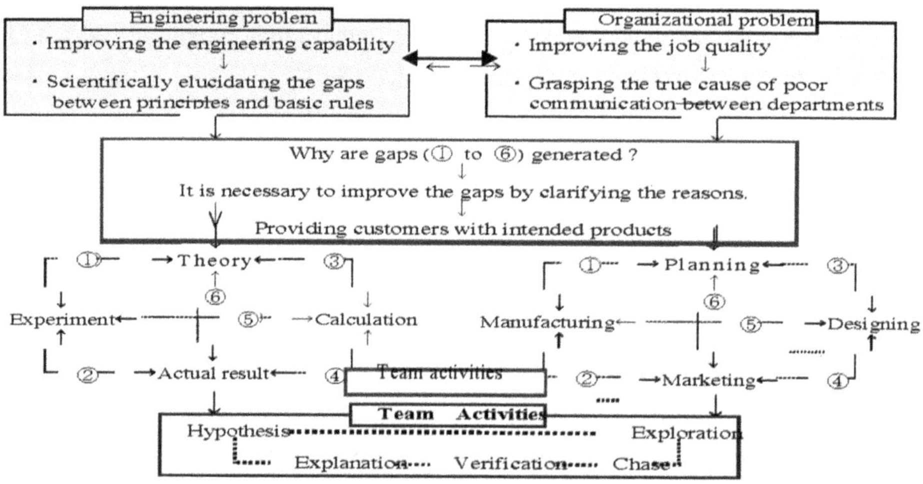

calculation (simulation), and actual result (market) as shown on the lower left of Figure 6. To accomplish this, the clarification of the six gaps (① to ⑥) in the business processes across the divisions, shown in the lower right of Figure 6. is of primary importance. By taking these steps, the intelligent technical information owned by the related divisions inside and outside the corporation will be fully linked, thus reforming the business processes involved in development design.

ESTABLISHMENT OF AN AUTOMOBILE OPTIMAL PRODUCT DESIGN MODEL FOR DEVELOPMENT DESIGN

Automobile Optimal Product Design Model (AOPDM)

In design and development for mass production, it is important to eradicate the repetitive trial-and-error testing of prototypes, and renovates low-productivity processes by introducing the latest CAE technology. To achieve this, the relevant departments must strategically cooperate to accumulate the necessary know-how (Steinberg, 1996; Amasaka, 2007, 2008).

Therefore, the author has constructed the Automobile Optimal Product Design Model (AOPDM) for the advanced product design in auto-manufacturers and other manufactures as shown in Figure 7 as a way of overcoming pressing bottleneck problems in development design (Amasaka, 2007, 2008, 2012, 2015b). As the figure shows, technical issues that must be resolved by development design departments include development design process evolution, high accuracy of the prediction and control, computerization of business processes, and optimization of development design specifications.

In Figure 7, in terms of a methodology for resolving these issues, the author has created four core models: the Stratified Intelligence CAE Management Model, Integrated Intelligence CAE System Approach Model, Highly Precise CAE Technology Element Model, and Highly Reliable CAE Analysis Approach Model. The organically integrated and intelligent application of these four models is essential. An overview of each is given below.

Stratified Intelligence CAE Management Model

The aim of the Stratified Intelligent CAE Management Model has created by the author is to enable intelligent CAE analysis as an idea generation support tool, and achieve highly-accurate CAE analysis equivalent to prototype testing results as shown in Figure 8 (Amasaka, 2008). Generally, at the design and development stage, there is a gap (discrepancy) between prototype evaluation results and CAE analysis results (Magoshi et al., 2003; Amasaka, 2007).

Figure 7. Outline of Automobile Optimal Product Design Model (AOPDM)

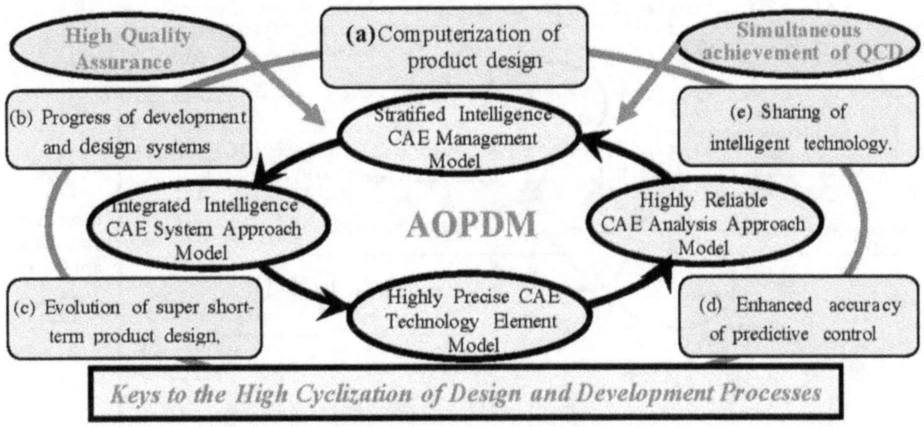

In Figure 8, it has become evident that some manufacturers are not fully confident in CAE results, and prefer to conduct survey tests with actual vehicles rather than CAE analysis at Step I on the bottom layer of this figure. This means that the application ratio of CAE is low at 25%, compared to the 75% application ratio of actual vehicle evaluation. Even among leading corporations, CAE analysis at Step II is limited to relative evaluation, and the application ratio of CAE is 50%, about the same as for actual vehicle evaluation. This is far from sufficient.

In order to break through this problem, the author has utilized visualization technology and statistical science in order to clarify the mechanisms involved, and focused their attention on the results of research that contributes to improving the accuracy of CAE analysis. Then, in Step III, the authors identified the causal relationships involved in bottleneck problems to create a generalized model, thereby enabling absolute evaluation.

As a result, it was confirmed that the accuracy of CAE analysis had improved and the CAE application ratio had increased to 75%. In Step IV, the CAE analysis technology derived from Steps I to III was incorporated, taking into consideration the influential factors and contribution ratio needed for a robust optimal CAE design capable of producing accurate results equivalent to actual vehicle evaluation. Thus, the accuracy of prediction and control was enhanced, demonstrating a remarkable increase in the ratio of CAE application to 100%. Solving similar problems in this way has made it possible to conduct design and development and related evaluation based on the results of CAE analysis.

This means that the evaluation of actual vehicles is now used to verify results, a role previously fulfilled by CAE analysis. As shown in the figure, the author has demonstrated the effectiveness of consistently applying statistical science at every step of CAE analysis (Amasaka, 2004, 2008, 2015a; Amasaka et al., 2012). The author therefore strongly recommends the utilization of SQC technical methods, effectively incorporating tools such as Q7 (Seven QC tools), N7 (New seven QC tools), RE (Reliability Engineering), MA (Multivariate Analysis), DOE (Design of Experiment), and other statistical science methods indicated in Figure 8.

Figure 8. Schematic Drawing of Stratified Intelligence CAE Management Model

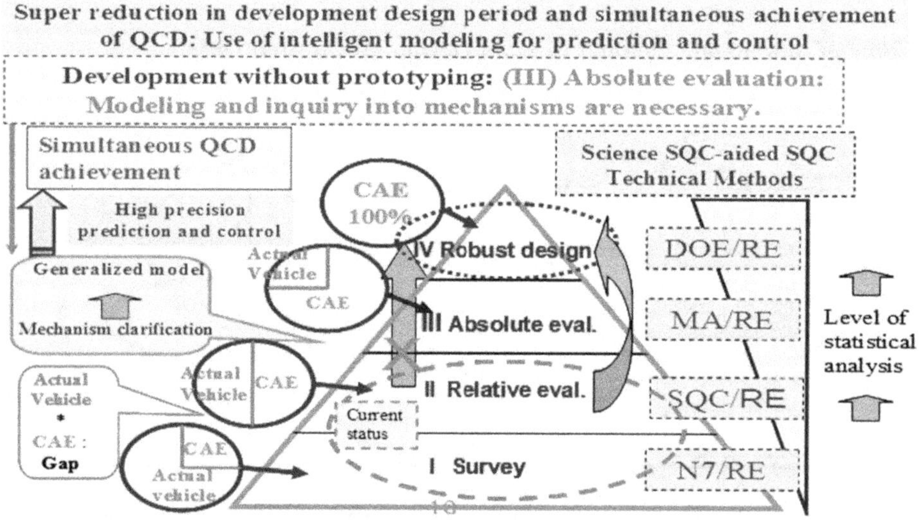

Integrated Intelligence CAE System Approach Model

Skilled CAE engineers are not generally experts in all the fields of the elemental technologies, but they understand their characteristics and interactions as "implicit knowledge" (rule of thumb, empirical knowledge), and are thus able to obtain favorable interactions and consequently the desired results by selecting and combining these technologies (Hashimoto, et al., 2005). The formulation of such "implicit knowledge" confined to the personal know-how of the engineers is an indispensable step in refining CAE as a problem solving method.

Therefore, the author has created the Integrated Intelligence CAE System Approach Model aimed at the development and intelligent operation of highly-reliable CAE software that generalizes these design and development behavior patterns and applies the aforementioned the Integrated Intelligence CAE System Approach Model as shown in Figure 9 (Amasaka, 2008).

For example, in the case of the ongoing problems with market claims concerning functional failures, the causes must be established by clarifying the relevant technological problems, with market claims concerning functional failures, the causes must be established by clarifying the relevant technological problems, such as why the failures occur and what kind of mechanisms are involved.

In Figure 9, to do this, (A) the actual vehicle must be evaluated to visualize the dynamic behavior of the problems. Next, it is important to cooperatively share the knowledge and know-how of internal and external specialists in order to (B) thoroughly investigate the cause and effect relationships to clarify the mechanisms involved in the failure, utilizing the latest SQC methods. The consistent application of N7, RE, MA, and DOE is highly recommended in order to ensure accurate failure analysis and factorial analysis. Any latent factors that may have previously been overlooked must be discovered at this stage, and theoretical thought processes applied to estimate the mechanisms. Then, it is necessary to (C) consolidate the findings and incorporate computer graphics (CG) to rationally reproduce the failure by visualizing the moment that the failure occurs (dynamic behavior) during testing.

Figure 9. Schematic drawing of Integrated Intelligence CAE System Approach Model

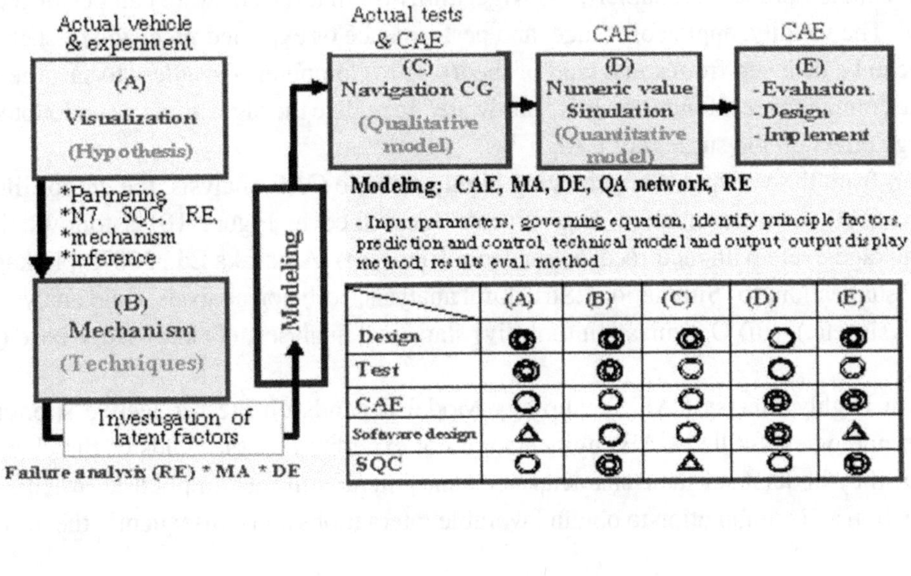

The author then has showed the use of CAE, CG, and navigation software (CAE-CG-NS) to model the problem on a qualitative level. During this CAE-CG-NS modeling stage for the highly-reliable CAE analysis, it is vital to conduct intelligent testing in order to properly model the cause and effect relationships involved in the unknown mechanisms. Through the use of CAE-CG-NS, it is extremely important to obtain new findings that can help to reduce the discrepancy (gap) in absolute values resulting from a combination of experiments and CAE analysis. Furthermore, (D) at the stage of developing highly-reliable CAE analysis, accurate testing must be conducted in order to make the implicit knowledge of the mechanisms sufficiently explicit.

It is necessary to consolidate the many findings obtained from these intelligent work processes and highly-reliable numerical simulation (quantitative modeling) to enable prediction and control through absolute values and, finally (E) validate the results through actual tests. For decentralized organizations and business processes, collective partnering through team activities (◎: main,○: sub, △: support) is indispensable among the specialists involved in design, testing, CAE analysis, CAE software development, and SQC throughout the process stages from (A) to (E) indicated in the Figure 8.

Highly Precise CAE Technology Element Model

Based on the above findings, the author has created the Highly Precise CAE Technology Element Model required for CAE analysis software in order to achieve highly-reliable CAE analysis as shown in Figure 10 (Amasaka, 2007; Amasaka Ed., 2007a). This model illustrates the techniques belonging to the domains of (1) Problem setting, (2) Modeling, (3) Algorithm, (4) Theory, and (5) Computer (calculation technology). These techniques are being used for the purpose of realizing the systemization or formulation of working level problems, development of the kind of algorithms which utilize calculation resources more efficiently, logical analysis of the algorithms, and improvement in hardware and software technology for accelerating the calculation speed.

In Figure 10, the process of CAE first starts with (1) "Problem"-Setting of problems to be solved, as well as (2) "Model"-Modeling of these problems as some type of mathematical formula. In CAE, when using calculators as a means to analyze the model, such a means of analysis needs to be provided in the form of a calculation procedure, namely, (3) Algorithms-So that the software can perform calculation. (4) "Theory"-The validity, applicable range, and performance or expected precision of such algorithms themselves can be deduced from some kind of theory. (5) "Computer"-Needless to say, the technology related to the computer itself functioning as "hardware" to realize the algorithms, is undoubtedly a factor having a large effect on the success of CAE.

Moreover, from the viewpoint of achieving highly-reliable CAE analysis, the author illustrates the "Intelligence CAE software creation requirements" described in Figure 10 as follows (illustration: Knowhow linkage-cycle with reciprocal action from (i) to (iv)) (Amasaka Ed., 2007a); linkage-cycle (i) Modelling visualization, (ii) Simulation (:Structural analysis, collision analysis, fluid analysis, chemical process analysis, etc.), (iii) Optimization tool, (iv) statistical analyses, (v) knowledge base (groupware weblog, etc.).

Success in Highly Precise CAE Technology Model depends on the "collective strengths" of the elemental technologies. Skilled CAE engineers are not experts in all the fields of the elemental technologies, but they understand their characteristics and interactions as "implicit knowledge" and thus conduct selection and combination to obtain favorable interactions and consequently the desired results.

Figure 10. Schematic Drawing of Highly Precise CAE Technology Element Model

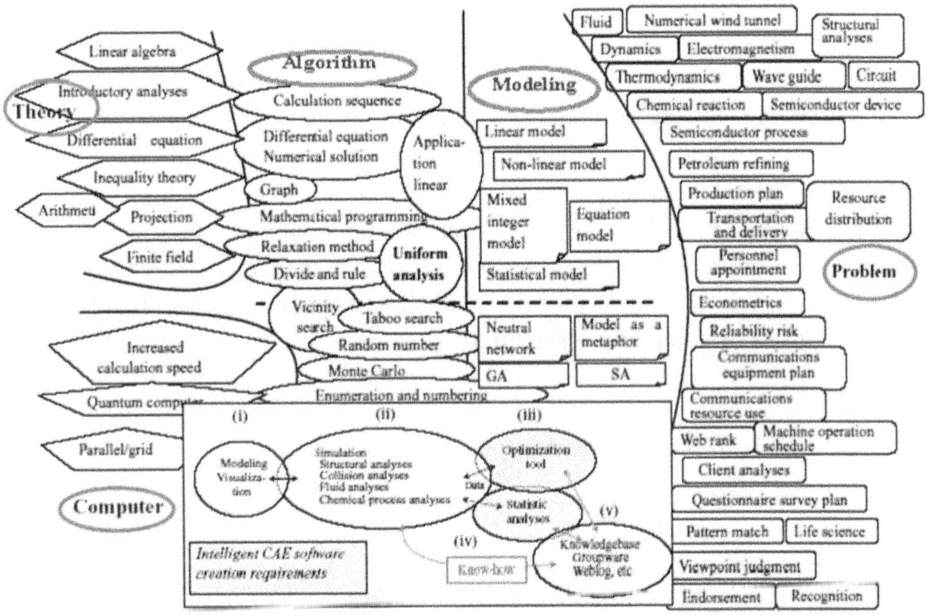

The formulation of such "implicit knowledge" confined to the personal know-how of the engineers is an indispensable step to be taken for sophistication of CAE as a problem solving method and therefore it is positioned as a major theme in author's work (Nonobe and Ibaraki, 2001; Enrique and Parallel, 2005; Whaley et al., 2000; Amasaka, 2008, 2010a)

Highly Reliable CAE Analysis Approach Model

Furthermore, in addition, the author has created the Highly-Reliable CAE Analysis Approach Model as shown in Figure 11, which incorporates numerical simulation and statistical science methods, in order to aid the intelligent operation of CAE analysis (Amasaka, 2012). The aim of this model was to incorporate statistical science to accurately determine the degree of influence of the technological elements required for design and development (principal design factors), which are vital for solving technological problems, and to provide approximate solutions such as factorial analysis, identification, control, and mechanism analysis, thereby enabling accurate structural modeling (Strassburger, et al., 2003: Leo, et al., 2004; Yamaji and Amasaka, 2008).

This methodology is designed to conduct CAE analysis through the use of three case methods (I, II, and III) to find the solutions to various problems related to development and designing.

- (I) Cases where design specification factors are identifiable through proper technology. Case Method (I) is a CAE analysis system approach method which utilizes statistical science focusing on "variation factor analysis" to make effective use of unique technologies. This case is generally implemented as a simplified model that contributes to the supplementary "survey" used for the prototyping and experimenting processes.

- (II) Cases where design specification factors are not clarified. Case Method (II) is a "relation between CAE and statistical science" approach in the case where the mechanism of the problem that occurs can be surmised to a certain extent through the use of unique technology. In the cases of univariate actual machine experiments, such design factor effects are often not identified with high precision, so it is realistic to conduct curve fitting by means of a neural network (NN) so as to reduce the deviance between the actual machine results and those of the CAE analysis.
- (III) Cases where the mechanism of technical problems is unclear. Case Method (III) proposes using a "relation between CAE and statistical science" approach in the case where the "mechanism of technological problems", the issue the development designers are most interested in, is not very well understood. This is done with a view to reflecting it specifically in actual business processes through the means of research and verification.

Figure 11. Outline of Highly Reliable CAE Analysis Approach Model

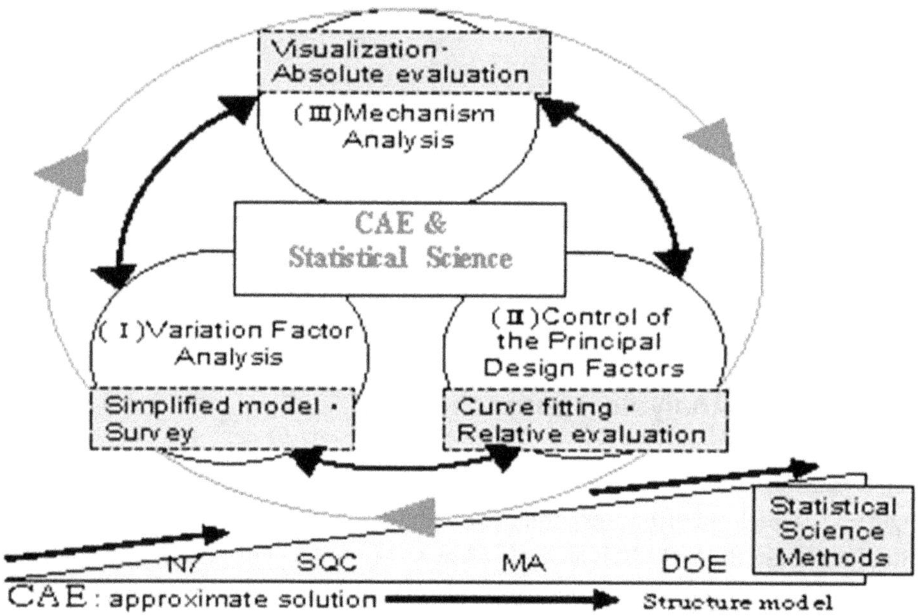

To ensure the effective deployment of this model, the authors advocate the utilization of mountain-climbing for problem-solving such as "SQC Technical Methods" (N7, RE, SQC, MA and DOE), the core principles of "Science SQC, new quality control principle" established by the author (Amasaka, 2004).

APPLICATION TO STUDY ON BOLT-NUT LOOSENING MECHANISMS

Creation of a Highly-Accurate CAE Analysis Approach Model

The number of bolts-nuts exceeds 3000 in an automobile. For many years, about 15% of automobiles' quality recall is the looseness of bolt-nut tightening around powertrain system (MLITT, 2005). In this section, therefore, the author has created a Highly-Accurate CAE Analysis Approach Model to explain undiscovered technological mechanisms (Ueno, et al., 2009; Takahashi, et al., 2010; Yamada and Amasaka, 2011; Kozaki, et al., 2012: Onodera and Amasaka, 2012; Amasaka et al., 2014; Hashimoto et al., 2014: Hashimoto, 2015; Nomura et al., 2015, 2016; Shimura and Sakurai, 2015; Amasaka, 2019b).

This created CAE model is no gap between its results and the results of actual machine tests (experiments), allows the realization of intelligent development design to the creation of drawings in manufacturing design described in Steps 1 through 5 utilizing the Mountain- Climbing for Problem-Solving Methods as shown in Figure 12 (Amasaka, 2004).

1. Experiments - Actual machine testing (Step 1)

In order to visualize the loosening mechanism of the bolt-nut tightening, it is necessary to make clear the dynamic behavior that accompanies occurrence of the problem as follows; The aim of Step 1-1 is to catch the fundamentals of actual bolt-nut tightening, and Step 1-2 is to verify the loosening mechanism of the bolts-nut tightening.

2. Modeling - Highly accurate simulation (Step 2)

In Step 2, to draw the information obtained in Steps 1, the author lists the specific components which make up this modelling as follows; The aim of Step 2-1 is to develop the intelligent CAE software by Finite Element Method (FEM), and Step 2-2 is to create of the Bolt-Nut Tightening Simulator for the optimization of highly accurate CAE analysis and comprehensive manner.

Figure 12. Highly-Accurate CAE Analysis Approach Model

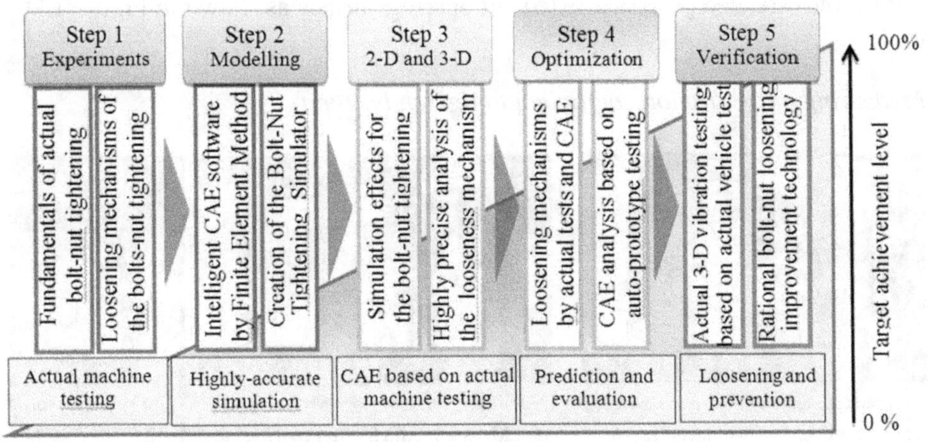

3. 2-D and 3-D analysis - CAE based on actual machine testing (Step 3)

In Step 3, to perform a highly accurate numerical simulation, the author develops the combination of 2-D and 3-D in Step 3-1 and 3-2 based on the investigation gained in Step 2, and articulates implicit knowledge about the bolt-nut loosening mechanism integrated on a qualitative level where the visualization produced through actual testing can be reproduced.

4. Optimization - Prediction and evaluation (Step 4)

In Step 4, the author conducts a highly reliable numerical simulation that enables the absolute values. Step 4-1 focuses on visualization of internal stress distribution of bolt-nut tightening by combination of actual tests and CAE analysis using photo-elastic experiment. Moreover, Step 4-2 develops the CAE analysis by comparing results of numbers of vibration cycles of axial force reduction between prototype testing and CAE analysis.

5. Verification – Loosening and prevention (Step 5)

Finally, Step 5-1 illustrates the actual 3-D vibration testing to observe the actual moment of *loosening behavior of bolt-nut* using a visualization device. In Step 5-2, furthermore, the author creates the new design nut having high cost performance which gave priority to mass-productivity by employing "Rational bolt-nut loosening improvement technology", and verifies the validity of developing AOPDM.

Example Applications of AOPDM

Experiments–Actual machine testing (Step 1)

1. Fundamentals of actual bolt-nut tightening experiments (Step 1-1)

The test piece is a M12 x 1.25 9T hexagon bolt and nut with flange that is often used to tighten parts of power-train system in automotive applications, and an experiment are conducted in order to confirm an important parameter of the friction coefficient based on the dynamic behavior of "angle * torque * axial force" of (a) the threaded portion and (b) nut bearing surface as shown in Figure 13.

Figure 13. Measuring of the friction coefficient to tighten bolt-nut

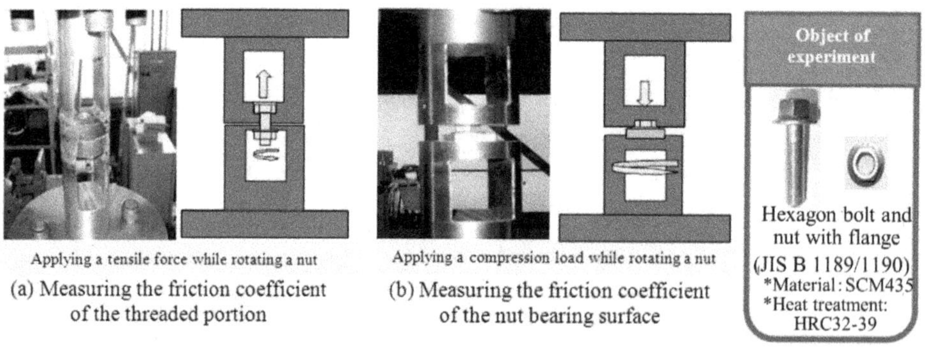

Specifically, Figure 14 below showed the relationship between angle and torque for 60KN of tensile force as well as compression load. In Figure 14(a), the friction coefficient of (a) the threaded portion is measured using a 2-axial fatigue testing machine, which is capable of applying axial force and twist force at the same time. The bolt head was pulled with the force of 20kN, 40kN and 60kN, conducting the experiment for each tensile force five times in total, while torque and axial force were measured. In Figure 14(b), the friction measurement for coefficient of (b) the flange (bearing) surface was similarly conducted using the 2-axial fatigue testing machine, applying a compression load of 20kN, 40kN and 60kN onto the substrate while rotating the nut so as to confirm the torque and axial force.

Figure 14. The relationship between angle and torque

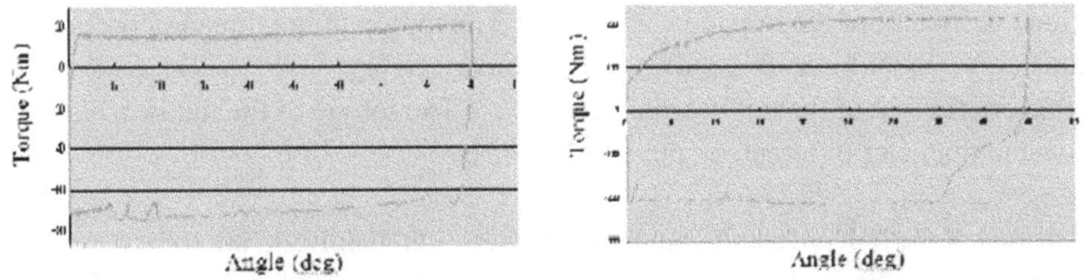

(a) Measuring the friction coefficient of the threaded portion

(b) Measuring the friction coefficient of the nut bearing surface

Based on the results of the friction coefficient measurement of (a) the threaded portion and (b) the nut bearing surface, torque and axial force were obtained. Applying theoretical equations to these experiment results, the friction coefficients were calculated. When calculating the friction coefficient of the threaded portion, μ_s equation (1) below was used. Also, the friction coefficient of the nut bearing surface μw was calculated using equation (2) (Tanaka et al., 1981; Suzuki, 2005). The bolt and nut dimensions necessary for calculation of these coefficients were given in Table 1.

Table 1. The bolt and nut measurements

	Bolt	**Nut**
Major diameter of external thread (mm)	12	12
Pitch diameter (mm)	11.19	11.19
Minor diameter of external thread (mm)	10.65	10.65
Pitch of threads (mm)	1.25	1.25
Width across flat (mm)	16.91	16.91
Flange diameter (mm)	26	26
Lead angle (deg)	2.03	2.03
Thread angle (deg)	30	30

*1 Source: ISO15071:1999, ISO15072:1999, ISO4161:1999 and ISO10663:1999

*2 Note: the author measured or calculated

$$\mu_s = \frac{\frac{2T_s}{d_2} - F\tan\beta}{\frac{2T_s}{d_2}\tan\beta + F}\cos\alpha$$

$$\mu_w = \frac{2T_w}{Fd_w}$$

Where:

μ_s: The friction coefficient of the threaded portion, T_s: The torque of the threaded portion,
d_2: Pitch diameter, F: Axial force, β: Lead angle, α: Thread angle,
μ_w: The friction coefficient of the nut bearing surface, T_w: The torque of the nut bearing surface,
d_w: The equivalent diameter of torque on nut bearing surfaces

The dimensions of the bolt are actually measured here, and the bolt and nut (units) are in millimeters. However, pitch and other dimensions that are difficult to measure are taken from the ISO standard (ISO 4161/15071/5072/10663, 1999). Using equations and dimensions such as those mentioned above, the friction coefficient of the threaded portion and bearing surface was then calculated.

As an example, the friction coefficients of the threaded portion and bearing surface when the tensile force and compression load in axial direction were both 60kN at the angle of 40°are shown in Table 2.

Using these calculated friction coefficients, bolt tightening simulation was conducted and the relationship between simulative axial force and torque was confirmed.

2. Loosening mechanisms of bolts-nut tightening (Step 1-2)

An external force was added in the bolt-nut vibration test to gauge changes to axial force, which was the bolt-nut tightening force, and in the stress distribution of the nut bearing surface and contacted surface of the base material as shown in Figure 15 and 16 (Test-A and Test-B).

Table 2. The friction coefficients

The friction coefficient of the threaded portion			The friction coefficient of the nut bearing surface		
angle (deg)	torque (Nm)	friction coefficient	angle (deg)	torque (Nm)	friction coefficient
40	18.63	0.02	40	215.26	0.35
40	23.05	0.03	40	221.63	0.37
40	35.30	0.06	40	198.09	0.33
40	28.44	0.04	40	208.39	0.34
40	32.85	0.05	40	226.53	0.37

Here, oscillation amplitude was applied to the bolt-nut joint, and the reduction in axial force of the joint and stress distribution at the nut bearing surface were measured by using the strain gauge equipped test bolt and the nut bearing surface pressure sheets for measuring the stress distribution.

The stress distribution is measured at the bolt and nut bearing surfaces using pressure sheets with 20kN, 35kN and 50kN at oscillation load of ±40%, ±60% and ±90% (±1.8kN, ±2.8kN and ±4.0kN) of the measured static release load (fall-off load of axial force) that pith of threads (hereinafter referred to as the pitch) is 1.25mm, respectively. Here, the author visualizes the

looseness behavior of bolt-nut tightening by using "Infrared *camera*". An example of Test-A showed the transition of bolt-nut load with the initial applied bolt-nut load of 20kN of external stress in a normal direction. Each measurement result was plotted with the bolt-nut load on the vertical axis, and the sampling number (5Hz) at ±1.8kN and ±2.8kN of oscillation load as the repetition number of times as described in Figure 15. In Test-A, rotation looseness of nut-tightening was confirmed at a stage of the beginning.

In same way, an example of Test-B showed the transition of nut-displacement with the bolt-nut load control of 50KN of external stress in a normal direction using load control by increasing load employing tensile load jig. The looseness of nut-tightening was confirmed at a stage after 4.4kN of the bolt-nut tightening load as described in Figure 16.

Next, the author checks the loosening mechanism of bolts-nut tightening in detail by the following tests (Test-C, -D and -E). An example of Test-C shows the comparison of flange surface stress distribution as the bolt and nut with the initial applied bolt-nut load of 20kN of external low-stress in a normal direction, and the sampling number (5Hz) at ±1.8kN and ±2.8kN of oscillation load on the vertical axis vibration as shown in Figure 17. In Figure 17(a), the flange (bearing) surface stress distribution of bolt was the uniform stress all-around the base material named substrate by using coloring type pressure gauge. In Figure 17(b), the bearing surface stress distribution of nut was the un-uniform stress all-around the base metal. The contact of around "b" surface area with "Nut-flange bearing surface and base material" showed the high-stress distribution under the influence of strong contact of spiral lead angle.

Figure 15. Looseness of nut-tightening (Test-A) (with the initial applied bolt-nut load "20kN" of external low-stress in a normal direction)

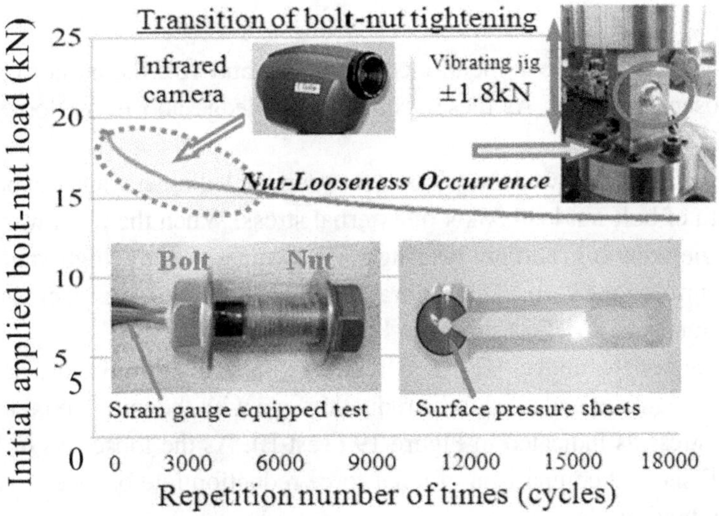

Figure 16. Looseness of nut-tightening (Test-B) (the bolt-nut load control of 50KN of external high-stress in a normal direction by the load increase method)

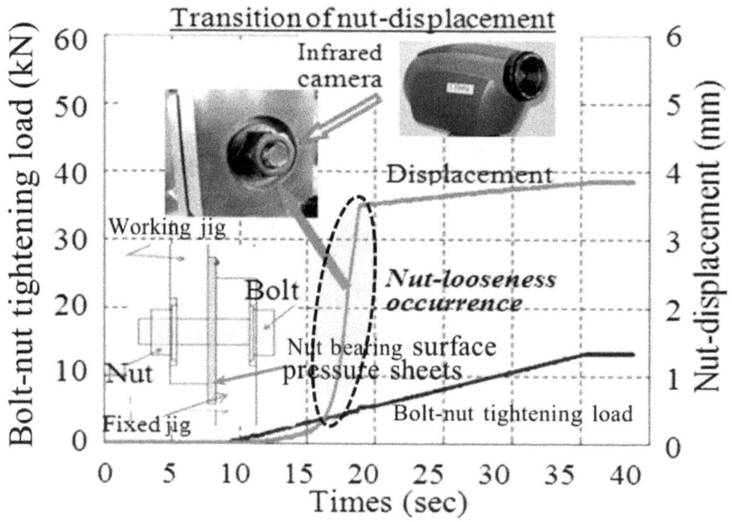

Figure 17. Comparison of flange surface stress distribution as the bolt and the nut (Test-C) (: with the initial applied bolt-nut load of 20kN of external low-stress in a normal direction)

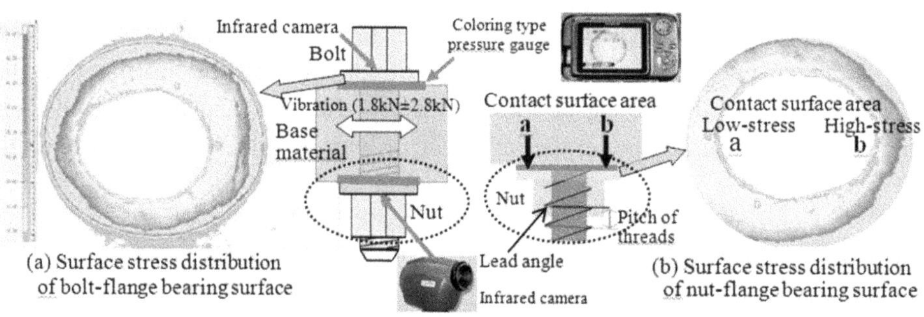

Therefore, (as shown in the above-mentioned Figure 15 and 16), the author checked by "Infrared camera" that nut-looseness occurs. As these acquired knowledge above, the looseness of bolt-flange surface was not checked.

Next, an example of Test-D showed the relation between pitch diameter and nut bearing surface stress with initial axial forth of bolt-nut load 35kN of external stress. When the pitch was

long, the lead angle grew big, and nut bearing surface stress became high value. In an example of pitch diameter "0.50mm" on the vertical axis vibration, initial axis forth was decreasing rapidly, and this example's reduction rate was 12.5% as shown in Figure 18.

From the knowledge of the above "Test-A, -B, -C and -D", in addition, the author researched the relation between pitch diameter and axial force reduction rate with the initial axial forth of bolt-nut load of 35kN of external stress as indicated in Figure 19 (Test-E). As the looseness of bolt-nut tightening, an example of Test-E showed comparison of axial force reduction rate between vertical axis vibration and horizontal axis vibration.

Figure 18. Relation between "Pitch" and "Nut bearing surface stress" (Test-D) (: with the relation between "Repetition number of times (cycles)" and "Initial axial forth" of bolt-nut load 35kN of external stress)

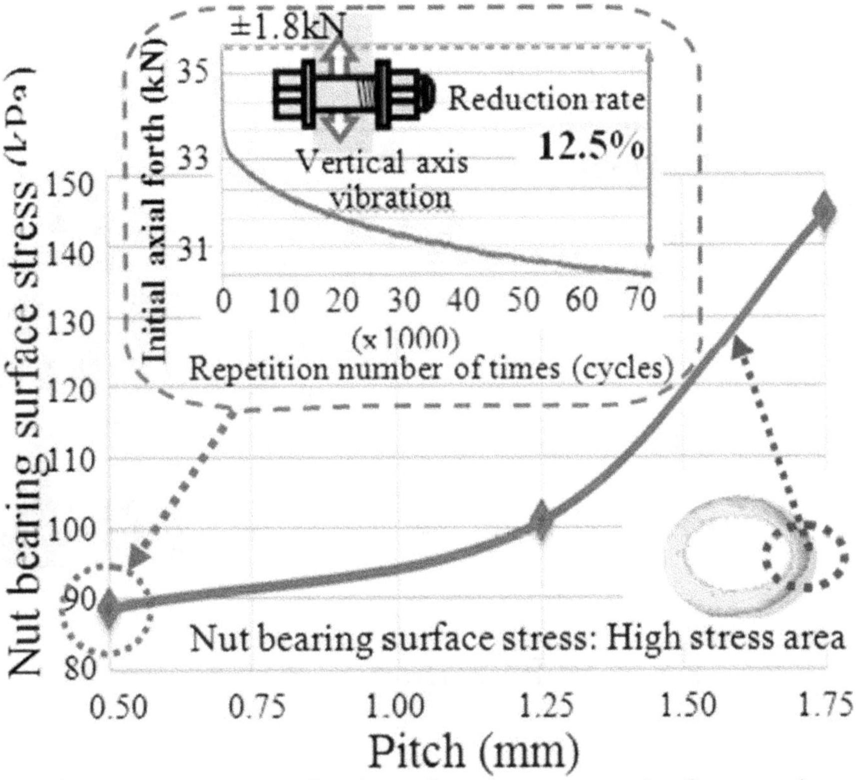

As the axial force reduction rate, in Figure 19, the test condition of vertical axis vibration was clearly larger than the test condition of horizontal axis vibration.

Modelling–Highly Accurate Simulation (Step 2)

1. Intelligent CAE software by Finite Element Method (Step 2-1)

The main issues in creating CAE software are grasping the actual state of contact between the threaded portion and grooves, and the friction coefficient of threaded portion and nut bearing surface based on the bolt and nut measurements (Table 1) and friction coefficients (Table 2). For structural analysis to function properly, there are two minimum requirements.

These are necessary to simulate the dynamic behavior of angle, torque, and axial force for both the threaded portion and nut bearing surface during bolt-nut tightening. They require the contact between the threaded portion and groove as well as contact between the threaded portion and bearing surface. These should be done on the basis of elastic static analysis and elastic dynamic analysis results, calculated using the Finite Element Method (FEM).

2. Creation of the Bolt-Nut Tightening Simulator (Step 2-2)

Figure 19. Relation between "Pitch" and "Axial force reduction rate" (Test-E) (: with the initial axial forth of bolt-nut load 35kN of external stress)

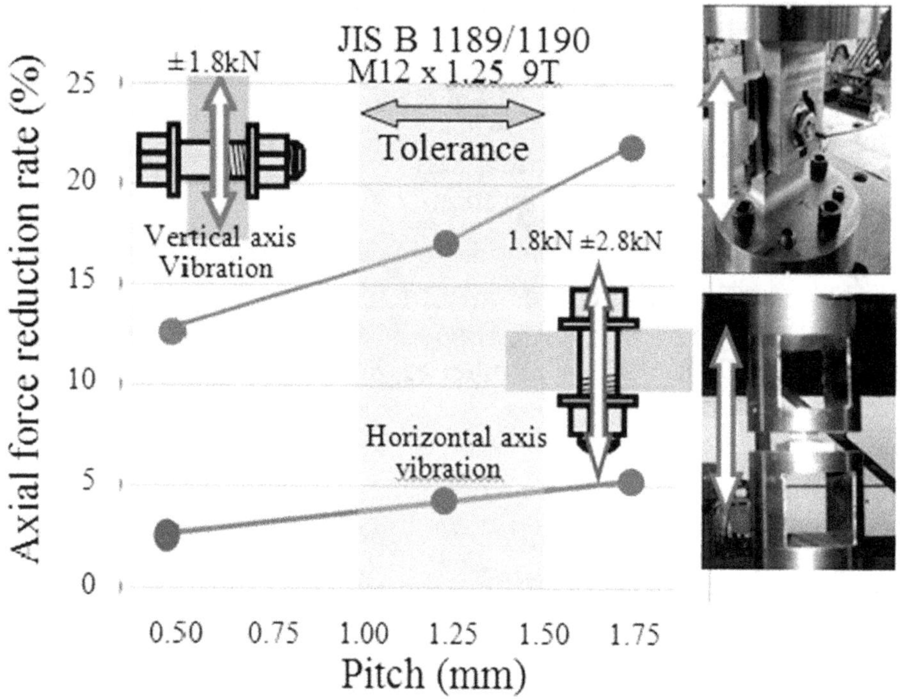

Then, the author creates a Bolt-Nut Tightening Simulator utilizing Highly Precise CAE Technology Element Model as shown in Figure 20 as follows;

(i) Relevant issues for conducting numerical simulation of physical chemical phenomena contain the (1) relationship between axial force and torque, (2) dynamic friction coefficient and static friction coefficient and (3) contact surface pressure on the threaded portion and nut bearing surface. (ii) Structuring models for solving these issues contain the (1) dynamic elemental model, (2) elastic-plastic model, (3) contact model and (4) material component rule model. (iii) Useful algorithms contain the (1) finite element method and (2) dynamic analysis method. (iv) Suitable theoretical equations contain the (1) structural mechanics and (2) equation of equilibrium. (v) Creative solutions for ensuring precision and realistic time calculation contain the (1) temporal integration method, (2) matrix function, (3) penalty method and (4) the Normal Lagrange Multiplier Method (Baggerly, 1996; Gamboa and Atrens, 2003).

To facilitate highly precise CAE analysis, the author has developed the bolt-nut tightening technical element model in order to allow accurate reproduction of actual machine tests. This model addresses the bolt-nut loosening mechanism through steps (1) to (5) below.

1. Problem-The author assessed the phenomenon by means of actual machine tests employing the Second Law of Thermodynamics, interpreting temperature changes detected using high speed camera and infrared camera as stress changes.

Figure 20. Bolt-Nut Tightening Simulator using Highly Precise CAE Technology Element Model

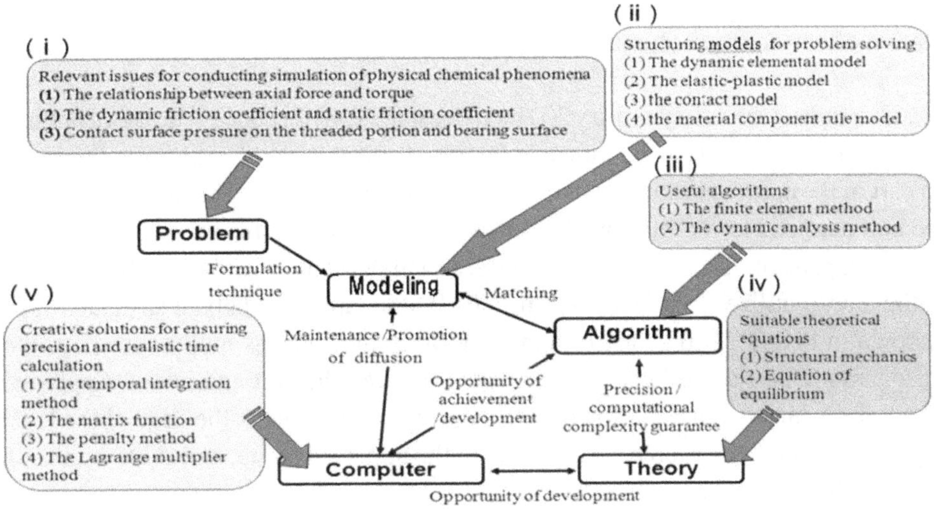

Figure 21. The axis symmetry 2-D model

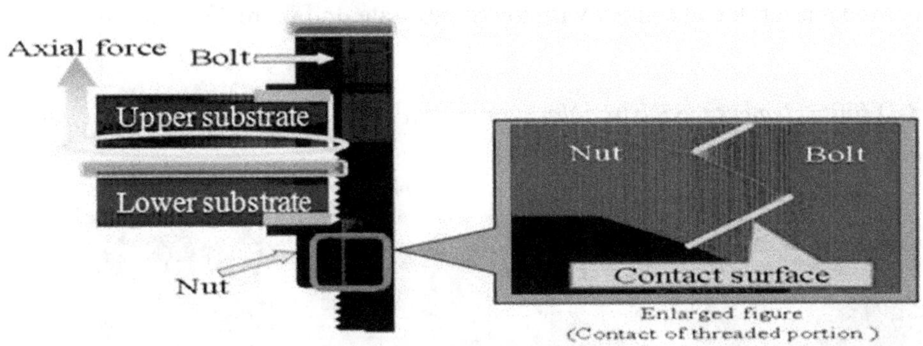

2. Modeling-To convert the entire nut being targeted in numerical analysis into a model that can work with CAE analysis, the author broke it down into elements and modeled the elements' material constitutive principle (component rule) as an equation.
3. Algorithms-The author synchronized important algorithms where the effects of external force were observed and eliminated gaps with actual machine tests so that the accuracy of FEM analysis and Nonlinear Analysis (Newton-Rraphson Method) increase.
4. Theory-Since the validity, application scope, and performance of the algorithms themselves can be derived from theory, the author calculated coefficients of friction using experimental values and a theoretical equation which vary with temperature, accurately by holding the temperature constant using visualization technology.
5. Computer-The author changed from the penalty method to the Augmented Lagrange Algorithm to enhance the engagement precision of the bolt and nut, which is characterized by numerical stability and a tendency to converge on solutions.

2-D and 3-D Analysis–CAE Based On Actual Tests (Step 3)

1. Simulation effects for the bolt-nut tightening (Step 3-1)

First, the author utilizes the axis symmetry 2-D model (using FEM) for contact surface of bolt-nut tightening using Bolt-Nut Tightening Simulator as shown in Figure 21. Regarding the analysis parameters, axial force is applied to part of the upper substrate and bolt bounded from all directions in the same way as it is applied to part of the bolt head and lower substrate. Concretely, the friction coefficient was calculated by conducting experiments on parts of the contact bearing surfaces and the contact surface of the threaded portions.

Second, the author utilizes 3-D model (using FEM) simulating the helical structure of the threaded portion as shown in Figure 22(a) and (b). In the diagrams, the analysis process involves the following steps: ① Place parts to be clamped using 2 substrates between the bolt and nut, ② Apply axial force to the bolt and nut determine the distribution of stress during contact, ③ Fix the edge of the lower substrate and apply upward perpendicular force (axial force) to the upper substrate, and ④ Determine the pressure on the contact nut bearing surface.

The results of 3-D analysis showed the examples of stress distribution of the nut surface and nut bearing surface in contact with lower substrate in the initial axial force of load 25kN and 35kN of external stress as shown in Figures 23. The diagrams of Mises stress shown in Figure 19(a) showed the stress distribution of the nut surface in contact with lower substrate. In Figure 23(a), the stress value of initial

Figure 22. 3-D finite element models simulating the helical structure of the threaded portion

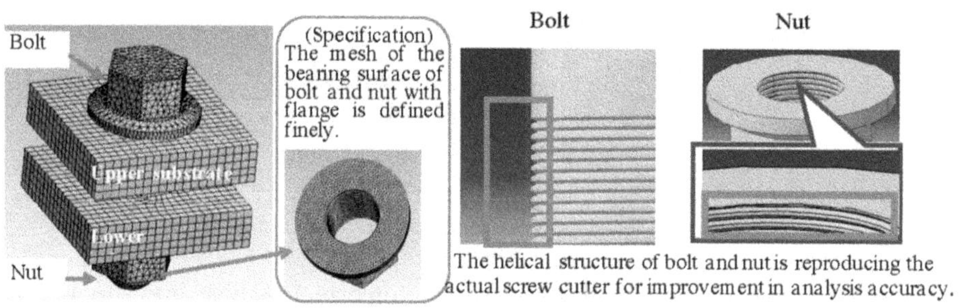

(a) 3-D Model (b) Reproducing the actual screw of the helical structure

Figure 23. Stress distribution of the nut surface and nut bearing surface in contact with lower substrate (: with the initial axial forth of bolt-nut load 25kN and 35kN of external stress)

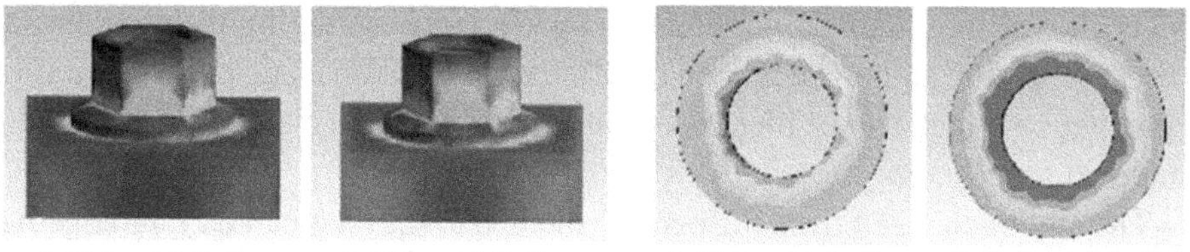

(a) Stress distribution of the nut surface in contact with lower substrate (b) Stress distribution of the nut bearing surface in contact with lower substrate

Figure 24. Comparison result between experiment and CAE simulation

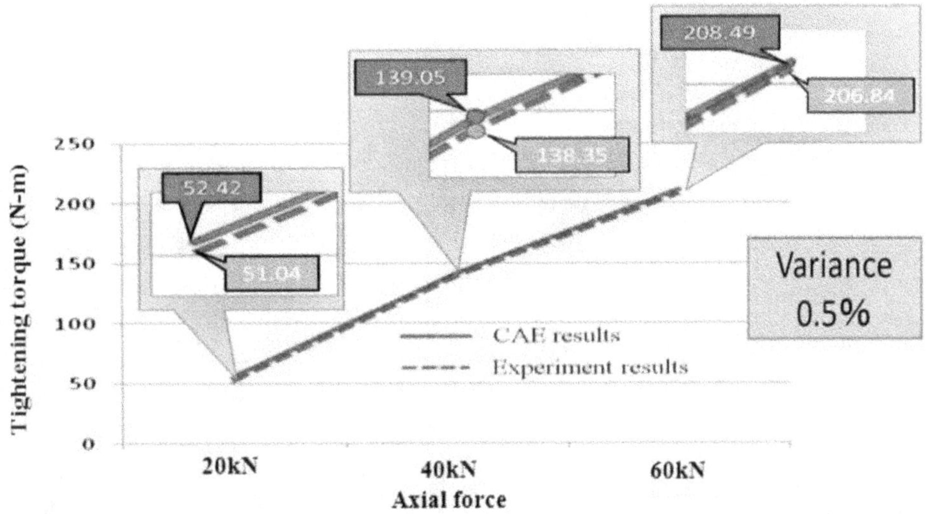

axial forth of load 35kN was a little bigger than the stress value of initial axial forth of load 25kN. In same way, Figure 23(b) showed the stress distribution of the nut bearing surface in contact with lower substrate. In Figure 23(b), the stress value of initial axial forth of load 35kN was much bigger than the stress value of initial axial forth of load 25kN.

Then, the author illustrates the comparison results of experiment and 3-D analysis through the relationship between torque and axial force of bolt-nut tightening as shown in Figure 24.

The results of experiment were represented by the dotted line (experiment results), and the results of the numerical simulation by CAE were represented by the solid line (CAE results). This diagram showed that the results of the CAE analysis closely match the results of the experiment.

2. Highly precise analyses of the bolt-nut loosening mechanism (Step 3-2)

Figures 25 showed the results of the 2-D analyses conducted as a stepping stone to conducting the 3-D analysis. The following stress distribution diagram indicated the presence of higher stress in

the inner portion of the nut as well as in the base material. Because the purpose of the axially symmetrical 2-D model was to understand the boundary conditions, model integrity, surfaces will be discussed in the 3-D model with stress values increasing as the colors change.

Moreover, the author will discuss the 3-D analysis results at the bolt-nut bearing surface when an axial force of 20kN was applied to the bolted joint along with the sampling number (5Hz) at ±1.8kN of oscillation load applied to the base material on the oscillation side (vertical axis vibration). Figure 26 shows the change in stress distribution at the nut bearing surface due to oscillation load. High stress was observed at the nut bearing surface, particularly at the inner portion (starting point and the end point) of the helix structure (Figure 26①).

This is similar to the observation made during the tightening analysis discussed earlier. Also, it is evident that the outer part of the nut bearing surfaces experience less stress (Figure 26②③④). This result

Figure 25. The results of axis symmetry 2-D model

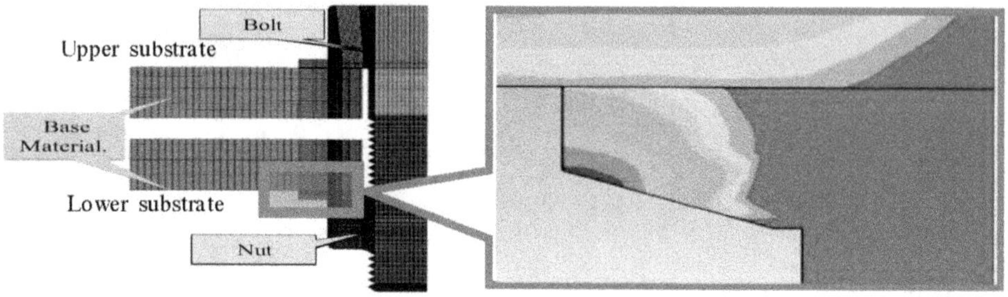

Figure 26. Example of transition of stress distribution at the nut bearing surfaces

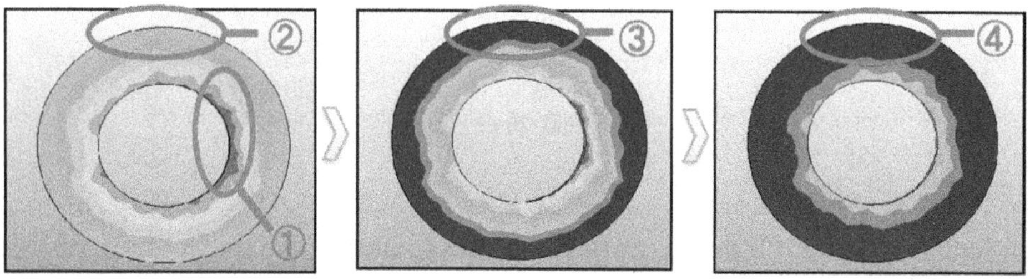

indicates that a reduction in contact force at the nut bearing surface of the area closer to the outer edge of a nut leads to slippage at the bearing surface when a bolt's axial force reduces with externally applied force.

Here, the author will compare the stress distribution of nut bearing surfaces during the vibration test and the stress distribution of nut bearing surfaces from the 2-D and 3-D analyses.

The stress at the nut bearing surface was higher in the area closer to the nut helix, and showed a stress distribution similar to the CAE simulation result. Although there are differences in the values that can be attributed to the distortion in the base materials, wear and roughness of the contact surfaces, the simulation was successful in reproducing similar stress values and stress distribution changes. Therefore, by conducting CAE analysis according to the Highly-Accurate CAE Analysis Approach Model created in this subsection 14.5.1, the author was able to show the effectiveness of the approach by reproducing an actual phenomenon. It is also plausible that this model can contribute to bolt loosening and bolt fracture analysis by understanding the changes in stress distribution at the nut bearing surfaces.

The 3-D analysis procedure is conducted in the next step. First, the two bolted workpieces are placed between the bolt and the nut using pitch 0.50 mm and 1.75 mm. The author will discuss the 3-D analysis results at the bolt bearing surface when an axial force of 35kN was applied to the bolted joint along with ±1.8kN of oscillation load applied to the base materials on the oscillation side (vertical axis vibration). Axial force is applied to the bolt (securing the edge of the lower substrate) and perpendicular to the upper substrate. Finally, the analysis looks at the pressure on the contact surface between the bolt-nut bearing surface and the base materials (lower substrate and upper substrate, and between the bolt threads and the nut).

Figure 27 showed a lack of uniformity in terms of nut bearing surface response (stress distribution) and a localized strong response where the nut thread structure begins. In looking at the differences between the two pitch values, the response distribution was more concentrated around the initial thread

Figure 27. 3-D analysis of pitch differences between two kinds (Ex. Stress distribution of nut bearing surface with initial axial forth of bolt-nut load 35kN of external stress by the sampling number (5Hz) at ±1.8kN of oscillation load employing nonlinear structural analysis (elastic analysis)) adapting nonlinear structural analysis (elastic analysis)

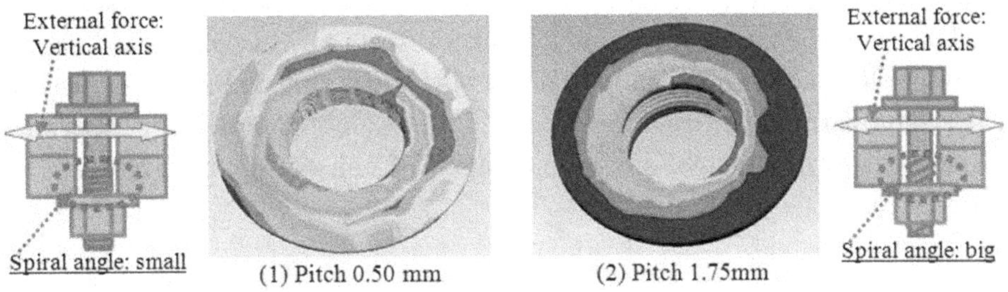

structure on the bolt with the longer pitch (1.75 mm) with stress values increasing as the colors change from blue to red.

These results suggested that differences in pitch also lead to differences in non-uniformity on nut bearing surfaces and a more pronounced gap between areas of strong and weak response. In terms of new information, the 3-D analysis revealed that the length of bolt and nut pitch impacts the reduction in contact force on contact surfaces.

Comparing the axial force reduction behavior measurements obtained through actual testing and those obtained through CAE analysis verified the precision of the CAE analysis results.

Figure 28 compares the results of actual testing and CAE analysis for the bolt and nut with 1.75 mm pitch under initial axial forth of 35 kN. The dashed line shows a margin of error of 3%, indicating that a high quality CAE analysis was achieved. Similar results were achieved for the 0.50 mm-pitch diameter bolt and nut as well.

Figure 28. Comparing the results of actual force reduction between actual testing and CAE

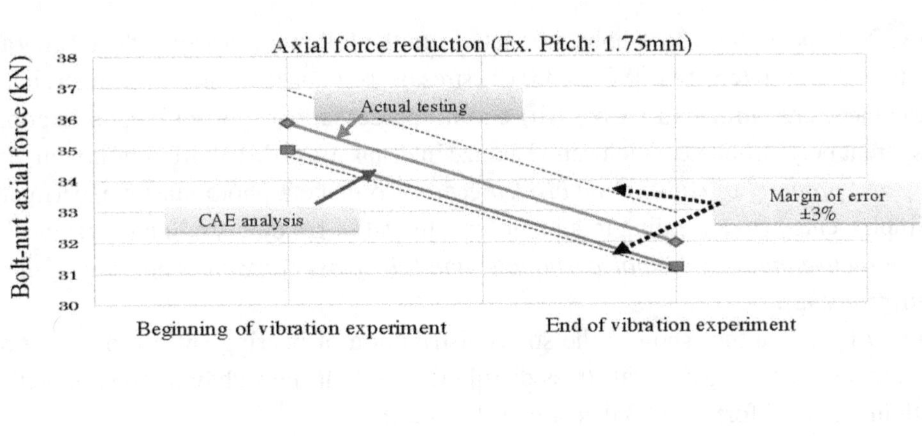

Optimization–Prediction and Evaluation (Step 4)

1. Loosening mechanisms by actual test and CAE analysis (Step 4-1)

Generally, internal stress distribution of screw engagement part made of the metal can't be measured. In actual test of Step 4-1, the author measured the stress distribution of bolt-nut tightening made from polycarbonate by interference fringes employing photo-elastic experimental device shown in Figure 29(a).

In 3-D analysis, furthermore, the author reproduced the result of photo-elastic experiment in highly-accurate CAE analysis as the internal stress distribution of bolt-nut tightening made from SCM435 shown in Figure 29(b).

Figure 29. Visualization of the internal stress of bolt-nut tightening by actual test and CAE

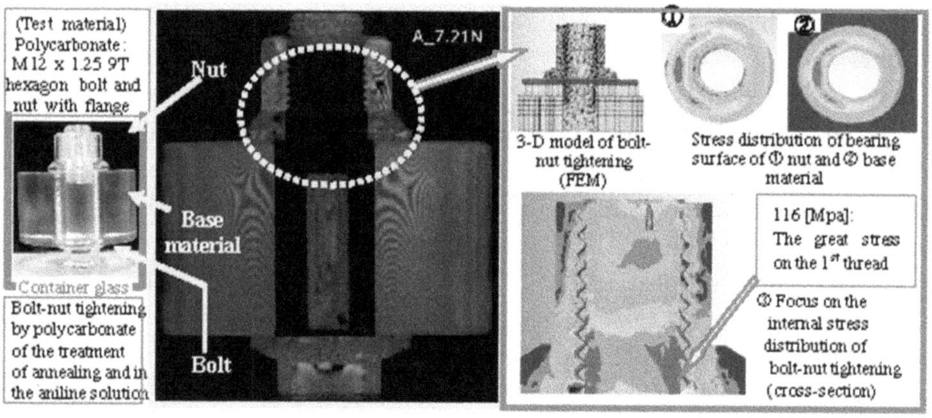

(a) Actual test-Stress distribution of bolt-nut tightening by interference fringes employing photo-elastic experiment device

(b) 3-D analysis - Stress distribution of bolt-nut tightening with initial axial forth load 35kN (Pitch: 1.25mm)

In Figure 29(a), the author chose polycarbonate from the following reasons; the (i) characteristic of polycarbonate had 1/20 intensity of SCM435, (ii) stress-strain curve of these two materials (SCM435 and polycarbonate) are similar in shape, (iii) cutting processing of polycarbonate is good, and (iv) highly transparent polycarbonate which can visualize internal stress distribution *by having the isotropic homogeneity and property of causing the birefringence.* To make a photo-elastic experiment succeed, the author implemented (v) annealing treatment for removal of residual strain and (vi) *aniline solution of the same refractive index as the polycarbonate, and (vii) glass containers not having the properties of optical birefringence.*

In Figure 29(b), the author showed the stress distribution of bearing surface of ① nut and ② base material, and focuses on the ③internal stress distribution of bolt-nut tightening (cross-section) by 3-D analysis with initial axial forth load 35kN (Pitch: 1.25mm).

From Figure 29(b)-③, the author has checked the transitions of internal stress distribution of bolt-nut tightening. Particularly, the author caught the existence of great stress on the 1st thread of engagement between the bolt and nut in detail. Furthermore, the author understood the state of change of internal stress distribution with sufficient accuracy through CAE analysis as the difference of initial axial forth load (20kN, 35kN and 50kN) of external stress, the difference of pitches (0.5mm, 1.25mm and 1.75mm), etc.

2. CAE analysis based on automobile prototype testing (Step 4-2)

In Step 4-2, the author implemented highly-accurate CAE analysis with no error (gap) compared to tests for ensure the optimization of prediction and evaluation of bolt-nut loosening mechanism. As the prototype testing and CAE analysis, Figure 30 showed a case of "Comparing the results of of numbers vibration cycles of actual force reduction" between prototype testing and CAE analysis. The author chose M12 9T flanged hexagonal bolts and nuts with three pitches (0.50mm, 1.25mm, 1.75mm) for automobile prototype testing using rear suspension arm with mount rubber-bush as follows;

① Accelerated test using 3-D vibration testing machine:

Concerning the equipment used in bolt-nut looseness tests, the author reproduced a working chassis designed to simulate prototype (bench) testing of a typical actual vehicle. These bolt-nut tightening with the mount and suspension were the automotive parts most prone to loosening. The author combined these parts to conduct tests using 3-D vibration.

In accelerated tests, it is possible to trigger a failure in a shorter amount of time (smaller number of vibration cycles) than usual by applying a large-stress amplitude. In Figure 26, A typical accelerated stress procedure consisted of creating an S-N curve based on the results of past tests conducted by the Amasaka-Laboratory, and then using Miner's rule to calculate the acceleration coefficient "4.4" employing test condition.

② Result of axial force reduction by prototype testing and CAE analysis:

1st, the author illustrated the overview of 2-D model and stress distribution of 2-D analysis with stress values increasing as the colors change from blue to red. 2nd, the author showed a typical result of prototype testing and 3-D analysis from the dual standpoints of time sequence and accuracy. As in the time sequence comparison in described Figure 30, axial force is shown on the vertical axis, and number of 3-D vibration cycles on the horizontal axis.

③ Actual machine test results are shown in blue, and CAE values in green:

This figure reveals that the author achieved an analysis with a good level of accuracy in terms of both the timing at which the bolt-nut loosened and in the extent of the decline in axial force.

Furthermore, to verify accuracy, the author confirmed that the broken circle delineates an error (gap) of 3% around the both test values of axial forth reduction "4.4kN" line in described Figure 30.

Figure 30. Comparing results of numbers vibration cycles of axial force reduction between prototype testing and 3-D analysis (Pitch: 1.25 mm)

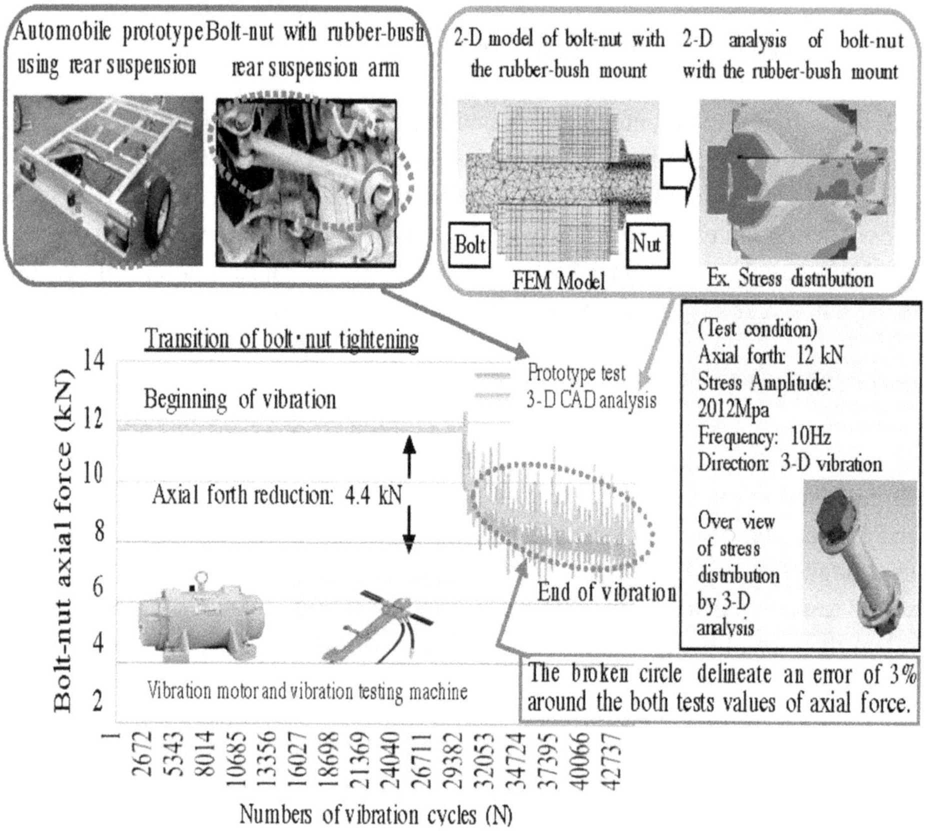

Verification–Loosening and Prevention (Step 5)

1. Actual 3-D vibration testing based on actual vehicle test (Step 5-1)

In Step 5-1, the author conducts 3-D oscillating experiment and CAE analysis. In order to clarify the loosening movement of bolt-nut joint, the author gave oscillating load to the bolting part for the vibration under actual market running with four kinds of combination of the flat road, winding road, intense gravel road of ups and downs, and intense bad road of ups and downs in the Japan National Route 16 over Tokyo and Kanagawa-Prefecture.

Figure 31 illustrated an example of actual 3-D vibration testing using actual vehicle test and CAE analysis as follows;

a. Figure 31(a) shows an example of actual vehicle vibration test using "Intense gravel road" based on "Oscillatory movement of rear suspension arm with shock absorber of Toyota Prius." In acceleration data of Figure 30(a), each of X-axis, Y-axis and Z-axis show front-back direction, left-right direction and up-down direction using wireless vibration recorder.

Figure 31. Example analysis of actual 3-D vibration testing using actual vehicle test and CAE based on "Oscillatory movement of rear suspension arm with shock absorber of Toyota Prius"

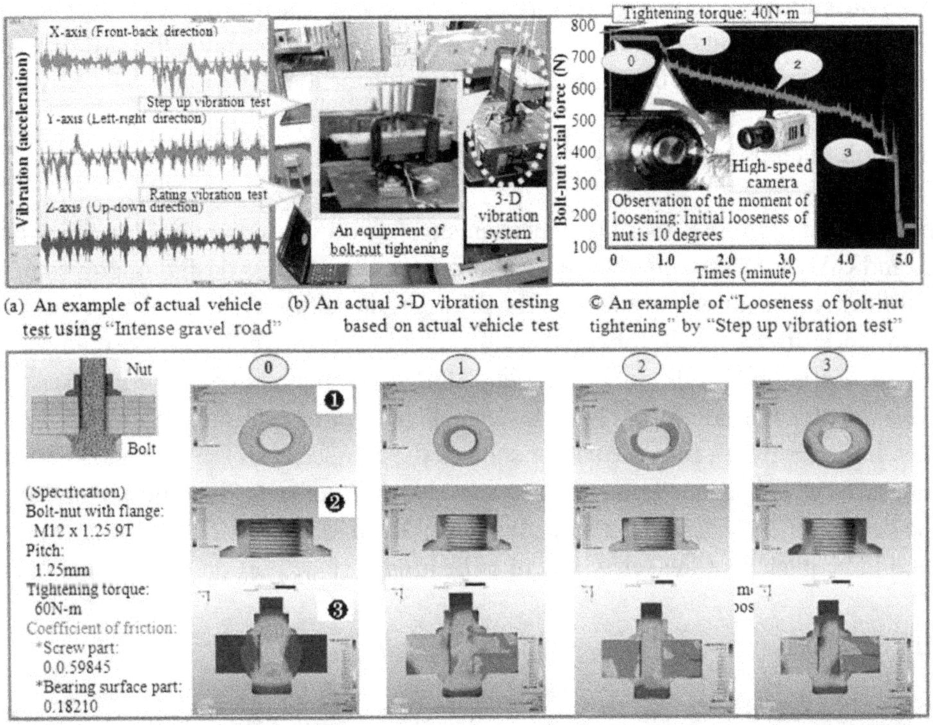

(a) An example of actual vehicle test using "Intense gravel road" (b) An actual 3-D vibration testing based on actual vehicle test © An example of "Looseness of bolt-nut tightening" by "Step up vibration test"

(d) An example of stress distribution of ①Nut bearing surface and ②Nut / ③Bolt-nut tightening by CAE analysis

b. Figure 31(b) shows an equipment of bolt-nut tightening using actual 3-D vibration system based on actual vehicle test in Figure 30(a). This 3-D vibration system contains 1. "Step up vibration test" named "Incremental vibration method, 0G→1G→3G→5G" and 2. "Rating vibration test" (Frequency: 3.3Hz, Acceleration: Max 5G, Exciting force: 4.9kN) and others.

c. In Figure 31(c), the author shows an example of looseness of bolt-nut tightening by "Step up vibration test" increasing 0.5G per 30 seconds about "the acceleration of each axis of x, yand z. Figure 31(c) expresses the movement of looseness of bolt-nut tightening as the relation between "Bolt-nut axial force and Time" in initial tightening torque 40N-m by using High-speed camera as the visualization technology. From transition of bolt-nut axial force, in this example, In Stage 0→1→2→3, initial loosening occurred in 1 minute after vibration beginning of stage 1, and complete loosening of bolt-nut has occurred 5 minutes after stage 3. In stage 1, especially, the author could observe the moment of nut loosening (: initial nut-loosening is 10 degrees) at the same time.

d. As a result of the experiment of 3-D vibration testing, the author illustrates an example of stress distribution of bolt-nut tightening by 3-D analysis based on stage 0→1→2→3 by step up vibration test. As a concrete instance, Figure 30(d) shows the stress distribution of 1. Nut bearing surface and cross-section of cross-section of the 2. Nut / 3. Bolt-nut tightening.

In Stage 0 the stress distribution of 1. Nut bearing surface is uniform distribution, and internal stress distribution of 2. Nut and 3. Bolt-nut-base material (cress-section) is uniform distribution. In Stage 1, 2 and the stress distribution of 1. Nut bearing surface, internal stress distribution of 2. Nut and 3. Bolt-nut-base material are un-uniformity distribution with the inclination. Especially, the author has confirmed that internal stress distribution of base material had large distortion.

2. Rational bolt-nut loosening improvement technology (Step 5-2)

Then, the author discerns the "loosening mechanism of a bolt-nut tightening" obtained in the various experiments and CAE analyses which were mentioned above, and tries design improvement of the nut form which is the main factor of looseness. In the 2nd stage, the author creates the high cost performance nut which gave priority to mass-productivity by utilizing rational bolt-nut loosening improvement technology, and verifies the validity of developing AOPDM from a viewpoint of looseness prevention.

Figure 32(a) illustrates a validity of "New design nut" preventing bolt-nut looseness by actual test and CAE analysis. In Figure 32(a), first, the author showed the comparison of "Form and stress distribution of nut bearing surface" of bolt-nut tightening between "Normal nut" and "New design nut" based on 3-D model. In the design of "New design nut", by "Boring" (Depth: 3.5-4.0mm / Inner diameter: φ14.0), the author deleted three pitches of the screw thread of bearing surface portion of "Normal nut" used by a

Figure 32. The validity of "New design nut" preventing bolt-nut looseness

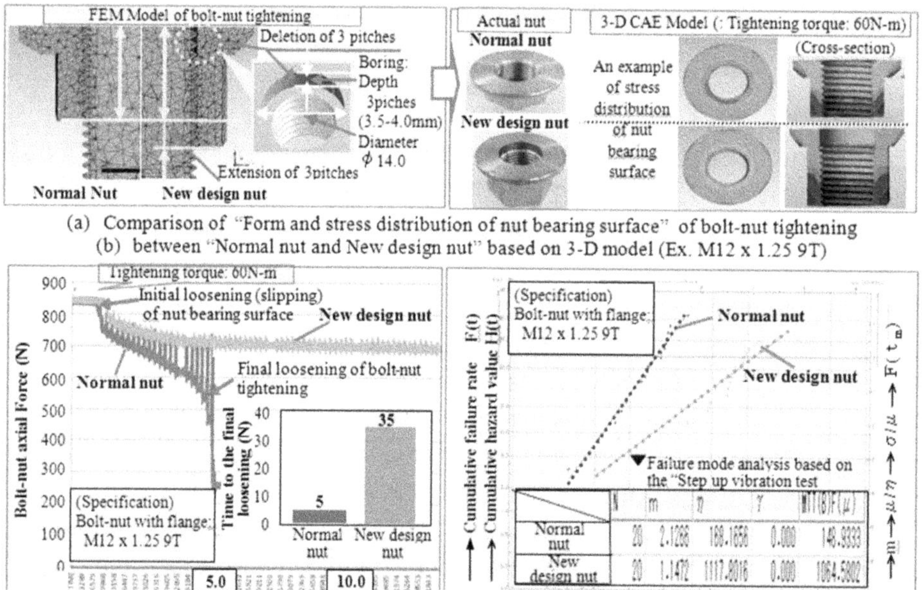

(a) Comparison of "Form and stress distribution of nut bearing surface" of bolt-nut tightening (b) between "Normal nut and New design nut" based on 3-D model (Ex. M12 x 1.25 9T)

(b) Comparison of "Time to the looseness occurrence" between "Normal nut and New design nut" based on the "Step up vibration test"

(c) Comparison of "Failure mode of bolt-nut loosening" between "Normal nut and New design nut" by using "Weibull type -Cumulative hazard paper"

mass-production vehicle, and lengthened three pitches for the full length of "Normal nut" for securing of screw strength as shown in Figure 32(a)-left.

In Figure 32(a)-right, furthermore, the author showed the "Normal nut" and "New design nut" which were actually manufactured, and the examples of both stress distribution of bearing surface and cross section by 3D analysis. Compared with the normal nut, the author checked that the bearing surface stress of "New design nut" was small by the effect of boring.

In Figure 32(b), 2nd, the author showed the comparison of "Time to the looseness occurrence" between "Normal nut" and "New design nut" based on the "Step up vibration test".

Especially, the author could check the sharp decline phenomenon of bolt-nut axial force stress through the "Transition of final loosening of bolt-nut tightening" as follows;

i. In normal nut, elapsed time from initial loosening to final loosening is 5 minutes.
ii. In New design nut, elapsed time from initial loosening to final loosening is 35 minutes.

From this study, the author could observe that the "New design nut" preventing bolt-nut looseness is 7 times compared with Normal nut.

In Figure 32(c), 3rd, the author showed the comparison of "Failure mode of bolt-nut loosening" between "Normal nut" and "New design nut" by using "Weibull type–Cumulative hazard paper" based on the Step up vibration test. In this failure mode analysis, the author could calculate "m" (shape parameter), "η" (scale parameter), "γ" (location parameter) and "MTTF" (Mean Time to Failure) by "Step up vibration test" of N=20 cases to each of "Normal nut" and "New design nut". From the comparison of MTTF, the author could check that "New design nut" preventing bolt-nut looseness is 7 time compared with Normal nut.

Although a detailed explanation is omitted, furthermore, the author checked that the well-known the Looseness prevent nut named "Hard-lock nut, U-nut and Self-locking nut" which are marketed (E.g., Hardlock Industry Co., Ltd., 2014 and Fuji Seimitsu Co., Ltd., 2014), and "New Design Nut" were equivalent performances as the preventing bolt-nut looseness. From the author's trial calculation, the manufacture cost of "New design nut" in the mass production is 25 yen/1peice, and is 1.2 times of "Normal nut" (21yen/1piece), however, is 1/6 of "Hard-lock nut" (150yen/1piece) (Hashimoto, 2015).

From the viewpoint of bottleneck solution of the market claim "looseness of bolt-nut tightening", the author concludes that "New design nut" has an excellent cost performance in the diffusion expansion to the mass production vehicle (At present, it is progressing).

Application to Similar Problems by Using AOPDM

The author was able to apply the AOPDM to critical development design technologies for automotive production, including predicting and controlling the special characteristics of "Urethane Foam Molding of seat pads", "Anti-vibration design of door mirrors", "Aerodynamics of body lifting power", and "Transaxle oil seal leakage" (Amasaka, 2010a, 2012, 2015a, 2020; Amasaka, et al., 2012: Nozawa, et al., 2012).

In each of these cases as well, discrepancy was 3–5% versus prototype testing. Based on the achieved results, the model is now being used as an intelligent support model for optimizing product design processes.

CONCLUSION

In this study, the author has established the AOPDM (Automobile Optimal Product Design Model) as part of principle - based research aimed at the innovation of development design processes in the automotive industry. As application of AOPDM, therefore, the author has created a Highly-Accurate CAE Analysis Approach Model by experiments and CAE utilizing AOPDM as part of principle-based research aimed at the evolution of product design processes.

This model's effectiveness for predictive evaluation method in design work has been demonstrated with various actual tests and precision CAE analysis to application to study on automotive bolt-nut loosening mechanism with no discrepancy between the experiment and CAE. Furthermore, the author has created the excellent "New design nut" prevention bolt-nut looseness in high cost performance from the viewpoint of bottleneck solution of the vehicle market claim "looseness of bolt-nut tightening".

ACKNOWLEDGMENT

The author would like to acknowledge the generous support received from the following researchers: all those at Study group of the Ideal Situation the Quality Management of Manufacturing Industry in Union of Japanese Scientists and Engineers (JUSE), Interim Report of Working Group No. 4 (WG 4) Studies Research on Simulation and SQC in Japanese Society for Quality Control (JSQC), and those connected with the Amasaka New JIT Laboratory at Aoyama Gakuin University that assisted with author's research, especially, Mr. Ueno, T., Mr. Takahashi, T., Mr. Yamada, H., Mr. Kozaki, T., Mr. Onodera, T., Mr. Hashimoto, K., Mr. Ebata, E., Mr. Nomura, R., Mr. Hori, K., Mr. Shimura, T., Mr. Sakurai, Y., Yamaki, M. and others.

REFERENCES

Amasaka, K. (2004). *Science SQC, New Quality Control Principle: The Quality Strategy of Toyota.* Springer-Verlag Tokyo. doi:10.1007/978-4-431-53969-8

Amasaka, K. (2007). Highly Reliable CAE Model, The key to strategic development of *Advanced TDS. Journal of Advanced Manufacturing Systems*, *6*(2), 159–176. doi:10.1142/S0219686707000930

Amasaka, K. (Ed.). (2007a). Establishment of a needed design quality assurance: Framework for numerical simulation in automobile production. Working group No. 4 studies in Japanese Society for Quality Control (JSQC).

Amasaka, K. (Ed.). (2007b). New Japan Model – Science TQM. Study group on the ideal situation of quality management in the manufacturing industry, Maruzen, Tokyo.

Amasaka, K. (2008). An Integrated Intelligence Development Design CAE Model utilizing New JIT. *Journal of Advanced Manufacturing Systems*, *7*(2), 221–241. doi:10.1142/S0219686708001589

Amasaka, K. (2010a). Proposal and effectiveness of a High Quality Assurance CAE Analysis Model: Innovation of design and development in automotive industry, *Current Development in Theory and Applications of Computer Science. Engineering and Technology*, *2*(1/2), 23–48.

Amasaka, K. (2010b). Product Design. In Quality Assurance Guidebook. The Japanese Society for Quality Control.

Amasaka, K. (2012). Constructing Optimal Design Approach Model: Application on the Advanced TDS. *Journal of Communication and Computer*, *9*(7), 774–786.

Amasaka, K. (Ed.). (2012). *Science TQM, New Quality Management Principle: The Quality Management Strategy of Toyota.* Bentham Science Publishers.

Amasaka, K. (2015a). New JIT, New Management Technology Principle. Taylor & Francis Group.

Amasaka, K. (2015b). Constructing a New Japanese Development Design Model "NJ-DDM": Intellectual evolution of an automobile product design. *Tem Journal Technology Education Management Informatics*, *4*(4), 336–345.

Amasaka, K. (2019a). Studies on New Manufacturing Theory, *Noble. International Journal of Scientific Research*, *3*(1), 1–20.

Amasaka, K. (2019b). Developing Automobile Optimal Product Design Model. *Japanese Operations Management and Strategy Association, The 9th International Symposium on Operations Management and Strategy 2019.*

Amasaka, K. (2019c). Establishment of an Automobile Optimal Product Design Model: Application to study on bolt-nut loosening mechanism. *Noble International Journal of Scientific Research*, *3*(9), 79–102.

Amasaka, K. (2022). New Manufacturing Theory: Surpassing JIT (2nd ed.). Lambert Academic Publishing.

Amasaka, K., Ito, T., & Nozawa, Y. (2012). A New Development Design CAE Employment Model. *The Journal of Japanese Operations Management and Strategy*, *3*(1), 18–37.

Amasaka, K., Onodera, T., & Kozaki, T. (2014). Developing a Higher-Cycled Product Design CAE Model: The evolution of automotive product design and CAE. *International Journal of Technical Research and Application*, *2*(1), 17–28.

Baggerly, R. (1996). Hydrogen-Assisted stress cracking of high-strength wheel bolts. *Engineering Failure Analysis*, *3*(4), 231–240. doi:10.1016/S1350-6307(96)00023-4

Enrique, A., & Parallel, M. (2005). *A new class of algorithms*. Wiley.

Fuji Seimitsu Co. Ltd. (2014). *U-Nut*. https://www.fun.co.jp/u_nut/u_nut.html/

Gamboa, E., & Atrens, A. (2003). Environmental influence on the stress corrosion cracking of rock bolts. *Engineering Failure Analysis*, *10*(5), 521–558. doi:10.1016/S1350-6307(03)00036-0

Hardlock Industry Co. Ltd. (2014). *Hard-lock Nut*. https://www.hardlock.co.jp/products/hln/

Hashimoto, H. (2005). Automotive Technological Handbook (3), Design and Body, Chapter 6, CAE. Society of Automotive Engineers of Japan.

Hashimoto, K. (2015). *Internal stress analysis of bolt with experiment and CAE analysis* (Master's thesis). Graduate School of Science & Engineering, Aoyama Gakuin University.

Hashimoto, K., Onodera, T., & Amasaka, K. (2014). Developing a Highly Reliable CAE Analysis Model of the mechanisms that cause bolt loosening in automobiles. *American Journal of Engineering Research*, *3*(10), 178–187.

ISO 4161/15701/15702/10663, (1991). BS (British Standards / ES (European Standards).

Kozaki, T., Yamada, H., & Amasaka, K. (2012). A Highly Reliable Development Design CAE Analysis Model: A precision CAE analysis approach To automotive bolt tightening. *International Business & Economics Research Journal*, *10*(1), 1–9.

Kume, H. (1999). *Quality Management in Design Development*. Union of Japanese of Scientist and Engineers.

Kume, H. (1999). *Quality Management in Design Development*. JUSE.

Leo, J. D. V., Annos, N., & Oscarsson, J. (2004). Simulation-based decision support for manufacturing system life cycle management. *Journal of Advanced Manufacturing Systems*, *3*(2), 115–128. doi:10.1142/S0219686704000454

Magoshi, R., & ... . (2003). Simulation Technology Applied to Vehicle Development. *Journal of Society of Automotive Engineers of Japan*, *57*(3), 95–100.

Ministry of Land, Infrastructure, Transport and Tourism. (2015). www.mlit.go.jp/jidosha/carinf/rcl/data.html

Nihon Keizai Shinbun. (2000). *Worst record: 40% increase of Vehicle Recalls*. Author.

Nihon Keizai Shinbun. (2012). *Toyota recalls 880,000 trucks.* Author.

Nomura, R., Hori, K., & Amasaka, K. (2015). Problem Prevention Method for product design based on predictive evaluation: A study of bolt-loosening mechanisms in automobile. *American Journal of Engineering Research, 4*(6), 174–178.

Nomura, R., Shimura, T., Sakurai, Y., & Amasaka, K. (2016). The elucidation of the loosening mechanism of automobile bolt nut conclusion by using experiments and CAE: Internal stress analysis which uses the photo-elasticity testing method and the three-dimensional testing method. *Japanese Operations Management and Strategy Association, The 6th Annual Technical Conference.*

Nonobe, K., & Ibaraki, T. (2001). An improved tabu search method for the weighted constraint satisfaction problem. *INTOR Information Systems and Operational Research, 39*(2), 131–151. doi:10.1080/03155986.2001.11732431

Nozawa, Y., Yamashita, R., & Amasaka, K. (2012). Analyzing Cavitation Caused by Metal Particles in the Transaxle: Application of High Quality Assurance CAE Analysis Model. *Journal of Energy and Power Engineering, 6*(12), 2054–2062.

Onodera, T., & Amasaka, K. (2012). Automotive bolts tightening analysis using contact stress simulation: Developing an Optimal CAE Design Approach Model. *Journal of Business & Economics Research, 10*(7), 435–442. doi:10.19030/jber.v10i7.7148

Shimura, T., & Sakurai, Y. (2015). *The elucidation of the nut loosening mechanism: Combined use of the three-dimensional system experiment by actual vehicle data, and CAE analysis* (Bachelor's thesis). School of Science & Engineering, Aoyama Gakuin University.

Steinberg, D. M. (1996). *Robust Design: Experiments for Improving Quality. In Handbook of Statistics 13.* North-Holland.

Strassburger, S., Schmidgall, G., & Haasis, S. (2003). Distributed manufacturing simulation as an enabling technology for the digital factory. *Journal of Advanced Manufacturing Systems, 2*(1), 111–126. doi:10.1142/S0219686703000253

Suzuki, M., Arafune, S., & Wadachi, M. (Eds.). (2005). *Encyclopedia of Physics.* Asakura-shoten.

Takahashi, T., Ueno, T., Yamaji, M., & Amasaka, K. (2010). Establishment of Highly Precise CAE Analysis Model using automotive bolts. *The International Business & Economics Research Journal, 9*(5), 103–113. doi:10.19030/iber.v9i5.574

Tanaka, M., Miyagawa, H., Asaba, E., & Hongo, K. (1981). Application of the finite element method of bolt-nut joints: Fundamental studies on analysis of bolt-nut joints using the finite element method. *Bulletin of the Japan Society of Mechanical Engineers, 24*(192), 1064–1071. doi:10.1299/jsme1958.24.1064

Ueno, T., Yamaji, M., Tsubaki, H., & Amasaka, K. (2009). Establishment of bolt tightening simulation system for automotive industry: Application of the Highly Reliable CAE Model, *International Business. Economic Research Journal, 8*(5), 57–67.

Whaley, R. C., Petitet, A., & Dongarra, J. J. (2000). *Automated empirical optimization of software and the ATLAS project. Technical report, University of Tennessee*. Department of Computer Science.

Yamada, H., & Amasaka, K. (2011). Highly-reliable CAE analysis approach-Application in automotive bolt analysis. *China-USA Business Review, 10*(3), 199–205.

Yamaji, M., & Amasaka, K. (2008). CAE analysis technology for development design utilizing statistical science. *The Open Industrial and Manufacturing Engineering Journal., 1*(1), 1–8. doi:10.2174/1874152500801010001

Chapter 15
Strategic Development of Automobile New Manufacturing Management Technology

ABSTRACT

The author considers the importance of strategic development for the new manufacturing management technology as the intelligence productivity improvement based on Advanced TPS employing NJ-AGPM. In this chapter, particularly, the author focuses on the typical dual technologies: (1) creation of the Working Value Evaluation Model (WVEM) to improve the performance of labor and (2) developing intelligence operators by employing the Human Integrated Assist System (HIA) based on the knowledge which could get it with WVEM. The author has verified the effectiveness of WVEM and HIA at an advanced car manufacturer Toyota and others.

INTRODUCTION

The Japanese manufacturing industry is now developing global production by establishing production sites in various countries. High quality assurance is regarded as the strong point of manufacturing in Japan (Abegglen, 1958). However, this situation is under threat (Hunt, 1991; Gabor, 1990). Therefore, the author considers it vital to make production operators more independent and creative in addition to their engineering capabilities and skills so as to become an "intelligence operator" for developing NJ-AGPM (New Japan Automobile Global Production Model) based on Advanced TPS (Amasaka, 2007; Amasaka and Sakai, 2011) (Refer to Chapter 5, 6 and 7).

To create products with superior quality, cost, and delivery (QCD) characteristics, the most important task for manufacturers is raising the quality of labor work performed by on-site operators (job performance), thus boosting the value of company labor employing typical dual technologies.

DOI: 10.4018/978-1-7998-8746-1.ch015

First, in this chapter, the author takes a fresh perspective on the issue, placing importance on the performance of labor itself developing Advanced TPS (Amasaka, 2007; Amasaka and Sakai, 2011). The author then identifies the relevance of key causal factors contributing to that performance. Having collected this information, the author then creates the Working Value Evaluation Model (WVEM) for labor valuation by using statistical science that allows manufacturers to visualize the performance of labor (Uchida et al., 2012) (Refer to Chapter 7).

Concretely, this model systematically covers 18 key factors, and is made up of five core models: reducing fatigue, preventing illness, comfort, knowledge and ability, organizations and roles/responsibilities (Amasaka, 2015, 2017, 2018, 2020).

Second, in a strategic development of Advanced TPS, the author considers the need to make production operators achieve challenges and creation in addition to engineering capabilities and skills so as to become "intelligence operator".

Concretely, in the wake of the recent rapid expansion of globalization, short-term training of production operators is an especially critical issue, particularly for ensuring productivity at the start-up of local production. To deal with this issue, it is urgent to apply this system to analyze the factors that contribute to the variations in the skill acquisition level of local operators. This is done with a view to establishing a training method that can support them to stably perform work despite the differences in their ability.

Specifically, in view of the need to develop a new creative human-oriented production system for meaningful working, the author constructs the Human Integrated Assist System (HIA), for creative, meaningful working leading to intelligence productivity improvement. It supports autonomous development of "*kaizen*" as the core of this system for the global production strategy (Sakai and Amasaka, 2008; Amasaka, et al., 2008, 2015, 2017, 2018, 2020).

CREATION OF A WORKING VALUE EVALUATION MODEL (WVEM)

Problems in Working Environments of Manufacturing

As a large manufacturing country, Japan is actively expanding its business overseas. On the other hand, the falling birth rate and the aging population are becoming serious problems in Japan (Kimura, 1999). Young people are said to have veered away from the manufacturing industry so the industry is now facing a shortage of workers. To cope with these problems, Japanese companies have eliminated hard labor in the working environment, and streamlined workplaces through the 5S (Seiri (tidiness), Seiton (orderliness), Seisou (cleanliness), Seiketsu (standardization) and Shitsuke (discipline)) (Toyota and Toyota Kyushuu, 1994; Sakai and Amasaka, 2005, 2006).

In the local manufacturing environment, however, the increase in the number of temporary workers and the acceptance of foreign trainees have caused a decline in autonomy in the workplaces, and workers have had difficulty in finding the value in working in such environments (Amasaka, 2003; Amasaka and Sakai, 2011). In such surroundings, there is an urgent need to help workers find meaning in their jobs and acquire high-level skills (Yamaji and Amasaka, 2007, 2008). If you look overseas, a new research field called Gerontechnology began in the Europe where, like Japan, the aging population has grown (Kinnunen-amoroso et al, 2009). In Gerontechnology, physical and mental aspects of old people are studied. Although Gerontechnology has yielded some results scientifically, it is still not applicable in an actual working environment.

Then the author thought that it is necessary to enhance the value in working to help workers be satisfied with their jobs and achieve self-realization, and thus build the Intellectual Working Value Improvement Model (IWV-IM) that systematizes factors contributing to enhance the value in working (Tsunoi, et al., 2010) (Refer to Appendix 15.A). IWV-IM clarified factors contributing to enhance the value in working that had previously been ambiguous and specific activities that companies have to work on. To make effective use of IWV-IM in each company, it is necessary for them to clarify which aspects are weak and which aspect should be improved first in an objective manner.

Working Value Evaluation Model (WVEM)

To improve the working value of workers from a comprehensive perspective, the author has created the Working Value Evaluation Model (WVEM) employing the Intellectual Working Value Improvement Model (IWV-IM), which quantitatively evaluates the awareness of the working value of workers by statistically analyzing data collected through actual condition survey on companies (Toyota Motor Corp., Nissan Motor Co., Ltd., and other three companies) (Tsunoi, 2010; Tsunoi et al., 2010; Amasaka, 2015, 2020).

1. Understanding the actual corporate condition

To delve deeper into the basic principles of working value, the author conducted a survey on actual workplaces. As the target industry, the author selected the automotive industry, which has a larger number of workers among manufacturing industries, and picked up 4 specific working processes (welding, painting, machining and assembling) that add a greater burden to human bodies.

Then, the author visited a plant and surveyed the actual conditions of a workplace by interviewing workers and taking videos of actual operation there. To improve work and working environments, the author found from the result of this survey that it is necessary to enhance work efficiency with the aid of teamwork, information sharing and statistical science. In the next subsection, the author explains information obtained through this survey in an organized way.

2. Arrangement of factors contributing to the improvement of working value

To organize data obtained from the actual condition survey, the author created a matrix diagram with 2 axes, namely one in a perspective of workload/working environment/skill and the other in a perspective of 4M-E (man, machine, method, material and environment) of field management. From the data summarized in the matrix diagram, the author extracted keywords that contribute to improve the working value in perspectives of workload, work environment and skill using Key-Graph.

The author added work efficiency factors obtained through the interviews to these keywords, and grouped the factors using an affinity diagram to see relationships between the factors. The result is shown in Figure 1. This diagram shows that factors contributing to working value enhancement can be divided into 3 groups, namely, workload reduction (disease prevention, fatigue reduction), working environment improvement (enhancement of organization, roles, and comfort) and skill improvement (intelligence / ability improvement). It also indicates that work efficiency affects each group.

3. Working value awareness survey

To understand how workers actually feel the value in working, the author conducted a survey on working value awareness. 20 factors contributing to working value enhancement described in the previous chapter are used as items in the awareness survey. This survey is targeted to workers who are working for safety & health and quality management sections in the manufacturing industry.

Figure 1. Factors contributing to the improvement of working value by the affinity diagram method

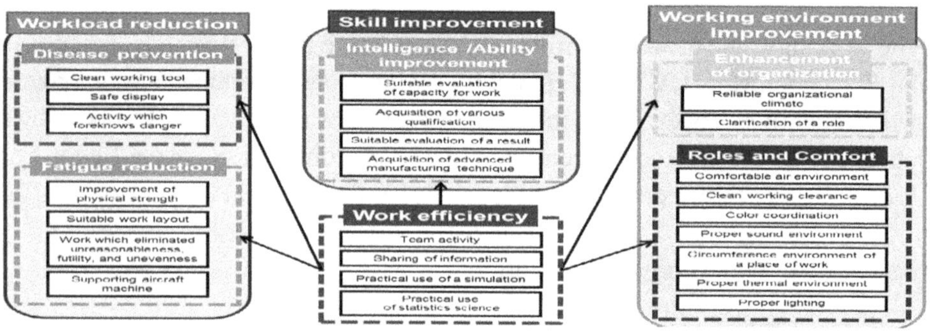

As shown in Appendix 15.B (Refer to appended Table 15.B, "Awareness survey sheet"), each item in the awareness survey was scored on a 1 to 7 scale, and the author received 25 sets of answers from workers in the manufacturing industry.

4. Data analysis (Interpretation of relationships between factors)

Based on the data obtained from the awareness survey, the authors investigate which working value factors that we should pay the most attention to enhance the value in working. Analysis is performed using principal component analysis and cluster analysis, because, by looking at the relationships between working value evaluation items perceived by the workers and aggregating the items, the authors can find out fundamental evaluation axes for the value in working.

As a result of the cluster analysis, the author confirmed that items are divided into 5 clusters as show in Figure 2. Working value items can be categorized into 5 groups (fatigue reduction, disease prevention, intelligence/ability, comfort, organization/roles) from their names and definitions, and the authors determine to use these 5 groups as the evaluation axes.

5. Weighting to the working value evaluation axes

To see what kind of relationships the 18 working value items have with the working value evaluation axes (primary latent factors), the author analyzed their weightings using covariance structure analysis and consider them by creating working value evaluation modeling formulas. As a result of cluster analysis, the authors already know that there are 5 working value evaluation axes: fatigue reduction, safety (disease prevention), comfort, organization/roles, and intelligence/ability.

The author assumes that these axes eventually lead to the value in working, and the author is analyzing the weightings of these 5 axes as the next step. As the estimation method of the covariance structure analysis, the author used maximum likelihood estimation, which is the most widely used estimation method. Figure 3 shows the result. The goodness of fit of this model is 0.623 and its interpretability exceeds 60%, which are fairly reliable values that indicate that this model can be trusted.

Figure 2. Cluster analysis

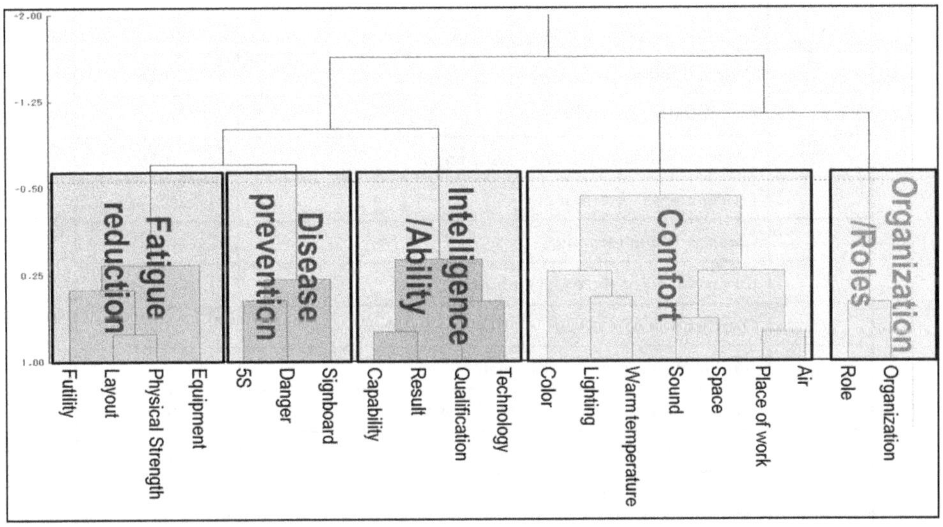

Figure 3. Weighting by covariance structure analysis

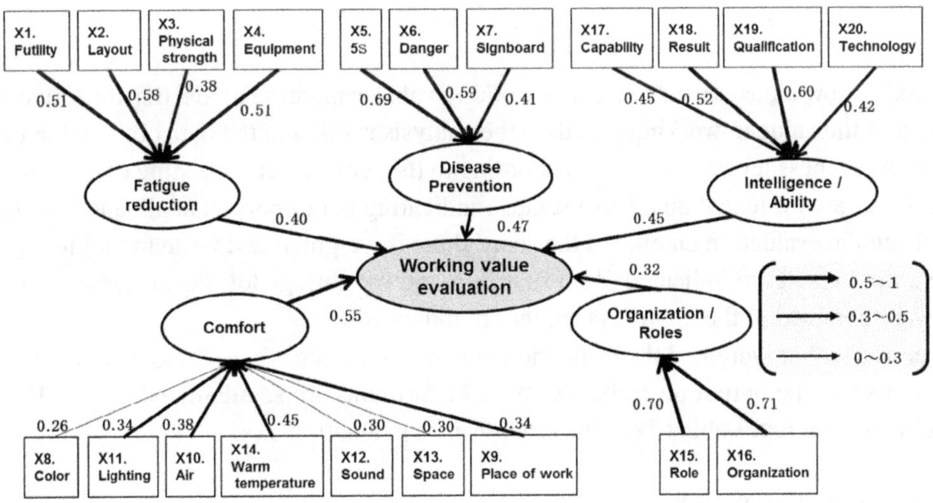

Table 1. Weightings of the working value evaluation items (1)

Variable	Working Value Evaluation Items	Point estimate
X_1	Reduction of futility, unreasonableness, and unevenness	0.36
X_2	A suitable work layout	0.51
X_3	Supporting aircraft machine	0.35
X_4	5S activity	0.34
X_5	Activity which foreknows danger	0.47
X_6	Conspicuousness of a signboard	0.36
X_7	Proper lighting	0.25
X_8	Comfortable air environment	0.30
X_9	Proper warm temperature environment	0.28
X_{10}	Proper sound environment	0.27
X_{11}	Clean working clearance	0.27
X_{12}	Environment of the on-site circumference	0.23
X_{13}	Clarification of a role	0.60
X_{14}	A reliable organizational climate	0.50
X_{15}	Suitable evaluation of capacity for work	0.36
X_{16}	Suitable evaluation of a result	0.35
X_{17}	Acquisition of qualification	0.32
X_{18}	Acquisition of advanced manufacturing technique	0.27

6. Formulation of Working Value Evaluation Model (WVEM)

Table 1 and 2 show indexes used to create a working value evaluation model that objectively evaluates the awareness of the value in working based on the analysis result and the data obtained in the previous sub-sections. Awareness levels are entered according to the score sheet consisting of 18 items presented in the table. Items are evaluated on a 1 to 7 scale: 1 indicating not important at all, and 7 indicating very important. Then the evaluation entered in the score sheet is weighted and write model formulas used to display the output result are indicated. As a first step, the weightings for the working value evaluation items that were obtained in the previous chapter are indicated.

Moreover, the author weighted the evaluation entered in the score sheet, and described a model formula used to display the output result below. WVEM formulas are standardized so that 100 is the full score, thereby making it possible to easily compare each evaluation axis.

$$L_1 = \left(0.36X_1 + 0.51X_2 + 0.35X_3\right) \times 11.7 \tag{i}$$

$$L_2 = \left(0.34X_4 + 0.47X_5 + 0.36X_6\right) \times 12.2 \tag{ii}$$

$$L_3 = (0.25X_7 + 0.30X_8 + 0.28X_9 + 0.27X_{10} + 0.27X_{11} + 0.23X_{12}) \times 8.93 \quad \text{(iii)}$$

$$L_4 = (0.60X_{13} + 0.50X_{14}) \times 13.0 \quad \text{(iv)}$$

$$L_5 = (0.36X_{15} + 0.35X_{16} + 0.32X_{17} + 0.27X_{18}) \times 11.0 \quad \text{(v)}$$

$$L_6 = (0.32L_1 + 0.39L_2 + 0.66L_3 + 0.20L_4 + 0.53L_5) \times 6.80 \quad \text{(vi)}$$

Table 2. Weightings of the working value evaluation items (2)

Variable	Working value evaluation axis	Dignity
L_1	Fatigue reduction	0.32
L_2	Disease prevention	0.39
L_3	Comfort	0.66
L_4	Organization / Roles	0.20
L_5	Intelligence / Ability	0.53
L_6	Working value	-

Figure 4. Radar chart for working value evaluation axe

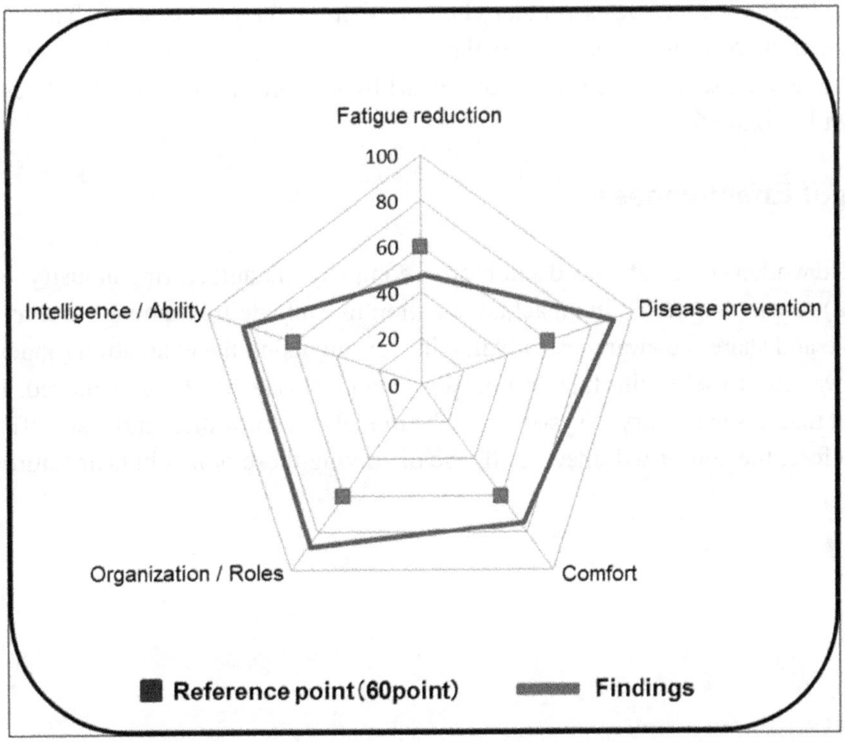

Figure 5. Radar chart by working value item

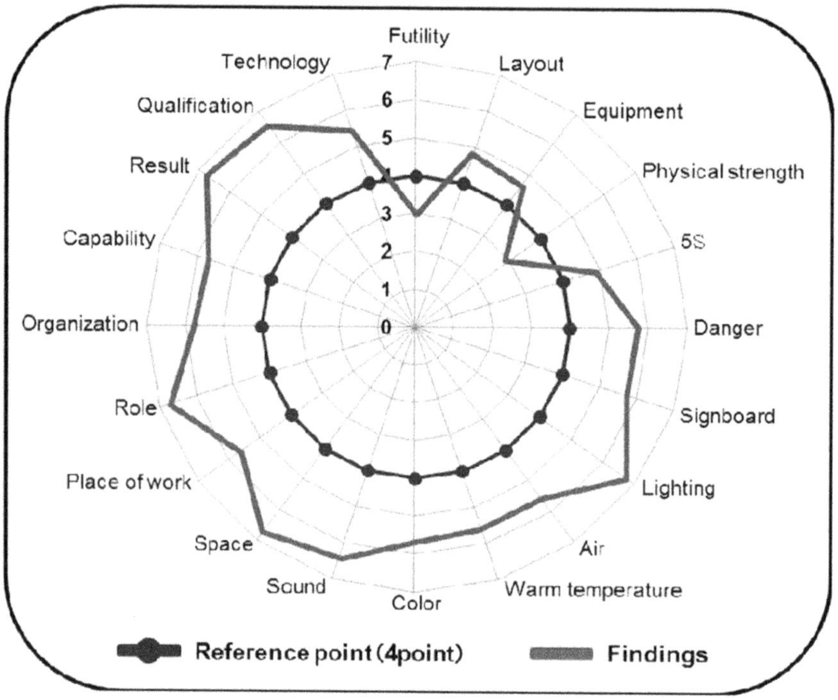

The above evaluation formulas allow us to describe the value in working in terms of figures. Also, standardization of evaluation formulas made it possible to compare the strength of each working value evaluation axis. Lastly, the author used radar charts to display the output result. The author created 2 radar charts. Radar chart for working value evaluation axes in Figure 4 shows the calculation results of the model formulas on a scale of 100, and Radar chart by working value item visualizes all evaluation scores as shown in Figure 5.

Verification of Effectiveness

The author asked workers of an advanced automotive company (manufacturing industry: quality control, safety & health) to use this model in an actual situation to evaluate this model. As a result, they were able to visualize and share the awareness of value in working using the evaluation model.

The author was able to determine that the goal presented in this research was achieved. They, however, also pointed out that it is necessary to systematize the model and show them more specific improvement methods. Therefore, the author will meet challenge of solving these points in near future research.

DEVELOPMENT OF HUMAN INTEGRATED ASSIST SYSTEM

The Necessity of Intelligence Operators for Highly Reliable Production

At present, the Japanese manufacturing industry is rapidly deploying global customer- oriented production throughout the world. However, this rapid spreading of production sites abroad, has brought about many new problems for Japanese production, which has developed a reputation in the past for assuring high quality. As seen in the case of automobiles, the "highly reliable production system" with target productivity equal to that in Japan is spreading worldwide, but the actual productivity is still often lower (Sakai and Amasaka, 2006) (Refer to Chapter 6 and 7).

The major cause of this situation, it has been revealed, is the dependence of conventional production system on operators' *kaizen* awareness or individual capabilities. This has limited its applicability to overseas operators familiar with different systems and having different cultural backgrounds. In Japan, for example, the reliability of a production line is gradually improved through repeated *kaizen* actions after a new start-up, resulting in possibilities for high product quality assurance. To solve such problems, early fostering of intelligence operators is the key to successfully achieving global production with high quality assurance. In order to attain high quality assurance worldwide, it is necessary to ensure all intelligence operators acquire a consistent level of manufacturing skill. In other words, correct *kaizen* and maintenance of the production equipment through fostering of intelligence operators is indispensable to worldwide application of the highly reliable production system (Sakai and Amasaka, 2008).

Furthermore for the improvement of production quality, "accelerated skill training", among other things, will have greater importance, and be a key to successful production activities. In connection with the recent increase of domestic and overseas production, a large number of new recruits and limited-term workers are being employed. Generally, these employees learn from their seniors by watching their work on an OJT (on the job training) or OFF-JT (off the job training) basis (Sakai and Amasaka, 2009; Amasaka and Sakai, 2011) Some acquire required skills quickly (within a week) and start to work at the production line immediately, whereas others cannot reach a required skill level even after three weeks, or perform unstable operation in building the product, resulting in being removed from the line until they reach the required skill level while working as supporting operators.

Such a situation where quality build-up, which plays a central role in QCD activities, cannot be sufficiently achieved has been observed from time to time. In order to realize the production strategy of "uniform quality worldwide and simultaneous start-up", it is urgent to carry out short-term training for production operators so as to level out the variations in their skill acquisition.

Strategic Implementation of Advanced TPS for Intelligence Operators

While manufacturing in workshops is being transformed thanks to digital engineering, the engineering capability in manufacturing workshops often drops, thereby weakening scientific production control for quality incorporation in processes (Amasaka, 2008). It is an urgent task to further Advance TPS strategically for higher-cycled next-generation production business processes, apart from the conventional experience in success from the viewpoint of global production (Amasaka, 2007).

The author, therefore, considered the necessity of including and organically integrating the four elements (production based on information: Information Technology, production based on management: Process Management, production based on technology: Production Technology, and production based on partnership: Human Management) with strategic application of Advanced TPS by using NJ-AGPM (New Japan Automobile Global Production Model) (Amasaka and Sakai, 2011) for the global production strategy (Refer to Chapter 6 and 7).

With respect to the requirements shown in Figure 1, Chapter 6 (Refer to Chapter 6), the mission of Advanced TPS in global deployment is to realize CS (customer satisfaction), ES (employee satisfaction), and SS (social satisfaction) through production that achieves high quality assurance. In implementing Advanced TPS for uniform quality worldwide and production at optimal locations (concurrent production), renewal of production management systems appropriate for digitized production and creating attractive workshop environments tailored to increasing the number of older and female workers are fundamental requirements.

In more definite terms, (a) requires strengthening the process capability maintenance and improvement by establishing an intelligent quality control system. (b) requires the establishment of highly reliable production system that achieves high quality assurance. (c) involves reformation of the work environment for enhancement of intelligent productivity. (d) requires developing intelligent operators (skill level improvement) and establishing an intelligent production operating system. These factors combined will realize higher-cycled next-generation business processes for early implementation of uniform quality worldwide and production at optimum locations.

HIA, Developing Intelligence Operators for Intelligence Productivity

Recently, to realize the higher productivity from production operators required for global production, the authors have paid attention to the need for a "new human-oriented production system" (Iiyoshi and Hannafin, 2002). This provides for creative, meaningful working, based on a production philosophy as the engineering nucleus of the Advanced TPS (Aspy and Wai, 2001; Sakai and Amasaka, 2005, 2006, 2007). Three basic requirements of production are as follows:

1. Establishing a production system that ensures overall line reliability, maintainability, and improves "advanced production equipment operation technologies" (fault diagnosis, maintenance and preventive maintenance of production equipment) to prevent availability degradation and quality defects;
2. Upgrading engineering and other skill levels to levels comparable with Japanese staff in a wide range of areas. This includes manual lines for small-lot production in automotive and other general assembly industries involving many hard-to-automate jobs, especially in developing countries; and
3. Attaining "mastered skills" equivalent to those of production operators in advanced countries equipped with sophisticated mass-production type equipment that allows intelligent diagnosis by individuals in the quality incorporating stage.

For systematization to satisfy these three requirements, it is necessary to improve the "sophisticated production equipment operating skills" and "mastered skills" of production operators themselves. Developing the intelligence operators for upgrading and unifying the production capabilities of worldwide operators is required before the "advanced production process", which is continuously driven by IT and digitization, creates a black box that depends on personal discretion (Chawla, 2002; Sakai and Amasaka, 2007).

The author, therefore, develops the Human-integrated Assist System (HIA) that realistically copes with these requirements (Sakai and Amasaka, 2008). Figure 6 shows the HIA development. As will be explained from the next section, the HIA covers system (tools, execution plan, skill requirements, and evaluation necessary) and methodology (formulating and establishing shortened training methods) for early fostering of operators with "mastered skills" as one of the two requirements explained earlier for a global production strategy.

Figure 6. Human-integrated Assist System (HIA)

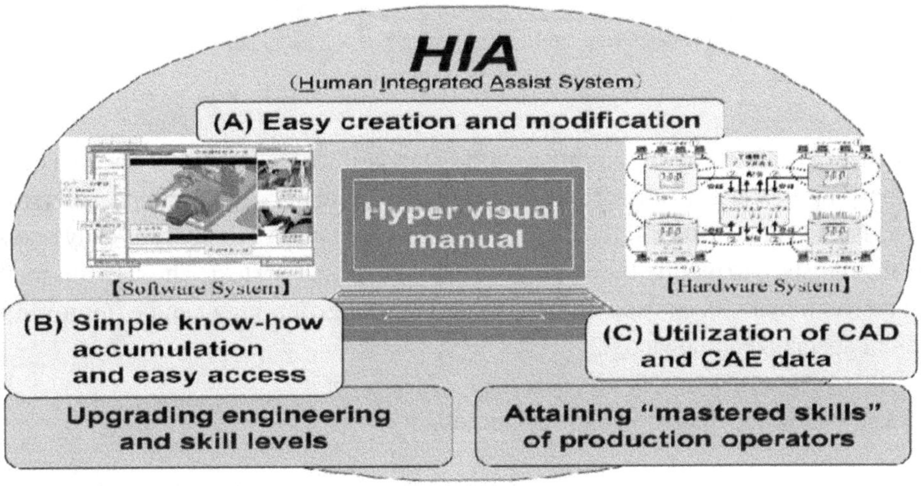

HIA Construction, the Key to Advanced TPS

Sharing of the same level of specialized job knowledge by worldwide intelligence operators with different cultural and language backgrounds is becoming increasingly important for global production (Hounshell, 1984; Roos et. al., 1990; Leonard-Barton, 2003). This makes it necessary to develop a user-friendly method with worldwide applicability.

The author, therefore, has devised the "*visual manual*" as a new communication tool. This is a key technology in the aforementioned HIA, of which the three basic requirements "(A), (B) and (C)" are summarized below.

1. Easy creation and modification

Conventional, hard-to-understand operation manuals written only in character text should be replaced with user-friendly intelligent manuals allowing easy understanding of the content by intelligence operators. The contents of such visual manuals should be revised as needed to present new ideas clearly. Figure 7 indicates the visual manual creation process.

Figure 7. "Hyper visual manual"

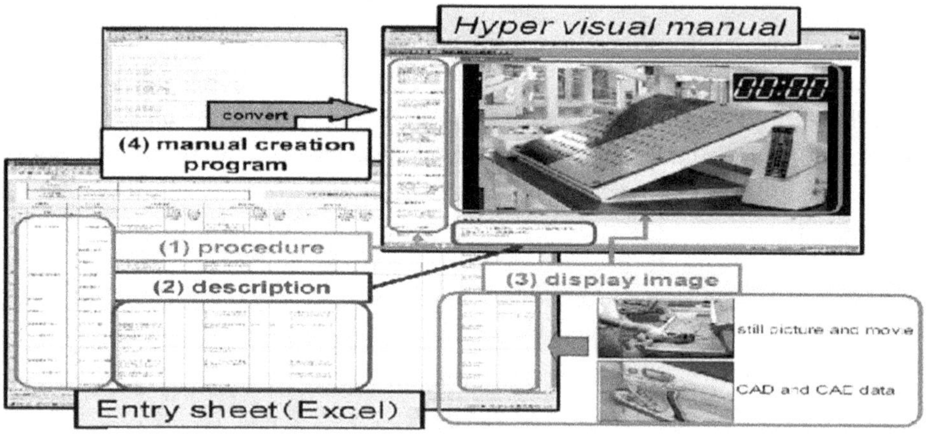

The entry sheet is created by modifying a world-standard Microsoft Excel sheet. This sheet is for the input of the (1) procedure, (2) description and (3) display image, and the input information is then converted to a visual manual using (4) the manual creation program. Anybody can easily revise the visual manual by using this sheet to modify the display image and explanatory text. Through this method, manuals that have conventionally been used only for basic knowledge learning can be improved to facilitate accumulation of specialized knowledge.

2. Simple know-how accumulation and easy access

It is necessary for intelligence operators at worldwide production sites to be able to have access to the necessary visual manual content for immediate use. Furthermore, revision of and additions to the visual manual requires simultaneous data storage and distribution. Figure 8 shows the system for visual manual selection. Depending on the selection method, a series of screens matching each particular situation can be selected. Method 1 clearly indicates the contents (title of each item is in a list) for the search of necessary content.

On the other hand, method 2 employs a search program using a key word for selection of content from the search result. The visual manual data is handled in the general HTML (Hyper Text Markup Language) format, enabling it to be used anywhere in the world, and the data can be delivered locally and globally through the internet. With regard to the hardware system, a plant server is installed at each plant to establish a server and client system.

It is used to view the data on each client system (PC) at each office or work-site through the internet, and a note can be written as required on the spot. Then, each plant server is controlled in synch with the central server so as to make the system simultaneously update and distribute any modifications. Thus, the intelligence operators at local and overseas plants can virtually experience the production method related to each production process and also obtain the related know-how, knowledge, and information concerning the same production process.

Figure 8. System for "Hyper visual manual" selection

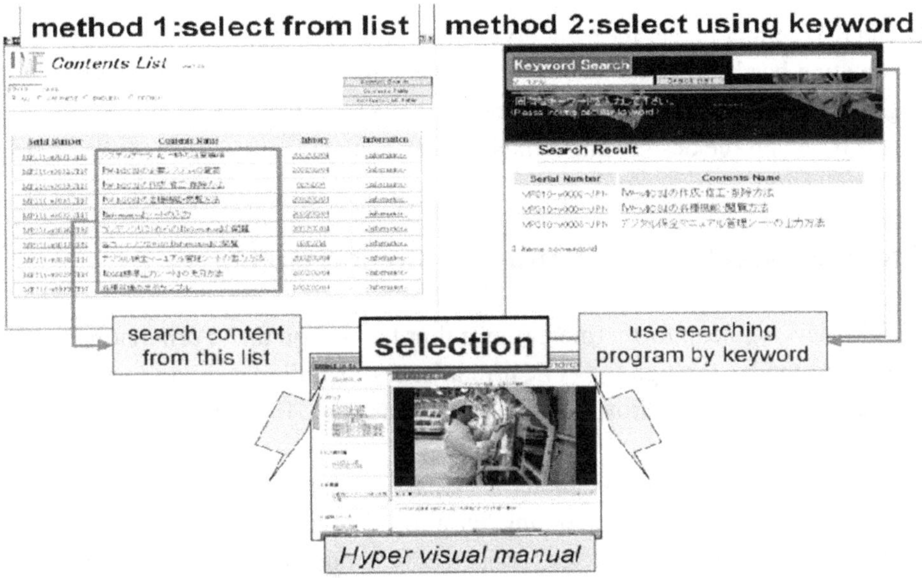

3. Utilization of CAD and CAE data

Explanation of work instructions by character text only creates problem such as lack of clarity and difficulty accessing the required item. On the other hand, visually appealing work instructions provide a perfect description of the scene so as to enable members that use different languages to obtain unified understanding of the same material. As the skill level and training method may vary from trainer to trainer, use of the still picture and movie images of the CAD and CAE data in the visual manual will convey consistent information at a higher level.

Figure 9. Flows of CAD and CAE data

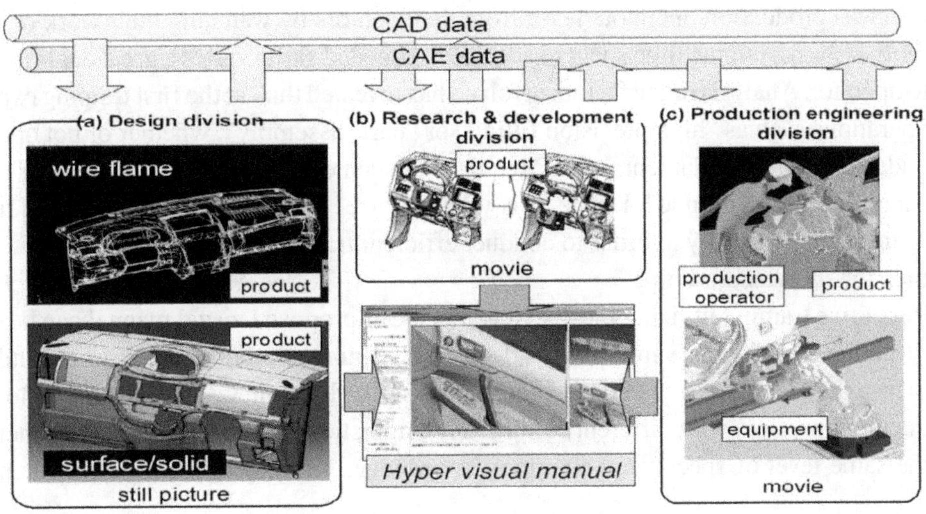

Figure 9 shows the flows of CAD and CAE data. The product data is mainly provided in still images for use by the (a) design division. Movie images, on the other hand, are used as visual manual data in the (b) R&D and (c) production engineering divisions and in the manufacturing shop. Thus, CAD and CAE data information has been made available on a network to production engineering and up to the manufacturing process, and it has become possible to instantaneously create procedures for the manufacturing process based on the design data, which in turn has made it possible to shrink the lead times from design to production.

Formulating and Establishing Shortened Training Methods

To realize the HIA development, furthermore, the author focuses on the "Formulating and establishing shortened training methods" through the (1) Current issues regarding training methods, (2) Measures for shortened training, (3) Optimization of training stage, and (4) HIA application examples.

1. Current issues regarding training methods
    (i) Advancement of HIA for overcoming variations in training methods-Up until now, "highly skilled trainers" with extensive experience have conducted technical training for production operators on a one to one basis. Consequently, the dissemination and deployment of operator training, particularly in Japan, has largely depended on the personal ability and qualifications of the trainers. However, replacement of these highly skilled trainers can easily cause confusion due to the different training methods provided. This factor accounts for the variation in the level of technique/skill acquisition of production operators. Therefore, the advancement of HIA is vital for training production operators around the world who speak different languages.
    (ii) Measures for countries with low retention rates-Conventionally, the unique Japanese-style training (experience-based learning) method on a man to man (face to face) basis where a sufficient amount of time is available has been successful. However, due to the low retention rate of employees in some countries, such methods do not seem effective for labor-intensive transmission of know-how (implicit knowledge). Against this background, a new tactic is needed to drastically shorten the training period compared to the conventional method.
    (iii) Overcoming the variation in skill levels of overseas production operators-Newly recruited overseas production operators learn from their seniors by watching their work on an OJT or OFF-JT basis, but the time spent to acquire the needed skills varies a great deal from operator to operator. Analysis of the factors involved has revealed that, at the first training experience in operations such as "high precision fitting" or "parts assembly", whether or not operators can understand the "fundamental skill" required of such operations is largely dependent on their "aptitude and inaptitude". Hence, it is vital to correctly assess the "aptitude and inaptitude" of individuals' ability in order to conduct efficient training.
2. Measures for shortened training
    a. Repetitive training utilizing the visual manual-Our proposed visual manual can be utilized as a training material that supports the off-the-line training of production operators and enhances their understanding of manufacturing-related skills. It is a new communication tool for production operators with different cultural and linguistic backgrounds. It enables them to share the same level of specialized operation knowledge, virtually experience the manufacturing

methods specific to each process as well as the related know-how, and also share knowledge and information regarding the production process with those working with the same process.

b. Intelligent IT system-Video based Intelligent IT System was created for the self-study of operators so that they can understand and recognize the work postures and other technical know-how (Nomiya and Uehara, 2004), which has been taught orally up until now. This system is designed for the accurate transmission of operation skills and repetitive training until the trainee fully understands the work procedure. Specifically, this system provides the footage of work operations performed after the repetitive image training via the visual manual mentioned above (a).

As shown in Figure 10, a series of work operations demonstrated by a "highly skilled trainer" are video-recorded and the same operations performed by a newly recruited production operator are also recorded and uploaded as video data. These two files are processed to be played side by side on a PC display. In this way, production operators can view their weak points objectively, and work on correcting them repeatedly so as to improve their skills to the desired level in a short period of time

Figure 10. Image comparisons of a highly skilled trainer and a newly employed operator

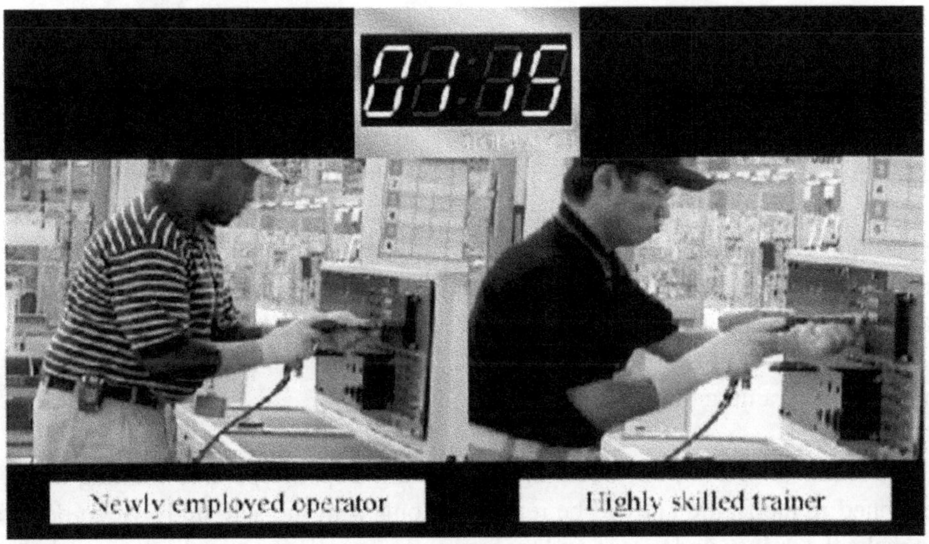

c. Assessment of aptitude / inaptitude by aptitude test-It has been determined that, of the production operators assigned to assembling processes, those who are assessed in advance as "apt" have a tendency to improve their skill in a short time after the assignment. The correlation between fundamental skill training items in the assembling process and skill acquisition on the site has also been identified. Based on these notions, the aptitude test sheet shown in Figure 11 was devised for the advanced assessment of aptitude and inaptitude.

Figure 11. Aptitude test sheets (ex. assembly process)

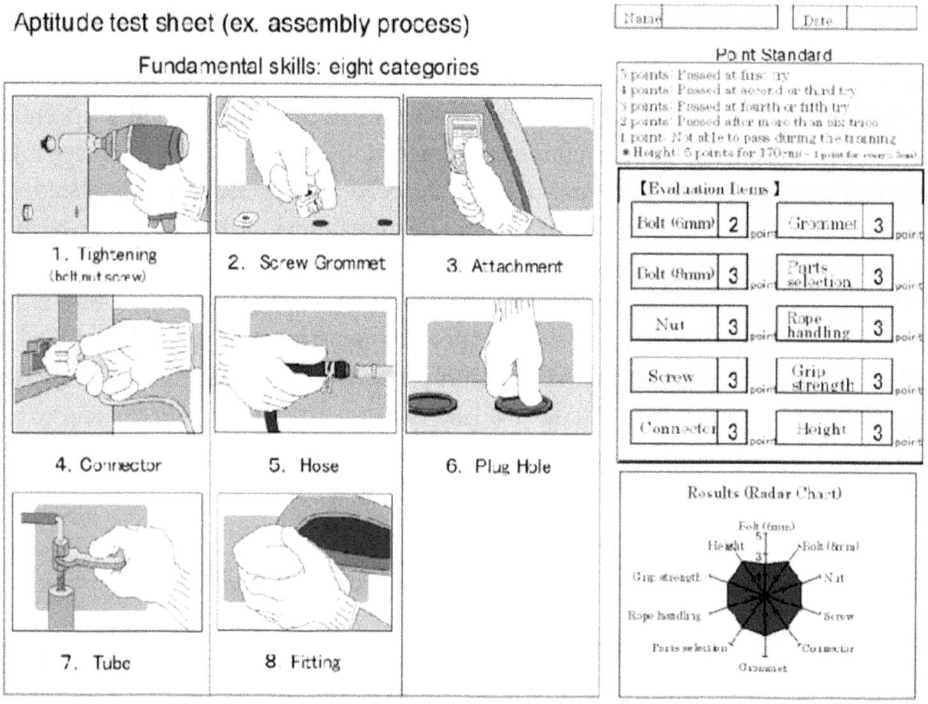

This illustrates the example of an assembling process in which a test is carried out for eight fundamental skill items, and the total points for each item are used for the assessment. Based on the results, those who are assessed as "apt" immediately start receiving training at the actual production line, whereas those who proved to be "inapt" go through repeated "dynamic training", which simulates a similar movement to the actual operations at the production line, to accelerate their skill development.

3. Optimization of Training Steps

Figure 12 presents the flow chart outlining the training steps. Repetitive training using the visual manual mentioned in the figure (1) will be repeated along with the self-study video described in the figure (2) to make the trainee understand and recognize their weak points until they reach the skill level designated for each process on the specified evaluation sheet.

Next, in accordance with the results of the aptitude test conducted earlier consisting of the eight fundamental skills discussed in the figure (3), assessment of aptitude and inaptitude will be made. Those who are assessed as "apt" immediately start receiving training at the actual production line. Those who proved to be "inapt" go through repeated "dynamic training", which simulates a similar movement until they reach the skill level designated on the evaluation sheet, after which training at the production line is given.

Figure 12. Flow chart of training program

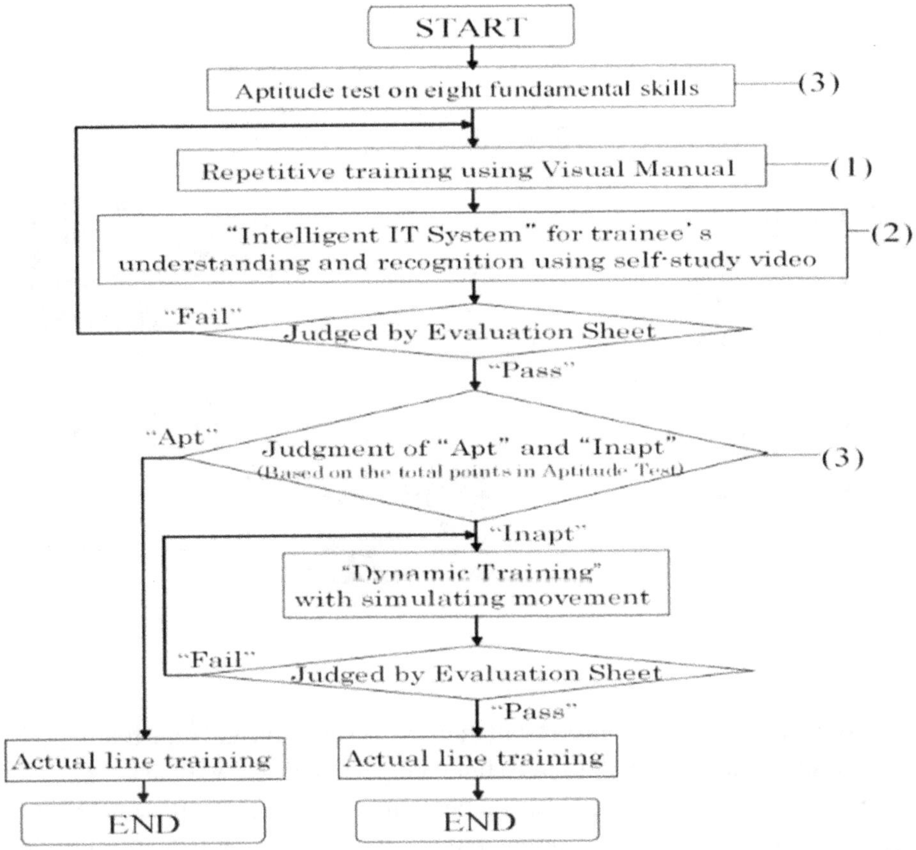

4. HIA application examples

This subsection explains the specific examples of the implementation of the HIA and the perceived effectiveness of this system at Toyota, an advanced automotive manufacturer.

a. Application case of skill training for newly employed production operators

The skill training for newly employed production operators in Japan and abroad was conducted in the production preparations stage using the developed HIA for startup with a stabilized regular production system. Skill training for assembly jobs is explained as an example here. Skill training is conducted for production operators so that they are able to operate correctly at the time of a new plant start-up or model change. Especially in the case of assembly jobs, accurate work completion within the specified time is required for target attainment at an early stage before start-up or changeover.

Since the conventional training used a group of operations for judgment of the training result based on completion in the specified cycle time, it brought about a disparity in the quality of final products. To be more definite, an example of a trimming process is shown in Figure 13. Fundamental skills are divided into eight items: bolt (6 mm) tightening, bolt (8 mm) tightening, nut tightening, screw tighten-

Figure 13. Example of skill levels between requirements and personal diagnosis

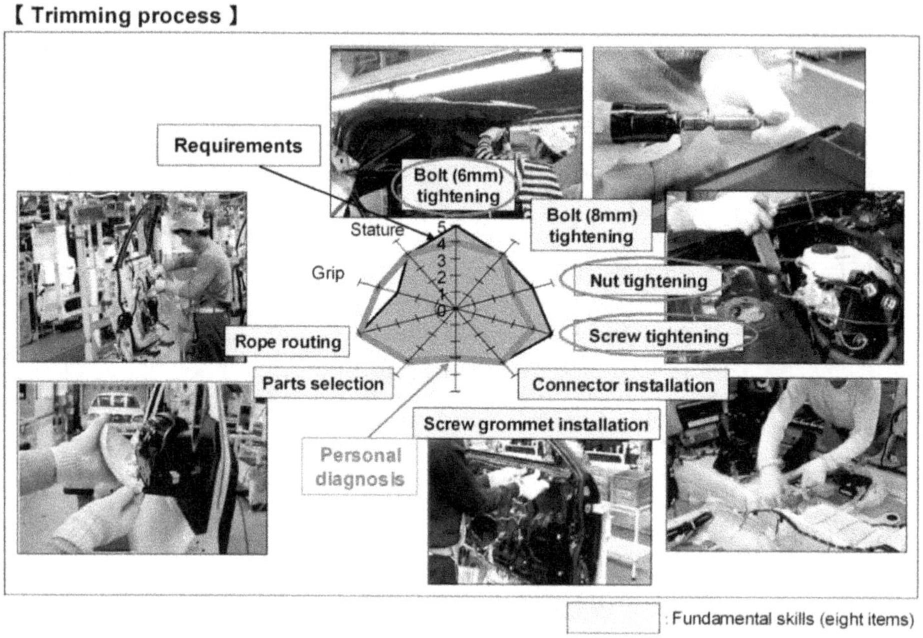

ing, connector installation, screw grommet installation, parts selection and rope routing. The training is conducted with the stress placed on bolt (6 mm) tightening and nut/screw tightening.

This radar chart shows the difference between the requirements and the personal diagnosis so as to make each person aware of, and able to overcome their weak points through training. The training is conducted repeatedly until attainment of the target level is determined by evaluation using the specified evaluation sheet. In Figure 13, the author shows an example of the visual manual concerning the bolt feeding operation.

First, the operational procedure is broken down into smaller operational movements.

Accurate motions are clearly indicated visually using still pictures, movie images, and animation. The visual manual is in a standardized form. The screen consists of a procedure block, description block, and a display image block, which has a main and a sub-screen. This manual is read by turning the page using the forwarding button according to the procedure.

Second, particularly in the description block, key points representing the know-how of each intelligence operator are written and visual information not displayed on the main screen is shown in detail in the sub-screen. The explanatory text under each image describes why the posture is needed, what role it plays in quality assurance, or other information from the intelligence operator so as to share the best practices in the world. This Figure 13 displays a movie showing the nut feeding procedure for assembling product parts on the main center screen. The sub-screen on the right side displays a still picture showing a key point of good posture by maintaining a right angle between the arm and the fingers.

Then, Figure 14 shows the learning evaluation conducted for new employees assigned this time to the trimming process. The learning curve for conventional training mainly consisting of OJT using the actual vehicle is compared with the new training using the visual manual. The degree of learning indicated in time series for the assigned trimming process job, according to the individual evaluation sheet (details are omitted), show that it took four weeks until satisfaction of the specified accuracy within the specified work time in the case of conventional training. However, this was reduced to one half (two weeks) with the new method.

The analytical results are as follows:

1. Training with the visual manual to detect primary individual weak points based on personal diagnosis has improved the understanding of the assigned job, and achieved faster learning compared to the conventional method.
2. When training with the visual manual is combined with OJT on the actual vehicle, it has been confirmed that the learning speed can be increased through repetition of training that places an emphasis on personal weak points.
3. Efficient training was attained without disparity in the degree of learning by teaching the same contents in the same manner according to the clarified teaching process and because the training procedure was not dependent on the quality of the trainers.

Figure 14. Learning evaluation for new employees assigned to trimming process

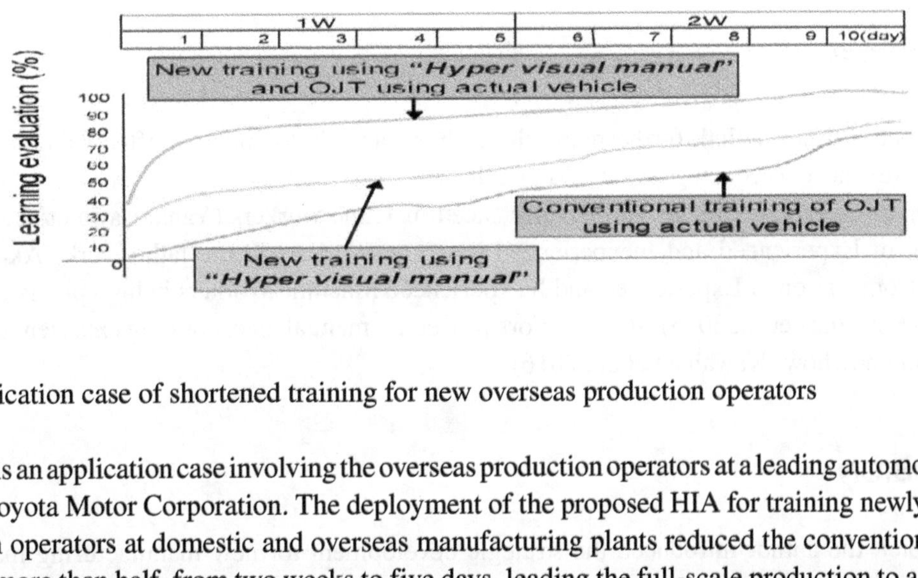

b. Application case of shortened training for new overseas production operators

Below is an application case involving the overseas production operators at a leading automotive manufacturer, Toyota Motor Corporation. The deployment of the proposed HIA for training newly employed production operators at domestic and overseas manufacturing plants reduced the conventional training period by more than half, from two weeks to five days, leading the full-scale production to a good start.

Figure 18, Chapter 7 (Refer to Chapter 7) specifically indicates the skill training curriculum for new overseas production operators. After conducting the aptitude test for fundamental skills, skill training utilizing the visual manual and Intelligent IT system was repeatedly carried out until the standard set out in the evaluation sheet was met. Those whose results on the aptitude test proved to be "inapt" went through "dynamic training" using the simulation training chart to simulate the movement repeatedly until the standard set out in the evaluation sheet was similarly met.

Afterwards, actual line training was finally given, and the designated skill level was reached in a period less than half compared to before. In this case, the launch of an overseas production plant, the target operating rate was achieved in four months after the start-up as shown in Figure 15.

Figure 15. Transition of operation rate after launch of production line

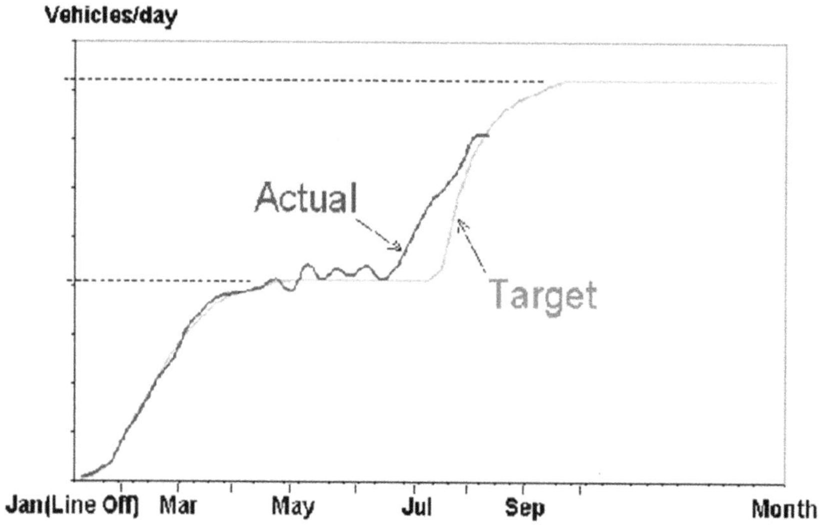

OTHER CASES

With its effectiveness verified, furthermore, the author was able to apply its effectiveness verified by developing Advanced TPS using NJ-AGPM as follows;

(i) Comparison of experienced and inexperienced machine workers (Yanagisawa et al., 2013), (ii) Comparison of Experienced and Inexperienced Machine Workers in the lathe work (Akaiwa et al., 2014), (iii) Comparison of Experienced and Inexperienced Machine Workers in high precision machine processing (Kawahara et al., 2015), and (iv) Work procedure manual incorporating experienced workers' intuition and knowhow (Kawahara et al., 2016).

CONCLUSION

In this chapter, the author introduced the strategic development for new manufacturing management technology as the intelligence productivity improvement developing Advanced TPS. First, as the concrete development examples, the author has created the WVEM that visualizes the awareness of the working value in the form of radar charts to understand workers' awareness of the value in working. Second, the author has developed HIA as a way forward in the creation of a new, people-centered production system that incorporates rich creativity and the motivation of those involved. As these results, the author has verified the validity of WVEM and HIA at an advanced car manufacturer Toyota and others.

ACKNOWLEDGMENT

The author would like to acknowledge the generous support of the following researchers: all those at Toyota Motor Corporation, and Amasaka New JIT laboratory at Aoyama Gakuin University that assisted with author's research, especially, Dr. Sakai, H., Mr. Uchida, K., Mr. Tsunoi, M., Mr. Yamaji, M. and others.

REFERENCES

Abegglen, J. C. (1958). *The Japanese factory: Aspects of its social organization.* The MIT Press.

Akaiwa, R., Sato, T., & Amasaka, K. (2014). Comparison of Experienced and Inexperienced Machine Workers in the lathe work. *The 6th Annual Technical Conference of the Japanese Operations Management and Strategy Association, Takushoku University,* 35-42.

Amasaka, K. (2003). Development of Science TQM, a new principle of quality management. *International Journal of Production Research, 42*(17), 3691–3706.

Amasaka, K. (2007). High Linkage Model "Advanced TDS, TPS & TMS": Strategic development of "New JIT" at Toyota. *International Journal of Operations and Quantitative Management, 13*(3), 101–121.

Amasaka, K. (2008). Strategic QCD studies with affiliated and non-affiliated suppliers utilizing New JIT. Encyclopedia of Networked and Virtual Organizations, 3(PU-Z), 1516-1527.

Amasaka, K. (2015). *New JIT, New Management Technology Principle.* Taylor & Francis, CRC Press.

Amasaka, K. (2017). *Toyota: Production system, safety analysis and future directions.* NOVA Publishers.

Amasaka, K. (2018). Innovation of automobile manufacturing fundamentals employing New JIT: Developing Advanced Toyota Production System. *International Journal of Research in Business, Economics and Management, 2*(1), 1–15.

Amasaka, K. (2019). Studies on New Manufacturing Theory. *Noble. International Journal of Scientific Research, 3*(1), 1–20.

Amasaka, K. (Ed.). (2019). *Fundamentals of manufacturing management: New manufacturing theory – Operations management strategy 21C.* Sankei-sha, Nagoya, Aichi-ken.

Amasaka, K., Kurosu, S., & Morita, M. (2008). *New Manufacturing Theory: Surpassing JIT- Evolution of JIT.* Morikita-shuppan.

Amasaka, K., & Sakai, H. (2011). The New Japan Global Production Model "NJ-GPM": Strategic development of Advanced TPS. *The Journal of Japanese Operations Management and Strategy, 2*(1), 1–15.

Aspy, P. P., & Wai, K. M. (2001). An online evaluation of the Compete Online Decision Entry System (CODES). *Developments in Business Simulation & Experimental Leaning, 28,* 188–191.

Chawla, R., & Banerjee, A. (2002). An automated 3D facilities planning and operations model: Generator for synthesizing generic manufacturing operations in virtual reality. *Journal of Advanced Manufacturing Systems, 1*(1), 5–17. doi:10.1142/S0219686702000039

Gabor, A. (1990). *The man who discovered quality: How Deming W. E. brought the quality revolution to America*. Random House Inc.

Hounshell, D. (1984). *From the American system to mass production*. Johns Hopkins University Press.

Hunt, V. D. (1991). *Quality in America: How to implement a competitive quality program*. Irwin Professional Pub.

Iiyoshi, T., & Hannafin, M. (2002). Cognitive tools and user-centered learning environments: Rethinking tools, functions, and applications. *World Conference on Educational Multimedia, Hypermedia and Telecommunications*, *1*, 831-836.

Kawahara, F., Kogane, Y., Amasaka, K., & Ouchi, N. (2016). Work procedure manual incorporating experienced workers' intuition and knowhow. *IOSR Journal of Business and Management*, *18*(12), 80–85.

Kawahara, F., Kogane, Y., Murakami, K., & Amasaka, K. (2015). Comparison of experienced and inexperienced machine workers in high precision machine processing. *The 7th Annual Technical Conference of the Japanese Operations Management and Strategy Association, Gakushuin University*, 261-276.

Kimura, F. (1999). *Illustration predict fear of Low birthrate and longevity*. Chukei Publishing Company.

Kinnunen-amoroso, M., Pasternack, I., Mattila, S., & Parantainen, A. (2009). Evaluation of the practice guidelines of finish institute of occupational health with agree instrument. *Industrial Health*, *47*(6), 689–693. doi:10.2486/indhealth.47.689 PMID:19996548

Leonard-Barton, D. A. (2003). The factory as learning laboratory. *MIT Sloan Management Review*, *34*(1), 23–28.

Nomiya, H., & Uehara, K. (2004). Visual learning by set covering machine with efficient feature selection. *Proceedings of 16th European Conference on Artificial Intelligence*, *110*, 525-529.

Roos, D., Womack, J. P., & Jones, D. T. (1990). *The machine that changed the world*. Rawson Associates Limited.

Sakai, H., & Amasaka, K. (2005). V-MICS, Advanced TPS for strategic production administration: Innovative maintenance combining DB and CG. *Journal of Advanced Manufacturing Systems*, *4*(6), 5–20. doi:10.1142/S0219686705000540

Sakai, H., & Amasaka, K. (2006). Strategic HI-POS, Intelligence production operating system: Applying Advanced TPS to Toyota's global production strategy. *WSEAS Transactions on Advances in Engineering Education*, *3*(3), 223–230.

Sakai, H., & Amasaka, K. (2007). Human Intelligence Diagnosis Method utilizing Advanced TPS. *Journal of Advanced Manufacturing Systems*, *6*(1), 77–95. doi:10.1142/S0219686707000905

Sakai, H., & Amasaka, K. (2008). Human-Integrated Assist Systems for intelligence operators. Encyclopedia of Networked and Virtual Iorganizations, 2(G-Pr), 678-687.

Toyota Motor Corporation & Toyota Motor Kyushu Corporation. (1994). *Development of a new automobile assembly line*. Author.

Tsunoi, M. (2020). *The creation and its validity of the valuation modeling of labor work value* (Master's thesis). Graduate School of Science and Engineering, Aoyama Gakuin Univetsity, Amasaka's New JIT Laboratory.

Tsunoi, M., Yamaji, M., & Amasaka, K. (2010). A study of building an Intellectual Working Value Improvement Model "IWV-IM". *International Business & Economics Research Journal*, *9*(11), 79–84. doi:10.19030/iber.v9i11.33

Uchida, K., Tsunoi, M., & Amasaka, K. (2012). Creating Working Value Evaluation Model "WVEM". *International Journal of Management & Information Systems*, *16*(4), 299–306.

Yamaji, M., & Amasaka, K. (2007). Evolution of technology and skills in production workplaces utilizing Advanced TPS. *Journal of Business & Economics Research*, *5*(6), 61–66.

Yamaji, M., & Amasaka, K. (2008). New Japan Quality Management Model: Implementation of New JIT for strategic management technology. *Journal of Business & Economics Research*, *7*(3), 107–114.

Yanagisawa, K., Yamazaki, M., Yoshioka, K., & Amasaka, K. (2013). Comparison of experienced and inexperienced machine workers. *International Journal of Operations and Quantitative Management*, *19*(4), 259–274.

APPENDIX 1

Intellectual Working Value Improvement Model

This study delves deeper into the basic principles of working value improvement and offers a step-by-step process for achieving that improvement for all workers—male or female, young or old. The author constructs the working value improvement model: Intelligent Working Value Improvement Model (IWV-IM) designed to improve working value and increase worker dedication as shown in Figure 16 (Tsunoi et al., 2010; Amasaka, 2015, 2020). The model shows the steps leading to working value improvement, each of which includes key factors. The balanced achievement of these different factors is what leads to working value improvement.

In Figure 16, more specifically, "working value" was defined from a 4M-E (Man, Machine, Method, Material and Environment) perspective by: 1) organizing the various factors underlying current issues using a matrix diagram, 2) using text mining while conducting a multivariate analysis, and 3) discovering and clarifying relationships among the identified factors. This analysis approach resulted in the identification of a group of three factors (work demands, psychological demands, and personal fulfillment) which were then used to formulate the different levels of the model.

Applying this model at worksites is thought to improve the quality of products and contribute to better quality management. This is achieved by increasing the motivation of individual workers, so that they pay more attention to preventing defective products and then enact that mindset by working together as a team to implement quality improvement measures. The effectiveness of the model was then verified at Toyota, a leading manufacturer (Refer to Tsunoi (2010) in detail).

Figure 16. Intellectual Working Value Improvement Model

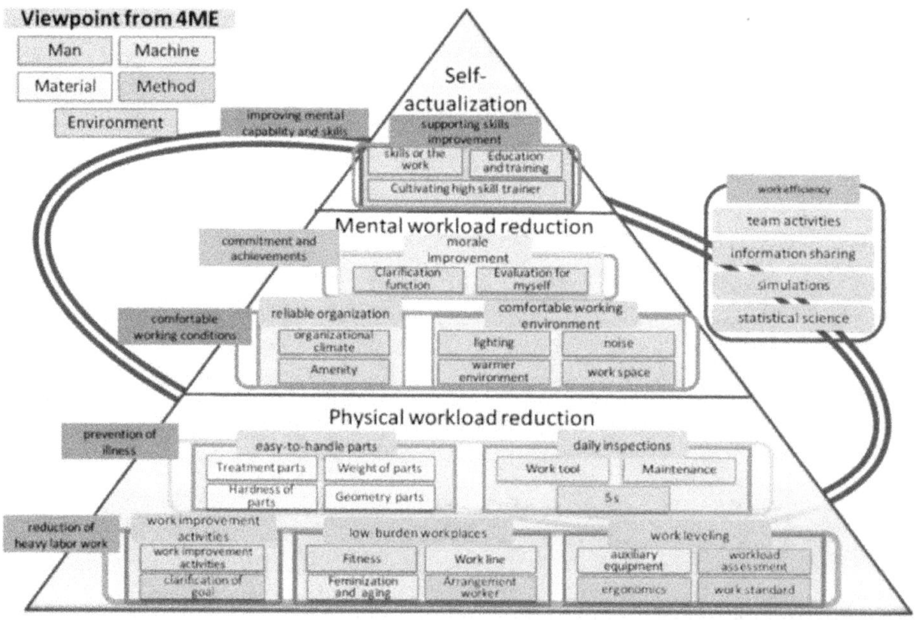

APPENDIX 2

A Survey on Working Value Awareness

Table 3. Awareness survey sheet

No.	Automobile Designs	Strongly agree	←--------------------→					Strongly disagree	Comment freely
1	Reduction of futility, unreasonableness, and unevenness	7	6	5	4	3	2	1	
2	A suitable work layout	7	6	5	4	3	2	1	
3	Making physical strength.	7	6	5	4	3	2	1	
4	Supporting aircraft machine	7	6	5	4	3	2	1	
5	5S activity	7	6	5	4	3	2	1	
6	Activity which foreknows danger	7	6	5	4	3	2	1	
7	Conspicuousness of a signboard	7	6	5	4	3	2	1	
8	Color coordination	7	6	5	4	3	2	1	
9	Environment of the on-site circumference	7	6	5	4	3	2	1	
10	Comfortable air environment	7	6	5	4	3	2	1	
11	Proper lighting	7	6	5	4	3	2	1	
12	Proper sound environment	7	6	5	4	3	2	1	
13	Clean working clearance	7	6	5	4	3	2	1	
14	Proper warm temperature environment	7	6	5	4	3	2	1	
15	Clarification of a role	7	6	5	4	3	2	1	
16	A reliable organizational climate	7	6	5	4	3	2	1	
17	Suitable evaluation of capacity for work	7	6	5	4	3	2	1	
18	Suitable evaluation of a result	7	6	5	4	3	2	1	
19	Acquisition of qualification	7	6	5	4	3	2	1	
20	Acquisition of advanced manufacturing technique	7	6	5	4	3	2	1	

Chapter 16
Developing New Japan Marketing Management Model for Customer Creation

ABSTRACT

In this chapter, the author develops the New Japan Marketing Management Model (NJ-MMM) named Advanced TMS (Total Marketing System) for customer creation in order to innovate in marketing process management by correctly identifying customer demands. To realize this, specifically, the author innovates the Japan's auto-dealers' sales activities employing Intelligent Customer Information Marketing Model (ICIMM) for the evolution of market creating. Concretely, the author focuses on the effectiveness of various advertising media using Science SQC based on the Customer Science approach. As a suitable example, particularly, the author develops the J-ANSMS (Japan's Automobile New Sales Marketing Management System) to improve the repeat customer ratio of Toyota vehicles as the Customer Retention (CR) activities employing SCCM (Scientific Customer Creative Model). The achievements of NJ-MMM are currently being applied at Toyota's Netz Chiba and other dealers.

INTRODUCTION

A future successful global marketer must develop an excellent quality marketing system (EQMS) that impresses users and continuously provides excellent, quality products in a timely manner through corporate management (Amasaka, 2005, 2007a). Then, in the light of recent changes of the marketing environment, the author believes it is now necessary to develop innovative business and sales activities that adequately take into account the changing characteristics of customer's who are seeking to break free from convention (Amasaka, 2002, 2009, 2011).

If they are to be successful in the future, those involved in global marketing must develop an EQMS that is impressive to users and that will enable the consistent and timely provision of excellent quality products through corporate management-Customer Science (CS) principle (Amasaka, 2002, 2005, 2007b).

DOI: 10.4018/978-1-7998-8746-1.ch016

Therefore, in particular, the author has developed the New Japan Marketing Management Model (NJ-MMM) named Advanced TMS so that the divisions responsible for the development and design of appealing products employing Intelligent Customer Information Marketing Model (ICIMM) based on the Scientific Customer Creative Model (SCCM) (Amasaka, 2007a,b, 2019;Amasaka, Ed., 2007) (Refer to Figure 1(3) and 9 in Chapter 6).

Moreover, NJ-MMM can easily acquire information on customer needs and preferences through the consistent application of objective data and scientific methodology using J-ANSMS (Japan's Automobile New Sales Marketing Management System) based on the CS-CIANZ (CS-Customer Information Analysis and Navigation System) (Amasaka, 2005, 2009, 2011, 2019; Yamaji and Amasaka, 2009) (Refer to Chapter 6 and Chapter 13: Figure 11 in 6 and Figure 4 in 11).

In this chapter, therefore, the author focuses on the effectiveness of various advertising media (mixed media) employing J-ANSMS called T-ANSMS (Toyota's Automobile New Sales Marketing Management System) (Amasaka, 2007a; Amasaka et al., 2013). As a suitable example of this study, particularly, the author develops the T-ANSMS (J-ANSMS) to improve the repeat customer ratio of Toyota vehicles as the Customer Retention (CR) activities by using Science SQC based on the Customer Science approach named Toyota Marketing SQC (Amasaka ret al., 1998; Amasaka, 2001a, 2004, 2015, 2022; Amasaka Ed. 2012).

Concretely speaking, this study deals with the subject of improving the sales rate for replacement Toyota vehicles, which involves setting up Toyota Netz dealers in a model case (Amasaka, 2001b, 2003).

First, specifically, Categorical Automatic Interaction Detector (CAID) and Cramer's analysis is used to identify characteristics and variations in customer orientation through the analysis of user questionnaire data. Second, accordingly, the author has analyzed the effects of the publicity and mixed media, and has developed the "Specific models for high replacement probability customers" trough researching the "Relationship between sales activities and publicity and advertising". Third, moreover the knowledge thus obtained is used to generate specific measures for increasing sales through CR based on customer type, enabling the development of T-ANSMS using CS-CIANZ) (Refer to Figure 11 in Chapter 6).

The achievements of a present model case are currently being applied at Netz Chiba and other Toyota dealers (Amasaka, 2009, 2011, 2015, 2022).

NEED FOR A MARKETING STRATEGY WHICH CONCIDERS MARKET TRENDS

Today's marketing activities require more than just short-term strategies, such as 4P (Product, Price, Place and Promotion) activities by the business and sales divisions. After the collapse of the bubble economy, the competitive environment in the market has drastically changed. Since then, companies that have implemented strategic marketing quickly and aggressively have been the only ones enjoying continued growth (Okada, et al., 2001). After close examination, it was said that strategic marketing activities must be conducted as company-wide, core corporate management activities that involved interactions between divisions inside and outside of the company (Jeffrey and Bernard, 2005; Amasaka, 2007a).

Therefore, a marketing management system needs to be established so that business/sales/ service divisions, which are carrying out development and design for appealing products projects, and which are also in the closest position to customers, can organizationally learn customers' tastes and desires by means of the continued application of objective data and scientific methodology (James and Mona, 2004; Amasaka, 2005). However, at present, the organizational system has not yet been fully established in these divisions; in some cases, even the importance of this system has not been commonly realized (Gary and Arvind, 2003; Amasaka, 2005).

The above research suggests that it is necessary to promote scientific activities involving sales and sales-related departments. That is, close observation of recent changes in the field of marketing by the author and other researchers has led us to the conclusion that it is necessary to place more emphasis on communicating with customers in order to gain an adequate understanding of their changing characteristics, unbiased by established concepts (Kotler, 1999; Niiya and Matsyoka, 2001; Okada et al., 2001; Amasaka, 2001a, 2007a).

This new understanding should form the basis of business and sales innovation. In particular, the author believes that a better quantitative understanding of the effect of publicity and advertising in automobile sales will enable more effective sales activities (Amasaka, 2001b, 2003, 2009). Although experience shows that, of the various types of advertising media, flyer advertising has been very effective in attracting customers, this has not yet been analyzed quantitatively (Gary and Arvind, 2003; James and Mona, 2004; James and Mona, 2004; Amasaka, 2009, 2011).

DEVELOPING NEW JAPAN MARKETING MANAGEMENT MODEL FOR CUSTOMER CREATION

Importance of Innovating Auto-Dealer's Sales Activities

Considering recent changes in the marketing environment, it is now necessary to implement innovation of business and sales activities to accurately grasp the characteristics and changes of customer preferences independently of convention. Contact with customers has never called for more careful attention and practice (Amasaka, 2011).

For example, it is now more important to construct and develop an intelligent customer information network "CS-CIANS" using Customer Science Principle that systematically improves know-how related to the application of customer information software with respect to users of various vehicle makes (Refer to Chapter 6 and 13). This information network turns customer management and service into a science by using Science SQC according to customers' involvement with their vehicles in daily life (Amasaka, 2002, 2003a, 2005).

To realize the innovation of business and sales activities as shown in Figure 1, the following three factors are important: merchandise, shop and selling power, and shop appearance and operation. Of these three factors, (a) innovation for building ties with customers is particularly important in innovating shop appearance and operation. It constitutes the base for the innovation of (b) business negotiation, (c) employee images, and (d) after-sales service (Amasaka, et al., 1998; Amasaka, 2011).

Concretely, One vital point of the strategic marketing structure is its definition; marketing activities should be defined from "Closed marketing activities" that are limited to the business and sales division to "Open marketing activities" that can be performed through steady linkage with all other divisions in a company-wide framework for realization of the "Modeling of Strategic Marketing System to reflect latent customer needs" (Amasaka et al., 2005; Shimakawa et al., 2006; Amasaka, Ed., 2007).

Figure 1. Innovation of the business and sales activities

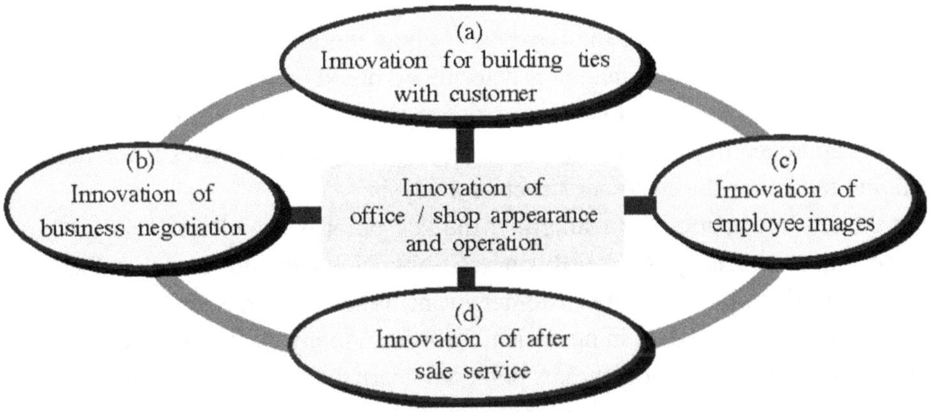

New Japan Marketing Management Model by Developing SCCM

Specifically, therefore, for the "Evolution of market creating" through "High quality assurance and innovating dealers' sales activities" by developing NJ-MMM (New Japan Marketing Management Model) named Advanced TMS as the realizing Strategic Marketing Development Model (SMDM) in Toyota based on TMS (Total Marketing System) as shown in Figure 2 (Amasaka, 2007a,d, 2011, 2015, 2019, 2022; Amasaka, Ed., 2012) (Refer to Chapter 5 and 6 in detail).

In Figure 2, NJ-MMM aims to achieve the high-cycle rate for market creation activities, and is composed of four core elements: the "New sales office image" (NSOI), "Intelligent Customer Information Network System" (ISINS), Rational Advertisement Promotion System (RAPS) and "Intelligent Sales Marketing System" (ISMS) by developing SCCM (Scientific Customer Creative Model) (Refer to Figure 9 in Chapter 6 in detail) By these elements, NJ-MMM innovates for bonding with the customer and reforms office-shop appearance and operation.

Figure 2. New Japan Marketing Management Model (NJ-MMM)

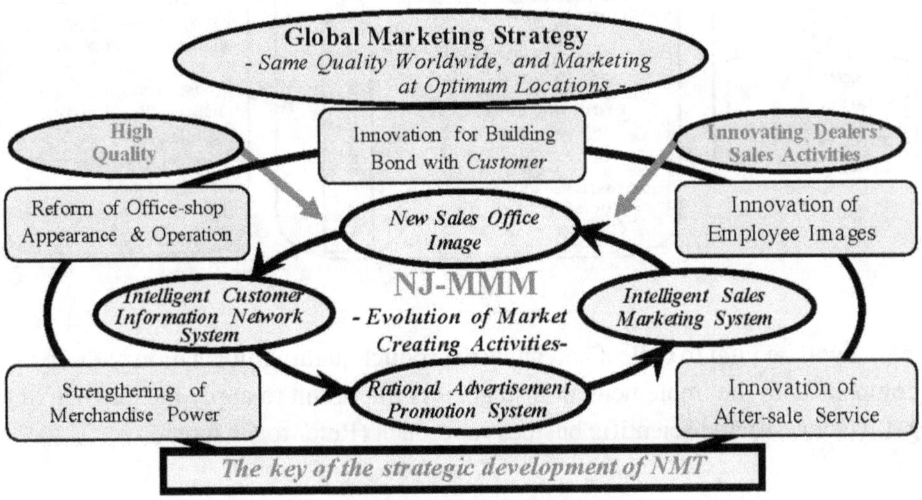

In Figure 9 in Chapter 6, to develop SCCMN strategy, the entire structure consists of three domains, (1) Input Information; (2) Information for marketing, and (3) Output information, as follows;

First, in the (1) Input Information, the key point is how the market segment and the target market are determined. In general, the target market is determined based on the company's core competencies, competition strategy, and resource strategy over the medium and long term basis. By introducing a scientific analysis approach that uses IT (Information technology), it clarifies a potential target market from the changing market or the customer structure analysis.

Second, in the (2) Information for marketing, the key point is to collect / analyze customers' demands and expectations precisely (Nikkei Business, 1999; Rickman and Cosenza, 2007). At this time, it is important to consider what value the customers want. When implementing information collection / analysis, customer value is described in numerical form from many different viewpoints.

Third, in the (3) Output information, the key point is to learn the structure of the customer's motivation to buy products, customer satisfaction. It is important to develop product planning, advertising and sales.

In each domain, the key marketing items are linked by paths to show how they are associated for realization of the "Strategic Marketing Model for customer value maximization" (Amasaka, et al., 2004: Shimakawa, et al., 2006).

Intelligent Customer Information Marketing Model for J-ANSMS Strategy

So, the author presents an Intelligent Customer Information Marketing Model (ICIMM) which takes the form of strategic marketing for J-ANSMS (T-ANSMS) strategy as shown in Figure 3 (Amasaka Ed., 2007; Amasaka, 2015, 2020) (Refer to Chapter 6).

Figure 3. Intelligent Customer Information Marketing Model (ICIMM)

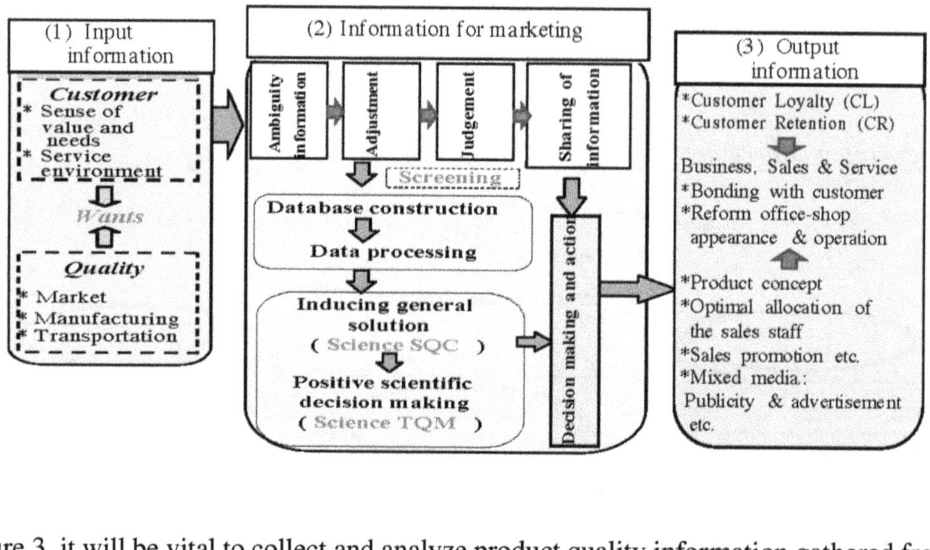

In Figure 3, it will be vital to collect and analyze product quality information gathered from outside and inside companies. In the implementation stage, it is important to apply the Science SQC based on Science TQM, via a verifiable scientific business approach (Refer to Chapter 5).

In particular, the process required for customer information development is as follows: (1) at the strategic customer concept stage (: Input information), "Wants" are created; (2) at the marketing stage (:Information for marketing), the concept is made into more concrete form; and (3) at the product planning and sales stage (: Output information), the development of high quality product concept is required. The new expectation for and role required of SCCM (Scientific Customer Creative Model) is the establishment of a new methodology to support the designing of strategic products from customer information in stages (1) and (2) (Amasaka Ed., 2007a: Amasaka, 2015, 2022).

DEVELOPING NJ-MMM FOR CUSTOMER CREATION USING ICIMM

As examples of research studies for innovating mode of business and sales operation, the author develops the NJ-MMM employing ICIMM based on the T-ANSMS (J-ANSMS) in order to improve the repeat customer ratio for Toyota vehicles as the scientific CR activities. The achievements of the present study are currently being applied at Netz Chiba and other Toyota dealers using ICIMM (Amasaka et al., 1998; Amasaka, 2001, 2007, 2009, 2010, 2012, 2015).

Trial for Increasing Sales through CR Based on Customer Type

The author implemented Customer Science to enable increased sales through CR based on customer type. For a model case, two Toyota A-dealers (Netz Chiba and one other) were selected and sales activities were enhanced by developing specific models for customers with a high probability of replacing their Toyota vehicle. Concretely speaking, this is a change from the current customer information-based uniform CR method to a CR method based on customer type for stratifying customers by ascertaining their orientation and/or changes from a wider area of selection of the conditions

Practical Studies on Science SQC

The author solves problems by using scientific approaches such as "Mountain climbing for problem-solving" (development of specific models for customers of high replacement probability) following the steps from (i) to (ix) shown in Figure 4. This involves application of SQC Technical Methods (demonstrative scientific methods using a combination of new seven tools (N7), multivariate analysis (MA), experimental design (DE), etc.), which is one of the core techniques of Science SQC (Amasaka, 2003a, 2004) (Refer to Chapter 5).

In steps (i) and (ii) shown in the figure, consideration was given to the development of specific models for high replacement probability customers as shown in Figure 5, an "Application type" association diagram. The aim was to increase sales through CR based on customer type, and the tools used include the N7 (affinity diagram, relation diagram, process decision program chart (PDPC), etc.). Then, in step (iii), a scenario of implementation plans for about a year was established (Amasaka et al., 1998; Amasaka, 2009; Amasaka Ed. 2012).

In steps (iv) through (vi), the graphical "Categorical Automatic Interaction Detector" (CAID) analytical method was implemented (Murayama, 1998; Amasaka, 2001a). This method has been developed as the new multivariate analysis, and was necessary for the qualitative and categorical data analysis required for questionnaire design, implementation and analysis. Based on the information thus obtained, models were established for high replacement probability customers.

Figure 4. Mountain climbing for Problem-Solving

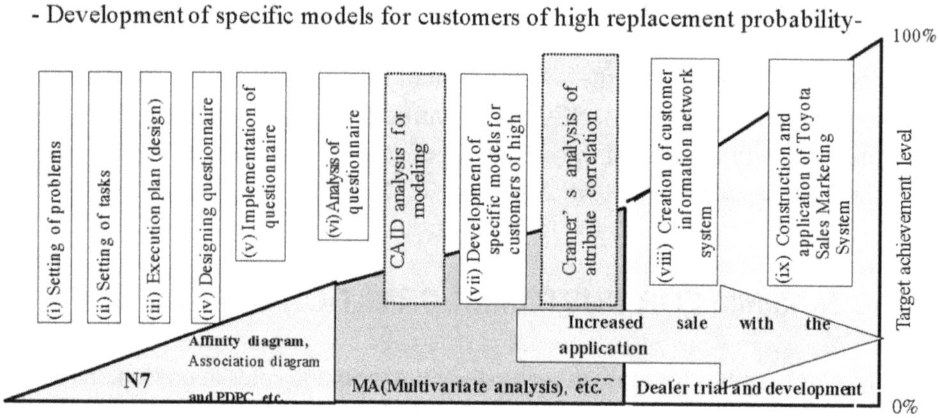

Figure 5. "Application type" association diagram (Step (i)-(iii))

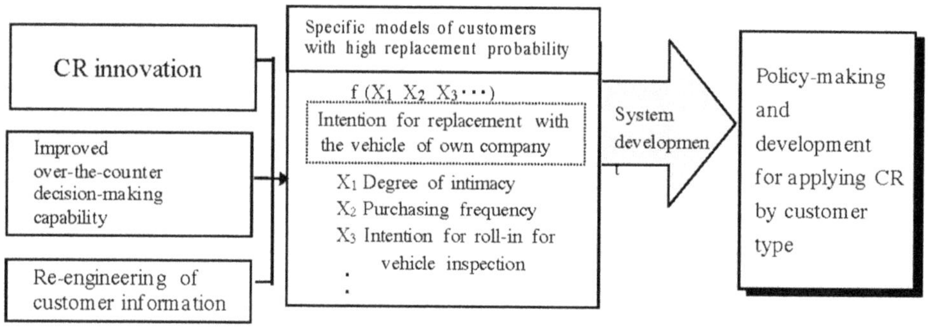

In the next step (vii), the sales method capable of deploying CR based on customer type was obtained using the "Cramer's analysis" of attribute correlation as the base for developing the customer information network system in step (viii). In the final step (ix), the scenario at Netz Chiba was examined as the basis for deployment to all Toyota dealers for the development of T-ANSMS (J-ANSMS) employing ICIMM in Toyota.

Development of Specific Models for High Replacement Probability Customers

1. Objective and explanatory variable for the planned questionnaire form
   a. Objective variable: Intention to replace with Toyota vehicle: (Yes, No)
   b. Explanatory variable: Records of roll-in (oil change, inspection and maintenance, fault repair, accident repair, vehicle inspection), number of new cars purchased, referral for new car purchase, voluntary insurance contract, degree of intimacy, degree of Toyota card usage, sex, age, etc. (categories 3 to 6).
2. Four measures to achieve design and implementation of effective questionnaire

Prior telephone notification was given to 4,000 customers who bought new Toyota vehicles within the five years on the planned questionnaire. To improve the recovery rate of the questionnaire, a simply-designed questionnaire was adopted with one section of questions laid out on one page as shown in Table 1 (Case-1). The subjects were required to answer methodically within about 15 minutes. Furthermore, introduction of a Questionnaire Information Box helped raise the recovery rate to over 40% (normally 20%) and the valid reply ratio to 98% (normally 70%).

Table 1. Example of questionnaire form (Case-1) Designing and implementation of questionnaire

—— We like to inquire on the after-sales services of your dealer. ——

Q1: Please let us know the present state of the maintenance, fault, repair and other your vehicle-related after-sales service (please give us an answer for each item from ① to ④).

	①Dealer used	②Reason for using	③Method of payment	④Method of roll-in
1. Oil change (please name a principal shop / station you use)	1. Dealer you purchased a new vehicle from 2. Other dealer 3. Vehicle maintenance service shop 4. Car shop 5. Gas station 6. Other ( )	1.Because of acquaintance 2. High level of technique 3. Low price 4. Privilege offered 5. Nearness of location 6. Other ( )	1. Cash 2. TOYOTA CARD 3. Other cards 4. Other ( )	1. Drive to the shop 2. Have the vehicle picked up 3. Other ( )
2. Inspection and maintenance service of your vehicle (Please name a principal shop you use)	1. Dealer you purchased a new vehicle from 2. Other dealer 3.Vehicle maintenance service shop 4. Car shop 5. Gas station 6. Other ( )	1.Because of acquaintance 2. High level of technique 3. Low price 4. Because of guidance 5. Nearness of location 6. Other ( )	1. Cash 2. TOYOTA CARD 3. Other cards 4. Other ( )	1. Drive to the shop 2. Have the vehicle picked up 3. Other ( )
3. Repair service of fault of your vehicle (please name a principal shop you use)	1. Dealer you purchased a new vehicle from 2. Other dealer 3.Vehicle maintenance service shop 4. Car shop 5. Gas station 6. Other ( )	1. Because of acquaintance 2. High level of technique 3. Low price 4. Good attending attitude 5. Nearness of location 6. Other ( )	1. Cash 2. TOYOTA CARD 3. Other cards 4. Guarantee 5. Other ( )	1. Drive to the shop 2. Have the vehicle picked up 3. Other ( )
4. Repair service of your vehicle after an accident (please name a principal shop you use)	1. Dealer you purchased a new vehicle from 2. Other dealer 3.Vehicle maintenance service shop 4. Car shop 5. Other ( )	1. Because of acquaintance 2. High level of technique 3. Low price 4. Good attending attitude 5. Nearness of location 6. Other ( )	1. Cash 2. TOYOTA CARD 3. Other cards 4. Guarantee 5. Other ( )	1. Drive to the shop 2. Have the vehicle picked up 3. Other ( )
5. Next vehicle inspection (what type of service shop would you select?)	1. Dealer you purchased a new vehicle from 2. Other dealer 3.Vehicle maintenance service shop 4. Car shop 5. Other ( )	1. Because of acquaintance 2. High level of technique 3. Low price 4. Because of guidance 5. Nearness of location 6. Other ( )	1. Cash 2. TOYOTA CARD 3. Other cards 4. Other ( )	1. Drive to the shop 2. Have the vehicle picked up 3. Other ( )
6. Purchase of a new vehicle (what type of shop would you select to purchase from?)	1. A shop you purchased your present car from 2. A shop other than one you purchased your present car from 3. Other ( )	1. Because of acquaintance 2. Sales staff is enthusiastic 3. Good attending attitude 4. Using the shop for the check-up and maintenance service of your vehicle 5. Good purchasing condition 6. Other ( )	1. Cash 2. Installment 3. Lease 4. Other ( )	1. Drive to the shop 2. Have a sales staff come to see me 3. Other ( )

3. Questionnaire analysis with CAID & Cramer's analysis of attribute correlation

After analysis of the questionnaire data, the results of analysis of causal relations were indicated graphically to accurately show the proposed measures and decision-making process that led to increased sales through the application of CR based on customer type.

Then, CAID analysis and Cramer's analysis of attribute correlation was applied to enable collation using empirical rules to form analysis I and analysis II as follows.

a. Analysis I:

Analysis I involves arranging customers having a high-probability of replacement with Toyota vehicles into a model using intelligent CAID analysis. Factors affecting replacement by high-probability customers are rearranged in the same manner as the variable designation method of multi regression analysis. This is conducted repeatedly based on empirical techniques of the staff and managers of business/sales divisions (so as to match their experience).

Then, the characteristics and changes in the customers' orientation are ascertained on the basis of actual contact with customers. Customers are stratified into customer types (customers of high, medium and low repeat business probabilities) from the customer CR point of view.

b. Analysis II:

Analysis II involves conducting factorial analysis using "creation of ties with customers" as the key point to map out our business and sales policies (Cramer's analysis of attribute correlation, etc.). In practice, correlation among influential factors is extracted by the intelligent CAID, including the degree of intimacy and roll-in for vehicle inspection and all other question items using the Cramer's analysis of attribute correlation.

For example, factors which improve the degree of intimacy with customers are identified from the sales activity and after-service activity viewpoints, aimed at deployment for sales policies.

4. Analytical result with CAID (Analysis I; from Step vi to step vii)

Figure 6 shows the legends of the analytical results. Analysis **a** in the figure indicates that 62% of 1,610 users who answered the questionnaire intend to replace their vehicles with a Toyota vehicle, while 38% do not. Next, analysis **b** is the division by the primary influential factor of the "degree of intimacy".

The upper setting of having "intimacy" (customers having good acquaintance with sales staff) indicates that 75% intend to buy Toyota for replacement, and the lower setting of having "no intimacy" (customers not having good acquaintance with the sales staff) indicates that 48% intend to buy Toyota. The difference between them is as much as 27%.

Thereafter, **c** indicates the analytical result for users who bought Toyota for the first time and those for two times and over (no significant difference among 2nd to 5th time purchasers). Similarly, analysis **d** stratifies the users by the "intention for roll-in for vehicle inspection service". From this figure it is known that 90% of customers of level 1 (regular customers) indicated in the top position of **d** intend to buy a Toyota vehicle for replacement.

Figure 6. CAID[1] Analysis (Step (vi)) *[1]: Multiple Cross-section Analysis (Categorical Automatic Interaction Detector)*

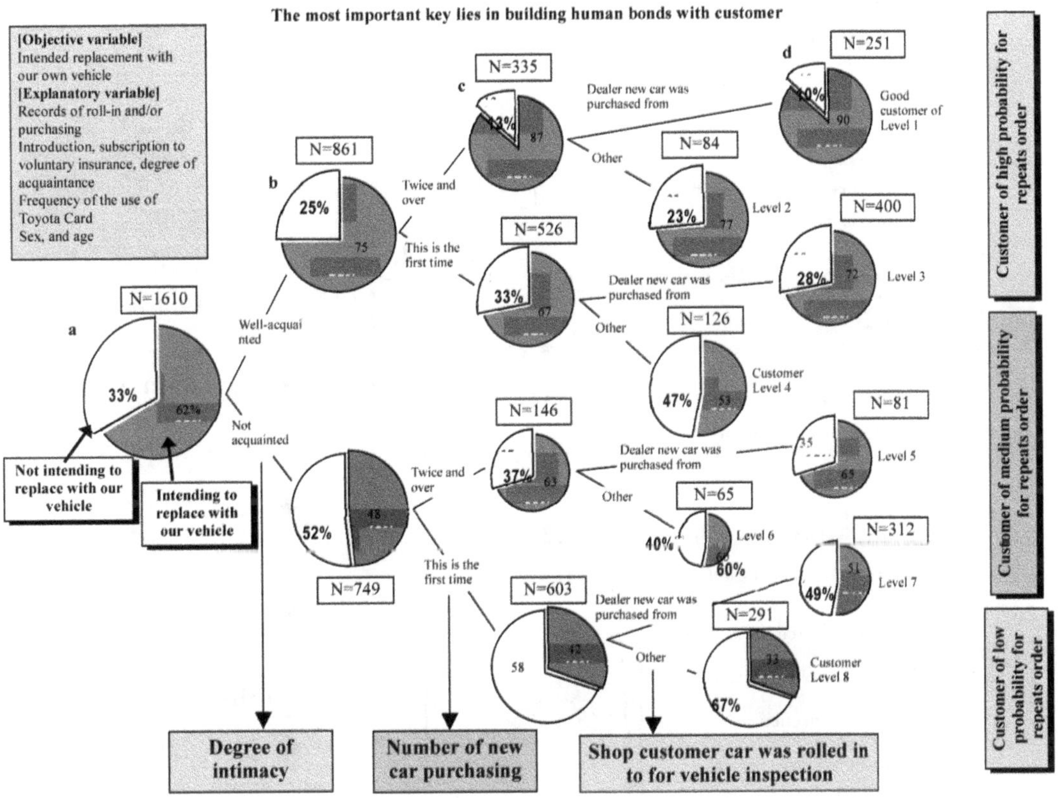

This figure combines customer types of whom 70% intend to buy Toyota (**b, c** and **d**) on customer levels 1 through 3 (regular customers), and classifies them as customers of high probability. Likewise, customer types of whom 50% intend to buy Toyota on the customer levels 4 through 7 (customers) are classified as customers of medium probability. Customers on level 8 are classified as customers of low probability since they fail to hold a majority. The author does not discuss other influential factors (such as **e**: introduction, **f**: sex, and so forth) where difference is noted between two dealers "Netz Chiba and Netz Ehime".

5. Analytical result with Cramer's analysis of attribute correlation (Analysis II: from Step vii to step viii)

Practical and detailed analysis is conducted from the sales policy standpoint aimed at increasing the frequency of contact with customers. Here, the correlation between the degree of intimacy extracted in step (vi) and all other questions is explained using a factor and result diagram based on the Cramer's analysis of attribute correlation as shown in Figure 7.

Figure 7. Factor analysis of Cramer's Analysis of attribute correlation (Example of Degree of Intimacy)

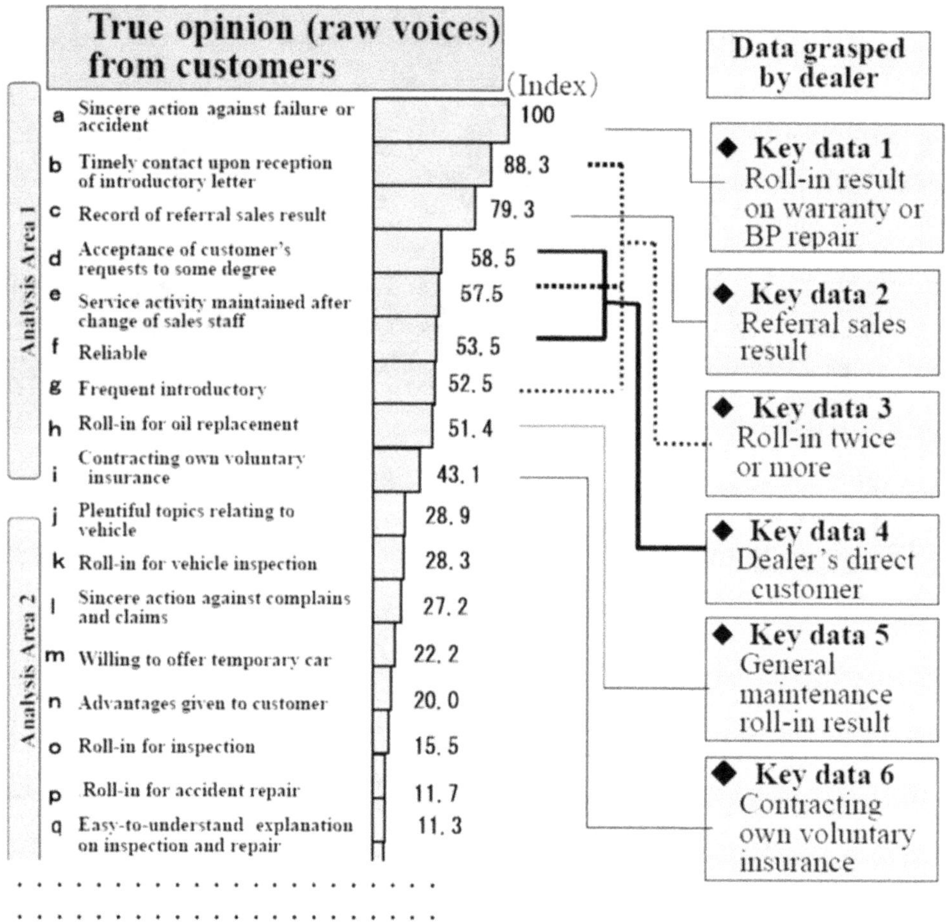

Area 1 in the figure contains factors a through i influential to the degree of intimacy and Area 2, factors j through w affecting the roll-in destination for vehicle inspection. "Index" in the figure represents the customer information numerically.

For example, the 0.14 of "sincere action against failure or accident" is an index when the Cramer's factor correlation coefficient is assumed to be 100. It is technically possible to correlate all factors in area 1 with the 6 key data shown in the figure. Based on the information obtained as a result of these analyses, practical policies can be established for promoting sales and after-service activities capable of improving the degree of intimacy with customers who can be handled by a dealer.

The information can also be used for simulation for sales expansion, which is the basis of innovation for creating strong contact between the dealer and its customers.

APPLICATION TO SCIENTIFIC AUTOMOBILE SALES INNOVATION AT TOYOTA

Dynamics of the Effect of Publicity and Advertising

The kind of information dealers need to know in order to continuously increase the number of customers attracted following the launch of a new model is (i) how many months the effect of the new model introduction lasts, (ii) the best timing (day of the week) and volumes for the most effective flyer advertising, (iii) the ratio of the "Purchase Intention Customers, (PIC)" who show an interest in purchasing a new car, (iv) the percentage of "PIC" who actually purchase new cars, and (v) variation among dealers. It is preferable to know the actual causes and effects involved (Amasaka, 2009, 2015; Amasaka, Ed., 2012).

Analytical methods have not been established for analyzing the dynamic effect of publicity and advertising due to the large scale and level of difficulty of market experiments for obtaining quantitative information in time series. Therefore, there are few reports on this subject relating to automobile marketing (Amasaka et al., 1998; Amasaka, 2001a,b). For this reason, the author presents in the next section factorial analysis conducted using Science SQC, in the hope that it will assist readers in strengthening their information-based marketing, and promoting the T-ANSMS (Amasaka, 2001a,b, 2011, 2015, 2022; Amasaka et al., 2013; Ogura et al., 2013).

Effectiveness of Advertising in Automobile Sales

This subsection demonstrates the effectiveness of the "flyer advertising effect", "day of the week effect", "new car effect". These effects are acknowledged among those on the front lines of automobile sales as having a high level of investment efficiency and resultant customer traffic, achieved through Science SQC called Marketing SQC (Amasaka et al., 1998; Amasaka, 2001a, 2003; Amasaka, Ed. 2012).

1. Publicity and advertising media and sales activities

Figure 8 shows a graphical representation of the causal relationship between sales and order taking activities (dealer visit ® PIC ® order placement), and publicity and advertising media (mixed media).

Figure 8. Relationship between sales activities and publicity and advertising

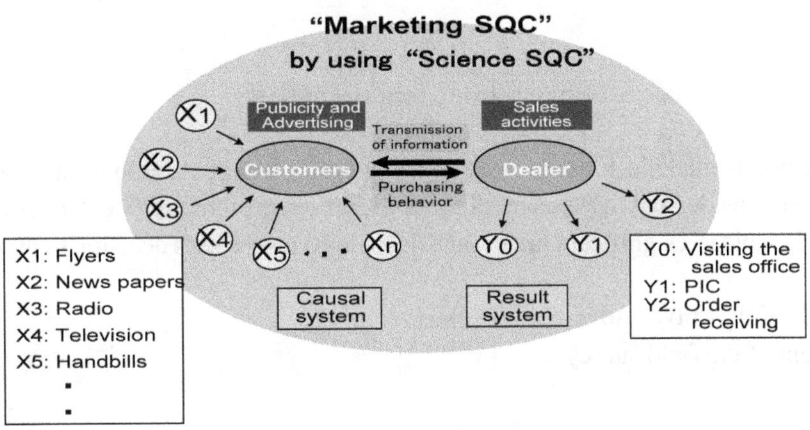

The diagram indicates that the dealer's publicity and advertising activities (causal system: X1 to Xn) attract customers' interest in purchasing, encourage them to visit the dealer (result system: Y0), and ultimately lead to the purchase of a vehicle (PIC: Y1®order placement: Y2).

2. Importance of mixed media

Next, the authors will comparatively evaluate the importance of the factorial effect of publicity and advertising on the basis of the subjective criteria (evaluation point: median) of representative sales staff from Toyota group dealers A and B. In Table 2, "Comparison of publicity and mixed media" indicates the extent of the effect gained from each of the respective media used to promote customer visits to dealers. This table suggests that the effect of mixed media delivered together with newspapers is expected to be significant, which agrees with the empirical knowledge (sales people's experience) fostered through years of sales activities

Table 2. Comparison of publicity and mixed media

	Flyer ad	News paper	Television	Radio	...
Information capacity	○	○△	△	×	...
Information quality	○	○△	△	×	
Frequency of acquiring information	○△	○△	△	○△	
Ease of acquiring information	○	○	△	△	
Residual effect	○	○	△	×	
Total point	174	144	60	30	...

Rating

- ◎ : 5 points
- ○ : 4 points
- ○△ : 3 points
- △ : 2 points
- × : 1 point
- ×× : 0 point

3. Survey on the effects of mixed media using factorial analysis

To verify the points made in subsection 16.3, analysis has been carried out on what customers say prompted them to consider buying a car at Toyota group's representative dealers A and B. Figure 9 shows that mixed media is a significant factor in influencing a customer's decision to purchase a new car.

4. An example of the "Flyer Advertising" effect
   a. Content of the field survey

Figure 9. Survey on what prompts customers to consider buying a car

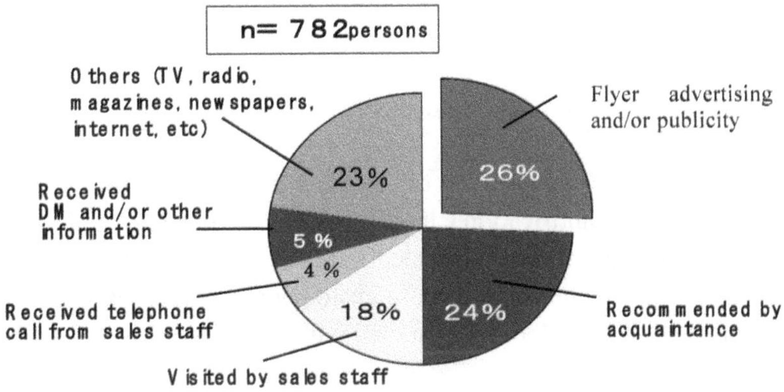

A field survey was conducted as follows by designating six sales offices of Toyota group's dealer B, which is located in an urban area.

i. A visitor questionnaire was used to determine customers' motives for visiting the dealer's sales office, and to create a customer profile (age, desired vehicle type, timing of purchase, budget, etc.)
ii. Analysis was carried out based on the results of the study in time series of distribution of the flyers (quantity, etc.) over the nine-month period starting before and ending after the latest introduction of a new car, and covering the order taking activities at the respective dealers (number of visitors ® number of PIC ® number of cars sold).
    b. Science SQC approach

The core techniques of Science SQC, SQC Technical Methods are used to objectify (modeling: explicit knowledge) the subjective evaluation (empirical knowledge: implicit knowledge) of the "flyer

Figure 10. Factorial analysis of the effect of "Flyer Advertising"

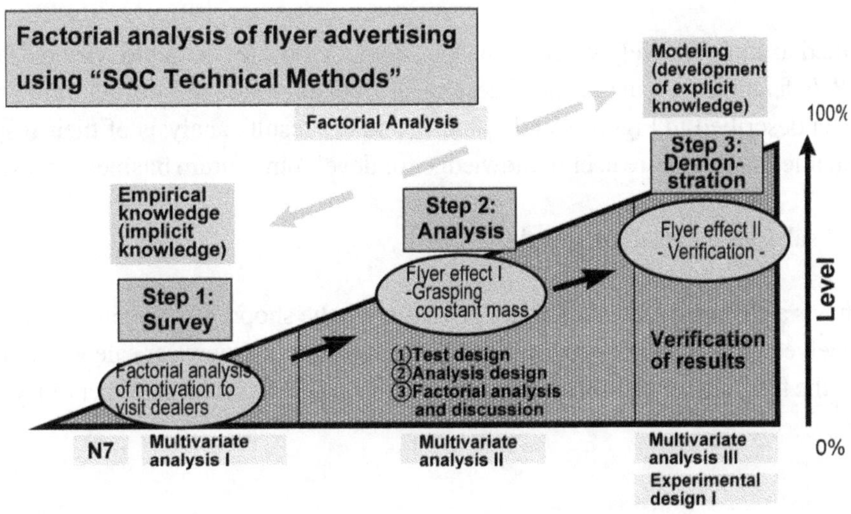

advertising" effect. Here, the Science SQC approach shown in Figure 10 is applied to conduct a factorial analysis on the effect of flyer advertising in the sequence of Step 1 (survey) and Step 2 (analysis). The author intends to report on Step 3 (demonstration) at a later time.

c. Analysis of customer motives for visiting dealers

Figure 11 represents graphically an analysis of customer motives for visiting dealers. This analysis was carried out on the basis of Quantification Class III in order to objectify subjective evaluations. The categorical quantities of publicity and advertising media such as flyers, newspapers and magazines shown in the diagram, lead us to the conclusion that those customers prompted by flyers to visit dealers are likely to at some time need to replace their old car, and will be on the lookout for a bargain.

Figure 11. Analysis of motives for visiting dealers (Quantification Class III scatter diagram showing category quantities)

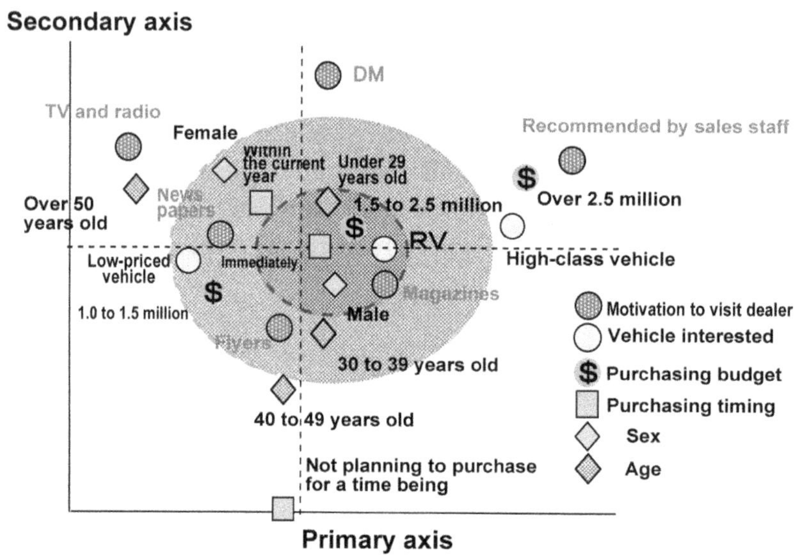

With other media, comparatively younger male customers may, for example, visit a dealer upon seeing some new RVs featured in a magazine. These results corroborate the information on publicity and advertising media described in Figure 8 and Table 2, and the results analysis of their respective effectiveness. This enables us to acquire useful knowledge for developing future business and sales activities.

d. Analysis of sales activities in time series

Figure 12 shows an overview of the number of visitors to the shop (Y0), the number of PIC (Y1) and actual orders received (Y2) in the two months following the start of a new car sale within the total nine-month period of the field survey. The chart gives an outline of the distribution effect of flyer advertising.

Figure 12. Example of the Records of Sales Activities

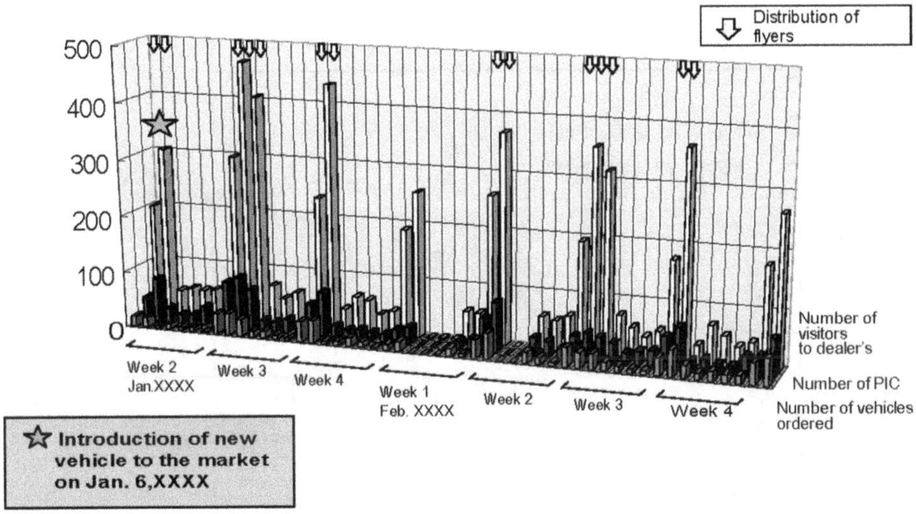

Figure 13. Relationship between the number of dealer visitors, PIC, and vehicle orders placed

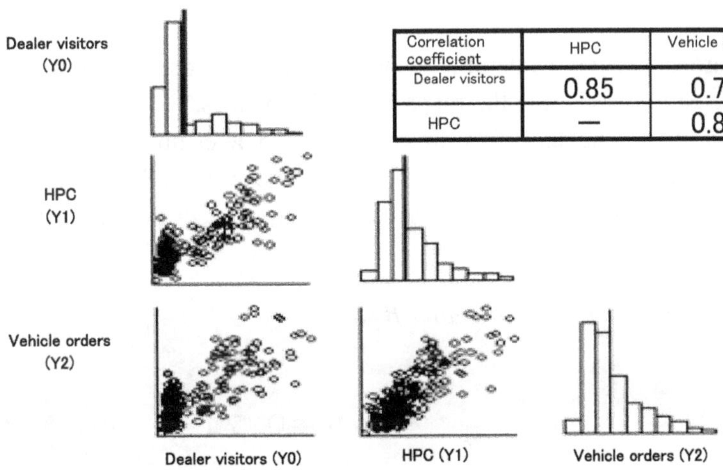

Correlation coefficient	HPC	Vehicle orders
Dealer visitors	0.85	0.78
HPC	—	0.82

Moreover, the author can assume from the multivariate association diagram in Figure 13, which covers the total nine-month survey period, that the number of visitors (Y0) is the principal factor in increasing the number of purchases (PIC (Y1) to order placement (Y2)).

Now let us look at the relationship between the number of visitors, number of HPC customers and the number of units sold, as shown in Figure 14. This diagram shows that (i) as the number of visitors (Y0) increases, the number of PIC (Y1) and the number of units sold (Y2) also increase on a regression slope of the respective exponents (regression coefficient) a 1 and a 2. Also, the diagram confirms that (ii) the ratio of the number of units sold is about one-half of the number of PIC. Further, the author can assume from the information in the diagram that (iii) due to the considerable dispersion in the data from

Figure 14. Scatter diagram showing the number of dealer visitors, PIC, and vehicles orders placed

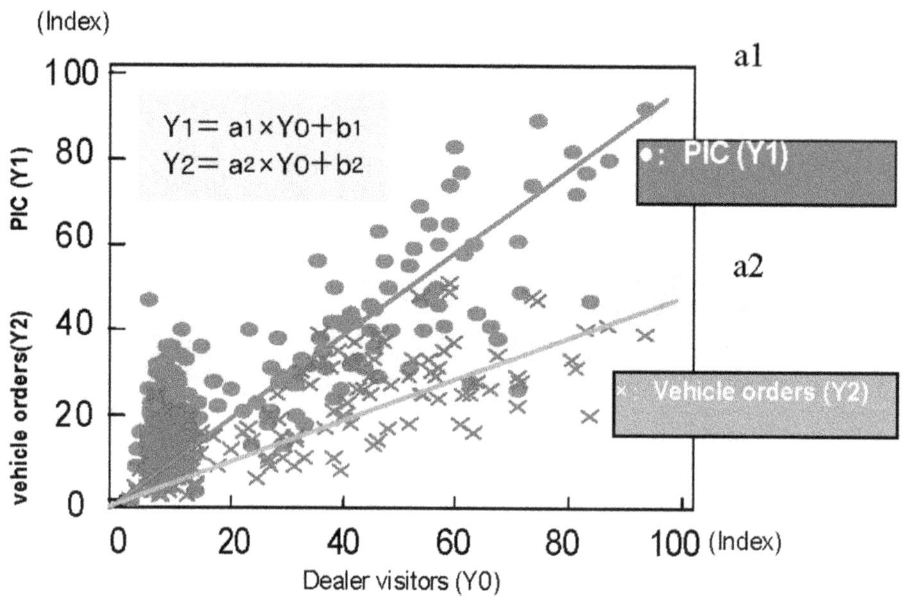

the regression line, there is also a considerable dispersion in the ratios of the number of PIC and units sold to the number of customers visiting the respective sales offices.

In this connection, a survey and analysis were carried out to determine whether such dispersion factors in the data are dependent on the characteristics of each sales office. Six representative sales offices were selected from dealer B and analysis was carried out on differences in flyer distribution, the number

Figure 15 Map showing location of Toyota dealer B sales

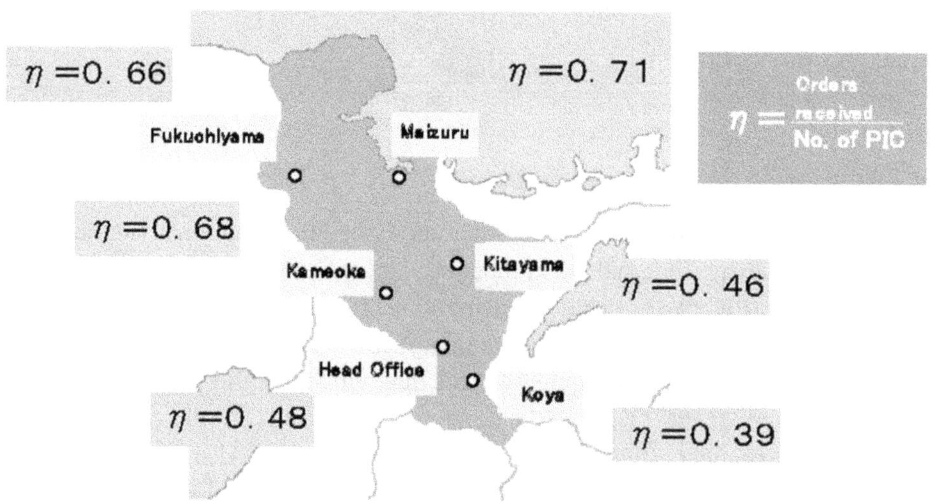

of visitors to each of the sales offices, the number of PIC, and the number of orders received for each office. The results of this analysis are summarized in Figure 15.

This figure indicates that there is considerable variation in the exponents of orders received among the sales offices. For example, in comparing the exponents of orders received (η= number of units ordered/number of PIC) between the main sales office located in an urban area and the Maizuru sales office located in an outlying area, the figure shows that the exponentηfor the Head Office is 0.48, while that for Maizuru sales office is 0.71.

Although it goes beyond the scope of this discussion, the author is able to obtain new activity guidelines for formulating new sales strategies by gaining an understanding of the data dispersion among the sales offices on the basis of such analysis.

e. Flyer effect, Day of the week effect, and New car effect

Due to time constraints in the object period for analysis, the author used quantification class I for the current factorial analysis of the survey data in time series. Figure 16 shows the "flyer effect", the "day of the week effect", and the "new car effect", which influence the number of visitors (Y0) to the sales office.

Confining the discussion to the current range of investigation, the following can be observed from Figure 16: (i) Item 1 shows that the greater the number of flyers distributed, the more customers visit the dealer. (ii) Item 2 shows that the effect is greater on Saturdays and Sundays, while the number of visitors is more or less constant on weekdays. (iii) Item 3 shows that the "new car effect" continued for two months in the current analysis, including the first month the new car went on sale. The effect contracted in the period from three to five months after the new car went on sale.

f. Considerations

As a result of the survey and analysis conducted thus far, the author has been able to quantitatively clarify the acknowledged opinions of sales staff (empirical knowledge) on the "flyer effect", the "day of the week effect" and the "new car effect." Based on this information the author believes that, in order to efficiently enhance the effectiveness of flyer advertising, it is necessary to carry out demonstrative research (Figure 10: Step 3 Demonstration) to determine the saturation point of flyer advertising (limit the number of flyers distributed), optimal timing (best days of the week for distribution), the elements of effective flyer design (layout and impact), and the location and scale of dealers.

Furthermore, the author intends to carry out a new demonstrative study on the effectiveness of similar mass media such as TV advertising, direct mail, and the internet, so that they can be applied as strategic steps in developing T-ANSMS.

Construction and Application of T-ANSMS

In Figure 11, Chapter 6 (Refer to Chapter 6), the author illustrates the T-ANSMS (Toyota's Automobile New Sales Marketing System) reflecting the contact between dealer and customers based on the information obtained above and containing the practical policies for sales and service activities in step (ix) of Figure 4. For practical application in Figure 4, Chapter 6, the questionnaire in step (vi) is reanalyzed at trial stages of the system in steps (vii) and (viii) of Figure 4 in order to ensure replacement by Toyota vehicles by adding the following strategies;

Figure 16. Quantification Class I (Graph of the category quantities)

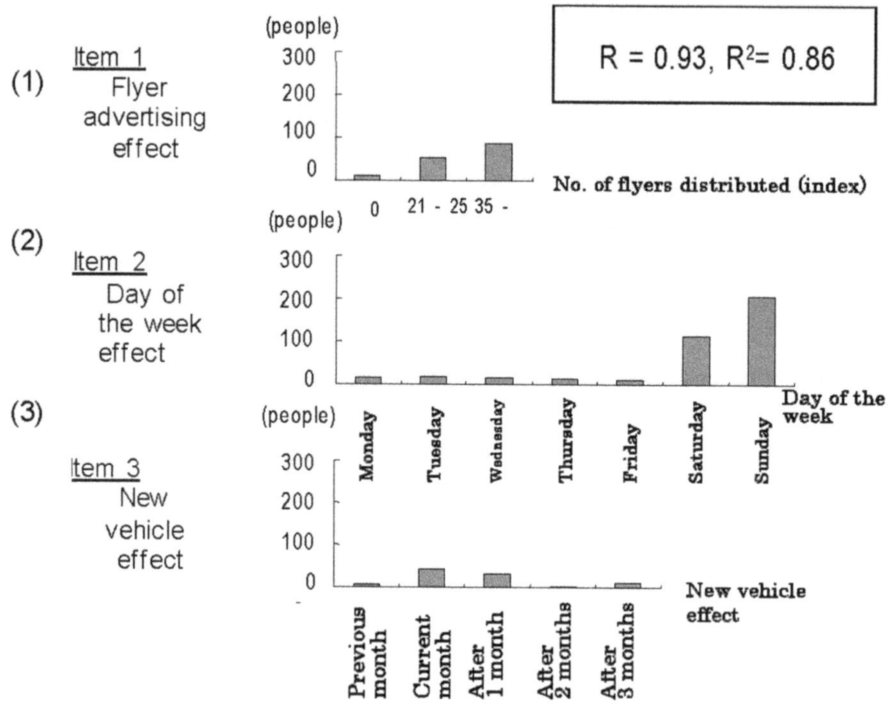

1. The CR activities based on customer type are adopted by classifying high- and middle-probability customers into those who visit the shop and those who must be visited by our staff, taking characteristics at new car purchase into account. A system is established so that the shop manager directly receives "Medium-Probability Customers (MPC)" upon their visit to the shop without fail in order to promote visits to the shop by "High-Probability Customers (HPC)". Thus, the frequency of contact with customers is increased. Further, sales and service activities focus on telephone calls for customers who visit the shop, and telephone calls and home visits for those who require visits by our staff, as shown in the figure.
2. As for "Low-probability customers (LPC)" who have less contact with the sales staff, a telephone call center is established within the dealer as shown in the figure to accumulate know-how related to the effective use of customer information software.

The two-step approach is adopted as the practical sales policy where telephone calls are used to follow up on the effect of publications, advertisements, catalogs, fliers and direct mail. As expected, excellent results have been reported at Netz Chiba and other Toyota dealers who introduced this system by applying the T-ANSMS constructed as above. In parallel to this study, the author recently studied so called "Database Marketing" where the effects of publications, advertisements, catalogs, fliers and direct mail are quantitatively analyzed to enable effective support for this system (Amasaka et al., 1998; Amasaka, 2003a, 2004).

The deployment of T-ANSMS, which involves strategic developments in the effective use of flyer advertising and other publicity media, has recently contributed to an increase in the sales share of Toyota vehicles in Japan (From 40% in 1988 to 46% in 2005) (Nikkei Business, 1999; Amasaka, 2001a,b, 2003b, 2009, 2011, 2015, 2022; Amasaka, Ed., 2012).

CONCLUSION

In this Chapter, the author has showed the effectiveness of various advertising media (mixed media) utilizing T-ANSMS named J-ANSMS employing NJ-MMM. As a suitable example of this study, particularly, the author has developed the T-ANSMS to improve the repeat customer ratio of Toyota vehicles as the CR activities by utilizing Science SQC based on Customer Science approach.

In this study, concretely, the author has dealt with the subject of improving the sales rate for replacement Toyota vehicles, which involves setting up Toyota Netz dealers in a model case. The achievements of the present study are currently being applied at Netz Chiba and other Toyota dealers.

Furthermore, as the concrete deployment of NJ-MMM the author introduces the Chapter 23 and 24 in detail based on the above Section 6.4.4 in Chapter 6.

ACKNOWLEDGMENT

The author would like to acknowledge the generous support of the following researchers: all those at Toyota Motor Corporation, and Amasaka New JIT laboratory at Aoyama Gakuin University that assisted with the research, especially, Mr. Yamaji, M., Mr. Ogura, M., Mr. Ishiguro, H., Mr. Kishimoto, M., Mr. Murayama, T., Mr. Ando, Y. and others.

REFERENCES

Amasaka, K. (2001a). Proposal of Marketing SQC to revolutionize dealers' sales activities. *Proceedings of the 16th International Conference on Production Research, Prague, Czech Public*, 1-9.

Amasaka, K. (2001b). A study of flyer advertising affect when TMS-S at Toyota. *Proceedings of the Twelfth Annual Conference of the Production and Operations Management Society, Orland, Florida*, 1-8.

Amasaka, K. (2002). New JIT, a new management technology principle at Toyota. *International Journal of Production Economics*, *80*(2), 135–144. doi:10.1016/S0925-5273(02)00313-4

Amasaka, K. (2003a). Proposal and implementation of the "Science SQC" quality control principle. *International Journal of Mathematical and Computer Modelling*, *38*(11-13), 1125–1136. doi:10.1016/S0895-7177(03)90113-0

Amasaka, K. (2003b). A demonstrative study on the effectiveness of "Television Ad." for the automotive sales. *Japan Society for Production Management, The 18th Annual Conference,* 113-116.

Amasaka, K. (2004). *Science SQC, New Quality Control Principle: The quality strategy of Toyota.* Springer-Verlag Tokyo. doi:10.1007/978-4-431-53969-8

Amasaka, K. (2005). Constructing a Customer Science Application System "CS-CIANS". *WSEAS Transactions on Business and Economics, 2*(3), 135–142.

Amasaka, K. (Ed.). (2007). New Japan Model: Science TQM. Study Group of the Ideal Situation on the Quality Management of the Manufacturing Industry, Maruzen, Tokyo.

Amasaka, K. (2007a). The validity of Advanced TMS, a strategic development marketing system utilizing New JIT. *The International Business & Economics Research Journal, 6*(8), 35–42.

Amasaka, K. (2007b). High Linkage Model "Advanced TDS, TPS & TMS": Strategic Development of "New JIT" at Toyota. *International Journal of Operations and Quantitative Management, 13*(3), 101–121.

Amasaka, K. (2009). The effectiveness of flyer advertising employing TMS: Key to scientific automobile sales innovation at Toyota, China-USA. *Business Review, 8*(3), 1–12.

Amasaka, K. (2011). Changes in marketing process management employing TMS: Establishment of Toyota Sales Marketing System, China & USA. *Business Review, 10*(7), 539–550.

Amasaka, K. (Ed.). (2012). Science TQM, new quality management principle: The quality management strategy of Toyota. Bentham Science Publishers.

Amasaka, K. (2015). *New JIT, new management technology principle*. CRC Press.

Amasaka, K. (2019). Studies on New Manufacturing Theory. *Noble. International Journal of Scientific Research, 3*(1), 1–20.

Amasaka, K. (2022). New Manufacturing Theory: Surpassing JIT (2nd ed.). Lambert Academic Publishing.

Amasaka, K., Kishimoto, M., Murayama, T., & Ando, Y. (1998). The development of "Marketing SQC" for dealers' sales operating system. *Journal of the Japanese Society for Quality Control*, 76-79.

Amasaka, K., Ogura, M., & Ishiguro, H. (2013). Constructing a Scientific Mixed Media Model for boosting automobile dealer visits: Evolution of market creation employing TMS. *International Journal of Engineering Research and Applications, 3*(4), 1377–1391.

Amasaka, K., Watanabe, M., Ohfuji, T., Matsuyuki, A., & Ebine, A. (2004). Toward the establishment of the quality management technology of the client extreme priority. *The Japan Society for Quality Control, The 74th Technical Conference*141-144.

Amasaka, K., Watanabe, M., & Shimakawa, K. (2005). Modeling of Strategic Marketing System to reflect latent customer needs and its effectiveness. *The Magazine of Research & Development for Cosmetica, Toiletries & Applied Industries Fragrance Journal, 33*(1), 72–77.

Gary, L. L., & Arvind, R. (2003). *Marketing Engineering: Computer-Assisted Marketing Analysis and Planning*. Pearson Education, Inc.

James, A. F., & Mona, J. F. (2004). *Service Management*. The McGraw-Hill Companies Inc.

Jeffrey, F. R., & Bernard, J. J. (2005). *Best face forward: Why companies must improve their service interfaces with customers.* Harvard Business School Press.

Kotler, P. (1999). *Kotler on Marketing - How to create, win, and dominate Markets.* The Free Press.

Murayama, T. (1992). Analyzing CAID. Marketing Review, 74-86.

Niiya, T., & Matsyoka, F. (Eds.). (2001). *Foundation lecture of the new advertising business.* Senden-kaigi, Co., Ltd.

Nikkei Business. (1999). Renovation of shop, product and selling method - Targeting young customers. *NETS.*

Ogura, M., Hachiya, T., & Amasaka, K. (2013). A Comprehensive Mixed Media Model for boosting automobile dealer visits. *The China Business Review, 12*(3), 195–203.

Okada, A., Kijima, M., & Moriguchi, T. (Eds.). (2001). *The mathematical model of Marketing.* Asakura-shoten.

Rickman, T., & Cosenza, R. (2007). The changing digital dynamics of multichannel marketing: The feasibility of the weblog: text mining approach for fast fashion trending. *Journal of Fashion Marketing and Management, 11*(4), 604–621. doi:10.1108/13612020710824634

Shimakawa, K., Katayama, K., Oshima, Y., & Amasaka, K. (2006). Proposal of strategic marketing model for customer value maximization. The Japan Society for Production Management, The 23th Annual Technical Conference, 161-164.

Yamaji, M., & Amasaka, K. (2009). Proposal and validity of Intelligent Customer Information Marketing Model: Strategic development of Advanced TMS. *China-USA Business Review, 8*(8), 53–62.

Section 4

Example Applications

Chapter 17
Strategic Patent Value Appraisal Model to Strengthen Corporate Technological Strategies

ABSTRACT

In this chapter, the author creates the strategic Patent Value Appraisal Model (PVAM) that contributes to corporate management technology. Improvement of "patent value" signifies engineers' value creation at work (invention). This model consists of several elements each for "inventive technique" and "patent right" in order to explain the indispensable elements of inventive technique and patent right for a strategic patent, and verified the validity of the model at Toyota and other leading corporations. Furthermore, standardization has been carried out in order to spread the effectiveness of PVAM, and Amasaka's Laboratory Patent Performance Model (A-PPM) has been created and its effectiveness will be investigated through trial application at major enterprises.

INTRODUCTION

Looking to attain a high performance business model for corporate management technology in Japanese companies, the author establishes and verifies the validity of the "New Japan Model" (NJM) using the five core elements "TDS, TPS, TMS, TIS & TJS" (Refer to Chapter 5). Among these, the intellectual property divisions are the think tank of corporate strategy and play a key role in acquiring patent rights and enhance the intellectual productivity of the company through collaborative activities employing SSTTM (Strategic Stratified Task Team Model) (Refer to Section 8.1).

In this section, therefore, the author proposes application of the strategic Patent Value Appraisal Model (PVAM) to corporate technological strategy (Amasaka, 2002, 2003a, 2007, 2009, 2015, 2022; Tsunoi et al., 2009; Anabuki, et al., 2011, Amasaka, Ed., 2012). It is generally stated that a "good patent" refers to an invention and/or a right that is useful for the entity that owns it for retaining their main business, while affecting the business of others. What is available in this field, however, is mere analysis

DOI: 10.4018/978-1-7998-8746-1.ch017

of simple metrical statistics that are available from patent information. In other words, no qualitative analysis is available of the engineers' level of consciousness about the depth of "what is a good patent?" for them, the patent inventors.

Specifically, the author undertook the task of formulating measures to define the concept of the PVAM. He defined it by grasping individual engineers' recognition of the present status of their patents as linguistic information and understanding it quantitatively utilizing Science SQC (Amasaka, 2003b, 2004). An improvement of patent value signifies engineers' value creation at work (invention). The author has established the PVAM that consists of several elements, each for a strategic patent. In recent years, the author has continued to apply the PVAM successfully and proved the validity of the proposal with advanced car manufacture Toyota and other leading corporations (Amasaka, 2009, 2015; Amasaka, Ed., 2012).

Furthermore, standardization has been carried out in order to spread the effectiveness of PVAM, and "A-PPM" (Amasaka's Laboratory Patent Performance Model) has been created and its effectiveness will be investigated through trial application at major enterprises; (Akimoto and Shimoda, 2000; Hirota and Miyamoto, 2000; Ishigaki and Niihara, 2001; Kaneta and Kuniyoshi, 2003; Amasaka, 2003a, 2009, 2015, 2022; Amasaka, Ed., 2012; Anabuki et al., 2011). This study provides new insight that contributes to the quality patent creation process for innovating intellectual property function and enhancing engineering strategy.

SIGNIFICANCE OF PATENT ACQUISITION IN CORPORATE STRATEGY

Current Situation of Patent Application in Japan

Patent application by companies accounts for a large percentage of total applications and is growing annually (Japan Patent Office, 2005). Japan had the highest share of global applications in 2005, with approximately 500,000 patent applications filed, which is about 10% of the total number of global applications. However, only 30% of the patent technology was utilized and the remaining 70% are so-called "sleeping patents".

In fact, over 40% of patent applications are "defensive patents" which does not assume any practical use of the patent. The present state, in which approximately 150,000 patents are registered annually, signifies an approximately 1 trillion yen deficit between patent maintenance costs and royalty income from patent utilization. On the other hand, although total patent application in the United States is only half that of Japan (second largest share in the world), its trade balance in the past ten years has resulted in a 17.5 trillion yen surplus. Compared with the 4.1 trillion yen deficit of the Japanese technical trade balance, the US surplus implies remarkably high patent quality (Amasaka, 2003a).

Corporate Innovation and the Significance of Patent Acquisition

The observation above confirms that the recent propagation of "Corporate innovation through competitive patents" is a matter of course (Nikkei, 2002). The current task for a company's technological strategy is to promote development of epoch-making innovative technology that will lead to quality patents and the acquisition of competitive, unique patents. A patent must be innovative and original.

Engineers should therefore develop strategic technology with epoch-making ideas (originality), which naturally necessitate the enhancement of the engineer's creativity. An engineer's pursuit of new technology toward the creation of "patent technology" encourages individual growth and corporate innovation and development (Amasaka, 2003a). As white-collar intellectual productivity also increases, "invention and acquisition of patent right" will serve as a core of the corporate strategy.

NEED FOR STRATEGIC VALUE APPRAISAL MODEL

Past Study of Qualitative Patent Value Appraisal

Generally, a "good, strategic patent" is an invention and right that advances the main business of the company, influences other companies and benefits the company itself (Amasaka et al. 1996). To the author's knowledge, no study has been presented for qualitative patent value appraisal (Kusama, 1992; Taketomi et al., 1997; Umezawa, 1999; Kevin and David, 2000; Ueno, 2003; Japan Patent Office, 2005). In many cases, evaluation of the patent application only involves statistical analysis, mainly classification and stratification of the technological development contents and characteristics of the company or inventor. There was one case of intellectual property value (cash flow) appraisal, but it only covered qualitative theory.

According to interviews (Japan Patent Attorneys Association, "Patent collateral value appraisal", 7major enterprises: Toyota, Fuji-Xerox, JFE Steel, Daikin Kogyo, NEC, Sanden and NHK Spring) and research (Japan Patent Office, "Patent evaluation index", 2005) by Kanerta (2005) and Amasaka (2007) of Amasaka New JIT Laboratory, most appraisal cases rely on intuitive and subjective evaluations and the results are likely to deviate. From this background, establishment of a consistent "patent value appraisal model" is strongly desired.

Challenge for Intellectual Property Divisions: "Qualitative Evaluation of Patent Value"

As already explained, the intellectual property divisions positioned on the outer circle play a key role in acquiring patent rights. The author researched and analyzed the example of a leading company, Toyota (97 engineers and managers from 7 divisions: 1 development, 1 design, 2 production engineering, 1 machinery, 1 research and 1 control) by using a questionnaire as shown in Table 1 and multivariate analysis (Amasaka, 2003a,b). This was done to discover the "expectations and roles of the intellectual property divisions", which are held by the managers and engineers of administrative divisions that create business model patents, and the engineering divisions that create technological patents for new technology, materials, production engineering and manufacturing methods

To clarify the question of "What is a good patent?" and how engineers and managers carry on their patent activities (what do they place priority on?) the authors conducted a questionnaire to study their consciousness. The author mainly divided questions into the "content of invented technology" and the "content of patent right." The questionnaire is based on a multiple choice reply form (marking method, 6 points: very important – 1 point: not needed at all) of eleven questions and one free opinion each. Each question consisted of a hearing conducted with the staff in charge of the intellectual property, the engineers, and the managers.

Table 1. Questionnaire on "What is a good patent?"

(Question A): What is a good patent for you? What do you routinely place priority and/or importance on to the patents?

* Please circle a number out of 1 to 6 in the following questions. (Questions may be similar to each other, but please answer them all. For any question, contact ________.)

If you have any other items than stated below you routinely feel the need for some action or measure, please state it in the space given to ⑫ and ㉔.

[1] The following are questions concerning the "Content of Inventions."

Item	Very important	Considerably important	Important	Neither important nor unnecessary	Not necessarily needed	Not needed at all
① Practicality (for the present and future)	6	5	4	3	2	1
② Cost (inexpensive, makes good profit)	6	5	4	3	2	1
③ Overthrowing established technologies (unexpectedness)	6	5	4	3	2	1
④ Merchandizability (sellable, marketable with high added value)	6	5	4	3	2	1
⑤ Can make good PR on our engineering capabilities	6	5	4	3	2	1
⑥ Performance (product performance, productivity)	6	5	4	3	2	1
⑦ Epoch-making (new, and much valuable)	6	5	4	3	2	1
⑧ Advancedness (ahead of competitors)	6	5	4	3	2	1
⑨ Idea and conception (not necessarily having to implement)	6	5	4	3	2	1
⑩ Uniqueness (differentiate others, pioneer)	6	5	4	3	2	1
⑪ General-purpose, developable and applicable	6	5	4	3	2	1
⑫ State your free opinion ( )	6	5	4	3	2	1

[2] The following are questions concerning the "Right."

Item	Very important	Considerably important	Important	Neither important nor unnecessary	Not necessarily needed	Not needed at all
⑬ Conceptual range of patent application and simple expression (unlimiting and can be widely interpreted)	6	5	4	3	2	1
⑭ Large system (combination of subsystems)	6	5	4	3	2	1
⑮ Rich with concrete cases and examples (many cases of embodiment)	6	5	4	3	2	1
⑯ Elementary technology (system component)	6	5	4	3	2	1
⑰ Coverage of patent right with multiple inventions (including improvements and peripheral points)	6	5	4	3	2	1
⑱ Possible prompt embodiment (early license fee receivable)	6	5	4	3	2	1
⑲ Toyota's embodiment technologies (confined to Toyota products)	6	5	4	3	2	1
⑳ Basic idea (nucleus of multiples, principle and rule)	6	5	4	3	2	1
㉑ Other companies are eager to acquire (others unable to bypass)	6	5	4	3	2	1
㉒ Internationally applicable (possible development overseas)	6	5	4	3	2	1
㉓ Embarrassing to others (effective in suppressing their development will)	6	5	4	3	2	1
㉔ State your free opinion ( )	6	5	4	3	2	1

As done previously, the author surveyed Toyota engineers who had acquired patents in the past in order to find out "what makes a strategic, good patent at a company" (Amasaka, 2003a). From the analysis of collected language data (cluster analysis and factor analysis), the author clarified the necessary factor structures. In general these consist of (1) Group (A): Realist (profit-minded), (2) Group (B): Advance (pioneer-minded) and (3) Group (C): Future (innovative-minded) as shown in Figure 1. Furthermore, depending on the divisions that the engineers belong to (R&D, production engineering, manufacturing) and also their job history (practicality, competitiveness, advancement), engineers' value (awareness) of patents differ. This new insight served as a stepping-stone to create the strategic Patent Value Appraisal Model (PVAM) to corporate technological strategy.

In order to achieve a breakthrough on these issues, NMT will be strategically incorporated. To be specific, the Intellectual Property Division and the engineers and managers of other indirect divisions will cooperate to (i) establish rational "patent value appraisal methods" utilizing a rule of thumb that can be shared by both divisions. As a result, the expected effect would be the establishment of a strategic patent acquisition process model to reduce the number of sleeping patents and the mistaken rejection of inventions filed by engineers and managers.

Figure 1. Grouping to common recognition of strategically "Good patent" (Cluster analysis and Factor analysis)

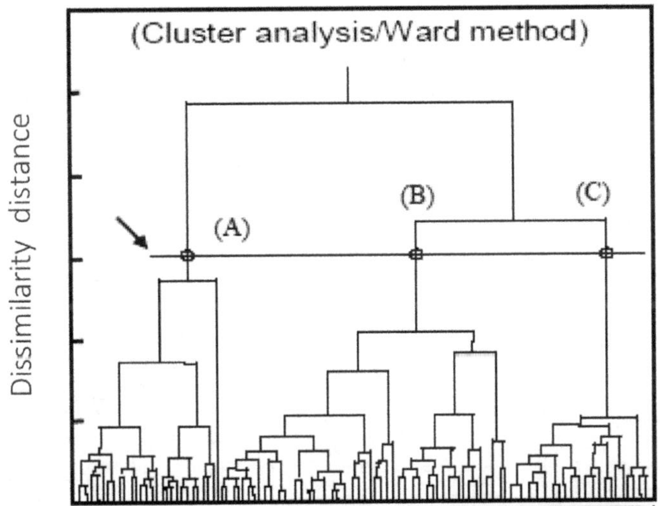

Cluster analysis	Group (A)	Group (B)	Group (C)
Total (N=97)	30%	48%	22%
A Div. (Control)	54	33	13
E Div. (Production Engineering)	30	60	10
D Div. (Development)	27	66	7
F Div. (Production Engineering)	33	42	25
C Div. (Design)	25	50	25
G Div. (Equipment Engineering)	1	56	33
B Div. (Research)	31	25	44
Factor analysis	(A) Realist group	(B) Preferential right group	(C) Futuristic group

Creation of Strategic Patent Value Appraisal Model (PVAM)

Based on the finding of the above analysis, the author has created and verified the strategic Patent Value Appraisal Model (PVAM) which assists creation of strategic patents as a core of the corporate strategy. To implement the method, the author has performed research and analysis by the same methods stated in section 17.3.2 above, targeting 248 engineers and managers of 16 divisions including research, development, design, production technology, production, and intellectual property, at 7 companies from a group of leading enterprises (Toyota, Fuji-Xerox, JFE Steel, Daikin Kogyo, NEC, Sanden and NHK spring) (Amasaka, 2003a).

Grasping the Relationship Between Good Invention and Good Patent Right

A patent is comprised of inventive technique (X) and patent right (Y). In order to identify the relationship between X and Y that is necessary for "strategic patents", the author extracted and summarized the necessary elements (explanatory variables: x_1 to x_{22}) from the language data obtained in the above survey and created a 6-point scale survey (6: extremely important, 5: very important, 4: important, 3: medium, 2: slightly unimportant, 1: unimportant) as described in Table 1.

Figure 2. Correlation between the contents of invented technology and the patent right
(Canonical correlation analysis: Scatter diagram of correspondence between components)

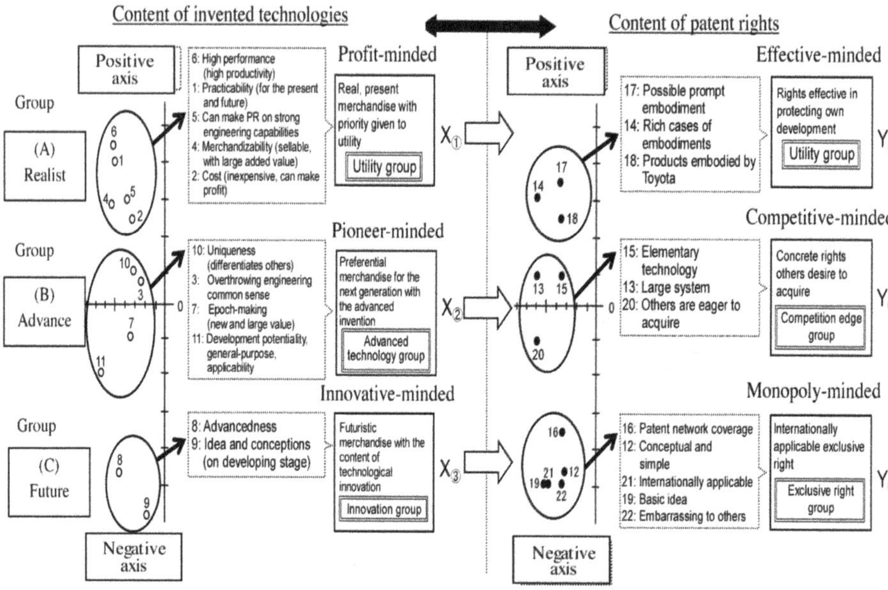

Aiming to understand the relationship between inventive technique (x_1: "practicality" to x_{11}: "expansive") and patent right (x_{12}: "scope of right is conceptual and simple" to x_{22}: prevent other companies), the author conducted a survey for Toyota engineers and managers (total 97 people from 7 divisions) and obtained the canonical correlation analysis results shown in Figure 2.

From the main component relation scatter diagram of the figure, "inventive technique" is classified into "Profit-minded: $X_{①}$ (prioritize profit with actual products at hand: x_1, x_2, x_4, x_5, x_6)," "Pioneer-minded: X (prioritize advanced technology with next-generation products: x_3, x_7, x_{10}, x_{11})," and "Innovative-minded: X_f (prioritize technical innovation with high-potential products: x_8, x_9)."

Corresponding to these groups, "patent right" is similarly classified into "effective- minded: $Y_{①}$ (effective right that protects company development: x_{14}, x_{17}, x_{18})", "competitive- minded: Y (practical right that attracts competitors: x_{13}, x_{15}, x_{20})", and "monopoly-minded: Y_f (exclusive right that is globally applicable: x_{12}, x_{16}, x_{21}, x_{22})." These findings were consistent with the experiences and techniques of the inventors, managers, patent evaluators, and patent attorneys.

Strategic Patent Appraisal Model (PVAM)

The Strategic Patent Appraisal Model (PVAM obtained from the canonical correlation analysis enabled qualitative patent value evaluation through an overall evaluation of inventive technique and patent right and also typifying the two elements into three clusters as follows:

1. Overall evaluation of inventive technique: $X=X_{\textcircled{1}}+X_{,}+X_{f}$
   (Standardization: Perfect score is 6)
   "Profit-minded": $X_{\textcircled{1}}=0.25x_{1}+0.22x_{2}+0.24x_{4}+0.20x_{5+}0.19x_{6}$
   "Pioneer-minded": $X_{,}=0.30x_{3}+0.32x_{7}+0.18x_{10}+0.20x_{11}$
   "Innovative-minded": $X_{f}=0.52x_{8}+0.48x_{9}$
2. Overall evaluation of patent right: $Y=Y\textcircled{1}+Y,+Yf$
   (Standardization:Perfect score is 6)
   "Effective-minded": $Y_{\textcircled{1}}=0.28x_{14}+0.35x_{17}+0.37x_{18}$
   "Competitive-minded": $Y_{,}=0.40x_{13}+0.38x_{15}+0.22x_{20}$
   "Monopoly-minded": $Y_{f}=0.20x_{12}+0.19x_{16}+0.18x_{19}+0.23x_{21}+0.20x_{22}$

Therefore, the author considered diffusion of the patent value appraisal model gained through the Toyota study and made revisions to the appraisal model in an approach similar to the above in cooperation with the 3 major enterprises (240 staff members in 16 divisions of Toyota, Xerox, and Daikin).

The example shown in Figure 3 is the evaluation by inventors at Xerox, JFE Steel, and Toyota (Evaluators: a, b, and c) of the inventive techniques and patent rights, expressed by radar chart. All of the inventions investigated possessed features of the contents of inventive techniques and patent rights, and received sufficient favorable comments from the inventors of the 3 enterprises.

Figure 3. Example of the qualitative evaluation map for visualized inventive technique/patent right using "PVAM"

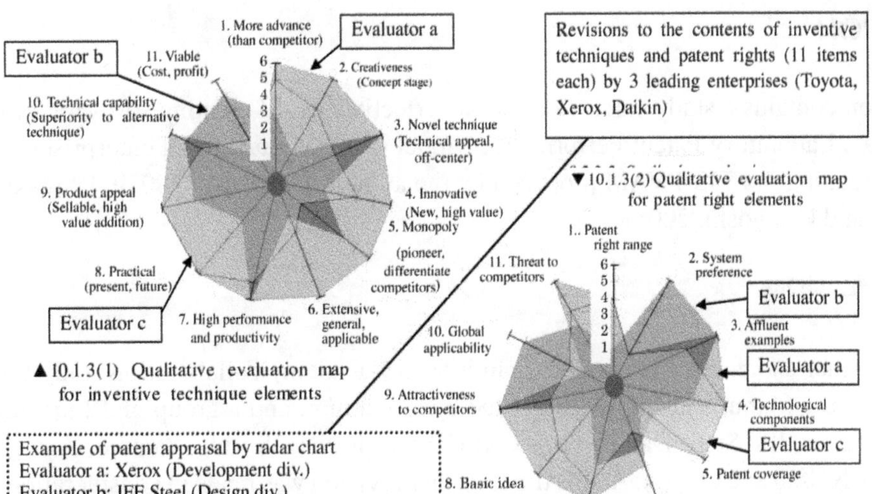

Verification of PVAM Validity

Therefore, the author will validate the effectiveness of PVAM with Toyota. Patent value evaluation can be strategically visualized from the appraisal model using PVAM as shown in Figure 4 (Amasaka, 2003a). Similarly, Figure 5 indicates an example of patent right evaluation. When the inventor applied the patent, the qualitative value of the patent had only a clearly above-average value for monopoly and competitive.

In order to raise the strategic value of the patent, the inventor revised the patent content with the support of the patent evaluator (intellectual property division) and patent attorney. Consequently, the patent's strategic value significantly increased.

Figure 4. Patent value appraisal model (PVAM) (Ex.1 Visualization of inventive technique)

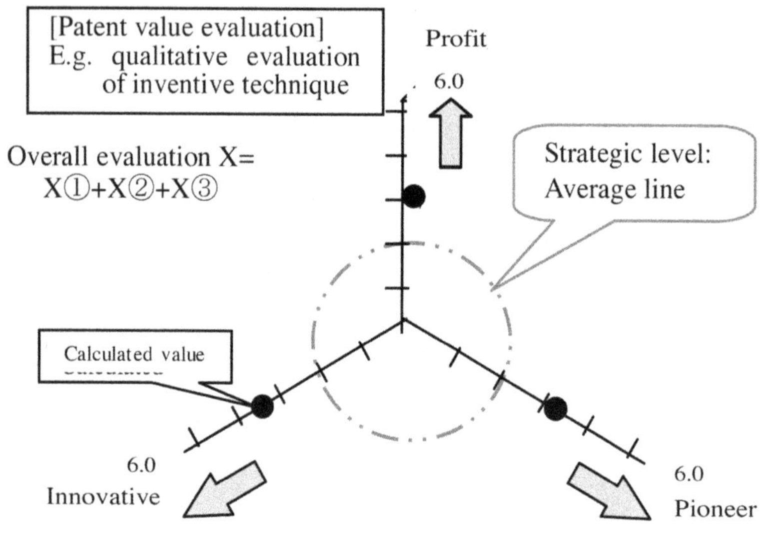

APPLICATION

This subsection contains a study carried out on the effectiveness of creating software for the standardized Amasaka's Laboratory Patent Performance Model (A-PPM) at leading enterprises, as a means of effectively spreading the TJS-PVAM proposed by the authors (Amasaka, 2003b, Ishigaki and Niihara, 2004, Kaneta and kuniyoshi, 2005).

Outline of "A-PPM"

PVAM was further expanded and applied in an industry-academy collaboration study group "Quality Management in the Manufacturing Industry" led by the author, and a group of 12 leading enterprises (Toyota, Fuji-Xerox, JFE Steel, Daikin Kogyo, NEC, Sanden, NHK Spring, Yanmar, Yokogawa-Electric, NTT-Docomo, Nissan and others). At this time, further revision was made in consideration of versatility and convenience (Amasaka, 2007).

Figure 5. Improved strategic value of patent right sing PVAM (Ex. 2 Visualization of patent right)

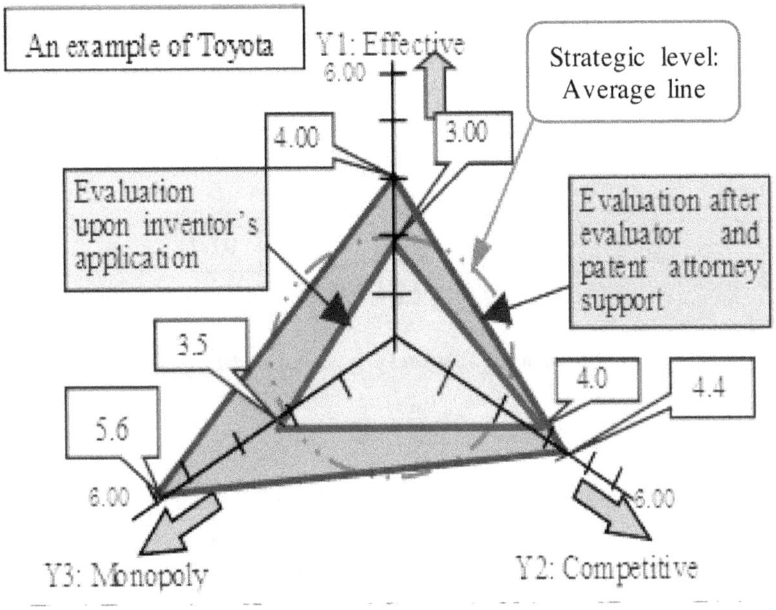

A proposal was made, as shown in Figure 6, and (1) standardized as A-PPM software. Its structure and features are clearly expressed. Reflecting the effectiveness stated previously, the contents of inventive techniques and patent rights are summarized and visualized in the combination of outer and inner circles.

For example, (2) the general evaluation of the "Effect of Technique" is specified in 3 representative items: (i) "Profit" is subcategorized as "Practical, Performance and Cost" and, in a similar manner, (ii) "Pioneer" is subcategorized into "Superior to competitor, Technique is advance and alterable," and (iii) "Innovative" is subcategorized into "Creative, Expansive, and innovation of Technique" and represented in a radar chart accordingly.

Similarly the general evaluation of (3) "Effect of Right Acquisition" is also expressed in 3 representative items: (iv) "Effective" is subcategorized into "Feasible, Product appeal, and contribution to innovation," (v) "Competitive" is subcategorized into "Attractive to competitor, Element technology, and Complete system," and (vi) "Monopoly" is subcategorized into "International, Patent coverage, and Principle discovery".

The 6 representative categories (i) to (vi) are appropriately placed under 3 well-balanced elements, which enhance the versatility and convenience of the A-PPM evaluation model. As described in Figure 3, (4) the 3 groups; namely (A) "Realist," (B) "Advanced", and (C) "Future," evaluated the contents of inventive techniques and patent rights, which are then totaled and their features (age aspect) visualized in a scale as shown in the figure.

"Realist" is the total of (i) Profit and (iv) Effective scores; "Advance" is the total of (ii) "Pioneer" and (v) "Competitive scores; and "Future" is the total of (iii) Innovative and (vi) Monopoly scores. Furthermore, these evaluations by the 3 groups were then totaled as (5) "Evaluation criteria," which is then placed on a 5-level scale (A: Excellent, B: Good, C: Fair, D: Poor and E: Bad). Rank C is the industrial average for patent application.

The A-PPM established in this manner automatically tabulates evaluation scores and expresses them in a radar chart, offering convenience to users. As a result, it is now possible to perform an appraisal of patent value for each invention in approximately 20 minutes.

Figure 6. Outline of A-PPM (Amasaka's Laboratory Patent Performance Model)

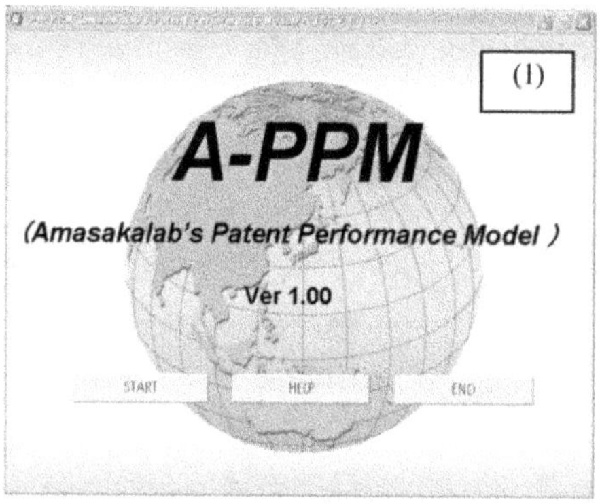

(a) Outline of "A-PPM" Software;
Data source: http://www.ise.aoyama.ac.jp/newjit/

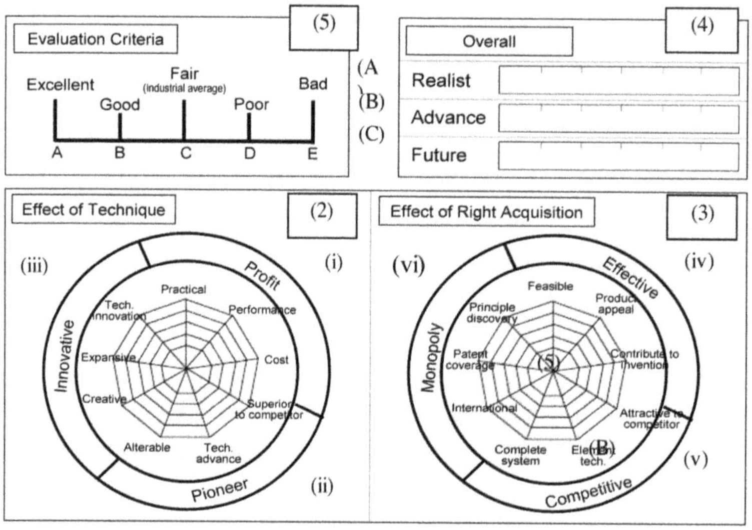

(b) "A-PPM" patent performance evaluation sheet

Validation of "A-PPM" Effectiveness

The author applied the established A-PPM and investigated its effectiveness at the previously mentioned 12 leading enterprises. Figure 7 shows the example of Fuji-Xerox. It shows in the figure that (a) evaluation upon inventor's application was later (b) supported by a patent attorney in the intellectual property division, thereby strategically enhancing the contents of inventive techniques and patent rights. Similarly, the authors are able to illustrate this effectiveness at other leading enterprises, confirming the results obtained.

CONCLUSION

In this Chapter, the author has created PVAM, a model that contributes to corporate strategy by utilizing Science TQM. In recent years, the author has continued to apply the PVAM successfully and proved the validity of the proposal at leading enterprises such as Toyota. Furthermore, in order to spread the effectiveness of PVAM, the author standardized A-PPM as software and validation of its effectiveness was made at 12 leading enterprises. This study provided a new insight that contributes to the quality patent creation process for innovating the intellectual property function and enhancing engineering strategy (Amasaka, 2007).

Figure 7. Example of improved strategic value of "Inventive Technique" and "Patent Right" using "A-PPM" by Fuji-Xerox

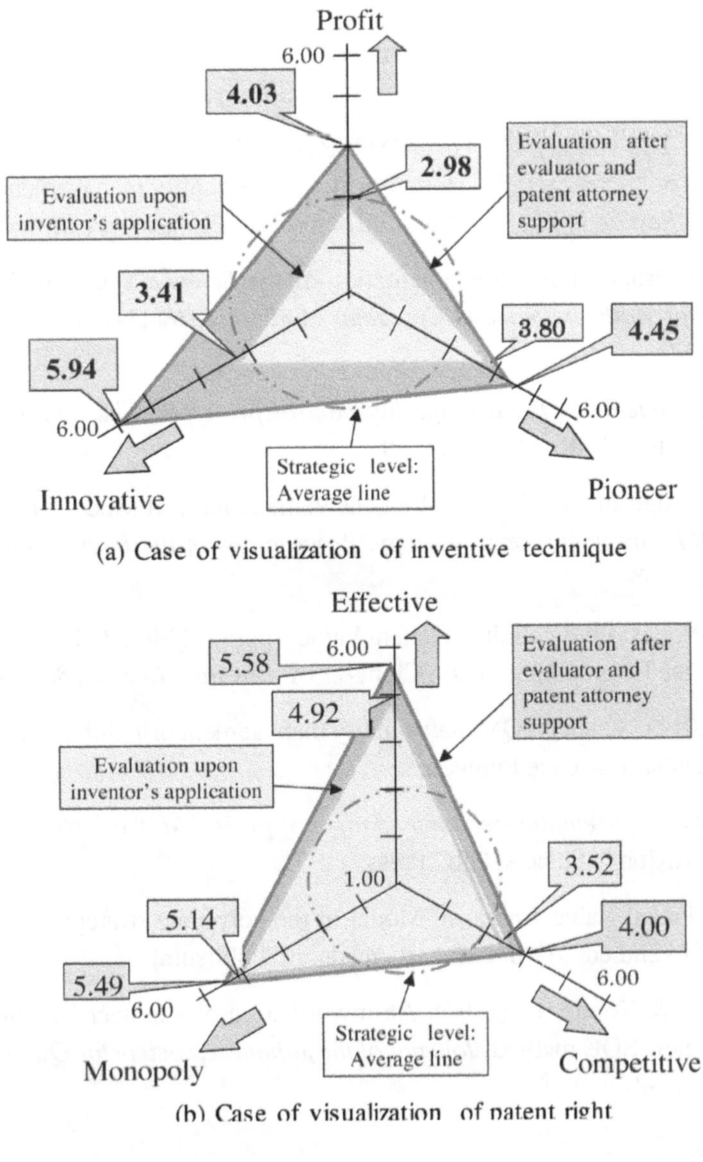

(a) Case of visualization of inventive technique

(b) Case of visualization of patent right

ACKNOWLEDGMENT

The author would like to acknowledge the generous support received from the following researchers: all those at Toyota Motor Corp., a group of 12 leading enterprises and those connected with the Amasaka New JIT laboratory at Aoyama Gakuin University that assisted with author's research, especially, Mr. Nitta, S., Kondo, K., Mr. Anabuki, K., Mr. Kaneta, T., Mr. Hirota, M., Mr. Miyamoto, T., Miss. Ishigaki, K, Mr. Niihara, K., Mr. Kuniyoshi, M., and others.

REFERENCES

Akimoto, S., & Shimoda, S. (2000). *Modeling of the conceptual composition of invention and right: Research on objectification of the patent value by opinion poll of engineers* (Bachelor thesis). School of Science and Engineering, Amasaka New JIT Laboratory.

Amasaka, K. (2002). *Quality of engineer's work and significance of patent application.* The 2nd patent seminar, Aoyama Gakuin University, Research Institute, Shibuya, Tokyo.

Amasaka, K. (2003a). The validity of "TJS-PPM", Patent Value Appraisal Method in the corporate strategy: Development of "Science TQM", a new principle for quality management (Part 3). *The Japan Society for Production Research, The 17th Annual Conference, Gakushuin University,* 189-192.

Amasaka, K. (2003b). Proposal and Implementation of the *Science SQC*, quality control principle. *International Journal of Mathematical and Computer Modelling*, *38*(11-13), 1125–1136. doi:10.1016/S0895-7177(03)90113-0

Amasaka, K. (2004a). *Science SQC, new quality control principle, The quality strategy of Toyota.* Springer-Verlag. doi:10.1007/978-4-431-53969-8

Amasaka, K. (2007). Proposal and Validity of Patent Value Appraisal Model "TJS-PVAM"- Development of "*Science TQM*" in the corporate strategy. *Proceedings of the International Conference Risk, Quality and Reliability*, 1-8.

Amasaka, K. (2009). Proposal and Validity of Patent Value Appraisal Model "TJS-PVAM"-Development of "Science TQM" in the Corporate Strategy, China-USA. *Business Review*, *8*(7), 45–56.

Amasaka, K. (Ed.). (2012). Science TQM, new quality management principle: The quality management strategy of Toyota. Bentham Science Publishers.

Amasaka, K. (2015). *Strategic employment of the Patent Appraisal Method: New JIT, new management technology principle.* Taylor & Francis, CRC Press.

Amasaka, K. (2022). Patent Value Appraisal Model in the corporate strategy. In New Manufacturing Theory: Surpassing JIT (2nd ed.). LAP Lambert Academic Publishing.

Amasaka, K., Nitta, S., & Kondo, K. (1996). An investigation of engineers' recognition and feelings about good patents by new SQC method. *Journal of the Japanese Society for Quality Control, The 52nd Technical Conference,* 17-24.

Anabuki, K., Kaneta, H., & Amasaka, K. (2011). Proposal and validity of Patent Evaluation Method "A-PPM" for corporate strategy. *International Journal of Management & Information Systems*, *15*(3), 129–137. doi:10.19030/ijmis.v15i3.4649

Hirota, M., & Miyamoto, T. (2000). *A proposal of the patent measuring model "A-PAT" (Ama-lab"s patent) as the corporate strategy* (Bachelor thesis). School of Science and Engineering, Aoyama Gakuin University, Amasaka New JIT Laboratory.

Ishigaki, K., & Niihara, K. (2001). *A study for objective evaluation of patent value – Proposal and validity of A-PPM* (Bachelor thesis). School of Science and Engineering, Aoyama Gakuin University, Amasaka New JIT Laboratory.

Japan Patent Office. (2005). *Patent Evaluation Index*. http:// www.jpo.go.jp/

Kaneta, H. (2005). *The research on construction of the patent evaluation model* (Master's thesis). Graduate School of Science and Engineering, Aoyama Gakuin University, Amasaka New JIT Laboratory.

Kaneta, Y., & Kuniyoshi, M. (2003). *A Study on Establishment of the Qualitative Valuation Modeling of Patent Value* (Bachelor thesis). School of Science and Engineering, Aoyama Gakuin University, Amasaka New JIT Laboratory.

Kevin, G. R., & David, K. (2001, July). Discovering New Value in Intellectual Property, Diamond. *Harvard Business Review*, 98–113.

Kusama, M. (1992). Analysis of Engineering Trend Utilizing Patent Information. *The 29th Information Science Technology Conference*, 177-182.

Nikkei. (2002). *Corporate Innovation through Competitive Patent*. Author.

Taketomi, T., Horiguchi, Y., & Hirabayashi, T. (1997). Evaluation of Intellectual Property Value and Recovery of Invested Resources. *R & D Management*, *2*, 32–43.

Tsunoi, M., Anabuki, K., Yamaji, M., & Amasaka, K. (2009). A study of Patent Evaluation Method "A-PPM" for Corporate Strategy. *The 11th Annual Conference of Japan Society of Kansei Engineering, Shibaura Institute of Technology*, 1-4.

Ueno, H. (2003). Formation of a Strategic Patent Group, and a Patent Portfolio Strategy. *Japan Marketing Journal*, *80*, 25–35.

Umezawa, K. (1999). Miscellaneous Impressions of Intellectual Property Rights. *Intellectual Property Management*, *49*(3), 353–36.

Chapter 18
Automobile Exterior Color Design Development Model:
Partnering of Both the Auto-Maker and the Paint-Maker

ABSTRACT

The idea of global quality competition in the auto industry has made developing body colors that best match the exterior design of vehicle models a critical factor in terms of product strategy, as color selection has the ability to affect consumer purchasing behavior. The rapid global advancement currently underway brings with it increasingly diverse and complex personal values and subjective impressions, which are difficult to fully grasp. In this chapter, the author has concluded that traditional design processes, which are implicit and rely heavily on designer intuition and experience-based rules of thumb, must be reformed. To achieve this, the author has created the Automobile Exterior Color Design Development Model (AECD-DM) partnering of auto-maker and paint-maker. Specifically, to affect purchasing customer behavior, the author has developed the AECD-DM to body color development at a specific company and has obtained the given results.

INTRODUCTION

The idea of global quality competition in the auto industry has made developing body colors that best match the exterior design of vehicle models a critical factor in terms of product strategy, as color selection has the ability to affect consumer purchasing behavior. The rapid global advancement currently underway brings with it increasingly diverse and complex personal values and subjective impressions, which are difficult to fully grasp. However, manufacturers that cannot accurately identify these consumer values and subjective impressions and incorporate the corresponding elements in their vehicle designs will find it difficult to remain competitive in the market.

In Chapter 13, the author developed and verified the effectiveness of their Customer Science Application System "CS-CIANS" (- Customer Information Analysis and Navigation System), a business

DOI: 10.4018/978-1-7998-8746-1.ch018

approach that scientifically indexes customer quality demands employing Advanced TDS through "Automobile Exterior Design Model using Customer Science principle" (Amasaka, 2002, 2005, 2007a,b) (Refer to Chapter 6 and 13).

The author has therefore concluded that traditional design processes, which are implicit and rely heavily on designer intuition and experience-based rules of thumb, must be reformed. To achieve this, the author creates the "Automobile Exterior Color Design Development Model" (AECD-DM) by partnering of both auto-maker and paint-maker using "Strategic Stratified Task Team: Joint Task 7" and Science SQC (Amasaka, 2003a,b; Miyake and Muto, 2010; Muto, et al., 2011, 2013) (Refer to Chapter 5 and 8).

On a concrete target, to affect purchasing customer behavior, the author first utilizes statistical modeling to visualize the factors involved in successfully meeting customer quality demands. Then, partnering (joint efforts) of auto-maker and paint-maker, they create indexes that allow auto-makers to develop a business approach that will align the concepts and approach of divisions involved in exterior design and color development. Second, linkages are forged between the identified factors of success and the indexes.

The author then develops the AECD-DM to body color development at a specific company and obtain the given results (Miyake and Muto, 2010; Muto, et al., 2011; Amasaka, 2015).

BACKGROUND

The author presented the study of "Automobile Exterior Design Model using "Customer Science Principle" which the author showed to Chapter 13. Then, the author focuses on the optimization of "Automobile exterior color design" (body color) which constitutes the typical core technologies in this study.

Prior research on this topic has been presented by Arima (2002), Kawamura (2003), Amasaka (2007a,b), Amasaka and Yamaji (2008), Takebuchi et al., 2012 and others (Amasaka, 1995; Amasak, et al., 1999; Amasaka & Nagaya, 2002; Fujieda et al., 2007: Yamaji et al., 2009).

However, the work of these authors focused on just a portion of the tasks associated with developing vehicle body colors. As clearly shown by "Chapter 13", in "Vehicle's exterior design" , the optimal matching with "Profile design (proportion) , Form and Color matching" is indispensable, Therefore, research that utilizes a comprehensive business approach involving both paint manufacturers and automakers has yet to be carried out.

Therefore, in an implementation stage, the author strategically applies the "Customer Science Principle" application system "CS-CIANS" constructed by Amasaka (2005). CS-CIANS is a method for generating customer value in a way that recognizes the necessity of reforming design work processes with product planning departments, with the aim of making customer intentions scientific. It is a networking system that includes a navigation system for analyzing customer information (via multivariate analysis) and analysis case examples.

The author expanded this model in order to create a business approach model from a perspective that includes both paint-maker manufacturers and automakers.

RESEARCH METHODS

To understand how vehicle body color development processes were currently being carried out, the authors conducted an on-site investigation of color designers at three auto-makers and three paint-makers (manufacturers) by "Partnering based on the Strategic Stratified Task Team: Joint Task 7" and Science SQC" (Miyake and Muto, 2010; Muto et al., 2010; Amasaka, 2015).

On-Site Investigations

The investigation revealed that vehicle body color development was carried out in six steps.

1. In first step, a market survey was conducted.
2. In second step, the product planning department came up with a product concept.
3. In third step, an exterior designer at the auto-maker then came up with the "exterior design and shape" (profile design and form) of the vehicle.
4. In fourth step, the automaker had a color designer come up with a color concept.
5. In fifth step, the automaker's color designer then sent a request to the color designer at the paint manufacturer asking them to develop the paint. This step involved repeated discussion about specific colors between the two color designers.
6. In six step, the designers communicate their color concept to a technician (a paint mixologist) who actually mixes and develops the paint.

However, there are problems with each process. Sometimes the designers cannot come to a subjective agreement about the paint, or there are variations in workflow because they are basing their decisions on intuition and rules of thumb. The reality is that designers find it quite difficult to gain a concrete understanding of customer needs.

Visualizing Problem Areas and Work Processes

Problems in the current work process identified through the on-site investigations were converted into binary data using problems as samples and keywords as variables, and then distributed using a "Cluster Analysis". The same data was also subjected to a "Principle Component Analysis" (PCA) using "First principle component (horizontal axes) and Second principle component" (vertical axes), where the distribution was plotted and grouped into clusters on the same scatter diagram as shown in Figure 1.

Data on the color development process was also grouped as shown in Figure 2, making the relationship between problem areas and the work process clear.

A closer look at the groups of relevant data in Figure 1 and Figure 2 reveals that problems with "Information (6)" occur during the "Market survey [1]" stage. The figures also show heavy overlap between the "Vehicle color designer [2]" and "Paint designer [3]" groups, indicating that both designers are grappling with the same problems.

Figure 1 reveals that those problems have to do with "Indicators and standards (3)", instincts, tricks of the trade, and "Personal experience (7)", and gaps between the roles of "Different departments (Gaps of department) (8)".

At the same time, it is clear that "Among color designers [4]" groups, there are problems associated with "Shared aims (1)" and "Gaps in subjective impression (4)". For "Paint mixologists [5]" and during the "Prototype evaluation [6]" stage, problems are occurring with "Technological constraints (2)" and "indicators and standards (3)".

Figure 1. Group into clusters

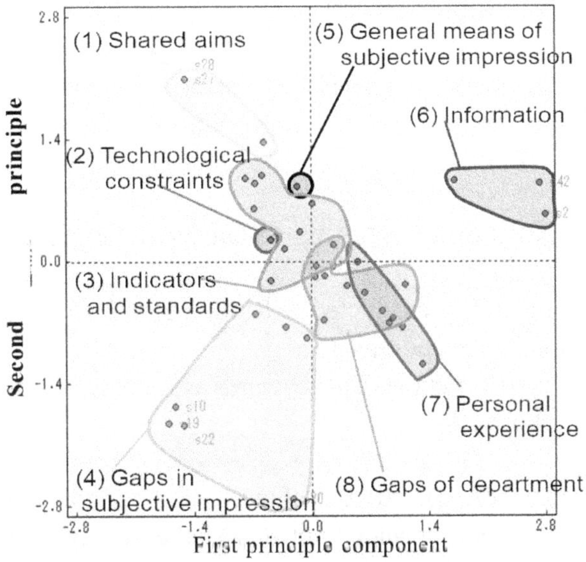

Figure 2. Group into the color development process

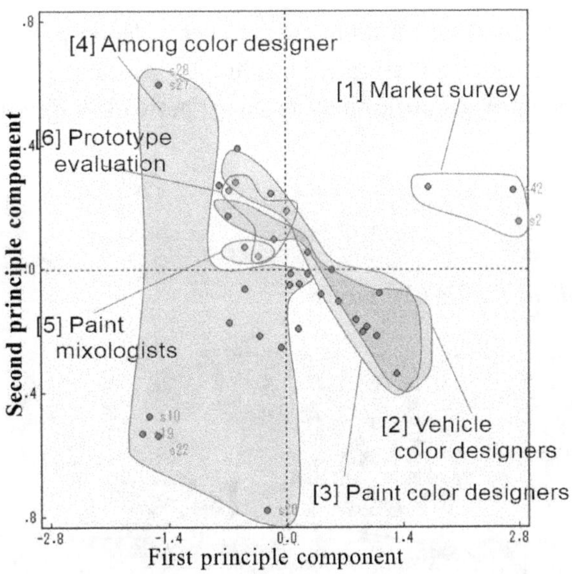

Visualizing success factors and elements

Fact-Finding Research at Manufacturers

A series of shared question items were developed for automakers and paint manufacturers based on each question. There were 7 valid responses collected from paint-makers (-manufacturers) and 12 collected from auto-makers.

Identifying Success Factors and Elements at Different Manufacturers

The results of the fact-finding survey conducted in Section 18.3.3.1 were converted into binary data using the same method outlined in Section 18.3.2.

Success key factors were used as samples and keywords as variables and then the data was distributed using a cluster analysis, as follows;

1. The analysis revealed that the five factors that allowed paint manufacturers to successfully create the product quality their customers demanded were (1) Market surveys, (2) Technological constraints, (3) Communication, (4) Scientific analysis, and (5) Collaboration with other departments.
2. Auto-makers identified six success factors: (1) Market surveys, (2) Technological constraints, (3) communication, (4) Scientific analysis, (5) Collaboration with other departments, and (6) Evaluations and standards.

Furthermore, "Text mining" was then used in order to get a clearer picture of the core elements involved in each success factor through an "Extraction example" as shown in Figure 3.

In Figure 3, the core elements of scientific analysis using "network diagram in Text mining" extracted the typical each factor as follows;

Figure 3. Extraction example of the Text Mining

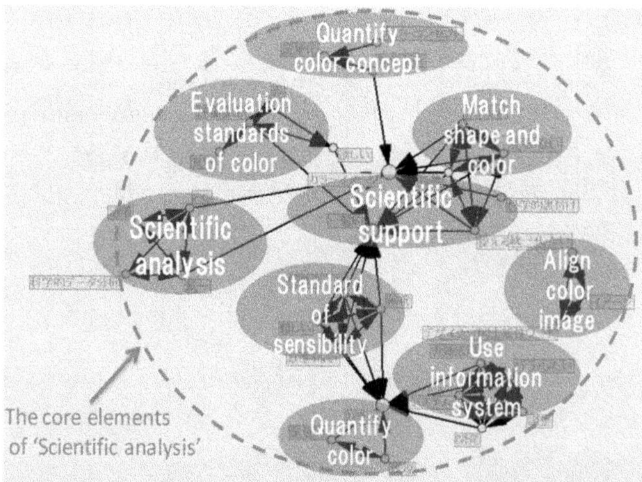

1. Quality: "Quality color concept", "Match shape and color", and "Align color image"
2. Methods: "Evaluation standards of color", "Standard of sensibility" and "Use information system" and "Support analysis"

In this way, a word network diagram was used to identify the connections among different elements and the strength of these different connections was calculated using partial correlation coefficients between the indicated elements. In Figure 3, a partial correlation coefficient of 0.7 or above was assigned the indicator +++, 0.6–0.7 was assigned a ++, and 0.5–0.6 a +.

Visualizing Success Factors and Elements at Both Manufacturers

In this subsection, the author shows the "Visualizing success factors and elements at both manufacturers". Figure 4 shows the results of scientific analysis for paint manufacturers as the typical network diagrams.

In Figure 4, the author shows the five factors: in order to successfully create the product quality for customers demanded: Market surveys, Technological constraints, Communication, Scientific analysis, and Collaboration with other departments.

Figure 4. Success factors and elements at paint manufactures using Text mining

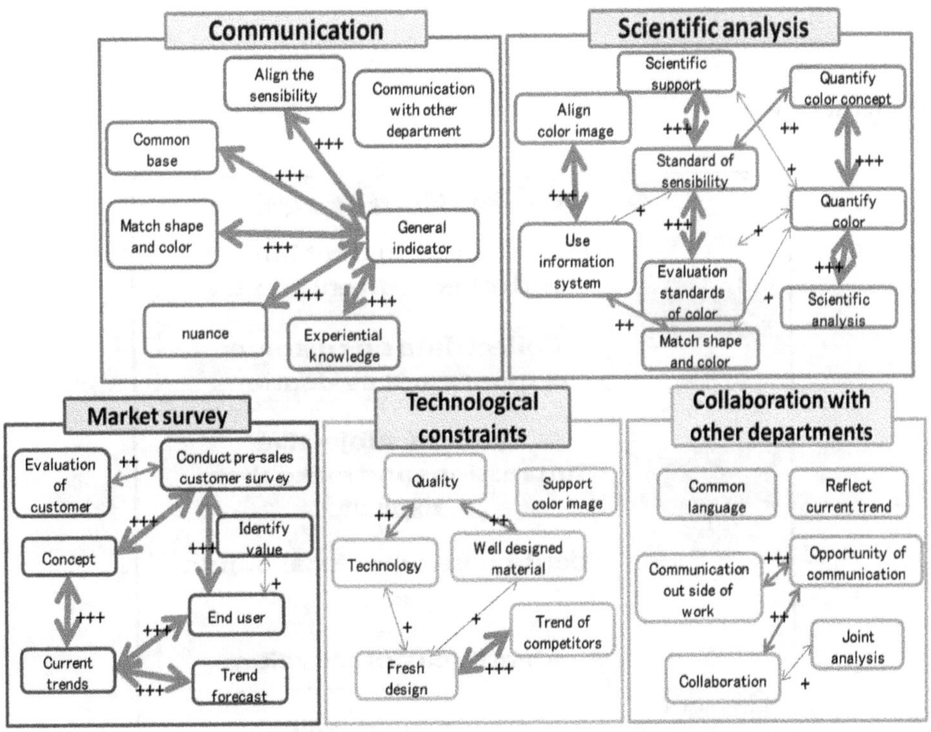

Actually, the author extracted the each success factor in Figure 3 as follows;

1. Market survy: Conduct pre-conduct customer survey, Evaluation of customer, Concept, Current trends, Trend forcast, End user and Identifyvalue
2. Technological constraints: Quality, Technology, Well design material, Fresh design Trend of competitors and support color image
3. Communication: Align the sensibility, Common base, Match shape and color, nuance, Experiential knowledge, General indicator and Communication with other department
4. Scientific analysis: Scientific support, Standard of sensibility, Evaluation standards of color, Match shape and color, Align color image, Use information system, Quality color concept, Quality color and Scientific analysis
5. Collaboration with other departments: Common langage, Communication out side of work, Collaboration, Jpint analysis, Oppotunity of communication and Reflect current trend

In this way, the success factors and elements identified at the different types of manufacturers were visualized using a single figure. They were then combined into one using all of the partial coefficients of 0.7 or greater (assigned the indicator +++).

Using the example of the scientific analysis indicated in Figure 4 for instance, partial correlation coefficients for "quantifying color concepts", "quantifying color", and "scientific data analysis" are 0.7 or more.

Figure 5. Market survey

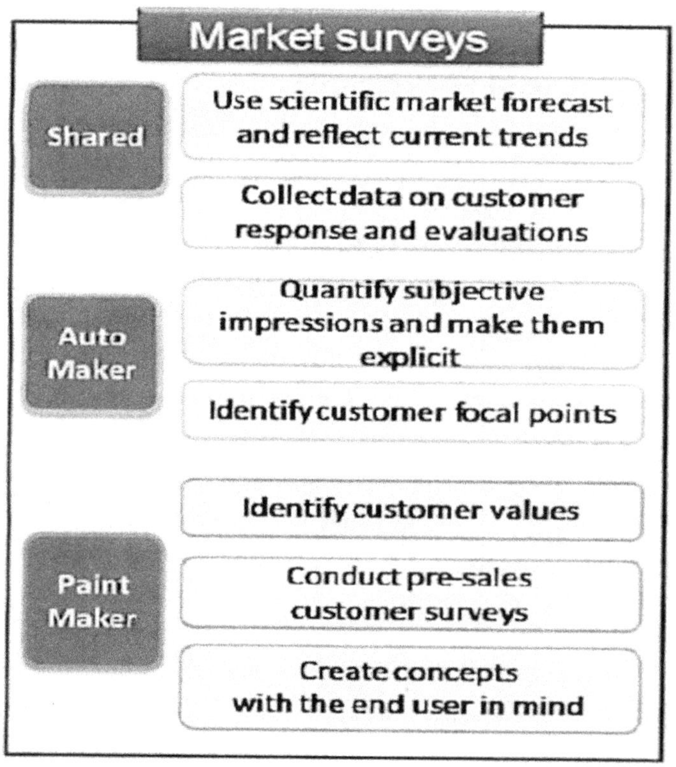

Figure 6. Communication

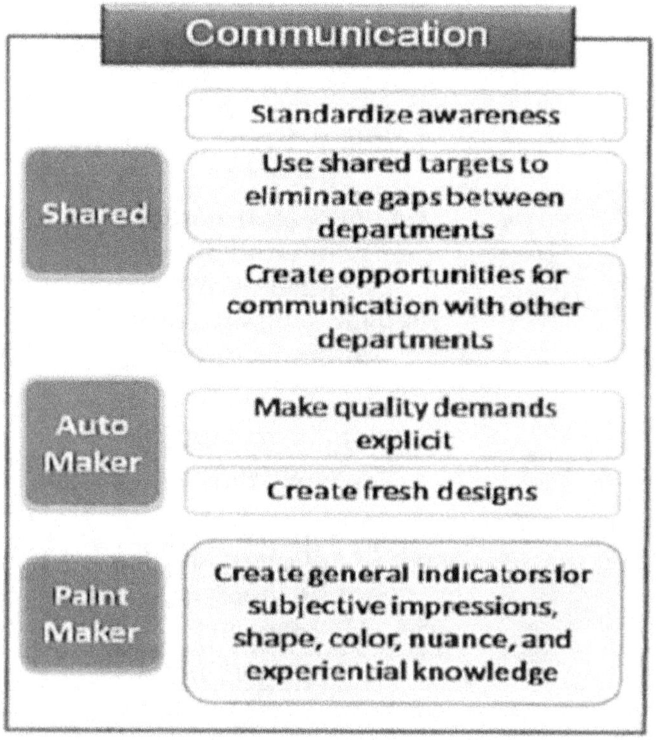

Figure 7. Scientific analysis

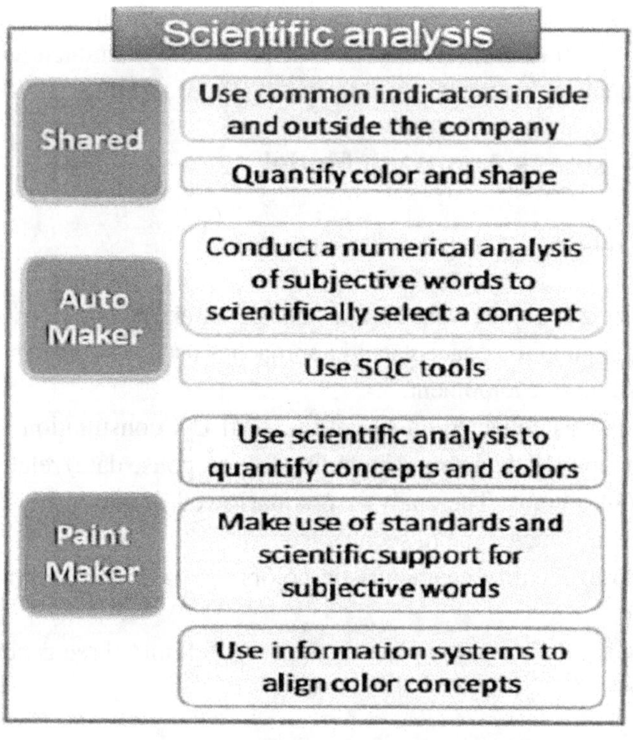

Figure 8. Collaboration with other departments

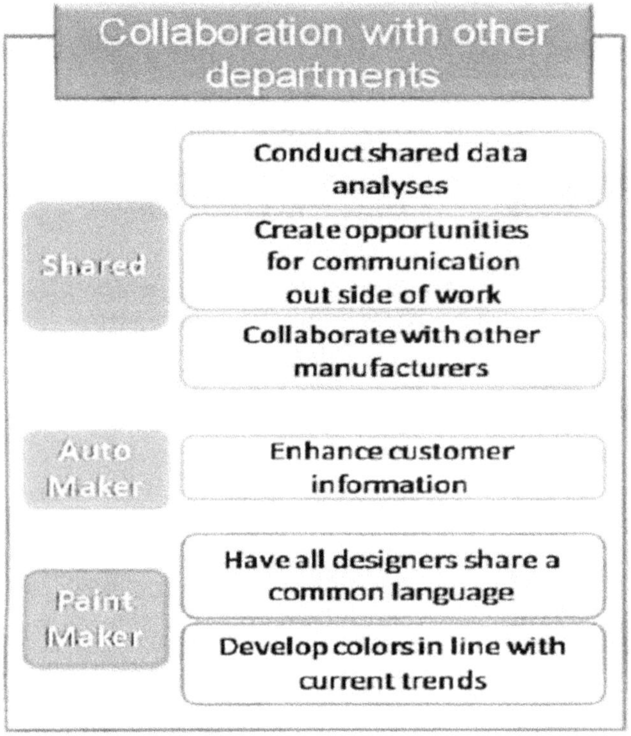

These are thus combined into a single success factor: "quantifying color concepts and colors through scientific analysis".

Next, the elements identified during this process are visualized in the three separate categories ((i)-(iii)) as shown in Figure 15-10 inside: (i) shared elements at both manufacturers, (ii) elements only at automakers, and (ii) elements only at paint manufacturers (Refer to Muto and Miyake (2010) in detail).

Constructing the Business Approach Model

1. Indexing customer values

In this subsection, customer values were used as a basis for an indexing procedure aimed at gaining a business approach that aligned the concepts and approaches used by departments involved in vehicle exterior design and body color development.

To do this, survey data was collected on-site at the AMLUX consultation space owned by Toyota Motor Corporation. A total of 417 data items (including free response data) related to vehicle body color were taken from about 6000 items. The analysis was narrowed down to the 134 free response items related to the most common vehicle type (a sedan).

Text mining was used to identify characteristic colors for each age group. An analysis was then conducted for each group.

The customer opinion results for participants in their 40s fell into three general groups:

Figure 9. Information / Technology

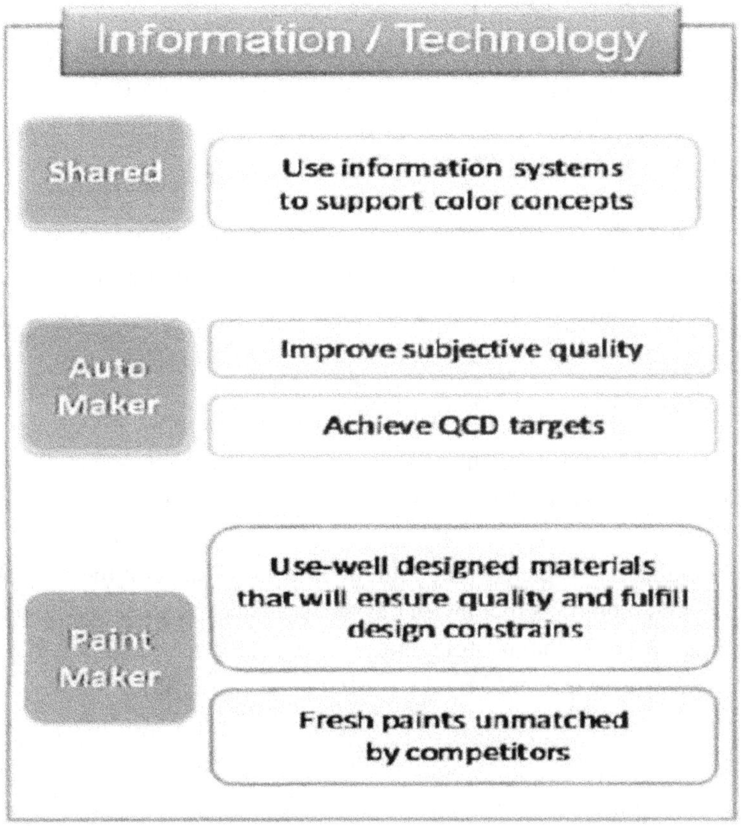

Figure 10. Evaluation / Standards

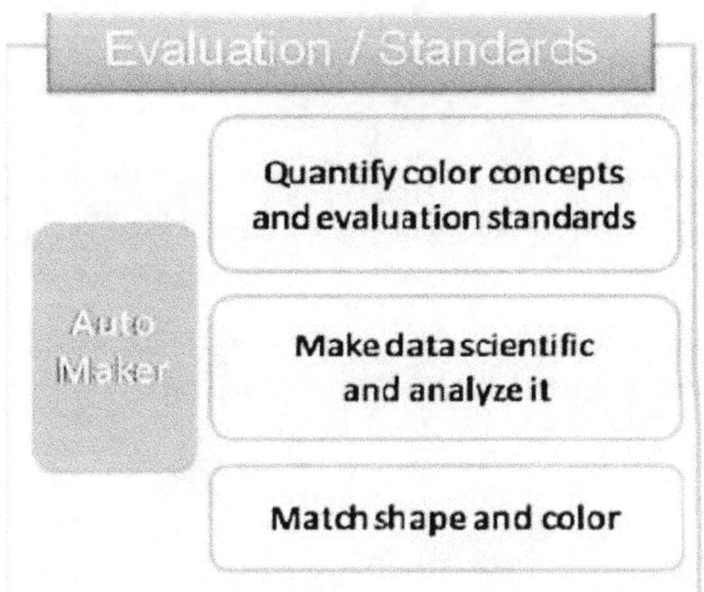

(1) opinions on existing colors, (2) color requests, and (3) awareness of color when purchasing a vehicle. An analysis of data from other age groups showed that all customer opinions could be divided into these three categories. These were converted into three indicators demonstrating customer values: (1) color evaluation, (2) color preference, and (3) focal points during purchase.

Organizing the opinions of huge numbers of customers into these three indicators should allow all departments to align their concepts and approaches.

Figure 11 shows the results of this analysis in its 40s.

2. Constructing an Automobile Exterior Color Development Approach Model by partnering both the auto-maker and paint-maker

Using the success factors and elements identified in Figure 5-Figure 10 inside and linking them using the three indicators developed in subsection 18..3.4(1), the Automobile Exterior Color Development Approach Model (AECD-AM) by partnering of auto-maker and paint-maker as shown in Figure 12 was developed with the aim of generating the quality that customers demand.

Then, the author describes the outline of AECD-AM in next Section 18.4. This business approach model adds three new indicators to the current vehicle body color development work process shown in the center of the figure, and then links them with the success factors and elements from Figure 5-Figure 10. The result is a set of guidelines that manufacturers can use to meet the quality needs of their customers (Amasaka, 2015) (Refer to Muto and Miyake (2010) in detail).

Figure 11. Analysis example in its 40s

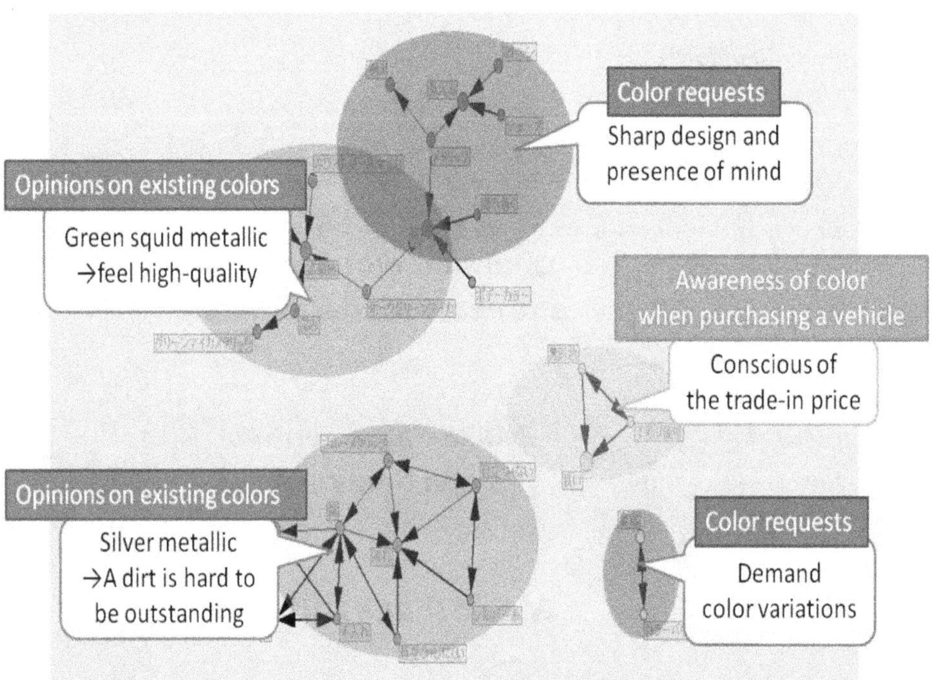

APPLICATION

Developing above-mentioned AECD-DM, the author has conducted a preference survey on young people's lifestyles and determined the elements most desired by young people when choosing automobile exterior colors.

Figure 12. Automobile Exterior Color Development Approach Model (AECD-AM) by partnering both the auto-maker and paint-maker

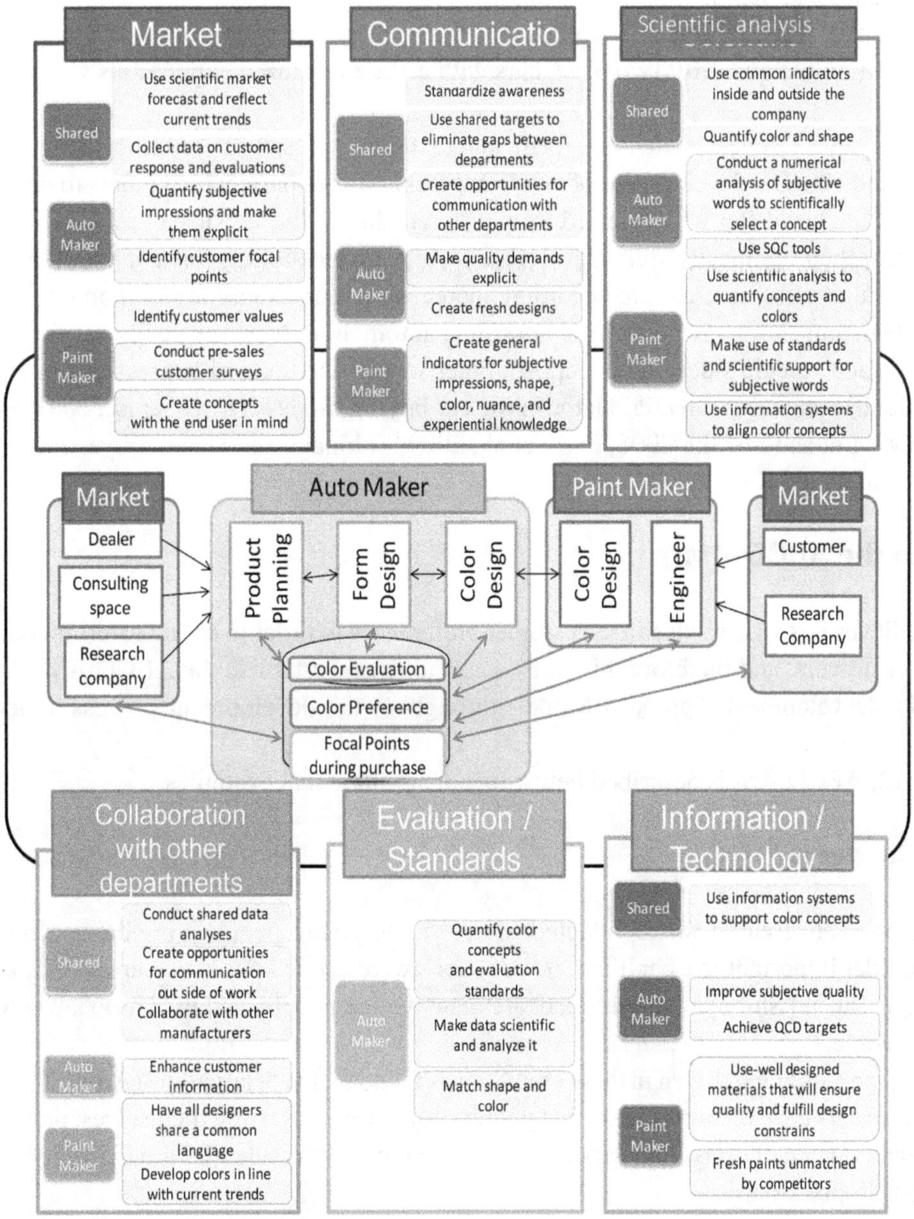

The author then determined the color elements that have most influence on customers aesthetically, and conducted correspondence analysis on the preferences and color elements using Science SQC (Amasaka, 2003a,b). The findings were subsequently used in the development of automobile exterior colors.

Importance of Textual Expressions of Automobile Exterior Colors

Color can be described in terms of three elements: hue, luminosity and intensity. However, automobile exterior colors are recognized not only in terms of these three elements, but also in terms of other qualities, including elements such as the intensity of reflected light, the cityscape reflected in the colors, metallic appearance and depth.

Qualities such as depth and metallic appearance are textural expressions that are unique to automobiles, and are difficult to quantify. Two black cars with different textural expressions will give different impressions.

Automobiles have a three-dimensional form, and textural expressions are important in making this unique form stand out. The development of new paint technologies has enabled paints to be designed so their brightness and hue differ when viewed from different angles through use of reflective materials in the paints to vary their luminosity. Such developments in paint technology make it possible to achieve a variety of textural expressions, and are becoming increasingly important for automobiles.

Automobile manufacturers seek to create appealing automobiles by strategically varying the textural expressions of each vehicle's design concept. In other words, the textural expressions in automobiles constitute a significant and influential factor in the car buying process (Koga, et al., 2003; Fujieda, etr al., 2007; Kawasumi and Suzuki, 2008; Park, et al., 2009; Tokinaga and Utsunomiya, 2009; Watanabe and Jo, 2009; Yamo and Kato, 2010).

Creation of the AECD-AM

The author believes it is vital to visualize customer preferences in order to create exterior colors that are appealing to customers, and therefore this study seeks to firmly establish the AECD-AM (Automobile Exterior Color Development Approach Model) throughout the development process as indicated in Figure 12.

In Figure 12, AECD-AM is described below together with actual examples.

1. Market Research (Step 1)

In Step 1, market research was conducted to determine young people's preferences and find out what they consider important in a car. First, observations were carried out in two areas of Tokyo, Japan: between "Harajuku and Shibuya", where there are many young people, and in "Hiroo", where there are fewer young people.

Comparing the cars being driven in these areas, it was found that in "Harajuku" (Around Omotesando, Shibuya-ku), the cars gave the impression that young people were asserting themselves, preferring vivid colors that stand out. In contrast, the cars in "Hiroo" (High class residential area, Shibuya-ku) gave a more luxurious impression.

Figure 13. Automobile Exterior Color Design Approach Model

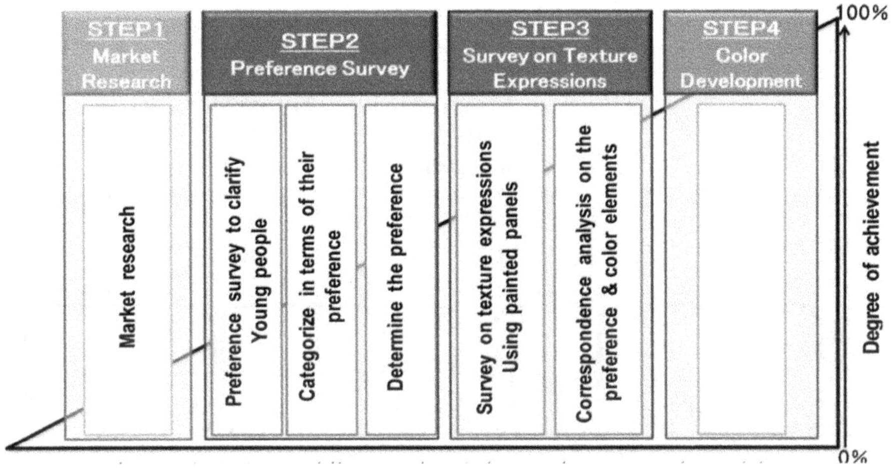

The cars had shiny surfaces displaying opaque, grainy colors with depth, and there was a preference for basic colors such as black and silver. In both cases, it was found that color preferences varied according to both cityscape and lifestyle.

2. Preference Survey (Step 2)

In Step 2, the authors conducted a preference survey to clarify young people's lifestyles and their perspectives concerning automobiles.

First, a preference survey sheet was created to determine the preferences of young people targeted by the survey. Participants were asked to evaluate the following items on a seven-point scale: (1) Four items concerning interest/enthusiasm for automobiles, and (2) 15 items concerning preferred automobile designs (preferences) (Refer to Appendix 18.A).

They were then asked to comment freely on (3) hobbies/interests, (4) most read fashion magazines, and (5) favorite colors. Four collage panels each were made for men and women based on fashion trends, and participants were asked which trends they most identified with. This survey was aimed at men and women in their twenties, and answers were obtained from a total of 74 men and women.

Based on the results of the preference survey, the following analysis was conducted to clarify car-related preferences. First, cluster analysis was conducted using the data on preferences gained from the seven-point evaluation as shown in Figure 13.

The differences in respondents' preferences were categorized into five groups and the groups were labeled as follows according to the respondents' particular interests and preferences: practicality, uninterested, self-expression, external appearance and functionality.

Based on the free opinions given, the characteristics of each group showed that respondents in the "practicality" group prefer practical compact cars, and those in the "uninterested" group show little interest in cars at all. Those in the "external appearance" group prefer stylish exteriors that stand out, while those in the "functionality" group focus more on performance. Respondents in the "self-expression" group show a strong tendency to prefer cars that help to express their own status or image, and members

Figure 14. Categorizing preferences using Cluster Analysis

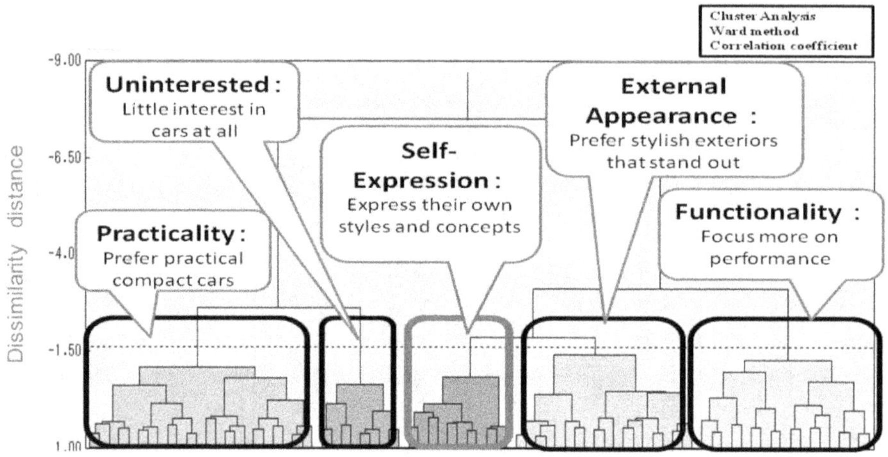

of this group tend to have the most interest in cars. This study focuses on developing exterior colors for people who value "self-expression".

Second, moreover, Principle Component Analysis (PCA) was conducted to clarify which aspects of automobile design are desired by each group. Having clarified each group's car-related preferences in this way, the author was able to determine the four preferences most important to people who value "self-expression" (classy, luxurious, dignified and sporty).

The author also found that respondents who said they value "self-expression" tend to have a "boy-ish or casual style" and prefer "red, black and brown". Accordingly, it is important to narrow down the colors to "red, black and brown", and focus on the above four preferences when developing exterior colors for people who value "self-expression". To successfully achieve this, it is necessary to determine the extent to which color influences customers aesthetically, and therefore a survey was conducted on textural expressions in Step 3.

3. Survey on Textural Expressions (Step 3)

A survey was conducted on textural expressions in order to quantify the extent to which automobile exterior colors influence customers aesthetically. First, the authors identified which of the many elements of color have the most influence on customers aesthetically. In addition to the three elements of color (hue, luminosity and intensity), the author also quantitatively identified three textural expressions unique to automobile colors (shine, opacity and graininess).

Shine is the intensity of reflected light, opacity is the variance in brightness between areas where light does or doesn't fall, and graininess is the size of particles giving the color its grainy appearance. Thus, a total of six elements of color (hue, luminosity, intensity, shine, opacity and graininess) were identified.

Next, the author conducted a survey using 11 painted panels with varying color elements to determine how customers are influenced aesthetically by color variations including the above textural expressions. For this study, the panels were shaped and painted like car panels to show the relevant textural expressions.

First, the painted panels were selected. Three panels were initially prepared for the survey, using three colors (red, black and brown) with minimal opacity and graininess. Then, a further eight panels

Table 1. Six elements of Color of Each Panel

Panel No.	Hue (H45°)	Luminosity (L45°)	Intensity (C45°)	Shine (60°)	Opacity (L15-110°)	Graininess (HG)
1	35.00	83.89	41.17	1.79	0	89.90
2	16.79	39.00	32.00	33.90	75.70	91.50
3	23.54	60.10	33.00	4.01	53.60	90.40
4	27.49	56.55	28.06	35.70	59.20	89.10
5	6.19	2.10	342.00	34.79	89.70	96.50
6	3.44	2.80	31.00	19.94	17.90	90.80
7	30.45	10.96	44.15	59.85	29.20	95.90
8	9.90	8.04	10.56	0.59	0	94.50
9	5.48	1.10	255.50	19.05	51.20	93.00
10	2.77	0.70	260.00	11.90	4.00	89.60
11	1.66	0.12	93.07	3.64	0	92.60

were prepared, varying the effect of the opacity and graininess equally to produce a total of 11 panels as shown in Figure 14(i), Chapter 13 (Refer to Chapter 13).

The six elements of color (hue, luminosity, intensity, shine, opacity and graininess) of each panel were measured. The results are shown in Table 1. Then, participants were asked to look at each painted panel and evaluate, according to a seven-point scale, the extent to which each panel gave the desired impression for the four preferences (classy, luxurious, dignified and sporty). Aesthetic evaluation data was obtained from the results.

The survey was aimed at men and women in their twenties, and answers were obtained from a total of 94 men and women as shown in Table 2. The results of the survey on textural expressions were used to determine the influence of variations in each color element in terms of the preferences.

Moreover, "Covariance Structure Analysis" was conducted to determine the correspondence relationship between color elements and preferences. The results were then used to provide information to contribute to the development of exterior colors appealing to people who value self-expression

Table 2. Aesthetic Evaluation Data (preference)

Participants	Panel No.	Classy	Luxurious	Dignified	Sporty
1	1	4	3	2	4
2	1	7	4	4	5
3	1	2	3	6	7
4	1	3	1	5	7
:	:	:	:	:	:
94	11	5	7	4	3

In the model diagram used for this "Covariance Structure Analysis", the "exterior color" latent variable was chosen as the latent variable that would satisfy the four vehicle design preferences of those who value self-expression. A path analysis using "AMOS 6.0" using IBM SPSS AMOS (Analysis of Moment Structures) was then conducted in order to determine the cause-and-effect relationship between the six color elements and exterior color.

Further paths were then drawn between the four preferences and a latent variable representing the exterior color. This exterior color variable consolidates the preferences of people in the self-expression group when evaluating automobiles and the paths enable the influences to be understood. The coefficients of each path are standardized coefficients.

The absolute values of these standardized coefficients indicate the degree of influence, while the direction of influence is indicated by positive or negative numbers as shown in Figure 14(ii), Chapter 13 (Refer to Chapter 13).

The model was subjected to a goodness-of-fit test once it was corrected using a modification index, resulting in reasonable scores of 0.979 GFI, 0.895 AGFI, 0.038 SRMR and 0.097 RMSEA. The results of the t test for each path coefficient showed that the path coefficient from graininess to exterior color was not significant, but that the remaining path coefficients were significant.

The standardized coefficients of paths shown on the model diagram can be used to determine which color elements are required and how they need to be altered to bring the color closer to the target preferences. For example, in developing a more classy color, the influence of luminosity is greatest at -0.37 (= -0.78*0.48). This shows that the degree of luminosity should be lowered to create a more classy color.

Table 3 shows the standardized coefficients for the effect of color elements desired for exterior colors. The highest values are for luminosity (-0.78), intensity (-0.41), and opacity (0.36), showing that these elements have the greatest influence.

The coefficients also show that the desired color can be achieved by lowering the degree of luminosity and intensity, and raising the level of opacity. Colors can then be developed based on these findings.

Table 3. Path from color elements to exterior color

Color elements	Standardized coefficients
Hue	-0.23
Luminosity	-0.78
Intensity	-0.41
Shine	0.15
Opacity	0.36
Graininess	-0.04

4. Color Development (Step 4)

In Step 4, the authors developed colors aimed at the self-expression group, based on the findings from Step 3.

Table 3 shows that colors preferred by people in the self-expression group can be achieved by lowering the degree of intensity and luminosity, and raising the level of opacity. Lowering the degree of intensity and luminosity results in subdued colors, giving a composed impression. Raising the level of opacity accentuates the color, giving a dignified impression.

Based on these findings, three painted panels were produced using the colors from the survey (red, black and brown). When developing the colors for the panels, the authors focused primarily on luminosity, intensity and opacity to produce colors to suit the preferences of people in the self-expression group as shown in Figure 14.

Figure 15. Exterior color designed for those pursuing "Self-expression"

5. Effectiveness of the AECD-AM

Respondents in the self-expression group were asked to freely evaluate the three developed colors. The respondents gave positive evaluations, saying they liked how classy the colors were and that they would like a car with colors such as these. This shows that the target users were satisfied with the exterior colors developed using this model.

Feedback was then obtained from designers at automobile and paint manufacturers to validate the effectiveness of the model. The feedback confirmed that quantifying the findings in this way makes it possible to gain an unbiased view of aesthetic influences on customers, thereby validating the model's effectiveness.

Verifying the AECD-AM

In order to confirm the effectiveness of the new business approach model, the authors requested that an automaker and a paint manufacturer evaluate it.

The model was favorably received, meriting the following responses: "this process is something I intuitively understand, but it's good to see all of these elements finally combined into a single model", "this model would be valuable as a tool for designing a checklist for each work process", and "the model is a good tool for developing a shared awareness of work approaches". The effectiveness of the model was thus confirmed.

CONCLUSION

In this study, the author used statistical science in the form of the Customer Science Application System "CS-CIANS" (a method for generating customer value, which they had previously created and verified) to construct the "AECD-DM" (Automobile Exterior Color Design Development Model). This represented a strategic expansion of Customer Science Principle by partnering of both the auto-maker and paint-maker. Specifically, data collected from companies was statistically analyzed in order to visualize success factors in meeting customer quality demands. Indicators reflecting customer values were then constructed. By linking these success factors and indicators, AECD-DM was created and its effectiveness confirmed.

In near future, the author applies this research to other than the automobile industry, and promote further expand of this business approach model.

ACKNOWLEDGMENT

The author would like to acknowledge the generous support received from the following researchers: all those at three auto-makers, three paint-makers (manufacturers), and those connected with the Amasaka New JIT laboratory at Aoyama Gakuin University that assisted with author's research, especially, Mr. Miss. Muto, M., Mr. Miyake, R., Takebuchi, S., Nakamura, T., Asami, H., Yamaji, M. and others.

REFERENCES

Amasaka, K. (1995). A Construction of SQC Intelligence System for Quick Registration and Retrieval Library. *Lecture Notes in Economics and Mathematical Systems, Springer, 445*, 318–336. doi:10.1007/978-3-642-59105-1_24

Amasaka, K. (2002). *New JIT*, A New Management Technology Principle at Toyota. *International Journal of Production Economics, 80*(2), 135–144. doi:10.1016/S0925-5273(02)00313-4

Amasaka, K. (2003a). Proposal and implementation of the "Science SQC" quality control principle. *International Journal of Mathematical and Computer Modelling, 38*(11-13), 1125–1136. doi:10.1016/S0895-7177(03)90113-0

Amasaka, K. (2003b). *Science SQC, new quality control principle: The quality strategy of Toyota.* Springer-Verlag.

Amasaka, K. (2005). Constructing a Customer Science Application System "CS-CIANS" -Development of a global strategic vehicle "Lexus" utilizing New JIT. *WSEAS Transactions on Business and Economics, 3*(2), 135–142.

Amasaka, K. (2007a). High Linkage Model "Advanced TDS, TPS & TMS": Strategic development of "New JIT" at Toyota. *International Journal of Operations and Quantitative Management, 13*(3), 101–121.

Amasaka, K. (2007b). The validity of "TDS-DTM": A strategic methodology of merchandise development of New JIT - Key to the Excellence Design "LEXUS". *International Business & Economics Research, 6*(11), 105–116.

Amasaka, K., & Nagaya, A. (2002). Automobile new Kansei engineering: Psychographics of the "Lexus" design profile (Chapter4). In *Product development involving Kansei: Methodology and practice* (pp. 55–72). Japan Publication Service.

Amasaka, K., Nagaya, A., & Matsubara, W. (1999). Studies on Design SQC with the application of Science SQC: Improving of business process method for automotive profile design. *Japanese Journal of Sensory Evaluations, 3*(1), 21–29. doi:10.9763/jjsse.3.21

Amasaka, K., & Yamaji, M. (2008). A study on construction of Automobile Design Concept Support Methods: Visualization of form and customer sensibility utilizing Design CAD. *The 38th Annual Conference of the Japanese Society for Quality Control*, 177-180.

Arima, M. (2002). (Description) Color Design Tosyoku Sekkei. *Readings: Techno Cosmos, 15*, 53–58.

Fujieda, S., Masuda, Y., & Nakahata, T. (2007). Development of Automotive Color Designing Process. *Journal of Society of Automotive Engineers of Japan, 61*(6), 79–84.

Kawamura, M. (2003). The charge of the color in fashion and color design which reflect a generation. *Automotive Engineering, 57*(5), 15–20.

Kawasumi, M., & Suzuki, S. (2008). Measurement of color discrimination ellipse for surface color with texture. *Journal of the Color Science Association of Japan, 32*(3), 166–174.

Koga, K., Takahashi, T., Yamane, T., & Abe, K. (2003). Automotive Basecoat with High Flip-Flop. *Journal of Society of Automotive Engineers of Japan, 57*(5), 31–35.

Miyake, R., & Muto, M. (2010). *Proposal of the business approach model to demand quality realization of a customer: The example of application to an automobile body color* (Bachelor's thesis). School of Science and Engineering, Aoyama Gakuin University, Amasaka New JIT Laboratory.

Muto, M., Miyake, R., & Amasaka, K. (2011). Constructing an Automobile Body Color Development Approach Model. *Journal of Management Science, 2*, 175–183.

Muto, M., Takebuchi, S., & Amasaka, K. (2013). Creating a New Automotive Exterior Design Approach Model - The relationship between form and body color qualities. *Journal of Business Case Studies, 9*(5), 367–374. doi:10.19030/jbcs.v9i5.8061

Park, S., Kamaike, M., & Nagao, T. (2009). Single picture impression structure and compound picture impression harmonization of user. *Environment and Car Design Science in Information Systems Research, 5*(6), 59–66.

Takebuchi, S., Nakamura, T., Asami, H., & Amasaka, K. (2012). The Automobile Exterior Color Design Approach Model. *Journal of Japan Industrial Management Association, 62*(6E), 303–310.

Tokinaga, I., & Utsunomiya, C. (2009). Advertising Strategy about Color Variation. *Design Science in Information Systems Research, 56*(4), 85–90.

Watanabe, A., & Jo, K. (2009). Consideration about the correlation nature of the cluster of a fashion, and the taste color of clothes. *Journal of the Color Science Association of Japan, 28*, 42–43.

Yamaji, M., & Amasaka, K. (2009). Intelligence Design Concept Method utilizing Customer Science. *The Open Industrial and Manufacturing Engineering Journal, 2*(1), 21–25. doi:10.2174/1874152500902010021

Yomo A. & Kato T. (2010). Grouping Tastes in Color by Personal Preference and Lifestyles. *The Institute of Image Information and Television Engineers) Technical Report, 34*(18), 59-61.

APPENDIX

Table 4. Q1. To what extent do you consider the following characteristics of automobile design to be important?

No.	Characteristic of automobile design	Very important						Not important at all	Comments
1	Sophisticated	7	6	5	4	3	2	1	
2	Traditional	7	6	5	4	3	2	1	
3	Chic	7	6	5	4	3	2	1	
4	Orthodox	7	6	5	4	3	2	1	
5	Originality	7	6	5	4	3	2	1	
6	Curving	7	6	5	4	3	2	1	
7	Advanced	7	6	5	4	3	2	1	
8	Sporty	7	6	5	4	3	2	1	
9	Classy	7	6	5	4	3	2	1	
10	Luxurious	7	6	5	4	3	2	1	
11	Fashionable	7	6	5	4	3	2	1	
12	Compact	7	6	5	4	3	2	1	
13	Practical	7	6	5	4	3	2	1	
14	Dignified	7	6	5	4	3	2	1	
15	Youthful	7	6	5	4	3	2	1	

Table 5. Q2. To what extent do you agree with the following statements?

No	Item	Strongly agree						Strongly disagree	Comments
1	An automobile is a mere transportation device.	7	6	5	4	3	2	1	
2	The economic burden accompanying possession and use of an automobile is large.	7	6	5	4	3	2	1	
3	An automobile is an indispensable item in life.	7	6	5	4	3	2	1	
4	Many color variations are necessary in an automobile.	7	6	5	4	3	2	1	

Chapter 19
Robot Reliability Design and Improvement Method Using Advanced TPS

ABSTRACT

T automobile industry uses many robots, and a practical scientific approach of reliability enhancing activities is the key to the realisation of a highly reliable production system of faster operating production robots. The reliability of the robots is improved not only by hardware designed to be more reliable on the supplier side, but also by collecting and analysing the user's observations at the production line over a long period of time. The author has established the Robot Reliability Design and Improvement Method (RRD-IM) by developing Advanced TPS. This method has been implemented worldwide in an advanced car manufacturer and has produced a better operating life cycle for industrial robots.

INTRODUCTION

To survive amidst severe competition, Japanese enterprises have recently been promoting global production, to achieve uniform quality worldwide, and increased production at optimal locations. This trend and a particular production environment have led the author to establish "Advanced TPS" (Advanced Total Production System) as the strategic development of "New Japan Model" named "New JIT" for manufacturing in the 21st century (Amasaka, 2002, 2007a, 2009, 2014, 2018; Amasaka and Sakai, 2010). This section concentrates on the strategic application of Advanced TPS and the creation of a highly reliable production system based upon it (Amasaka and Sakai, 2009).

Nowadays, the automobile industry uses many robots, and a practical scientific approach of "reliability enhancing activities" is the key to the realisation of a highly reliable production system faster operating production robots. The reliability of the robots is improved not only by hardware designed to be more reliable on the supplier side (Craig, 1988), but also by collecting and analysing the user's observations at the production line over a long period of time (Kitano, 1996; Atkeson and McIntyre, 1985; Atkeson *et al.*, 1986). The author has established a strategic manufacturing technology for the robots named

DOI: 10.4018/978-1-7998-8746-1.ch019

"Robot Reliability Design and Improvement Method" (RRD-IM) (Sakai and Amasaka, 2007a) (Refer to Chapter 7). RRD-IM contains three core methods of evaluating robot reliability: initial failure (-IF), random failure (-RF) and wear failure (-WF). The author has implemented RRD-IM at an advanced car manufacturer A and achieved the anticipated results. Then, based on these three failure modes, they have implemented the reliability design to ensure better line availability.

The author has also suggested a methodology to increase reliability through defining the target value of MTBF (mean time between failure), in preparation for a global production strategy. They have simultaneously achieved a QCD (quality, cost, delivery) programme enabling manufacturers to offer high product assurance (Sakai and Amasaka, 2007a,b, 2013, 2014; Amasaka and Sakai, 2009; Amasaka, 2015, 2017, 2022).

DEVELOPMENT OF ADVANCED TPS

In recent years, the technical manufacturing capability in the Japanese manufacturing industry has declined as the result of production transfers to overseas locations. Yet high quality assurance at PPM (parts per million) level is needed in the domestic plants, and the following requirements have emerged: (1) Worldwide quality assurance (2) Uniform productivity all over the world

The Key to Success in Global Production using Advanced TPS

The author addressed the requirements above and organically integrated four core technologies to develop Advanced TPS as an effective manufacturing technology for global production, Figure 1(2), Chapter 6 (Sakai and Amasaka, 2005, 2013, 2014; Amasaka, 2006, 2007a,b) (Refer to Chapter 6 and 15).

The mission of Advanced TPS is to achieve epoch-making improvements in productivity, cost, quality, and workability. The four core elements are: (a) Integrated Quality Control System, (b) Highly Reliable Production System, (c) Rational Advertisement Promotion System and (d) Intelligent Operator Development System.

In the near future, the reformation of production workshops by the production facilities administration, ideal maintenance, and the advancement of traditional Toyota Production System for high quality assurance and a highly reliable production system, will be required (Amasaka, 2015, 2017, 2022) (Refer to Chapter 3).

The Necessity of a Scientific Approach

The necessary requirements for a highly reliable production system are, 1) Fast repair of facilities in the event of a breakdown (maintainability), and 2) Speed of production (productivity) (Kelly, 1997). Regarding maintainability, the primary objective of maintenance is to provide quality products promptly (Wang and Marvin, 2000). For this, it is essential to improve the administration of the production facilities to enhance availability (Smith, 1993; Modarres et al., 1999).

The author therefore structured and developed ARIM-BL (Availability Reliability Information Monitor - Body Line) at an advanced car manufacturer A, with excellent results. ARIM-BL consists of two systems, (a) a body measurement system and (b) a line information administration system, which allows data to be accessed in real time from the facility (Amasaka and Sakai, 1996, 1998).

The first issue, maintenance instructions are one way of conveying maintenance skills, but their written nature gives them disadvantages such as complexity and the difficulty of searching for specific information quickly. It is crucial to establish a new universal means of transmitting skills easily. Using database technology and computer graphics, the authors have developed new and more general approaches. In addition, systems to help visualize maintenance instructions and new media to transmit skills are needed.

The author creates a new system using the visualization-maintenance innovated computer system (V-MICS) (Sakai and Amasaka, 2005), and effectiveness has been verified in Toyota.

The second issue, productivity, benefits from "reliability enhancing activities" that improve the operation rate of production robots. Therefore, the rest of this paper contains a proposal for a model for robot "reliability enhancing activities".

ROBOT RELIABILITY DRSIGN AND IMPROVEMENT METHOD AS THE KEY TO ADVANCED TPS

To develop a highly reliable production system for global purposes, the author establishes the "Robot Reliability Design and Improvement Method" (RRD-IM) by developing Advanced TPS as shown in Figure 1 (Sakai and Amasaka, 2007a; Amasaka, 2015).

Figure 1. Robot Reliability Design and Improvement Method (RRD-IM)

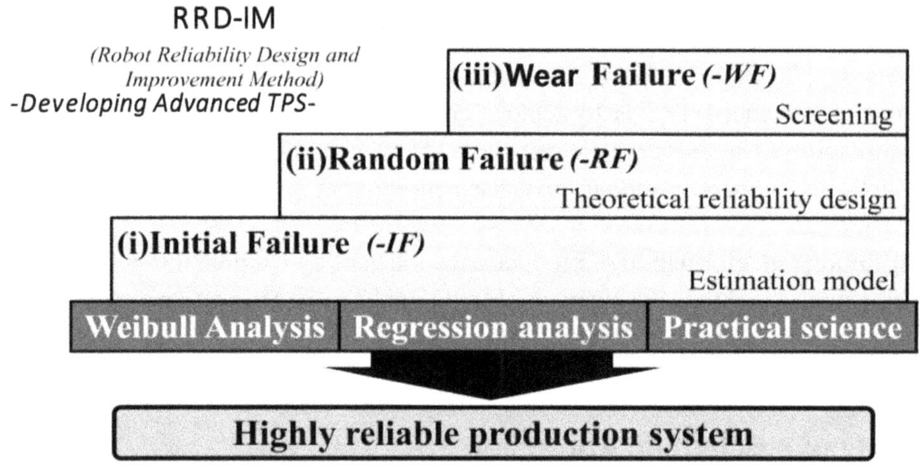

Concept and Structural Elements

This incorporates Weibull Analysis, multiple linear regression analysis, and practical science, and is composed of three main elements corresponding to the three failure modes as indicated in Figure 2. The model proceeds through the following stages, (1) Initial Failure (-IF), (2) Random Failure (-RF) and (3) Wear Failure (-WF). There are three basic countermeasures for the failure forms, as follows:

1. Eliminate the initial failure factors by screening before placing into line operation.
2. Evaluate the MTBF for random failures, and theoretically predict the relation between the number of units to be introduced to the line and the availability of the production line. When the production line availability requirement is not satisfied, revisit the hardware design of the robot to improve the MTBF.
3. To address wear-out failure, accurately specify the worn out parts and the expected lifetime of the parts. Carry out part replacement and robot overhauls as preventative measures

To detect defective elements that could lead to initial failure, the authors generally recommend screening via heat-accelerated testing. By a theoretical examination of the MTBFs in the random failure mode, the number of units to be introduced, availability, and the investigation of the validity of MTBF of 3,000 hours, the author implements a design review on the use of the elements if necessary. The author establishes a more accurate degradation model that focuses on gear wear in the wear-out failure mode and construct the part-life estimation system based on this model.

1. Initial failure

In screening for the defective elements, the author must first find appropriate conditions for the acceleration test on the printed circuit board in the robot. Screening is difficult under gentle conditions, but on the other hand, even normal elements are destroyed under excessively severe conditions. The author therefore carried out an accelerated life test to find the conditions under which failure forms do not change (Myers et al., 1998).

Taking T=20 °C as the environmental temperature for initial failure, a Weibull form modulus m=0.58 is obtained as a result of Weibull analysis of the holding time and accumulated failure rate F(t). Heating to T=60 °C shows that the form modulus stays at m=0.6 up to the accumulated failure rate of 70%, demonstrating that since the **m** value is almost constant, acceleration is possible. However, the gradient of the line gradually increases after F(t)=70%, which indicates the possibility of a change in the failure form. The author therefore concludes that the time showing the accumulated failure rate of 70% is the life span of the defective parts in the initial failure form. The results mentioned above are shown on the left of Figure 2.

Next, to find the proper heating and holding time, the authors made an Arrhenius plot (Shiomi, 1970) of life span against temperature change. The results, on the right of Figure 2, reveal the lifespan. This allows us to determine the tolerance time (L1) in the acceleration test for temperature T1, which is determined by the heating equipment.

2. Random failure
    a. Reliability design for the robot line

In the random failure mode, robots have a constant failure rate regardless of their operating time. Hence, it is possible to theoretically predict the availability of a production line using multiple robots.

First, the author implemented the theoretical reliability design for the line, using robots to define the MTBF. Then the author tried to find the countermeasures through the comparison body assembly line adopting the series model (Matsubara, 1981) where multiple units of robots are arranged as shown in Figure 3.

Figure 2. Accelerated Life via High Temperature (left) / Arrhenius Plot between Temperature and Holding Time (right)

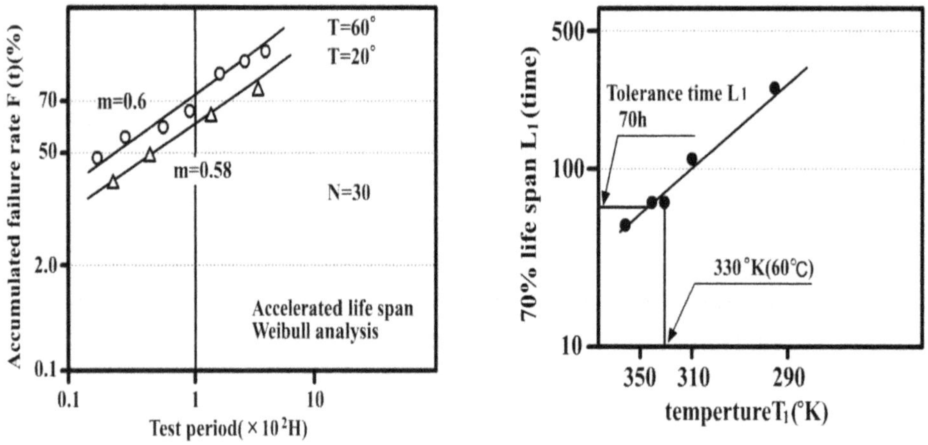

Figure 3. Body Assembly Model Line

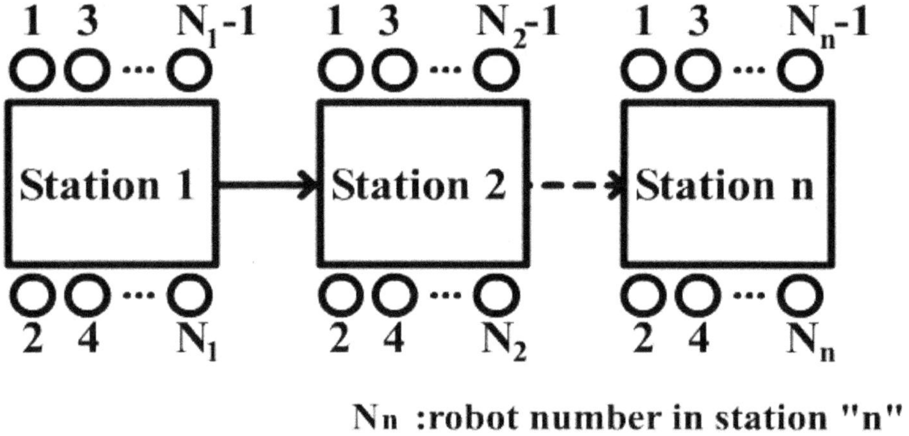

The line availability is therefore decided by the number of robots introduced. Where the number of robots is N, the MTBF of a robot is t, the failure recovery time of a robot is R, the total number of robots in failure is n, and the line operating time is T, the robot availability A will be calculated as follows:

$$A = (T - n \bullet R) / T \tag{1}$$

Where the average number of failures in the line is ‘n’,

$$m = N \bullet T / t \tag{2}$$

The number of failed robots n in random failure mode follows the Poisson distribution (Nakamura et al, 1997). P is the probability of n failed robots:

$$P = m^n \cdot e^{-m} / n! \tag{3}$$

The line availability A is secured if the failure number is less than 'n', so the condition to secure A with a significance level α is calculated as follows:

$$\sum_0^n P(n) < 1 - \alpha \tag{4}$$

The expression (4) can be changed by using Chi square distribution as follows;

$$m = \chi_\varphi^{\ 2}(1-\alpha)/2 \tag{5}$$

$$N \cdot T = 1/2t \cdot \chi^2_{2(t(1-A)/r+1)}(1-\alpha) \tag{6}$$

Where χ is the Chi square distribution, and φ is the degree of freedom, φ=2(n+1). Furthermore, the expression (6) can be changed as follows;

$$t = 2N \cdot T / \chi^2_{2(T(1-A)/r+1)}(1-\alpha) \tag{7}$$

b. Reliability improvement for the robots

The author mentioned that a design review is necessary for some defective elements that appear in the random failure mode. It is well known that the failure rate of a system of elements in random failure mode is the sum of the failure rate of each element (Taki, 1994). Hence, the design review is possible by finding the failure rate and the number of elements used for the robot controller (Valter, 1993; Balestrino *et al.*, 1983; Koivo and Guo, 1983; Slotine and Li, 1987).

3. Wear failure

As mentioned above, wear failure in robots is caused by gear wear. The authors recommend periodic overhaul as the appropriate preventative measure. Nevertheless, failures still occur during line operation, and it is necessary to make a life estimation based on deterioration due to wear, to implement an effective overhaul régime. The author therefore decided to investigate the wear phenomenon, and propose a life estimation based on the deterioration model.

The author implemented an acceleration test under oil-less conditions to investigate the wear phenomenon on the robot gear as shown in Figure 4.

Figure 4. Checking wear under No Lubrication Conditions

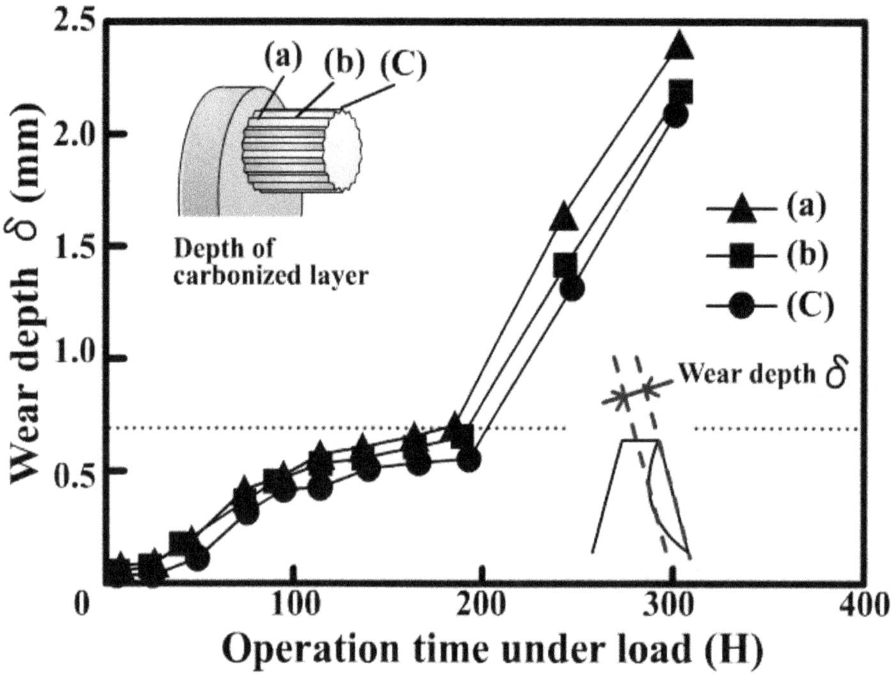

This shows that the wear developed rapidly after 200 hours of operation, and we also found the carbonized layer did not remain. A ferrograph revealed a flake structure in the wear powder, confirming that wear was caused by adhesive wear.

It is well known that adhesive wear can be found by the expression (8), where the load on the gear tooth is P, the slippage of the tooth face is L and the amount of wear is Δ:

$$\Delta = k \bullet P \bullet L \tag{8}$$

If the wear depth of the gear is δ and the engaging time is S, expression (8) can be changed as follows;

$$\delta = a \cdot \ln(P \cdot S) + b \tag{9}$$

'a' and 'b' in the above expression are coefficients that vary depending on the lubrication condition (Nakamura et al, 1997).

RRD-IM APPLICATION EXAMPLE

In the robot system used on the production line shown in Figure 5, the processing tool is mounted on the main body of the control unit (Shiomi, 1970; Amasaka and Sakai, 1996). The processing tool in the body assembly line is surveyed to evaluate the reliability of the facility.

Figure 5. Overview of body assembly line utilizing many robots

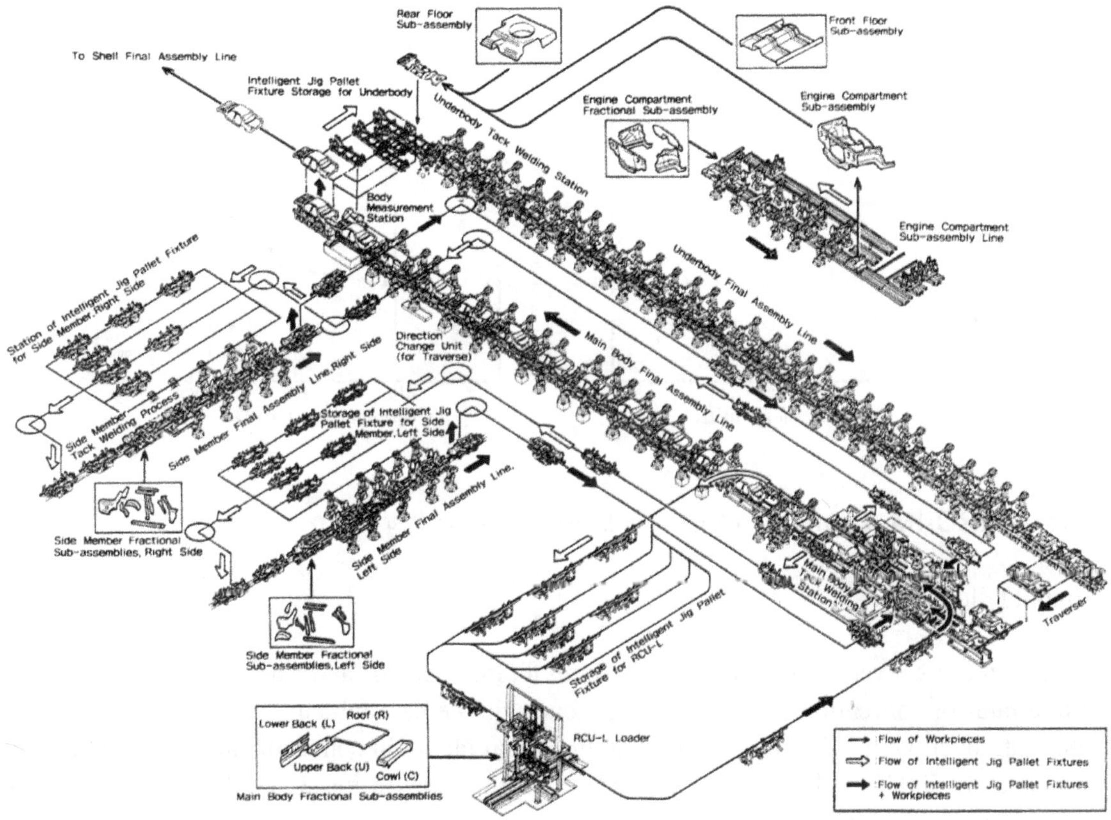

A line that has a high maintenance coefficient has difficulty achieving a high line availability.

The result of the evaluation shows that the robot body has an overwhelmingly high maintenance coefficient. Thus, the reliability of the production line depends on the reliability of the robot body.

Practical Robot Failures

The author investigated the failure rate of the robot body in the 1980s over an eight-year period without overhaul since introduction, and found the results showed a typical bath-tub curve.

The result after Weibull analysis of this curve is shown on the left of Figure 6, and indicates that the initial failure period (m=0.6) is 500 hours, and the random failure period (m=0.97) comes after that time, although this is not always clear because it is affected by the working conditions of the robots. Also, the MTBF at the random failure period is found to be 8,000 hours.

The author carried out a Weibull analysis for each robot defect factor. The results showed that the initial failure (m=0.55, 0.7) factor was mostly defective elements such as an IC chip mounted in the print circuit board of the robot's controller or position detector. Defective elements are found in the random failure (m=1.1) factors too. For this, the design factor will be estimated.

The wear failure (m=2.5) factor is gear wear, resulting from incomplete preventative maintenance. These results are shown on the right of Figure 6.

Figure 6. Weibull Analysis results for robots in the 1980's (left) / Weibull Analysis Results of Robot Defect Factors (right)

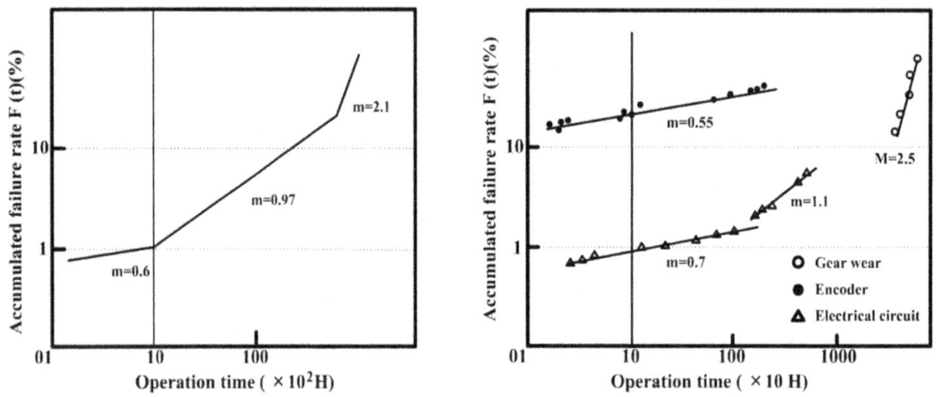

Result of RRD-IM Application in the Body Assembly Line

1. Initial failure

To assess the effectiveness of the countermeasures for initial failure and random failure, we compared the failure rates of conventional robots with new ones via the bath-tub curve that we have used since the robot introduction in 1987. This proves that the initial failure in conventional robots that occurred at approximately 500 hours has almost been solved, and the MTBF for the random failure period has satisfied the required 30,000 hours.

2. Random failure
   a. Reliability design for the line robots

Where the operating time is one month T=400 hours, the significance level α=0.05, the failure recovery time r=1.2 hours, and the required line availability A=98%, the relationship between the number of robots N and the robot MTBF t is found from expression (7) and is plotted on the left of Figure 7..

If the number of robots to be introduced to the body assembly line is 300 units, the graph shows that the required MTBF is 30,000 hours, so it is necessary to improve the MTBF of 3,000 hours per robot by one order of magnitude.

b. Reliability improvement for the robots

The author investigated the total failure rate of the elements used for the robot controller and decided to stop the use of elements with a high failure rate. At the same time, we tried to reduce the element number from 1,100 to 770 by integration of the control circuit. Furthermore, by studying the printed circuit boards with failed elements, the author found that at high frequency, metal parts evaporated and the failed element was destroyed and blackened by over-voltage.

Figure 7. Robot Number and Necessary MTBF (left) / Linear Line Showing the Relation between Load and Wear depth (right)

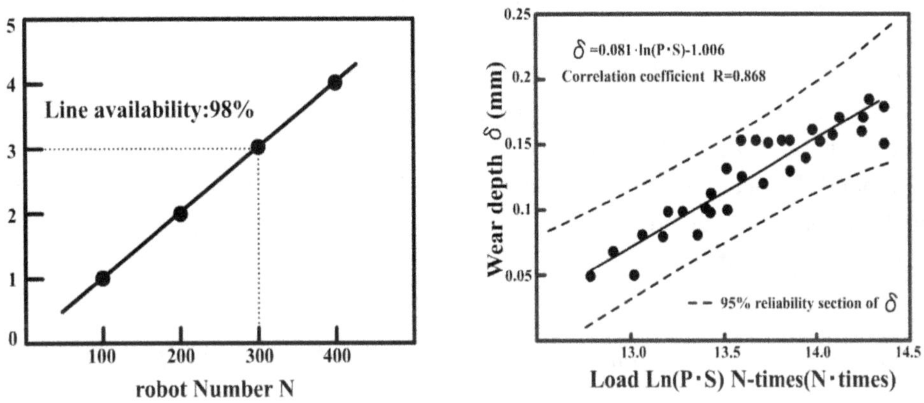

The mechanism generating the over-voltage in the line was partially determined through FTA (fault tree analysis) and included 'wraparound of the surge voltage', 'defect in the self-discharge circuit', and 'mistaken operation' (Takada, 1999), but the underlying cause was difficult to ascertain. So, after investigating the voltage margin for all elements, The author installed an electronic circuit using a Zener diode to protect against over-voltage.

3. Wear failure

The depth of the gear wear δ can be estimated by using expression (9) above as the deterioration model. When this value is over the depth of the carbonized layer, the wear failure can be predicted, making it possible to apply preventative maintenance measures.

To find the 'a' and 'b', coefficients in expression (9), the relationship of δ, P and S is found by using a particular robot developed to improve lubrication by the attachment of an automatic oil feeder.

The relationship is plotted on the right of Figure 8 and given by the empirical formula below:

$$\delta = 0.081 \bullet \ln(P \bullet S) - 1.006 \quad (10)$$

This shows that the load exerted on the gear P, and the engaging time S can be found by measuring the phase between the motor current and the position transducer of the robot. However, this estimation is made at the start of the operation. Recently, robot programming is often carried out off-line. The off-line programming system simulates the motion of the robot using mechanical modelling of its kinematics and dynamics. Therefore, the P and S loads on each tooth of the robot's gear are easily predictable.

So, the author decided to construct a system to estimate the life span using expression (10) during programming, to ascertain the overhaul time, and then use this for preventative maintenance after robot introduction (Walker and Orin, 1982).

Evaluation on the Actual Line

The author evaluated the robot on the line used to practise reliability design and improvement methodology discussed in Subsection 19.3.1(2). To evaluate the countermeasures for initial failure and random failure, the failure rates for conventional robots and new ones were compared using the bath-tub curve.

This proves that the initial failure in conventional robots that occurred at approximately 500 hours has almost been solved, and the MTBF for random failure has achieved the required 30,000 hours. In addition, we applied the overhaul time-régime calculated from loads P and S for each robot, through the life-estimation system presented in Subsection 19.3.1(3). As a result, the wear failure also has been solved, as shown in the left of Figure 8.

Figure 8. Reliability Achieved Situation (left) / Line Availability Tendency (right)

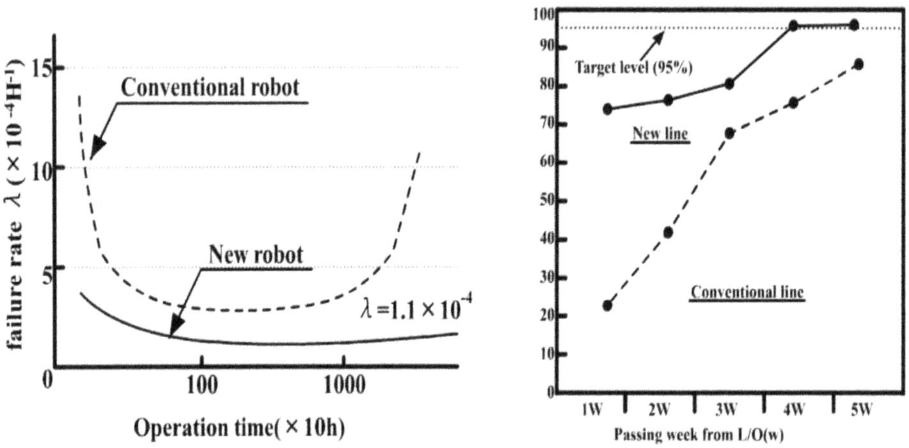

Furthermore, the author found that we could reduce the overhaul cost by half by changing from the conventional method of setting wear depth at 0.2mm as the gear replacement standard, to the new method of replacing only the gears predicted to reach their limit of use (carbonized layer thickness; generally 0.7mm), when shifting the vehicle model year.

The change in the availability of the line that introduced 300 units of robots is shown on the right of Figure 8. This indicates that the target level for line availability, of 95%, has been achieved successfully soon after starting the line operation.

CONCLUSION

Through long-term observation and analysis of robot failure in the vehicle body assembly line, the authors achieved a great improvement in reliability. The author considers it significant that these activities have been driven by robot users who are involved in the management of the production line, rather than just by the robot vender. The conclusions drawn from this study include:

ACKNOWLEDGMENT

The author would like to acknowledge the generous support of the following researchers: all those at Toyota Motor Corporation, and Amasaka New JIT laboratory at Aoyama Gakuin University that assisted with the research, especially, Dr. Sakai, H., and others.

REFERENCES

Amasaka, K. (2002). A New Management Technology Principle at Toyota. *International Journal of Production Economics, 80*(2), 135–144. doi:10.1016/S0925-5273(02)00313-4

Amasaka, K. (2007a). High Linkage Model "Advanced TDS, TPS & TMS": Strategic development of "New JIT" at Toyota. *International Journal of Operations and Quantitative Management, 13*(3), 101–121.

Amasaka, K. (2007b). Applying New JIT - Toyota's global production strategy: Epoch-making innovation in the work environment. *Robotics and Computer-integrated Manufacturing, 23*(3), 285–293. doi:10.1016/j.rcim.2006.02.001

Amasaka, K. (2009). The Foundation for Advancing the Toyota Production System Utilizing New JIT. *Journal of Advanced Manufacturing Systems, 80*(1), 5–26. doi:10.1142/S0219686709001614

Amasaka, K. (2014). New JIT, New Management Technology Principle: Surpassing JIT. *Journal of Procedia Technology, 16*(Special issues), 1135–1145. doi:10.1016/j.protcy.2014.10.128

Amasaka, K. (2015). New JIT, new management technology principle. Academic Press.

Amasaka, K. (2017). *Toyota, Production system, safety analysis and future directions*. Nova Science Publishers.

Amasaka, K. (2018). Innovation of automobile manufacturing fundamentals employing New JIT: Developing Advanced Toyota Production System. *International Journal of Research in Business, Economics and Management, 2*(1), 1–15.

Amasaka, K. (2022). New Manufacturing Theory: Surpassing JIT (2nd ed.). Lambert Academic Publishing.

Amasaka, K., & Sakai, H. (1996). Improving the Reliability of Body Assembly Line Equipment. *International Journal of Reliability Quality and Safety Engineering, 3*(1), 11–24. doi:10.1142/S021853939600003X

Amasaka, K., & Sakai, H. (1998). Availability and Reliability Information Administration System ARIM-BL by methodology in Inline-Online SQC. *International Journal of Reliability Quality and Safety Engineering, 5*(1), 55–63. doi:10.1142/S0218539398000078

Amasaka, K., & Sakai, H. (2009). TPS-QAS, New Production Quality Management Model: Key to New JIT-Toyota's global production strategy. *International Journal of Manufacturing Technology and Management, 18*(4), 409–426. doi:10.1504/IJMTM.2009.027774

Amasaka, K., & Sakai, H. (2010). Evolution of TPS fundamentals utilizing New JIT strategy–Proposal and validity of Advanced TPS at Toyota. *Journal of Advanced Manufacturing Systems*, *9*(2), 85–99. doi:10.1142/S0219686710001831

Atkeson, C. G., An, C. H., & Hollerbach, J. M. (1986). Estimation of Inertial Parameters of Manipulator Links and Loads. *The International Journal of Robotics Research*, *5*(3), 101–119. doi:10.1177/027836498600500306

Atkeson, C. G., & McIntyre, J. (1985). Robot Trajectory Learning through Practice. *Proceedings of IEEE International Conference on Robotics and Automation*, 1737-1742.

Balestrino, A., Maria, G. D., & Sciavicco, L. (1983). An Adaptive Model Following Control for Robot Manipulators, *ASME. Journal of Dynamic Systems, Measurement, and Control*, *105*(3), 143–151. doi:10.1115/1.3140646

Craig, J. J. (1988). *Adaptive Control of Mechanical Manipulators*. Addison-Wesley.

Kelly, A. (1997). *Maintenance Strategy*. Butter Worth Heinemann.

Kitano, M. (1996). New Flexible Automation: A Process Planner's View. *Proceedings of the Japan/USA Symposium on Flexible Automation*, 1-8.

Koivo, A. J., & Guo, T. H. (1983). Adaptive linear controller for robotic manipulators. *IEEE Transactions on Automatic Control*, *AC-28*(2), 162–171. doi:10.1109/TAC.1983.1103211

Matsubara, K. (1981). *Tripology*. Sangyo Library.

Modarres, M., Mark, K., & Vasiliy, K. (1999). *Reliability Engineering and Risk Analysis*. Marcel Dekker Inc.

Myers, E. A., Trinh, J. V., & Myyers, T. R. (1998). Structure and function of the ovine type 1 corticotrophin releasing factor receptor and a carboxv1-terminal variant. *Molecular and Cellular Endocrinology*, *144*, 21–35.

Nakamura, H., Sakai, H., Miura, H., & Sakamoto, Y. (1997). Construction of Life Estimation based on Deterioration Model. *Precision Technology Bulletin*, *63*(11), 1620–1624.

Sakai, H., & Amasaka, K. (2005). V-MICS, Advanced TPS for Strategic Production Administration: Innovative Maintenance Combining DB and CG. *Journal of Advanced Manufacturing Systems*, *4*(6), 5–20. doi:10.1142/S0219686705000540

Sakai, H., & Amasaka, K. (2006). Strategic HI-POS, Intelligence Production Operating System. *WSEAS Transactions on Advances in Engineering Education*, *3*(3), 223–230.

Sakai, H., & Amasaka, K. (2007a). The Robot Reliability Design and Improvement Method and the Advanced Production System. *International Journal of Industrial and Service Robotics*, *6*(8), 310–316. doi:10.1108/01439910710749636

Sakai, H., & Amasaka, K. (2007b). Development of a Robot Control Method for Curved Seal Extrusion for High Productivity in an Advanced Toyota Production System. *International Journal of Computer Integrated Manufacturing*, *20*(5), 486–496. doi:10.1080/09511920601160262

Sakai, H., & Amasaka, K. (2013). Establishment of Body Auto Fitting Model "BAFM" using "NJ-GPM" at Toyota. *The Journal of Japanese Operations Management and Strategy*, *4*(1), 38–54.

Sakai, H., & Amasaka, K. (2014). How to build a linkage between High Quality Assurance Production System and Production Support System. *The Journal of Japanese Operations Management and Strategy*, *4*(2), 20–30.

Shiomi, H. (1970). *Introduction to destructible physics*. Union of Japanese Scientist and Engineering, JUSE Press LTD.

Slotine, J. J., & Li, W. (1987). On the Adaptive Control of Robot Manipulators. *The International Journal of Robotics Research*, *6*(6), 49–59. doi:10.1177/027836498700600303

Smith, A. H. (1993). *Reliability centered maintenance*. McGraw-Hill.

Takada, S. (1999). Life Cycle Maintenance. *Precision Technology Bulletin*, *65*(33), 349–353.

Taki, T. (1994). Influence of Differences in Material on the Endurance Limit of Gearing. *Proceedings of the JSLE, Trib Conference*.

Valter, L. (1993). *Handbook in Design of Reliable Equipment*. DELTA Danish Electronics, Light & Acoustics.

Walker, M. W., & Orin, D. E. (1982). Efficient Dynamic Computer Simulation of Robotic Mechanisms", *ASME. Journal of Dynamic Systems, Measurement, and Control*, *104*(3), 205–211. doi:10.1115/1.3139699

Wang, J. X., & Marvin, L. R. (2000). *What Every Engineer Should Know about Risk Engineering and Management*. Marcel Dekker Inc. doi:10.1201/9781482293579

Chapter 20
Body Auto Fitting Model "BAFM": Developing NJ-GPM

ABSTRACT

In this chapter, the author has established the Body Auto Fitting Model (BAFM) developing NJ-GPM (New Japan Global Production Model) based on the innovative deployment of Advanced TPS, Strategic Production Management Model. Therefore, the author has realized innovative unmanning of the fitting line by integrating the technologies utilizing BAFM, a model designed to achieve worldwide uniform quality and production at optimal locations. The keys to successful global production such as robotics, vision systems, bolt tightening, product quality management, and the ability to automatically fit and fasten door, hood, and luggage compartment panels to the car body was achieved. This study shows the development of the following three items: (1) panel fitting accuracy, (2) automatic bolt tightening, and (3) integration into flexible assembly line at an advanced car manufacturer Toyota.

INTRODUCTION

The leading Japanese management technology that has contributed most to worldwide manufacturing from the second half of the 20th century is the Japanese Production System, which is typified by the Toyota Production System (Ohno, 1977). This system has been further developed and spread in the form of internationally shared global production systems.

With this in mind, the author has created the "New Japan Global Production Model, NJ-GPM" to enable the strategic development based on the innovative deployment of "Advanced TPS, Strategic Production Management Model" employing NJM (New Japan Model) (Amasaka, 2007a,b,c: Amasaka and Sakai, 2011) (Refer to Chapter 5, 6 and 7).

The aim of this model is to realize a highly reliable production system suitable for global production by reviewing the production process from production planning and preparation through production itself and process management. The newly-created NJ-GPM is fundamental to the strategic development of global production (Amasaka and Sakai, 2010).

DOI: 10.4018/978-1-7998-8746-1.ch020

Therefore, the author has established the "Body Auto Fitting Model" (BAFM) developing NJ-GPM, and has verified the effectiveness of this research through example application (Sakai and Amasaka, 2013). Specifically, this study focuses on the fitting line by integrating the technologies using BAFM at an advanced car manufacturer Toyota.

BACKGROUND

The Current Condition and Problems of Conventional Production System

Today's manufacturers in Japan are globally expanding their operations at a full speed to be price competitive and need to establish a new production system to suit their global strategies. Conventionally, well-experienced and highly-skilled trainers go to local production sites and provide local production operators hands-on training one-on-one.

The quality of trainings for production operators greatly rely on personal capabilities of the highly-skilled trainers. Different trainers would give different trainings, which may confuse trainees and result in unevenness in production operators' skill acquisition processes. Production operators in Japan also have experienced the same problems while passing down the Japanese manufacturing technology.

Ideas for Three Important Points for Global Production

The author has proposed that there are three important points to assure high quality and high efficiency, and shorten lead time: (1) Production equipment using industrial robots, (2) Skilled workers who operate the equipment (production operators), and (3) Production systems including production data systems to activate the equipment and workers

The main factors for global production are to build a linkage among individual processes in production planning, production preparation, actual production and process control, to make those processes as perfect as possible, and to raise reliability in the manufacturing technology for global production (Sakai and Amasaka, 2007b,c).

DEVELOPING THE "NEW GLOBAL PRODUCTION MODEL" (NJ-GPM), STRATEGIC DEVELOPMENT OF ADVANCED TPS

Global production must be developed in such a way as to establish the kind of manufacturing that is required to gain the trust of customers around the world. It must achieve a high level of quality assurance and efficiency and shortening lead times to reinforce the simultaneous achievement of QCD requirements. The vital key to achieving this is the introduction of a production system that incorporates production machinery automated with robots, skilled and experienced workers (production operators) to operate the machinery, and production information to organically combine them (Brooks, 1986; Raibert, 1986).

Having recognized the need for a new production system suitable for global production, the author has created the "NJ-GPM" (New Japan Global Production Model) to realize the strategic development of the "Advanced TPS, Strategic Production Management Model" (Amasaka and Sakai, 2011). This model eradicates ambiguities at each stage of the production process not only from production planning and preparation through production itself and process management, but also between the processes. NJ-GPM is to achieve a highly reliable production system for global production which will improve the reliability of manufacturing through the clarification and complete coordination of these processes (Refer to Chapter 6).

ESTABLISHMENT OF "BODY AUTO FITTING MODEL" (BAFM)

The author has established the "Body Auto Fitting Model" (BAFM) using the development of NJ-GPM. The aim of BAFM is to realize a highly reliable production system suitable for global production by reviewing the production process from production planning and preparation through production itself and process management. The missions of BAFM for global production are (i) solve technical problems in advance in a production planning process by simulating technical problems with computer graphics created in CAE (Computer Aided Engineering), (ii) improve production operators' skills to operate automated equipment and the manufacturing technology, (iii) create production data that network and visualize the above objectives by the aid of IT (Information Technology).

To fulfill those missions, one requirement is that production operators must create a combination of processes in process planning and be well-prepared so that they can easily do the processes. Digital engineering will lead to building a linkage among production processes to prevent technical problems including: (1) Integrity between advanced equipment and its operators' skills, (2) Integrity between production operators' skills and their movements, (3) Integrity among facility, its production operators' skills, and parts, and (4) Another requirement is network systems that enable production operators to build the linkage. It is required urgently to build the linkage that disperses and integrates information globally while respecting local independence.

Four Essential Techniques to Build the Linkage among Production Processes in BAFM for Global Production

The idea in Figure 1 to build the linkage among production processes in BAFM for global production consists of the following four essential techniques; (1) PSCS: Production Support CAE System, (2) PSAS: Production Support Automated System, (3) OTAS: Operator Training Application System and (4) HQAS: High Quality Assurance Production System.

To use PSCS and PSAS, it is important to plan precisely from production planning stages and prevent problems by simulating. (i) Reforming production planning: CAE data simulation will optimize production requirements regarding production lines (logistic and transportation), robots (placing arrangement) and production operators (allocation and workability) for the entire plant and (ii) reforming production preparation: Highly accurate robot production system will replace heavy load processes that are currently done manually by workers.

For OTAS and HQAS, it is inevitable to improve, visualize and systemize workers' skills (iii) in production processes. For those purposes above, skill-mastering support systems will improve and judge workers' skills and place workers in the most appropriate positions in production processes. (iv) In process control, intelligent quality control systems will use IT control charts based on statistics and assure process capacity (Cp) and machine capacity (Cm). It is vital to reform these stages in production planning, production preparation, mass production and process control.

Figure 1. Outline of the "Body Auto Fitting Model" (BAFM)

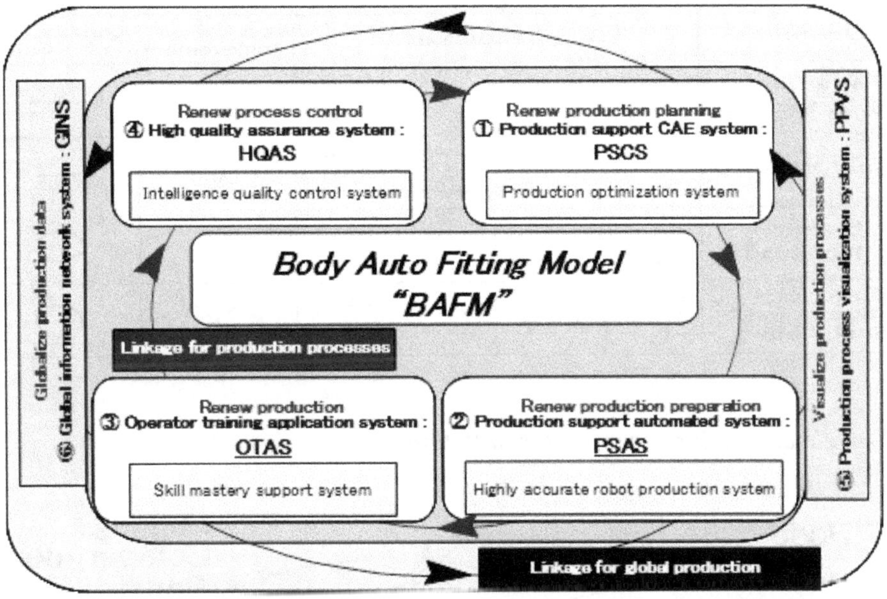

Two Essential Techniques to Build the Linkage to Globally Develop BAFM

The following two systems will support building the linkage to globally develop BAFM among production operators. To use PPVS (Production Process Visualization System), and GINS (Global Information Network System), in Figure 1, Chapter 21, the additional, following two systems are required.

1. Systems to visualize production processes in planning, preparation and process control and gain better results of QCD activities
2. Servers and client systems to use production data globally

All of these above will implement BAFM for global production to immediately establish the manufacturing technology that assures high quality (Sakai and Amasaka, 2006). In this paper, the authors verify the effectiveness of highly reliable robot production system for PSAS using the development of BAFM.

EMPLOYING THE FITTING LINE USING BAFM

Necessity of the Fitting and Fastening Automation

The recent labor shortage in Japan has been imposing ever increasing pressure on manufacturing sectors to reduce the dependence on manual labor. In body assembly plants, automation of spot welding and similar operations will be reaching nearly 100% as shown in Figure 2.

On the other hands, automation of setting, fitting and fastening of door, hood and luggage compartment panels requiring highly skilled operators is the next important step in complete automation of the body shop as shown in Figure 3. Furthermore, in the overseas body assembly plant, the quality problem has occurred, once the operator has fired for every time.

Figure 2. Operations in body assembly plant and level of automation

Operation	Automation Level	Level of Achievement	Quality Importance
Parts Setting S/A Setting	30	△	—
Spot Welding	88	◎	—
Brazing–Finishing	10	○	○
Exterior Component Installation	8	×	○

Figure 3. Schematic of exterior component installation

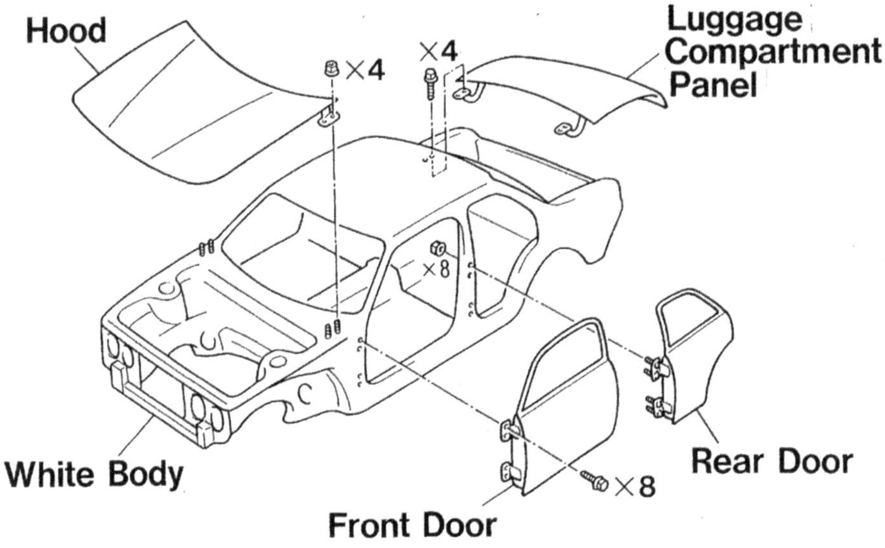

Therefore, the author has realized innovative unmanning of the fitting line by integrating the technologies utilizing BAFM. Such as robotics (Sakai and Amasaka, 2007b, 2007c), vision systems, bolt tightening and product quality management, the ability to automatically fit and fasten door, hood and luggage compartment panels to the car body was achieved.

This section shows the development of the following three items: (1) panel fitting accuracy, (2) automatic bolt tightening, and (3) integration into flexible assembly line at Toyota, a leading international corporation (Sakai and Yasumatsu, 1993; Sakai et al., 1993).

Strategic Project Target

First, the strategic project target and the specific requirements were established at Toyota.

1. **Fitting Quality Requirements:** To ensure fitting accuracy, which provides a sleek exterior surface, strong emphasis was placed on the control of the gaps and surface disparity between panels. Recent worldwide emphasis on quality required that high fitting accuracy requirements were set at 3σ: ±1.0mm (typical: 3σ: ±1.5mm).
2. **Equipment Requirements (Bolt and Nut Supply and Tightening):** The most important basic technology regarding the installation equipment was supply of the bolts, nuts and their tightening processes. Achieving the target operational availability of 95% required the reliability of tightening (success rate per bolt) to be as high as 99.99%.
3. **System Requirements:** For the overall line side system, achievement of high reliability and space efficiency were considered a must. Also, an overall control system combing all the individual technologies and high system flexibility was required.

Engineering Aspects

Engineering aspects to be cleared in order to meet the requirements described above are shown in Table 1. The following sections will describe how we overcame these hurdles.

Table 1. Technical Goals in Development of Automated Body Fitting line

	Requirement	Technical Goals	
Ⓐ Fitting Accuracy	3σ:±1.0mm (Variation in Gap and Surface Disparity)	[A−1]	· Setting the Fitting Quality Standards
		[A−2]	· Selecting the Fitting Adjustment Method
		[A−3]	· Establishing the Means of Measuring the Fitting Position
Ⓑ Assembly Reliability	Tightening Success Rate : 99.99%	[B−1]	· Analysis of Tightening Mechanisms
		[B−2]	· Study of Bolt and Nut Designs
		[B−3]	· Defining the Equipment Specifications

EXAMPLE APPLICATIONS

In this section, the author introduces example application "body auto fitting system" of pioneering technology as applications of the BAFM, which has contributed to the advancement of management technology at Toyota (Amasaka and Sakai, 2011).

A: Fitting Accuracy

1. [A-1]: Setting the fitting quality standards

Standards for the fitting of luggage compartment panel and doors were defined as follows;

a. **Luggage compartment panel:** The panel is fitted into opening the determined by several parts; right and left side member panels, upper back panel and lower back panel.

Configuration of the opening is not necessarily precise or consistent but has certain errors in the longitudinal and lateral dimensions.

To achieve high fitting accuracy, the gaps (s_1~s_4) and surface disparity (d_1~d_4) between the side member panels and luggage compartment panel are measured with sensors attached to the robot which holds and "fits" the luggage compartment panel. The gaps distributed between the left and right were equalized while the surface disparity is corrected to the target value; $s_1=s_2$, $s_3=s_4$ and $d_1=d_2$, $d_3=d_4=d'$ respectively as shown in Figure 4.

b. **Doors:** To determine the orientation of the body, initially the measurement datum was taken from an underbody panel. This was because the underbody pallet carries the white body and an underbody panel was assumed to be "held" in the most accurate position.

These measurements led to a deviation of σ=0.2~0.4mm in relation to the door opening. However, if two holes on the side member panel are used as the datum, the dimensional deviation is σ=0.1~0.2mm for the door opening as shown in Figure 5.

Figure 4. Luggage fitting standards

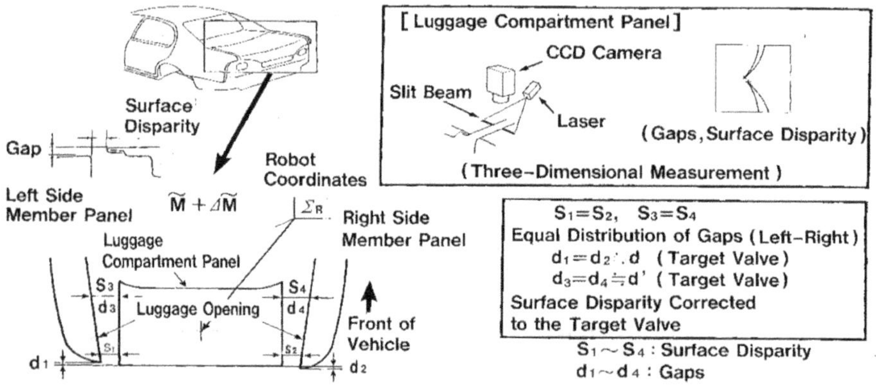

The two datum holes are measured via CCD cameras attached to the door panel jig. The jig is in turn attached to the robot via a tool changer and two dimensional measurements are then possible through coordinate conversion algorithms.

2. [A-2]: Selecting the fitting adjustment method (gap, surface disparity and datum hole measurement)
   a. **Measurement system:** The measurement of the gaps and surface disparity between the luggage compartment panel and the opening essentially requires three-dimensional measurement (Aloimonos, 1988). While there are several methods of three-dimensional measurement such as holography and interference fringe pattern analysis, we chose triangulation which could be done with a simple instrument and considered to be the most practical method.

Figure 5. Standards for door fitting

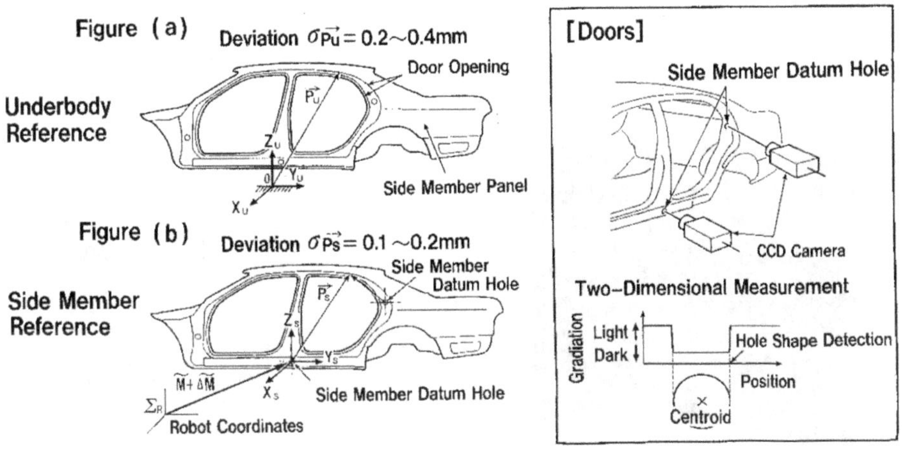

In triangulation, a slit shaped laser beam is applied to the object of measurement and the reflected light is monitored by a CCD camera. For the two-dimensional measurement of the door fitting datum holes, a CCD camera which measures light intensity variation and then digitizes the image data to recognize the contour of the object (circle) was implemented.

The digitized data was then used to calculate the object centered as shown in Figure 6.

Figure 6. Outline of measurement system

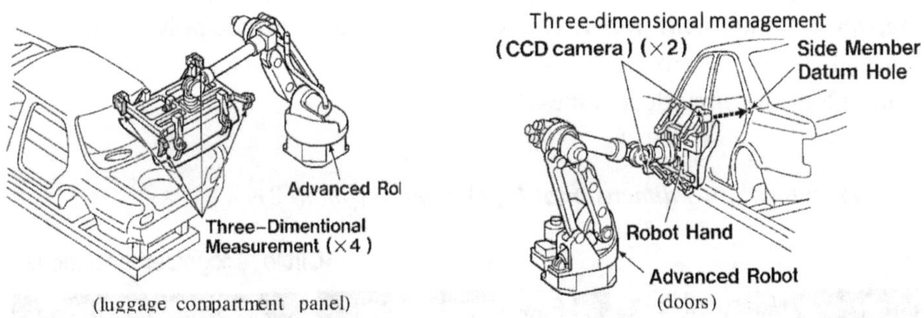

b. Preliminary study and initial problems
   i. **Luggage compartment panel**: In Figure 7(1), photo shows the result of preliminary gap and surface disparity measurements, indicating that a mid-point on the curvature is mistakenly recognized as the true end point. This error was caused by the logic, which as the surface was being scanned recognized the point where the slit image disappeared. For example, on scanning line 11, a slight change in the gloss of the body surface can be misconceived as an end point. In Figure 7(2), the software was revised to counteract these types of errors.

Figure 7. Measurement system for luggage compartment panel and doors

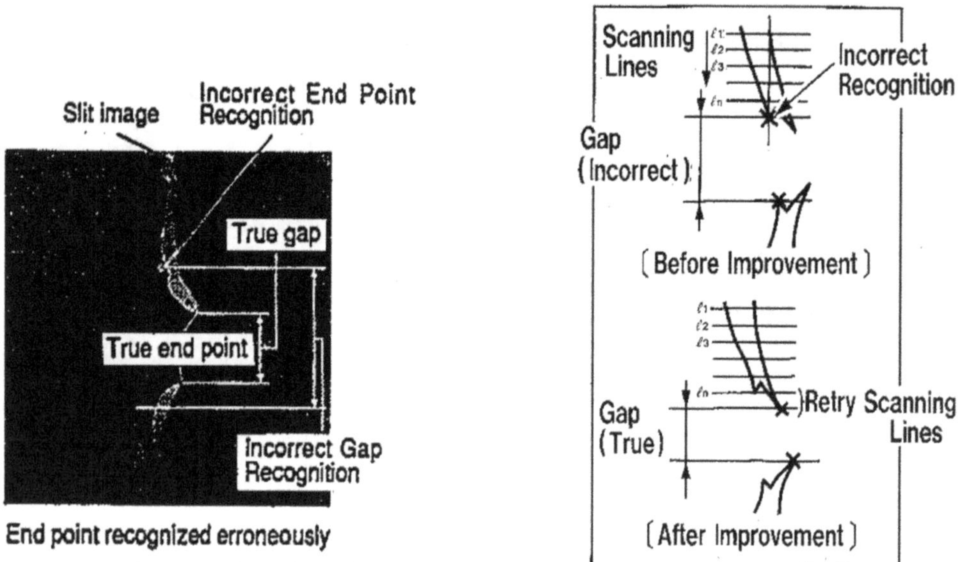

photo1: measurement of gap and surface disparity (2) end point detection logic

ii. **Doors:** The result of a test operation with the two-dimensional sensor is shown in Figure 8, photo 2 shows (a) normally detection, (b) a case where there was a surface flaw (surface scratch). The resulting hole centered offset causes an error which lowers measurement accuracy and (c) a measurement failure where the measurement system stopped operation. The prototype measurement system described above was improved by introducing the following ideas.

1. **Luggage compartment panel:** 1. development of a electronic noise reduction program
2. **Doors:** 1. statistical processing of the image recognition data, 2. development of centered location logic for imperfect circles

Figure 8. Measurement with two-dimensional CCD camera (photo 2)

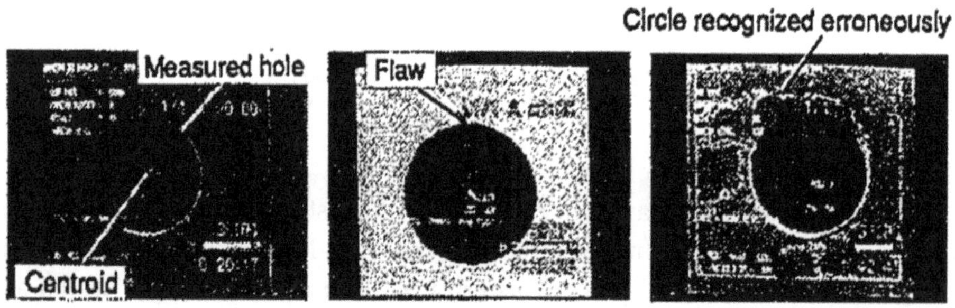

(a). Normally detection (b) Presense of Flaw (c) Blurred Image

c. Problem solutions

The following description uses the two-dimensional hole recognition sensor as an example.

1. The selected method quantitatively represents the characteristic properties f(μ, σ) of the image. These characteristic properties are then statistically confirmed using a pattern recognition process that utilizes 18 typical patterns stored in a database as shown in Figure 9.

The logic was developed by first assuming the image pattern which corresponds to $\mu + n\sigma$ is image A' and the pattern which corresponds to $\mu - n\sigma$ is image A'' with regards to one characteristic property f(μ, σ) (where μ is the mean value of the characteristic property, σ is the deviation, and threshold level is set at $\mu \pm n\sigma$). These two images are then used to determine a characteristic property C which is determined by $\mu - n\sigma < C < \mu + n\sigma$ which then denotes a particular pattern A.

Figure 9. Statistical processing of image recognition data

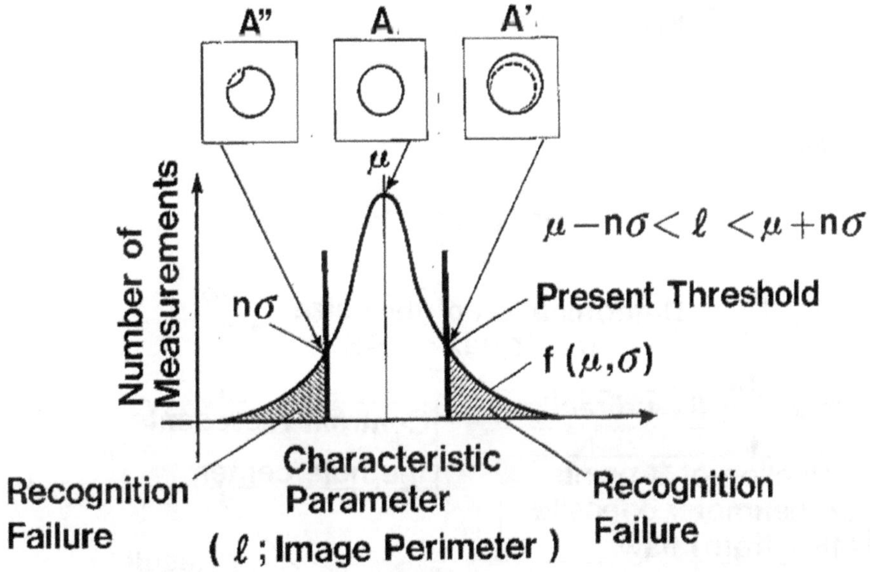

2. Accurate hole location by the algorithm described in (a) may be adversely effected by minute impurities such as changes in the surface gloss, existence of flaws or deformations around the hole. To compensate for such effects, we developed the following detection algorithm. Centered G of the image is first determined as shown in Figure 10.

Then distances $r = \overline{Gi_n}$ (from G to the point i_n), which divide the perimeter into n equal parts, are checked to determine three points corresponding to the value of r which most frequently appears, denoting them as i_a, i_b and i_c. The center of a circle defined by these three points is determined to be true center of the hole. This algorithm is shown in Figure 11.

Figure 10. Hole center detection

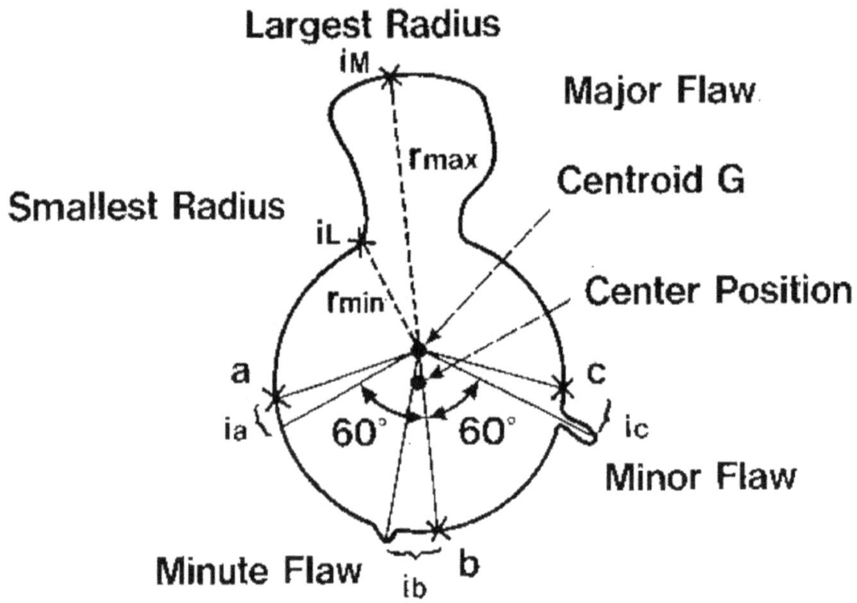

Figure 11. Algorithm

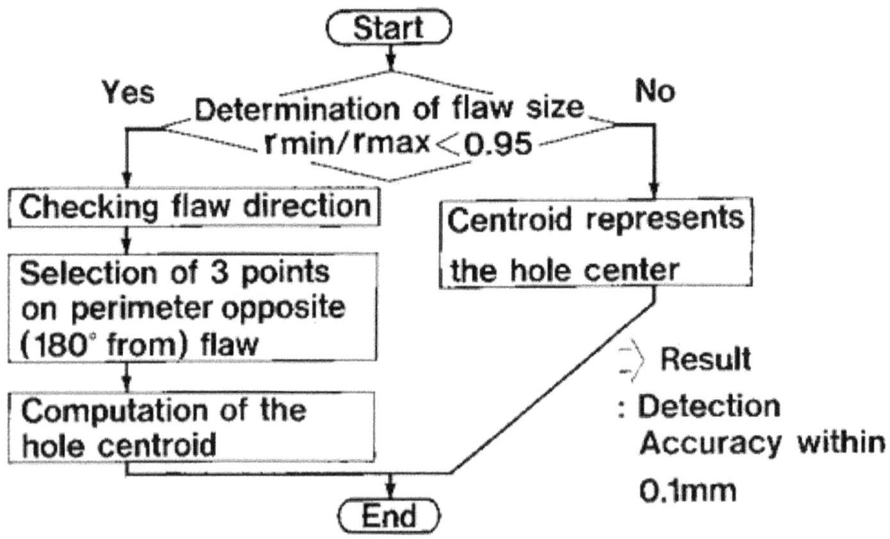

Through both the statistical processing additions and the software improvements, both 100% recognition success rate and detection accuracy within 0.1mm were achieved.

3. [A-3]: Establishing the means of measuring the fitting position

A robot with coordinate conversion function capability was chosen to be utilized by the fitting system. As the robot "fits" the panels to their respective openings, the fitting position was corrected by using coordinate data obtained from the sensors mounted on the robot hand. The algorithm selected to determine **F**, the coordinate conversion technique for the luggage compartment panel, will be described below.

Gap measurement is denoted by S_i, surface disparity by d_i (i=1~4) and the position vector matrix of the hand coordinate viewed from the base coordinate of the robot by $\tilde{M}$. The target values of S_i and d_i are defined as S_{io} and d_{io} respectively, while $\mathbf{g}_i(S_{io}, d_{io})$ are the ideal functions. Let positions on the side member be $\vec{p}_{bi}$ (i=1~4) and the positions on luggage side be $\vec{p}_i$ (i=1~4). Allowing $\Delta\tilde{M}$ representing the displacement of the robot, the least squares method can be applied to approach S_{io} and d_{io}. $\Delta\tilde{M}$ can then be obtained by solving the following equation:

$$\frac{\partial\left\|\tilde{M}\cdot\Delta\tilde{M}\cdot\vec{p}_{li}-\vec{p}_{bi}-g_i\left(S_{i0},d_{i0}\right)\right\|}{\partial_{aj}}=0 \qquad (1)$$

where a_j (j=1,2,3…6) are elements of $\Delta\tilde{M}$ and || ||indicates the absolute function.

Defining $\tilde{M}_0 * \Delta\tilde{M} \equiv \mathbf{F}$, determines the algorithm which determines the optimum gaps and surface disparities at each location, as shown in Figure 12.

Figure 12. Coordinate conversion algorithm

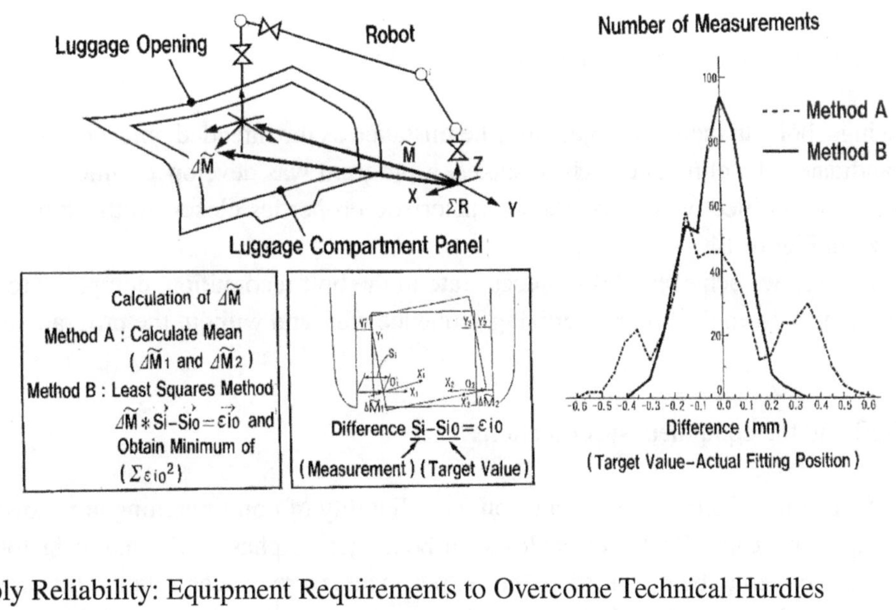

B: Assembly Reliability: Equipment Requirements to Overcome Technical Hurdles

1. [B-1]: Study of bolt and nut designs (bolt type review)

Especially for the bolt type review, bolt designs were studied because of its significant influence on the reliability of tightening. Flat tip, round tip and self locating tip bolt types were studied with regards to the allowance for approach misalignment of bolt β and the bolt inclination allowance α, as shown in Figure 13.

Figure 13. Bolt design influences

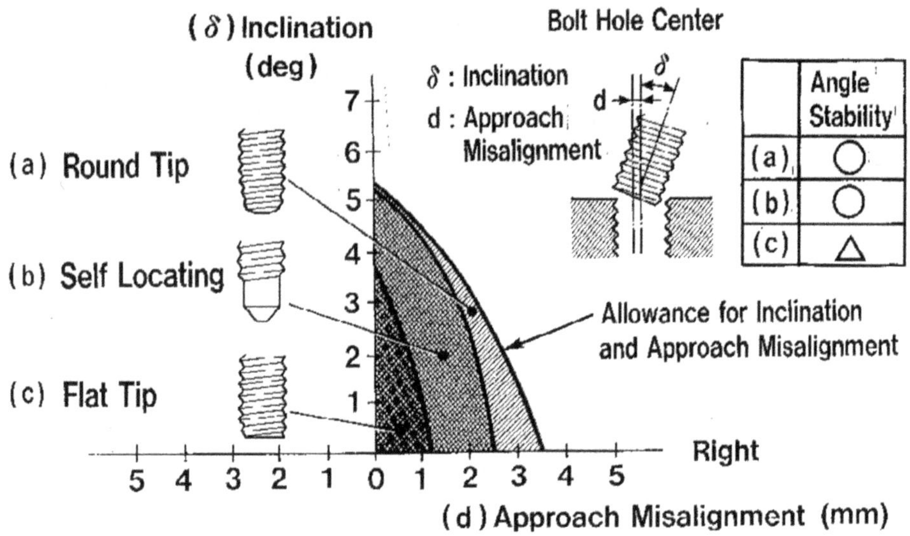

This study revealed that the round tipped bolt and the best tightening reliability.

2. [B-2]: Bolt position measurement study (rear door application)

When viewing a bolt, an incorrect object may be mistaken as the intended object due to the presence of multiple candidates. To eliminate such mistakes, a program was developed which chooses among multiple candidates an object which has the characteristic properties closest to those of the intended object, as shown in Figure 14.

With this program, we achieved 100% success rate in the bolt recognition, compared to 70% in the trial operation. Images from the bolt recognizing sequence with and without the program are shown in Photo 3.

3. [B-3]: Defining the equipment specifications

Characteristic factors which have influence on the reliability of bolt tightening are shown in Figure 15. Those having significant effects are enclosed in boxes for emphasis. The major factor related to tightening was determined to be thrust force, thus experiments were concentrated in this area.

Initially the thrust force provided by a spring, but it provided excessive force in the early stage of tightening. Ultimately, the thrust force was provided by the robot which was synchronized with the progress of the tightening, as shown in Figure 16 and Figure 17.

Figure 14. Bolt Recognition Program

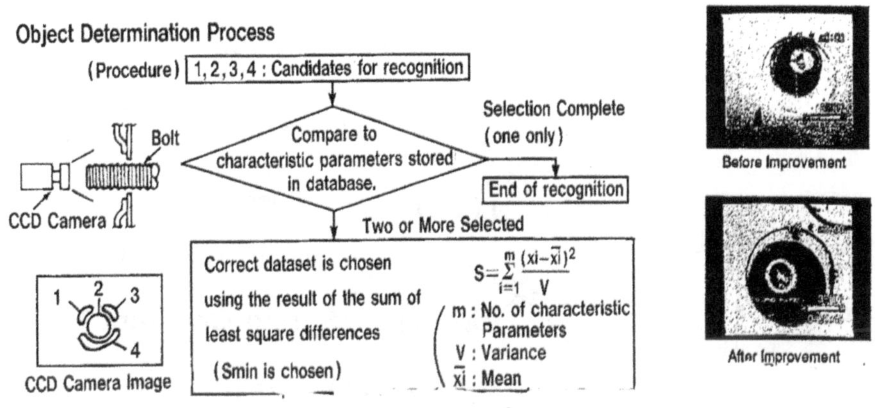

Figure 15. Tightening reliability Cause and effect diagram

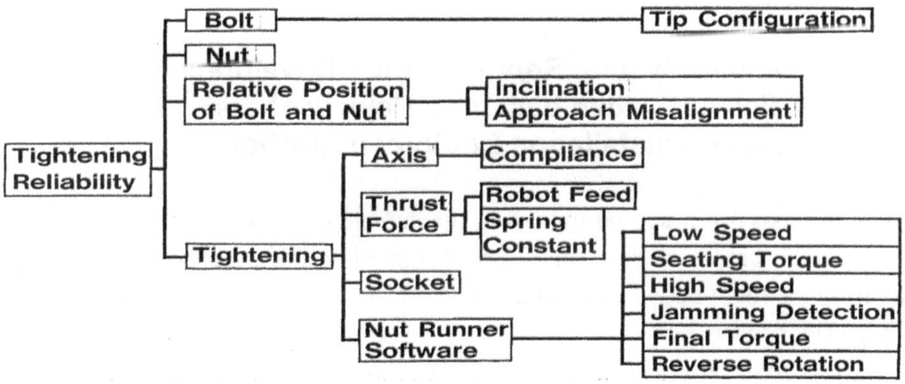

Figure 16. Trust force control

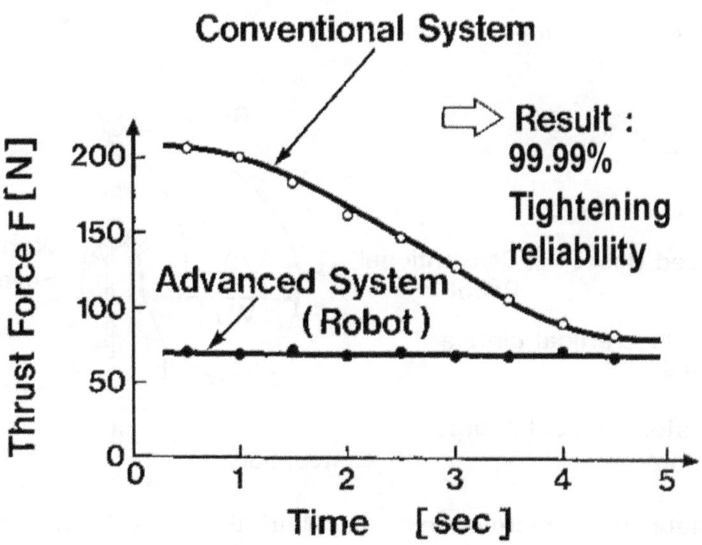

Figure 17. Trust Force Control Method

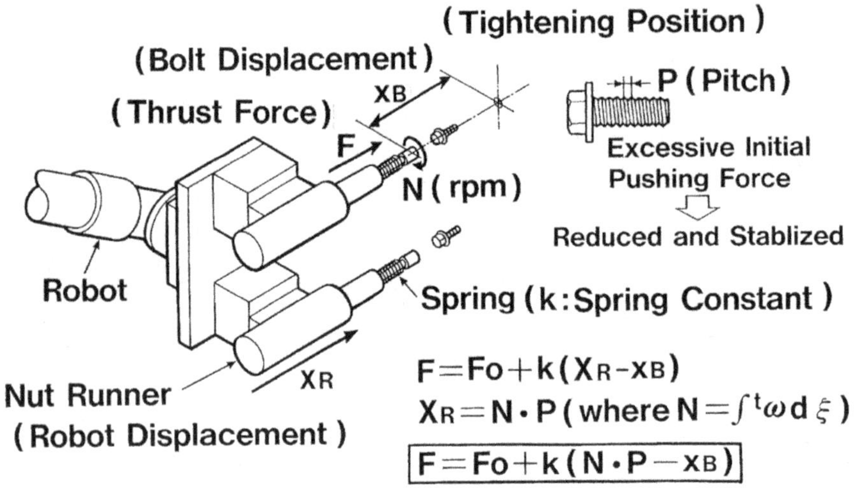

Engineering Aspects of System Requirements: Development of Floor Space-Efficient System based on Review of the Transfer Equipment and Installation Equipment (Robots)

The explanation in this system will be limited to the subject of floor space efficiency. With the conventional robots on the simple mechanism of movable parallel links, the work envelope is confined to a region away from the robot body by predetermined offset. This forces the assembly line to require an undesirably large floor space.

The author reviewed the arm mechanism of the robot and employed a fixed parallel link mechanism which enabled the robot envelope to include an area very near the robot body, as shown in Figure 18. The effect of floor space reduction achieved with this type of robot is shown in Figure 19.

Figure 18. Advanced robot illustration

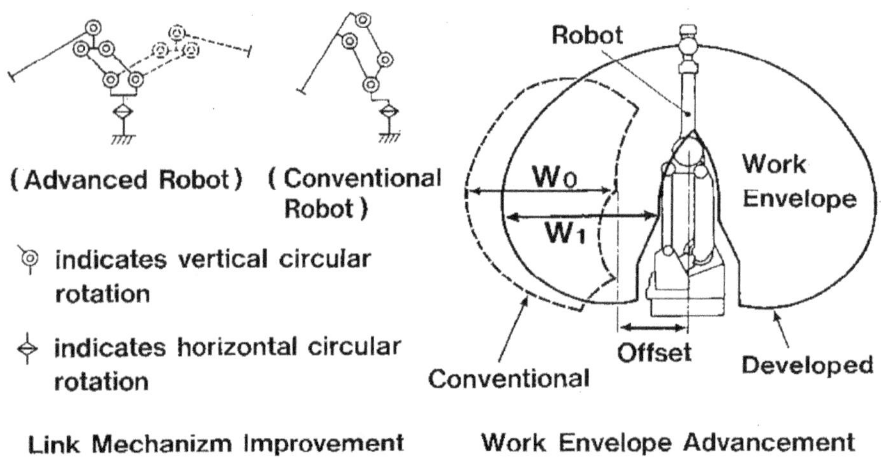

Figure 19. Effect of floor space reduction

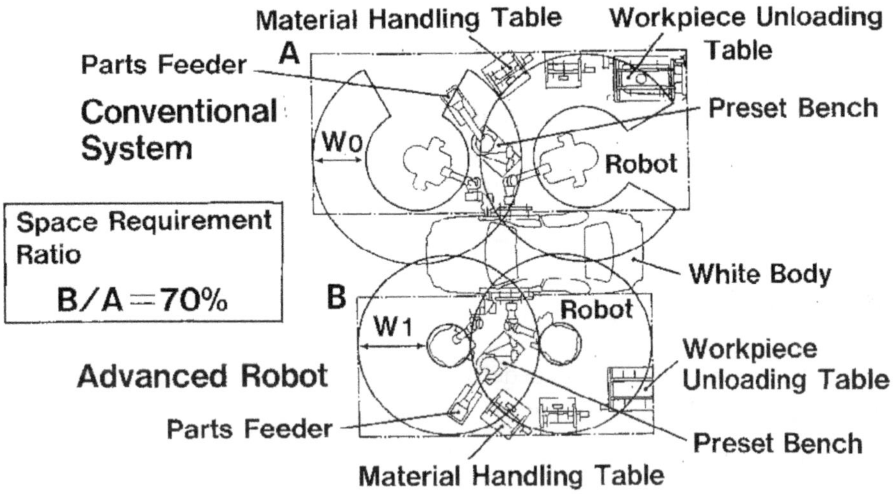

Results

This system is currently integrated in to the body assembly line located in the domestic plant. Conventional robot control method is the fixed point control, such as handling, spot-welding an arc-brazing. On the other hand, this newly method is the actual manufacturing point control, which the robot is synchronized with the tightening progress. Remarkable improvements were achieved in this line, such as the 95% line operation availability and replacement of approximately 10.6 workers, as shown in Table 2. These results were made possible by achieving the target reliability of bolt tightening (99.99%) and the target fitting accuracy (3σ:±1.0mm).

Table 2. System evaluation

	Fitting Quality 3σ (mm)	Tightening Reliability (%)	Labor Savings (persons/day)
Conventional System	±1.5	99.00	——
Advanced System	±1.0	99.99	10.6

CONCLUSION

Automation in its true sense was successfully realized without need to correct the fitting in the downstream processes satisfying the major design stipulation. Success may attribute to the mastering of basic technologies and combining them into a complete system integrated into a flexible production line. In this chapter, the author has established the "BAFM" (Body Auto Fitting Model) using NJ-GPM, and its effectiveness has been verified at an advanced car manufacturer Toyota.

ACKNOWLEDGMENT

The author would like to acknowledge the generous support of the following researchers: all those at Toyota Motor Corporation, and Amasaka New JIT laboratory at Aoyama Gakuin University that assisted with the research, especially, Dr. Sakai, H., Mr. Yasumatsu and others.

REFERENCES

Aloimonos, J., Weiss, I., & Bandyopadhyay, A. (1988). Active vision. *International Journal of Computer Vision, 1*(4), 333–356. doi:10.1007/BF00133571

Amasaka, K. (2007a). New Japan Production Model, an advanced production management principle: Key to strategic implementation of New JIT. *The International Business & Economics Research Journal, 6*(7), 67–79.

Amasaka, K. (2007b). Applying New JIT-Toyota's global production strategy: Epoch-making Innovation in the work environment. *Robotics and Computer-integrated Manufacturing, 23*(3), 285–293. doi:10.1016/j.rcim.2006.02.001

Amasaka, K. (2007c). High Linkage Model "Advanced TDS, TPS & TMS": Strategic development of "New JIT" at Toyota. *International Journal of Operations and Quantitative Management, 13*(3), 101–121.

Amasaka, K., & Sakai, H. (1996). Improving the reliability of body assembly line equipment. *International Journal of Reliability Quality and Safety Engineering, 3*(1), 11–24. doi:10.1142/S021853939600003X

Amasaka, K., & Sakai, H. (1998). Availability and Reliability Information Administration System, ARIM-BL by methodology in Inline-Online SQC. *International Journal of Reliability Quality and Safety Engineering, 5*(1), 55–63. doi:10.1142/S0218539398000078

Amasaka, K., & Sakai, H. (2010). Evolution of TPS fundamentals utilizing New JIT strategy–Proposal and validity of Advanced TPS at Toyota. *Journal of Advanced Manufacturing Systems, 9*(2), 85–99. doi:10.1142/S0219686710001831

Amasaka, K., & Sakai, H. (2011). The New Japan Global Production Model "NJ-GPM": Strategic development of Advanced TPS, *JOMS. Journal of Japanese Operations Management and Strategy, 2*(1), 1–15.

Brooks, R. A. (1986). A robust layered control system for a mobile robot. *IEEE Journal of Robotics and Automation, Ra, 2*(1), 14–23. doi:10.1109/JRA.1986.1087032

Ohno, T. (1977). *Toyota Production System*. Diamond-Sha.

Raibert, T. (1977). *Legged robots that balance*. MIT Press.

Sakai, H., & Amasaka, K. (2003). Construction of "V-IOS" for Promoting Intelligence Operator – Development and Effectiveness for "Visual Manual Format. *The Japan Society for Production Management, The 18th Annual Conference, Nagasaki Institute of Applied Science,* 173-176.

Sakai, H., & Amasaka, K. (2005). V-MICS, Advanced TPS for strategic production administration: Innovative maintenance combining DB and CG. *Journal of Advanced Manufacturing Systems*, *4*(6), 5–20. doi:10.1142/S0219686705000540

Sakai, H., & Amasaka, K. (2006a). TPS-LAS model using Process Layout CAE System at Toyota, Advanced TPS: Key to Global Production Strategy New JIT. *Journal of Advanced Manufacturing Systems*, *5*(2), 1–14. doi:10.1142/S0219686706000790

Sakai, H., & Amasaka, K. (2006b). Strategic HI-POS, intelligence production operating system - Applying Advanced TPS to Toyota's global production strategy. *WSEAS Transactions on Advances in Engineering Education*, *3*(3), 223–230.

Sakai, H., & Amasaka, K. (2007a). Human Digital Pipeline Method using total linkage through design to manufacturing. *Journal of Advanced Manufacturing Systems*, *6*(2), 101–113. doi:10.1142/S0219686707000929

Sakai, H., & Amasaka, K. (2007b). Development of a robot control method for curved seal extrusion for high productivity for an Advanced Toyota Production System. *International Journal of Computer Integrated Manufacturing*, *20*(5), 486–496. doi:10.1080/09511920601160262

Sakai, H., & Amasaka, K. (2007c). The Robot Reliability Design and Improvement Method and the Advanced Toyota Production System. *Industrial Robot: International Journal of Industrial and Service Robotics*, *34*(4), 310–316. doi:10.1108/01439910710749636

Sakai, H., & Amasaka, K. (2013). Establishment of Body Auto Fitting Model "BAFM" using "NJ-GPM" at Toyota. *The Journal of Japanese Operations Management and Strategy*, *4*(1), 38–54.

Sakai, H., & Yasumatsu, S. (1993). Development of body auto fitting system. *Proceedings of the 26th International Symposium on Automotive Technology and Automation*, 1-8.

Chapter 21
Comparing Experienced and Inexperienced Machine Workers:
Improving the Skills of Technicians

ABSTRACT

Toward the firm development of Advanced TPS based on the NMT (New Japan Model), this chapter aims to clarify the factors involved in improving the skills of technicians by conducting a comparison of experienced and inexperienced workers engaged in lathe work, using statistical science and electro-encephalography (EEG). First, a fact-finding survey concerning skill transfer in machining work was conducted to determine the kind of lathe work tasks undertaken by skilled workers. Second, a survey comparing worker's cognition was conducted using EEG analysis. Third, the decision-making criteria used by experienced workers were identified. Fourth, decisions related to the workpiece were visualized. The findings thus obtained were then used to clarify the necessary factors for efficiently and effectively improving the skills of inexperienced workers, and the required results have been achieved.

INTRODUCTION

The Japanese manufacturers today are operating for global production strategy. To overcome this, the authors believed it crucial to improve the intelligence skill level of the production operators who are the foundation of manufacturing. The author recognized the requirement for creating a new production system: Advanced TPS based on the NMT (New Japan Model) (Amasaka, 2002, 2007: Amasaka and Sakai, 2011) (Refer to Chapter 5, 6, 7 and 15).

As a solution, especially, the author suggested the improvement in value of the labor work of automobile manufactures (Sakai and Amasaka, 2006, 2007 and 2008; Tsunoi et al., 2010; Amasaka and Sakai, 2011: Uchida et al., 2012) (Refer to Chapter 6, 7, 15 and 21). Then, toward the firm development of "Advanced TPS", this research aims to clarify the factors involved in improving the skills of technicians

DOI: 10.4018/978-1-7998-8746-1.ch021

by conducting a comparison of experienced and inexperienced workers engaged in lathe work (Yamazaki and Yoshioka, 2011; Yanagisawa, et al., 2013).

With the amount of production from the machining and assembly industries increasing year-on-year, machining technology is becoming increasingly important because machining is the fundamental process underpinning the industry. However, while the global level of technology is improving in line with machine-related companies' expansion of overseas production, the stagnant level of Japanese technology has become a matter for concern. Particularly evident is the sluggish pace at which the technical skills of inexperienced workers improve. This is thought to be due to the implicit style of training, which relies upon the intuition and know-how of experienced workers.

Thus, the author used electroencephalography (EEG) and statistical science to conduct a comparison of experienced and inexperienced workers engaged in lathe work, which is the foundation of machining work, and analyze the skills possessed by experienced workers. The findings were used to analyze the factors involved in improving the skills of inexperienced workers, and the required results have been achieved by using Science SQC (Yamazaki and Yoshioka, 2011; Yanagisawa et al., 2013; Amasaka, 2015) (Refer to Chapter 5).

SKILL TRANSFER PROBLEM IN THE MANUFACTURING INDUSTRY

In Japan, occupations in the service industry are by far the most popular, and the number of employees engaged in this kind of work is increasing year-on-year. Employment in the manufacturing industry continued to decline during the 10 year period between fiscal 1992, which was the peak, and fiscal 2002.

During this period, the figure fell 22% from 15.69 million people to 12.22 million people, resulting in fewer opportunities to transfer skills. For large companies, such a reduction in the number of employees places a greater burden on individual workers, which itself leads to an increase in the rate of people leaving. For businesses operating on a smaller scale such as small and medium sized companies and small factories, this leads to a lack of successors and ultimately to bankruptcy. Thus, Japan's manufacturing industry will begin to shrink.

In addition to the lack of successors, another problem faced by Japan's manufacturing industry is that of "skill transfer", or training. Although the manufacturing industry—which relies heavily on specialist technology—is becoming increasingly mechanized, there are still many products where a human touch is required in order to maintain quality.

As is the case with traditional crafts, workers need many years of experience to become able to produce quality products and the lack of established training methods makes it difficult to train new employees. Thus, the two major challenges for Japan's manufacturing industry are a lack of successors and problems with training new employees.

The World Skills Competition (formerly known as the "Skill Olympics") is run by World Skills International (WSI: World Skills International). The organization's committee is made up of official and technical delegates from member countries. The purpose of the competition is to promote occupational training in the participating countries and to encourage international exchange and goodwill among young technicians. Japan has been participating since the 11th competition in 1962.

Although Japan placed first or second from about the 11th competition to the 20th competition, Korea is recently going from strength to strength as shown in Table 1. In Korea, the large number of technical colleges means that training for machining skills is well organized and therefore technical skills are improving. Japan's manufacturing industry, which was once at a global top class level, is currently deteriorating and it is now vital to quickly find solutions to the problems associated with skill transfer within the industry.

Table 1. Top three ranking countries in world skills competition

Competition number	**The top three countries that won the gold medal**		
	First rank	Second rank	Third rank
40	South Korea	Switzerland	Japan
39	Japan	South Korea	France
38	Japan, Switzerland, South Tyrol, Italy	Germany, Finland	
37	South Korea	Switzerland	Japan
36	South Korea	Germany	Japan
35	Chinese Taipei	South Korea	Japan
34	South Korea	Chinese Taipei, Switzerland	
33	South Korea		Japan, Germany, Switzerland
32	Chinese Taipei	South Korea	Germany
31	South Korea	Chinese Taipei	Australia
30	South Korea	Chinese Taipei	Australia
29	South Korea	Japan	Chinese Taipei
28	South Korea	Japan	Chinese Taipei
27	South Korea	Chinese Taipei	Australia
26	South Korea	Japan	Germany
25	South Korea	Japan	Switzerland
24	South Korea	Switzerland	Australia
23	South Korea	Germany	Japan
22	Switzerland	South Korea	Spain
21	Germany	South Korea	Japan
20	Japan	Spain	Switzerland
19	Japan	Germany	South Korea
18	Japan	Switzerland	Germany
17	Switzerland	Japan	South Korea
16	Spain	Japan	West Germany
15	Japan	Netherlands	UK, Italy
14	UK	Japan	Spain
13	Japan	UK	Portugal, Spain
12	Japan	Ireland	West Germany
11	Spain	Japan	

PRIOR RESEARCH

Similar research has been conducted on visualizing the knowledge possessed by experienced workers, such as "Development of Knowledge Visualization System for Knowledge Transfer" (Watanuki and Tanaka; 2003), which visualized knowledge related to metal casting. With the aim of supporting the effective and efficient gaining of knowledge for inexperienced workers, Watanuki and Tanaka developed a system to systematize metal casting-related knowledge.

First, the work was broken down into processes such as planning, mold making, and mold filling. These general work processes were then further broken down into more detailed processes to produce an overview of the tools, terminology, and techniques related to each process. Furthermore, similar research has also been conducted on visualizing skills, such as "Detailed Design and Improvement of a Manual Assembly Task Incorporating How to Efficiently Handle Uncertainties" (Murakami and Mizuyama; 2007).

This research suggests that efficiency during assembly work relies upon skillfully handling uncertainties. Uncertainties in the contact state during work processes are expressed as an aggregate (called a "conceptual state") of more than one contact state possessing a degree of probability, not necessarily limited to those perceived by the worker, and the work undertaken by workers is classified into several work elements. Thus, assembly work is expressed as "a series of work elements whereby the initial conceptual state is caused to transition into the target conceptual state". Murakami and Mizuyama therefore propose a method of designing assembly work processes which focuses on the transition between conceptual states, while taking into account the lack of clarity concerning the conceptual states that relate to the contact states and applying the distance from the target conceptual state, providing a yardstick for deciding which conceptual states a product should pass through.

Research concerning the comparison of experienced workers and inexperienced workers has also been conducted by Miyamoto, "Comparison of Body Movement and Muscle Activity Patterns During Sharpening a Kitchen Knife Between Skilled and Unskilled Subjects" (Miyamoto, et al; 2006). This research suggests that knife sharpening, which is fundamentally a grinding process, involves grinding work and decision-making that relies heavily upon implicit factors such as experience and intuition developed over many years. The research clarifies the distinctive movement of the upper limbs and the muscle activity of the key muscle groups during grinding work performed by experienced workers and inexperienced workers, and studies the correspondence relationships between the movements and muscle activity to determine the stipulated factors affecting the finished state of the blade.

The above clearly demonstrates the fact that there is little research concerning the comparison of experienced workers and inexperienced workers engaged in machining work, and that more research in this field is urgently required in order to prevent the current state of the manufacturing industry in Japan from ultimately falling into decline. Thus, based on the example of the application of statistical science called "Science SQC, new quality control principle" provided by the author (Amasaka, 2004), the author has employed statistical science to visualize the unconscious "decision-making" processes applied by experienced workers in order to enable the experienced workers to train inexperienced workers effectively and efficiently.

VISUALIZING THE SKILLS OF EXPERIENCED WORKERS AND INEXPERIENCED WORKERS

Comparing the Working Efficiency of Workers

When comparing experienced workers and inexperienced workers, the first thing to be compared is working efficiency. "Lathe work" involves processes such as rough cutting, semi-finishing, making adjustments, and finishing. For the comparison, videos were taken of experienced workers and inexperienced workers while working, and the time taken (seconds) for each processes' tasks was noted. This helped to clarify the differences in working efficiency. Observing the processes separately, the initial setup tasks and actual work tasks were represented with different colors and the work times were noted in seconds as shown in Table 2.

Next, the total times for initial setup and actual work were compared. It was found that, while there was little difference in the amount of time taken by experienced workers and inexperienced workers for the actual work tasks due to the use of automated machines, there was a significant difference for the initial setup tasks as shown in Table 3.

Because the machining conditions differ depending on the workpiece, it takes longer for inexperienced workers to make decisions due to their lack of experience and knowledge, which impacts upon their working efficiency. The author investigated what forms the basis of efficient and effective working practices for experienced workers, and found that their work practices were based on logical cognition, and therefore decisions were influenced more by logic than by physical movements while working as shown in Figure 1.

Comparing Experienced and Inexperienced Workers' Cognition using Electroencephalography

Electroencephalography was used to clarify differences in the cognition of experienced workers and inexperienced workers. The respective workers' Beta waves (waves that occur when the brain is particularly active) were monitored while they were performing lathe work, and an $X\text{-}R_S$ control chart was used to identify the response points and determine the data that deviates from the control limit lines. The analysis focused on the median control limit (CL), upper control limit (UCL), and lower control limit (LCL) for the left brain, which performs logical cognition, and the right brain, which performs sensible cognition as shown in Table 4 and Figure 2.

Points where the left brain and right brain cognition of experienced workers and inexperienced workers deviate from the control limit lines were identified and compared. There are three main types of work: cutting during lathe work, checking measurements using a micrometer, and checking the finish of a completed product. The results of the comparison reveal that a strong left brain response is common to both (a) Experienced workers and (b) Inexperienced workers as shown in Table 5(a) and Table 5(b).

Therefore, it is clear that both types of workers frequently use logical cognition while working. Much right brain activity is found in experienced workers, while almost no right brain activity is found in inexperienced workers. It was determined from these results that, due to their lack of experience, inexperienced workers concentrate only on knowledge and techniques they have been taught.

Thus, it can be seen that the application of logical cognition as well as differences in logical content have a significant influence on completed products in machining work.

Table 2. Work tasks and work times for experienced workers and inexperienced workers

Experienced				Inexperienced		
Work tasks	**Time (s)**	**Work times (s)**		**Work tasks**	**Times (s)**	**Work times (s)**
Scaling	0-3	4		Scaling	0-5	5
Peel off black skin	3-22	20		Peel off black skin	5-24	20
Micrometer	22-27	6		Escape	24-25	2
Escape	27-28	2		Micrometer	28-36	9
Scaling	29-41	13		Scaling	37-48	12
Rough cutting	42-75	34		Rough cutting	49-92	44
Escape	75-76	2		Escape	92-94	3
Scaling	76-78	3		Scaling	94-98	5
Rough cutting	78-111	33		Rough cutting	99-133	35
Escape	111-113	3		Escape	133-136	4
Scaling	113-115	3		Scaling	136-140	5
Rough cutting	115-149	35		Rough cutting	140 175	36
Escape	149-153	4		Escape	175-179	5
Scaling	153-155	3		Scaling	180-188	9
Rough cutting	155-181	26		Rough cutting	188-216	29
Escape	181-183	3		Escape	216-217	2
Scaling	183-185	3		Scaling	217-225	9
Rough cutting	185-210	26		Rough cutting	225-254	30
Escape	211-212	2		Escape	254-255	2
Scaling	213-215	3		Scaling	255-259	5
Rough cutting	216-244	29		Rough cutting	259-285	27
Escape	244-247	4		Escape	285-292	8
Scaling	247-249	3		Scaling	292-300	9
Rough cutting	250-263	14		Rough cutting	300-316	17
Escape	263-263	1		Escape	317-317	1
Scaling	264-267	4		Scaling	318-322	5
Rough cutting	268-283	16		Rough cutting	322-339	18
Escape	283-286	4		Escape	339-345	7

Table 3. Total times for initial setup and actual work

	Experienced	**Inexperienced**
Setup	622s	1061s
Work	936s	962s

Figure 1. Points considered by experienced workers during lathe work

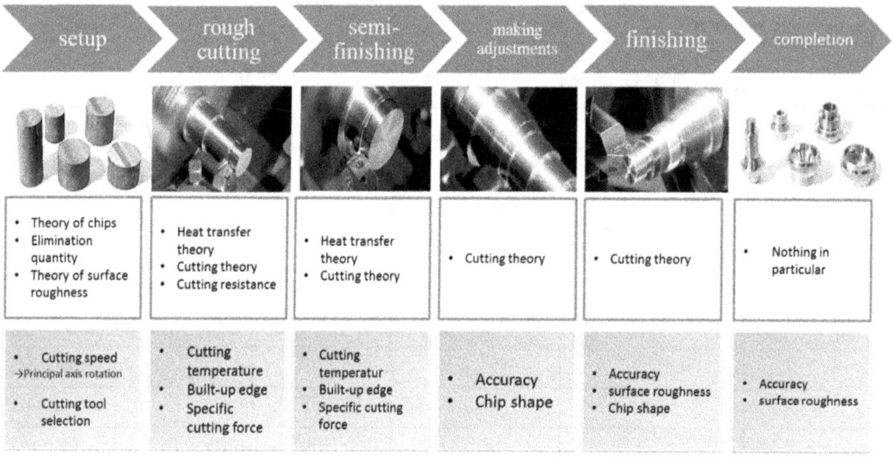

Table 4. Left brain and right Brain control lines

	Median control limit (CL)	Upper control limit (UCL)	Lower control limit (LCL)
Left brain of experienced	27.6836	31.8045	23.5627
Right brain of experienced	27.3690	30.7490	23.9889
Left brain of inexperienced	26.6430	30.1310	23.1550
Right brain of inexperienced	26.5407	29.5164	23.5650

Figure 2. X-Rs Control Chart

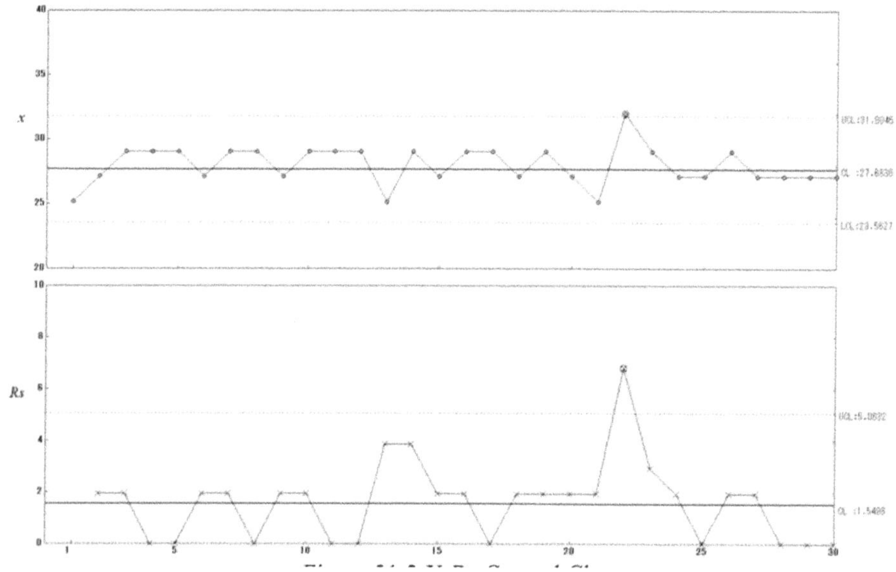

Table 5. Correspondence table for experienced workers' left/ right brain response points and work tasks

Seconds	Work	Left brain	Right brain		Seconds	Work	Left brain	Right brain
3	Cutting	O	-		1	Cutting	-	O
6	Cutting	O	-		4	Cutting	-	O
20	Cutting	O	-		22	Cutting	O	-
111	Micrometer	-	O		119	Micrometer	O	O
152	Micrometer	O	-		126	Micrometer	-	O
238	Cutting	O	-		168	Micrometer	O	-
250	Cutting	O	-		240	Cutting	O	-
272	Cutting	O	O		254	Cutting	O	O
310	Micrometer	O	-		256	Cutting	O	-
331	Checking	O	-		288	Cutting	O	O
359	Checking	O	-		312	Micrometer	O	-
					313	Micrometer	O	O
					329	Checking	O	-
					338	Checking	O	-
					360	Checking	O	-
					363	Checking	O	O
(a) **Experienced workers**					(b) **Inexperienced workers**			

Table 6. Workpieces and cutting speeds

Work pieces	Tensile strength [N/mm^2]	Elongation [%]	Hardness [HV]	Thermal conductivity [w/m/°C]	Density [kg/m^3]	Young's modulus [GPa]	Shear elasticity modulus [G]	Yield strength [MPa]	Cutting speeds [m/min]
A5056	299	40	95	238	2.6	700	26	195	135
C1100	245	14	50	400	8.9	130	48	200	220
SUS304	520	55	200	16	8	197	74	205	200
SS400	400	20	125	80	7.9	206	79	240	250
Ti-6Al-4V	980	14	318	22	4.4	106	41	920	60
Industrial pure iron	196	60	100	67	7.9	205	81	98	150
SUS410	540	25	230	28	7.8	200	75.8	345	200
SUS430	450	22	90	25.6	7.8	200	76.9	205	300
S45C	828	22	170	44	7.8	205	82	727	250
Nickel	335	28	638	90	8.9	204	81	58	60
Magnesium alloy (MB1)	230	6	52	30.8	1.8	40	17	140	150
Industrial pure titanium (C.P.Ti)	320	27	200	21.9	4.6	106	45	170	80

Identifying Decision-Making Criteria of Experienced Workers using Statistical Analysis

Workers perform the initial setup work, then begin the actual machining work, and finally perform the finishing work to complete the product. There are two types of decisions that experienced workers are required to make during this workflow: decisions that arise during the initial setup stage before the main work commences, and decisions that arise after the main work commences.

During the initial setup stage, workers must visually and tactually check the workpiece and its characteristics in order to make decisions concerning the most suitable cutting speed and cutting tool for the workpiece, and also use the visual and other senses to determine whether the cutting work is satisfactory. Thus, statistical analysis was used to clarify the criteria that are applied by experienced workers when making such decisions.

It was confirmed by Dr. Hosoda, Y. (a professor at the Institute of Technologists, Saitama, Japan) that experienced workers determine the suitable cutting speed based on the physical and mechanical characteristics of the workpiece. The physical and mechanical characteristics of a workpiece are its tensile strength, elongation, hardness, thermal conductivity, density, Young's modulus, shear elasticity modulus, and yield strength, and the relative influence of these characteristics are clarified in accordance with the cutting conditions as shown in Table 6.

Multiple regression analysis was conducted in order to determine the relationship between the optimum cutting speed and the physical and mechanical factors as shown in Table 7. Values were selected for the variables using the stepwise method, and the partial regression coefficients resulting from the analysis revealed that the shear elasticity modulus, hardness, elongation, and Young's modulus have a significant influence on the rough machining cutting speed (in the order of hardness > shear elasticity modulus > elongation > Young's modulus).

Table 7. Multiple regression analysis results for rough machining cutting speed objective variable

	Objective variables	**Residual sum of squares**	**Multiple correlation coefficient**	**Contribution ratio R^2**	**R*^2**	
	Cutting speeds	8388.941	0.937	0.877	0.807	
No	Explanatory variables	Residual sum of squares	Variation	Variance ratio	Partial regression coefficient	Standard partial regression coefficient
1	Constant Term	21056.002	12667.06	10.5698	108.931	
2	Tensile strength	8385.841	-3.099	0.0022	-	
3	Elongation	18375.675	9986.735	8.3333	-2.313	-0.478
4	Hardness	49807.393	41418.45	34.5609	-0.401	-0.825
5	Thermal conductivity	8388.933	-0.008	0	-	
6	Density	7970.62	-418.321	0.3149	+	
7	Young's modulus	11366.074	2977.133	2.4842	0.116	0.243
8	Shear elasticity modulus	45024.054	36635.11	30.5695	2.94	0.885
9	Yield strength	7957.383	-431.557	0.3254	-	

To conduct the same multiple regression analysis with respect to cutting work for finishing, which is performed after the rough machining process, the rough machining cutting speed was added as an explanatory variable as shown in Table 8.

Table 8. Rough machining / Finishing cutting speeds for each workpiece

	Tensile strength [N/mm^2]	Tensile strength [%]	Hardness [HV]	Thermal conductivity [w/m/°C]	Density [kg/m^3]	Young's modulus [GPa]	Shear elasticity modulus [G]	Yield strength [MPa]	Cutting speeds [m/min]	Finishing cutting speeds [m/min]
A5056	299	40	95	238	2.6	700	26	195	135	300
C1100	245	14	50	400	8.9	130	48	200	220	300
SUS304	520	55	200	16	8	197	74	205	200	500
SS400	400	20	125	80	7.9	206	79	240	250	300
Ti-6Al-4V	980	14	318	22	4.4	106	41	920	60	100
Industrial pure iron	196	60	100	67	7.9	205	81	98	150	300
SUS410	540	25	230	28	7.8	200	75.8	345	200	500
SUS430	450	22	90	25.6	7.8	200	76.9	205	300	500
S45C	828	22	170	44	7.8	205	82	727	250	500
Nickel	335	28	638	90	8.9	204	81	58	60	200
Magnesium alloy(MB1)	230	6	52	30.8	1.8	40	17	140	150	300
Industrial pure titanium (C.P.Ti)	320	27	200	21.9	4.6	106	45	170	80	150

Values were again selected for the variables using the stepwise method, and the partial regression coefficients resulting from the analysis revealed that the rough machining cutting speed and elongation had a significant influence (rough machining cutting speed > elongation) as shown in Table 9.

Next, the author investigated the criteria for selecting the cutting tool. The physical and mechanical characteristics were set as the explanatory variables, while the cutting tool material used during rough machining and finishing were set as the objective variables. Discriminant analysis was conducted and, when the discriminant coefficients were converted to absolute values and averages were calculated, the results showed that the influence occurred in the order of density > tensile strength > elongation as shown in Table 10.

When the same analysis was conducted concerning selection of the cutting tool for finishing, the results showed that the influence occurred in the order of thermal conductivity > density > elongation.

Next, the important decision-making factors applied by experienced workers when making decisions during work processes were clarified. It was found that, in order to ensure satisfactory cutting, experienced workers change variable factors such as the tool type and cutting speed in accordance with decision-making factors such as the chips, lathe vibration, and air temperature.

Table 9. Multiple regression Analysis Results for finishing cutting speed objective variable

	Objective variables	**Residual sum of squares**	**Multiple correlation coefficient**	**Contribution ratio R^2**	**R*^2**	
	Finishing cutting speeds	60238.617	0.854	0.729	0.669	
No	Explanatory variables	Residual sum of squares	Variation	Variance ratio	Partial regression coefficient	Standard partial regression coefficient
1	Constant Term	60343.498	104.881	0.0157	9.277	
2	Tensile strength	55432.865	-4805.75	0.6936	+	
3	Elongation	75709.123	15470.51	2.3114	2.307	0.264
4	Hardness	53781.995	-6456.62	0.9604	+	
5	Thermal conductivity	52619.435	-7619.18	1.1584	-	
6	Density	60014.957	-223.66	0.0298	-	
7	Young's modulus	60236.063	-2.553	0.0003	+	
8	Shear elasticity modulus	59967.696	-270.921	0.0361	+	
9	Yield strength	59117.164	-1121.45	0.1518	+	
10	Cutting speeds	212160.113	151921.5	22.698	1.494	0.828

Table 10. Discriminant Coefficients for cutting tool materials during rough cutting

		Group1-Group2	**Group1-Group3**	**Group1-Group4**	**Group2-Group3**	**Group2-Group4**	**Group3-Group4**
		Discriminant coefficient	**Discriminant coefficient**	**Discriminant coefficient**	**Discriminant coefficient**	**Discriminant coefficient**	**Discriminant coefficient**
	Mahalanobis distance	75.419	40.154	8.69	9.435	38.974	17.092
	Determine the error rate (%)	0.001	0.077	7.025	6.229	0.09	1.936
1	Constant Term	86.422	52.761	17.174	-33.661	-69.248	-35.587
2	Tensile strength	4.32	2.94	1.24	1.37	3.08	1.71
3	Elongation	3.97	3.59	0.84	0.37	3.13	2.75
4	Hardness	0.173	0.121	0.048	-0.052	-0.125	-0.073
5	Thermal conductivity	-0.158	-0.097	-0.048	0.061	0.11	0.049
6	Density	-4.558	-3.592	-1.035	0.966	3.524	2.558
7	Young's modulus	0.057	0.034	0.022	-0.023	-0.034	-0.012
8	Shear elasticity modulus	0.031	0.025	0.003	-0.005	-0.027	-0.022
9	Yield strength	0.304	0.203	0.086	-0.101	-0.219	-0.117

For this research, chip color and chip shape—which are the keys to making appropriate decisions—are used as decision-making factors, while the tool type, cutting speed, feed rate, cutting depth, presence/absence of cutting oil, escape angle, and shear angle are the variable factors.

Furthermore, the analysis conducted for this research uses a material called S45C as an example. This material was selected because, as a kind of carbon steel, S45C is the most commonly used material and also the material used for the World Skills Competition. The authors clarified the important criteria used by experienced workers for making decisions based on the chip color and chip shape when cutting S45C.

The color of chips varies depending on the cutting temperature, and the shape of the chips also varies significantly. Covariance structure analysis was used to clarify what kind of influence these elements receive from each factor. This was done separately with respect to cutting work for the rough machining process and cutting work for the finishing process.

The results of the covariance structure analysis are as follows. The chip color during rough machining as shown in Figure 3, where surface roughness and subsurface damage are not a consideration, is strongly influenced by the cutting speed.

Figure 3. Chip color during rough machining

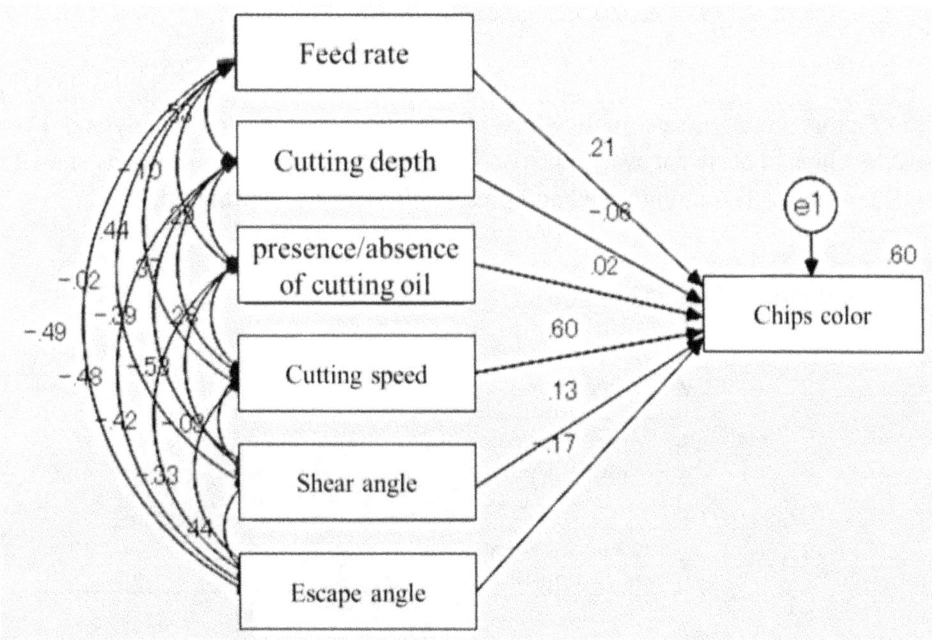

Due to the emphasis on efficiency, the cutting speed is the only factor to have a significant influence. The chip shape during rough machining as shown in Figure 4 is influenced by the cutting speed and the escape angle. This is because chips can become wedged between the workpiece and the lathe jaws during cutting. This may cause the chips to melt due to the heat and adhere to the tool blade, resulting in the formation of a built-up edge.

Figure 4. Chip shape during rough machining

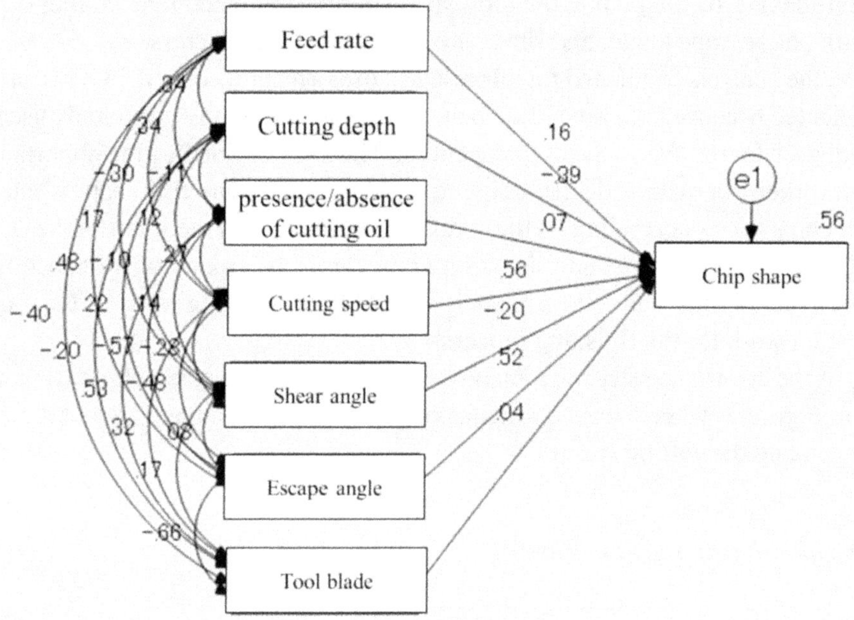

Significant factors are an escape angle which allows chips to flow away easily and a cutting speed which causes the chips to be swept away quickly. The chip color during finishing as shown in Figure 5 is strongly influenced by the cutting speed and presence/absence of cutting oil.

Figure 5. Chip color during finishing

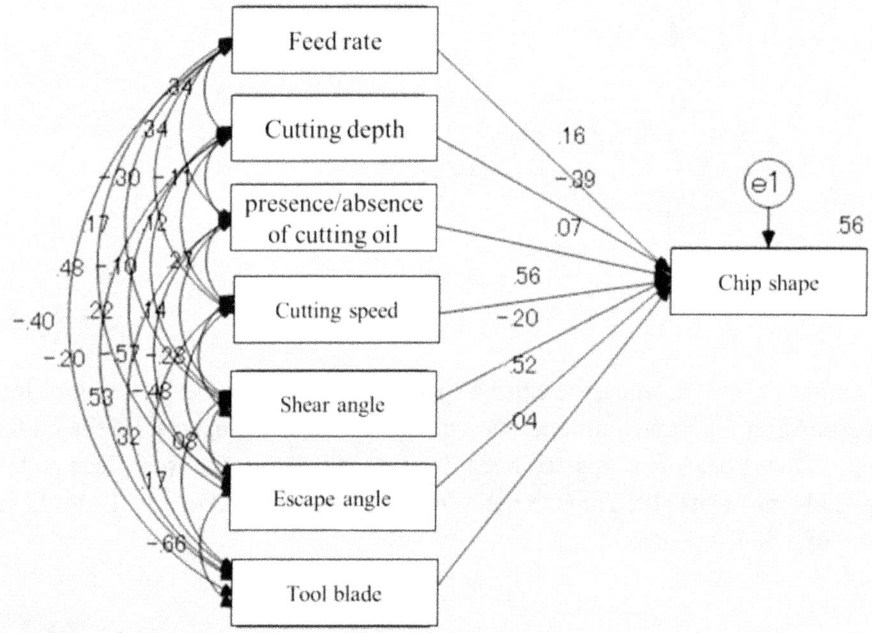

This is because damaged layers can occur during finishing due to the heat generated as the cutting speed is changed. The chip shape during finishing as shown in Figure 6 is strongly influenced by the escape angle and the feed angle. This is because chips can easily become caught during the finishing process, which is required for lowering the surface roughness, and these factors must be adjusted to avoid the occurrence of this. Thus, the above analysis reveals the decision-making factors applied by experienced workers when selecting the cutting speed and selecting the cutting tool.

Figure 6. Chip Shape during Finishing

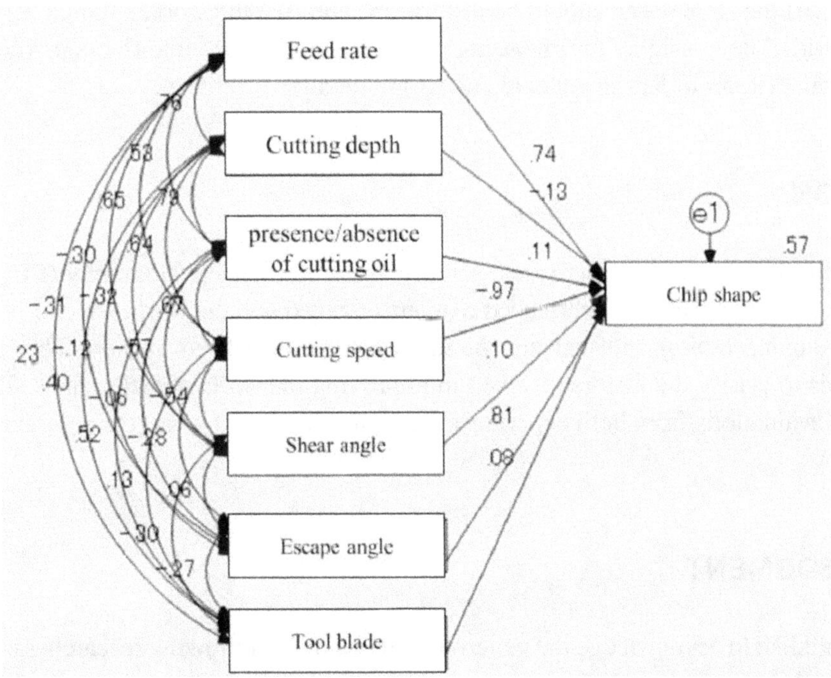

EVALUATION OF THIS RESEARH

The decision-making factors and factors involved in improving technical skills that have been made explicit by this research were evaluated by Dr. Hosoda, a professor at the Institute of Technologists, and 10 students (with lathe experience) from the institute's department of manufacturing technologies.

Opinions from an experienced worker's perspective such as the following were received: "The research clarifies points where inexperienced workers need guidance such as cutting tool selection, which is beneficial for both the person giving guidance and the person receiving guidance".; "Comparing workers' cognition using brain waves is an innovative research method, and I rate it highly". Opinions from an inexperienced worker's perspective such as the following were received: "Logic-based research such as this makes the subject easy to understand and easy to learn about".

APPLICATION TO SIMILAR ISSUE

With its effectiveness verified, the author was able to apply as the similar issue "Work procedure manual incorporating experienced workers' intuition and knowhow" as follows. The author considered the working of a lathe and identified the difference in skills of experienced and inexperienced workers by analyzing (i) the workers' brainwaves, (ii) the vibration of the workpieces, and (iii) the odor emitted during the work. This analysis demonstrated that experienced workers (i) relaxed and concentrated at appropriate times, (ii) adjusted the slide speed appropriately, and (iii) oiled the machine adequately, depending on the odor. Subsequently, the created a work procedure manual to teach when (i) the worker should relax or concentrate, (ii) the slide speed should be fast or low, and (iii) the worker should oil the machinery. The author provided new insights for imparting experienced workers' intuition and knowhow to inexperienced workers. (Refer to Kawahara et al., (2016) in detail).

CONCLUSION

For this research, the authors used statistical science and electroencephalography (EEG) to conduct a comparison of experienced and inexperienced workers engaged in lathe work, which is the fundamental process involved in machining, and analyzed the skills of the experienced workers. They then conducted factorial analysis to clarify the factors involved in improving the skills of technicians. The research received positive evaluations from both experienced and inexperienced workers, and the required results were achieved.

ACKNOWLEDGMENT

The author would like to acknowledge the generous support of the following researchers: Amasaka New JIT laboratory at Aoyama Gakuin University that assisted with the research, especially, Miss. Yamasaki, M., Mr. Yoshioka, K., Mr. Yanagisawa, K., and others. Further, Part of this research is supported by Dr. Yasuhiro, H (a professor at the Institute, Japan) and students.

REFERENCES

Amasaka, K. (2002). New JIT, a new management technology principle at Toyota. *International Journal of Production Economics*, *80*(2), 135–144. doi:10.1016/S0925-5273(02)00313-4

Amasaka, K. (2004). *Science SQC, new quality control principle: The quality strategy of Toyota*. Springer-Verlag. doi:10.1007/978-4-431-53969-8

Amasaka, K. (2007). High linkage model "Advanced TDS, TPS & TMS": Strategic development of "New JIT" at Toyota. *International Journal of Operations and Quantitative Management*, *13*(3), 101–121.

Amasaka, K. (2015). New JIT, new management technology principle. Taylor and Francis Group.

Amasaka, K., & Sakai, H. (2011). The New Japan Global Production Model "NJ-GPM": Strategic development of Advanced TPS. *The Journal of Japanese Operations Management and Strategy*, *2*(1), 1–15.

Kawahara, F., Kogane, Y., Amasaka, K., & Ouchi, N. (2016). Work procedure manual incorporating experienced workers' intuition and knowhow. *IOSR Journal of Business and Management*, *18*(12), 80–85.

Miyamoto, N. (2006). Comparison between expert and non-expert in sharpening a kitchen knife. *Symposium on Sports Engineering: Symposium on Human Dynamics*, 187-192.

Murakami, Y., & Mizuyama, H. (2007). Detailed design and improvement of a manual assembly task incorporating how to efficiently handle uncertainties. *Journal of the Society of Plant Engineers Japan*, *19*(3), 177–188.

Sakai, H., & Amasaka, K. (2006). Strategic HI-POS, Intelligence Production Operating System: Applying Advanced TPS to Toyota's global production strategy. *WSEAS Transactions on Advances in Engineering Education*, *3*(3), 223–230.

Sakai, H., & Amasaka, K. (2007). Human Intelligence Diagnosis Method utilizing Advanced TPS. *Journal of Advanced Manufacturing Systems*, *6*(1), 77–95. doi:10.1142/S0219686707000905

Sakai, H. & Amasaka, K. (2008). *Human-Integrated Assist System for intelligence operators.* Academic Press.

Tsunoi, M., Yamaji, M., & Amasaka, K. (2010). A Study of Building an Intellectual Working Value Improvement Model, IWV-IM. *International Business & Economics Research Journal*, *9*(11), 79–84. doi:10.19030/iber.v9i11.33

Uchida, K., Tsunoi, M., & Amasaka, K. (2012). Creating Working Value Evaluation Model "WVEM". *International Journal of Management & Information Systems*, *16*(4), 299–306.

Watanuki, K., & Tanaka, S. (2003). Development of Knowledge Visualization System for knowledge transfer. The Japan Society of Mechanical Engineers, 23, 111-112.

Yamasaki, M., & Yoshioka, K. (2011). *Study on comparing experienced and inexperienced machine workers: The example of lathe work* (Bachelor's thesis). School of Science and Engineering, Aoyama Gakuin University, Amasaka New JIT Laboratory.

Yanagisawa, K., Yamasaki, M., Yoshioka, K., & Amasaka, K. (2013). Research on comparing experienced and inexperienced machine workers. *International Journal of Operations Production Management& Information Systems*, *1*(4), 241–250.

Chapter 22
CS and CL for Boosting Marketing Effectiveness to Strengthen Japanese Auto-Dealerships

ABSTRACT

Faced with a sluggish economy, car sales have been disappointing in recent years. Given this situation, it is critical that auto-dealerships shift the focus of their sales and marketing activities from attracting new customers to keeping the customers they already have. This move can be expected not only to reduce sales costs, but also contribute to healthy profits. Therefore, the author proceeds with researching Customer Satisfaction (CS) and Customer Loyalty (CL) as a way of boosting marketing effectiveness, clarifying the key factors that comprise customer loyalty and help improve the marketing strategy. Then, as an application example, the author focuses on the development and effectiveness for CS and CL describing Video Unites Customer Behavior and Maker's Designing Intentions (VUCKMIN) and Total Direct Mail Management Model (TDMM).

INTRODUCTION

Relationships between auto-dealerships and their customers typically change and develop over time. Analyzing this phenomenon through a customer's lifecycle framework allows us to assess the financial rewards a company receives over the course of these developments; in other words, figure out how much profit is generated over time.

When sales and new customer acquisition rates begin to fall, dealers start shifting their attention to how they can keep their existing core customers (Customer Retention, CR) and how they can get these customers to purchase additional related or different products.

The auto-industry is already mired in this situation and must find ways to deal with it. Customer loyalty (CL) is a concept that will become increasingly critical in the future.

DOI: 10.4018/978-1-7998-8746-1.ch022

It requires that auto-dealerships work to boost satisfaction among their core customers by continuing to offer the products and services that these loyal customers want to take advantage of and purchase (Amasaka, 2007, 2009, 2011; Okutomi, 2011; Okutomi and Amasaka, 2012, 2013; Amasaka et al., 2013).

Then, in previous research, many studies have already been done across a variety of industries dealing with the analysis methods and processes that can be used to clarify the components involved in customer satisfaction and customer loyalty (Ex. Yamamoto and Enkawa, 2000).

Several of these studies, particularly one by Kawasaki and Yoshizawa (2001), customer satisfaction (CS) using customer data marketing to increase satisfaction levels.

At the same time, though structural analysis tools have been applied to customer loyalty in some studies, the author knows of no studies that have been done on auto sales from a multidisciplinary perspective.

In this section, therefore, the author looks to statistics as it focuses on CS as a way of boosting marketing effectiveness, clarifying the key factors that comprise CL, and helps to improve the marketing strategy employing NJ-MMM (New Japan Marketing Management Model) as indicated in Figure 2, Chapter 16 (Refer to Chapter 16). This model was developing SCCM (Scientific Customer Creative Model) based on "Advanced TMS, strategic customer creation model" in NJ-AGMM (New Japan Automobile Global Manufacturing Model) as described in Figure 1(3) and 9 (Okutomi, 2011; Okutomi and Amasaka, 2012, 2013, 2019) (Refer to Chapter 6 and Chapter 16).

Then, as application examples using those knowledge acquired above, the author focuses on the development and effectiveness for CS and CL describing "Video Unites Customer Behavior and Maker's Designing Intentions" (VUCKMIN) and "Total Direct Mail Management Model" (TDMM) (Kimura et al., 2007; Kojima et al., 2010; Murato et al., 2008; Yamaji et al., 2010; Ishiguro et al., 2010; Ishiguro and Amasaka, 2012a,b; Amasaka et al., 2012; Amasaka, 2015).

SITUATION AND PROBLEM OF JAPAN'S AUTO-SALES

The author shows five customer lifecycle stages (Prospect - First time buyer - Initial repeater - Core customer - Withdrawal) as they apply to auto sales (dealerships) as shown in Figure 1 (Okutomi, 2011; Okutomi and Amasaka, 2012, 2013).

Generally speaking, the Japanese auto industry has now maximized new vehicle sales—meaning that the market has fully matured when it comes to traditional auto sales methods.

Faced with a sluggish economy, car sales have been disappointing in recent years. Given this situation, it is critical that dealerships shift the focus of their sales and marketing activities from attracting new customers to keeping the customers they already have.

This move can be expected not only to reduce sales costs, but also contribute to healthy profits. A dealership's best (core) customers took on that designation through a process of satisfactory purchases with that company.

They are familiar with the features of their dealership's products and services, know how purchases are made, and know the best way to take advantage of how the dealership runs.

For this reason, marketing activities that target these core customers will help create a customer base that is superior to that of competitors working in the same industry. Core customers are an auto dealer's most priceless asset.

Figure 1. Customer lifecycle

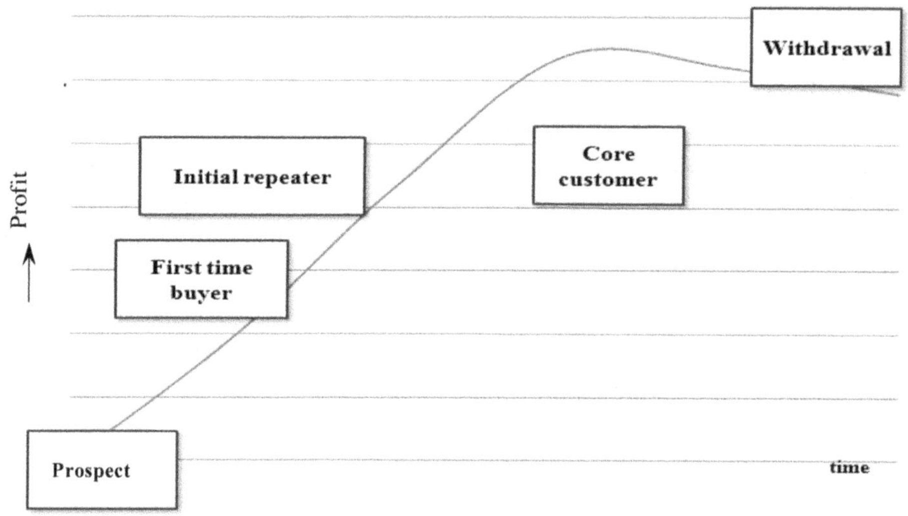

CS AND CL TO BOOST MARKETING EFFECTIVENESS AT JAPAN'S AUTO-DEALERSHIPS

Sales and Marketing at Auto-Dealerships

The author conducted interviews with six auto-dealerships, each of whom represent major automakers - four Japanese (A, B, C, and D) and two foreign (E and F) (Okutomi, 2011; Okutomi and Amasaka, 2012, 2013).

Based on these interviews and the resulting analysis, it was found that sales and marketing activities at auto dealerships were not particularly focused on boosting satisfaction and loyalty among core customers - and an unexpected majority had no awareness of these concepts.

At the same time, even if auto-dealerships were aware of the need for improvements in these areas, it was common for sales staff to simply rely on their personal knowledge (experiential data), so that related activities tended to be completely different for each person.

As a result, when it came to CS and CL, problems (issues) were arising from the mismatch between managers' intentions, salesperson activities, and customer experiences (preferences) at auto-dealers.

CS and CL to Boost Marketing Effectiveness for CR Activities

To help resolve the sales and marketing issues outlined in the previous section and simultaneously achieve higher satisfaction among core customers, the author employed statistical methods to make explicit (objectify) the operations currently being implicitly carried out at auto-dealerships based on employees' personal knowledge.

The goal was to make sales and marketing activities more effective by having them accurately reflect the needs of core customers employing "Visualization of experienced - based implicit knowledge"

(Figure 3, Chapter 4) and "Customer Science Principle" (Figure 2, Chapter 13) (Refer to Chapter 4 in Parr I and Chapter 13 in Part III).

The specific procedure shown in Figure 1 used to do this was as follows;

1. In Step 1, the author specified the key factors that make up CS and CL
2. In Step 2, the author collected customer information and subjected it to an analysis of covariance structure. The insights gained from this analysis were then used to determine the degree to which each key factor impacts CS and CL (Okutomi, 2011; Okutomi and Amasaka, 2012, 2013).
3. In Step 3, concretely, the key factors comprising satisfaction and loyalty among core customers at the six target dealerships - four Japanese (A, B, C, and D) and two foreign (E and F) were identified in order to determine the level of impact each carries.

(1) Specify the Key Factors (Step 1)

In Step 1, the author collected and analyzed sales information from core customers to identify the components of satisfaction and loyalty among them. One way they did this was by actually going to dealerships to participate in new car (vehicle) presentations and collecting the required information from customers.

The author put together their own questionnaire for the information collection process, with items that not only has reflected the personal knowledge of salespeople and managers, but also information has gained from direct interviews with customers. As a result of these information collection efforts, the author was able to add survey items that accurately reflected how important service was to customers - both before and after a new car purchase.

Working from these insights as a basis, the author has added in the SERVQUAL framework (a service quality evaluation measurement tool) to create a new evaluation and measurement scale that was ultimately used to generate the questionnaire.

Because the SERVQUAL method is not limited to a specific industry, it has some issues in terms of applicability to individual business activities (including auto-sales) (Ex. Parasuraman et al., 1988).

To eliminate these issues, the author used the aforementioned interviews to ensure that they had a complete grasp of the factors specific to the auto- industry. (Okutomi, 2011; Okutomi and Amasaka, 2012, 2013)

(2) Collecting and Analyzing the Customer Information (Step 2)

Once the items extracted from these interviews were integrated with the SERVQUAL framework, the authors were able to specify 29 individual factors. These included 17 product factors, 3 employee factors, 6 dealership factors, and 3 corporate factors.

In Step 2, the 29 factors listed in Table 1 were rated on a seven-point scale along with CS and CL to identify the kinds of things that customers were looking for. As the table indicates, core customers from six auto-dealers were asked to complete a survey (questionnaire form) covering four key topics (factors): products, dealership, employees, and company. A total of 226 valid responses were received from 138 men and 88 women.

After collecting the survey data, the author subjected it to an analysis of covariance structure in order to find out the degree of impact each factor had on CS and CL.

Table 1. Survey (Questionnaire form)

factor	Question items	Rating scales						
		Very dissatisfied	dissatisfied	A little dissatisfied	neutral	A little satisfied	satisfied	Very satisfied
product	exterior						○	
	interior						○	
	Safety device				○			
	Handling					○		
	Cornering						○	
	Straight-line stability				○			
	High-speed stability				○			
	Durability				○			
	pedal			○				
	seat							○
	Engine displacement			○				
	fuel efficiency		○					
	Interior noise					○		
	Body shaking				○			
	Car navigation system				○			
	audio				○			
	price				○			
employee	polite						○	
	knowledge					○		
	Prompt customer service						○	
dealership	Appearance				○			
	Opening Hours			○				
	location			○				
	mandatory inspection services					○		
	Emergency measure							○
	Periodic contact					○		
corporate	pamphlet・Website				○			
	TV commercials				○			
	corporate image					○		
	Customer Satisfaction						○	
	Customer Loyalty					○		

(3) Finding out the Degree of Impact Each Factor (Step 3)

The author showed the cause-and-effect model created by the author based on the four key factors specified in the previous section as shown in Figure 2.

This diagram was used as a structural model of "Customer satisfaction (CS) and Customer loyalty (CL)" at auto-dealerships. The four key factors (first-order compositional factors) represented in the figure are comprised of individual, or second-order compositional factors, which impact "Customer satisfaction (CS) and Customer loyalty (CL)".

In the cause-and-effect model, "CS and CL" was assumed to independent relationship as shown in Figure 3, 4 and 5, as follows;

Figure 2. Cause-and-effect model of key factor

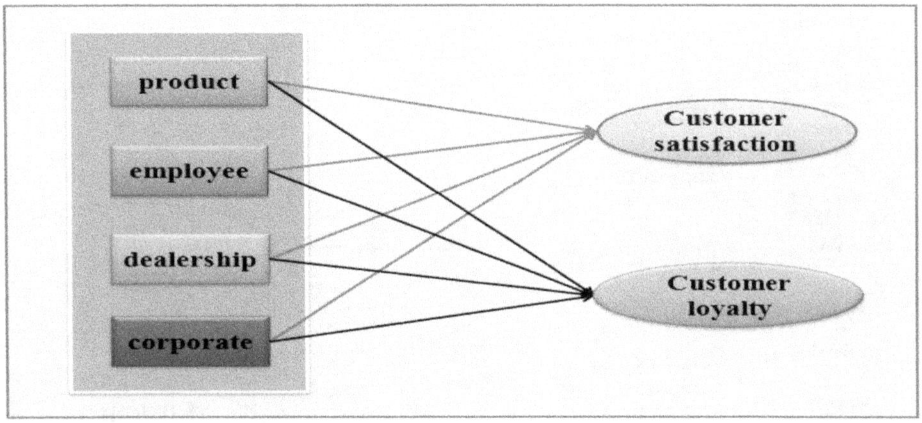

Figure 3. Cause-and-effect model of individual factor

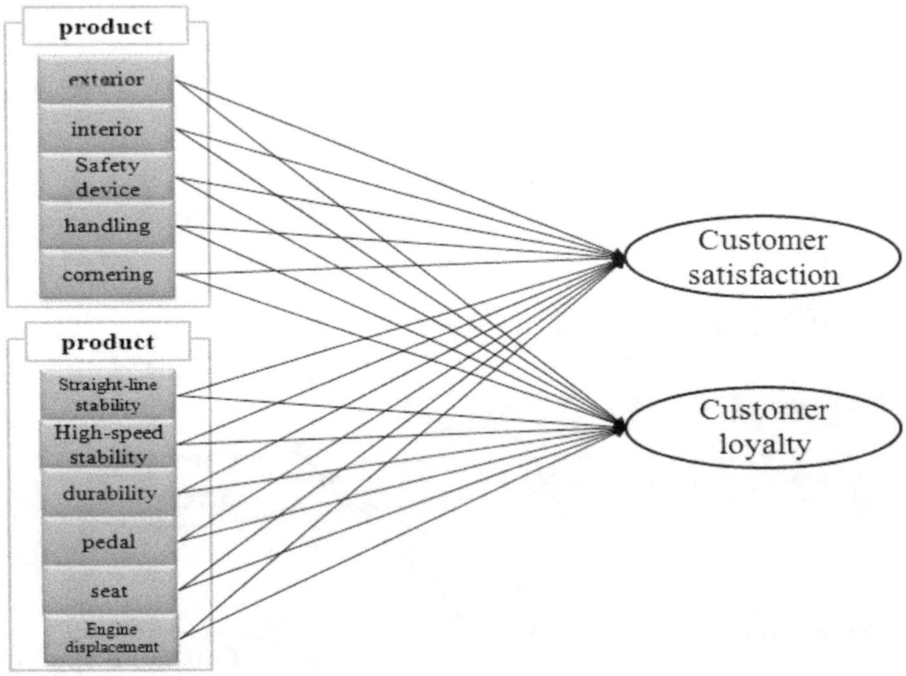

Each figure with (products, dealership, employees, and company) showed (i) Cause-and-effect model of individual factor, (ii) Cause-and-effect model of individual factor, and (iii) Cause-and-effect model of individual factor.

Then, Table 2 showed the results of the "Covariance Structure Analysis" on each individual factor that makes up the four key factors as they relate to "CS and CL)".

Figure 4. Cause-and-effect model of individual factor

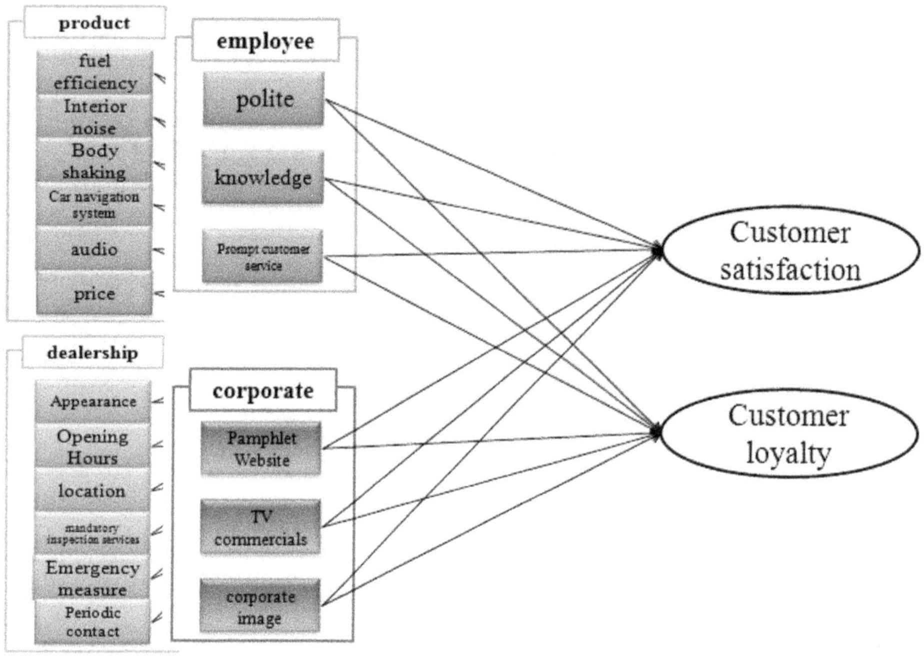

Figure 5. Cause-and-effect model of individual factor

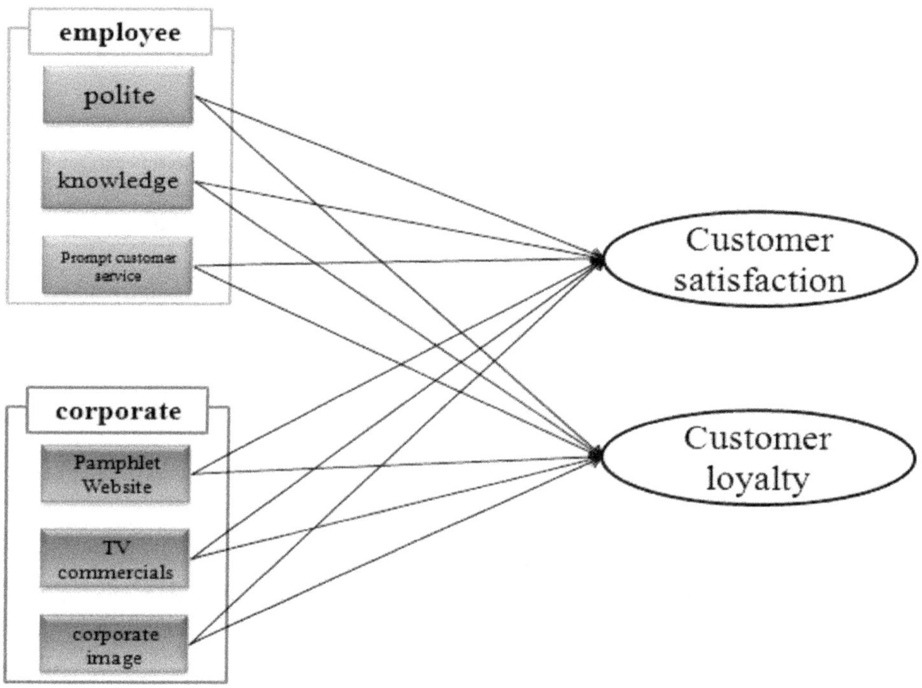

Under product, this table showed that the individual factors with the greatest impact on "CS and CL" were aspects of driving performance quality (engine displacement, fuel efficiency, handling stability, etc.) as well as subjective quality factors like exterior features and seats.

The analysis results indicated that if auto manufacturers are to prioritize "Customer satisfaction (CS) and Customer loyalty (CL)" during their sales and marketing activities, they need to enhance product development so that it focuses on performance quality, design quality (including exterior design quality like body shape and paint color), and subjective qualities like seat comfort. At the same time, affili-

Table 2. Results of the covariance structure analysis

product	Customer Satisfaction	Customer Loyalty
exterior	.612	.470
interior	.198	.217
Safety device	-.034	-.109
Handling	.087	.026
Cornering	.190	.149
Straight-line stability	.207	.213
High-speed stability	.106	-.077
Durability	-.045	-.064
pedal	-.458	-.257
seat	.519	.694
Engine displacement	.600	.343
fuel efficiency	.475	.270
Interior noise	.136	.188
Body shaking	.254	.506
Car navigation system	-.045	-.120
audio	.181	-.099
price	-.024	.119
dealership	**Customer Satisfaction**	**Customer Loyalty**
Appearance	.115	-.041
Opening Hours	.024	-.048
location	-.098	.169
mandatory inspection services	.208	.086
Emergency measure	.659	.559
Periodic contact	-.294	.278
employee	**Customer Satisfaction**	**Customer Loyalty**
polite	.291	.552
knowledge	.154	.316
Prompt customer service	.464	.077
corporate	**Customer Satisfaction**	**Customer Loyalty**
pamphlet・Website	.205	.057
TV commercials	.128	.502
corporate image	.776	.511

ated dealerships need to work to enhance customer handling during emergencies as well as mandatory inspection services.

Similarly, it can be inferred that because corporate image and TV (television) commercials also have a powerful effect on customers, vehicles are an important factor in generating trust towards a company. Under the topic of employees, prompt, polite customer service was found to have the greatest impact on CL. This point is to a customer mindset whereby those looking to replace an existing vehicle have a desire to go back to the dealership where they purchased their old car because they have a lasting impression of the courteous manner with which a salesperson treated them before.

Similarly, it can be inferred that because corporate image and TV commercials also have a powerful effect on customers, vehicles are an important factor in generating trust towards a company (Refer to Okutomi, (2011), and Okutomi and Amasaka (2012, 2013 in detail). The analysis results obtained above provide clues as to how more logical sales and marketing activities might be carried out in the future.

By making explicit underlying employee knowledge on the degree to which certain factors affect CS and CL that makes buyers want to come back for repeat purchases, the author was able to visually present a structural model of impact outlining the relative strength of both the key and individual factors that can help boost CS and CL.

Then, in the following section, the effectiveness of the knowledge acquired by this research is described.

APPLICATION EXAMPLES

In this subsection, as application examples using those knowledge acquired above, the author focuses on the development and effectiveness for CS and CL describing "Video Unites Customer Behavior and Maker's Designing Intentions" (VUCMIN) and "Total Direct Mail Model" (TDMM) (Murato et al., 2008; Yamaji et al., 2010; Ishiguro and Amasaka, 2012a; Amasaka et al., 2012; Amasaka, 2015, 2020).

A New Strategic Advertisement Model "VUCMIN" Designed to Enhance the Desire to Visit Auto-Dealers

1. Outline

In the 21st century, one of the important issues in the industrial world is how to create desirable and influential products. The created method VUCMIN (Video Unites Customer Behavior and Maker's Designing Intentions) uses video advertisement, and was developed based on scientific approaches and analyses that focus on the standard behavioral movements of customers who visit dealers when choosing an automobile (Yamaji et al., 2010; Amasaka et al., 2012; Amasaka, 2015).

VUCMIN, which is based on the different approaches identified in target customer profiles, aims to increase the desire of customers to visit dealers. After creating this video advertisement, customers were verified as having a positive opinion towards visiting dealers with a plan to purchase the vehicle featured in the video.

2. Need for a New Advertising Approach in the Automobile Industry

Advertising expenses in the Japanese automotive industry are trending to around 6 trillion Japanese Yen (Dentsu, 2003). Despite these high advertising expenses, the number of vehicle sales is stagnant (JAMA, 2005).

Further, it is thought that retaining existing customers and gaining new customer profiles will be difficult unless researchers construct a new advertising policy; therefore, the author creates a new advertisement approach (Amasaka, 2007).

From the manufacturers' perspective, new designs must be created to grasp the heart of customers and find out how sale advertisements can deal with new customer intentions in the future. When looking at media-based advertising expenses, there has been an increase in internet advertising expenses recently (Dentsu, 2003).

The automobile industry has also been expected to use internet video as a new advertising method.

3. Approach of the VUCMIN Study

Figure 6. The process of VUCMIN study

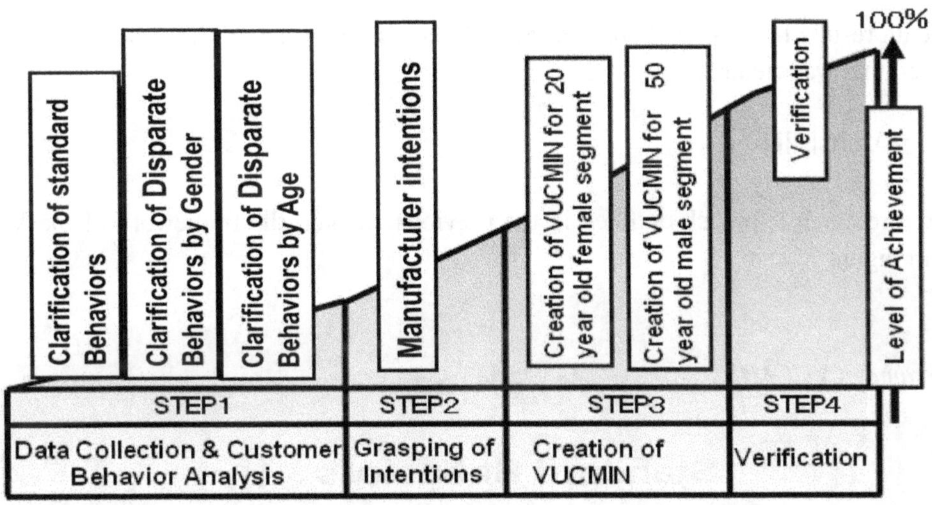

The purpose of the "Video Unites Customer behavior and Maker's designing Intentions, VUCMIN" study is to effectively generate fascination with a product, resulting in an increase in the desire of customers to visit dealers and growth in the number of vehicle sales.

The author generated the following solution to the current situation outlined in Subsection 23.1(1): distribution of a video 1 to 2 minutes in length to a particular age group and gender segment. The video takes customer preferences and the intentions of the product planning and design departments into account.

Figure 6 represents the steps (Step 1–Step 4) of the VUCMIN study, utilizing the specific concept methods outlined in "SQC Technical Methods" (Amasaka, 1999, 2004, 2007).

These steps cover preparation of internet video distribution, which unites customer preferences and behaviors with the manufacturer's design intentions.

a. Analysis of Customer Behavior and Data Collection (Step 1)

This step aims to provide an up-to-date inquiry as to deep-seated customer wants in terms of customer behavior analysis (James, et al., 2006). Disparate behaviors by gender and age segment will be clarified in the analysis of standard behaviors.

b. Perception of Intentions (Step 2)

In this step, the intentions of the product planning department and designers are scientifically analyzed in terms of product design. Identifying which aspects of the vehicle the designers and manufacturer want to express to customers is an important step in preparing the video.

c. Creation of VUCMIN (Step 3)

An advertising video is created, targeting females in their 20s and males in their 50s using the results of Step 1 and Step 2. With this final step, the authors try to reach a solution based on the above research.

d. Verification (Step 4)

Using the data results from Steps 1 through Step 3, the authors verified the validity of the VUCMIN internet video that was created.

4. Frame of VUCMIN

Based on the research approach outlined in the previous chapter, the framework of the VUCMIN is created as in Figure 7.

Figure 7. Frame of VUCMIN

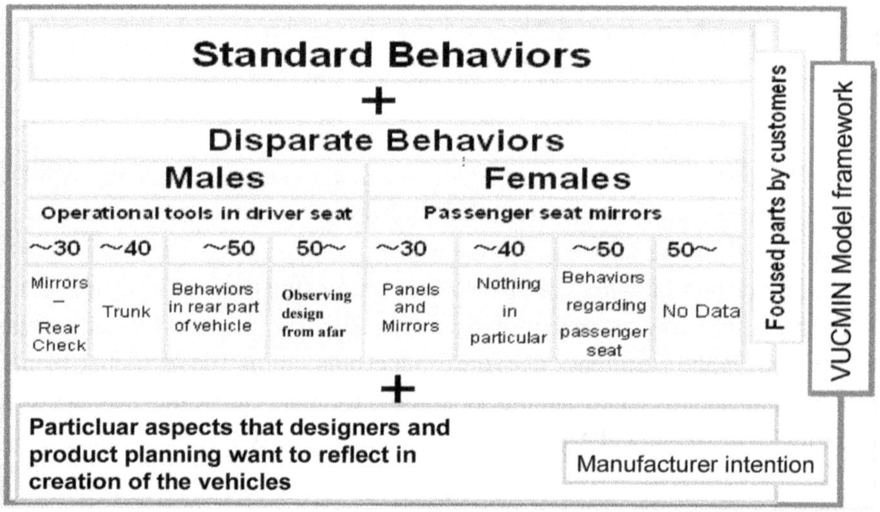

In this figure, i) standard behaviors and ii) disparate behaviors by gender are identified and classified. After classifying the subjects by age, the details of disparate behaviors are identified mainly in terms of the front seat of the vehicle (driver's seat tools, passenger rearview mirror, etc.) and the rear seat (not shown in figure).

This knowledge of customer behaviors and knowledge of the parts that product planning and designers wish to show to customers are taken into consideration as the basis for the VUCMIN framework.

5. The Process of VUCMIN Creation

In this subsection, the authors explain the process of video creation using VUCMIN.

a. Data Collection From "Customer Behaviors"

In this subsection, customer behaviors are analyzed while customers are facing the vehicle from the front. This allows collection of customer information used to create the video. It is thought that customers' desire to visit the dealer can be increased via video distribution when the customer is in the stage "prior to dealer visit".

The author therefore conducted the following survey in order to investigate customer behaviors. The author prepared the survey table in Figure 8 (: Figure 8(a) shows the outline of Sample 1, 2 and 3, and Figure 8(b) shows the enlargement of Sample 1 by indicated by dotted red circle).

Figure 8. Survey samples (Outline of Sample 1, 2, and 3)

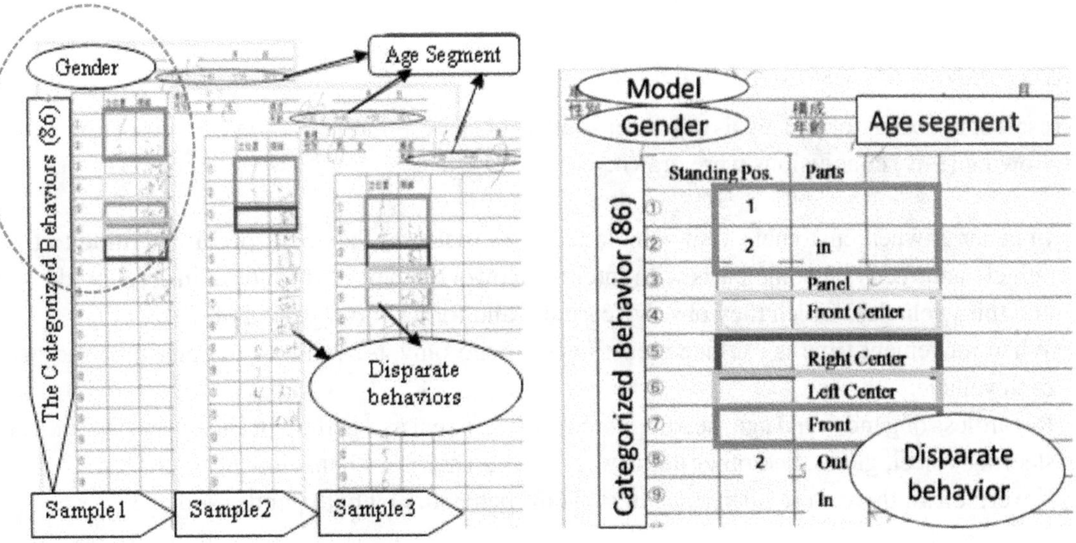

Then, the survey item categories were decided as follows.

In the survey table, the target car (vehicle) model is 1, gender 2, age 3, standing positions 4, and vehicle part focused on is 5. Among those items, standing positions are categorized as in Figure 9.

Front is 1, front fender (driver seat) 2, rear fender (driver seat side) 3, trunk is 4, rear fender (passenger seat side) 5, front fender (passenger seat) 6, handle 7, shift lever 8, near passenger seat is 9. In total, all customer behaviors (standing positions, getting in and out, operation, walking time, etc.) are categorized into 85 distinct types of behaviors.

The survey was conducted on customers visiting the "Toyota Exhibition Hall" (Tokyo) in the 2 months from August 2006 to September 2006 between 12:00 and 17:00 p.m., according to age and gender group. 316 data items were collected.

Figure 9. Samples of customer standing positions

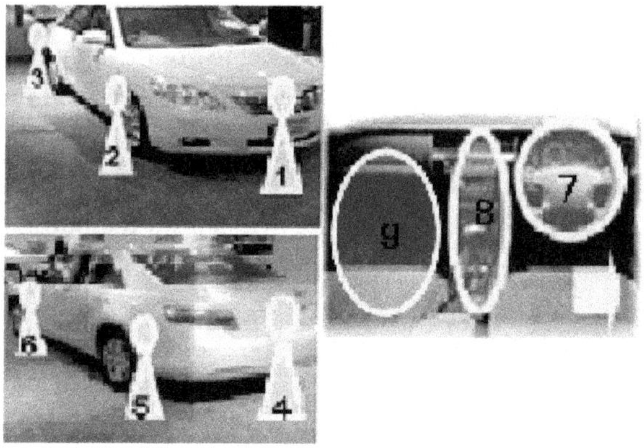

b. Data Analysis of Customer Behaviors

As a result of the behavioral analysis of how customers observe vehicles outlined in Subsection 22.4.1(3), the following (i~iv) conclusions were drawn:

i. In general, when customers visit vehicle galleries (dealers) they pay special attention to the first vehicle and focus on some parts with interest. However, they start to loose interest by the second and third vehicles, which they observe casually and for a shorter period of time.
ii. When movement time is excluded, customers spend only 1-2 minutes to determine the value of each vehicle.
iii. Regardless of gender and age, heading for the driver's seat and getting in and observing the interior, steering wheel, gages, and other items was common standard behavior.
iv. Nevertheless, there were disparities in standard behaviors by both gender and age.

6. Detailed Analysis for Creation of VUCMIN

a. Standard Behaviors for Creating the Video

Toyota's Mark X was the vehicle model used in creating the video, and analyses regarding standard behavior were conducted as follows.

As seen in Figure 9 above, survey sheets are taken on each customer sample while they are observing the vehicle. Sample 1 is a 20 year old male, sample 2 is a 30 year old female, and sample 3 is a 40 year old male. Samples of each of the three customers are different according to their age and gender.

For further analysis, TMS (Text Mining Studio) is conducted on all categorized customer behaviors and the results are shown in Figure 10, numbers 1 to 86. The numbers in the inner circle of the figure (1, 9, 12, 16, 22, 29, 31, 32, 85) represent the nine standard behaviors

(I) (observing front area ® sitting in the driver's seat ® driver operation system (control system) → leaving the driver's seat, etc.). Element resolution of the standard behaviors are also shown in Figure 11.

Next, the numbers in middle circle of the figure (17, 35, 40, 49, 53, 59, 73) represent the seven standard behaviors (II) (observing rear seat from driver's seat → moving to rear seat → leaving driver's seat and observing side of trunk → getting into rear seat of passenger seat → moving into passenger seat).

Moreover, the remaining 70 attached behaviors from the outer circle of Figure 8.1.11 specify individual behaviors. For example, 2 through 8 are looking at the vehicle entirely from behind, tires, and engine; 18 to 28 are passenger seat storage, side mirror, and lights: 42 to 48 are looking at vehicle diagonally from 45 degree angle, looking under the vehicle, etc.

Finally, as a result of detailed analyzes, a pattern of standard behaviors was identified regardless of age or gender. Front →moving to driver's seat → entering driver's seat → looking out the front view → observing steering operation systems and instrument panel → looking to passenger seat side →looking at operation systems on driver's side and checking side mirrors → leaving the vehicle.

Figure 10. TMS analysis of standard behavior

Figure 11. Standard customer behaviors

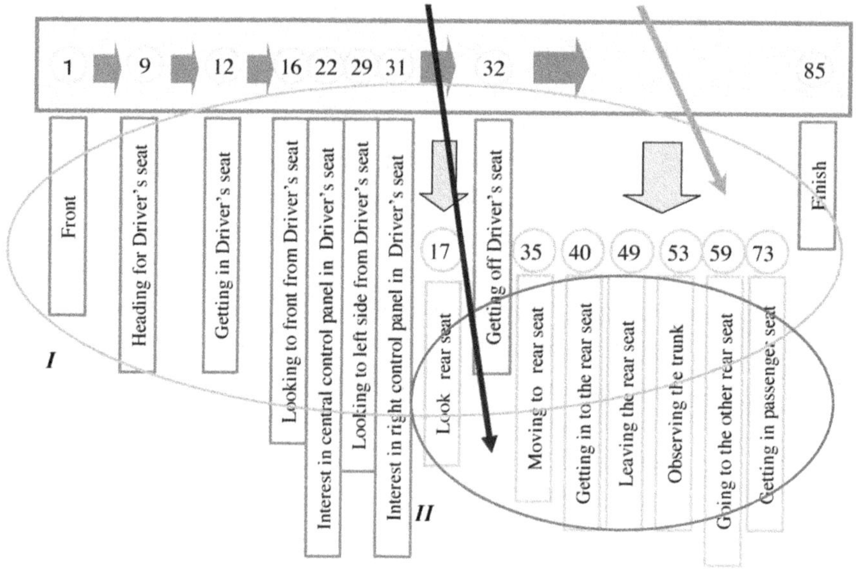

b. Disparate Customer Behavior by "Gender and Age" for Creating Video

In this subsection, the following analyses of disparate behavior are conducted regarding age and gender.

i. Explanation of Disparate Behaviors by "Gender"

On the basis of the data collected above, a "Correspondence Bubble Analysis" was then conducted as seen in Figure 12 to identify disparities in behavior by gender.

Correspondence Bubble Analysis is an analysis technique generally known as correspondence analysis. This method distributes area maps related to attributes (gender, age) and texts (customer behaviors). Items with stronger relationships are closely distributed.

In Figure 12, the difference in distributed texts (behaviors) by age and gender can be seen. (The blue line in the figure shows behaviors by gender, and the green line shows behaviors by age). Moreover, the authors identified male and female behaviors as follows.

1. **Female behaviors**

According to the results of the Correspondence Bubble Analysis, female customer behaviors indicate that they are especially concerned with the area around the passenger seat in addition to the front fender and rear-view mirror, door opening and closing, the dashboard, sun visor (make-up mirror), etc.

2. **Male behaviors**

However, males do not show concern the with passenger seat, and instead were focused on the driver seat position, shift lever, door switches, air conditioner, operating tools, and switches around the driver seat such as audio parts.

Figure 12. Disparate customer behaviors by "Age and Gender"

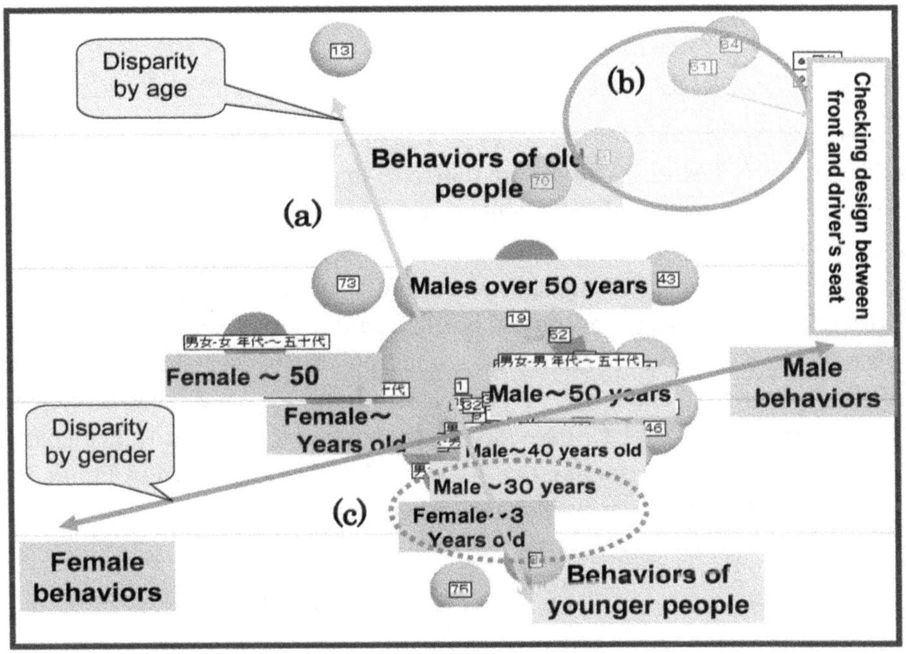

ii. Explanation of Disparate Behaviors by "Age"

In this subsection, disparate behaviors are investigated by conducting a "Correspondence Bubble Analysis", on both gender and age attributes.

For example, the following behaviors are seen for (a) males over 50 years old (the numbers from orange areas (b) in the figure, 8, 51, 84: (i) looking towards the driver's seat from far behind, (ii) observing the design between the front and driver's seat, (iii) looking to the driver's seat from a distance, etc.). In particular, disparate behaviors are not evident until (c) the age of 30 for both male and female profiles.

Moreover, males in their 20s look at (i) the rear seats from the driver's seat, (ii) the rearview mirror, and (iii) the side mirrors. Similarly, profile behaviors of females in their 20s are looking at (i) the side mirror on the opposite side, (ii) rearview window, (iii) instrument panel, (iv) the dashboard, and lastly, focusing on (v) the operation and sound of the passenger seat door while opening and shutting.

In the creation of VUCMIN, the basis of this knowledge will be explained in the next Subsection 22.4.1(7).

7. The Creation of VUCMIN

a. Identifying of the Intentions of Product Designers

This chapter will explain the influence of product planning and designer intentions in VUCMIN creation. The Toyota mid-size passenger car "Mark X" (named USA "Cressida") is used as a target vehicle in design inquiries. According to common opinions from designers and product planning at Toyota Motor Corporation, the parts that are focused on to be demonstrated to customers are:

(i) Front Proportions, (ii) Streamlined Side proportions, (iii) Tri-beam Headlamps (lenses), (iv) Widened Console Box, and (v) Sharpened Rear

b. The Creation of VUCMIN for Males in Their 50s and Females in Their 20s

In this subsection the video created for the target profile of males in their 50s will be explained using the timetable in Figure 13. The timetable figure indicates that video time is set at 90 seconds. Video shooting order is composed specifically of scenes from 1 to 11 starting from the front, driver's seat, side, and rear of the vehicle.

Scenes are 1. direct front scene, 2. diagonally front view scene, 3. door opening scene of the driver's seat, 4. entire driver's seat view scene, 5. console box and shift lever scene, 6. Steering handle scene, 7. Operation tools of driver's seat scene, 8. side view scene from driver's seat, 9. rear side view scene, 10. entire view of vehicle from rear, and lastly, moving back to front, 11. entire view of the vehicle scene.

The composed scenes form the VUCMIN video on the basis of the standard and disparate behaviors of customers. Example photos representing these scenes (1 to 11) are shown in Figure 14. Using the same approach, VUCMIN is created regarding age and gender.

Figure 13. VUCMIN (Males in their 50s, Mark X) Creation Timetable

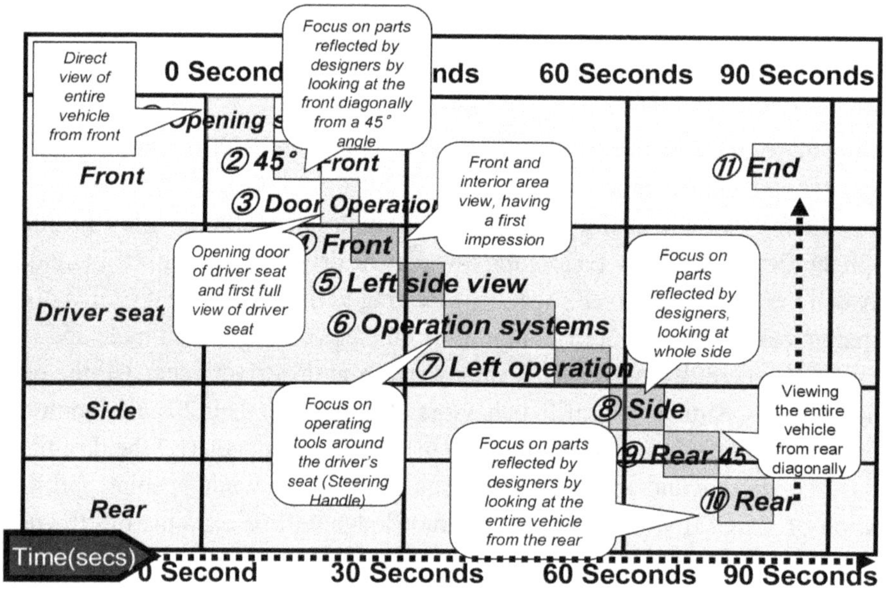

8. Effectiveness of VUCMIN

In this subsection, customer surveys were executed in order to test the effectiveness of VUCMIN. Specifically, this was done by asking customers, after seeing the "Mark X" video, approximately when do you plan to purchase one by visiting a Toyota dealer?" in order to verify their desire to visit dealers (high, low).

Figure 14. Example of representative photos for VUCMIN video

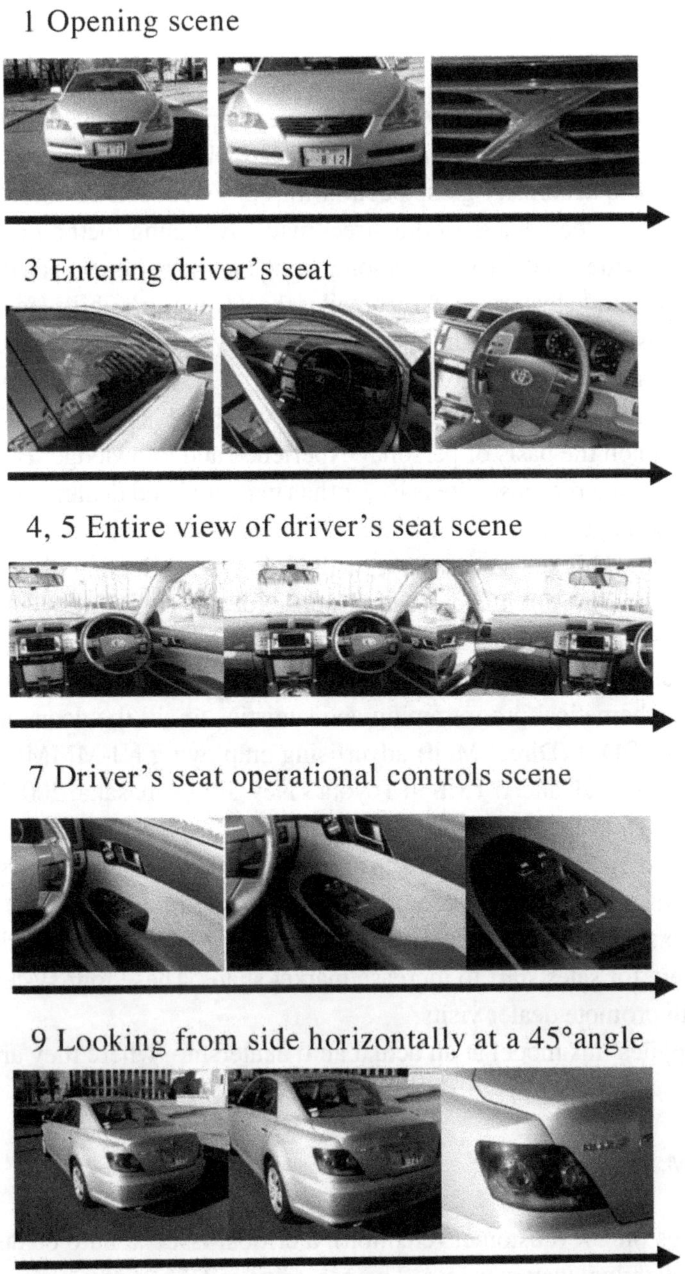

According to the survey results, the desire to visit dealers (early stage consideration of "Mark X" purchase) was not only increased for current Toyota vehicle owners but also for customers who own vehicles from other manufacturers.

The author has verified currently the effectiveness of this study as part of the strategic advertising method "VUCMIN", which utilizes internet interface with the collaboration of universities and industries (Refer to Kimura et al., 2007; Kojima et al., 2010; Murat et al., 2008 and Yamaji et al., 2010 in detail).

Total Direct Mail Model (TDMM) to Attract Customer

1. Outline

Recent changes in the marketing environment have made the personal relationship between businesses and their customers even more critical. Businesses are faced with the task of constructing sales schemes that are able to flexibly and accurately grasp peculiarities and trends in customer preferences.

This study looks at the effectiveness of the direct mail advertising method in bringing customers to auto dealers, based on the idea that forming personal bonds with customers is a core component of successful sales. One of the unique features of direct mail is the advertiser's ability to select which customers will receive the mailings. This point is the focus of this study, which attempts to identify an optimum decision-making process for selecting target customers.

The way that dealers currently select which customers will receive direct mail is by having individual salespeople choose them on the basis of personal experience and knowledge. Because there is no clear decision-making process, the response rate is lower than expected and dealers do not achieve the targets set forth in their sales strategies.

To address these issues, this study presents a methodology for selecting direct mail (DM) recipients from the dealer pool that will result in increased response (dealer visit) rates. The proposed mechanism for selecting these optimum recipients is a strategic "Total Direct Mail Model" (TDMM) with the aim of bringing more customers into auto dealerships (Murat et al., 2008; Ishiguro and Amasaka, 2012a).

This model uses mathematical programming and statistics to aid the decision-making process and boost the effectiveness of DM (Direct Mail) advertising employing NJ-MMM (New Japan Marketing Management Model named Advanced TMS in Toyota's New JIT (Amasaka, 2007b,c, 2011, 2015, 2019) (Refer to Chapter 6 and 16 in Part I and III).

The core systems used in the model are (1) a customer purchase data analysis system to increase dealer visits, (2) a DM content optimization system to target customer preferences, (3) a system for strategically determining who should be sent direct mail based on who actually visits the dealership, and (4) a DM promotion system for sales staff to increase market share. These four systems are integrated and strategically applied to promote dealer visits.

The author then applies this model at an actual auto dealership, where they are able to successfully increase dealer visits.

2. Necessity of DM

This subsection focuses on CR (customer retention), a critical issue at auto dealerships, and discusses a methodology for preventing customer loss. The necessity of DM (direct mail) as a tool for retaining premier customers is discussed below.

a. DM and CR

Auto-dealerships typically store customer attributes, purchase history, and other information on their clients in a database or similar storage system (Amasaka, 2004).

The database is used to identify premier customers, and pinpointing their preferences is critical if the dealership is to prevent them from taking their business elsewhere.

The author considers using a database to help find premier customers and then sending them DM to be an effective method of sales promotion.

In references of DM effects, (i) Kotler and Keller (2006) identified the ability to select your recipients and the ability to offer personalized content as the advantages of DM, and (ii) Piersma and Jonker (2004) studied how often to send DM to individual customers in order to establish long-term relationships between the direct mailer and the customers. Furthermore, (iii) Jonker et al. (2006) provided a decision support system to determine mailing frequency for active customers based on their behavioral data: their recency, frequency, and monetary (RFM) values, (iv) Bell et al. (2006) applied experimental designs to increase direct mail sales. (v) Beko and Jagric (2011) presented demand models for direct mail and periodicals market using time series analysis, and (vi) DM is notable as an effective way of targeting specific premier customers for sales promotions (Bult and Wansbeek, 2005).

b. DM and AIDA Model

The AIDA (attention-interest-desire-action) model is a well-known advertising information management model developed by St. Elmo Lewis. The model presents the psychology of consumer purchase behavior as a series of four steps: *attention*, *interest*, *desire*, and *action* (Ferrell and Hartline, 2005; Shimizu, 2004).

The author has created a model of customer response for use in auto sales (Amasaka, 2007b, 2009). This model is based on the AIDA model and presented in Figure 15. The model allows dealerships to boost the percentage of customers that visit the showroom by using mass media advertising, flyers, magazine ads, and DM (direct mail) and others (DH (direct hand9, Train cars ads., internet etc.).

Figure 15. AIDA Model

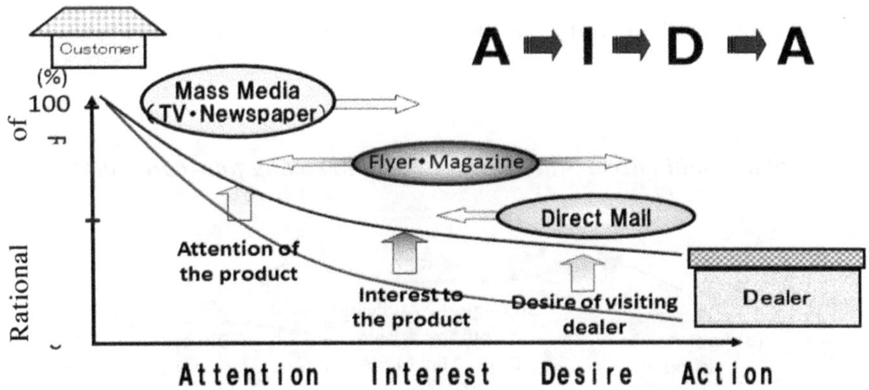

c. Current Research on DM Activities

In studying the current status of direct mail activities at dealerships, the author identified the following issues:

1. Strategy formulation: target customers and sales concepts are unclear
2. Direct mail content: customer preferences are not accurately identified

3. Recipients: recipients are determined based on experiential knowledge of sales staff, which leads to a high degree of variation in the quality of work performed
4. Approach to customers who visit the dealership: purchase behavior characteristics of individual customer are not well understood

Given these problems, direct mail cannot currently be thought of as effective in all cases. The author has demonstrated that the percentage of direct mail recipients that visit the dealers is as low as 1–5%, and that the profitability of those customers that do come in is not very high (Ishiguro and Amasaka, 2012a,b; Ishiguro et al., 2010).

It is critical that these issues be resolved so that direct mail activities are more efficient (sophisticated). This will help dealerships retain their premier customers and boost their sales. A survey of the literature did not reveal any prior research that successfully addresses these problems.

1. Strategically Creating a "Total Direct Mail Model" (TDMM)

Based on previous direct mail research and studies done on the actual state of direct mail activities, the author created a "Total Direct Mail Model" (TDMM) as the strategic DM application. This concept model is shown in Figure 16.

As the figure indicates, the model consists of the following four core functions:

a. Direct mail strategy formulation: Scientific identification of premier customers (Amasaka, 2011).
b. Direct mail content: Development of content based on customer preferences (Kimura et al., 2007).
c. Mailing process: Establishing a process for determining recipients based on customer information and other data (Ishiguro et al., 2010; Ishiguro and Amasaka, 2012b).
d. Customer handling: Clearly identifying customer purchase behavior characteristics (Kojima et al., 2010).

Figure 16. Creation of a "Total Direct Mail Model" (TDMM) using four core functions

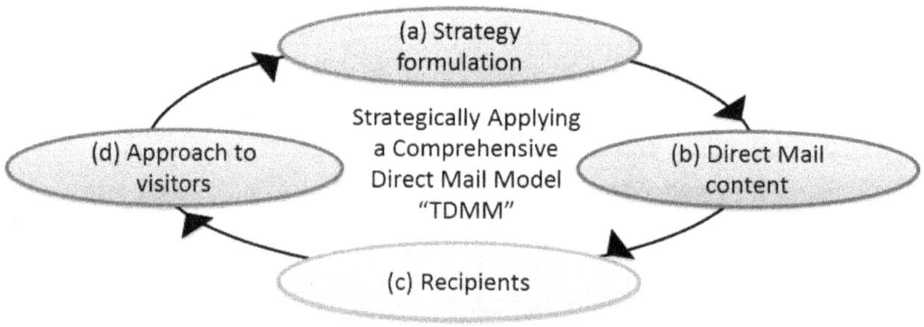

Then, Figure 17. shows the strategically "TDMM Approach Model" to practically implementing the above strategies. The related systems for realizing four core functions are described below.

Figure 17. Strategically TDMM Approach Model for realizing four core functions

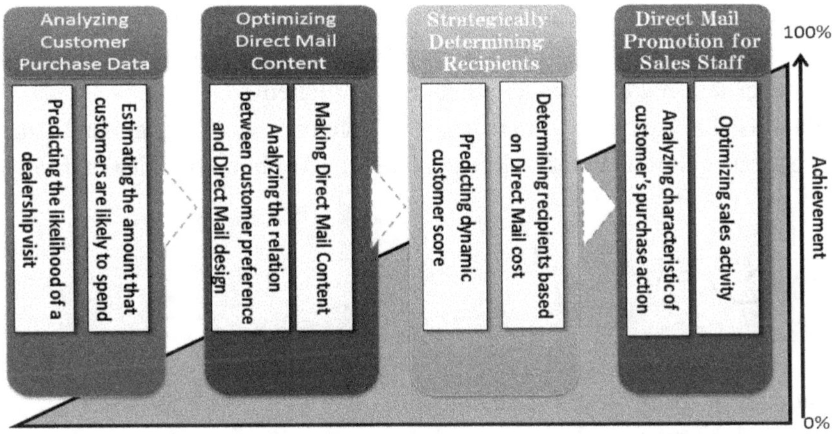

a. System for Analyzing Customer Purchase Data

As Table 3 describes, the system for analyzing customer purchase data supports dealers in formulating a direct mail strategy by identifying different premier customer segments.

Table 3. System for analyzing customer purchase data

		Likelihood of spend	
		High	**Low**
Likelihood of visit	High	Preferred customer Luxury car intention Own customer	Basic car intention Own customer
	Middle	Semi-preferred customer Luxury car intention Own/other customer	Basic car intention Own/other customer
	Low	Luxury car intention Other customer	Not preferred customer Basic car intention Other customer

i. Identifying Premier Customer Segments

Premier customers are first defined according to two different criteria: the likelihood that they will visit the dealership, and the amount of money they can be expected to spend on purchases. This information is based on the purchase process (whether they buy vehicles after coming to the dealer). These two indicators are then combined and used to define the level of the premier customer.

ii. Predicting the Likelihood of a Dealership Visit

Discriminant analysis is used to score each customer in terms of how likely he or she is to visit the dealership. Past visit data is used to arrive at a discriminant score, using whether the direct mail will lead to a visit as the external criterion and customer attributes as the items.

The score is then used to carry out a logistic regression analysis (Tsujitani and Amasaka, 1993) in order to get a regression equation (1) that will calculate the likelihood of a dealership visit.

$$P_i = \frac{1}{1+\exp\{-(\alpha_0 + \sum_j \alpha_j \delta_{ij})\}}, \quad i = 1, 2, \ldots, n \tag{1}$$

i : Customer ID number (n: Number of the customers)
j : Customer attribute (J: Number of the attributes)
P_i : Likelihood that customer i will visit the dealer
α_j : Discriminant coefficient
δ_{ij} : Indicates whether or not customer i has attribute j (0 or 1)

i. Estimating the Amount that Customers are Likely to Spend

Regression analysis is used to obtain a regression equation (2) for this calculation, with customer purchase amount as the external criterion and customer attributes as the items.

This equation is then used to estimate the amount that customers are likely to spend based on their specific attributes.

$$V_i = \beta_0 + \sum_j \beta_j \delta_{ij}, \quad i = 1, 2, \ldots, n \tag{2}$$

V_i : Amount that customer i is likely to spend
β_j : Partial regression coefficient

b. System for Optimizing DM Content

The system for optimizing direct mail content is used to analyze how customer preferences change in response to changes in direct mail design. To get this information, a Key Graph is used to collect free-response customer feedback on different direct mail designs.

Figure 18 shows an example of a Key Graph. In this example, the authors were able to determine that using a black background gives the design a high-end feel and causes it to stand out.

By referring to concepts arrived at using these new insights as well as the system for analyzing customer purchase data, direct mail designers can now create designs that accurately reflect sales strategies and customer preferences.

Figure 18. Key Graph

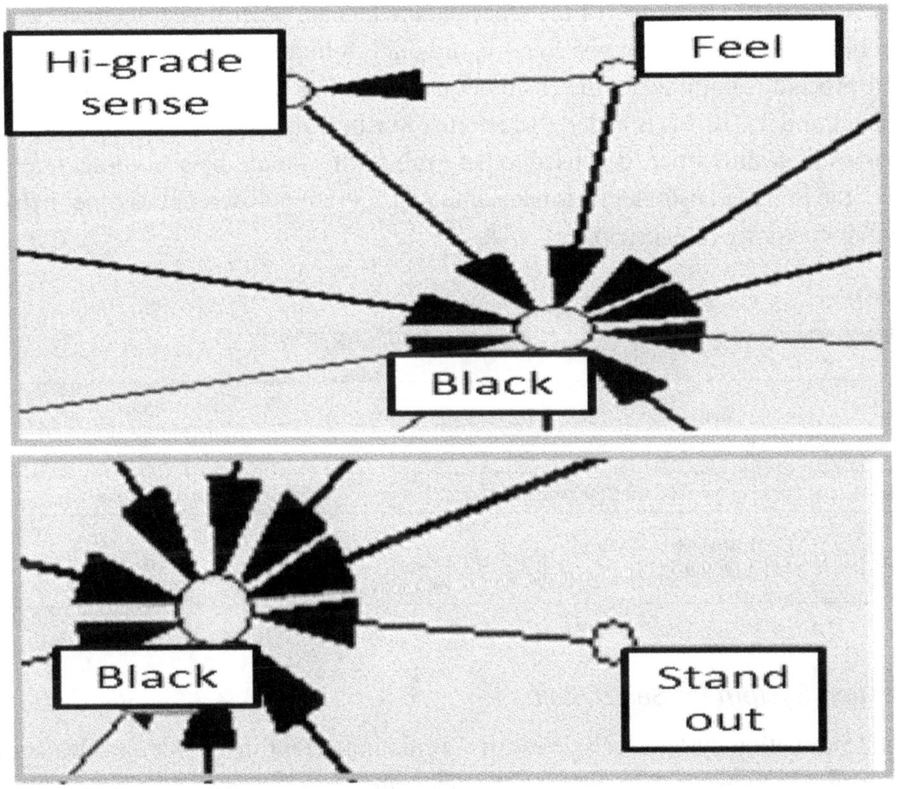

c. System for Strategically Determining DM Recipients

The system for strategically determining direct mail recipients identifies who direct mail should be sent to among the premier customer categories identified using the system for analyzing customer purchase data. Equations (3) to (5) are used to determine the recipients.

$$\underset{x_1,x_2,\ldots,x_n\in\{0,1\}}{Maximize}\sum_i P_i V_i x_i \tag{3}$$

$$s.t.\sum_i x_i = N \tag{4}$$

$$L_j N \le \sum_i \delta_{ij} x_i \le H_j N,\ j = 1,2,\ldots,J \tag{5}$$

x_i : Whether customer i is flagged as a direct mail recipient (0 or 1)
N : Total number of direct mailings sent
L_j/H_j : Lower/Upper limit for the percentage of direct mailings sent to customers with attribute j

Mathematical programming is used to solve the above equations and determine who customer *i* should be targeted as a recipient. The values of the other parameters are determined in advance.

P_i (the likelihood of a dealership visit) and V_i (amount of money likely to be spent) are determined using the same procedure outlined for the customer purchase data analysis system (Subsection 22.4.2(2-1)), once behavioral data (RFM) is added to customer attribute data.

Table 4 shows their difference. It is used to determine who should be sent direct mail based on the current level of the premier customer (this takes into consideration different customer behaviors among different premier customer categories).

Table 4. Difference between static customer and dynamic customer

Static (Analyzing customer purchase data)	Dynamic (Strategically determining direct mail recipients)
Customer segment who like target car during the promotion term	Customer segment who like target car most now
Life stage Life style	Life stage Life style RFM

d. DM Promotion System for Sales Staff

The direct mail promotion system for sales staff reveals important insights that sales staff can use in order to handle customers when they come to the dealership.

Specifically, the system surveys dealerships to determine what elements are prioritized when someone from the premier customer category purchases a vehicle.

As Figure 19 describes, survey data is then subjected to a cluster analysis and principle component analysis to identify characteristics of customer purchase behavior. These results are then communicated to the sales staff.

Figure 19. Characteristic of customer's purchase action

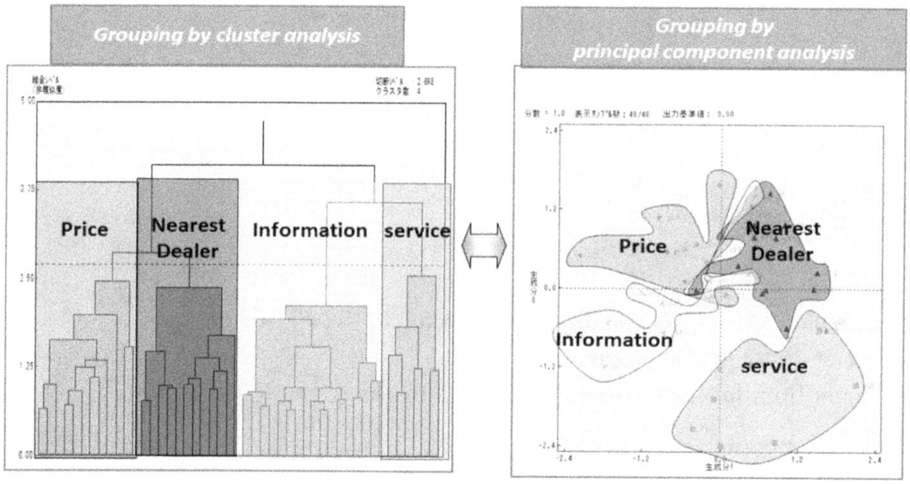

e. Effectiveness of TDMM

As Figure 20 shows, the author is currently using the "Strategic development of TDMM application for auto-dealers" presented here at Company A in an attempt to increase the percentage of customers that visit the dealer as well as the amount of money they spend when they come in.

Specifically, they are using the four systems described above based on Company A's customer information and sales data as well as on customer preferences collected via surveys. Then, to realize of TDMM effectiveness for improving business process of auto-dealers using "Strategically TDMM Approach Model" (Figure 17), the author has proceeded the actual application examples based on the four core functions ((a), (b), (c) and (d) in Figure 16, Chapter 8) as follows;

a. "Changes in marketing process management: Establishment of Toyota Sales Marketing System" to develop the scientific identification of premier customers (Amasaka, 2011).
b. "Creation of Scientific Approach Method for DM (SAM-DM): Effectiveness of attracting customer" for the development of content based on customer preferences (Kimura, 2007),
c. "Effectiveness of a highly compelling DM method "PMOS-DM" to bring customers into auto-dealerships" to establish a process for determining recipients based on customer information (Ishiguro et al., 2010; Ishiguro and Amasaka, 2012b).
d. "Development of DM method "PMCI-DM" for effectively attracting customers" aiming clearly identifying customer purchase behavior characteristics (Kojima et al., 2010)

Developing VUCMIN and TDMM for CS and CL to Boost Automobile Marketing

In this study, for CS and CL to boost automobile marketing, the author has developed the created "VUCMIN and TDMM" in order to enhance the desire to visit stores in the automobile industry.

Then, taking advantage of those acquired knowledge by the validity "VUCKMIN and TDMM", moreover, the author illustrates the typical studies for the "Progress of automobile marketing for business and sales" by using next Chapter 23 based on the above Section 6.4 in Chapter 6 and Section 16.3 in Chapter 16, as follows;

Chapter 6: "Change in automobile marketing for developing customer creation" in Section 6.4
Chapter 16: "Developing New Japan Marketing Management Model for customer creation" in Section 16.3
Chapter 23: "Scientific Mixed Media Model employing Advanced TMS: For boosting auto-dealer visits"

CONCLUSION

Faced with a sluggish economy, car sales have been disappointing in recent years. In this section, therefore, the author focused on CS as a way of boosting marketing effectiveness, clarifying the key factors that comprise CL, and helps to improve the marketing strategy employing NJ-MMM (New Japan Marketing Management Model).

Specifically, the author has developed with researching CS and CL as a way of boosting marketing effectiveness, clarifying the key factors that comprise customer loyalty, and help improve the marketing strategy. Then, as application examples using those knowledges acquired above, the author illustrated the development and its effectiveness for CS and CL describing VUCMIN (Video Unites Customer Behavior and Maker's Designing Intentions) and TDMM (Total Direct Mail Management Model).

ACKNOWLEDGMENT

The author would like to acknowledge the generous support of the Amasaka New JIT Laboratory at Aoyama Gakuin University that assisted with the research, especially, Mr. Okutomi, H., Yamaji, M., Hifumi, S., Sakalsis. M. M., Ishiguro, H., Kojima, T., Kimura, T. and others.

REFERENCES

Amasaka, K. (1999). A study on Science SQC by utilizing Management SQC- A demonstrative study on a New SQC concept and procedure in the manufacturing industry. *Journal of Production Economics, 60-61*, 591–598. doi:10.1016/S0925-5273(98)00143-1

Amasaka, K. (2004). *Science SQC, new quality control principle*. Springer-Verlag. doi:10.1007/978-4-431-53969-8

Amasaka, K. (2007a). Proposal of Marketing SQC to revolutionize dealers' sales activities-A demonstrative study on Customer Science by utilizing Science SQC. *Proceedings of the 16th International Conference Production Research. Praha Czech Public*, 1-9.

Amasaka, K. (2007b). The validity of Advanced TMS, A strategic development marketing system–Toyota's Scientific Customer Creative Model utilizing New JIT. *The International Business & Economics Research Journal*, *6*(8), 35–42.

Amasaka, K. (2007c). High Linkage Model "Advanced TDS, TPS & TMS": Strategic development of "New JIT" at Toyota. *International Journal of Operations and Quantitative Management*, *13*(3), 101–121.

Amasaka, K. (2009). The effectiveness of flyer advertising employing TMS: Key to scientific automobile sales innovation at Toyota, China-USA. *Business Review*, *8*(3), 1–12.

Amasaka, K. (2011). Changes in marketing process management employing TMS: Establishment of Toyota Sales Marketing System, China-USA. *Business Review*, *10*(6), 539–550.

Amasaka, K. (Ed.). (2012). Science TQM, new quality management principle: The quality management strategy of Toyota. Bentham Science Publishers.

Amasaka, K. (2015). *New JIT, new management technology principle*. Taylor and Francis, CRC Press.

Amasaka, K. (2019). Studies on New Manufacturing Theory, *Noble*. *International Journal of Scientific Research*, *3*(1), 1–20.

Amasaka, K., Ogura, M., & Ishiguro, H. (2013). Constructing a Scientific Mixed Media Model for boosting automobile dealer visits: Evolution of market creation employing TMS. *International Journal of Engineering Research and Applications*, *3*(4), 1377–1391.

Beko, J., & Jagric, T. (2011). Demand models for direct mail and periodicals delivery services: Results for a transition economy. *Applied Economics*, *43*(9), 1125–1138. doi:10.1080/00036840802600244

Bell, G. H., Ledolter, J., & Swersey, A. J. (2006). Experimental design on the front lines of marketing: Testing new ideas to increase Direct Mail sales. *International Journal of Research in Marketing*, *23*(3), 309–319. doi:10.1016/j.ijresmar.2006.05.002

Bult, J. R., & Wansbeek, T. (2005). Optimal selection for direct mail. *Marketing Science*, *14*(4), 378–394. doi:10.1287/mksc.14.4.378

Dentsu Inc. (2003). *Dentsu Online, Total Advertisement Expenses Total of Japan*. https://www.dentsu.co.jp/marketing/adex/adex2005/media.html

Ferrell, O. C., & Hartline, M. (2005). *Marketing Strategy*. Thomson South-Western.

Hifumi, S. (2006). *A study on a strategic advertising and publicity (animation): The proposal of "A-VUCMIN" for raising the volition of coming to the dealers' shop* (Master's thesis). Graduate School of Science and Engineering, Aoyama Gakuin University, Amasaka New JIT Laboratory.

Ishiguro, H., & Amasaka, K. (2012a). Establishment of a Strategic Total Direct Mail Model to Bring Customers into Auto Dealerships. *Journal of Business & Economics Research*, *10*(8), 493–500. doi:10.19030/jber.v10i8.7177

Ishiguro, H., & Amasaka, K. (2012b). Proposal and effectiveness of a highly compelling direct mail method: Establishment and deployment of PMOS-DM. *International Journal of Management and Information Systems*, *16*(1), 1–10.

Ishiguro, H., Kojima, T., & Matsuo, I. (2010). A Highly Compelling Direct Mail Method "PMOS-DM": Strategic applying of statistics and mathematical programming. *The 4th Spring Meeting of Japan Statistical Society Poster Session.*

Japan Automobile Manufacturers Association (JAMA). (2005). *Automobile Sale Numbers of Japan*. https://www.jama.or.jp/stats/product/index.html

Jonker, J. J., Piersma, N., & Potharst, R. (2006). A Decision Support System for direct mailing decision. *Decision Support Systems*, *42*(2), 915–925. doi:10.1016/j.dss.2005.08.006

Kawasaki, S., & Yoshizawa, N. (2011). *Customer database marketing for the improvement in CS: The multivariate analysis of the customer information for raising commodity value* (Bachelor thesis). School of Science and Engineering, Department of Industrial and System Engineering, Aoyama Gakuin University, Tokyo.

Kimura, T., Uesugi, Y., Yamaji, M., & Amasaka, K. (2007). A study of Scientific Approach Method for Direct Mail, SAM-DM: Effectiveness of attracting customer utilizing Advanced TMS. *Proceedings of the 5th Asian Network for Quality Congress, Hyatt Regency*, 938-945.

Kojima, T., Kimura, T., Yamaji, M., & Amasaka, K. (2010). Proposal and development of the Direct Mail Method "PMCI-DM" for effectively attracting customers. *International Journal of Management & Information Systems*, *14*(5), 15–22. doi:10.19030/ijmis.v14i5.9

Kotler, P., & Keller, K. L. (2006). *Marketing Management (12th ed.).* Prentice Hall.

Murat, S. M., Hifumi, S., Yamaji, M. & Amasaka, K. (2008). Developing a Strategic Advertisement Method "VUCMIN" to enhance the desire of customers for visiting dealers. *Proceedings of the International Symposium on Management Engineering,* 248-257.

Okutomi, H. (2011). *A study on establishment of the structure model on relationship between CS and CL: An example of Japan's auto-dealerships* (Bachelor thesis). School of Science and Engineering, Department of Industrial and System Engineering, Aoyama Gakuin University, Amasaka New JIT Laboratory, Sagamihara, Kanagawa, Japan.

Okutomi, H., & Amasaka, K. (2012). Researching Customer Satisfaction and Loyalty to boost marketing Effectiveness A look at Japan's auto dealerships. *Proceedings of the 2nd International Symposium on Operations Management Strategy 2012*, 124-131

Okutomi, H., & Amasaka, K. (2013). Researching Customer Satisfaction and Loyalty to boost marketing effectiveness: A look at Japan's auto-dealerships. *International Journal of Management & Information Systems*, *17*(4), 193–200. doi:10.19030/ijmis.v17i4.8093

Parasuraman, A., Zeihaml, V. A., & Berry, L. L. (1988). SERVQUAL: A multiple-item scale for measuring consumer perceptions of service quality. *Journal of Retailing*, *64*(1), 12–40.

Piersma, N., & Jonker, J. J. (2004). Determining the Optimal Direct Mailing Frequency. *European Journal of Operational Research*, *158*(1), 173–182. doi:10.1016/S0377-2217(03)00349-7

Roger, D. B., Paul, W. M., & James, F. E. (2006). *Consumer Behavior*. The Dryden Press.

Shimizu, K. (2004). *Theory and Strategy of Advertisement*. Sousei-Sha.

Tsujitani, M., & Amasaka, K. (1993). Analysis of enumerated data (1): Logit transformation and graph analysis. *Quality Control*, *44*(4), 61–66.

Yamaji, M., Hifumi, S., Sakalsis, M. M., & Amasaka, K. (2010). Developing A Strategic Advertisement Method "VUCMIN" to Enhance the Desire of Customers for Visiting Dealers. *Journal of Business Case Studies*, *6*(3), 1–11. doi:10.19030/jbcs.v6i3.871

Yamamoto, Y., & Enkawa, T. (2000). Structural analysis on relationship between customer satisfaction and loyalty. *Journal of Japan Industrial Management Association*, *51*(2), 143–152.

Chapter 23
Scientific Mixed Media Model Developing NJ-MMM for Boosting Auto-Dealer Visits

ABSTRACT

In this chapter, the author has constructed the Scientific Mixed Media Model (SMMM) for boosting automobile dealer visits by developing NJ-MMM (New Japan Marketing Management Model) named Advanced TMS, Strategic Customer Creation Model in order to realize the automobile market creation. Specifically, SMMM develops and validates the effectiveness of putting together four core elements—(1) Video that Unites Customer behavior and Manufacturer Design Intentions (VUCMIN), (2) Customer Motion Picture-Flyer Design Method (CMP-FDM), (3) Attention-Grabbing Train Car Advertisements (AGTCA), and (4) Practical Method using Optimization and Statistics for Direct Mail (PMOS-DM)—into new strategic advertisement methods designed to enhance marketing and the desire in the automotive industry. At present, SMMM is applied to a dealership representing an advanced car manufacturer Toyota, where its effectiveness is verified.

INTRODUCTION

Recently, in light of recent changes in the marketing environment, the author believes it is now necessary to develop innovative business and sales activities that adequately take into account the changing characteristics of customers who are seeking to break free from convention (Amasaka, 2011). If they are to be successful in the future, those involved in global marketing must develop a marketing system of the highest quality.

A marketing management system needs to be established particularly so that business, sales, and service divisions, which are developing and designing appealing products and are also closest to customers, can organically learn customer tastes and desires by means of the continued application of objective data and scientific methodology. At present, however, a system for applying scientific analytical methods to

DOI: 10.4018/978-1-7998-8746-1.ch023

customer data has not been satisfactorily established. In some cases, its importance has not even been recognized.

In this chapter, therefore, the author has constructed the "Scientific Mixed Media Model" (SMMM) for boosting automobile dealer visits by developing NJ-MMM (New Japan Marketing Management Model) named "Advanced TMS, strategic customer creation model" in order to realize the automobile market creation (Amasaka et al., 2013) (Refer to Section 4.2 in Chapter 4). This model that enables the sales, marketing and service divisions nearest the customer to systematically identify their tastes and desires is critical. The aim of SMMM is for an evolution of market creation through innovative advertisements promoting dealer sales activities (Amasaka et al., 2008, 2013; Amasaka, 2013, 2019).

To achieve this goal, the author presents SMMM, which takes the form of strategic marketing and has four core elements: (1) Video that Unites Customer behavior and Manufacturer Design Intentions (VUCMIN), (2) Customer Motion Picture–Flyer Design Method (CMP-FDM), (3) Attention-Grabbing Train Car Advertisements (AGTCA), and (4) Practical Method using Optimization and Statistics for Direct Mail (PMOS-DM).

The effectiveness of SMMM using four core elements has been applied to a dealership representing an advanced car manufacturer Toyota, where its effectiveness was verified (Amasaka et al., 2013; Ogura et al., 2013a; Amasaka, 2015, 2020).

NEED FOR A MAEKETING STRATEGY THAT CONSIDERS MARKET TRENDS

Today's marketing activities require more than just short-term strategies by the business and sales divisions. In a mass-consumption society, when the market was growing in an unchanging way, sales increases were achieved by means of simple mass marketing through huge corporate investments in advertising (Nikkei Business, 1999: Amasaka, 2005).

However, after the collapse of the bubble economy, the competitive market environment changed drastically. Since then, companies that have implemented strategic marketing quickly and aggressively have been the only ones enjoying continued growth (Okada, et al., 2001). Upon close examination, it was determined that strategic marketing activities must be conducted as company-wide, core corporate management activities that involve interactions between each division inside and outside of the company (Jeffrey and Bernard, 2005).

Therefore, a marketing management model needs to be established so that business, sales, and service divisions, which are developing and designing appealing products and are also closest to customers, can organizationally learn customer tastes and desires (Amasaka et al., 2005; Shimakawa, et al., 2006). Specifically, pursuing improvements in product quality by means of the continued application of objective data and scientific methodology is increasingly important (James and Mona, 2004: Amasaka, 2005).

At present, the organizational system and rational methodology that allows them to analyze data on each customer using a scientific analysis approach has not yet been fully established in these divisions; in some cases, the importance of this system has not even been widely recognized (Niiya and Matsuoka, 2001; Gray and Arvind, 2003; Ikeo, 2006; Amasaka, 2007).

EVOLUTION OF MARKET CREATION DEVELOPING NJ-MMM

Significance of NJ-MMM Based on TMS

TMS (Total Marketing System) as the key of the strategic development of NJM (New Japan Model) shown in Figure 1 and 2, Chapter 5, is composed of these technological elements: (a) market creation activities through collection and utilization of customer information, (b) strengthening of merchandise power based on the understanding that products are supposed to retain their value, (c) establishment of marketing systems from the viewpoint of building bonds with customers, and (d) realization of the customer focus utilizing customer information network for CS (Customer Satisfaction), CD (Customer Delight) and CR (Customer Retention) elements needed for the corporate attitude (behavior norm) to enhance customer values (Amasaka, 2019) (Refer to Section 5.3 in Chapter 5).

Therefore, to realize market creation with an emphasis on the customer by developing CL (Customer Royalty), the significance of NJ-MMM (New Japan Marketing Management Model) based on TMS is to promote market creation and to realize quality management through scientific marketing and sales, not by sticking to conventional concepts as shown in Figure 2, Chapter 16 (Amasaka, Ed., 2012; Okutomi and Amasaka, 2013; Amasaka, 2015, 2020) (Refer to Chapter 16 and 23 in detail).

Specifically, NJ-MMM aims to achieve the high cycle rate for market creation activities by employing SCCM (Scientific Customer Creative Model), and is composed of four core elements: the NSOI (New sales office image), ISINS (Intelligent Customer Information Network System), RAPS (Rational Advertisement Promotion System) and ISMS (Intelligent Sales Marketing System) indicated in Figure 9, Chapter 6 (Refer to Section 6.4.4 in Chapter 6). By these elements, NJ-MMM innovates for bonding with the customer and reforms office-shop appearance and operation.

Developing Customer Science Principle for the Strengthening of NJ-MMM

Then, the author develops the Customer Science Principle using Science SQC for the strengthening of NJ-MMM (Amasaka, 2002, 2003, 2004, 2005, 2019), Supplying products that satisfy consumers (customers) is the ultimate goal of companies that desire continuous growth. Customers generally evaluate existing products as good or poor, but they do not generally have concrete images of products they will desire in the future. For new product development, it is important to precisely understand the vague desires of customers.

To achieve this goal, the author has created the "Customer Science Principle" to help systematize SMMM shown in Figure 2, Chapter 13 (Amasaka, 2002, 2005) (Refer to Chapter 13). To plan and provide customers with attractive products is the mission of companies and the basis of their existence. This principle is particularly important to convert customer opinion (implicit knowledge) to images (linguistic knowledge) through market creation activities, and to accurately reflect this knowledge in creating products (drawings, for example) using engineering language (explicit knowledge).

This refers to the conceptual diagram that rationally objectifies subjective information (y) and subjectifies objective information $\left(\hat{y}\right)$ through the application of correlation technology. Then, the author applies the statistical science methodology "Science SQC", which has four core principles (Scientific SQC, SQC Technical Methods, Integrated SQC Network (TTIS), and Management SQC) as shown in Figure 3, Chapter 5, and which is designed to develop Customer Science Principle in business and sales divisions to make changes to marketing process management (Amasaka, 2003, 2004, 2015, 2020; Amasaka et al., 2012) (Refer to Chapter 5).

CONSTRUCTING A SCIENTIFIC MIXED MEDIA MODEL FOR BOOSTING AUTOMOBILE DEALER VISITS

Publicity and Advertising as Automobile Sales Promotion Activities

For many years, automobile dealers have been employing various publicities and advertising strategies in cooperation with automobile manufacturers in order to encourage customers to visit their shops.

Figure 1 shows a graphical representation of the relationship between publicity and advertising media—a relationship that helps draw customer traffic to dealers (Amasaka, 2009, 2011). Area A represents multimedia advertising (the internet, CD-ROMs, etc.), Area B represents direct advertising (catalogs, direct mail, handbills (directly handed to customers), telephone calls, etc.), and Area C represents mass media advertising (TV and radio broadcasting, flyers, public transportation (train cars), newspapers, magazines, etc.).

There appear to be few cases where scientific research methods have been applied to the effect of mixed media (areas A to C) and used to study the ways in which such sales activities actually draw customers to automobile dealers (Kubomura and Murata, 1969).

However, the rational effects of the media-mix are insufficient as advertisement methods, and the author therefore considers the need to scientifically promote a new advertisement media mixed model (Melewar and Smith, 2003: Amasaka, 2007: Smith, 2009: Ogura, et al., 2013a; Amasaka et al., 2013).

Figure 1. Graphical representation of customer motives for visiting automobile dealers

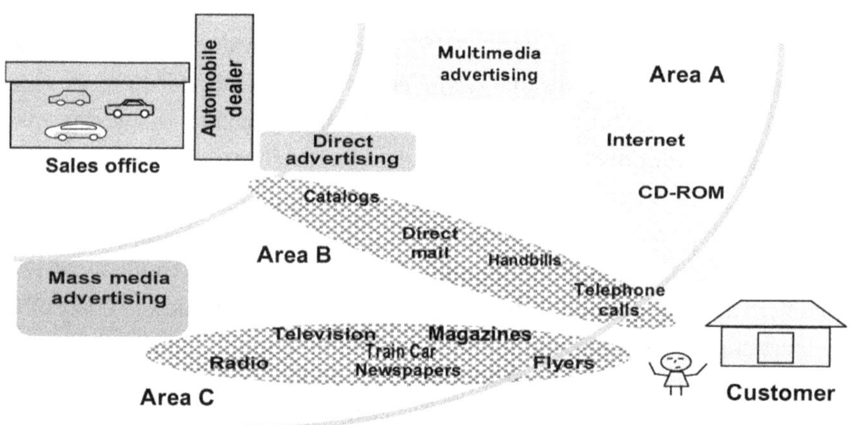

Creation of a Scientific Mixed Media Model

As part of an organization's market creation activities, it is important to gain a quantitative understanding of the effect of publicity and advertising, which are the principal methods involved in sales promotion and order taking, in order to aid the development of future business and sales strategies (Kobayashi and Shimamura, 1997: Kishi, et al., 2000: Shimizu, 2004: Ferrell and Hartline, 2005: Amasaka, 2007, 2009, 2011; Amasaka et al., 2013).

After recent changes in the marketing environment, what is needed now is to develop innovative business and sales activities that are unconventional and correctly identify the characteristics of and changes in customer tastes. There have never been a greater need for careful attention and practice in customer contact, and in order to continuously offer an appealing and customer-oriented marketing strategy, it is important to evolve current market creation activities to strengthen commercial viability and reform office/shop appearance and operations using the Customer Science approach (Amasaka, 2002, 2005).

Therefore, the author wants to construct a "Scientific Mixed Media Model" (SMMM) for boosting automobile dealer visits employing TMS for the innovation of (a) Market Creation Activities, (b) Product Value Improvement, (c) Building Ties with customers and (d) Customer Value Improvement for improving mass media and multimedia, direct advertising, internet, CD-ROM (TV, newspapers, flyers, direct mail, radio, magazines, train cars, etc.) as shown in Figure 2.

Specifically, SMMM aims to achieve a "high cycle rate for market creation activities", and is composed of four core elements (1)-(4) by developing "Evolution of market creation activities" for the "Contact with customers", "Strengthening of merchandise power" and "Reform of office/shop appearance and operations" (Yamaji et al., 2010; Koyama et al., 2010; Ishiguro and Amasaka, 2012a,b; Ogura et al., 2013b), as follows;

1. "Video that Unites Customer behavior and Manufacturer Design Intentions" (VUCMIN)
2. "Customer Motion Picture–Flyer Design Method" (CMP-FDM)
3. "Attention-Grabbing Train Car Advertisements" (AGTCA)
4. "Practical Method using Optimization and Statistics for Direct Mail" (PMOS-DM)

These four core elements aim to provide an up-to-date inquiry as to deep-seated customer wants in terms of customer behavior analysis (James, et al., 2006). Disparate behaviors by gender and age segment will be clarified in the analysis of standard behaviors.

SMMM for the evolution of market creation activities improves "innovative automobile dealer sales activity knowhow" regarding repeat users of various manufacturers' vehicles.

Its characteristics are described below.

1. VUCMIN

The created VUCMIN uses video advertisements, and is developed based on scientific approaches and analyses that focus on the standard behavioral movements of customers who visit dealers when choosing an automobile (Hifumi, 2006: Murat, et al., 2008: Yamaji, et al., 2010).

Figure 2. A Scientific Mixed Media Model for boosting automobile dealer visits

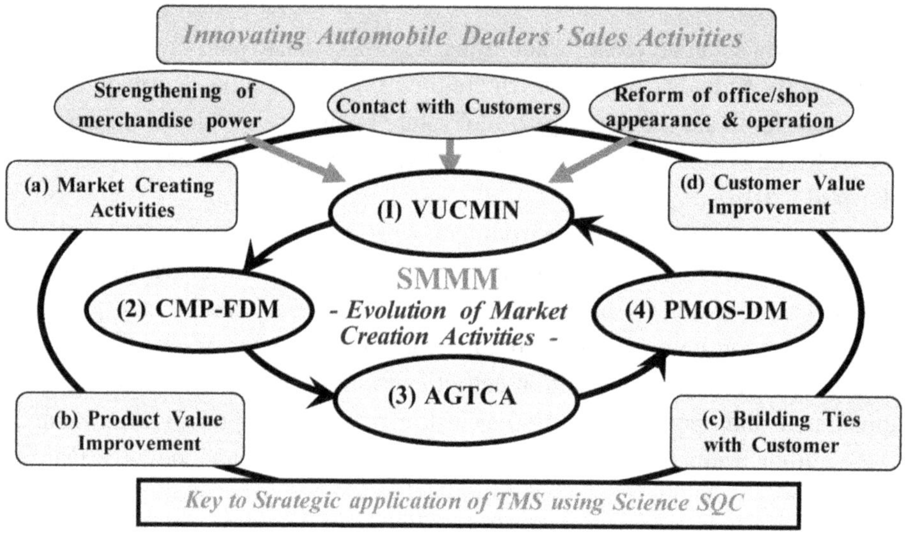

This method, which is based on the different approaches identified in target customer profiles, aims to make customers more eager to visit automobile dealers. After creating this video advertisement, customers are verified as having a positive opinion towards visiting dealers with a plan to purchase the vehicle featured in the video.

More concretely, based on the research approach outlined in the previous chapter, the framework of VUCMIN was established as shown in Figure 7 (Amasaka, 2015, 2020) (Refer to Chapter 23 in detail).

2. CMP-FDM

In this study, the author establishes a method of creating attractive flyer designs while using customer behavior analysis with videos that help dealers attract customers and aim to reform conventional marketing activities.

CMP-FDM analyzes how customers see flyers, and the authors create attractive designs that guarantee each customer's satisfaction. Next, the authors integrate the design elements into one that will satisfy all types of customers (universal type) by organizing the design features (design elements), and then validating the method (Koyama, et al., 2010).

More concretely, the author shows the steps (1 to 5) for establishing CMP-FDM as shown in Figure 3. The created CMP-FDM utilizing SQC Technical Methods (Amasaka, 2003, 2004) consists roughly of two processes: research and flyer design (Amasaka, 2015, 2020).

In the first process, the author checks the current state of flyers as preliminary research as follows;

In step 1, the author analyzes customer behavior towards the flyers using video recordings in order to understand how to the materials are actually viewed. Then, the author proves that customers can be classified into three types: active customers, collection-first customers, and indifferent customers.

In step 2, to address problems with the current flyer design (information appearing on the flyer, such as exterior photos, price, car name, loan information, and interior photos), the authors clarify what each customer type wants to know from the content. One problem is the provision of a lot of unnecessary information and a lack of necessary information.

In step 3, to solve problems in flyer layout, the authors clarify what kind of layout each customer group wants. One problem is typeface that is too small to see or information that is too varied to understand.

In step 4, based on the results of steps 2 and 3, the authors incorporate the design elements into one flyer that it is attractive to all customer type.

In step 5, the authors conduct a survey to compare the composite flyer developed in step 4.

Figure 3. Steps of establishing CMP-FDM

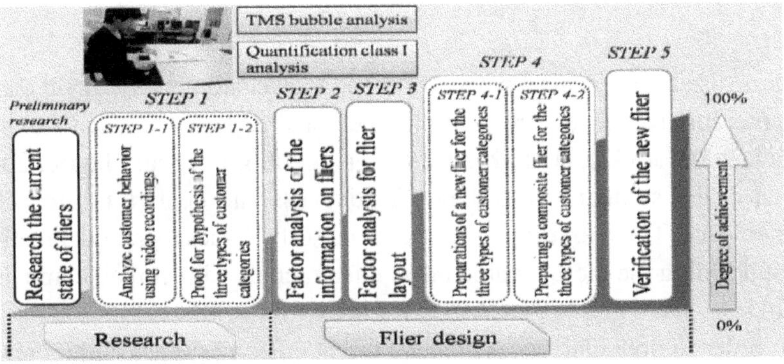

3. AGTCA

This study deals with train car advertisements (hanging posters, above-window posters, and sticker ads) that have become increasingly popular in recent years.

Focusing on transit advertising, which has a good contact rate and provides long-term contact, the authors decided to examine customer relationships and how they relate to train car advertising with the aim of defining the ideal format for this type of media.

The goal was to first quantify the way passengers pay attention to train car advertisements, and then propose the ideal form that in-car train advertising should take based on a visual representation of passenger information.

More concretely, the purpose of AGTCA is to examine the correlations between passenger information and riding conditions in train car advertising in order to discover the ideal way to advertise inside passenger trains, using the same research steps as CMP-FDM employing SQC Technical Methods (Refer to Ogura et al., (2013b) in detail), as follows;

Specifically, to examine and the survey data for the "Visualizing causal relationships between passenger information and riding conditions", the author analyses the procedure and goals using statistical analysis, as follows;

i. Look at overall trends in passenger information using a cross-tabulation method that focuses on whether passenger attention turned to hanging posters, above-window posters, or sticker advertisements and others.
ii. Perform a cluster analysis on riding conditions and group the results using Quantification Theory Type III. Then, look at the relationship between (1) the riding conditions grouped in the cross tabulation and (2) whether passenger attention turned to hanging posters, above-window posters, or sticker advertisements.
iii. Research the grouped riding condition data and basic passenger information to determine how it relates to attention rates established for the three types of advertising using a Categorical Automatic Interaction Detector (CAID) analysis (Murayama, et al., 1982: Amasaka, et al., 1998: Amasaka, 2011).

4. PMOS-DM

No clear processes are used at car dealers when deciding target customers for direct mail campaigns, and individual sales representatives tend to rely on their personal experience when making such decisions (Bult and Wansbeek, 2005; Jonker, et al., 2006; Bell, et al.,2006; Beco and Jagric, 2011).

This means that dealer strategies lose their effectiveness and dealers fail to achieve the desired increase in customer visits. Thus, for this study, the author establishes a practical method using PMOS-DM as a method of deciding the most suitable target customers for direct mail campaigns (Ishiguro and Amasaka, 2012a,b).

Specifically, in order to both clarify the dealer's target customer types and increase the number of customer visits, the author applies mathematical programming (combinatorial optimization) using statistics to establish a model for determining the most suitable target customers for direct mail campaigns.

More concretely, this model was created using the same research steps as CMP-FDM employing SQC Technical Methods: a three-pronged approach to resolving dealers' current problems with direct mail activities, as follows;

Step 1 is to increase the response rate, or the percentage of customers who visit the dealer as a result of receiving direct mail. To achieve this, the PMOS-DM uses statistical analysis to determine which customers are most likely to respond.

Step 2 is to reflect dealer aims in the recipient selection process. This is achieved by using a simulation driven by mathematical programming to optimize the selection of target customers (refer to Appendix 3: Optimal selection using a model formula).

Step 3 is to clarify the recipient selection process by providing dealers with a model that outlines a specific approach.

Following an explicit model informed by statistics and mathematical programming keeps inconsistency among salespeople to a minimum. The three-pronged approach proposed in this study therefore provides a direct mail method that allows dealers to both target their desired customer segment and boost response rates at the same time.

In short, PMOS-DM uses statistics and mathematical programming to create an objective decision-making process that does not rely on the current selection methods used by salespeople, which are based on personal knowledge and experience and therefore vague and implicit. At the same time, the model aims to boost the direct mail response rate in line with dealer targets (Amasaka, 2015, 2020).

EXAMPLE APPLICATIONS

This subsection validates the effectiveness of SMMM for effective advertising designed to bring customers into auto dealerships by use of four core elements (VUCKMIN, CMP-FDM, AGTCA, PMOS-DM), and the Customer Science approach to quantitatively assess the effectiveness of various advertising (mass media, direct advertising, and multimedia) (Amasaka, 2015, 2020).

Visualizing Causal Relationships in Customer Purchase Behavior

SMMM was developed in order to draw more attention to the vehicle, spark interest in the vehicle, and make customer want to visit the dealer.

To achieve the purpose of this research, a field survey on vehicle advertising was conducted to identify the core elements of each media type and to visualize the relationship between those elements and the media as well as the causal relationships between each media type and (a) vehicle awareness, (b) vehicle interest, and (c) desire to visit dealers (sales shops).

A survey was conducted in order to better understand the causal relationships among different types of media, media elements, and customer (consumer) purchase behavior.

The advertising and marketing division at an advanced car manufacturer A (Toyota Motor Corporation), Japan Toyota Dealer Y of an advanced car manufacturer A, and the Z market survey company helped to conduct an in-person survey on advertising and marketing by visiting male and female licensed drivers age 18 and older living in Tokyo, Fukuoka, and Sapporo of Japan.

A total of 318 valid responses (197 male and 121 female, generally uniform age balance) were collected. The investigation period was the five months leading up to the release of the new Q model by an advanced car manufacturer A.

Based on the author's existing research and knowledge (Amasaka, 2007, 2009, 2011), they were able to identify media mix effects in each form of media using a purchasing action model, TV ads, radio ads and newspaper ads (early June 2005), as well as internet ads (early July) and train car (transportation) ads (mid-August) before the new car sale, and flyer and magazine ads (late August), DM ads (early September) and DH (Direct Hand) ads. (mid-September) issued by Japan Toyota dealer Y.

Participants were shown TV commercials and newspaper ads promoting Japan Toyota's new Q car and then asked questions inquiring about their purchase behavior and about the media and media elements. The collected data was analyzed and the causal relationships between media, media elements, and consumer purchase behavior were outlined (Ogura et al., 2013a).

The questions that the authors used in the survey are listed in Table 1. The questionnaire was multiple choice and asked respondents to describe their opinion (item ① was yes-no, and the five-point scale in items ③ and ④ was converted into binary data).

Elements in each form of media were identified using multivariate analysis (cluster analysis, quantification theory type III) and other statistical methods as shown in Figure 4.

Table 1. Survey questions

①	Are you aware of the Japan Toyota Q model?
②	What media did you see advertising this vehicle?
③	Are you interested in this vehicle?
④	Do you want to or did you actually visit a dealer to inquire about this car?
⑤	What kind of influence does each type of media have on you in terms of your attention, interest, and desire?
⑥	What was your impression of the advertisement?
⑦	Which advertising elements do you consider most important?

As the example in the figure shows, the critical elements in terms of generating the distinct promotional outcomes that consumers expect are: impact, contact frequency, newsworthiness, informativeness, and memorability (Ogura, et al., 2013a; Amasaka et al., 2013).

Figure 4 also positions TV ads, transportation ads, internet ads, newspaper ads, DM in order to identify the expected advertising effectiveness of each.

Finally, the insights gained through scientific analysis were used to describe specific chracteristics of the four core elements of the proposed SMMM (VUCMIN, AGTCA, CMP-FDM, and PMOS-DM) below so that more customers would be drawn to visit auto-dealers.

Figure 4. A scatter diagram with the principle component scores using Quantification Theory Type III

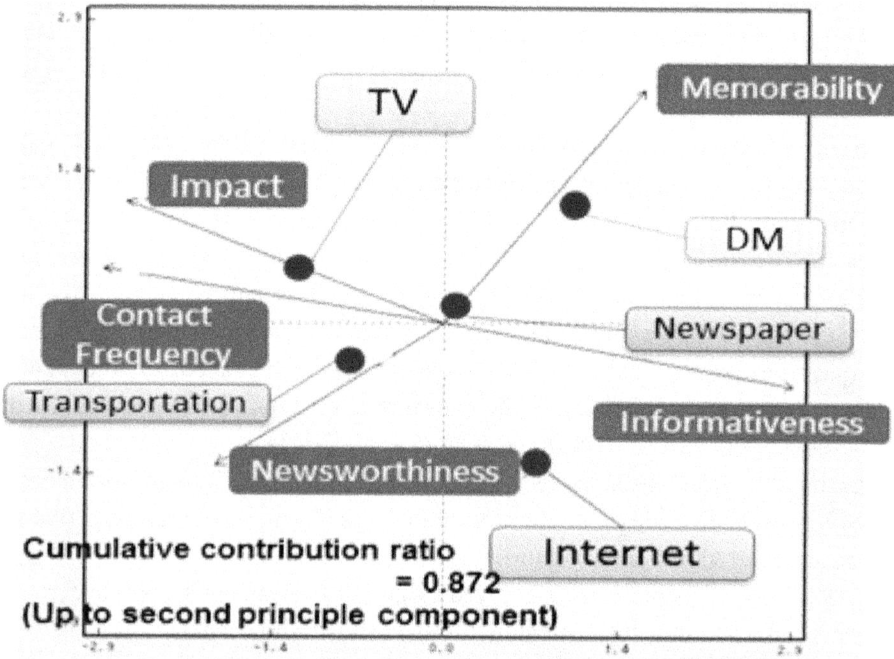

Application of VUCMIN

In their previous research, the author identified behavioral patterns of customers as they focus on the exterior of a vehicle (Refer to Chapter 13). Insights gained during this research were used to explain the influence of product planning and designer intentions in VUCMIN creation (Hifumi, 2006; Yamaji et al., 2010).

The Toyota vehicle "Mark X" named "Cressida" in USA was used as a target vehicle in design inquiries. According to "common opinions from designers and product planning at an advanced car manufacturer A, the parts that are given the most attention when the vehicle is shown to customers are the (i) front proportions, (ii) streamlined side proportions, (iii) tri-beam headlamps (lenses), (iv) widened console box, and (v) sharpened rear.

More concretely, the video created for the target profile of males in their 50s is explained using the timetable in Figure 13 (Refer to Chapter 23). The timetable shows video time as set to 90 seconds. Video shooting order is composed specifically of scenes from 1 to 11 starting from the front, driver seat, side, and rear of the vehicle.

Scenes are: (1) direct front scene, (2) diagonal front view scene, (3) driver side door opening scene, (4) entire driver seat view scene, (5) console box and shift lever scene, (6) steering wheel scene, (7) driver seat operational scene, (8) side view scene from driver's seat, (9) rear side view scene, (10) entire view of vehicle from rear, and lastly, (11) moving from back to front, the entire view of the vehicle scene.

The scenes that form the VUCMIN video were composed on the basis of the standard and disparate behaviors of customers. Example photos representing these scenes (1 to 11) are shown in Figure 14 (Refer to Chapter 23). Using the same approach, VUCMIN was created for each age and gender. In this section, customer surveys were executed in order to test the validity of VUCMIN.

This was done by asking customers, "After seeing the Mark X video, when do you think you might visit an advanced car manufacturer A dealer to consider purchasing one?" to verify their desire to visit dealers (high, low). According to the survey results, the desire to visit dealers (early consideration of Toyota Mark X purchase) not only increased for current Toyota vehicle owners but also for customers who own vehicles from other manufacturers.

The author is currently promoting the results of this research as part of the strategic advertising method VUCMIN, which utilizes an internet interface in collaboration with universities and industrial players.

Application of CMP-FDM

Flyers are a form of advertising media important for raising the customer-attraction effect. However, the results of an interviews by the author at to six dealers (national and foreign-affiliated) and two advertising agencies specializing in flyers showed that the dealers did not think that designing flyers was important—their only priority was distribution, and they outsourced the design.

Moreover, they did not understand actual customer behavior (how customers looked at flyers and what they paid attention to). Therefore, customer behavior is not reflected into the creation of flyers, and the resulting design is not attractive to customers who want to visit dealers.

The author studied how customers view flyers by analyzing browsing behavior (Koyama, et al., 2010). To resolve the problems with the information contained in current flyer designs, the authors identified which information each consumer type focuses on. In step 1 and 2, the purchase group is taken up as an example of the factor analysis results, with the Text Mining Studio corresponding bubble analysis results focusing on the purchase group as shown in Figure 5.

Figure 5. Results for the information on flyers for the purchase group using Text Mining Studio "Corresponding Bubble Analysis"

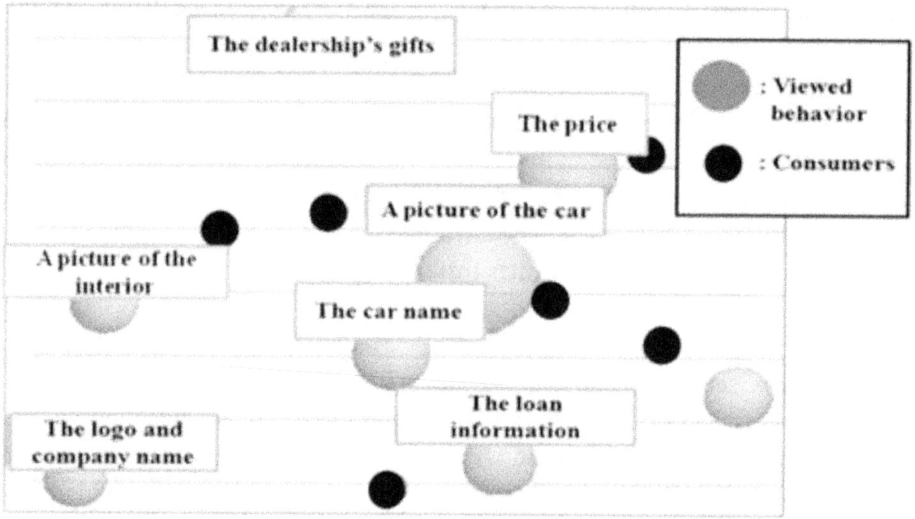

From this figure, it can be seen that the purchase group strongly correlated with viewing behaviors in the following order:

(1) Looking at a picture of the car, (2) looking at the price, (3) looking at the car name, (4) looking at the loan information, (5) looking at a picture of the interior, (6) looking at dealer gifts, and (7) looking at the logo and company name. Through this analysis we were able to clearly reveal the information on flyers that consumers actually focus their attention on, which dealers had previously been unable to grasp.

Through this analysis the authors were able to clearly reveal the information on flyers that consumers actually focus their attention on, which dealers had heretofore been unable to grasp.

In step 3, in order to resolve problems with the flyer layout, the author clarified the position and size of the information on flyers that each consumer type focuses their attention on. In step 4 an attractive flyer design is created based on the knowledge gained in steps 1 to 3.

An example of a new attractive flyer design for Toyota's new vehicle as shown in Figure 11. This design was intended to be appealing for a universal type of consumer.

The effectiveness of the CMP-FDM method for creating the appealing flyer design shown in Figure 6 was confirmed from the survey procedures and analysis obtained from steps 1 through 5, as well as the acquired results.

Application of AGTCA

Firstly, the author researched the causal relationship between basic passenger information and ad awareness (Ogura, et al., 2013a) as follows;.

Figure 6. Example of new attractive flyer design

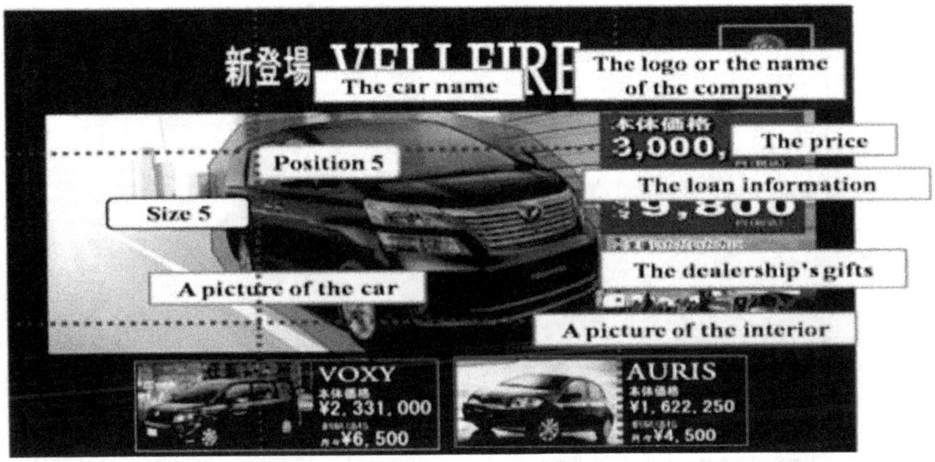

Firstly, in step 1, the author performed a cross tabulation on the survey data and researched the correlations between whether passengers notice each form of train car advertising and passenger information (age and gender) in order see how passenger information relates to attention rates.

Secondly, the author researched the causal relationship between riding conditions and ad awareness of passengers. In step 2, the author used the survey data gathered to represent current in-train advertising conditions, and subjected it to a Cluster Analysis of group riding conditions as shown in Figure 7. Similar results were obtained when the Quantification Theory Type III was used on the survey data shown in Figure 8. Since the first group consisted of standing passengers who ride the train for 0–15 minutes, they were labeled “short-distance passengers”. The second group rode the train for a longer period of time and tended to sit, so this group was called the “long-distance passengers”.

Thirdly, the author researched the causal relationships among basic passenger information, riding conditions and ad awareness of passengers. In step 3, Figure 9 shows the results of the awareness rate for hanging posters among short-term riders, which was used as a criterion variable in the CAID analysis. The results indicate that the highest awareness rate in this group is among men in the youngest age category (15–25).

Barring a few exceptions, the results indicate an overall trend where awareness rates are higher among younger people. Comparing the two groups, the authors found that the short-term passengers (who tended to stand when riding) had higher awareness rates in general. Passengers who sat, on the other hand, had more opportunities to engage in different activities during their ride, such as reading or doing work, which probably contributed to their paying less attention to advertisements than the passengers who were standing.

The analysis revealed that women passengers 26 and older in particular did not look at in-car advertisements. It also indicated that older passengers frequently paid attention to advertisements located above windows. Based on these conclusions, firstly, the author’s recommendation is for existing train car advertising.

Because hanging posters, stickers, and other in-car advertisements are likely to attract younger riders, this space should be used to advertise weekly manga magazines, fashion magazines, sales, or other products likely to appeal to this generation.

Figure 7. Cluster analysis of the ride condition

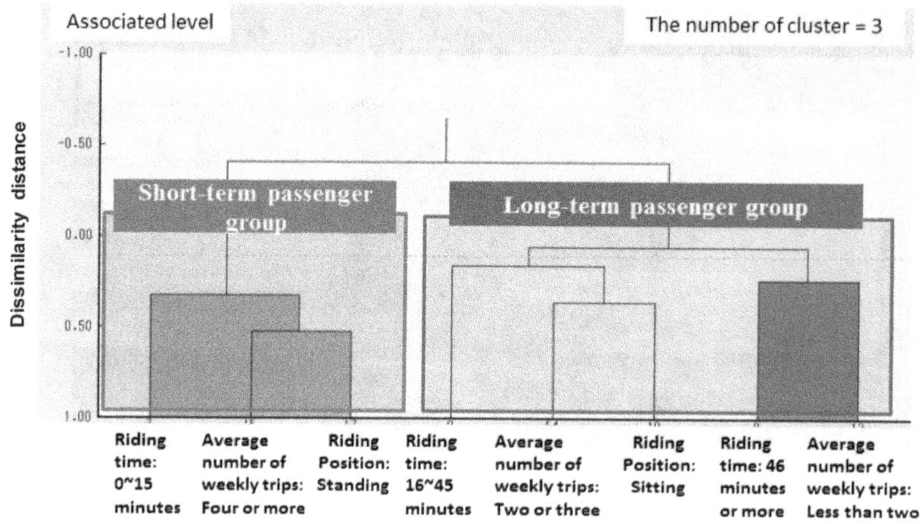

Figure 8. Quantification Theory Type III of the ride

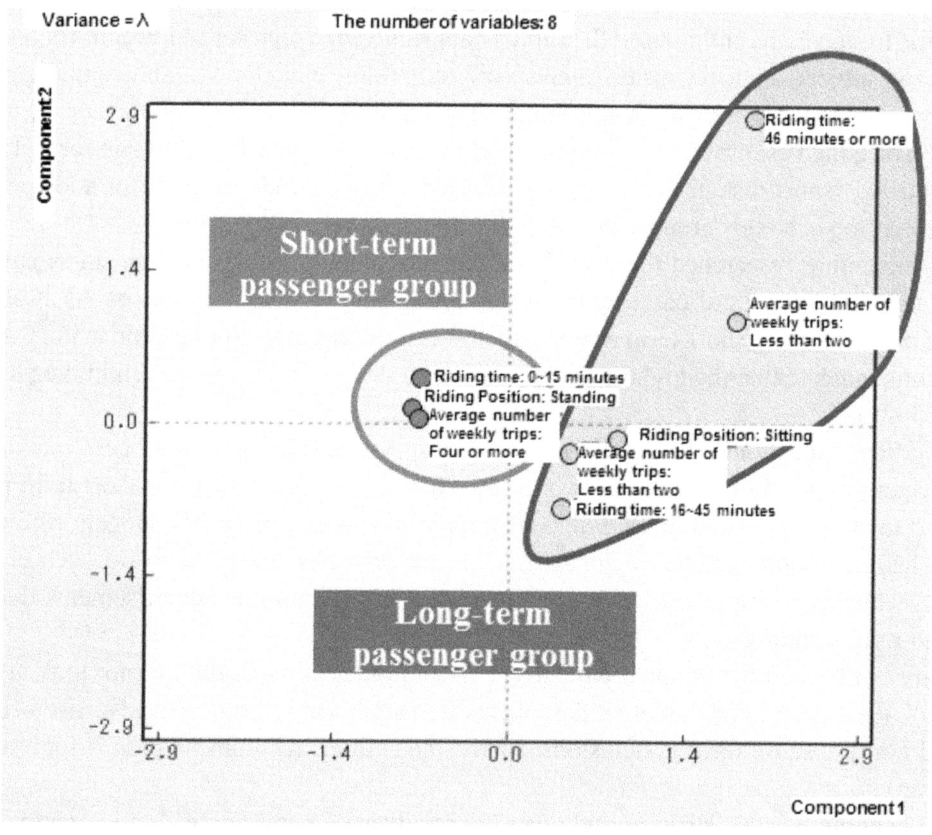

Figure 9. Results of the CAID analysis on the short-term passenger group

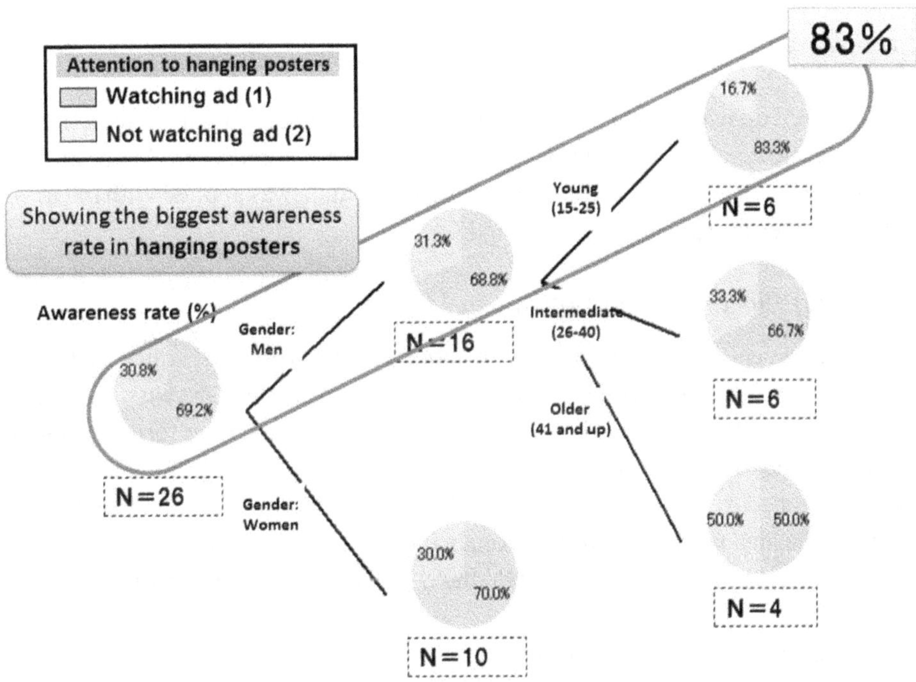

Another important consideration is using popular celebrities to catch the eye of these passengers. Above-window advertising space, on the other hand, may be better used to appeal to those of the older generation. These passengers are more likely to be married and have children, so it may be beneficial to feature family-friendly topics.

Specifically, posters advertising events for families or travel may be ideal in this location. Also, because it was found that standing passengers tend to look at advertisements frequently, riders may pay attention not only to ads that help them pass the time while standing, but also those that stimulate their interest or desire. Instead of showing just a picture, a magazine ad, for example, could feature headlines or other clever designs aimed at stimulating purchase behavior. It is important that other advertisements do not simply catch the eye, but encourage viewers to linger.

Secondly, the author suggests that trains adopt new forms of advertising media. The analysis results indicated that passengers who stand tend to have high awareness rates when it comes to in-car advertising, but advertisements on the floor may be easier for sitting passengers to see. Riders who sit naturally allow their eyes to fall downward, making a floor advertisement an eye-catching option. Those who sit and read are also looking downward as well, increasing the chances that they may see these advertisements.

Focusing on train car ads, which have a good contact rate and long-term contact, the authors decided to examine those relationships and how they relate to train car advertising with the aim of defining the ideal format for this type of media.

Application of PMOS-DM

1. Putting POMS-DM to work

The researchers teamed up with Company M to guide direct mailing efforts in conjunction with an event showcasing multiple new vehicle models (Kojima, et al., 2010: Ishiguro and Amasaka, 2012a,b). The following steps show how optimal selection using a model formula was applied with the formulas shown in (24.1) to (24.5) (Refer to Appendix 24.A, B and C).

(Step 1) Organizing Customer Information

In Step 1, participating dealers had information on a total of 391 customers, which included data on sex (male/female), age (20s, 30s, 40s, 50s, 60+), and age of current vehicle (3-5 years, 6-8 years, 9+ years).

There were a total of 391 values assigned to j: Customer number in the formula, and a total of 10 different values assigned to m (customer attributes: e.g. sex, age, age of current vehicle). A binary code (0 or 1) was then assigned to the collected customer information in order to analyze it. This resulted in values for the f_j^m (Indicates whether or not customer j has attribute m (0 or 1)) variable. Recipients of direct mailing could now be determined based on the dealers' customer information.

(Step 2) Determining Response Likelihood

Step 2 was to conduct a survey and analyze the data to determine which customer attributes were most likely to lead customers to visit a dealer as a result of receiving DM. The survey method used in this study was to ask customers of varying attributes (sex, age, vehicle age, etc.) whether receiving direct mail had ever caused them to visit the dealer.

Once the results were collected, they were quantified and subjected to the multivariate analysis (Quantification Theory Type II) analysis to determine which customers had the highest likelihood of responding to DM. This made it possible to analyze customer attributes in terms of whether or not they were likely to lead to a dealer visit in terms of an external standard.

These response likelihood values were then assigned the variable E^m (Effect of customer attribute (m) on the likelihood that the customer will visit the dealer).

Formula (1) below shows the results of this analysis. The discriminant ratio for the analysis results was 77.36%, indicating that they were fairly reliable. The linear discriminant formula produced from the analysis results is as follows;

$$y = 0x_{11} - 1.4x_{12} + 0x_{21} + 0.9x_{22} + 2.1x_{23} + 3.7x_{24} + 1.7x_{25} + 0x_{31} - 1.3x_{32} - 0.9x_{33} - 1.4 \quad (1)$$

If the linear discriminant is greater than 0, the customer is likely to visit the dealer as a result of receiving direct mail.

If it is less than zero, it indicates that they are not likely to visit. Therefore, the coefficient produced by this formula indicates the response likelihood for the customer attribute as expressed by E^m. The results of this analysis, which allowed us to identify which customers were likely to visit the dealer, are summarized in Table 2.

Table 2. Response likelihood by attribute

	Customer attribute	Response likelihood
x11	Men	0
x12	Women	-1.4
x21	22-29 years old	0
x22	30-39 years old	0.89
x23	40-49 years old	2.1
x24	50-59 years old	3.7
x25	60+ years old	1.7
x31	Currently driving a vehicle 3–5 years old	0
x32	Currently driving a vehicle 6–8 years old	-1.3
x33	Currently driving a vehicle 9+ years old	-0.9

(Step 3) Selecting DM Recipients

In Step 3, the customer information collected in Step 1 is plugged into f_j^m, and the information on response likelihood for each customer attribute is plugged into E^m. The number of direct mailings to be sent is plugged into C (total number of direct mailing sent).

The upper and lower limits for the percentage of direct mailings to go to customers with each attribute is set at the dealer's discretion using the variables H^m (upper limit for the percentage of direct mailings sent to customers with attribute *m*) and L^m (lower limit for the percentage of direct mailings sent to customers with attribute *m*). Once all the parameters are set, the simulation is carried out.

During this process, formulas (2) through (7) are solved as a weighted constraint satisfaction problem (Refer to Appendix 1, 2, and 3). In the weighted constraint satisfaction problem, the weighted constraints are moved to the target function as in formula (2),

Where they are added as a way of minimizing the level of deviation outside of the given limits. Even if a feasible solution that satisfies the constraints does not exist, the formula allows dealers to come as close as possible to meeting the constraints.

Here, in constraining the number of mailings sent to customers with the attributes defined in formula (7), it is difficult to set customer attributes L^m and H^m, ensuring that a feasible solution is more likely to exist. Therefore, when approaching the issue as weighted constraint satisfaction problem, it is best to find a solution that best satisfies formula (7).

In other words, this allows dealers to send direct mail to those customers most likely to come into the shop based on dealer strategy.

$$MIN - \sum_m (E^m \sum_j (f_j^m x_j)) + \sum_m W^m (L^m C - f_j^m x_j) + \sum_m W^m (H^m C - f_j^m x_j) \quad (2)$$

m Customer attributes (e.g. sex, age, age of current vehicle)
j Customer number
Wm Weighting for customers with customer attributes *m* in direct mail target group
f_j^m Indicates whether or not customer *j* has attribute *m* (0 or 1)

x_j Marks customer j for direct mailing (0 or 1)
R^m Ideal percentage with customer attributes m in direct mail target group
C Total number of direct mailings sent
L^m Lower limit for the percentage of direct mailings sent to customers with attribute m
H^m Upper limit for the percentage of direct mailings sent to customers with attribute m

(Step 4) Evaluating the Results

Once the recipients of direct mailings are selected based on the simulation, whoever is sending out the direct mail checks the simulation results to make sure that they accurately reflect the dealer's marketing strategy.

If the desired results are not achieved, the causes for the discrepancy are identified, the parameters are adjusted, and the simulation is run again.

2. Effectiveness of PMOS-DM

The effectiveness of the PMOS-DM was assessed by comparing the response rates (percentage of DM recipients who visited the dealer as a result) when salespeople selected DM recipients based on personal knowledge and experience and when recipients were selected using the model.

Five new models were showcased at the event held. Four of the design concepts targeted female buyers, and one targeted male buyers. As a result, the dealer's marketing strategy was to target women in particular throughout a wide range of age groups. This strategy was thus taken into account when verifying the effectiveness of the model. These verification results are summarized in Table 3.

The response rate when DM recipients were selected on the basis of personal knowledge and experience of the sales staff was 19%. When selection was made using the PMOS-DM model, the rate was 20.4%.

Table 4 shows the same information for female customers only (those targeted in the dealer's marketing strategy). Salespeople generated a 4.2% response rate using their personal knowledge and experience, while the model generated a 19.8% response rate, signaling a significant improvement.

The effectiveness of the model was thereby verified in the course of this study.

Table 3. Verification results (all)

	Dealer	PMOS-DM
Number of direct mailings sent	269	269
Number of resulting dealer visitors	51	59
Response rate	19.0%	20.4%

Table 4. Verification results (women)

	Dealer	PMOS-DM
Number of direct mailings sent	**48**	**61**
Number of resulting dealer visitors	**2**	**12**
Response rate	**4.2%**	**19.8%**

Verification Results

Using the analysis results obtained in the previous section (Visualizing causal relationships in customer purchase behavior), a follow-up survey using questionnaire data from Table 1 was then conducted to verify whether the research achieved its aim of bringing more customers into the dealers by means of raising the percentage of people affected.

Figure 10 shows the verification results from application of new mixed media "New-SMMM" for raising the percentage of people affected. New-SMMM is effective due to its composition of four core elements (VUCMIN, CMP-FDM, AGTCA and PMOS-DM) and use as a new strategic advertisement in nine media elements (TV, radio, newspapers, internet, train cars, flyers, magazines, DM and handbills) designed by the author (Amasaka et al., 2013).

The figure shows the result of a follow-up survey "New Q car" using application of new SMMM, where 16 people (percentage of people affected: 11.8%) actually visited the dealer, while 8 people signed a sales contract. Comparative verification was done by looking at the results of the "usual experience of mixed media" when the dealer in the figure announced the old model "Q car" of 4 years ago in a survey of similar size. In this case, the percentage of people affected was just 1.1%, thus validating the effectiveness of SMMM.

Figure 10. Verification results

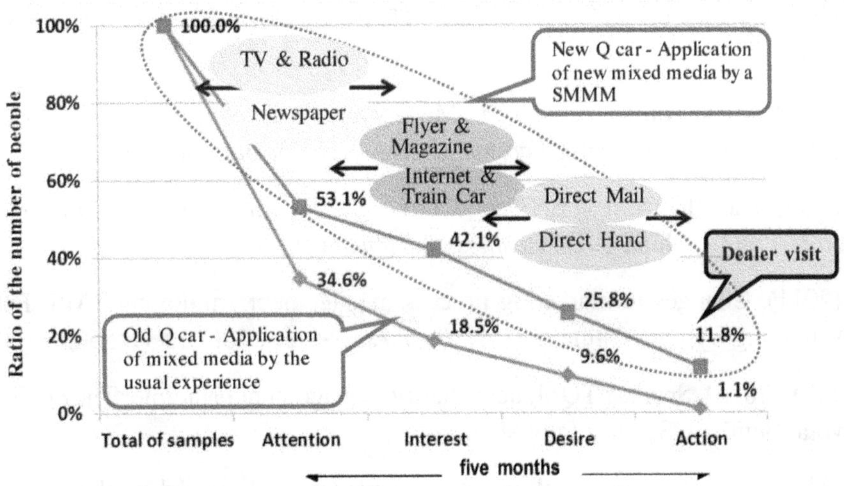

CONCLUSION

The aim of this research study was to bring more customers into auto dealers. In order to achieve this, A SMMM (Scientific Mixed Media Model) was developed as a way to improve the quality of the consumer purchase behavior model in terms of vehicle awareness, vehicle interest, and desire to visit dealers. The collected research results are now being widely distributed as part of Toyota's current sales strategy.

ACKNOWLEDGMENT

The author would like to acknowledge the generous support of the Amasaka New JIT Laboratory at Aoyama Gakuin University, Toyota Motor Corporation and other companies that assisted with the research, especially, Mr. Hifumi, S., Mr. Murat, S. M., Yamaji, M., Mr. Ogura, M., Mr. Ishiguro, H., Mr. Kojima, T., Mr. Koyama, H., Mr. Okajima, R., Mr. Todokoro,T., Mr. Kimura,T., Mr. Mr. Hachiya, T., Mr. Ando, Y., Mr. Masubuchi, K., Mr. Kishimoto, Mr. Murayama, T., and others.

REFERENCES

Amasaka, K. (2002). New JIT, a new management technology principle at Toyota. *International Journal of Production Economics*, *80*(2), 135–144. doi:10.1016/S0925-5273(02)00313-4

Amasaka, K. (2003). Proposal and implementation of the "Science SQC" Quality Control Principle. *International Journal of Mathematical and Computer Modelling*, *38*(11-13), 1125–1136. doi:10.1016/S0895-7177(03)90113-0

Amasaka, K. (2004). *Science SQC, New Quality Control Principle: The Quality Strategy of Toyota*. Springer-Verlag. doi:10.1007/978-4-431-53969-8

Amasaka, K. (2005). Constructing a Customer Science Application System "CS-CIANS": Development of a global strategic vehicle "Lexus" utilizing New JIT. *WSEAS Transactions on Business and Economics, 2*(3), 135-142.

Amasaka, K. (2007). The validity of Advanced TMS, a strategic development marketing system utilizing New JIT. *The International Business & Economics Research Journal*, *6*(8), 35–42.

Amasaka, K. (2009). The effectiveness of flyer advertising employing TMS: Key to scientific automobile sales innovation at Toyota, China-USA. *Business Review*, *8*(3), 1–12.

Amasaka, K. (2011). Changes in marketing process management employing TMS: Establishment of Toyota Sales Marketing System, China & USA. *Business Review*, *10*(7), 539–550.

Amasaka, K. (Ed.). (2012). Science TQM, new quality management principle: The quality management strategy of Toyota. Bentham Science Publishers.

Amasaka, K. (2013), The strategic development of Advanced TPS based on the New Manufacturing Theory (Plenary Lecture). *The 1st WSEAS International Conference on Industrial and Manufacturing Technologies*, 248-261.

Amasaka, K. (2015). New JIT, new management technology principle. Taylor and Francis Group.

Amasaka, K. (2019). Studies on New Manufacturing Theory. *Noble. International Journal of Scientific Research*, *3*(1), 1–20.

Amasaka, K., Kishimoto, M., Murayama, T., & Ando, Y. (1998). The development of Marketing SQC for Dealers' Sales Operation System. *Journal of the Japanese Society for Quality Control, The 58th Technical Conference*, 76-79.

Amasaka, K., Kurosu, S., & Morita, M. (2008). *New Manufacturing Theory: Surpassing JIT - The evolution of Just-In-Time*. Maruzen.

Amasaka, K., Ogura, M., & Ishiguro, H. (2013). Constructing a Scientific Mixed Media Model for boosting automobile dealer visits: Evolution of market creation employing TMS. *International Journal of Business Research and Development, 3*(4), 1377–1391.

Amasaka, K., Watanabe, M., & Shimakawa, Y. (2005). Modeling of Strategic Marketing System to reflect latent customer needs and its effectiveness. *The Magazine of Research & Development for Cosmetica, Toiletries & Applied Industries Fragrance Journal, 33*(1), 72–77.

Beco, G. H., & Jagric, T. (2011). Demand models for direct mail and periodicals delivery services: Results for a transition economy. *Applied Economics, 43*(9), 1125–1138. doi:10.1080/00036840802600244

Bell, G. H., Ledoher, J., & Swersey, A. J. (2006). Experimental design on the front lines of marketing: Testing new ideas to increase direct mail sales. *International Journal of Research in Marketing, 23*(3), 309–319. doi:10.1016/j.ijresmar.2006.05.002

Bult, J. R., & Wansbeek, T. (2005). Optimal selection for direct mail. *Marketing Science, 14*(4), 378–394. doi:10.1287/mksc.14.4.378

Ferrell, O. C., & Hartline, M. (2005). *Marketing Strategy*. Thomson South-Western, Mason.

Gary, L. L., & Arvind, R. (2003). *Marketing Engineering: Computer-assisted marketing analysis and planning*. Pearson Education, Inc.

Hifumi, S. (2006). *A study on a strategic propaganda advertisement (animation): The proposal of "A-MUCMIN" Which raises the volition of coming to the auto shop* (Master's thesis). Aoyama Gakuin University, Graduate School of Science and Engineering. Amasaka New JIT Laboratory.

Ikeo, K. (2006). Feature-marketing innovation. *Japan Marketing Journal.*

Ishiguro, H., & Amasaka, K. (2012a). Proposal and effectiveness of a Highly Compelling Direct Mail Method: Establishment and deployment of PMOS-DM. *International Journal of Management & Information System, 16*(1), 1–10.

Ishiguro, H., Matsuura, S., & Amasaka, K. (2012b). Establishment of a Strategic Total Direct Mail Model to bring customers into auto dealerships. *Journal of Business & Economics Research, 10*(8), 493–500. doi:10.19030/jber.v10i8.7177

James, A. F., & Mona, J. F. (2004). *Service Management*. McGraw-Hill Companies Inc.

James, F. E., Roger, D. B., & Paul, W. M. (2006). *Consumer Behavior*. Dryden Press.

Jeffrey, F. R. & Bernard, J. J. (2005). Best face forward. *Diamond Harvard Business Review*, 62-77.

Jonker, J. J., Pielsma, N., & Potharst, R. (2006). A decision support system for direct mailing decision. *Decision Support Systems, 42*(2), 915–925. doi:10.1016/j.dss.2005.08.006

Kishi, S., Tanaka, H. & Shimamura, K. (2000). *Theory of modern advertising*. Yuhikaku Publishers.

Kobayashi, T., & Shimamura, K. (1997). *New edition new Ad*. Dentsu.

Kojima, T., Kimura, T., Yamaji, M., & Amasaka, K. (2010). Proposal and development of the Direct Mail Method "PMCI-DM" for effectively attracting customers. *International Journal of Management & Information Systems, 14*(5), 15–22. doi:10.19030/ijmis.v14i5.9

Koyama, H., Okajima, R., Todokoro, T., Yamaji, M., & Amasaka, K. (2010). Customer behavior analysis using motion pictures: Research on attractive flyer design method. *China-USA Business Review, 9*(10), 58–66.

Kubimura, R., & Murata, S. (1969). *Theory of PR*. Yuuhikaku.

Melewar, T. C., & Smith, N. (2003). The internet revolution: Some global marketing implications. *Marketing Intelligence & Planning, 21*(6), 363–369. doi:10.1108/02634500310499220

Murayama, Y. (1982). *Analyzing CAID marketing review*. Japan Research Center.

Niiya, Y., & Matsuoka, F. (Eds.). (2001). *Foundation Lecture on the New Advertising Business*. Sendenkaigi.

Nikkei Business. (1999). *Renovation of Shop, Product and Selling Method-targeting Young Customer by Nets*. Author.

Ogura, M., Hachiya, T., & Amasaka, K. (2013a). A Comprehensive Mixed Media Model for boosting automobile dealer visits. *The China Business Review, 12*(3), 195–203.

Ogura, M., Hachiya, T., & Amasaka, K. (2013b). Attention-grabbing train car advertisements. *The China Business Review, 12*(3), 195–203.

Okada, A., Kijima, M., & Moriguchi, T. (Eds.). (2001). *The mathematical model of marketing*. Asakura-shoten.

Okutomi, H., & Amasaka, K. (2013). Researching Customer Satisfaction and Loyalty to boost marketing effectiveness: A look at Japan's auto dealerships. *International Journal of Mangement & Information Systems, 17*(4), 193–200. doi:10.19030/ijmis.v17i4.8093

Sakalsis, M. M., Hifumi, S., Yamaji, M., & Amasaka, K. (2008). Developing a Strategic Advertisement Method "VUCMIN" to enhance the desire of customers for visiting dealers. *Proceedings of the International Symposium on Management Engineering*, 248-257.

Shimakawa, K., Katayama, K., Oshima, K., & Amasaka, K. (2006). Proposal of Strategic marketing model for customer value maximization. *The Japan Society for Production Management, The 23th Annual Technical Conference,* 161-164.

Shimizu, K. (2004). *Theory and Strategy of Advertisement*. Sousei-Sha.

Smith, D. A. (2009). Online accessibility concerns in shaping consumer relationships in the automotive industry. *Online Information Review, 33*(1), 77–95. doi:10.1108/14684520910944409

Yamaji, M. S., Hifumi, S., Sakalsis, M. M., & Amasaka, K. (2010). Developing a Strategic Advertisement Method "VUCMIN" to enhance the desire of customers for visiting dealers. *Journal of Business Case Studies, 6*(3), 1–11. doi:10.19030/jbcs.v6i3.871

APPENDIX 1

Optimal selection using a model formula

Using numerical simulation, the PMOS-DM model uses a mathematical formula to select target customers for direct mail. In coming up with a formula to determine who should be targeted by direct mail, the author referred to the formulas shown in formula (3) and (4), which were developed by Kojima et al. (2010) and Ishiguro and Amasaka (2012a).

$$Min\ L^m C \leq \sum_j f_j^m x_j \leq H^m C \tag{3}$$

subject to

$$Min \sum_m (E^m \sum_j (f_j^m x_j)) \tag{4}$$

m Customer attributes (e.g. sex, age, age of current vehicle)
j Customer number
Wm Weighting for customers with customer attributes m in direct mail target group
f_j^m Indicates whether or not customer j has attribute m (0 or 1)
x_j Marks customer j for direct mailing (0 or 1)
R^m Ideal percentage with customer attributes m in direct mail target group
C Total number of direct mailings sent

The target function of formula (3) is to minimize the gap between the ideal number of direct mailings sent to customers with attribute m (CR^m) and the number actually sent to customers with that attribute ($\Sigma f_j^m x_j$). In other words, the formula expresses the concept of setting a target value when sending out direct mail. Accordingly, the formula can be adapted to cases where a clear, rational target value can be set. However, the formula cannot be used when it is difficult to set a logical target value for the number of direct mailings to be sent—and a dozen or so of the dealers that the authors studied did not set one.

For those dealers, the authors set up a formula that would clarify the process that senior sales staff used to determine who should be targeted by a given direct mail campaign.

In the process of conducting interviews, the authors learned that senior sales staff use an abstract method of targeting those customers who seem like they would have an easy time coming into the dealer.

The author then constructed a makeshift definition of this group of customers as follows.

Each group of customers defined by a given attribute (male, female, 20s, 30s, etc.) has different preferences that would motivate them to come into the dealer. Each customer's willingness to come in can be assigned a cumulative value based on that person's attributes. Those with a high cumulative value can be considered the ones who are likely to come into the shop.

With this line of thinking, the authors developed a formula for calculating the total willingness for customers targeted by direct mail. They then constructed a model for optimizing those values. Finally, the authors came up with a set of constraints in order to put limits on the number of mailings dealers would send, with the aim of maximizing the effectiveness of those that were sent.

APPENDIX 2

Model Formula

This is the model formula used in the numerical simulation.

$$Max\ L^m C \leq \sum_j f_j^m x_j \leq H^m C \tag{5}$$

subject to

$$\sum_j x_j = C \tag{6}$$

$$L^m C \leq \sum_j f_j^m x_j \leq H^m C \tag{7}$$

m Customer attributes (e.g. sex, age, age of current vehicle)
j Customer number
E^m Effect of customer attribute (m) on the likelihood that the customer will visit the dealer
f_j^m Indicates whether or not customer j has attribute m (0 or 1)
x_j Marks customer j for direct mailing (0 or 1)
C Total number of direct mailings sent
L^m Lower limit for the percentage of direct mailings sent to customers with attribute m
H^m Upper limit for the percentage of direct mailings sent to customers with attribute m

This mathematical formula is designed to determine a value for the variable x_j. If the value is 1, mailings should be sent to the customer number indicated by j. If it is 0, a direct mailing should not be sent.

The other variables are parameters that must be given values before solving the formula. C, L^m, and H^m are set at the discretion of whoever is sending out the direct mail.

The value f_j^m is determined based on the customer information that the dealer has. E^m is determined later via statistical analysis. The roles of the individual formulas are as follows.

The objective function in formula (5) is used to maximize the customer response rate (the percentage of customers that come to the dealer as a result of the direct mail).

The constraint in formula (6) determines the number of direct mailings that are to be sent out. The constraint in formula (7) determines how many direct mailings are to be sent to each customer segment, which is how dealer aims are incorporated into the model.

The mathematical formula is designed so that the number of customer attributes it handles (m) can be increased at will.

Depending on what customer information dealers have, they can limit these attributes to basic life stages or expand them to include hobbies, preferences, and other lifestyle characteristics.

APPENDIX 3

Recipient Selection Process

The authors describe the procedure for using the mathematical formula provided to select direct mail recipients.

First, a "response likelihood" value must be set for each customer using the variable E^m. The list of customers is then reordered with those with the highest likelihood of responding at the top.

The purpose of the objective function in formula (24.5) is to order customers according to their likelihood of responding (visiting the dealer as a result of direct mail).

Next, this list is used to select the number of customers equal to the number of direct mailings (the constraint) to be sent out, starting with those most likely to respond.

For example, if 50 direct mailings are to be sent, they would be sent to the top 50 customers most likely to respond to them. This is the basic principle behind the development of the formulas.

In addition, when the dealer has a specific aim in mind (e.g. sending a large number of direct mailings to women), the constraint function in formula (24.7) can be used to incorporate that aim in the calculations.

For example, if the dealer wanted at least 60% of the 50 mailings to go to women, the women customers would be listed in order of response likelihood and the top 30 customers would be selected to receive direct mail.

The remaining 20 recipients would be selected from the entire pool of target customers in order of their response likelihood as well. The purpose of this function is to allow dealers to use their marketing strategies to boost response rate.

Chapter 24
Conclusion

ABSTRACT

This book focused on the theory and application of strategic management technology through the application of NAGMS for the evolution of Japan automobile manufacturing foundation. Developing NAGMS has proven to be effective in actual implementations. Concretely, the author introduces the application examples through expanding Japanese automobile uniform quality and production at optimum locations through SCM strategy in the world. Moreover, through automobile simultaneous QCD fulfilment for customer value creation with application examples, the validity of NAGMS is then verified at an advanced car manufacturer Toyota and others. In recent years, NAGMS has been applied at many leading Japanese companies where its effectiveness has been verified, and it is now known as strategic global management technology model as the authored New Manufacturing Theory.

A future successful global marketer must develop an advanced management system that impresses users and continuously provides excellent products of high quality in a timely manner through corporate management. To succeed in global production, achieving worldwide uniform quality and simultaneous launch (production at optimal locations) is an urgent task. The simultaneous achievement of QCD requirements that reinforce the product appeal is required to realize this global production system.

Against this background, in this book, by predicting the form of next generation automobile manufacturing, the author hereby has examined a "New Automobile Global Manufacturing System" (NAGMS) that contains the hardware system with five core elements - "TDS, TPS, TMS, TIS and TJS" (Total Development System, Total Production System, Total Marketing System, Total Intelligence Management System and Total Job Quality Management System) for transforming management technology into automobile management strategy—Surpassing JIT.

To realize automobile manufacturing strategy that places top priority on customers with a good QCD, the author, therefore, a high linkage model "Advanced TDS, TPS, TMS, TIS and TJS" for expanding "uniform quality worldwide and production at optimum locations". Then, this book focused on the theory and application of strategic management technology through the application of NAGMS for the "Evolution of Japan automobile manufacturing foundation". As these results, developing of NAGMS has proved to be effective in actual implementations.

DOI: 10.4018/978-1-7998-8746-1.ch024

Concretely, the author introduces the application examples through "Expanding Japanese automobile uniform quality and production at optimum locations through SCM strategy in the world".

Moreover, through "Automobile simultaneous QCD fulfilment for customer value creation" with "Application examples", the validity of NAGMS is then verified at an advanced car manufacturer Toyota and others.

In recent years, NAGMS has been applied at many leading Japanese companies where its effectiveness has been verified, and it is now known as strategic global management technology model as the authored "New Manufacturing Theory". It is hoped that this book will contribute to the evolution of management technology for expanding global manufacturing.

Appendix

Figure 1. Advance Type Vehicle; Strategic Vehicle in near Future by creating Amasaka New JIT Laboratory

References:

K. Amasaka, Automobile Exterior Design Model: Framework Development and Supporting Case Studies, *Journal of Japanese Operations Management and Strategy* (2018), Vol. 8, No.1, pp. 67-89.

K. Amasaka, (Plenary Lecture) Attractive automobile design development: Study on customer values), *Executive Lecture* in *Rotary Club, Tokyo, June 06, 2017.*

T. Kobayashi, R. Yoshida, K. Amasaka, N. Ouchi, A Study for Creating an Exterior Vehicle Design Attracting Indifferent Customers, *Hong Kong Int. Conf. on Engineering and Applied Sciences*, December 17, 2015, Hong Kong.

T. Kobayashi, R. Yoshida, K. Amasaka, N. Ouchi, A Statistical and Scientific Approach to Deriving an Attractive Exterior (December. 2016), pp. 74-79

Appendix

Figure 2. Elegant Type Vehicle; Strategic Vehicle in near Future by creating Amasaka New JIT Laboratory

References:

K. Amasaka, Automobile Exterior Design Model: Framework Development and Supporting Case Studies, *Journal of Japanese Operations Management and Strategy* (2018), Vol. 8, No.1, pp. 67-89.

K. Amasaka, (Plenary Lecture) Attractive automobile design development: Study on customer values), *Executive Lecture* in *Rotary Club, Tokyo, June 06, 2017.*

T. Kobayashi, R. Yoshida, K. Amasaka, N. Ouchi, A Study for Creating an Exterior Vehicle Design Attracting Indifferent Customers, *Hong Kong Int. Conf. on Engineering and Applied Sciences*, December 17, 2015, Hong Kong.

T. Kobayashi, R. Yoshida, K. Amasaka, N. Ouchi, A Statistical and Scientific Approach to Deriving an Attractive Exterior (December. 2016), pp. 74-79

Figure 3. Progress Type Vehicle; Strategic Vehicle in near Future by creating Amasaka New JIT Laboratory

References:

K. Amasaka, Automobile Exterior Design Model: Framework Development and Supporting Case Studies, *Journal of Japanese Operations Management and Strategy* (2018), Vol. 8, No.1, pp. 67-89.

K. Amasaka, (Plenary Lecture) Attractive automobile design development: Study on customer values), *Executive Lecture* in *Rotary Club, Tokyo, June 06, 2017.*

T. Kobayashi, R. Yoshida, K. Amasaka, N. Ouchi, A Study for Creating an Exterior Vehicle Design Attracting Indifferent Customers, *Hong Kong Int. Conf. on Engineering and Applied Sciences*, December 17, 2015, Hong Kong.

T. Kobayashi, R. Yoshida, K. Amasaka, N. Ouchi, A Statistical and Scientific Approach to Deriving an Attractive Exterior (December. 2016), pp. 74-79

About the Author

Kakuro Amasaka was born in Aomori Prefecture, Japan, on May 5, 1947. He received a Bachelor of Engineering degree from Hachinohe National College of Technology, Hachinohe, Japan, in 1968, and a Doctor of Engineering degree specializing in Precision Mechanical and System Engineering, Statistics and Quality Control from Hiroshima University, Hiroshima, Japan, in 1997. Since joining Toyota Motor Corp., Japan, in 1968, Dr. Amasaka worked as a quality management consultant for many divisions. He was an engineer and manager of the Production Engineering Div., Quality Assurance Div., Overseas Engineering Div., Manufacturing Div., and TQM Promotion Div. (1968-1997), and the General Manager of the TQM Promotion Div. (1998-2000). Dr. Amasaka became a professor of the College of Science and Engineering, and the Graduate School of Science and Engineering at Aoyama Gakuin University, Tokyo, Japan in April 2000. Now, he is a professor emeritus of Aoyama Gakuin University (2016-present). His specialties include production engineering (Just in Time and Toyota Production System), statistical science, multivariate analysis, reliability engineering and information processing engineering.

Index

E

F

G

H

I

J

L

M

N

O

P

Q

R

S

T

V

W

www.ingramcontent.com/pod-product-compliance
Lightning Source LLC
LaVergne TN
LVHW062104300926
849161LV00010B/2373
* 9 7 8 1 7 9 9 8 8 7 4 6 1 *